UNDERSTANDING PROPERTY LAW

By

John G. Sprankling
Professor of Law
McGeorge School of Law
University of the Pacific

LEXIS Publishing™

LEXIS°NEXIS°· MARTINDALE-HUBBELL°
MATTHEW BENDER°· MICHIE°· SHEPARD'S°

Library of Congress Cataloging-in-Publication Data

Sprankling, John G., 1950–
  Understanding property law / by John G. Sprankling.
    p. cm.
  Includes index.
  ISBN 0-8205-4058-7 (softcover)
  1. Property—United States. I. Title.

KF561 .S67 2000
346.7304—dc21
                                                                00—031333

Editorial Offices
2 Park Avenue, New York, NY 10016-5675 (212) 448-2000
201 Mission Street, San Francisco, CA 94105-1831 (415) 908-3200
701 East Water Street, Charlottesville, VA 22902-7587 (804) 972-7600
www.lexis.com

For Gail, Tom, and Doug.

PREFACE

This book is designed to help the reader in understanding property law. It is primarily oriented toward law students enrolled in the introductory "Property" course who need a concise and readable treatise. Thus, the book (a) explains the basic principles of property law and (b) discusses the policy concerns and historical currents that have shaped this law. At the same time, I hope that the book will be useful to attorneys and scholars as a general survey of property law doctrine, history, and theory.

I welcome your comments, criticisms, and suggestions about the book. Please write to me at McGeorge School of Law, University of the Pacific, 3200 Fifth Avenue, Sacramento, CA 95817 or e-mail me at jsprankling@uop.edu.

John G. Sprankling
June, 2000

ACKNOWLEDGMENTS

I owe thanks to many people who assisted in preparing this book. Dean Gerald Caplan of McGeorge School of Law, University of the Pacific, provided constant support. My colleagues Ira Bloom, Ray Coletta, George Gould, and Brian Landsberg reviewed portions of the draft manuscript and offered valuable suggestions. Pat Cannon, Anne Heindel, and the entire Matthew Bender team were a pleasure to work with throughout the editorial and publication process. Finally, I thank my wife Gail Heckemeyer for her loving encouragement and careful proofreading.

TABLE OF CONTENTS

PART III: ESTATES AND FUTURE INTERESTS

PART IV: LANDLORD AND TENANT

CHAPTER 15   Introduction to Landlord-Tenant Law

CHAPTER 16   Creation of the Tenancy

CHAPTER 17   Condition of Leased Premises

PART V: THE SALE OF LAND

CHAPTER 20   **The Sales Contract**

☑CHAPTER 25   The Recording System

☐CHAPTER 26   Methods of Title Assurance

PART VI: OTHER TRANSFERS OF LAND TITLE

PART VII: OWNERS AND NEIGHBORS

PART VIII: LAND USE CONTROLS—PRIVATE

CHAPTER 32   Easements

CHAPTER 33   Real Covenants

Chapter 1

WHAT IS "PROPERTY"?

SYNOPSIS

§ 1.01 An "Unanswerable" Question?

What is "property?"[1] The term is extraordinarily difficult to define. One of America's foremost property law scholars even asserts that "[t]he question is unanswerable."[2] The problem arises because the legal meaning of "property" is quite different from the common meaning of the term. The ordinary person defines property as *things*, while the attorney views property as *rights*.

Most people share an understanding that property means: "*things* that are *owned* by persons."[3] For example, consider the book you are now

---

[1] *See generally* John E. Cribbet, *Concepts in Transition: The Search for a New Definition of Property*, 1986 U. Ill. L. Rev. 1; Francis S. Philbrick, *Changing Conceptions of Property in Law*, 86 U. Pa. L. Rev. 691 (1938); Charles A. Reich, *The New Property*, 73 Yale L.J. 733 (1964); Joseph L. Sax, *Some Thoughts on the Decline of Private Property*, 58 Wash. L. Rev. 481 (1983); Jeremy Waldron, *What Is Private Property?*, 5 Oxford J. Legal Stud. 313 (1985).

[2] John E. Cribbet, *Concepts in Transition: The Search for a New Definition of Property*, 1986 U. Ill. L. Rev. 1, 1.

[3] Thomas C. Grey, *The Disintegration of Property*, in Nomos XXII 69, 69 (J. Roland Pennock & John W. Chapman eds., 1980).

1

reading. The book is a "thing." And if you acquired the book by purchase or gift, you presumably consider it to be "owned" by you. If not, it is probably "owned" by someone else. Under this common usage, the book is "property."

In general, the law defines property as rights[4] among people[5] that concern things. In other words, property consists of a package of legally-recognized rights held by one person in relationship to others with respect to some thing or other object. For example, if you purchased this book, you might reasonably believe that you own "the book." But a law professor would explain that technically you own legally-enforceable rights concerning the book.[6] For example, the law will protect your right to prevent others from reading this particular copy of the book.

Notice that the legal definition of "property" above has two parts: (1) *rights* among people (2) that concern *things*. The difficulty of defining "property" in a short, pithy sentence is now more apparent. Both parts of the definition are quite vague. What are the possible *rights* that might arise concerning things? Suppose, for example, that A "owns" a 100-acre tract of forest land. What does it mean to say that A "owns" this land? Exactly what are A's rights with respect to the land? The second part of the definition is equally troublesome. What are the *things* that rights may permissibly concern? For example, could A own legal rights in the airspace above the land, in the wild animals roaming across the land, or in the particular genetic code of the rare trees growing on the land? Indeed, can A own rights in an idea, in a graduate degree, in a job, or in a human kidney? In a sense, this entire book is devoted to answering these and similar questions.

§ 1.02 Property and Law

[A] Legal Positivism

Law is the foundation of property rights in the United States. Property rights exist only if and to the extent they are recognized by our legal system. As Jeremy Bentham observed: "Property and law are born together, and die together. Before laws were made there was no property; take away laws, and property ceases."[7] Professor Felix Cohen expressed the same thought more directly: "That is property to which the following label can be attached. To the world: Keep off X unless you have my permission, which I may grant or withhold. Signed: Private citizen. Endorsed: The state."[8] This view that

---

[4] While property is commonly discussed in terms of "rights," perhaps "relationships" would be a better term. *See* § 1.03[C].

[5] "People" is used here in a broad sense to include business and governmental entities as well as individuals.

[6] Still, even attorneys and legal scholars loosely refer to someone "owning" a particular parcel of land or other thing if the person owns *all* the legal rights to it. While convenient, this shorthand adds to the semantic confusion.

[7] Jeremy Bentham, The Theory of Legislation 69 (Oceana Publications, Inc. 1975) (1690).

[8] Felix S. Cohen, *Dialogue on Private Property*, 9 Rutgers L. Rev. 357, 374 (1954).

rights, including property rights, arise only through government is known as *legal positivism*.

[B] An Illustration: *Johnson v. M'Intosh*

The Supreme Court's 1823 decision in *Johnson v. M'Intosh*[9] reflects this approach. Two Native American tribes sold a huge parcel of wilderness land to a group of private buyers for $55,000. The federal government later conveyed part of this property to one M'Intosh, who took possession of the land. Representatives of the first buyer group leased the tract to tenants, and the tenants sued in federal court to eject M'Intosh from the land. The case revolved around a single issue: did Native Americans have the power to convey title that would be recognized by the federal courts? The Court held the tribes lacked this power and ruled in favor of M'Intosh.

Writing for the Court, Chief Justice Marshall stressed that under the laws of the United States, only the federal government held title to the land before the conveyance to M'Intosh, while the Native Americans merely held a "right of occupancy" that the federal government could extinguish. The title to lands, he explained, "must be admitted to depend entirely on the law of the nation in which they lie."[10] The Court's decision could not rely merely on "principles of abstract justice" or on Native American law, but rather must rest upon the principles "which our own government has adopted in the particular case, and given us as the rule for our decision."[11] In short, under the laws established by the United States, must a United States court hold that the United States owned the land? For Marshall, the answer was easy: "Conquest gives a title which the Courts of the conqueror cannot deny."[12] Property rights, in short, are defined by law.

[C] Natural Law Theory

In contrast to legal positivism, *natural law theory* posits that rights arise in nature as a matter of fundamental justice, independent of government. As John Locke observed, "[t]he Law of Nature stands as an Eternal Rule to all Men, *Legislators* as well as others."[13] The role of government, Locke argued, was to enforce natural law, not to invent new law. Natural law was a central strand in European philosophy for millennia, linking together Aristotle, Christian theorists, and ultimately Locke, and heavily influencing American political thought during the eighteenth century. As the Declaration of Independence recited, the "unalienable Rights" of "Life, Liberty, and the Pursuit of Happiness" were endowed upon humans "by their Creator"; governments exist merely "to secure these rights."

---

[9] 21 U.S. (8 Wheat.) 543 (1823). *See also* Tee-Hit-Ton Indians v. United States, 348 U.S. 272 (1955) (holding federal government was not obligated to pay for removal of timber from lands claimed by Native Americans).

[10] Johnson v. M'Intosh, 21 U.S. (8 Wheat.) 543, 572 (1823).

[11] Johnson v. M'Intosh, 21 U.S. (8 Wheat.) 543, 572 (1823).

[12] Johnson v. M'Intosh, 21 U.S. (8 Wheat.) 543, 588 (1823).

[13] John Locke, Two Treatises of Government 358 (Peter Laslett ed., student ed. 1988) (3d ed. 1698).

The Declaration of Independence was the high-water mark of natural law theory in the United States. The Constitution firmly directed the young American legal system toward legal positivism, subject only to the Ninth Amendment's vague assurance that certain rights are "retained by the people." The influence of natural law theory steadily diminished thereafter. By 1823, when deciding *Johnson v. M'Intosh*,[14] the Supreme Court could easily dismiss the natural law argument that "abstract justice" required recognition of Native American land titles.

§ 1.03 Defining Property: What Types of "Rights" Among People?

[A] Scope of Property Rights

Suppose that O "owns" a house commonly known as Redacre. If we asked an ordinary person what O can legally do with Redacre, the response might be something like this: "O can do anything he wants. After all, it's *his* property. A person's home is his castle." This simplistic view that property rights are *absolute*—that an owner can do "anything he wants" with "his" property—is fundamentally incorrect.

Under our legal system, property rights are the product of human invention. As one court explained: "Property rights serve human values. They are recognized to that end, and are limited by it."[15] Thus, property rights are inherently *limited* in our system. They exist *only to the extent* that they serve a socially-acceptable justification.

As discussed in Chapter 2, the existence of private property rights is supported by a diverse blend of justifications. These justifications share two key characteristics. Each recognizes the value of granting broad decision-making authority to the owner. Under our system, a high degree of owner autonomy is both desirable and inevitable. But none of these justifications supports unfettered, absolute property rights. On the contrary, each requires clear limits on the scope of owner autonomy. Indeed, in a sense we can view property law as a process for reconciling the competing goals of individual owners and society in general. Society's concerns for free alienation of land, stability of land title, productive use of land, and related policy themes sometimes outweigh the owner's personal desires.

[B] Property As a "Bundle of Rights"

[1] Overview

It is common to describe property as a "bundle of rights"[16] in relation to things. But which "sticks" make up the metaphorical bundle? We

---

[14] 21 U.S. (8 Wheat.) 543 (1823).

[15] State v. Shack, 277 A.2d 369, 372 (N.J. 1971).

[16] *See, e.g.,* Kaiser Aetna v. United States, 444 U.S. 164, 176 (1979) (referring to the "bundle of rights that are commonly characterized as property").

traditionally label these sticks according to the *nature* of the right involved. Under this approach, the most important sticks in the bundle are:

(1) the right to exclude;

(2) the right to transfer; and

(3) the right to possess and use.

The rights in the bundle can also be divided in other ways, notably by *time* and by *person*. For example, consider how we could subdivide the right to possess and use based on time (*see* Chapters 8–9, 12–14). Tenant T might have the right to use and possess Greenacre for one year, while landlord L is entitled to use and possession when the year ends. Or we could split up the same right based on the identity of the holders (*see* Chapters 10–11). Co-owners A, B, and C might all hold an equal right to simultaneously use and possess all of Blueacre.

[2] Right to Exclude

One stick in the metaphorical bundle is the right to exclude others from the use or occupancy of the particular "thing." If O "owns" Redacre, O is generally entitled to prevent neighbors or strangers from trespassing (*see* Chapter 30). In the same manner, if you "own" an apple, you can preclude others from eating it. Of course, the right to exclude is not absolute. For example, police officers may enter Redacre in pursuit of fleeing criminals; and O probably cannot bar entry to medical or legal personnel who provide services to farm workers who reside on Redacre.[17]

Is the right to exclude a necessary component of property? Not at all. O might own title to Redacre subject to an easement that gives others the legal right to cross or otherwise use the land (*see* Chapter 32). Or O might lease Redacre to a tenant for a term of years (*see* Chapter 15), thus surrendering the right to exclude. Similarly, a local rent control law might prevent O from ever evicting his tenant from Redacre, absent good cause (*see* § 16.03[B][2]).

[3] Right to Transfer

A second stick in the "bundle of rights" is the right to transfer the holder's property rights to others. O, our hypothetical owner of Redacre, has broad power to transfer his rights either during his lifetime or at death. For example, O might sell his rights in Redacre to a buyer, donate them to a charity, or devise them to his family upon his death. In our market economy, it is crucial that owners like O can transfer their rights freely (*see* § 9.08[A]).

But the law imposes various restrictions on this right. For example, O cannot transfer title to Redacre for the purpose of avoiding creditors' claims. Nor is O free to impose any condition he wishes incident to the transfer; thus, a conveyance "to my daughter D on condition that she never sell the land" imposes an invalid condition (*see* § 9.08[B]). Similarly, for example, O cannot refuse to sell his rights in Redacre because of the buyer's race,

---

[17] State v. Shack, 277 A.2d 369 (N.J. 1971).

color, national origin or gender (*see* § 20.01).[18] Some types of property are *market-inalienable*,[19] essentially meaning that they cannot be sold at all (e.g., human body organs),[20] while other types of property cannot be transferred at death (e.g., a life estate).

Is the right to transfer essential? No. For example, although certain pension rights and spendthrift trust interests cannot be transferred, they are still property.[21]

[4] Right to Possess and Use

A third stick is the right to possess and use. As owner of Redacre, O has broad discretion to determine how the land will be used. For example, he might live in the house, plant a garden in the backyard, play tag on the front lawn, install a satellite dish on the roof, and host weekly parties for his friends, all without any intervention by the law. Similarly, if you "own" an apple, you can eat it fresh, bake it in a pie, or simply let it rot.

Traditional English common law generally recognized the right of an owner to use his land in any way he wished, as long as (a) the use was not a nuisance (*see* Chapter 29) and (b) no other person held an interest in the land (*see* Chapters 8–19, 32–34). Today, however, virtually all land in the United States is subject to statutes, ordinances, and other laws that substantially restrict its use (*see* Chapter 36).[22] For example, local ordinances typically provide that only certain uses are permitted on a particular parcel; if Redacre is located in a residential zone, O cannot operate a store or factory there. If the Redacre home is a historic structure, the local historic preservation ordinance may bar O from destroying the building or even altering its appearance.[23] Similarly, Redacre might be subject to private restrictions that dramatically curtail permitted uses; for example, such restrictions might ban gardens, satellite dishes, or even noisy games of tag (*see* Chapter 35).

The right to possess and use is a common—but not a necessary—component of property. If O leases Redacre to tenant T for a 20-year term, O temporarily surrenders his right to possess and use the land; but O still holds property rights in Redacre.

---

[18] *See also* Jones v. Alfred H. Mayer Co., 392 U.S. 409 (1968) (upholding constitutionality of statute prohibiting racial discrimination in sale or other transfer of property).

[19] *See* Margaret J. Radin, *Market-Inalienability*, 100 Harv. L. Rev. 1849 (1987).

[20] *See also* Andrus v. Allard, 444 U.S. 51 (1979) (upholding constitutionality of statute prohibiting sale of endangered species).

[21] *See, e.g.,* Broadway Nat'l Bank v. Adams, 133 Mass. 170 (1882) (holding beneficiary's interest in spendthrift trust was not transferable).

[22] *See also* Schild v. Rubin, 283 Cal. Rptr. 533 (Ct. App. 1991) (overturning trial court decision that enjoined neighbors from playing basketball during specified hours).

[23] *See also* Eyerman v. Mercantile Trust Co., 524 S.W.2d 210 (Mo. Ct. App. 1975) (refusing to enforce instructions in decedent's will that her home be destroyed).

[C] From "Rights" to "Relationships"

Attorneys, judges, and even law professors customarily define property in terms of *rights*. But what about *duties*? Suppose landowner L is required by law to preserve the habitat of endangered species, even though this limits her ability to use the land. We might explain this requirement either as a restriction on L's rights or as a duty that L owes. In recent decades, the law has increasingly recognized that property owners both hold rights and owe duties. Perhaps it is more accurate to define property as *relationships* among people that concern things.

Professor Wesley Newcomb Hohfeld revolutionized property law theory in the early twentieth century by envisioning property as a complex web of legally-enforceable relationships.[24] He developed an analytical framework for precisely classifying these relationships. Under this view, a property owner may hold four distinct entitlements: rights, privileges, powers, and immunities. Each entitlement is linked to a "correlative" counterpart: right-duty; privilege-no right; power-liability; and immunity-disability. Although Hohfeld's system was partially adopted by the first Restatement of Property in 1936, it enjoys less influence today. His insight that property consists of relationships among people, however, remains important.

§ 1.04 Defining Property: Rights in What "Things"?

[A] The Problem

What can permissibly be the subject of property rights? In other words, if "property" consists of legal rights or relationships among people that concern "things," what is the universe of "things"?

The concepts of *value* and *scarcity* are useful tools in thinking about these questions, but do not go far enough. An ordinary person might define property as "things worth money"—land, jewels, cars, and so forth. Yet property rights can exist in things that have no monetary value (e.g., letters from a loved one) or even a negative value (e.g., land heavily contaminated with toxic wastes). Scarcity is a more promising theme. Indeed, one scholar defines property as "a system of rules governing access to and control of scarce material resources."[25] Certainly, property rights are more likely to develop in things that are scarce (e.g., paintings by Leonardo da Vinci) than in things that are common (e.g., mosquitos).[26] Yet scarce things may remain unowned (e.g., an idea for a new television series), while property rights might exist in ubiquitous things (e.g., air space).

So what "things" can be the subject of property rights? The law's traditional reply to this question is simple: all property is divided into two

---

[24] *See* Wesley N. Hohfeld, *Some Fundamental Legal Conceptions as Applied in Judicial Reasoning*, 23 Yale L.J. 16 (1913).

[25] Jeremy Waldron, *What Is Private Property?*, 5 Oxford J. Legal Stud. 313, 318 (1985).

[26] *See generally* Harold Demsetz, *Toward A Theory of Property Rights*, 57 Am. Econ. Rev. 347 (1967).

categories, *real property* (rights in land) and *personal property* (rights in things other than land). Yet this reply is remarkably unhelpful. The universe of "things" in which property rights can exist does not extend to all "land" or to all "things other than land."

[B] Real Property

Real property consists of rights in land and anything attached to land (e.g., buildings, signs, fences, or trees). It includes certain rights in the land surface, the subsurface (including minerals and groundwater), and the airspace above the surface (*see* Chapter 31).

But how extensive are these rights? If F owns exclusive property rights in 100 acres of land known as Greenacre, does he also own rights in all the airspace 1,000 miles above the land? Or in the soil 1,000 miles below Greenacre? If the wind blows across Greenacre, does F own rights in the wind? Or in the wild bee hive in a Greenacre tree?

Historically, property law was almost exclusively concerned with real property. In feudal England—the birthplace of our property law system— land was the source of political, social, and economic power (*see* Chapter 8). Control over land provided the basis for political sovereignty, the foundation of social status, and the principal form of wealth; accordingly, disputes concerning real property were resolved in the king's courts. Personal property, in contrast, was relatively unimportant in the feudal era; when a person died, the distribution of his personal property was supervised by church courts. Under these conditions, two distinct branches of property law evolved. Real property law, the dominant branch, became complex and often arcane; in contrast, personal property law remained relatively simple and straightforward. Thus, the property law that the new United States inherited from England mainly consisted of real property law.

Even today, the standard first year law school course on "property" mainly examines real property law. This focus may appear anachronistic in our technological age; stocks, bonds, patents, copyrights, and other forms of intangible personal property are increasingly valuable. Yet land remains the single most important resource for human existence. All human activities must occur somewhere. As our population increases and environmental concerns continue, disputes about property rights in our finite land supply will escalate.

[C] Personal Property

[1] Chattels

Items of tangible, visible personal property—such as jewelry, livestock, airplanes, coins, rings, cars, and books—are called *chattels*. Virtually all of the personal property in feudal England fell into this category. Today, property rights can exist in almost any tangible, visible "thing." Thus, almost every moveable thing around you now is a chattel owned by someone.

There are two particularly prominent exceptions to this general observation. Even though human kidneys, fingers, ova, sperm, blood cells, and other body parts might be characterized as "tangible, visible things," most courts and legislatures have proven reluctant to extend property rights this far (*see* Chapter 6). Similarly, deer, foxes, whales, and other wild animals in their natural habitats are deemed unowned (*see* Chapter 3).

[2] Intangible Personal Property

Rights in intangible, invisible "things" are classified as intangible personal property. Stocks, bonds, patents,[27] trademarks, copyrights, trade secrets, debts, franchises, licenses, and other contract rights are all examples of this form of property.[28] The importance of intangible personal property skyrocketed during the twentieth century, posing new challenges that our property law system was poorly equipped to handle.[29]

What are the other intangible "things" in which property rights may exist? The answer to this question is changing quickly. Consider the example of a person's name. Traditionally, property rights could not exist in a name, unless it was used in a special manner (e.g., as a trademark). Today, however, the law protects a celebrity's "right of publicity"—the right to the exclusive use of the celebrity's name and likeness for commercial gain (*see* § 7.05[F]).[30] But the answers to other questions are less clear. If spouse A works to finance spouse B's law school education, is B's law degree deemed marital "property" such that A is entitled to a share when he and B divorce? If A works for C for 30 years, does A have a property right in his job?[31] Upon retirement, does A have a property right in social security benefits?[32] The universe of intangible things is seemingly endless, and the law in this area will continue to evolve rapidly.

---

[27] *See, e.g.,* Hughes Aircraft Co. v. United States, 717 F.2d 1351 (Fed. Cir. 1983).

[28] The fact that intangible personal property is sometimes evidenced by a document (e.g., a stock certificate or promissory note) does not convert it into a chattel.

[29] For example, can property rights exist in computer time? *See* Lund v. Commonwealth, 232 S.E.2d 745 (Va. 1977) (overturning defendant's conviction for larceny on the basis that computer time is not a "good" or "chattel").

[30] *See, e.g.,* Midler v. Ford Motor Co., 849 F.2d 460 (9th Cir. 1988).

[31] *See, e.g.,* Perry v. Sindermann, 408 U.S. 593 (1972); Local 1330, United Steel Workers v. United States Steel Corp., 631 F.2d 1264 (6th Cir. 1980); *see generally* Joseph W. Singer, *The Reliance Interest in Property*, 40 Stan. L. Rev. 614 (1988).

[32] *See* Flemming v. Nestor, 363 U.S. 603 (1960) (finding no property right in social security benefits for purposes of Due Process Clause); *but cf.* Joy v. Daniels, 479 F.2d 1236 (4th Cir. 1973) (holding tenant in federally-subsidized apartment had property right to continue occupancy, absent good cause for eviction, for purposes of Due Process Clause).

Chapter 2

JURISPRUDENTIAL FOUNDATIONS OF PROPERTY LAW

§ 2.01 Why Recognize Private Property?

Consider a 100-acre tract of prairie grassland in the American Midwest known as Goldacre, the perfect site for a wheat field. What alternative models of ownership might apply to this land? One option might be called *no property*: no one has any rights in the parcel. Another possibility is *common property:* every person holds equal rights in the land. A third model is *state property*: the state owns all rights in the tract. The final option is *private property*: one or more persons hold rights in the land. Under our legal system, Goldacre is probably governed by the private property model.

Why does American law recognize private property?[1] We view property as a cluster of legally enforceable rights among people concerning things. But why should government enforce those rights in the first place? In other words, what is the *justification* for private property? The answer to this

---

[1] *See generally* Lawrence C. Becker, Property Rights: Philosophic Foundations (1977); Robert C. Ellickson, *Property in Land*, 102 Yale L.J. 1315 (1993); Carol M. Rose, *Property as the Keystone Right?*, 71 Notre Dame L. Rev. 329 (1996).

question is crucial because the *justification* for private property will necessarily affect the *substance* of property law. For example, suppose that we recognize private property solely in order to reward useful labor; if so, all property law rules will be devoted toward implementing this end. In short, the scope and extent of property rights logically turn on the underlying justification for private property.

In reality, American property law is based on a subtle blend of different—and somewhat conflicting—theories. No single approach is accepted as the complete justification for private property. The dominant theory is undoubtedly traditional utilitarianism (*see* § 2.04). However, other major theories—including first occupancy (*see* § 2.02), labor-desert theory (*see* § 2.03), the law and economics variant of utilitarianism (*see* § 2.05), civic republican theory (*see* § 2.06), and personhood theory (*see* § 2.07)—also influence the evolution of property law. Of course, this is far from a complete list. A variety of other perspectives—including such diverse examples as libertarian theory,[2] the "green property" movement,[3] the critical legal studies approach,[4] and John Rawls's theory of distributive justice[5] —are also important.

Rather than a uniform theory of property, these diverse approaches form a kind of jigsaw puzzle whose pieces do not fit neatly together. As Lawrence Becker laments, each approach is "typically embedded in a general moral theory which makes it difficult to use one argument to support, augment, or restrict another."[6] Accordingly, while these theories all support the existence of private property in the abstract, they differ widely on how property rights should be defined and allocated.

§ 2.02 First Occupancy (aka First Possession)

[A] Nature of Theory

Who was first? The first occupancy theory reflects the familiar concept of first-in-time: the first person to take occupancy or possession of something owns it.[7] Suppose fisherman A uses his fishing gear to catch a wild

---

[2] *See generally* Robert Nozick, Anarchy, State, and Utopia (1974).

[3] *See, e.g.,* J. Peter Byrne, *Green Property*, 7 Const. Commentary 239 (1990); Christopher D. Stone, *Should Trees Have Standing?—Toward Legal Rights for Natural Objects*, 45 S. Cal. L. Rev. 450 (1972); *see also* Sierra Club v. Morton, 405 U.S. 727 (1972) (Douglas, J., dissenting) (arguing that concern for environmental protection should lead to the conferral of standing upon "environmental objects" such as trees, rivers, and valleys to sue for their own preservation).

[4] *See, e.g.,* Roberto M. Unger, *The Critical Legal Studies Movement*, 96 Harv. L. Rev. 561 (1983).

[5] *See generally* John Rawls, A Theory of Justice (1971).

[6] Lawrence C. Becker, Property Rights: Philosophic Foundations 3 (1977).

[7] *See, e.g.,* Pierson v. Post, 3 Cai. R. 175 (N.Y. 1805) (discussing rights in wild fox); *cf.* Johnson v. M'Intosh, 21 U.S. (8 Wheat.) 543 (1823) (discussing rights as among European nations to conquer lands occupied by non-Europeans).

fish. Under this approach, A owns property rights in the fish simply because he was the first person to capture it. Or suppose F, a farmer in the nineteenth-century West, diverts irrigation water to her land from a nearby river; over time, F acquires water rights under the prior appropriation doctrine merely because she used the water first.

First occupancy theory seeks to explain how rights of private property arise in unowned natural resources. William Blackstone—whose *Commentaries on the Laws of England* quickly became the most popular legal treatise in the young United States—described the process as follows. When the world was in a state of nature, blessed with abundant food and other natural resources but only a small human population, everything was held "in common" by the inhabitants as "the immediate gift of the creator;" thus, any person could take "from the public stock to his own use such things as his immediate necessities required."[8] If early inhabitant A was hungry, for example, he could simply eat a wild nut from any tree. In a second phase, Blackstone argued, "by the law of nature and reason, he who first began to use it, acquired therein a kind of transient property, that lasted so long as he was using it, and no longer."[9] Thus, if A picked nuts off the tree, and sat down to eat them, he acquired property rights in the nuts for as long as he continued eating them. Blackstone concluded that as the human population increased, this custom of first occupancy ripened into permanent property rights. Now, if A labored to pick nuts off the tree, he owned the nuts, whether he ate them immediately or stored them for future use. The same principle applies to property rights in land. Person P acquires ownership rights in the 100-acre prairie tract known as Goldacre simply by occupying it first.

The principle of first occupancy is a fundamental part of American property law today, though in practice it is often blended together with other theories, particularly utilitarianism and the labor theory. First occupancy theory was particularly influential during the nineteenth century, when it was used to allocate property rights in such diverse resources as wild animals and fish (*see* § 3.02), oil and gas (*see* § 31.06[B]) and surface water (*see* § 31.02[A]). Even today, the first-in-time principle is still the basic rule for determining the respective priority of competing title claims to real property (*see* § 24.02).

[B] Critique of Theory

Most legal scholars hold the same opinion of first occupancy theory: while it helps to *explain* how property rights evolved, it does not adequately *justify* the existence of private property. Suppose vagrant V accidentally kicks over a rock and discovers a gold mine. V's claim is first in time, but why should this make a difference? Why should V own the gold, rather than, for example, the residents of the region or the parents of handicapped children?

---

[8] 2 William Blackstone, Commentaries on the Laws of England 3 (Bell ed., 1771).

[9] 2 William Blackstone, Commentaries on the Laws of England 3 (Bell ed., 1771).

Further, the first occupancy approach is counterproductive because it encourages the waste of natural resources. Consider hunting. If property rights in wild animals are allocated to the first successful hunter, then long-term conservation is impossible. Because no hunter can control the conduct of other hunters, each hunter has an incentive to protect his or her individual self-interest by killing as many animals as possible as quickly as possible. What about oil? If property rights in subsurface oil are acquired by the first person to pump it out of the ground, then no one has an incentive to preserve oil resources for future use. Suppose A, B and C all own parcels of land overlying an underground oil deposit. If A begins to pump out oil, B and C will rationally do the same; otherwise, A will pump out all the oil, leaving B and C with no rights at all.

Richard Epstein offers at least a lukewarm defense. Assuming that some system of property rights is necessary, "if only to organize the world in ways that all individuals know the boundaries of their own conduct,"[10] he argues that first occupancy is superior to a system that recognizes original common ownership in all citizens. First, it places wealth in private hands, which leads to more efficient utilization of resources. Second, the first occupancy rule has become a well-established custom for centuries; whatever its original merits may be, any attempt to abandon the rule now would upset the stability of private property ownership.

The first occupancy approach is a valuable tool in one setting: it serves as a low-cost "tie breaker." All other things being equal, it offers a quick, clear, and inexpensive method to resolve competing claims to property rights and thereby avoid conflict.[11] In other words, if the positions of two competing claimants are otherwise identical, the law usually breaks the tie by recognizing the rights of the first-in-time claimant.

§ 2.03 Labor-Desert Theory

[A] Nature of Theory

The labor-desert theory posits that people are entitled to the property that is produced by their labor. Under this approach, fisherman A owns property rights in the fish he caught because the catch resulted from his labor; A baited the hook, waited patiently, and reeled in the fish. Or suppose sculptor B utilizes her creative powers to transform unowned clay into a valuable statue; again, B owns rights in the statue because of her labor. The respective property rights of A and B arise as a matter of natural justice because they mixed their labor with unowned raw materials, not simply because they were first in time.

As developed by its foremost exponent, the seventeenth-century philosopher John Locke, the labor theory assumes a world in a state of nature, without private property ownership.[12] It seeks to explain how unowned

---

[10] Richard A. Epstein, *Possession as the Root of Title*, 13 Ga. L. Rev. 1221, 1238 (1979).

[11] *See* Carol M. Rose, *Possession as the Origin of Property*, 52 U. Chi. L. Rev. 73 (1985).

[12] *See generally* Walton H. Hamilton, *Property—According to Locke*, 41 Yale L.J. 864 (1932).

natural resources (e.g., wild nuts, game, or unoccupied land) are transformed into private property owned by one person. The theory proceeds in four basic steps:

(1)   every person owns his body;

(2)   thus, each person owns the labor that his body performs;

(3)   so, when a person labors to change something in nature for his benefit, he "mixes" his labor with the thing; and

(4)   by this mixing process, he thereby acquires rights in the thing.

Consider an example. P owns his body, and thus owns his own labor. When P picks wild nuts from a tree and places them in his sack, he mixes his labor (which he owns) with the nuts (which are unowned), and thereby obtains property rights in the resulting mixture (nuts in the sack). In the same fashion, Locke concludes: "*As much Land* as a Man Tills, Plants, Improves, Cultivates, and can use the Product of, so much is his *Property*. He by his Labour does, as it were, enclose it from the Common."[13] Thus, P can acquire ownership rights in our hypothetical prairie tract, Goldacre, simply by cultivating and harvesting wheat on the land.

Strong traces of the labor theory linger in American property law today, often intermixed with first occupancy theory.[14] Perhaps the clearest example is accession: one who in good faith applies labor to another's chattel receives title to the resulting product if, for example, the labor greatly increases the value of the original item (*see* § 7.01). Other examples include adverse possession (*see* Chapter 27), the good faith improver doctrine (*see* § 30.07), and various intellectual property rules (*see* § 7.05).

[B] Critique of Theory

Legal scholars are almost uniformly critical of Lockean labor theory as a justification for private property rights.[15] At best, critics observe, the theory should permit a person to receive the value that his or her labor adds to a thing, not title to the thing itself. If P's labor adds only 1% to the value of a thing, why should P receive 100% of the thing? Similarly, if P plants, nurtures, and harvests wheat on unowned land commonly known as Goldacre, at most P should hold rights to the resulting wheat, not to the land itself.

Another line of attack focuses on time. Suppose P acquires title to Goldacre through his labor. P then hires farm workers F and G to grow the next wheat crop on the land. Even though F and G mix their labor with the land, they cannot acquire ownership, because the land is already owned

---

[13] John Locke, Two Treatises of Government 290–291 (Peter Laslett ed., student ed. 1988) (3rd ed. 1698).

[14] *Cf.* Haslem v. Lockwood, 37 Conn. 500, 507 (1871) (holding that plaintiff, who raked abandoned horse manure into piles and thus "greatly increase[d] its value by his labor," could recover the value of the manure from the defendant who carried away the piles).

[15] *See generally* Lawrence C. Becker, Property Rights: Philosophic Foundations 36–56 (1977).

by P. Thus, the labor theory honors only first labor, not all labor. In this sense, it seems to suffer from the same defects as first occupancy theory.

Finally, the labor theory assumes an unlimited supply of land and other natural resources. Thus, if P appropriates Goldacre through his labor, he theoretically causes no harm to other people. Assuming an infinite supply of natural resources, F, G and others could freely occupy unowned land. However, the twentieth century has taught us that the world is finite. Thus, if the law recognizes P's title to Goldacre, F, G, and others do suffer harm.

§ 2.04   Utilitarianism: Traditional Theory

[A]   Nature of Theory

Utilitarian theory views property "as a means to an end."[16] This is—by far—the dominant theory underlying American property law. Under this approach, private property exists in order to maximize the overall happiness or "utility" of all citizens. Accordingly, property rights are allocated and defined in the manner that best promotes the general welfare of society. As the New Jersey Supreme Court observed in *State v. Shack*:[17] "Property rights serve human values. They are recognized to that end, and are limited by it."

The modern fathers of utilitarianism were David Hume and Jeremy Bentham, both eighteenth-century English philosophers. For Hume, property rights stemmed not from morality or natural justice, but rather from human invention. Mankind recognizes the existence of private property, he suggested, simply as a convention that promotes social utility. Bentham, in turn, both refined and popularized Hume's thesis. He observed: "Property and law are born together, and die together. Before laws were made there was no property; take away laws, and property ceases."[18] In crafting property law, the role of the legislator was to do "what is essential to the happiness of society; when he disturbs it, he always produces a proportionate sum of evil."[19]

Suppose fisherman A catches a wild fish. According to utilitarian theory, society recognizes that A owns rights in the fish because this result promotes overall public happiness. In general, fishermen derive pleasure from catching fish, and obtain sustenance from eating the fish they catch. Accordingly, society recognizes the ownership rights of all fishermen who successfully catch fish. Perhaps catching the fish made A grumpy or even mad. But the facts relating to A's personal situation are irrelevant. A's property rights stem from a general rule applicable to all citizens. Conversely, human happiness might require that society restrict or ban fishing, in order to allow an endangered species to recover from over-fishing and thus be available for future generations of fishermen.

---

[16] Lawrence C. Becker, Property Rights: Philosophic Foundations 57 (1977).

[17] 277 A.2d 369, 372 (N.J. 1971).

[18] Jeremy Bentham, The Theory of Legislation 69 (Oceana Publications, Inc. 1975) (1802).

[19] Jeremy Bentham, The Theory of Legislation 69 (Oceana Publications, Inc. 1975) (1802).

The same analysis applies to our hypothetical wheat field, Goldacre. The law recognizes farmer P as the owner of property rights in Goldacre because this result best promotes overall societal happiness, not because P has any natural or moral entitlement. How so? In general, recognizing private property rights in land produces public benefits. Without private property rights, farmers in general could not bar trespassers from removing their crops; under these conditions, farmers would not invest the time, money, and energy needed to supply society with wheat. Property rights thus provide farmers with the investment security that induces them to grow wheat to help feed the public. And—as a general matter—farmers presumably derive personal satisfaction and pleasure from owning and farming their lands.

[B] Critique of Theory

How can human happiness be measured? Are the appropriate yardsticks love, wealth, respect, intelligence, leisure time, dignity, self-esteem, health, or other factors? Critics charge that utilitarian theory is effectively meaningless because it is impossible to assess happiness. For example, a particular law might bring more wealth to one group of citizens, but lessen the self-esteem of another equal-sized group. Alternatively, a law might increase the dignity, but impair the health, of all citizens. Although there is widespread agreement that utilitarian theory supports the existence of private property as a general matter, critics argue that it offers no guidance about how property rights should be allocated or defined.

One important implication of utilitarian theory is that property rights are not "written in stone," but rather are subject to change. If property is merely a tool used to engineer maximum human happiness, then new social, economic, or political conditions may require that property rights be reallocated or redefined. Even assuming that happiness can be measured, are courts and other governmental institutions competent to decide what changes in traditional property rights are necessary or appropriate for the welfare of society?

§ 2.05 Utilitarianism: Law and Economics Approach

[A] Nature of Theory

The law and economics approach incorporates economic principles into utilitarian theory.[20] While traditional utilitarianism defines human happiness in rather vague terms, the law and economics view essentially assumes that happiness may be measured in dollars. Under this view, private property exists in order to maximize the overall wealth of society.

---

[20] *See generally* Guido Calabresi & A. Douglas Melamed, *Property Rules, Liability Rules, and Inalienability: One View of the Cathedral*, 85 Harv. L. Rev. 1089 (1972); R.H. Coase, *The Problem of Social Cost*, 3 J.L. & Econ. 1 (1960); Harold Demsetz, *Toward a Theory of Property Rights*, 57 Am. Econ. Rev. 347 (1967).

Richard Posner, the preeminent law and economics scholar, begins by defining property as "rights to the exclusive use of valuable resources."[21] The law enforces property rights in order to motivate individuals to utilize resources "efficiently." In this sense, an "efficient" allocation of resources is one in which "value"—defined as an individual's willingness to pay—is maximized. For example, if A is willing to pay $100 for a particular widget, while B is willing to pay only $30, value is maximized if A obtains the widget. For Posner, the key to efficient allocation is a truly free market in goods and services. Accordingly, the principal role of property law is to foster voluntary commercial transactions among private parties.

Posner postulates a world filled with economically-rational actors, all constantly seeking to maximize their self-interests. In this setting, an efficient property law system must have three central components: universality, exclusivity, and transferability. *Universality* simply means that all property is owned by someone. The second component, *exclusivity*, denotes that the law recognizes the absolute right of an owner to exclude all members of society from the use or enjoyment of the owned resource. Finally, *transferability* means that property rights are freely transferable, so that a resource can be devoted to the most highly-valued use. Of course, even if these components are present, the free exchange of property rights may be impaired by *transaction costs* (e.g., the costs of investigating a potential purchase, negotiating a purchase contract, or dealing with the *free rider*—the group member who receives benefit but refuses to pay). The Coase Theorem holds that property will eventually be devoted to its highest value use, regardless of how property rights are initially allocated, if no transaction costs exist.

Consider again our hypothetical prairie tract Goldacre. Farmer P is deciding whether to plant wheat on Goldacre. Society will gain wheat—and thus added wealth—if P and similarly-situated farmers have adequate incentive to invest the time, energy, and money necessary to raise crops. In a world without property law, P will worry: strangers might appropriate the harvest, or P might fall ill and be unable to tend the crop. How can property law encourage P to grow wheat? Posner would answer the question in three steps. First, recognize that P holds property rights in Goldacre. Second, define P's rights so that P has the exclusive right to the use and enjoyment of Goldacre; in this manner, the law will enforce P's exclusive rights to the wheat he grows. Third, allow P to freely transfer his rights in Goldacre to others, so that illness or other calamity does not impair wheat production.

The law and economics approach to utilitarian theory has been quite influential in recent decades, affecting academic debate (and, to a lesser extent, case law) in areas ranging from tenants' rights to land use law.[22] In particular, the concept of *externalities*—that is, economic costs or benefits caused by a person's failure to consider the full impacts of his use of

---

[21] Richard A. Posner, Economic Analysis of Law 31 (4th ed. 1992).

[22] *See, e.g.,* Chicago Bd. of Realtors, Inc. v. City of Chicago, 819 F.2d 732 (7th Cir. 1987) (Posner, J., concurring).

resources—has offered important insights into nuisance law (*see* Chapter 29).

[B] Critique of Theory

The law and economics approach is, to put it mildly, controversial. One major concern is its assumption that social utility or value is appropriately measured by willingness to pay. Not all human desires or satisfactions can be quantified in dollar terms. Such basic human needs as dignity, love, self-esteem, respect, and honor carry no price tag.

Even if all human happiness could be reduced to dollars, the "willingness to pay" standard is still fundamentally flawed. Why? The existing distribution of wealth in our society is unequal. Posner tells a parable of two families, each interested in purchasing a very expensive type of pituitary extract that increases the height of children. The poor family is unable to afford the extract, even though without it their son will be a dwarf forever. Conversely, the rich family can afford to purchase the extract, so that their son—a boy of otherwise normal height—can grow a few inches above normal. For Posner, the rich family places more "value" on the extract because it is willing to pay more than the poor family. Thus, value is maximized by allowing the rich family to receive the extract.

Implicit in the law and economics approach is an assumption that increasing overall social wealth will benefit all members of society, a view characterized by some critics as "trickle-down economics." In other words, if the size of the "pie" increases, the size of each piece of the pie will also increase. However, critics charge that the minimal government intervention championed by law and economics advocates tends to perpetuate the existing unequal distribution of wealth.

Even Posner acknowledges that law and economics theory presents profound moral questions. He concedes that economic analysis cannot answer "the ultimate question of whether an efficient allocation of resources would be socially or ethically desirable."[23] Still, Posner insists that efficiency should be considered an important factor in legal decision making.

§ 2.06 Liberty or Civic Republican Theory

[A] Nature of Theory

Liberty theory argues that the ownership of private property is necessary for democratic self-government.[24] As it developed before the American Revolution, this approach posited that property rights provided citizens with the economic security that allowed independent political judgment. Citizen C1, owning 1,000 acres of land, could support his family by farming

---

[23] Richard A. Posner, Economic Analysis of Law 13 (3d ed. 1986).

[24] *See generally* Gregory S. Alexander, *Time and Property in the American Republican Legal Culture*, 66 N.Y.U. L. Rev. 273 (1991); William H. Simon, *Social-Republican Property*, 38 UCLA L. Rev. 1335 (1991).

his own land, without any external assistance. He was accordingly free to serve the common good through voting, political discussion, holding office, and so forth. In contrast, landless citizen C2 would be dependent on the good will of others for sustenance, somewhat like the feudal serf; C2 was thus subject to manipulation, bribery, or other economic pressure. If offered a bribe to vote for a particular candidate, for example, C2 might well prefer his private self-interest over the common good.

For this reason, Thomas Jefferson advocated the distribution of federally-owned public lands to landless citizens.[25] Jefferson envisioned a nation of yeoman farmers, virtuous and independent enough to pursue the public good. His dreams contributed to the generous federal land distribution policies of the eighteenth and nineteenth centuries—notably the Homestead Act of 1862—by which most of the lands now comprising the United States were transferred into private ownership.[26]

[B] Critique of Theory

The influence of liberty theory waned during the nineteenth century in the face of changing economic, political, and social conditions. Modern scholars are skeptical of the original assumption that property ownership is essential to political freedom. Developments over the last 40 years—notably the civil rights movement—demonstrate that even our poorest citizens have the political courage to fight for the common good. Moreover, even assuming that economic security is vital for political independence, today most citizens derive that security not from "property" in the traditional sense, but rather from wages earned through relatively secure employment.

Further, taken to its logical conclusion, liberty theory seems to support a redistribution of property from the rich to the poor. If property exists only to ensure democratic government, then each citizen must be allocated a share of society's wealth.[27] Yet the Takings Clause of the Fifth Amendment—included in the Constitution partly in response to Madison's concerns about potential wealth redistribution (*see* § 39.02[B])—bars this outcome.

§ 2.07 Personhood Theory

[A] Nature of Theory

Personhood theory justifies private property as essential to the full development of the individual. Under this approach, certain things—for

---

25 *See* Stanley N. Katz, *Thomas Jefferson and the Right to Property in Revolutionary America*, 19 J.L. & Econ. 467 (1976).

26 *Cf.* Joy v. Daniels, 479 F.2d 1236 (4th Cir. 1973) (holding tenant in quasi-public housing had property right to continue occupancy there even after termination of lease absent good cause for eviction).

27 *Cf.* Frank I. Michelman, *Property as a Constitutional Right*, 38 Wash. & Lee L. Rev. 1097 (1981); Charles A. Reich, *The New Property*, 73 Yale L.J. 733 (1964).

example, a wedding ring—are seen as so closely connected to a person's emotional and psychological well-being that they virtually become part of that person.[28] Thus, a person should have broad property rights over such things.

Over two centuries ago, the German philosopher Georg Hegel argued that a "person has as his substantive end the right of putting his will into any and every thing and thereby making it his."[29] More recently, Margaret Radin addressed the same theme; she observed that most people "possess certain objects they feel are almost part of themselves," objects that are "closely bound up with personhood because they are part of the way we constitute ourselves as continuing personal entities in the world."[30] In short, people define their selves through objects. The emotional and psychological link between a person and certain "things"—for example, a love letter or a family home—is so great, Radin suggests, that a person should be able to control the thing through enhanced property rights.

[B] Critique of Theory

Personhood theory might be classified as a variant on utilitarian theory. It seeks to maximize utility by protecting a person's emotional or psychological happiness. Yet, at best, it explains the existence of private property rights only in those "things" seen as central to personhood. It does not seek to justify the existence of what Radin terms "fungible property," that is, rights in money, stocks, bonds, commercial real estate, and other "things" that are less connected to personhood.

Like traditional utilitarian theory, the personhood approach also offers little guidance on the allocation or definition of property rights. Radin argues that when a property right is personal, a prima facie case exists that it should be protected to some extent against conflicting fungible property rights held by others. To what extent? Suppose landlord A leases one of the apartments in his 10-unit building to tenant B on a month-to-month basis. Two years later, A seeks to evict B in order to sell the land to a computer manufacturing company, which will build a factory on the site and provide jobs for 400 neighborhood residents. Assuming the apartment unit is "personhood" property, is B entitled to reside there for as long as she pays rent and otherwise performs the lease terms? In other words, will B's personhood interest override A's "fungible" interest?

---

[28] *Cf.* Joseph W. Singer, *The Reliance Interest in Property*, 40 Stan. L. Rev. 614 (1988) (stressing the importance of individual reliance as a basis for recognizing property rights).

[29] Georg W. F. Hegel, The Philosophy of Right 23 (T. Knox ed., 1952) (1821).

[30] Margaret J. Radin, *Property and Personhood*, 34 Stan. L. Rev. 957, 959 (1982).

Chapter 3

PROPERTY RIGHTS IN WILD ANIMALS

SYNOPSIS

§ 3.01   The Origin of Property Rights

Property courses often begin with a surprising topic—ownership of wild animals. In a sense, the topic seems almost irrelevant. Modern disputes about who owns a particular squirrel or fish, for example, are uncommon. And it is simply too expensive to litigate the rare dispute that does arise. So why study the topic?

The law governing ownership of wild animals helps answer a key question—how do property rights originate?[1] Today, virtually everything around us is owned by someone. But because wild animals in nature are considered unowned, they occupy a unique niche in property law. The legal principles governing acquisition of title to wild animals shed light on the policies that influenced the development of American property law. More

---

[1] *See generally* Richard A. Epstein, *Possession as the Root of Title*, 13 Ga. L. Rev. 1221 (1979); Carol M. Rose, *Possession as the Origin of Property*, 52 U. Chi. L. Rev. 73 (1985).

directly, the principles governing ownership of wild animals were ultimately extended by analogy to the ownership of other resources, including water, oil, and natural gas (*see* Chapter 31).

§ 3.02 The Capture Rule in General

[A] Basic Rule

As a general principle, no one owns wild animals—in Latin, *ferea naturae*—in their natural habitat.[2] Under the common law "capture rule," property rights in wild birds, fish, and other animals are obtained only through physical possession. The first person to capture or kill a wild animal acquires title to it.[3] For example, suppose that F finds and pursues a deer, only to have it escape; F has no rights to the deer. If G now traps the deer in a net, he "owns" the deer. But even G's ownership rights are limited. If the deer escapes from the net, G loses his rights and another hunter may acquire title through capture.

Understandably, this rule does not apply to domesticated or tame animals (*domitae naturae*). Suppose that F's cow strays onto G's land, where G captures it. Because the cow is considered a domestic animal, the capture is irrelevant. The rules concerning domestic animals are grounded in policies quite different from those relevant to wild animals. F still owns the cow, absent adverse possession by G.[4]

[B] *Pierson v. Post*

[1] Facts

The landmark case illustrating the capture rule—and much more—is *Pierson v. Post*.[5] It is still celebrated as one of the most famous decisions in American law. The facts of the case are deceptively simple. One day in the early 1800s, Post was hunting in the New York wilderness with his dogs. On a patch of "unpossessed" land, he found and pursued a fox. Pierson, fully aware that Post was chasing the fox, killed it himself to prevent Post from catching it. Although not clear from the case, this incident sparked or worsened a feud between the Post and Pierson families. The ensuing litigation was more about offended honor than the monetary value of the fox carcass.

Post sued Pierson for the value of the fox, claiming trespass on the case. Post won and Pierson appealed to the New York Supreme Court. Both

---

[2] Douglas v. Seacoast Prods., Inc., 431 U.S. 265, 284 (1977).

[3] *See, e.g.,* Pierson v. Post, 3 Cai. R. 175 (N.Y. 1805); Missouri v. Holland, 252 U.S. 416, 434 (1920) ("Wild birds are not in the possession of anyone; and possession is the beginning of ownership.").

[4] *See, e.g.,* Conti v. ASPCA, 353 N.Y.S.2d 288 (City Civ. Ct. 1974) (owner still held title to trained parrot after its escape, because parrot was a domesticated animal).

[5] 3 Cai. R. 175 (N.Y. 1805).

Post vs. Pierson (probable capture standard) (actual capture standard)

parties agreed that property rights in wild animals were obtained only by "occupancy," that is, by first possession. Thus, as the court phrased it, the issue was "what acts amount to occupancy" of a wild animal?[6] Pierson maintained that only killing or other *actual capture* of the animal constituted possession. Post argued for what might be called a *probable capture* standard: a pursuing hunter with a reasonable chance of success has sufficient "possession" to create ownership. No prior English or American decision had addressed the issue.

[2] Majority Opinion *(went w/ actual capture standard in favor of Pierson.)*

The majority adopted the actual capture test in a somewhat mechanical opinion. Writing for the court, Justice Tompkins examined ancient treatises on Roman, European, and English law to locate an applicable rule. Finding that these authorities uniformly endorsed the actual capture standard, he concluded that the fox "became the property of Pierson, who intercepted and killed him."[7] To a lesser degree, Tompkins also relied on public policy factors. He suggested that the actual capture standard rewarded successful hunters, ensured certainty in property rights, and minimized quarrels.

[3] Dissent *(wanted probable capture so as to eliminate foxes)*

In his sometimes facetious dissent, Justice Livingston criticized the majority's blind application of ancient rules to the fundamentally different conditions prevailing in the United States: "[I]f men themselves change with the times, why should not laws also undergo an alteration?"[8] He observed that the fox was a "noxious beast," akin to a pirate, that caused damage to farmers. Viewing the law as an instrument of social change, he argued that the court should select the standard that provided "the greatest possible encouragement"[9] for the destruction of foxes. He reasoned that the better rule required only continued pursuit together with a "reasonable prospect . . . of taking" the fox (i.e., a probable capture standard).

[4] *Pierson* in Context

Pierson is important at several levels. It established the actual capture rule as the American standard for acquiring title to wild animals. As a prominent decision in a legal system with little case law, it also provided a bridge for extending the capture rule by analogy to other natural resources.[10] More fundamentally, *Pierson* symbolizes the struggle between two theories of jurisprudence—formalism and instrumentalism. The majority opinion reflects the older, formalistic approach to judging; the judge mechanically derives the appropriate rule from existing authorities,

---

[6] Pierson v. Post, 3 Cai. R. 175, 177 (N.Y. 1805).

[7] Pierson v. Post, 3 Cai. R. 175, 178 (N.Y. 1805).

[8] Pierson v. Post, 3 Cai. R. 175, 181 (N.Y. 1805) (Livingston, J., dissenting).

[9] Pierson v. Post, 3 Cai. R. 175, 180 (N.Y. 1805) (Livingston, J., dissenting).

[10] *See, e.g.,* Hammonds v. Central Kentucky Natural Gas Co., 75 S.W.2d 204 (Ky. Ct. App. 1934); Elliff v. Texon Drilling Co., 210 S.W.2d 558 (Tex. 1948).

however remote. The dissent represents the then-emerging view of the American judiciary that the law should serve as an instrument of social change. The dissent's insistence that law must "change with the times" still resonates today.

[C] Defining "Capture"

[1] The Actual Capture Standard

Pierson recognizes that a hunter who actually kills or captures a wild animal, and immediately takes possession of it, acquires title. It also suggests that the mortal wounding of an animal "by one not abandoning his pursuit"[11] may constitute capture. Later decisions have somewhat relaxed the *Pierson* standard. For example, if F sets a trap that catches a wild muskrat in his absence, the muskrat still belongs to F. Similarly, if G begins chopping down a tree housing a wild bee hive, he has acquired sufficient title to the hive to prevail over H, a stranger who drives him away.[12]

[2] Two Fish Stories

A well-known pair of decisions involving ownership of fish illustrates the capture standard. In *State v. Shaw*,[13] a long funnel-shaped net directed fish into a holding net about 28 feet square; the narrow end of the funnel entering the holding net was less than 3 feet wide. Although fish could both enter and exit the holding net through this opening, under normal conditions few, if any, fish actually escaped. Finding that it was "practically . . . impossible" for fish to escape, the *Shaw* court held that the net owners had captured the fish.

Conversely, in *Young v. Hichens*,[14] the court held that plaintiff did not possess a school of fish that was virtually surrounded by his net. The lengthy net was drawn around the fish in almost a complete circle, leaving a gap of only about 40 feet. Before plaintiff's employees could close the gap with a second net, defendant's boat sailed through the gap into the circle and captured the fish. Lord Denman concluded that even though it was "almost certain" plaintiff *would have* obtained possession but for defendant's intervention, it was "quite certain" that plaintiff *did not* actually obtain possession.[15]

Both decisions turn on the likelihood that fish might escape from the net. In *Shaw,* the facts established that fish rarely escaped from the trap. But the net circle in *Young* was incomplete, creating a small risk that fish could escape before the gap was plugged.

---

[11] Pierson v. Post, 3 Cai. R. 175, 178 (N.Y. 1805).

[12] Adams v. Burton, 43 Vt. 36 (1870).

[13] 65 N.E. 875 (Ohio 1902).

[14] 115 Eng. Rep. 228 (Q.B. 1844).

[15] Young v. Hichens, 115 Eng. Rep. 228, 230 (Q.B. 1844).

[3] Role of Custom

Custom may also help define capture, as reflected in a series of decisions concerning property rights in whales, notably *Ghen v. Rich*.[16] There, Ghen shot a bomb lance into a fin-back whale off the Cape Cod coast, killing it instantly. The whale immediately sank, presumably to the sea bottom. Three days later a beachcomber found the carcass stranded on a beach 17 miles away, and sold it to Rich who extracted its valuable oil. *Pierson* might suggest that Ghen had no rights in the whale. Although he killed it, he failed to take immediate possession of the carcass and in fact left the area, thus arguably "abandoning his pursuit."

The custom in the Cape Cod region, however, was that a whale killed in this manner belonged to the fisherman, while the finder of the carcass received a small reward for his help. Judicial acceptance of this custom was critical to the survival of the local whaling industry.[17] The court awarded the value of the whale to Ghen under the custom, noting that if a fisherman does "all that it is possible to do to make the animal his own, that would seem to be sufficient."

[D] Release or Escape After Capture

In general, ownership rights end when a wild animal escapes or is released into the wild.[18] Suppose K captures a wild rabbit; one week later, the rabbit escapes back into the forest, where it is instantly killed by L. L owns the rabbit. Once K's qualified property rights lapsed, the rabbit was again unowned and subject to capture by another. If the law were otherwise, hunters like L might be deterred from hunting at all. How could they distinguish an "owned" rabbit from an "unowned" rabbit?

But suppose a wild animal escapes onto land that is far from its native habitat. If O's giraffe flees into the Colorado mountains, for example, P cannot acquire title by capturing it. The exotic nature of the animal effectively puts P on notice that it is already owned by another.[19] O's investment in the giraffe is protected.

An interesting problem arises when a captured wild animal is tamed and then released back into nature. For example, suppose that K allows his captured rabbit to roam the forest during the daytime, knowing that it will faithfully return each night. L cannot shoot the rabbit. A captured animal that has the habit of occasionally returning to its captor (*animus revertendi*)

---

[16] 8 F. 159 (D. Mass. 1881).

[17] *See* Robert C. Ellickson, *A Hypothesis of Wealth-Maximizing Norms: Evidence from the Whaling Industry*, 5 J.L. Econ. & Org. 83 (1989).

[18] *See, e.g., In re* Oriental Republic Uruguay, 821 F. Supp. 950 (D. Del. 1993) (owner who released wild ducks into marshland could not obtain damages when they were later killed by an oil spill); Mullett v. Bradley, 53 N.Y.S. 781 (App. Div. 1898) (owner's rights ended when undomesticated sea lion escaped).

[19] The classic illustration is E.A. Stephens & Co. v. Albers, 256 P. 15 (Colo. 1927), where the court held that the escape of a non-native silver fox in Colorado did not end the owner's rights.

is still considered property. In this instance, the law's interest in motivating owners to tame wild animals for productive use outweighs the concern for certainty.

§ 3.03 Evaluation of the Capture Rule

[A] Rationale for the Rule

American law has traditionally viewed wild animals in nature as either dangerous or worthless. The primary policy underlying the capture rule is to encourage the killing or capture of wild animals for the benefit of society, consistent with utilitarian theory. For example, if H is aware that he can acquire title to any deer he can kill, he has an incentive to invest his money and time in deer hunting. As a result, society will obtain additional venison and skins. But if title could be obtained merely by chasing deer, H might not be willing to devote his time to hunting. Any wild deer H finds might be already owned by someone else who had pursued it unsuccessfully. If H killed the deer, the prior pursuer might claim it as his property. Thus, the capture rule rewards success, not mere effort.

In addition, the rule creates a clear, "bright line" standard for determining ownership which provides several benefits. Possession provides notice to the world of the owner's rights. Consider the example of property rights in a wild duck. Under the capture rule, it is simple to determine who has possession of—and thus owns—the duck. Accordingly, the rule tends to avoid disagreement and thus prevent quarrels which may erupt into violence. Further, from the perspective of law and economics, the rule is an efficient mechanism for resolving any disputes that do occur; ownership can be established with minimal expenditure of society's resources (e.g., attorneys fees, judicial time). Finally, the certainty of title stemming from the rule encourages an owner to invest time and energy in making the captured animal more useful to society (e.g., training a wild parrot to perform tricks).

[B] Criticism of the Rule

Today the capture rule is uniformly condemned by legal scholars for the very reason that once supported it: the rule encourages the destruction of wild animals. It is seen as an anachronism from the era when the United States was a vast wilderness.[20]

Advocates of the law and economics movement observe that the capture rule results in over-intensive hunting.[21] Because no person can control hunting by others, each person has an incentive to protect his or her individual self interest by killing animals as rapidly as possible. As Harold

---

[20] *See generally* John G. Sprankling, *The Antiwilderness Bias in American Property Law,* 63 U. Chi. L. Rev. 519 (1996).

[21] A related law and economics theme is that the capture rule encourages overinvestment, which wastes societal resources.

Demsetz observed in a landmark article, "it is in no person's interest to invest in increasing or maintaining the stock of game."[22] Under such a system, conservation of wild animals for prudent, long-term human use is impossible.

Environmental law scholars view the capture rule—and the ethic it reflects—as an unmitigated tragedy that devastates natural ecosystems.[23] They observe that the modern capture rule threatens the continued existence of uncounted species, just as unregulated nineteenth-century hunting eradicated the American passenger pigeon.

§ 3.04 Rights of Landowners

[A] No Ownership of Animals

Does the owner of land also own the wild animals on the land? Under the English doctrine of *ratione soli,* wild animals were considered to be in the "constructive possession" of the landowner. But the landowner did not acquire title to such an animal until and unless it was captured, whether by the landowner or by someone else. Thus, if poacher P killed a deer on O's land, O now owned the deer.[24] Yet attempts to transplant the *ratione soli* principle to the United States were ineffective. Early American courts viewed the rule as both undemocratic and inconsistent with the policies underlying the capture rule.

Accordingly, in the United States a landowner generally owns no rights in wild animals on the land. For example, in one case[25] a group of Wyoming landowners asserted that the state's refusal to grant them licenses to hunt elk and other wild animals on their own lands was an unconstitutional "taking" of property. The court reasoned, however, that mere ownership of the animals' habitat did not confer property rights in the animals: "[N]o one 'owns' wild animals, in the proprietary sense, when they are in their

---

[22] Harold Demsetz, *Toward a Theory of Property Rights,* 57 Am. Econ. Rev. 347, 351 (1967); *see also* Garrett Hardin, *The Tragedy of the Commons,* 162 Sci. 1243 (1968); Richard A. Posner, Economic Analysis of Law 36 (4th ed. 1992); Richard J. Agnello & Lawrence P. Donnelley, *Property Rights and Efficiency in the Oyster Industry,* 18 J.L. & Econ. 521 (1975).

[23] *See, e.g.,* Lynton K. Caldwell, *Land and the Law: Problems in Legal Philosophy,* 1986 U. Ill. L. Rev. 319; Eric T. Freyfogle, *Ownership and Ecology,* 43 Case W. Res. L. Rev. 1269 (1993); Carol M. Rose, *Given-ness and Gift: Property and the Quest for Environmental Ethics,* 24 Envtl. L. 1 (1994); Steven M. Wise, *The Legal Thinghood of Nonhuman Animals,* 23 B.C. Envtl. Aff. L. Rev. 471 (1996).

[24] Keeble v. Hickeringill, 103 Eng. Rep. 1127 (Q.B. 1707), was cited by the *Pierson* court as illustrating the *ratione soli* principle. In *Keeble,* the plaintiff owned a "decoy pond"—a pond specially constructed to lure wild ducks so that plaintiff could capture them. On three occasions, the defendant discharged guns near the pond for the purpose of frightening away the wild ducks that had landed there. Yet the *ratione soli* principle does not satisfactorily explain why plaintiff prevailed in his later damages action. Although the ducks were in his constructive possession, he had not yet captured them and thus did not own them. *Keeble* is best explained under tort law, not property law: defendant maliciously interfered with the plaintiff's business.

[25] Clajon Prod. Corp. v. Petera, 854 F. Supp. 843 (D. Wyo. 1994).

natural habitat unless and until the animals are reduced to something akin to possession."[26] The relatively narrow exception to this rule involves immobile animals such as clams, mussels, and oysters. Permanently affixed to the land (much like trees and other vegetation), these immobile animals are usually deemed the property of the landowner.[27]

[B] Right to Exclude Hunters

The trespass doctrine provides an American landowner with protection similar to *ratione soli*. A landowner may bar hunters and others from trespassing on his land.[28] As a practical matter, to the extent consistent with hunting laws, this doctrine gives the landowner the exclusive opportunity to capture wild animals on the property.[29]

§ 3.05 Regulation by Government

[A] State and Federal Restrictions

Modern game laws and other government restrictions have substantially eroded—though not erased—the capture rule. States routinely regulate hunting and fishing within their borders to protect wild animals on behalf of the public in general. For example, under the police power, states may ban hunting altogether, or regulate its frequency, duration, and manner.[30] Federal law similarly protects wild animals to some extent; for example, the Endangered Species Act[31] prohibits the killing of certain protected species. When hunting is permitted, government regulations are usually consistent with the capture rule—the first successful captor acquires title to the wild animal.

[B] No Proprietary Ownership of Animals

Despite the breadth of these regulatory powers, state and federal governments do not "own" wild animals in a proprietary sense. During the nineteenth century, states uniformly declared ownership over the wild animals within their territories, usually by enacting statutes to the effect that the state held wildlife in trust for its residents. A substantial body of case law embraced this state ownership theory. With its 1977 decision

---

[26] Clajon Prod. Corp. v. Petera, 854 F. Supp. 843, 852 (D. Wyo. 1994).

[27] *See, e.g.,* McKee v. Gratz, 260 U.S. 127, 135 (1922) (mussels in stream bed with "a practically fixed habitat" were held possessed by landowner).

[28] In order to bar hunting on undeveloped land, statutes in most states require that the owner "post" appropriate "no hunting" signs on his land. The lack of such posting may imply permission from the owner to use his land for hunting. McKee v. Gratz, 260 U.S. 127 (1922).

[29] Some decisions suggest that a landowner is entitled to wild animals killed on his land by a trespasser. *See, e.g.,* State v. Repp, 73 N.W. 829 (Iowa 1898).

[30] *See generally* George C. Coggins & Robert L. Glicksman, Public Natural Resources Law § 18.01 *et seq.* (1990).

[31] 16 U.S.C. §§ 1531–1544.

in *Douglas v. Seacoast Products, Inc.*,[32] however, the Supreme Court rejected this claim as "no more than a 19th-century legal fiction."[33] Writing for the Court, Justice Brennan restated the capture rule: "Neither the States nor the Federal Government, any more than a hopeful fisherman or hunter, has title to these creatures until they are reduced to possession by skillful capture."[34] Thus, most courts hold that government entities are not liable for damage to private property caused by wild animals.[35] For example, if wild turkeys eat O's corn crop, O cannot obtain damages from the government.

[32] 431 U.S. 265 (1977).

[33] Douglas v. Seacoast Products, Inc., 431 U.S. 265, 284 (1977).

[34] *See also* Hughes v. Oklahoma, 441 U.S. 322 (1979) (an Oklahoma statute barring transportation of lawfully-caught wild minnows out of state violated the Commerce Clause; because Oklahoma had never owned the minnows, it did not have a special right to the property within its jurisdiction).

[35] *See, e.g.,* Sickman v. United States, 184 F.2d 616 (7th Cir. 1950), *cert. denied,* 341 U.S. 939 (1951) (geese); Moerman v. State, 21 Cal. Rptr. 2d 329 (Ct. App. 1993) (elk).

Chapter 4

FINDERS OF PERSONAL PROPERTY

SYNOPSIS

§ 4.01 Finders As Owners

Suppose that F finds a gold ring. Does she own it? Over the centuries, finders' claims to jewelry, currency, gold, shipwrecks, ancient artifacts, and other valuable personal property have produced an immense (and somewhat inconsistent) body of case law in England and the United States. As one court noted, "[t]hese cases . . . have long been the delight of professors and text writers, whose task it often is to attempt to reconcile the irreconcilable."[1] Many states have simplified the area through legislation.

This chapter explores the law concerning finders of personal property.[2] American decisions often recite pithy formulas intended to summarize this law, e.g., "A finder of property acquires no rights in mislaid property, is entitled to possession of lost property against everyone except the true owner, and is entitled to keep abandoned property."[3] Yet the law is substantially more complicated than these efforts suggest, turning on artificial distinctions and muddled policy rationales that have long been criticized by legal scholars.

The discussion below is organized around three factors that dominate the judicial analysis of finders' rights:

(1)   the presumed intent of the original owner, reflected in four categories of "found" property;

(2)   the identity of the competing claimants; and

(3)   the location where the item is found.

§ 4.02   Who Is a "Finder"?

[A]   Definition of "Finder"

The first person to take possession of lost or unclaimed property is a "finder." Possession requires both (1) an intent to control the property and (2) an act of control.[4] In cases involving portable personal property, application of this standard is simple. For example, if F picks up a lost gold ring and places it in her pocket, she has exhibited both intent and actual control and is deemed a finder. Conversely, if F merely sees the ring and passes by, she has not become a finder. As in the case of wild animals (*see* § 3.02), discovery alone is insufficient to confer title.

[B]   Finders of Nonportable Objects

The application of this standard to nonportable personal property is more complex, as illustrated by a series of decisions involving finders of sunken ships. What constitutes "possession" of a shipwreck? In *Eads v. Brazelton*,[5]

---

[1] Hibbert v. McKiernan, 2 K.B. 142, 149 (1948).

[2] *See generally* Edward R. Cohen, *The Finders Cases Revisited*, 48 Tex. L. Rev. 1001 (1970); Richard H. Helmholz, *Wrongful Possession of Chattels: Hornbook Law and Case Law*, 80 Nw. U. L. Rev. 1221 (1986); Richard H. Helmholz, *Equitable Division and the Law of Finders*, 52 Fordham L. Rev. 313 (1983); David Reisman, Jr., *Possession and the Law of Finders*, 52 Harv. L. Rev. 1105 (1939).

[3] Michael v. First Chicago Corp., 487 N.E.2d 403, 409 (Ill. App. Ct. 1985).

[4] *See, e.g.,* Powell v. Four Thousand Six Hundred Dollars ($4,600.00) U.S. Currency, 904 P.2d 153 (Okla. Ct. App. 1995) (motorists who spotted currency scattered across road, notified sheriff, and then returned to area to prevent third parties from recovering it had "possession," even though—at the sheriff's request—they refrained from touching the money).

[5] 22 Ark. 499 (1861).

for example, plaintiff located a wreck under the Mississippi River, attached buoys to the wreck, and blazed shoreline trees to mark its location; although plaintiff intended to return to recover the wreck's cargo, he failed to do so. About eight months later, defendants found the wreck, and began removing the cargo. In the ensuing litigation, the court concluded that plaintiff had never acquired possession of the wreck. Certainly, the buoys and blazes indicated plaintiff's intent to take possession. But they were not accompanied by any acts of control, such as "placing his boat over the wreck, with the means to raise its valuables and with persistent efforts directed to raising [the cargo]."[6]

§ 4.03   Categories of "Found" Property

[A]   Four Traditional Categories

The common law recognizes three basic categories of "found" property:

    (1)   abandoned property;

    (2)   lost property; and

    (3)   mislaid property.[7]

English law traditionally included a fourth category—known as "treasure trove"—which most jurisdictions have not adopted. "Found" property is assigned to one of these categories according to the presumed intent of its original owner. The rights of a finder and other claimants turn in part on how the property is categorized. Broadly speaking, if a "found" object does not fit within these categories, it is not subject to the law of finders.[8]

[B]   Definitions

[1]   Abandoned Property

Property is *abandoned* when the owner intentionally and voluntarily relinquishes all right, title, and interest in it.[9] For example, if O deposits a broken toy on the sidewalk so that it can be removed by garbage collectors, he has abandoned it. On the other hand, if O merely leaves the toy on the sidewalk overnight, intending to reclaim it in the morning, no abandonment has occurred. Thus, one illustrative decision held that the owners of "up to one billion dollars in gold" sunk in an 1857 shipwreck did not abandon their rights merely by failing to recover the gold.[10]

---

[6] Eads v. Brazelton, 22 Ark. 499, 512 (1861).

[7] *See, e.g.,* Benjamin v. Lindner Aviation, Inc., 534 N.W.2d 400 (Iowa 1995).

[8] *See, e.g.,* Goodard v. Winchell, 52 N.W. 1124 (Iowa 1892) (meteorite that was found by defendant after it "fell from the heavens" onto plaintiff's land was not subject to the law of finders).

[9] Ritz v. Selma United Methodist Church, 467 N.W.2d 266 (Iowa 1991).

[10] Columbus-America Discovery Group v. Atlantic Mutual Ins. Co., 974 F.2d 450 (4th Cir. 1992).

[2] Lost Property

Property is deemed *lost* when the owner unintentionally and involuntarily parts with it through neglect or inadvertence and does not know where it is.[11] Thus, if O's lucky silver dollar accidentally falls through a hole in his pocket onto the ground, it is considered lost.

[3] Mislaid Property

Property is considered *mislaid* when the owner voluntarily puts it in a particular place, intending to retain ownership, but then fails to reclaim it or forgets where it is.[12] For example, if O momentarily places his wallet on a store counter while paying for a purchase, and then leaves the store without it, the wallet is mislaid.

[4] Treasure Trove

Finally, *treasure trove* consists of gold, silver, currency, or the like intentionally concealed by an unknown owner for safekeeping in a secret location (e.g., buried underground or hidden in a house) in the distant past. As one court described the concept, "it carries with it the thought of antiquity."[13]

[C] Criticism of the Category System

In theory, the category system helps implement the wishes of the object's original owner. For example, if O intends to relinquish his rights in a toy left on the sidewalk (abandoned property), the law will vest title in finder F. Conversely, if O left the toy there temporarily, intending to reclaim it (mislaid property), F has no rights. In practice, however, proving the owner's intent is difficult in most cases, because the typical dispute is between a finder and the landowner or other occupant of the land where the object is found; the object's true owner is usually unknown and thus not a party to the dispute. The court must attempt to discern the missing owner's intent by the only evidence available—the nature of the item and the circumstances under which it was found.

Commentators generally agree that this approach is an unreliable method for determining intent.[14] For example, suppose that F finds a gold ring near a gopher hole in City's park. If F and City dispute ownership, their respective rights pivot on how the ring is classified. What was the intent of the original ring owner? Four conclusions are possible:

(1) the ring accidentally fell off the owner's finger (lost property);

(2) fearing an accidental loss, the owner placed the ring there for temporary storage but then forgot it (mislaid property);

---

[11] Benjamin v. Lindner Aviation, Inc., 534 N.W.2d 400 (Iowa 1995).

[12] Ritz v. Selma United Methodist Church, 467 N.W.2d 266, 269 (Iowa 1991).

[13] Ritz v. Selma United Methodist Church, 467 N.W.2d 266, 269 (Iowa 1991).

[14] *See, e.g.*, Richard H. Helmholz, *Equitable Division and the Law of Finders*, 52 Fordham L. Rev. 313, 316 (1983).

(3)   following a failed marriage, the heartbroken owner dropped the ring on the ground and walked away (abandoned property); or

(4)   the owner hid the ring underground years ago for safekeeping (treasure trove).[15]

§ 4.04 Rights of Finder Against Original Owner

[A] Rights to Lost or Mislaid Property

Suppose that O's valuable watch accidentally slips off his wrist while he is strolling down the sidewalk and is later found by F. O demands its return; F refuses. Who owns the lost watch? The childhood refrain "finders keepers, losers weepers" suggests that F now owns it. Yet—as between these two claimants—all American courts would conclude that O is still the owner. F holds the watch as a mere bailee for O's benefit (*see* § 7.03). Thus, F may be liable to O for damages if he delivers the watch to another person who falsely claims to be the true owner.[16]

As a general rule, an owner retains title to lost or mislaid property found by another.[17] In *Ganter v. Kapiloff*,[18] for example, the defendant discovered rare stamps worth over $150,000 in a dresser he had purchased at a used furniture store for $30. When the true owners of the stamps brought a replevin action to regain possession, the defendant finder claimed ownership under a "finders keepers" theory. Affirming summary judgment in favor of the true owners, the court dismissed the finder's theory as a mixture of " 'hot air,' folklore, and wishful thinking."[19]

The policy rationale for preferring the true owner over the finder is straightforward. Under utilitarian theory, the law seeks to encourage the productive labor that an owner undertakes to acquire property, not to reward a finder's minimal effort. Similarly, the rule provides an owner with the security of title that is necessary to use property for maximum social benefit, rather than keeping it hidden and idle for fear of loss. In addition, a contrary rule would tend to encourage theft because a thief might obtain title by pretending to be a finder.

---

[15] For example, in Hendle v. Stevens, 586 N.E.2d 826 (Ill. App. Ct. 1992), a child playing with friends on undeveloped land kicked a small mound of earth near two animal burrows, revealing $6,061 in currency fastened together with string or a rubber band; the court was unable to conclude from this evidence whether the currency was lost, mislaid, or abandoned.

[16] *See, e.g.,* Fisher v. Klingenberger, 576 N.Y.S.2d 476 (City Ct. 1991) (finder's agent who mistakenly delivered found tools to third party claiming ownership, but failed to check claimant's identity, held liable in damages to true owner).

[17] In other words, "owners keepers, finders weepers"! However, for example, a finder may acquire title to personal property through adverse possession. *See* § 7.02.

[18] 516 A.2d 611 (Md. Ct. Spec. App. 1986).

[19] Ganter v. Kapiloff, 516 A.2d 611, 612 (Md. Ct. Spec. App. 1986).

[B] Rights to Abandoned Property

In contrast, the first person who takes possession of abandoned property acquires title that is valid against the world, including the prior owner.[20] For example, suppose that O suddenly throws his watch on the sidewalk and hurries away shouting: "I never want to see that watch again." This conduct would be considered abandonment; it demonstrates that O has voluntarily and intentionally relinquished his title to the watch. When bystander F picks up the watch and places it in his pocket, his possession confers title. O has no legal right to demand its return.

When an owner releases his or her rights through abandonment, the property becomes unowned. Much like an escaped wild animal (*see* § 3.02[D]), the property is now available for "capture" by another who will place it in productive use, thereby benefiting society in general.

§ 4.05 Rights of Finder Against Third Persons Generally

[A] "Finders Keepers"?

Decisions often proclaim that the finder of lost property obtains title sufficient to prevail over every other claimant except the true owner. This is a vast oversimplification. The owner or occupant of land where the object is found often receives title (*see* § 4.06), despite the finder's claim. Setting aside this special situation, however, as a general rule the finder acquires title to lost property that is superior to the claims of all other persons except the owner.[21] Thus, broadly speaking, if F finds O's lost watch, F obtains title to the watch that prevails over the claims of everyone *except O*. Thus, if F now loses the watch and it is found by X, F can recover the watch from X.

[B] *Armory v. Delamirie*

The leading case illustrating this rule is *Armory v. Delamirie*.[22] Plaintiff, a poor "chimney sweeper's boy," found a "jewel" in 1722 and took it to the defendant's goldsmith shop for identification. After an apprentice removed the "stones" from their socket, the defendant refused to return them to the boy. The court concluded that by finding and possessing the jewel the boy had acquired "such a property as will enable him to keep it against all but the rightful owner." The defendant was accordingly held liable in trover[23] for the value of the jewel.

---

[20] *See, e.g.*, Haslem v. Lockwood, 37 Conn. 500 (1871) (manure dropped on public street by passing animals was abandoned property; plaintiff acquired ownership by an act of possession—raking the manure into piles).

[21] Indeed, as a general rule, even one who acquires possession of property through theft acquires title that is superior to that of others except the true owner.

[22] 93 Eng. Rep. 664 (K.B. 1722).

[23] "Trover" is a common law theory to recover damages for interference with personal property that is owned or possessed by another person.

The facts in *Armory* help illustrate the justifications for the general rule preferring the finder over third parties. The rule allows a finder like the sweeper's boy to return a "found" item to productive use, rather than encouraging him to keep it hidden. Moreover, the boy's prior possession is an efficient standard for determining ownership, with minimal expenditure of societal resources. Finally, this result honors the reasonable expectations of the competing parties; the goldsmith is the moral equivalent of a thief.

[C] Relativity of Title

The respective rights of competing claimants in cases like *Armory* illustrate the doctrine of "relativity of title," which extends to both real and personal property. It is a basic precept of American property law that title is relative, not absolute.

Suppose that the jewel in *Armory* was lost by O. As between O and F, the boy finder, the law would hold that O owned the jewel. Yet, as the case demonstrates, as between F and the goldsmith, the court held that F was the owner. *How can O and F both "own" the jewel at the same time?* The answer is found in relativity of title. Depending on the circumstances, the law may choose to recognize different persons as the "owner" of the same property. O is still an "owner." But until O reclaims the ring, the law also recognizes F as an "owner."

§ 4.06 Rights of Finder Against Landowner

[A] The Issue

Suppose F finds a diamond ring on land owned by L. As between F and L, who owns the ring? Most of the complexity (and inconsistency) in the law of finders stems from judicial efforts to resolve this thorny question. Some courts assert that the finder of lost property prevails over all claimants except the object's true owner; under this view, F owns the ring. In practice, however, this approach has been virtually swallowed by a series of exceptions that tend to vest title in the person who owns or occupies the land where the object is found. In short, an American court is more likely to award the ring to L than to F.

[B] Rights to Objects Found on Private Land Generally

[1] Location of Object

In general, objects found either within a house[24] or embedded in the soil on private land[25] are awarded to the landowner, not the finder. For

---

[24] *But see* Hannah v. Peel, 1 K.B. 509 (1945) (under English law, brooch found by lawful occupant of home awarded to finder, rather than to landowner who had never lived in the home).

[25] *See, e.g.,* Favorite v. Miller, 407 A.2d 974 (Conn. 1978) (portion of statue buried in swamp); Allred v. Biegel, 219 S.W.2d 665 (Mo. Ct. App. 1949) (ancient Indian canoe); South Staffordshire Water Co. v. Sharman, 2 Q.B. 44 (1896) (gold rings in mud at bottom of pond).

example, in *Favorite v. Miller*[26] defendant believed that pieces of a 200-year-old lead statue of King George III hacked apart during the chaos of the Revolutionary War might be located on swamp land owned by plaintiff. Without seeking plaintiff's permission, defendant entered the land, used his metal detector to locate a statue fragment buried 10 inches below the soil surface, removed the fragment, and sold it to a museum. Applying the rule for objects "embedded in the earth" and stressing that defendant was a trespasser, the court awarded the fragment to the landowner.

The rationale for this rule is somewhat elusive. Courts often recite that such objects were already in the "constructive possession" of the landowner before the find, but this fiction explains little. Similarly, some courts rely on the distinction between "mislaid" and "lost" property, suggesting that vesting possession in the landowner will facilitate its return to the true owner; yet, as *Favorite* illustrates, the true owner may never return. These cases are better explained by focusing on the reasonable expectations of the parties. Consistent with the traditional rule that title to land carries with it title to everything attached to or under the land, landowners would reasonably expect that they own objects within their house or under their land. In general, persons entering onto the land of another should have no expectation that the law will award them title to objects they find there.

This focus on expectations helps decipher the well-known case of *Hannah v. Peel*.[27] Defendant acquired title to a house in England, but never entered into occupancy. The house was requisitioned by the government for quartering soldiers during World War II. Plaintiff, a soldier stationed at the house, discovered a brooch covered with "cobwebs and dirt" loose in a crevice in his bedroom wall; he turned the brooch over to the police, who delivered it to the defendant landowner. In a remarkably vague opinion, the court ruled for plaintiff.

If the doctrine of constructive possession is to be taken seriously, one might try to explain this outcome by pointing out that the defendant landowner in *Hannah* had never physically occupied the house and thus never held possession. But this explanation cannot suffice. For example, if the brooch had been found by a plumber who entered the house at the landowner's request to fix a leaky pipe, the court would have awarded it to the absentee landowner, not the plumber. The key lies in the expectations of the landowner. Once possession of the house was lawfully transferred to the government, the landowner's expectation of owning objects later found within the house was greatly diminished; after all, an object like the brooch might have been hidden in the crevice by another soldier after the government took possession.

Given the judicial focus on awarding objects found *within a house* or *embedded in the soil* to the landowner, one might expect to encounter a line of authority holding that objects found elsewhere on private land (i.e., *outside on the land surface*) are awarded to the finder. Yet this scenario rarely

---

[26] 407 A.2d 974 (Conn. 1978).

[27] 1 K.B. 509 (1945).

arises; and even when it does, the finder's status may be enough to defeat the claim.

[2] Status of Finder

The status of the finder also plays an important role. For example, the successful plaintiff in *Hannah v. Peel* was a lawful occupant, akin to a tenant, with broad rights to use and enjoy the land. In contrast, if the finder is a mere employee of the landowner (e.g., a gardener) or is present on the land for a special purpose (e.g., to deliver mail), the claim of the landowner normally prevails.

Trespassers pose special problems. Treatises and courts sometimes broadly assert that even the trespassing finder prevails over the landowner. But many courts are concerned about endorsing a rule that would encourage trespass. They hold that a trespassing finder acquires no rights in found objects, unless the trespass is merely trivial or technical.[28] Indeed, Professor R.H. Helmholz concludes that courts routinely rule against the trespassing finder: "[A] trespassing finder can acquire no rights in the fruits of his wrong."[29]

[C] Rights to Treasure Trove

Under English law, neither the finder nor the landowner owned treasure trove; rather, it belonged to the king. American courts uniformly reject the English approach, but differ on what standard should replace it. Some older authorities treat treasure trove like any form of lost property, vesting title in the finder. But modern courts—seeking to deter trespass by would-be finders—increasingly award treasure trove to the landowner, either treating it as an object embedded in the soil[30] or as mislaid property.[31]

[D] Rights to Objects Found in Public Places

A valuable object left in a public place such as a store, bank, or restaurant is usually considered mislaid property and awarded to the owner or occupant of the premises, not the finder.[32] The rule rests on the legal fiction

---

[28] *See, e.g.,* Favorite v. Miller, 407 A.2d 974 (Conn. 1978); Bishop v. Ellsworth, 234 N.E.2d 49, 52 (Ill. App. Ct. 1968).

[29] Richard M. Helmholz, *Wrongful Possession of Chattels: Hornbook Law and Case Law,* 80 Nw. U. L. Rev. 1221, 1231 (1986).

[30] *See, e.g.,* Morgan v. Wiser, 711 S.W.2d 220 (Tenn. Ct. App. 1985) (buried gold coins awarded to landowner, on rationale that "the discouragement of trespassers contributes to a preservation of the peace in the community").

[31] As Professor Helmholz has observed, it "makes little sense to award what may be intentionally buried property to the finder and yet maintain the distinction between lost and mislaid property for the avowed purpose of protecting the true owner." Richard M. Helmholz, *Equitable Division and the Law of Finders,* 52 Fordham L. Rev. 313, 318 n.26 (1983).

[32] *But see* Bridges v. Hawkesworth, 21 L.J.Q.B. 75 (1851) (banknotes in parcel found on floor of shop were not "intentionally deposited" there by owner; they were thus considered "lost" property and awarded to finder, not shopkeeper).

that mislaid property has been entrusted to the custody of the owner or occupant.

In *McAvoy v. Medina*,[33] for example, a customer claimed title to a "pocket-book" containing money that he had discovered on a table in defendant's barbershop. The parties agreed that the true owner was a prior customer who had "voluntarily placed" the pocketbook on the table. The court concluded that it had been mislaid, not lost; thus, arguably it was already in the barber's "constructive possession" before its discovery. The pocketbook was awarded to the barber on the basis that this result would best ensure its return to the true owner. Remembering his loss, the owner would presumably return to the shop and demand his property. As a bailee, the barber was obligated to "use reasonable care for the safe keeping of the same until the owner should call for it."[34]

[E] Ensuring Return to the True Owner?

Are the rules governing the respective rights of the finder and the landowner designed to ensure a "found" object's safe return to its original owner, as the mislaid property cases suggest? This explanation seems to falter somewhat when applied to lost property. For example, the true owner is more likely to return and reclaim property accidentally left on the land surface (recent loss, easy to locate) than property embedded in the soil (old loss, difficult to locate). If so, then a "return to owner" principle would tend to support awarding possession of objects found on the surface to the landowner (as custodian until the owner's probable return), but awarding possession of embedded objects to the finder (because the owner is unlikely to return). But the law is just the reverse; objects embedded in the land belong to the landowner, while courts continue to imply that objects found on the land surface should be awarded to the finder.

§ 4.07 Statutes Defining Rights of Finders

In many states, statutes governing rights in "found" property supersede the confusing common law. These statutes commonly adopt two simplifying reforms. First, either expressly or implicitly, most of these statutes abolish the traditional distinctions between lost property, mislaid property, and treasure trove; some extend to abandoned property as well. Second, they replace the tangled common law doctrines governing the respective rights of landowners and finders with a clear rule: *the finder wins.*[35]

---

[33] 93 Mass. (11 Allen) 548 (1866).

[34] McAvoy v. Medina, 93 Mass. (11 Allen) 548, 549 (1866).

[35] Hurley v. City of Niagara Falls, 289 N.Y.S.2d 889 (App. Div. 1968), illustrates the operation of such a statute. Defendants hired plaintiff, a contractor, to build a recreation room in the basement of their home; while trying to remove a pipe, plaintiff found $4,990 in currency hidden behind a sink partition. Under the common law approach, a court would presumably have awarded the money to the landowners as mislaid property, while stressing that finder was on the premises only for a limited purpose. Relying on the New York statute, however, the court vested title in the finder as "the person who first took possession of the money."

These statutes usually follow the same basic pattern. Typically, the finder must turn over the "found" item to the local police department or other law enforcement agency, often with a written description of the circumstances of the find.[36] Either the finder or the local authority may be required to advertise the find. The true owner of the item may recover it within an established time period (generally ranging from 90 days to one year); some jurisdictions require that the owner pay a reward to the finder. If no one claims the item within the required time period, it becomes the property of the finder.

The most remarkable feature of this statutory approach is its departure from the common law tendency to award "found" property to the landowner or occupant. The approach is designed to maximize the likelihood of returning property to its true owner by giving the finder an incentive to turn it over to local authorities.

§ 4.08 Special Issue: Native American Artifacts

Suppose amateur archaeologist F accidentally discovers Native American pottery and other artifacts that were ceremonially buried with deceased tribal members in the distant past. Do the standard rules governing finders apply to this situation? The artifacts cannot be deemed lost property because they were intentionally buried in a particular location, not lost involuntarily through neglect. Similarly, a burial is not necessarily an abandonment. In one recent decision, for example, a Louisiana court held that ancient Indians did not abandon jewelry, pottery, and other items buried with the dead because they did not intend to relinquish all ownership rights; thus, the tribe still held title to these objects over the claim of the archaeologist who "found" them.[37]

One solution to such ownership disputes is to view the entire tribe as the original owner of buried Native American cultural artifacts, not particular deceased tribal members or their descendants.[38] Under this approach, newly discovered artifacts always have a current owner who can assert prior ownership rights and thus supersede the finder's claim. The Native American Graves Protection and Repatriation Act of 1990[39] adopts this analysis for Native American cultural items found at burial sites on lands owned or controlled by the federal government.[40] Such cultural items belong to the tribe as a whole where either (1) the items have ongoing

---

[36] See, e.g., Cal. Civ. Code §§ 2080–2080.2; N.Y. Pers. Prop. Law §§ 251–257.

[37] Charrier v. Bell, 496 So. 2d 601 (La. Ct. App. 1986).

[38] See, e.g., Charrier v. Bell, 496 So. 2d 601 (La. Ct. App. 1986) (awarding ownership of buried artifacts to tribe); cf. Chilkat Indian Village IRA v. Johnson, No. 90-01 (Chilkat Tribal Court, Nov. 3, 1993) (enforcing tribal ordinance that requires approval by the tribal council before "traditional Indian artifacts" and similar objects can be sold or removed from the village).

[39] 25 U.S.C. §§ 3001–3012. See also David G. Bercaw, Comment, Requiem for Indiana Jones: Federal Law, Native Americans, and the Treasure Hunters, 30 Tulsa L.J. 213 (1994).

[40] But see Wana the Bear v. Community Constr., Inc., 180 Cal. Rptr. 423 (Ct. App. 1982) (Native American burial ground on land under development not covered by California statute that prohibits the disinterment of human remains in public cemeteries).

religious, historical, or cultural importance to the tribe or (2) the lineal descendants of the dead cannot be identified.

Chapter 5

GIFTS OF PERSONAL PROPERTY

§ 5.01   Gifts in Context

The right to transfer property by gift is uniformly recognized as a fundamental right.[1] From the utilitarian perspective, legal recognition of a gift provides mutual benefits to both parties, thus optimizing social happiness; the donor derives altruistic satisfaction, while the donee receives the value of the item.[2]

This chapter examines gifts of personal property—both tangible personal property such as artwork, jewelry, and antiques, and intangible personal property such as copyrights and choses in action—made during the donor's lifetime; Chapter 28 examines the transfer of property at death. The rules governing gifts—once remarkably rigid—have been in transition for several decades, torn between the conflicting policies of certainty and donor

---

[1] *See* Carol M. Rose, *Giving, Trading, Thieving, and Trusting: How and Why Gifts Become Exchanges, and (More Importantly) Vice Versa,* 44 U. Fla. L. Rev. 295 (1992).

[2] *See generally* Richard A. Posner, *Gratuitous Promises in Economics and Law,* 6 J. Legal Stud. 411 (1977); Steven Shavell, *An Economic Analysis of Altruism and Deferred Gifts,* 20 J. Legal Stud. 401 (1991).

autonomy. Concerned that judicial enforcement of the traditional "delivery" requirement may frustrate a donor's intent, modern courts increasingly ignore or circumvent this standard. Under this emerging view, clear evidence of the donor's intent obviates the need for formal delivery.

§ 5.02 What Is a Gift?

A gift is a voluntary, immediate transfer of property without consideration from one person (the *donor*) to another person (the *donee*). Consider a hypothetical party celebrating B's birthday. Each party guest (donor) voluntarily presents a colorfully-wrapped package (gift) to B (donee), without receiving payment or other consideration; the transfer of ownership rights in the package to B is immediately effective. A transfer that takes effect in the future is not a valid gift; for example, a transfer effective upon the donor's death is governed by the law of wills, not the law of gifts.

The law recognizes two categories of gifts. The *gift inter vivos* is an ordinary gift made by one living person to another, as in the birthday example above; once made, it is irrevocable. The *gift causa mortis* is also a present gift between living persons, but one made in anticipation of the donor's imminent death; thus, if the donor survives the anticipated peril, the gift is revoked.

One scholar suggests that the boundaries between gift and two other types of property transfers—larceny (involuntary transfer without consideration) and sale (voluntary transfer for consideration)—may overlap.[3] If elderly R "gives" a valuable jewel to her young friend E, was the jewel given in exchange for the services that E has provided in caring for R, and hence more like a sale than a true gift? Or was this transfer the product of undue influence that E exerted over R, and thus like larceny?

§ 5.03 Gifts Inter Vivos

[A] General Rule

There are three requirements for a valid gift inter vivos:

(1) *intent* (the donor must intend to make an immediate gift);

(2) *delivery* (the donor must deliver the gift); and

(3) *acceptance* (the donee must accept the gift).

In practice, intent is usually the most important element. The requirement of delivery is controversial; while still significant, it is being increasingly eroded by courts concerned that it may frustrate the donor's intent. Finally, acceptance of a valuable gift is usually presumed and thus rarely becomes an issue.

---

[3] Carol M. Rose, *Giving, Trading, Thieving, and Trusting: How and Why Gifts Become Exchanges, and (More Importantly) Vice Versa*, 44 U. Fla. L. Rev. 295, 303 (1992).

[B] Intent

The donor must intend to make an immediate transfer of ownership to the donee. The statements and actions of the donor usually provide the best evidence of intent. In *Gruen v. Gruen*,[4] for example, the donor's intent to transfer rights in a painting to his son as a birthday present was established in part by a letter that expressly stated: "I therefore wish to give you as a present the oil painting by Gustav Klimpt of Schloss Kammer."[5] Alternatively, intent may be inferred from the donor's act of giving possession of the item to the donee, the nature and value of the item, the relationship between the parties, and other circumstances.

If the donor intends the "gift" to take effect in the future (e.g., upon the donor's death), it is a nullity that confers no rights on the donee. Suppose R plans to produce a musical comedy, and tells E: "After my musical is produced, I'll give you 5% of my share of the profits." Because R intends a future transfer only, no gift results. But the requisite intent for a present transfer will be found if R states instead: "I give you 5% of my share of the future profits from the musical."[6]

Under the same logic, if a condition precedent must be fulfilled before a gift becomes effective, no immediate transfer has occurred and thus no gift will be found. But an invalid conditional gift may be enforceable as a valid contract. If R tells E, "when you bring me that photograph, I'll give you that rare stamp we discussed," R's statement could be seen as an offer for a unilateral contract, which E can accept through the act of bringing R the photograph. However, a gift that takes immediate effect may be made subject to a condition subsequent (e.g., "I give you this rare stamp, but if you don't visit me next week the gift will be void.").

Conditional gift issues arise most commonly in the special context of engagement presents. Suppose that M gives W an engagement ring, the engagement is later broken, and W refuses to return the ring. Who is entitled to the ring? Courts uniformly agree that an engagement ring is given subject to the implied condition subsequent of future marriage. Most courts still cling to the traditional view that the donor can recover the ring only if the engagement were dissolved by agreement or if the donee were at fault in breaking the engagement.[7] But a growing minority of courts follows a "no fault" approach to the issue, always allowing the donor to recover the ring.[8] Three rationales underpin this modern view: (1) because

---

[4] 496 N.E.2d 869 (N.Y. 1986).

[5] Gruen v. Gruen, 496 N.E.2d 869, 871 (N.Y. 1986).

[6] Speelman v. Pascal, 178 N.E.2d 723 (N.Y. 1961) (letter demonstrated donor's intent to make a present gift of 5% of future profits from the musical "My Fair Lady"); *see also* Gruen v. Gruen, 496 N.E.2d 869 (N.Y. 1986) (father intended the immediate transfer of a remainder interest in a painting to his son, even though the father retained a life estate).

[7] Vann v. Vehrs, 633 N.E.2d 102 (Ill. App. Ct. 1994) (agreement); Coconis v. Christakis, 435 N.E.2d 100 (Ohio County Ct. 1981) (recognizing rule, but finding no fault by donee).

[8] *See, e.g.,* Fierro v. Hoel, 465 N.W.2d 669 (Iowa Ct. App. 1990); Aronow v. Silver, 538 A.2d 851 (N.J. Super. Ct. Ch. Div. 1987) (condemning majority rule as "sexist and archaic"); Gaden v. Gaden, 272 N.E.2d 471 (N.Y. 1971).

the engagement period is intended to allow a couple to test the permanency of their mutual feelings, the donor should not be penalized for avoiding an unhappy marriage; (2) it is extraordinarily difficult to assess fault in this setting; and (3) just as fault has become irrelevant to divorce proceedings, it should be irrelevant to breaking an engagement.

[C] Delivery

[1] The Requirement of Delivery

The second traditional requirement for the validity of a gift is delivery.[9] The United States inherited the English common law rule that words alone were insufficient to effect a gift of personal property. As a leading English decision explained: "[I]n order to transfer property by gift . . . there must be an actual delivery of the thing to the donee. Here the gift is merely verbal."[10] Under this early view, "delivery" meant physically handing over the chattel to the donee. Over time, three additional types of delivery have been accepted: constructive delivery, symbolic delivery, and delivery through a third person.[11]

Why require delivery at all? Its genesis is found in the feudal mind set which inextricably linked title and possession; title to a chattel could be transferred only by transferring possession. The requirement survived the centuries because—as Philip Mechem summarized in a famous article[12]—it arguably serves three policy goals. First, the donee's possession helps to demonstrate the donor's intent to make a gift. Second, the delivery requirement warns the donor about the legal significance of the act, preventing impulsive conduct that the donor might later regret. Finally, the donee's possession provides prima facie evidence that a gift was made.

English law recognized one exception to the delivery requirement: if title to a chattel was transferred by a *deed of gift,* manual delivery was unnecessary. In this context, a deed of gift meant a formal written instrument that:

(1)   contained language reflecting the donor's intent to make a gift;

(2)   described the subject matter of the gift;

(3)   identified the donee; and

(4)   was "sealed" (that is, bore a wax impression of the donor's personal seal).

---

[9] *See, e.g.,* Irvin v. Jones, 832 S.W.2d 827, 827 (Ark. 1992) (finding no gift of certificates of deposit where the alleged donee had "retained sole possession of the certificates at all times and . . . never delivered them to appellants"); *see also* Irons v. Smallpiece, 106 Eng. Rep. 467 (R.B. 1819) (the landmark English decision imposing the delivery requirement).

[10] Irons v. Smallpiece, 106 Eng. Rep. 467, 468 (R.B. 1819).

[11] There are, of course, various exceptions to the delivery requirement (e.g., property already in the possession of the donee need not be delivered).

[12] Philip Mechem, *The Requirement of Delivery of Gifts in Chattels and of Choses in Action Evidenced by Commercial Instruments,* 21 Ill. L. Rev. 341 (1926).

The American reaction to this exception was mixed; some states followed the English approach, while others permitted the use of a deed of gift only if manual delivery was impractical. Since then, virtually all states have eliminated the traditional distinction between sealed and unsealed instruments. In light of this, would an unsealed, informal writing such as a letter obviate the need for manual delivery even if such delivery could easily be made? Certainly the main current of American law is flowing in this direction, though with a semantic twist. Rather than relying on deed of gift terminology, modern courts refer to the use of a writing as *symbolic delivery*.

[2] Methods of Delivery

[a] Manual Delivery

Traditionally, "delivery" connoted *manual delivery*, sometimes called *actual delivery*. In order to deliver an item of personal property, the donor physically transferred possession of the item to the donee. If the item was small and portable—like a ring—the donor usually handed it directly to the donee. For example, R, a guest at E's birthday party, delivers her wrapped present by placing it into E's outstretched hands. Manual delivery is the main method of delivery today for items of tangible personal property.

The limitations of manual delivery, however, are readily apparent. Some items of tangible personal property are too cumbersome and bulky to be handed to a donee (e.g., a large marble statue), while others may not be readily available (e.g., located in a distant state or pledged to a creditor). And manual delivery is impracticable when the donee receives less than complete title to the item (e.g., a one-tenth interest or a remainder interest). Finally, intangible personal property—by definition—cannot be manually delivered.

[b] Constructive Delivery

All jurisdictions permit *constructive delivery* when manual delivery is impracticable or impossible. Under the conventional view, constructive delivery occurs when the donor physically transfers to the donee the means of obtaining access to and control of the property, most commonly by handing over a key. For example, in *Newman v. Bost*[13] the donor effected constructive delivery of a bureau and other household furniture by handing the donee the keys that unlocked these items. Similarly, buried coins are constructively delivered when the donor informs the donee of their location, while range cattle are deemed delivered when the donor rebrands them with the donee's brand.

Suppose that R receives a check, endorses it in favor of her apartment roommate E, places it on the kitchen table during E's absence, and then abandons the apartment. Is this constructive delivery of the check to E? Because manual delivery of the check was possible, the traditional answer

---

[13] 29 S.E. 848 (N.C. 1898).

is "no." In the landmark decision of *Scherer v. Hyland*,[14] however, the New Jersey Supreme Court dramatically expanded the definition of constructive delivery and found a valid gift on these facts. As the *Scherer* court explained, this approach "would find a constructive delivery adequate to support the gift when the evidence of donative intent is concrete and undisputed, there is every indication that the donor intended to make a present transfer . . . and when the steps taken by the donor . . . must have been deemed by the donor as sufficient to pass the donor's interest."[15]

[c] Symbolic Delivery

Most jurisdictions also permit *symbolic delivery* when manual delivery is difficult. Under this approach, an object that represents or symbolizes the gift is physically handed to the donee. Although in theory virtually any symbol might suffice (e.g., a Rolls-Royce hood ornament might symbolize the car), in practice this type of delivery is almost always effected by giving the donee some type of writing. In *Speelman v. Pascal*,[16] for example, the donor's letter giving the donee a share in future profits from the musical "My Fair Lady" was held an effective symbolic delivery.

The modern trend is to recognize an informal writing as symbolic delivery even when manual delivery is possible,[17] as evidenced by the well-known New York decision of *In re Cohn*.[18] There, the donor signed and dated a memorandum that recited "I give this day to my wife . . . five hundred shares of American Sumatra Tobacco Company common stock," but failed to hand over the stock certificates to her.[19] As the dissent protested, "there was no physical or other impossibility to the actual delivery of the stock."[20] Reasoning that the delivery requirement was intended to guard against fraud, mistake, or undue influence—and finding none—the majority found the memorandum to be effective symbolic delivery.[21]

[d] Delivery to Third Person

Delivery of a gift may be effected through a third party intermediary. Suppose that R manually delivers a gold watch to T, with instructions that T in turn deliver it to E; T then hands over the watch to E. This is a complete gift. But which transfer constituted delivery: R's transfer to T or T's transfer to E? The answer turns on T's status. If T was an agent of R (and thus

---

[14] 380 A.2d 698 (N.J. 1977).

[15] Scherer v. Hyland, 380 A.2d 698, 701 (N.J. 1977).

[16] 178 N.E.2d 723 (N.Y. 1961).

[17] While most states reach this result through case law, others have adopted statutes that provide that symbolic delivery is always permitted. *See, e.g.*, Cal. Civ. Code § 1147.

[18] 176 N.Y.S. 225 (App. Div. 1919).

[19] *In re* Cohn, 176 N.Y.S. 225, 225 (App. Div. 1919).

[20] *In re* Cohn, 176 N.Y.S. 225, 232 (App. Div. 1919) (Page, J. dissenting).

[21] Gruen v. Gruen, 496 N.E.2d 869, 874 (N.Y. 1986) (letter from donor to donee constituted valid symbolic delivery of vested remainder in painting; physical delivery of painting to donee not required because "it would be illogical for the law to require the donor to part with possession of the painting when that is exactly what he intends to retain").

subject to R's control), then the gift was not complete until T handed the watch to E. Conversely, if T was an agent of E, the gift was complete when T obtained possession.

What if R changes her mind while T still possesses the watch and demands its return? The central question is again T's status. If T is R's agent, then the gift has never been completed and R may revoke it; but if T is E's agent, the gift is irrevocable.

It is well-settled law that the status of the third party intermediary turns on the donor's intent. Thus, the donor's express statement of intent at the time of the transfer to the intermediary is usually controlling (e.g., suppose R handed the watch to T, saying: "Hold this watch as trustee for E.") All too commonly, however, the donor's intent is unclear and must be judicially determined from the circumstances of the case.

A donor may use third party delivery to create a valid conditional gift. For example, assume that R hands the watch to T, saying: "Deliver this watch to E when he passes the state bar examination and hold it as his trustee until then." Because T is E's agent, the transfer to T constituted immediate delivery of the watch, completing the gift. But E is not entitled to possession of the watch until he passes the state bar examination.

[3] Demise of the Delivery Requirement

Enforcement of the delivery requirement may defeat the donor's intent. Suppose that R tells her friend E, in the presence of ten witnesses: "I hereby give you the Rembrandt painting hanging on my living room wall; I wouldn't want my greedy nephew N to get it." E replies: "Thanks, I accept." Ignorant of the law, R fails to hand over the painting to E and dies the next day, leaving no will. Under the rules of intestate succession, all the property R owned at her death is inherited by N, her only living relative. Many courts would invalidate R's attempted gift on these facts due to lack of delivery and award the painting to N, even though R's contrary intent was clear.

The delivery requirement is slowly disappearing. Over 70 years ago, a farsighted legal scholar criticized delivery as a feudal anachronism and predicted its demise.[22] Since then, judicial expansion of constructive and symbolic delivery has eroded the traditional rule.[23] Thus, although the 1992 Restatement (Second) of Property: Donative Transfers formally asserts that delivery is required,[24] it concludes in a comment: "It is here suggested that the law should recognize, to the extent it has not already done so, that a completed gift of personal property may be accomplished

---

[22] Harlan F. Stone, *Delivery of Gifts in Personal Property*, 20 Colum. L. Rev. 196 (1920); *see also* Chad A. McGowan, *Special Delivery: Does the Postman Have to Ring at All—The Current State of the Delivery Requirement for Valid Gifts*, 31 Real Prop. Prob. & Tr. J. 357 (1996); Patrick J. Rohan, *The Continuing Question of Delivery in the Law of Gifts*, 38 Ind. L.J. 1 (1962).

[23] *See, e.g., In re* Drewett, 34 B.R. 316 (E.D. Pa. 1983) (finding a valid gift of diamond ring, even though donor continued to wear ring and never executed any writing).

[24] Restatement (Second) of Property: Donative Transfers § 31.1 (1992).

without a delivery by proof of the donor's manifested intention to make a gift."[25]

The law of gifts will remain unsettled while the delivery requirement lingers. In the interim, courts will continue the trend of subordinating delivery to intent. When evidence of donor intent is compelling, many courts will ignore delivery; if evidence of donor intent is weak, however, courts may rely on a lack of delivery to invalidate a gift.

[D] Acceptance

The third element for a valid gift—acceptance by the donee—is easily established in almost all instances. Even absent any affirmative statements or conduct by the donee indicating acceptance, courts universally presume acceptance of a gift that is unconditional and valuable to the donee.[26] Thus, if R intends to give an antique vase to E and delivers it to him, E's acceptance of the vase is presumed. The gift will fail only if E expressly refuses to accept it.[27]

§ 5.04 Gifts Causa Mortis

[A] General Rule

A gift causa mortis may be defined as a gift of personal property in anticipation of the donor's imminently approaching death.[28] Unlike a gift inter vivos, a gift causa mortis is revocable. The donor may revoke such a gift at any time before his death. In addition, if the donor does not die from the anticipated peril, the gift is automatically revoked as a matter of law.[29] A valid gift causa mortis requires all three gift inter vivos elements (intent, delivery, and acceptance) plus a fourth element: the donor's expectation of imminent death.

The gift causa mortis is best viewed as an emergency substitute for a will. Suppose that D collapses and is rushed to the hospital by her niece N, where the doctor advises D that her death is only minutes away; there is insufficient time for D to prepare and execute a will. D privately hands her diamond ring to N, saying: "I give you this ring." Under these circumstances, it makes sense to enforce D's gift.[30]

---

[25] Restatement (Second) of Property: Donative Transfers § 31.1 com. k (1992).

[26] Scherer v. Hyland, 380 A.2d 698 (N.J. 1977); Restatement (Second) of Property: Donative Transfers § 31.1 cmt. l.

[27] Why might a donee like E refuse a valuable gift? Possible reasons include: (1) to avoid adverse tax consequences; (2) to thwart creditors; and (3) to avoid moral obligation to the donor.

[28] Coley v. Walker, 680 So. 2d 352 (Ala. Civ. App. 1996).

[29] Most American courts view the gift causa mortis as a gift subject to a condition subsequent that the donor die from the anticipated peril.

[30] See, e.g., Newman v. Bost, 29 S.E. 848 (N.C. 1898) (former manager of opera house, on deathbed and stricken with paralysis, made gift causa mortis to housekeeper).

[B]　Donor's Anticipation of Imminent Death

Although the classic gift causa mortis occurs at the donor's deathbed, the doctrine also extends to other situations where death may be weeks or even months away. Most gift causa mortis decisions involve a donor confronting the substantial certainty of death in the near future from a particular illness or affliction, such as a cardiac patient about to undergo a risky operation. A gift made by a donor contemplating suicide may also meet this standard.[31] A donor's natural apprehension of death in the distant future, however, does not support a gift causa mortis.

[C]　Criticism of Doctrine

The typical gift causa mortis lacks the formal safeguards that the law requires for a valid will (e.g., a writing, disinterested witnesses). Thus, courts have traditionally viewed the doctrine with disfavor (and even hostility), fearing that it encourages fraud, perjury, and undue influence.

For example, assume that after A dies, his brother B begins wearing A's valuable ring; when questioned, B asserts that A gave him the ring when they were alone in A's hospital room a few moments before A died. How can a court now determine if A actually intended a gift? In a case involving a claimed gift inter vivos, the donor is usually alive to testify concerning intent; if the donor is dead, evidence that the donee held long-term possession of the item without any objection allows an inference of donor intent. In contrast, here both A's testimony and evidence of A's acquiescence in B's possession of the ring are unavailable. B is the only witness to the alleged gift, raising concerns that his story is a tangle of lies. Or was the gift the product of undue influence that B exerted while A was in a highly vulnerable condition?

§ 5.05　Restrictions on Donor's Autonomy

Suppose that R exchanges some of his property for a stack of $100 bills and begins handing the bills to strangers passing by on the sidewalk. Assuming that the elements of intent, delivery, and acceptance are all present, the legal system will not question R's actions. The competing jurisprudential theories that underpin American property law agree that R has the right to give his property away to anyone he chooses.[32]

Statutory exceptions have somewhat eroded this general rule in extreme situations. For example, elderly parent P cannot freely give away assets to her child C in order to impoverish herself and thus qualify for federal Medicaid benefits.[33] Similarly, most states restrict lifetime gifts by one

---

[31] *See, e.g.,* Scherer v. Hyland, 380 A.2d 698 (N.J. 1977). In some states, however, a gift in contemplation of suicide is void as against public policy.

[32] Moreover, public policy encourages charitable donations, as evidenced by the charitable deduction available under the Internal Revenue Code.

[33] 42 U.S.C. § 1396p(c); *see also* Jan Ellen Rein, *Misinformation and Self-Deception in Recent Long-Term Care Policy Trends,* 12 J.L. & Pol. 195, 219–227 (1996).

spouse that are intended to nullify the property rights that the law accords to a surviving spouse (*see* § 11.03[D]).

Chapter 6

PROPERTY RIGHTS IN HUMAN BODIES

SYNOPSIS

§ 6.01 The Controversy

A wishes to sell her kidney to B. C and D, a married couple in the middle of divorce proceedings dispute "custody" of a frozen embryo. E and F, another couple, contract for G to bear the E-F child. All three situations raise the question: can property rights exist in human bodies or body parts?

The United States seemingly answered this question with a firm "no" when the Thirteenth Amendment[1] abolished slavery in 1865 for moral, religious, and philosophical reasons.[2] In the post-Civil War era, one human being could no longer own another. The same rationale suggested that one person could not own *part* of another, but the issue rarely surfaced. To the contrary, human hair and blood—once removed from the body—were routinely treated as property and regularly sold. While the law did not allow people to sell themselves into slavery,[3] it permitted them to sell certain replenishable body parts.

But extraordinary leaps in medical technology in recent decades have reopened the issue. When organ transplants became feasible, for example,

---

[1] U.S. Const. amend. XIII, § 1.

[2] Prior to the Thirteenth Amendment, the American legal system viewed slaves as property. *See, e.g.,* Dred Scott v. Sandford, 60 U.S. (19 How.) 393 (1857) (observing that the "right of property in a slave is distinctly and expressly affirmed in the Constitution"); State v. Mann, 13 N.C. (2 Dev.) 263 (1829) (dismissing criminal indictment based on shooting a slave, because the "power of the master must be absolute to render the submission of the slave perfect"); *see also* Cheryl I. Harris, *Whiteness as Property,* 106 Harv. L. Rev. 1709 (1993); Aviam Soifer, *Status, Contract, and Promises Unkept,* 96 Yale L.J. 1916 (1987).

[3] For a discussion of the economic justifications of the prohibition on self-enslavement, see Anthony T. Kronman & Richard A. Posner, The Economics of Contract Law 253–260 (1979).

the need for human organs skyrocketed. Similarly, the development of in vitro fertilization and other reproductive technologies designed to help infertile couples have created a growing demand for human genetic materials (ova and sperm), embryos, and surrogacy arrangements. The use of body parts (and bodies) for these purposes raises troubling questions that our legal system has only begun to address.

Two principal issues emerge: (1) who has decision-making authority over the human body or body parts? and (2) to what extent can government restrict or condition this authority?[4] Property law may help answer these questions, either directly or by analogy.

§ 6.02 Rights in Body Parts Generally

[A] The Role of Property Law

The law generally acknowledges the authority of all persons to control the destiny of their body parts. Replenishable body parts such as hair, blood, and bone marrow present the clearest illustration.[5] For example, A may cut her hair and then (a) transfer it (e.g., as a token given to a loved one), (b) use it (e.g., in making a wig), and (c) exclude others from its possession (e.g., by keeping it in a drawer).

The same principle applies, though with somewhat less force, to nonreplenishible body parts. Suppose B has two kidneys, while his brother C needs a kidney transplant to survive. The law would allow B to donate one kidney to C, and indeed society would applaud this decision. It saves C's life, while allowing B's own life to continue unimpaired. B thus has the authority to decide the future of his kidney; he can transfer it to C, or continue to use it himself and exclude others from its use. Yet B's decision-making authority is limited by law. Presumably B could not donate both of his kidneys to C, since this would be the equivalent of suicide. Moreover, while B may undeniably donate a kidney to C or anyone else,[6] he probably cannot sell his kidney for transplantation. The National Organ Transplant Act prohibits the sale in interstate commerce of any human organ "for use in human transplantation."[7] There is, however, a flourishing international market in body organs.

How should we characterize the respective rights of A and B? From the perspective of property law, their rights closely resemble the traditional property rights that comprise the "bundle of rights," including the rights

---

[4] *Cf.* John A. Robertson, *In the Beginning: The Legal Status of Early Embryos,* 76 Va. L. Rev. 437 (1990).

[5] *See, e.g.,* United States v. Garber, 607 F.2d 92, 97 (5th Cir. 1979) (noting that blood plasma, like any other salable part of the human body, is tangible property).

[6] The Uniform Anatomical Gift Act, 8A U.L.A. 19, which authorizes the gift of body organs, has been adopted in all fifty states.

[7] 42 U.S.C. § 274e.

to transfer, use, and exclude.[8] Yet many courts have proven reluctant to adopt a pure property law approach to the question.

[B] *Moore v. Regents of the University of California*

[1] The Issue

The most prominent decision in the area—*Moore v. Regents of the University of California*[9] —involved extreme facts. While treating plaintiff Moore for leukemia, physicians at the UCLA Medical Center discovered that some of his white blood cells ("T-lymphocytes") possessed an unusual quality: they overproduced certain proteins ("lymphokines") that regulate the body's immune system. This quality would make it easier for researchers to identify the genetic material that produced a particular lymphokine; large quantities of the lymphokine might then be manufactured and then used to help in the treatment of disease. Moore's cells were not genetically unique; rather, this overproduction was apparently caused by his leukemia. In short, Moore's cells had potential commercial value; yet no one informed Moore of this.

Removal of Moore's spleen was necessary to save his life. Moore consented to the operation, but was unaware that the physicians had retained his spleen (and other bodily fluids and tissues extracted during follow-up visits) for research purposes. Eventually, the physicians were able to use Moore's cells as raw material to produce a "cell line" (i.e., a "culture capable of reproducing indefinitely"); they received a patent on the cell line.

Moore sued the Regents (as owners of the Medical Center), the physicians, and others for damages, on various causes of action including conversion. To sustain a cause of action in conversion, a plaintiff must show wrongful interference with ownership or possession of personal property. Defendants demurred to Moore's complaint, asserting that he could not meet this standard as a matter of law. Moore, on the other hand, alleged that he continued to own the cells after they were removed from his body. The issue ultimately reached the California Supreme Court.

[2] The Decision

The majority held that Moore retained no ownership interest in the cells after removal, and thus could not sue on a conversion theory. Interestingly, the court seemed to assume that Moore had decision-making control over his cells before removal, consistent with the general principle that a person has broad autonomy over his body. While sometimes seeming to follow a

---

[8] *See, e.g.,* Brotherton v. Cleveland, 923 F.2d 477 (6th Cir. 1991) (holding that wife has a "property interest" in deceased husband's corneas).

[9] 793 P.2d 479 (Cal. 1990). For case notes on *Moore*, see Laura M. Ivey, Comment, Moore v. Regents of the Univ. of California: *Insufficient Protection of Patients' Rights in the Biotechnological Market*, 25 Ga. L. Rev. 489 (1991); Jennifer Lavoie, Note, *Ownership of Human Tissue: Life After* Moore v. Regents of the Univ. of Cal., 75 Va. L. Rev. 1363 (1989); Stephen A. Mortinger, Comment, *Spleen for Sale:* Moore v. Regents of the Univ. of California *and the Right to Sell Parts of Your Body,* 51 Ohio St. L.J. 499 (1990).

property rights analysis, however, the court was unwilling to characterize the removed cells as Moore's property for two main reasons.[10]

First, it concluded that a California statute governing the disposition of human body parts following scientific use drastically preempted the patient's control over removed cells. "[T]he statute eliminates so many of the rights ordinarily attached to property that one cannot simply assume that what is left amounts to 'property' or 'ownership' for purposes of conversion law."[11] The implication here is that Moore effectively "owned" his cells until removal, when his property rights were eliminated by a specialized statute.

Second, striking a utilitarian theme, the court reasoned that recognizing conversion liability would harm society by discouraging vital medical research. Fearing strict liability in conversion—regardless of all good faith—scientists and biotechnology companies would be reluctant to conduct such research because "clear title" to human cells could never be established. The key to understanding the majority opinion is the unusual context from which the case arises: the surgical removal of body parts ultimately used for medical research.

The decision sparked a mixture of concurring and dissenting opinions. For example, one concurring justice raised moral and ethical objections to any sale of the "sacred" human body. Adopting a formalistic "bundle of rights" analogy, a dissenting justice argued that Moore at least retained one property right despite the statute—the *"right to do with his own tissue whatever the defendants did with it."*[12]

[3] Reflections on *Moore*

Moore provoked a firestorm of critical legal commentary, more directed toward the rationale than the result.[13] If Moore owned his cells before their removal, which the majority seems to assume, it is not at all clear how he lost ownership. More to the point, how did the physicians and other defendants *obtain* ownership? It is tempting to dismiss the decision as counterintuitive: Moore cannot own his cells, but the defendants can own them?

Much of the difficulty stems from the court's reluctance to concede that property rights can exist in human cells. Certainly, once the cells were removed from Moore's body, they were a type of property for some purposes. If a thief had stolen the cells from the Medical Center laboratory, he could have been sued in conversion by the Regents and criminally prosecuted for larceny; and if the laboratory had burned down, the fire insurance policy would logically cover the loss of the cells.

---

[10] Even if Moore owned the cells, the majority asserted, he did not own the patented cell line; the cell line was a distinctly new type of property—the product of creative effort applied to fungible raw materials.

[11] Moore v. Regents of the Univ. of Cal., 793 P.2d 479, 492 (Cal. 1990).

[12] Moore v. Regents of the Univ. of Cal., 793 P.2d 479, 510 (Cal. 1990) (Mosk, J., dissenting).

[13] *See, e.g.,* E. Richard Gold, Body Parts: Property Rights and the Ownership of Human Biological Materials (1996); Stephen R. Munzer, *An Uneasy Case Against Property Rights in Body Parts, in* Property Rights (Ellen F. Paul *et al.*, eds. 1994).

On the other hand, if the cells were deemed property, then the majority must explain why Moore lost ownership. Some observers question the court's interpretation that the statute eliminated *all* of Moore's rights. The statute on its face is merely a health and safety measure, intended to protect the public from disease caused by the improper disposal of human tissue, not a statute intended to abridge property rights. Moreover, the statute merely restricts the final disposal of such tissue "following conclusion of scientific use." It does not purport to restrict the use or transferability of human tissue *before* or *during* scientific use. Thus, as a dissenting justice points out, Moore logically retained at least one stick in the metaphorical bundle: the control of the future scientific use of his cells. But why didn't Moore lose his rights by abandoning the cells? This finding was not available to the court due to the procedural posture of the case. The case arose on demurrer, where all facts alleged in the complaint are presumed to be true; Moore (unsurprisingly) did not plead facts establishing an abandonment.

The court might have reached the same result by conceding that Moore owned the cells, but that his property rights did not include the right to sell them or otherwise profit from their commercial use. Just as body organs cannot be sold for transplantation purposes, many other forms of property are "market-inalienable." They can be given away, but for reasons of public policy they cannot be sold.[14]

[C] Should Human Organs Be Sold?

The demand for human organs in the United States far outstrips the supply. Thousands of patients who desperately need kidney transplants, for example, will not receive them due to a chronic shortage of available kidneys. Many law and economics scholars argue that the federal ban on interstate sale of human organs should be lifted. The central core of this view is that a free market serves as an efficient system for allocating all types of scarce resources. From this perspective, the shortage of organs is easily explained: potential providers have no incentive to supply organs because they cannot receive payment. Allowing the sale of human organs would solve this problem. Suppose A wishes to sell her extra kidney to B, who will die without an immediate transplant. Permitting the proposed A-B sale maximizes the utility of each; B continues living and A receives payment. Under this view, a free market in human organs maximizes overall social utility.

The sale of human organs is extraordinarily controversial, raising some of the same concerns surrounding legal restraints on abortion or prostitution.[15] Personhood theory would object to organ sales as incompatible with human dignity. The same moral, religious, and philosophical reasons that supported the abolition of slavery suggest that the human body—and

---

[14] Margaret J. Radin, *Market-Inalienability,* 100 Harv. L. Rev. 1849 (1987).

[15] *See generally* Henry B. Hansmann, *The Economics and Ethics of Markets for Human Organs,* 14 J. Health Pol. Pol'y & L. 57 (1989).

therefore body organs—cannot be treated as mere property, but must be seen as legally unique. Under this view, the state should intervene to protect A and other potential sellers, even over their objections. Conversely, sales of body organs would be consistent with libertarian theory: if A and B, as competent adults, voluntarily agree to a kidney sale, the state should not restrict their autonomy. Even as all persons have the fundamental right to control their own bodies, this approach holds that all persons have complete decision-making authority over parts of their bodies, without any need for the societal paternalism inherent in the current ban.

Some utilitarian theorists argue that the social cost of organ sales may outweigh any benefit. Under the current regime, organs are available for transplantation at no cost. Permitting organ sales would tend to increase the overall cost of medical care. Moreover, a market approach would exacerbate the division between rich and poor. Today the patient's wealth is largely irrelevant in the allocation of available organs. But under a market approach, organs would tend to be allocated to the rich (who could, by definition, afford to pay) rather than to the poor (who could not). For the same reason, the poor (who need the money) would be more likely suppliers of organs than the rich (who do not), presenting concerns of human exploitation.

A final concern is the social burden caused by unregulated organ sales. Suppose A sells not only her kidney, but—in a future era of transplantation technology—also sells her corneas, arms, legs, and other nonrenewable body parts. If A is both immobile and blind, society will presumably bear the cost of her lifetime care. In this sense, organ sales pose the same dangers that justify regulation of gambling, drug use, and other self-destructive activities.

§ 6.03 Rights in Human Eggs, Sperm, and Embryos

[A] Genetic Material As Property

The issue of rights in human eggs, sperm, and embryos is particularly complex because such genetic materials have the potential to create a human being. Of course, the likelihood that any particular egg, sperm, or even embryo will successfully develop into a living person is extremely slim. Commentators have advanced three alternative legal approaches to genetic material: (a) treating it as "property," (b) treating it as "life," and (c) according it a middle status of "special respect."[16]

Genetic materials are effectively treated as property for most routine purposes, although the property label is infrequently used. Since human beings "own" their own bodies, the argument goes, they similarly "own"

---

[16] See, e.g., Patricia A. Martin & Martin L. Lagod, The Human Preembryo, the Progenitors, and the State: Toward a Dynamic Theory of Status, Rights, and Research Policy, 5 High Tech. L.J. 257 (1990); John A. Robertson, In the Beginning: The Legal Status of Early Embryos, 76 Va. L. Rev. 437 (1990).

whatever their bodies produce.[17] Thus, for example, the law permits a man to sell his sperm. The legal status of embryos also illustrates the point. Suppose that W and H, a married but infertile couple, contract with an in vitro fertilization clinic to help them produce a child. The clinic will require them to execute advance instructions governing the status of future embryos. Utilizing eggs from W and sperm from H, the clinic creates embryos which are frozen and stored for later implantation in W's uterus. W and H now have decision-making control over the embryos, at least as far as the clinic is concerned, and are thus treated as co-owners. In disputes arising between "parents," on the one hand, and third parties such as clinics or storage facilities, on the other, property law principles provide a tool for resolving disputes.[18]

[B] A Right to Destroy Embryos?

The most challenging legal and ethical issues involve the destruction of embryos. The property law model applies with lesser force in this context. Suppose W and H—due to divorce, death, or financial difficulties—jointly instruct the storage facility to discard (and thus destroy) the embryos. Acknowledging the decision-making authority of W and H as progenitors, courts would enforce this directive.[19] Similarly, where W and H have reached an advance agreement between them concerning the disposition of the embryos, courts would presumably find the contract to be binding.[20]

But suppose W and H never reached an advance agreement; now divorcing, they disagree about the fate of the embryos. In the leading case on point,[21] W sought "custody" of the embryos in order to donate them to an infertile couple, while H (anxious to avoid the financial and psychological burdens of fatherhood) argued that they should be destroyed. The Tennessee Supreme Court was forced to decide the legal status of the embryos under these unusual circumstances. It concluded that embryos were neither "persons" or "property," but rather occupied an "interim category that entitles them to special respect because of their potential for human life."[22]

---

[17] See, e.g., Hecht v. Superior Court, 20 Cal. Rptr. 2d 275, 283 (Ct. App. 1993) (holding that man who stored sperm in sperm bank for future use had "an interest, in the nature of ownership, to the extent that he had decision making authority as to the use of his sperm for reproduction," and thus that upon his death the sperm became part of his estate).

[18] See, e.g., York v. Jones, 717 F. Supp. 421 (E.D. Va. 1989) (holding that an agreement between an embryo storage facility and the biological parents that recognized the parents' property interest in the embryo should be considered a bailment, such that the facility was required to release the embryos to the parents upon their request).

[19] Cf. Davis v. Davis, 842 S.W.2d 588 (Tenn. 1992) (noting that a joint agreement regarding disposition of embryos would be enforced as between the progenitors).

[20] But see La. Rev. Stat. Ann. § 9:129 (forbidding the intentional destruction of embryos in Louisiana).

[21] Davis v. Davis, 842 S.W.2d 588 (Tenn. 1992); see also Jennifer L. Carow, Note, Davis v. Davis: An Inconsistent Exception to an Otherwise Sound Rule Advancing Procreational Freedom and Reproductive Technology, 43 DePaul L. Rev. 523 (1994); Kristine E. Luongo, Comment, The Big Chill: Davis v. Davis and the Protection of "Potential Life"?, 29 New Eng. L. Rev. 1011 (1995).

[22] Davis v. Davis, 842 S.W.2d 588, 597 (Tenn. 1992).

Yet the court seemed to accord little weight to this finding; for example, it largely ignored the interests of third parties who might ultimately receive the embryos. Rather, it proceeded to analyze the rights of W and H in property-like terms. The court recognized that W and H had "an interest in the nature of ownership" in that they had joint decision-making authority over the embryos. Because W and H disagreed over the fate of the embryos, however, the court reasoned that the outcome hinged on balancing the respective interests of W and H for and against procreation. It observed that ordinarily the party seeking to avoid procreation should prevail, as long as the other party has a reasonable possibility of achieving parenthood by other means. Here W still had an opportunity to achieve parenthood through a future IVF procedure. More importantly, W's interest in procreation was weak because she merely intended to donate the embryos, not to use them herself. Thus, H's interest in avoiding procreation prevailed.

§ 6.04 Surrogate Parenting: The Sale of Babies?

A logical extension of the law and economics approach to body parts would support the unrestricted sale of babies. Indeed, Richard Posner advocated this course in a famous (and somewhat facetious) article.[23] The potential sale of a living human being, of course, invokes the same policies that resulted in the prohibition of slavery, in addition to the general concerns surrounding property rights in body parts discussed above.

The modern phenomenon of surrogate parenting raises somewhat related concerns.[24] Suppose A donates an egg that is fertilized by B's sperm and implanted in surrogate mother C, all pursuant to a contract under which the future baby will belong to D and E. Should the surrogacy contract be enforced?[25] Or is this arrangement the functional equivalent of selling a living child? Alternatively, one might ask whether this complex web of relationships should be governed by property law, contract law, adoption law, or some other set of legal principles.

The leading decision of *In re Baby M*[26] posed an even more difficult problem. A and B, a married couple, could not have children due to B's infertility. A entered into a surrogacy contract with C, a third party. A and C agreed that A's sperm would be used to artificially inseminate C, who would carry the child to term and then deliver it to A, in return for a $10,000 payment to C; C further agreed to forever surrender any claim to custody

---

[23] Elisabeth M. Landes & Richard A. Posner, *The Economics of the Baby Shortage*, 7 J. Legal Stud. 323 (1978); *see also* J. Robert Prichard, *A Market for Babies?*, 34 U. Toronto L.J. 341 (1984); Margaret J. Radin, *What, if Anything, Is Wrong with Baby Selling?*, 26 Pac. L.J. 135 (1995).

[24] *See generally* Richard A. Posner, *The Ethics and Economics of Enforcing Contracts of Surrogate Motherhood*, 5 J. Contemp. Health L. & Pol'y 21 (1989); Marjorie M. Shultz, *Reproductive Technology and Intent-Based Parenthood: An Opportunity for Gender Neutrality*, 1990 Wis. L. Rev. 297.

[25] *Cf.* Johnson v. Calvert, 851 P.2d 776 (Cal. 1993) (enforcing surrogacy contract where egg and sperm from third parties were implanted into surrogate mother).

[26] 537 A.2d 1227 (N.J. 1988).

of the child. After the birth, however, C refused to relinquish the baby to A. When A sued, the New Jersey Supreme Court refused to enforce the contract. Observing that the contract was essentially a consensual adoption, the court ruled that it violated both the statutory provisions governing adoption and the strong public policy that adoption decisions be based on the best interests of the child, not the wishes of the prospective parents. The court similarly expressed concern that the contract purported to sever the mother's connection to the child without adequate safeguards to protect her rights; if legalized, such contracts might subject poor mothers to economic duress. Ultimately, the court concluded that the mother's consent was irrelevant: "There are, in a civilized society, some things that money cannot buy."[27]

---

[27] *In re* Baby M, 537 A.2d 1227, 1249 (N.J. 1988).

Chapter 7

OTHER PERSONAL PROPERTY RULES

SYNOPSIS

§ 7.01 Accession

[A] Basic Rule

When one person uses labor or materials to improve a chattel owned by another, the doctrine of accession determines who receives title to the resulting product.[1] The original owner of the chattel almost always retains title where the improver acted in bad faith (e.g., stole the chattel). Under some circumstances, however, the accession doctrine may vest title in the good faith improver. If title is awarded to the improver, he or she is obligated to compensate the original owner for the value of the chattel in unimproved condition.

Accession illustrates the strong influence of Lockean labor theory on American property law. Locke posited that each person owns his own body, and thus his own labor; if one mixes his labor with raw materials found in a "state of nature" to produce a new item, it is owned by the laborer (see § 2.03[A]). It was simple for common law courts to extend this principle to the analogous situation where the improver mistakenly believes that he or she owns the raw materials. As between the industrious improver and the idle owner, accession assigns title to the improver, thereby rewarding and encouraging productive labor.

[B] Addition of Labor Only

One branch of the doctrine involves adding *only labor* to a chattel owned by another. Suppose that S uses O's clay to create a valuable sculpture, mistakenly believing that O agreed to this use. Who owns the sculpture? As a general rule, one who in good faith applies labor to another's property acquires title to the resulting product if this process either (1) transforms the original item into a fundamentally different article (e.g., seeds planted to produce a crop)[2] or (2) greatly increases the value of the original item (e.g., timber made into barrel staves).[3] Under this doctrine, S owns the sculpture; O is entitled to damages equal to the fair market value of the original clay.[4]

[C] Addition of Labor and Materials

The other branch of accession involves adding *both labor and materials* to another's chattel. When materials owned by two different owners are combined together in good faith, the owner of the "principal" materials

---

[1] *See generally* Richard A. Epstein, *Possession as the Root of Title,* 31 Ga. L. Rev. 1221 (1979); Carol M. Rose, *Possession as the Origin of Property,* 52 U. Chi. L. Rev. 73 (1985).

[2] *But see* Bank of Am. v. J & S Auto Repairs, 694 P.2d 246, 249 (Ariz. 1985).

[3] *Compare* Wetherbee v. Green, 22 Mich. 310 (1871) (when standing trees worth $25 were converted into barrel hoops worth about $700, the innocent trespasser owned the hoops) *with* Isle Royale Mining Co. v. Hertin, 37 Mich. 332 (1877) (when standing trees worth about $1 per cord were converted into firewood worth $2.87 per cord, no accession occurred).

[4] B.A. Ballou & Co. v. Citytrust, 591 A.2d 126 (Conn. 1991).

acquires title to the final product. For example, suppose M innocently installs a custom truck body on a bare truck frame owned by O. If M's materials add more value to the finished truck than O's frame, M owns the truck; O receives only the fair market value of the frame.[5]

§ 7.02 Adverse Possession of Personal Property

[A] Traditional Approach

Title to personal property can be acquired through adverse possession.[6] Most courts apply the adverse possession standards for real property (*see* Chapter 27) to chattels as well, either directly or by analogy. Thus, under the traditional view, one whose possession of a chattel is *actual, adverse, hostile, exclusive, open and notorious,* and *continuous* for the appropriate statute of limitations period obtains title to it, subject to the qualifications discussed below. The limitations period for recovery of a chattel (usually 2-6 years) is shorter than the parallel period for real property (usually 5-20 years). In most states, the limitations period begins running when the adverse possessor obtains possession of the chattel.

[B] Critique of Traditional Approach

Application of the real property adverse possession standards to chattels is troublesome. Suppose that for six years X possesses a valuable antique vase owned by Z; X displays the vase prominently in his living room during this period. Is this conduct sufficiently "open and notorious"? If the elements of adverse possession are intended to give adequate notice to the true owner of the chattel so as to start the statute of limitations running, one might argue that X's acts are insufficient because Z is unlikely to receive notice.[7]

Under the traditional approach, however, X has probably acquired title to the vase. After all, X has used the vase in the same manner that any normal owner would. What more could X do? The difficulty here stems from the fundamental difference between real and personal property. Because real property is immobile, its ordinary use by an adverse possessor may provide notice to the true owner; the law presumes that owners periodically inspect their lands. Yet because a chattel is portable, the adverse possessor's ordinary use will normally not put the true owner on notice.

---

[5] Eusco, Inc. v. Huddleston, 835 S.W.2d 576 (Tenn. 1992).

[6] *See generally* J.B. Ames, *The Disseisin of Chattels,* 3 Harv. L. Rev. 23 (1889); Patty Gerstenblith, *The Adverse Possession of Personal Property,* 37 Buff. L. Rev. 119 (1989); R.H. Helmholz, *Wrongful Possession of Chattels: Hornbook Law and Case Law,* 80 Nw. U. L. Rev. 1221 (1986).

[7] *Cf.* O'Keeffe v. Snyder, 416 A.2d 862 (N.J. 1980).

[C] Emerging Approaches

[1] Discovery Approach

A small group of states has responded to the inadequacy of the traditional standard by adopting a "discovery'" approach, particularly where the chattel has artistic, historic, or other special importance. In these states, the statute of limitations begins running only when the true owner actually knows (or reasonably should know) that the adverse possessor holds the item. Thus, as a practical matter, the limitations period does not commence unless the conduct of the adverse possessor is obvious enough to place a diligent owner on notice.

The New Jersey Supreme Court's decision in *O'Keeffe v. Snyder*[8] illustrates the discovery approach.[9] Three pictures painted and owned by plaintiff Georgia O'Keeffe disappeared from an art gallery in 1946; O'Keeffe learned in 1976 that defendant Snyder had acquired the paintings and brought a replevin action against him. Snyder claimed ownership by adverse possession, asserting that the applicable six-year limitations period had expired in 1952. Observing that the traditional adverse possession standard may not be sufficient to put the original owner on actual or constructive notice when art or other chattels are merely displayed in a private home, the court adopted the discovery rule in its stead. Thus, "if an artist diligently seeks the recovery of a lost or stolen painting, but cannot find it or discover the identity of the possessor, the statute of limitations will not begin to run."[10]

The discovery approach imposes a significant burden on the adverse possessor. For example, in order to commence the limitations period for recovery of a painting, the adverse possessor might be required to maintain the painting on public display in a museum or to publish periodic newspaper advertisements seeking the true owner. Ironically, the good faith adverse possessor who is unaware of any competing claimant will be unlikely to take these steps and thus will not acquire title. Yet the bad faith adverse possessor who knowingly complies with the law will obtain title from the negligent owner.

[2] "Demand and Refusal" Approach

The "demand and refusal" approach adopted by New York affords owners even greater shelter than the discovery approach. Under this view, the limitations period for a replevin action against the good faith purchaser of a stolen chattel does not commence until the purchaser receives and refuses the owner's demand to turn over possession of the item.[11]

---

[8] 416 A.2d 862 (N.J. 1980).

[9] The case is analyzed in Paula A. Franzese, *"Georgia on My Mind"—Reflections on* O'Keeffe v. Snyder, 9 Seton Hall L. Rev. 1 (1989).

[10] O'Keeffe v. Snyder, 416 A.2d 862, 872 (N.J. 1980).

[11] Solomon R. Guggenheim Found. v. Lubell, 569 N.E.2d 426 (N.Y. 1991).

§ 7.03   Bailments

[A]   Bailments in Context

Broadly defined, a bailment is the rightful possession of chattels by someone other than the owner.[12] Bailments are ubiquitous in everyday life. For example, bailments are created when: A borrows B's book; A leases B's trailer; B stores her furniture in A's warehouse; and A finds B's lost watch. In each instance, A is a *bailee* (the person holding possession of the item) and B is a *bailor* (the owner of the item). The bailee is obligated to care for the item, and ultimately to redeliver it to the bailor.

The law governing bailments is extraordinarily complex. Over the last century, a property-based approach to bailments has slowly eclipsed the traditional contract approach. Certainly, many bailments stem from contract (e.g., A leases a car from Avis). The resulting impetus to explain bailments in contract terms was understandable; and decisions in some states still recite the necessity for an express or implied contract before a bailment may be found. Yet two types of bailments do not fit neatly into the contract model: many gratuitous bailments arise from agreement, but do not involve consideration; and involuntary bailments are imposed by law, in the absence of agreement. The property approach is broad enough to encompass all bailment categories. Yet the influence of the contract model lingers in some jurisdictions.

[B]   Creation

[1]   Possession of Chattel

Under the property-based approach, a bailment arises when the bailee has rightful possession of a chattel owned by another person. Possession means (1) physical control over the chattel and (2) the intent to exercise that control. For example, suppose O obtains a safe deposit box at B Bank; both O and B Bank have a separate key to the box, and both keys are required to open the box. These facts create a bailment because B Bank, as bailee, exercises control over the vault in which the safety deposit box is located. O, the bailor, cannot obtain access to her box without B Bank's consent.

[2]   "Park and Lock" Arrangements

One of the most intriguing bailment issues concerns the status of cars parked pursuant to "park and lock" arrangements. Assume O drives his car into the entrance to L's parking lot, takes a ticket from L's machine that causes the barrier gate to raise, parks and locks the car, and retains

---

[12] Recent scholarship on bailment includes R.H. Helmholz, *Bailment Theories and the Liability of Bailees: The Elusive Uniform Standard of Reasonable Care*, 41 U. Kan. L. Rev. 97 (1992); Kurt P. Autor, Note, *Bailment Liability: Toward a Reasonable Standard of Care*, 61 S. Cal. L. Rev. 2117 (1988).

his keys. Exit from the lot is controlled by L's employee, a cashier in a booth; L's security employees patrol the lot periodically. O returns to find that his car has been stolen. Can O now sue L for breach of the bailee's duty of care?

Cases are almost evenly split on the point. A bailment was found in the leading case of *Allen v. Hyatt Regency-Nashville Hotel*. [13] There the Tennessee Supreme Court emphasized that the car owner had utilized an indoor commercial garage located in a hotel. In addition to the hotel employee who monitored the exit, hotel security personnel patrolled the area regularly. The court concluded that these facts created the requisite control for a bailment to exist, even though the car owner retained his keys and chose his own parking space.

Ellish v. Airport Parking Company of America, Inc. [14] illustrates the opposing viewpoint. The New York appellate court explained that the airport parking lot at issue was designed to provide temporary storage space for cars in an urban area, quite unlike the "traditional warehouses of the professional bailee with their stress on security and safekeeping." [15] It observed that the plaintiff retained as much control as possible over the car; she chose her own parking space, retained her keys, and did not expect the defendant to move the car during her absence. Further, plaintiff was warned when she entered the lot that it was not attended. The court reasoned that she had no expectation that the defendant would take special precautions on her behalf. Thus, the relationship was one of license, not bailment.

[C] Duties of Bailee

[1] Basic Standard of Care

The legal principles defining the bailee's duty of care are in transition. During the nineteenth century, most states adopted a rather intricate approach developed by Supreme Court Justice Joseph Story, under which the bailee's duty of care varied according to the type of bailment involved. [16] If the bailment was solely for the benefit of the bailor (e.g., when a finder finds a lost article), the bailee was liable only for gross negligence. If the bailment was for the mutual benefit of bailor and bailee (e.g., when a customer test drives a dealer's car), the bailee was held to the ordinary negligence standard. Finally, if the bailment was solely for the benefit of the bailee (e.g., when a neighbor borrows a lawn mower), the bailee was liable for damage caused by even slight negligence.

Today almost all states have replaced this elaborate system with the ordinary negligence standard. [17] Regardless of the category of bailment

---

[13] 668 S.W.2d 286 (Tenn. 1984).

[14] 345 N.Y.S.2d 650 (App. Div. 1973).

[15] Ellish v. Airport Parking Co. of Am., Inc., 345 N.Y.S.2d 650, 653 (App. Div. 1973).

[16] Peet v. Roth Hotel Co., 253 N.W. 546 (Minn. 1934).

[17] For criticism of the traditional approach, see Kurt P. Autor, Note, *Bailment Liability: Toward a Standard of Reasonable Care*, 61 S. Cal. L. Rev. 2117 (1988).

involved, this modern view requires a bailee to exercise the same degree of care that a reasonable person would exercise under the circumstances. [18] For example, in *Peet v. Roth Hotel Co.* [19] a hotel was held liable for the value of a ring that was lost after the plaintiff bailor entrusted it to the hotel's cashier for delivery to a hotel guest. [20] As is typical in bailment disputes, the plaintiff was unaware of the circumstances surrounding how the hotel lost the ring, and thus unable to prove negligence. The Minnesota Supreme Court followed the modern solution to this proverbial dilemma; it ruled that plaintiff established a prima facie case by proving only that the bailment existed and the ring was not returned to him. This shifted to the hotel the burden of providing evidence that the ring was lost without any negligence on its part, a burden it could not meet. [21]

[2] Misdelivery

In contrast, the bailee who delivers the item to the wrong person is usually held strictly liable, on the theory that this constitutes conversion. If O leaves his rare book behind in R's restaurant where it is later destroyed by flooding, R will be liable only if the damage was caused R's own negligence. But if R, in complete good faith and after exercising all due care, instead delivers the book to T (a third party who has no legal right to it), then R is strictly liable. Most commentators agree that this distinction makes little sense. [22] The bailee's liability should be governed by a uniform standard, not by a standard that varies according to the type of event that causes the loss. [23]

[3] Exculpatory Contracts

Bailees often attempt to exculpate themselves from future negligence by contract, using a variety of methods (e.g., language on claim check or sign on wall). In general, American courts will not enforce a provision that limits the bailee's liability if the bailor is not actually aware of the provision. Even where the bailor is so aware, many courts refuse to uphold such provisions on public policy grounds, especially where there is a disparity of bargaining power between the parties.

---

[18] *See generally* R.H. Helmholz, *Bailment Theories and the Liability of Bailees: The Elusive Uniform Standard of Reasonable Care,* 41 U. Kan. L. Rev. 97 (1991).

[19] 253 N.W. 546 (Minn. 1934).

[20] *See also* Shamrock Hilton Hotel v. Caranas, 488 S.W.2d 151 (Tex. Civ. App. 1972) (hotel liable when its cashier delivered lost purse to wrong person).

[21] *See also* Buena Vista Loan & Sav. Bank v. Bickerstaff, 174 S.E.2d 219 (Ga. Ct. App. 1970) (applying common law rule); Singer Co. v. Stott & Davis Motor Express, Inc., 436 N.Y.S.2d 508 (App. Div. 1981) (applying parallel rule in Uniform Commercial Code § 7-204 to dispute between merchants).

[22] *See, e.g.,* R.H. Helmholz, *Bailment Theories and the Liability of Bailees: The Elusive Uniform Standard of Reasonable Care,* 41 U. Kan. L. Rev. 97 (1992).

[23] Shamrock Hilton Hotel v. Caranas, 488 S.W.2d 151 (Tex. App. 1972) (adopting negligence standard for bailee's misdelivery of restaurant customer's mislaid purse).

§ 7.04   Bona Fide Purchasers

[A]   General Rule

Suppose T steals 20 bags of wheat from O, and then sells them to B, who pays fair value and believes in good faith that T owns the wheat. As between O and B, who owns the wheat? As a general rule, a seller of personal property cannot pass on better title than he or she possesses, even to a bona fide purchaser. Thus, O still owns the wheat. Because T's mere possession of the wheat gave him no rights to it, he could not transfer title to B. This common law principle is codified in Uniform Commercial Code § 2-403(1): "A purchaser of goods acquires all title which his transferor had or had power to transfer."[24] This approach places a heavy burden on the buyer to investigate the validity of the seller's title, and presumably serves the policy goal of deterring theft. In theory, as the difficulty of selling stolen goods increases, the rate of theft should decline.

[B]   Exceptions

[1]   Rationale

Common law courts recognized that strict adherence to the rule would greatly impair legitimate commerce. Suppose O recovers his wheat and seeks to sell it to M. O may be unable to prove his ownership to M's satisfaction; during the era when the rule evolved (and still today, in most instances), there were no public records that identified the owner of a particular chattel. In addition, from the perspective of law and economics, even if O's ownership could be proven, the transaction costs might be high. Prospective buyers like M might be reluctant to purchase O's wheat for either reason.

As a result, courts developed several exceptions that protect the title of a bona fide purchaser of personal property under limited circumstances. In order to qualify as a bona fide purchaser, a buyer must both (1) pay valuable consideration and (2) believe in good faith that the seller holds valid title. The same principles are incorporated into the Uniform Commercial Code, which protects the good faith purchaser for value in specific situations.[25]

[2]   Entrustment of Goods to Merchant

One exception involves the owner who entrusts goods to a merchant.[26] Suppose that O breaks her diamond bracelet, and brings it to J, a jeweler, for repair; J then sells the bracelet to B, a bona fide purchaser. B now owns the bracelet. Under the Uniform Commercial Code, one who entrusts possession of goods to a merchant who deals in goods of that kind gives the

---

[24] U.C.C. § 2–403(1).

[25] U.C.C. § 1–201.

[26] U.C.C. § 2–403.

merchant power to transfer title to a bona fide purchaser in the ordinary course of business. The common law rule is substantially the same.

The conventional rationale for this doctrine is estoppel. By placing her bracelet in the hands of J, a merchant who regularly sells jewelry, O impliedly represents to the world that J is authorized to sell it. In other words, by her conduct O is estopped to deny J's authority when the rights of a bona fide purchaser are involved.

[3] Goods Obtained by Fraud or Duress

Another exception concerns goods that a buyer procures from an owner by fraud or duress. The buyer's title to the goods is not void, but merely voidable if and when the owner successfully litigates the issue. Until then, the buyer can transfer valid title to a bona fide purchaser.[27] Suppose O sells his ancient Roman statue to F in exchange for a painting that F fraudulently claims was painted by Picasso; F then sells the statue to B. If B is a bona fide purchaser, she now owns the statue. As between the wholly innocent bona fide purchaser, on the one hand, and the original owner who could have prevented harm by exercising due care, on the other, justice imposes the loss on the more culpable party, the original owner

[4] Money and Negotiable Instruments

Finally, the bona fide purchaser of money or negotiable instruments (including checks, promissory notes, and the like) prevails over the original owner.[28] For example, if T steals a $1,000 bill from O's safe, and gives it to bona fide purchaser B in exchange for a used car, B owns the bill. The reason for this exception is apparent: commerce would be paralyzed if the recipient of money or other forms of payment bore the burden of investigating the payor's title.

§ 7.05 Intellectual Property

[A] Common Law Hostility

The common law traditionally provided little protection for intellectual property. Even today, absent a special common law right or a statute, "a man's property is limited to the chattels which embody his invention."[29] Suppose O creates an innovative pattern for a men's tie. After O has sold several hundred ties, his competitor C begins selling the same pattern of tie at a lower price. At common law, O has no recourse; C can imitate O's pattern freely.

Why? Much of the answer stems from the traditional judicial reluctance to recognize ideas as property at all, reflecting a societal mind set that

---

[27] U.C.C. § 2–403.

[28] U.C.C. § 3–305.

[29] Cheney Bros. v. Doris Silk Corp., 35 F.2d 279, 280 (2d Cir. 1929); see also Smith v. Chanel, Inc., 402 F.2d 562 (9th Cir. 1968).

equated property with interests in land and other tangible objects; a tie could be property, but not the idea for the tie. Contemporary authorities typically defend the common law approach with a wholly different argument: it encourages competition that in turn lowers prices for the consumer. Yet the flaw in this approach is obvious: it discourage creative effort.

[B] Modern Utilitarian Approach

Today, the exceptions have largely swallowed the common law rule. Our legal system extends substantial protection to many forms of intellectual property including copyrights, patents, trademarks, and rights of publicity. Reflecting utilitarian theory, the law attempts to balance two competing goals: (1) providing an incentive to invest time and resources in creative effort that produces new goods, and (2) encouraging competition to reduce the price of goods.

The classic solution to this dilemma is to give the creator a limited monopoly in the creation. For instance, O, the inventor of a new product, receives a patent—an exclusive property right to use and sell her product. The patent rewards her effort and encourages the creative endeavors of others. Yet O's patent lasts only for 20 years. When it expires, O's competitors may sell the same product without her consent, thus lowering the price for consumers.

All four types of intellectual property discussed below are based on a first-in-time approach. In a broad sense, the property right is assigned to the first person who both labors to create the idea and gives appropriate notice of the creation.

[C] Copyrights

Federal copyright law protects rights in original books, articles, songs, paintings, sculptures, pictures, and related artistic creations. To qualify as "original," the work must exhibit at least some minimal creativity on the part of the author. [30] In addition, the work must also be "fixed" in tangible, physical form. For example, a sound recording of a speech qualifies for protection, but not an unrecorded speech. New works receive copyright protection for the length of the author's life plus 70 years after death. [31] There are a number of exceptions to the scope of this protection. Most notably, under the "fair use" doctrine, limited use of copyrighted materials for teaching, scholarship, news reporting, parody, and similar purposes is permitted without authorization. [32]

A copyright is effectively the grant of a limited monopoly that serves important public purposes. As the Supreme Court has explained: "It is

---

[30] *See, e.g.,* Feist Publications v. Rural Tel. Serv. Co., 499 U.S. 340 (1991) (listings of names, towns and telephone numbers in "white pages" telephone directory not sufficiently original for copyright).

[31] 17 U.S.C. § 302(a). Works created after 1977 are governed by this standard, while earlier works are governed by more complex provisions.

[32] *See, e.g.,* Sony Corp. of Am. v. Universal City Studios, 464 U.S. 417 (1984).

intended to motivate the creative activity of authors . . . by the provision of a special reward, and to allow the public access to the products of their genius after the limited period of exclusive control has expired."[33]

Copyright protection extends only to the particular form or manner in which a fact or idea is expressed, not to the fact or idea itself.[34] Yet under limited circumstances the common law may protect mere information, regardless of its form. The leading case adopting this view is *International News Service v. Associated Press*,[35] where plaintiff Associated Press complained that defendant INS was pirating and reselling news that plaintiff had gathered. The articles that plaintiff distributed to its customers could be copyrighted, but not the information that they contained. Stressing that defendant was appropriating material that plaintiff had acquired through the investment of labor, skill, and money and thus "endeavoring to reap where it has not sown," the Supreme Court held that plaintiff had a temporary "*quasi*-property" right in its news for so long as the news retained commercial value.[36]

[D] Patents

Exclusive property rights in certain types of inventions may be secured under a federal patent. A person who invents or discovers any "new and useful" process, machine, or other invention[37] and meets other statutory requirements may obtain a patent upon application to the federal Commissioner of Patents and Trademarks.[38] Once issued, a patent is effective for a term of 20 years from the application date.[39] During this period, the patent holder owns the exclusive right to make, use, or sell the invention in the United States.[40]

Yet the property rights of a patent holder are not absolute. In order to obtain a patent, the applicant must publicly disclose enough information to allow others "skilled in the art" to make and use the invention.[41] Competitors may use this data to create new, non-infringing inventions; moreover, once the patent term ends, they may freely manufacture and sell the formerly patented invention.

---

[33] Sony Corp. of Am. v. Universal City Studios, 464 U.S. 417, 429 (1984).

[34] A few states, most notably New York, recognize a common law property right in original ideas. *See, e.g.,* Werlin v. Reader's Digest Ass'n, Inc., 528 F. Supp. 451 (S.D.N.Y. 1981) (idea for magazine article protected).

[35] 248 U.S. 215 (1918).

[36] International News Serv. v. Associated Press, 248 U.S. 215, 239, 242 (1918). For an analysis of this decision, see Douglas G. Baird, *Common Law Intellectual Property and the Legacy of* International News Service v. Associated Press, 50 U. Chi. L. Rev. 411 (1983).

[37] For example, Moore v. Regents of the University of California, 793 P.2d 479 (Cal. 1990), involved a patent for a "cell line" (that is, a group of human cells) used to produce particular proteins.

[38] 35 U.S.C. §§ 101, 102.

[39] 35 U.S.C. § 154(a)(2).

[40] 35 U.S.C. § 154(a)(1).

[41] 35 U.S.C. § 112.

[E] Trademarks

A trademark is a word, name, symbol, or device used to identify and distinguish the products of a particular manufacturer or retailer.[42] Statutory trademark protection is obtained by registering the mark with the federal Patent and Trademark Office and using the mark in interstate commerce. The holder of a registered trademark holds the exclusive right to use the mark for specific types of products throughout the United States for ten years; the trademark may be renewed for additional ten-year terms. Even without registration, the first-in-time user of a trademark acquires common law rights to continue this use in the affected region. Similar statutory and common law protection is provided to the holder of a service mark, defined as any word, name, symbol, or device used to identify and distinguish the services provided by a particular business.

Trademark protection both encourages competition and fosters product quality.[43] For example, assume that B Corporation manufactures and sells a line of power tools (saws, drills, etc.), each bearing the symbol of a bee wearing a carpenter's outfit. B Corporation now has a greater incentive to invest in research and development to improve its product, and thereby compete more effectively, because customers will be able to identify its products easily. The trademark serves as a label of quality, allowing customers to avoid purchasing shoddy goods.

[F] Rights of Publicity

The last fifty years have witnessed the evolution of a new form of intellectual property: a celebrity's "right of publicity." In most jurisdictions, an actor, politician, or other famous person has a property right to the exclusive use of his or her name and "likeness" for financial gain. Thus, for example, if L renames his liquor store "Bill Clinton's Liquor Store," Bill Clinton could sue to enjoin this unauthorized use of his name.[44]

Some courts have extended this protection to the more amorphous concept of a celebrity's "identity" or "persona." An example is *White v. Samsung Electronics America, Inc.*,[45] where Vanna White, hostess of the television game show "Wheel of Fortune," claimed that defendant's advertisement appropriated her identity. The advertisement showed a robot (with hair and attire similar to White's) near a copy of the "Wheel of Fortune" game board, with the legend "Longest-running game show. 2012 A.D." Even though White's name and likeness were not used, the Ninth Circuit concluded that her right of publicity had been invaded because the robot figure would remind a reasonable viewer of White.

---

[42] 15 U.S.C. § 1127.

[43] *See generally* Park 'N Fly, Inc. v. Dollar Park & Fly, Inc., 469 U.S. 189 (1985).

[44] *See, e.g.,* Martin Luther King, Jr. Center for Social Change v. American Heritage Products, 296 S.E.2d 697 (Ga. 1982); State *ex rel.* Elvis Presley Memorial Found. v. Crowell, 733 S.W.2d 89 (Tenn. Ct. App. 1987).

[45] 971 F.2d 1395 (9th Cir. 1992).

Recognition of a celebrity's right of publicity presents troubling questions. All creative effort builds on the foundation of the past. As the definition of intellectual property is extended to encompass more of that foundation, we may impair creativity in the future. As Judge Kozinski observed in a later chapter in the *White* saga, "[o]verprotection stifles the very creative forces it's supposed to nurture."[46]

Another concern is interference with free speech. Famous people are part of the fabric of American culture and history. Even as the scope of protected intellectual property expands, the right of free speech contracts. In *Martin Luther King, Jr. Center for Social Change v. American Heritage Products,*[47] for example, the Georgia Supreme Court held that the defendant could not manufacture and sell plastic busts of Dr. Martin Luther King, Jr. A concurring justice wondered—and rightly so—whether this rule would similarly prohibit other uses of King's name or likeness, such as a portrait for the state capitol, a statue for a local park, or a newspaper story about his life.[48]

[G] Property Rights in Cyberspace

The Internet poses complex and fascinating intellectual property law issues. One illustrative dispute concerns property rights in domain names. Suppose A registers a domain name that includes a trademark already owned by B, hoping that this will force B to purchase the name from A. Can B enjoin A's use of the domain name? After an initial period of uncertainty, a tidal wave of litigation has established that such use violates the rights of the trademark owner.[49]

Beyond the confines of trademark law, the "cybersquatter" poses a more difficult issue. Suppose C registers 50 domain names, none of which interferes with a trademark, and establishes a skimpy web page for each one, but does not actually place the names in normal use; C plans to sell the names to interested parties in the future. Should this be enough to confer ownership of the domain names on C, so as to preclude later registrant D from using the name? To date, domain names are assigned on a first-in-time basis, with no requirement of substantial use to perfect the registrant's property right. Thus, cypersquatters like C have an incentive to register multiple names, in the hope that they will be able to profit from them in the future.[50]

---

[46] White v. Samsung Electronics America, Inc., 989 F.2d 1512, 1513 (9th Cir. 1993) (Kozinski, J., dissenting).

[47] 296 S.E.2d 697 (Ga. 1982).

[48] Martin Luther King, Jr. Center for Social Change v. Am. Heritage Products, 296 S.E.2d 697, 708–709 (Ga. 1982) (Weltner, J., concurring).

[49] *See, e.g.,* Panavision Int'l v. Toeppen, 141 F.3d 1316 (9th Cir. 1998) (defendant violated plaintiff's trademark in "Panavision" by registering "PanaVision" as domain name for web page that merely showed photographs of Pana, Illinois; defendant, who had registered over 100 other trademarks as domain names, attempted to sell the name to plaintiff for $13,000 before litigation began).

[50] *See, e.g.,* Avery Dennison Corp. v. Sumpton, 999 F. Supp. 1337 (C.D. Cal. 1998) (defendants registered over 12,000 domain names).

Chapter 8

HISTORY OF THE ESTATES IN LAND SYSTEM

§ 8.01 The Estates System

What does it mean to "own" property? O, a layman, might believe that he "owns" his home. But technically O owns only an "estate" in the home, probably fee simple absolute. O's estate consists of a cluster of legally-enforceable rights concerning the home.

Estates and *future interests* are the traditional building blocks of property law. The United States largely inherited the system of estates and future interests that evolved in England. Understanding the historical context in which this system arose—the focus of this chapter—is crucial to understanding modern property law. The current law governing estates is discussed in detail in Chapters 9–11, while future interests are covered in Chapters 12–14.

§ 8.02 Defining "Estate" and "Future Interest"

A *present estate* (sometimes called a *possessory estate* or just abbreviated as *estate*) is a legal interest that entitles its owner to the immediate possession of real or personal property. For example, if A owns a present estate in the farm known as Greenacre, he may now reside on Greenacre, cultivate its fields, harvest its crops, exclude other persons, and otherwise use the land. A does not "own" the land that comprises Greenacre. Rather, A owns an estate "in" Greenacre. The cluster of legal rights that constitute A's estate is seen as conceptually different from the land.

What if B now has a legal right to take possession of Greenacre in the future (e.g., "five years from now" or "upon A's death")? B does not hold a present estate because he is not entitled to immediate possession. Instead, his right is classified as a *future interest*. A future interest is a non-possessory interest that will or may become a present estate in the future.

The universe of estates and future interests concerns only the basic rights and duties of an owner in relationship to other private persons. It does not address the separate subject of land use regulation: the rights and duties between an owner and the state in relation to land (*see* Chapters 36–40).

§ 8.03 Property Law in Feudal England

[A] The Feudal Foundation

The English property law system may be traced backward in time to a single defining event: the Norman Conquest of 1066.[1] William the Conqueror became the King of England after leading his invading Norman army to victory over the ruling Saxons at the Battle of Hastings. However, as one historian observed, "[f]or nearly twenty years after the Battle of Hastings, the chances were against survival of the Anglo-Norman monarchy."[2] William's reign was threatened by continued domestic rebellion and

---

[1] For detailed discussion of the development of the feudal property system in England, see generally Cornelius J. Moynihan, Introduction to the Law of Real Property 1–21 (2d ed. 1988); Powell on Real Property ¶¶ 16–33 (Michael Allan Wolf ed., Matthew Bender); Theodore F.T. Plucknett, A Concise History of the Common Law 507–545 (5th ed. 1956).

[2] Frank M. Stenton, The First Century of English Feudalism, 1066–1166 148 (1932).

by the risk of foreign invasion. How could a small group of Normans occupy and defend the whole of England? William met this challenge by creating a complex military and governmental organization resting on principles of feudal *tenure* borrowed from Europe.

The heart of the new feudal system was a huge redistribution of land under terms imposed by the crown. William, as king, was quickly deemed to "own" all land in England. The Saxon nobles who had opposed William forfeited their lands to him; and other landowners—more or less voluntarily—ceded ownership to William in a process known as commendation. Over time, William transferred control over large tracts of land to approximately 1,500 supporters known as *tenants in chief*, in return for military service and other carefully-defined duties that were seen as a burden on the land itself. The results of this land redistribution were chronicled in the Domesday Book of 1086, which catalogued the landholdings of each tenant in chief.

The relationship between William and his tenants in chief was not a commercial, arms-length one, as is found in a modern sale of land. Rather, the feudal relationship between a lord and his vassal was intensely personal. In an elaborate ceremony known as *homage*, the vassal knelt and swore personal allegiance to the lord, creating mutual obligations of loyalty and support. Thus, when William, as lord, granted land to his tenants in chief, as vassals, they were considered to "hold" the land "of" the king. The tenants in chief did not "own" land in the modern sense. Rather, they essentially had the right to use, possess, and enjoy the land, but on the king's behalf. Initially, William granted land only for the lifetime of the tenant in chief. When the holder died, William might regrant the land to the holder's eldest son as a favor, but had no obligation to do so. In a sense, the tenant in chief was more akin to a well-trusted provincial governor than to a contemporary landowner.

The relationship between William and his tenants in chief became the basic model for landholding arrangements throughout feudal England. Through a process called *subinfeudation*, the tenants in chief created similar arrangements with their own vassals, who in turn created similar relationships with others, and so forth.

[B] Feudal Tenures

[1] Free Tenure and Unfree Tenure

Over time, feudal England recognized two categories of landholdings: *free tenures* and *unfree tenures*. The free tenures could be held only by the upper classes, essentially nobles and gentry, whose dignity and social position were incompatible with physical labor. The unfree tenures were held by the peasants or *villeins* who actually worked on the land. The king's courts protected only the rights of tenants holding free tenures, and thus set the stage for the later development of the common law of property.

The free tenures—based on the relationship between William and his tenants in chief—were by far the most important category. All of these tenures shared a common core: each tenant owed the lord both *service* and *incidents*. And the obligation to provide service and incidents was considered to be attached to the land, thereby binding the tenant's successors in perpetuity.

[2] Services

Four free tenures were recognized in feudal England, each characterized by the type of service the tenant owed to the lord. The Normans had four basic needs: "safety, subsistence, salvation, and splendor."[3] Each need was met by a different type of tenure.

Knight service was the most honorable (and initially the most important) form of tenure. Most of the tenants in chief held their lands in knight service, which required them to provide a specified number of fully equipped knights to the king for 40 days of military service each year.

Socage tenure addressed the subsistence element. It required the tenant to periodically furnish to his lord a specified money payment (e.g., 20 pence), a fixed quantity of a particular agricultural product (e.g., 20 hens), or a defined labor (e.g., plowing a field two days each week).

Frankalmoign tenure involved a grant of land to a priest, church, or other religious body, accompanied by the service of praying for the grantor's salvation. Almost half of England was once held in frankalmoign tenure.

Finally, *serjeanty tenure* usually required the tenant to perform ceremonial or personal services to the king.

[3] Incidents

[a] Incidents During the Tenant's Lifetime

In addition to service, each free tenant owed the lord various other obligations, together called the *incidents* of tenure. Like service, the incidents were considered to burden the land. Four incidents existed during the tenant's lifetime:

(1) *homage* (the ceremony by which the tenant became a vassal);

(2) *fealty* (the oath by which the tenant promised to be loyal to the lord);

(3) *aids* (the tenant's duty to provide financial support to the lord on specified occasions, e.g., ransoming the lord from imprisonment); and

(4) *forfeiture* (the return of the land to the lord if the tenant was disloyal or failed to perform the required service).

[b] Incidents at Tenant's Death

At the tenant's death, four other incidents might arise: escheat, relief, wardship, and marriage. Over time, these incidents became far more

---

[3] Powell on Real Property ¶ 20 (Michael Allan Wolf ed., Matthew Bender).

valuable than the tenurial service or the lifetime incidents, and this development in turn influenced the law's evolution.

Suppose tenant in chief A held land of the king in knight service. If A died without heirs, the land would return or *escheat* to the king, who could then grant it anew to another noble. Modern law recognizes the same basic concept; if a person dies intestate without heirs today, his or her property escheats to the state.

Alternatively, suppose that A was survived by two grown sons, B and C. Although initially the king could regrant the land to whoever he pleased in this situation, over time the custom arose—later converted into an obligation—that the land would pass to the tenant's eldest son.[4] However, the heir was required to pay the king a fixed sum, called a *relief*, to obtain the land. The modern counterpart to the relief is the inheritance tax.

Wardship and marriage, the two remaining incidents, applied only to knight service and serjeanty tenure. Suppose A died leaving D, a five-year-old boy, as his only heir. The incident of *wardship* allowed the king, as overlord, to have possession of A's lands until D reached the age of 21; during this period, the king was entitled to the rents and profits from the land. The incident of *marriage* allowed the lord to sell the right to marry the heir. D, the minor heir, could refuse the marriage, but was then required to pay the lord a substantial fine.

[C] Subinfeudation and the Feudal Pyramid

Each tenant holding "of" a lord could create subtenures through a process called *subinfeudation*. Over time, this produced a complex pyramid of landholding arrangements that evolved into the Anglo-American system of estates in land.

Suppose again that tenant in chief A holds of the king in knight service the modern equivalent of 50,000 acres of land; A is required to provide five equipped knights for the king. A might grant the use of 5,000 acres to K, one of his knights, in knight service; K would be required to provide one knight to A, and would also owe to A the feudal incidents. K, in turn, might subinfeudate 1,000 acres to F in socage tenure, receiving in return the fixed sum of 1,000 pence per year and feudal incidents. The result is a chain of feudal relationships among the king, A (tenant in chief), K (called a *mesne lord*), and F (called a *tenant in demesne*). Each occupies a particular niche or *status* in the feudal pyramid. K, for example, owes service and incidents to A, but receives them from F.

As a result of subinfeudation, one parcel of land could simultaneously be the subject of many different tenures. F's 1,000-acre parcel, for example, is burdened by two tenures in knight service and one socage tenure. Thus, in effect, multiple persons could "own" property rights in the same land at the same time. Under this example, F holds the right to present possession

---

[4] The principle that the eldest son inherits, called *primogeniture*, dominated English law until its abolition in 1925.

of the 1,000-acre tract. Yet K, A, and the king all hold rights in the same tract that may give them possession in the future. For instance, if F dies without heirs, the land will escheat to K.

[D] Evolution of the Estates in Land System

[1] Problems Produced by Subinfeudation

Over time, the feudal tenures withered away under the pressure of social and economic changes, to be replaced by the modern estates in land. The transformation was initially sparked by a decline in the value of the feudal services. As changes in the technology of warfare rendered knights obsolete, knight service became irrelevant. Further, as inflation eroded the purchasing power of money, the socage tenures which required fixed monetary payments lost most of their value. However, because the value of land rose with the prevailing inflation, the feudal incidents that were tied to the possession of land—escheat, marriage, and wardship—retained their value.

As incidents became far more valuable than services, subinfeudation increasingly undercut the rights of the lords. Suppose that F is about to die without heirs, and realizes that his land will then escheat to his lord, K. Due to inflation, the fixed rent of 1,000 pence has minimal value; assume that the reasonable rental value of the land is 10,000 pence annually. F might altruistically subinfeudate to B, a worthy but poor young farmer, in socage tenure for 10 pence per year. When F dies, the land does not escheat to K. Rather, K is entitled to the service due from F (1,000 pence per year) and succeeds to F's rights against B (10 pence per year). But the worth of this service to K is comparatively small. K loses the opportunity to receive the current rental value, 10,000 pence, because F has circumvented the incident of escheat. In this manner, tenants like F used subinfeudation to avoid the valuable incidents of escheat, marriage, and wardship.

[2] Statute Quia Emptores

The lords responded in 1290 with the enactment of the Statute Quia Emptores,[5] which abolished subinfeudation, and thus, in the short run, shored up the feudal system. Yet in the long run Quia Emptores ensured the disintegration of the system for two reasons. First, Quia Emptores greatly simplified landholding arrangements. No new tenures could be created and the existing tenures slowly disappeared with escheat or forfeiture. Over time, the middle layers of the feudal pyramid vanished, until most tenants in possession of land held directly of the king. Second, in exchange for banning subinfeudation, the lords allowed each free tenant to substitute another tenant in his stead without securing the lord's approval. In effect, a tenant could freely alienate his interest in land. No longer would each tenant and lord be bound together in the personal obligations of loyalty and support that characterized the early feudal

---

[5] 18 Edw. I, ch.1 (1290).

system. Instead, the relationship between tenant and lord was increasingly viewed in economic terms.

[3] From Tenures to Estates

With the principle of free alienation firmly established by Quia Emptores, it became possible to transfer—and thus create—different forms of land ownership known as estates. Each free person occupied a niche or *status* in the feudal pyramid; as feudalism waned, the related term *estate* was used to describe these new forms of landholdings. The estate system was built on the basic feudal contours. Multiple persons could hold interests in the same land at the same time. One person could hold the right to immediate possession of land, while others could hold a right to acquire possession in the future.

Over time, the king's courts recognized and protected three basic *freehold* estates—the life estate, the fee tail, and the fee simple (*see* § 9.05). In a sense, each estate was an echo of the feudal past. The life estate endured for the life of a specific person or persons, like the original grants of William the Conqueror. The fee tail endured from generation to generation as long as the bloodline of the original holder continued; like William's later grants, it expired if a holder died without closely-related heirs. Finally, as the logical consequence of Quia Emptores, the fee simple was freely transferable and endured literally forever; it escheated to the king only if the holder died without any heirs.

Even as these new estates developed, an intricate network of future interests arose (*see* § 12.04). By definition, if an owner holding fee simple transferred a lesser estate, such as the life estate or the fee tail, one or more future interests were created.

§ 8.04 Property Law in Post-Feudal England

[A] New Economic and Social Conditions

Between 1500 and 1700, evolving economic and social conditions opened a new chapter in the development of English property law. Agriculture shifted from subsistence crops to farming for national and foreign markets, as innovative techniques enhanced production and transportation facilities improved. With increased demand for manufactured woolen goods, sheep-raising efforts expanded. In turn, as ownership of land became more profitable, new tensions arose that shaped the law's future evolution.

Two themes dominated the era. One was the demise of feudalism. Over the kings' stubborn objections, the remaining feudal remnants were slowly swept away by a rising tide of private property law centered on estates in land. The other, somewhat overlapping theme, was an epic battle to determine the future course of the new estates in land system. Would it tilt toward protecting the autonomy of existing landowners to transfer their lands on whatever terms they chose? Or would it tilt toward restricting such rights in order to ensure that land was freely alienable, as the newly-wealthy commercial interests desired?

[B] The Demise of Feudalism

Feudalism was an anachronism in England long before 1500. In particular, landowners resented the burdensome feudal incidents—which were by now usually owed directly to the king—just as modern landowners dislike taxation. Beginning in the 1300s, landowners sought to avoid the incidents through a creative technique known as the *use*. O, an owner, could convey his land to T, a trusted person, for the use or benefit of B, a relative or friend of O. This arrangement deprived the lord of the incidents that would otherwise arise on O's death; and B could enforce T's obligation in chancery court. In 1535, King Henry VIII was able to protect his revenues by abolishing the use through the famous Statute of Uses,[6] a temporary reprieve for the feudal system.

Yet almost immediately, the collapse of feudalism continued. An initial step was the enactment of the Statute of Wills[7] in 1540. Under prior law, an estate in land could not be devised; if a tenant died without an heir, it escheated to the lord. The Statute of Wills permitted the tenant to devise his rights, thus narrowing the incident of escheat.

In 1660, the Statute of Tenures[8] effectively ended feudalism. It abolished the feudal incidents of aids, homage, marriage, relief, and wardship, and converted all lingering knight service tenures into socage tenures. After 1660, if O, an English landowner held fee simple, he could be said to hold the modern equivalent of full ownership. Certainly, the concept of tenure remained in theory; O was still deemed to "hold" "of" someone else, not to "own" land directly. But with the demise of the feudal incidents, tenure had no practical significance other than the residual incident of escheat if O *both* died without heirs *and* failed to devise his estate.

[C] The Battle Between Autonomy and Free Alienation

[1] The Basic Tension

As feudalism waned, a second epic struggle developed: would the emerging property law system favor owner autonomy or free alienation? The basic battle lines were drawn between large landowners, on the one hand, and newly-wealthy trading and commercial interests, on the other.

Large landowners sought unfettered autonomy to transfer their rights on whatever terms they deemed appropriate, regardless of the impact on society in general. In an era when land was the principal form of wealth, these owners wished to control the disposition of their property long after death in order to protect the economic, political, and social power of

---

[6] 27 Hen. VIII, ch. 10 (1536).

[7] 32 Hen. VIII, ch. 1 (1540).

[8] 12 Car. II, ch. 24 (1660).

successive family generations. For example, suppose O devises Redacre, a large farm, "to my elder son G and his heirs, on condition that Redacre is always used for growing turnips, and if not so used, then to my younger son H and his heirs." G holds a special form of fee simple called fee simple subject to an executory limitation, while H owns a future interest called an executory interest; if G or any of G's successors ceases using Redacre for growing turnips, then H or his successor acquires fee simple absolute in Redacre. From O's perspective, the restriction makes sense; it encourages G and his successors to continue the currently desirable use of growing turnips on Redacre, which will provide income for their support without risking the family wealth in speculative ventures.

The trading and commercial forces, on the other hand, tended to view land as an economic investment. They argued that land should be freely transferable or *alienable* (like iron, fish, timber, and other commodities) to maximize its profitability. Accordingly, this group opposed future interests that tended to restrict the free transfer of rights in land. Consider again the farming restriction that O imposed on Redacre in the hypothetical above. Suppose that 100 years after O's death, raising turnips on Redacre no longer makes economic sense; the land is more valuable for other uses (e.g., as a factory site). Yet G's successor M is effectively locked into the low-value use of turnip farming. M cannot sell the land to an investor seeking a factory site; nor can M mortgage it in order to develop a factory on the land. Why? Because any buyer or lender would lose all rights once the turnip growing use terminated. If all English land could be burdened with similar restrictions, national economic development would be impaired.

[2] A Swinging Pendulum

The evolution of English property law between 1500 and 1700 can be broadly described as a pendulum swinging first toward owner autonomy and then back toward free alienability.

The period began with an explosion in future interests. In 1472, the decision in *Taltarum's Case*[9] ended the practical effectiveness of the fee tail by allowing a collusive lawsuit to end the entail. As a result, the landed gentry increasingly turned to various types of future interests—particularly contingent remainders held by transferees—to control future inheritances. During the early 1500s, courts expanded the types of remainders that could be created in real property.

This trend accelerated with the enactment of the Statute of Uses[10] in 1535, which similarly enlarged the categories of permissible interests in land. It permitted the creation of a second major type of contingent future interest that could be held by transferees: the executory interest. It also allowed the creation of trusts, and thus authorized a new layer of future interests in equity. Finally, the Statute of Wills[11] in 1540 allowed owners

---

[9] Y.B. 12 Edw. IV, fol.19, pl. 25 (1472).

[10] 27 Hen. VIII, ch. 10 (1536).

[11] 32 Hen. VIII, ch. 1 (1540).

to transfer rights in property by devise. This provided an efficient vehicle for creating the broad range of future interests that was now authorized.

The swing of the pendulum back toward free alienability is symbolized by a series of common law restrictions that progressively curtailed future interests, such as the Rule in Shelley's Case [12] (1581) (*see* § 14.13) and the Rule Against Perpetuities (*see* §§ 14.10, 14.11), which effectively began with the *Duke of Norfolk's Case* [13] (1681).

[D] The New Estates in Land System

By 1700, the English common law of property was relatively settled. Almost all of this body of law dealt with estates in land and their accompanying future interests. Little or no attention was devoted to areas that today form major components of modern property law, such as sales, financing, and public land use restrictions. Rather, the common law was primarily concerned with classifying different estates and interests held by private owners and describing the legal effects that flowed from these classifications.

As the product of over 600 years of legal evolution since the Norman Conquest, the estates in land system was extraordinarily complex. A few of its components were meaningless relics of feudalism. Others were products of the struggle against feudalism. Still other aspects were compromises forged in the tug of war between supporters of owner autonomy and advocates of free alienabilility.

§ 8.05 Estates in Land in the Early United States

[A] The "Reception" of English Property Law

Independence confronted our new nation with a dilemma: should we follow traditional English property law or create a uniquely American property law system? In the short run, necessity compelled the states to continue the use of relatively familiar English common law, which had been employed during the colonial era, despite the prevailing revolutionary antipathy toward the crown. This process is called the *reception* of English common law.

Thus, the states largely adopted the English principles governing estates in land and future interests. The feudal relic of tenure, however, was rejected. The Revolution was seen as severing all ties between American landowners and the king, including the traditional (although already irrelevant) notion of tenure. Although some states viewed themselves as successors to the crown, most states abolished tenure. In addition, other factors narrowed the influence of the English system. [14]

---

[12] 1 Co. Rep. 93b, 76 Eng. Rep. 206 (K.B. 1581).

[13] 22 Eng. Rep. 931 (1681).

[14] *See* John G. Sprankling, *The Antiwilderness Bias in American Property Law*, 63 U. Chi. L. Rev. 519, 521–556 (1996) (discussing the early development of American property law).

[B] Simplification Due to Lack of Legal Resources

As a practical matter, the states were able to implement only a simplified version of English property law due to a lack of legal resources. English-trained lawyers were quite rare; most American lawyers and judges had learned the law through a combination of self-education and apprenticeship. Also, English law books were relatively scarce in America. Blackstone's eminently readable—but oversimplified—*Commentaries on the Laws of England* became the standard legal treatise, perhaps even more popular in the United States than in England. Accordingly, much of the complexity and nuance that characterized the English system was lost in the transplantation process.

[C] Express Exception for Local American Conditions

In embracing the common law, each state added a major exception: English principles would apply only to the extent consistent with local American conditions. In terms of property law, one fundamental difference between England and the new United States was geography. Most of the English land surface was devoted to agricultural use, and its property law system was accordingly attuned to a mature agrarian economy. Applying English rules to the vast, unowned wilderness of the United States often made little sense. For example, in England the holder of a mere life estate had only a limited right to cut timber due to the shortage of remaining forest. This rule was unnecessary (and indeed, counterproductive) in the United States, where the vast forests were considered the equivalent of weeds—obstacles to agricultural development.

[D] Little Demand for English Complexities

The surplus of "unowned" American land meant that much of the English system was irrelevant. The key feature of the system was that multiple persons could own simultaneous interests in the same property. There was little demand for this multilayered structure in the United States, where fee simple absolute land was abundant but labor was scarce. Why should citizen C hold land as a mere life tenant or tenant for years when fee simple land was freely available in the West?

[E] Democratic Concerns

Finally, certain feudal aspects of English property law were rejected outright as inconsistent with the goals of American democracy. For example, the states rejected the English rule of *primogeniture*, which restricted inheritance to the eldest son, as inconsistent with social equality. States similarly abolished the estate in fee tail—which allowed an owner to transmit property through generations of descendants without any sale to third parties—due to the fear of creating a landed aristocracy that would dominate American political life.

§ 8.06 Trends in Modern Law Governing Estates in Land

[A] The Victory of Fee Simple Absolute

The modern law governing estates in land is a jigsaw puzzle consisting of both new and archaic pieces. Developments in the United States have eroded away much of the elaborate English system in favor of fee simple absolute, the most basic estate. Because of changing cultural attitudes, freehold estates other than fee simple absolute are rarely created today. Moreover, contemporary legislatures and courts are typically hostile toward such other estates for two reasons. First, the future interests that accompany other estates tend to limit the free alienation of property, anathema in a society that increasingly views land as a commodity. Second, there is a clear movement toward disregarding "dead hand" control of land, in favor of protecting the good faith expectations of living property owners.

Today, virtually all land in the United States is held in fee simple absolute, unencumbered by any future interests. The law governing the fee simple absolute is relatively straightforward. Accordingly, the importance of estates in land as a discrete area of property law is slowly declining. Many of the traditional freehold estates in land—and the intricate future interests that accompanied them—are now increasingly obsolete (*see* Chapter 9). Yet remnants of the common law complexity linger, causing confusion to judges, attorneys, and law students alike.

[B] Developments in Communal Ownership

Communal ownership was a central feature of English property law. Multiple persons could share a concurrent estate in land, each having an equal right to possession and enjoyment of the entire parcel. American states largely adopted the English system of concurrent estates. Two of these estates—the tenancy in common and the joint tenancy—remain in widespread use today with only minor modifications from their common law ancestors, particularly as vehicles for owning family property (*see* Chapter 10). Beginning in the 1960s, the rise of condominium development produced an explosion in the use of concurrent estates among non-family members, which continues today.

[C] Toward Gender Equality in Marital Property Ownership

The modern law governing marital property largely ignores the traditional English common law approach (*see* Chapter 11). Driven by feudal principles, the English system was premised on gender inequality; it vested virtually total control over family property in the husband. Modern American law has steadily moved toward gender equality.

Chapter 9

PRESENT ESTATES

SYNOPSIS

§ 9.01   A Byzantine System

American property law has long been dominated by a byzantine system of estates in land. Precise, elaborate, and sometimes arbitrary rules are used to classify estates and future interests into various categories. For decades the study of property law was almost exclusively devoted toward mastering this system of classification. Yet this complex system is increasingly irrelevant. Virtually all land sales transactions today involve only fee simple absolute, the most basic estate. The other historic estates and future interests discussed in this chapter are rarely if ever created in land. In addition, statutes in many states have greatly simplified the subject.

Modern law recognizes only certain types of estates that are equated with "ownership," traditionally called *freehold estates*. Accordingly, if the language of a deed, trust, or will creates a freehold estate, it will be deemed to be one of the following:

(1) fee simple absolute (often abbreviated as "fee simple") (*see* § 9.05[B]);

(2) fee simple determinable (*see* § 9.06[C][2]);

(3) fee simple subject to a condition subsequent (*see* § 9.06[C][3]);

(4) fee simple subject to an executory limitation (*see* § 9.06[C][4]);

(5) life estate absolute (usually abbreviated as "life estate") (*see* § 9.05[D]);

(6) some form of defeasible life estate (*see* § 9.06[C][5]); or

(7) fee tail (*see* § 9.05[C]).

§ 9.02   Creation of Estates

Estates and their accompanying future interests originate in two main sources: deeds (*see* Chapter 23) and wills (*see* Chapter 28). Certainly, estates and future interests can arise from a trust (*see* Chapter 28), but inevitably either a deed (if an inter vivos trust) or a will (if a testamentary trust) is employed to transfer the property into the trust. Similarly, estates and future interests that already exist may be transferred (but not created) through intestate succession.

Suppose that O holds fee simple absolute—the largest estate recognized by law—in Brownacre; he wants to create a present estate in P for the duration of P's life and a future interest in Q that matures into a present estate when P dies. O could accomplish this goal by executing a deed that immediately conveys Brownacre "to P for life, and then to Q and his heirs." Or O might execute a will that (effective upon O's death) devises Brownacre "to P for life, and then to Q and his heirs."

§ 9.03 Classifying Estates

The central challenge that estates present is classification. English common law developed a number of specific types of estates, together with an intricate system for determining which language in a deed, trust, or will created each type. American law inherited and somewhat modified this system. Thus, our law is preoccupied with rules designed to determine the *precise* name of a particular estate. Which legal pigeonhole does particular language fit into? Once the type of estate is identified, it is usually simple to determine the resulting rights and duties of the affected parties.

Three main variables are used in classifying an estate: (1) is it freehold or nonfreehold?, (2) is it absolute or defeasible?, and (3) is it legal or equitable? Depending on the answer to each of these inquiries, additional variables may become important.

§ 9.04 Estates: Freehold or Nonfreehold?

The law traditionally recognized six basic types of estates: three *freehold* estates (fee simple, fee tail, and life estate) and three[1] *nonfreehold* estates (term of years tenancy, periodic tenancy, and tenancy at will). Modern law generally retains this system, although some of these estates are rare or obsolete. There appears to be a judicial consensus that no new estates may be created; thus, any language creating an estate will be interpreted to mean one of the traditional types. The basic permissible estates are shown on Table 1 below.

The freehold/nonfreehold distinction was a product of English feudalism. Freehold estates were held by the powerful: the nobles, gentlefolk, and others with a niche on the feudal pyramid. In early England, such estates could be created only through an intricate ceremony (*feoffment with livery of seisin*), which was performed on the land to be transferred. The holder of such an estate was said to have an almost mystical form of possession known as *seisin.* He was benefited from the social, political, and economic facets of the feudal pyramid and obligated to perform feudal duties to a superior. In contrast, nonfreehold estates were held by the powerless—common people who typically farmed the land. A nonfreehold estate could be created informally by agreement; its holder did not have seisin and owed no feudal duties.

Modern law still reflects the freehold/nonfreehold split, even though its feudal rationale ended long ago. Perhaps predictably, the branch of English law governing freehold estates evolved quite differently from that relating

---

[1] Scholars sometimes identify a fourth type of nonfreehold estate, known as the tenancy at sufferance, which arises when a tenant holds over after his legal right to possession ends (*see* § 15.05[E]).

to nonfreehold estates. Today we view freehold estates as forms of "owning" land, while nonfreehold estates are merely seen as forms of "leasing" land. The balance of this chapter covers freehold estates; nonfreehold estates are discussed in Chapter 15.

TABLE 1: PRESENT ESTATES

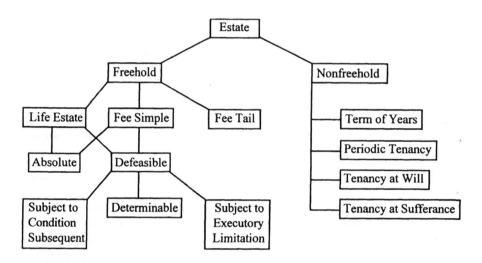

§ 9.05 Basic Categories of Freehold Estates

[A] Duration of Estates

The technical distinction between the three basic freehold estates is premised on *duration*. For example, the duration of the fee simple is potentially infinite, while the life estate lasts only for the lifetime of a particular person.

Each type of estate creates different rights and duties in its holder. The fee simple absolute stands alone as the largest "bundle" of permissible property rights, unencumbered by any future interest. By definition, all other freehold estates are accompanied by a future interest in another person, and the rights of the estate owner are accordingly diminished. Thus, if A holds only a life estate in Greenacre, someone else must hold the right to possession of Greenacre after A's death. A's rights over Greenacre are limited by this future interest. For example, A cannot destroy the productive apple orchard on Greenacre because this would permanently interfere with future enjoyment of the property and thus constitute waste.

[B] Fee Simple

[1] Characteristics

Fee simple roughly corresponds to the layperson's understanding of "ownership." The most common type of fee simple—called fee simple absolute—is the largest aggregation of property rights recognized under American law. It is also—by far—the most common estate utilized for ownership of land. Over 99% of all privately-owned land in the United States is held in fee simple absolute.[2] If you "own" a home, farm, or other real property, your estate is almost certainly fee simple absolute.

Technically, fee simple is a freehold estate whose duration is potentially infinite.[3] Thus, if O holds this estate it may endure forever. It does not end if O conveys it to another person; nor does it end if O dies. Rather, it endures over time, being transferred in multiple transactions by wills, deeds, or intestate succession to perhaps an infinite number of new owners.

Despite the conventional definition, the risk that a fee simple absolute might end is more theoretical than real. In theory at least, this estate might be terminated by escheat. Suppose O dies without leaving a will (in other words, "intestate") and leaves no legal heirs who are entitled to his property under the rules governing intestate succession. Under these circumstances, his fee simple absolute is transferred to the state by operation of law, a process called escheat. In a few states, escheat is seen as ending a fee simple absolute and other estates. In most states, however, the escheat process simply transfers a continuing estate to the state as another new owner.

[2] Creation

Under the common law approach, a fee simple estate could be conveyed only if a precise legal formula was used. In large part, this result reflected the law's early preference for the life estate. Unless the correct wording was employed to convey a fee simple or fee tail, the resulting estate would be considered a life estate.[4]

If O held fee simple in Greenacre, he could convey his estate to A by using a formula that included the phrase: "to A and his heirs." The words "to A" are termed *words of purchase*; they identify the person who now owns the estate. The words "and his heirs" are called *words of limitation.* They serve only to signal the type of estate A receives, here fee simple absolute, and do not create any property rights in anyone else. Thus, if A has three children (B, C, and D) at the time of O's conveyance, the children have no interest at all in Greenacre despite use of the phrase "and his heirs." A can convey or devise his rights in Greenacre to anyone and exercise all of his

---

[2] In practice, "fee simple absolute" is commonly abbreviated as "fee simple."

[3] Restatement of Property § 14 (1936) (defining an "estate in fee simple").

[4] Under the Statute of Wills adopted in 1540, inclusion of specific words of inheritance such as "and his heirs" was not required if the language of the will evidenced the testator's clear intent to devise a fee simple estate.

other rights concerning the property regardless of the wishes of B, C, and D.

In contrast, modern American law assumes that an owner normally intends to convey the entire estate rather than a lesser estate. This produces a constructional preference for the fee simple. Suppose O holds fee simple absolute in Greenacre, and executes a conveyance to A. Unless O uses language that clearly evidences his intent to create a lesser estate, his conveyance will be construed as transferring fee simple absolute to A. For example, if O grants Greenacre "to A" today, A receives fee simple absolute. It is no longer necessary for O to add the traditional verbiage "and his heirs."[5]

This fee simple preference mirrors several concerns. First, in everyday life most grantors both hold fee simple absolute and actually intend to transfer their entire estate. Construing ambiguous language in a deed or will as transferring fee simple absolute implements this intent and respects the autonomy of the grantor. Second, the fee simple preference serves the interrelated goals of marketability and efficiency.

[3] Rights and Duties of Estate Owner

Fee simple absolute provides an owner with the maximum quantum of rights recognized under American law. Suppose H, an unmarried man, owns fee simple absolute in Greenacre, consisting of ten acres of apple orchards. By definition, no one has a future interest in the property, and thus H owes no duties to other interest holders. Nonetheless, like all property rights, H's rights are affected by various utilitarian restrictions imposed to benefit society as a whole. As one court commented, "[a] man's right in his real property of course is not absolute."[6] What are H's basic rights?

First, H is entitled to the use of Greenacre forever. Accordingly, he may harvest the apples or allow them to rot; he may nurture the trees or chop them all down. No private person has the right to challenge this conduct. Of course, H's right is not absolute, for government might regulate the manner in which H uses the land (see Chapters 36–40). While H could chop the trees down, he might not be able to burn them down; states often regulate open burning on private land to protect nearby properties against fire danger. Similarly, the smoke produced by H's fire might drift across adjacent land owned by N, a neighboring owner; if this smoke unreasonably interferes with N's use and enjoyment of his property, N could successfully sue H on a private nuisance theory (see Chapter 29). But absent such unusual circumstances, H is relatively free to use Greenacre as he wishes simply because he owns all of the private property rights in the metaphorical "bundle of rights" that represents title.

Second, H is entitled to sole possession of Greenacre, which generally allows him to exclude all other persons from the land (see Chapter 30).

---

[5] See, e.g., Cole v. Steinlauf, 136 A.2d 744 (Conn. 1957). Only South Carolina still clings to the outmoded "and his heirs" formula. McLaurin v. McLaurin, 217 S.E.2d 41 (S.C. 1975).

[6] State v. Shack, 277 A.2d 369, 373 (N.J. 1971).

Suppose T, a hungry stranger, wishes to enter Greenacre to obtain an apple; H may legally prevent T's entry. If T enters without H's consent, T is liable to H in damages for trespass and might also face criminal trespass charges. Yet the right to exclude is not absolute. A wide range of nonpermissive entries is sanctioned by the law (e.g., police officers may enter in pursuit of a fugitive). In the celebrated *State v. Shack*[7] decision, the New Jersey Supreme Court extended this principle by holding that employees of publicly-funded health and legal services organizations could enter a farm to meet with workers living there despite the vehement protests of the employer-owner.

Finally, H may transfer his rights in Greenacre. During his lifetime, H may convey his estate by deed to whoever he wishes; alternatively, H may devise his rights by will to the devisees of his choice. In either case, H can opt to transfer either all or part of his estate. For example, H could grant a life estate to his sister S, retaining a reversion.[8] Even H's right to transfer, however, is somewhat restricted. A variety of doctrines limit the types of future interests that H can create; other rules curtail restraints on alienation and similar conditions that H may impose on his successors.

[C] Fee Tail

[1] Characteristics

The *fee tail*[9] is a largely-obsolete freehold estate whose duration was measured by the lives of the lineal descendants of a designated person.[10] For example, if O granted Greenacre "to A and the heirs of his body," this language created an estate that would endure as long as A's bloodline continued. Assume A had only one child, B, who in turn had only one child, C. Upon A's death, B automatically received the right to possession of Greenacre; upon B's death, the right to possession passed in turn to C. This cycle continued until the family line expired.[11]

Today the fee tail is virtually extinct in the United States. Yet fee tail remains a subject of academic interest, principally because the reasons for

---

[7] 277 A.2d 369 (N.J. 1971).

[8] Of course, if H retains rights in Greenacre at his death that are not devised (for example, because he left no will), these rights will pass by intestate succession to his heirs or, if he has no heirs, will escheat to the state (*see* Chapter 28).

[9] Literally, fee tail means a "cut" or "limited" fee simple. "Tail" stems from the Norman French term "talliare," meaning "to cut" or "to limit." The word "curtail" is derived from the same source.

[10] Restatement of Property § 59 (1936) defines fee tail as an estate "in favor of a natural person as to whom the conveyance contains words of inheritance" and "in specific words confines the succession to the issue of the first taker or to a designated class of such issue."

[11] An estate even more esoteric than fee tail is the *fee simple conditional*, which survives only in Iowa and South Carolina. The fee simple conditional is an estate that may only be inherited by the heirs of the first taker. Even where it survives, this estate has been limited by judicial interpretation; once issue are born to the first taker, he may circumvent the restriction simply by conveying fee simple absolute to another.

its rejection help explain the foundational principles of American property law.

[2] Creation

Why create a fee tail? Early English landowners wanted the ability to ensure that their land would be passed on to successive generations of their descendants, and thus remain within the family. In feudal England, ownership of land was central to both social identity and personal wealth. If a landowner could limit the alienability of family lands over the long term, he could safeguard the prestige and honor of his descendants. Suppose L owned fee simple absolute in Redacre. If L were about to die, he could of course convey fee simple absolute to his son M. What if M proved an incompetent manager and was forced to convey Redacre to his creditors? Or, even worse, what if M fell into a drunken stupor and gambled Redacre away? Landowners like L sought a method to prevent incompetent or dissipated descendants from alienating the family lands.

The fee tail was born in 1285 with the enactment of the statute De Donis Conditionalibus.[12] Under this statute, lands could be restricted so that they would pass only to lineal descendants of the first taker. Eventually, specialized forms of fee tail emerged, including fee tail male (limited to male lineal descendants) and fee tail special (limited to lineal descendants from a particular wife). If a landowner like L conveyed fee tail in Redacre to M (e.g., "to M and the heirs of his body"), M could not endanger future generations by transferring fee simple. At most, M could transfer the right to use Redacre during his lifetime; upon M's death, his eldest child would automatically be entitled to possession of the land.

Over the ensuing centuries, English land was increasingly "entailed," that is, held in fee tail. Indeed, the entailed family manor became a stock feature in English novels,[13] until the estate was formally abolished there in 1925. But long before then, fee tail owners were able to circumvent the entail through either of two ingenious and complex procedures, the common recovery (a collusive lawsuit that allowed the successful fee tail holder to convey fee simple)[14] and the fine.

[3] Accompanying Future Interests

Suppose O conveyed Greenacre "to A and the heirs of his body." By definition, two future interests arose: (a) one in the lineal descendants of A for as long as A's bloodline continued; and (b) one in O that would become possessory when A's bloodline ended. A's living lineal descendants (and prospective future descendants) all received a remainder. Thus, for example, if A had one living son, S, when O's conveyance became effective, S received a vested remainder in fee tail. But if A then had no living children,

---

[12] 13 Edw. I, ch. 1 (1285).

[13] *See, e.g.,* Daphne Du Maurier, Rebecca (1938).

[14] *See* Taltarum's Case, Y.B. 12 Edw. 4, fol. 19, pl. 25 (1472).

his unborn, potential descendants would hold a mere contingent remainder in fee tail.

A separate future interest became possessory when the fee tail ended, here when A's bloodline expired. The classification of this interest turned on who acquired it when the fee tail was first created. The future interest was a reversion if it was created in the transferor. Suppose O conveyed Greenacre "to A and the heirs of his body"; O retained a reversion by operation of law simply because he conveyed less than his entire estate. If O later conveyed his reversion to his daughter D or another successor, it would still be considered a reversion.

On the other hand, if O conveyed the property "to A and the heirs of his body, and then to B and her heirs," O transferred all of his rights. Because ultimate future interest was held by B, who received it in the same conveyance that created the fee tail itself, B's future interest was considered a remainder.

[4] Rights and Duties of Estate Owner

The rights of a fee tail owner were quite restricted when compared to those of the fee simple owner. The holder of fee tail was entitled to the use and enjoyment of the land involved, but not to the extreme of committing waste (*see* § 9.09). For example, if A held fee tail in Greenacre, A could harvest the apples from its orchards or allow them to rot, like a fee simple owner. But—unlike the fee simple owner—A could not chop down the trees because this would unreasonably interfere with the ability of future interest holders to enjoy their rights.

More importantly, the fee tail owner had only a limited right of transfer. Because the owner's possessory right ended at death, it could not be devised or inherited. At most, the owner could convey the right to possess the property during his lifetime. Thus, if A (trying to settle his gambling debts) purported to convey Greenacre to B in fee simple in 1500, B received only what A had—the right to possession of Greenacre until A died. If A died in 1501, B's rights ended and the possessory estate in Greenacre automatically passed to A's eldest son.

[5] The Demise of Fee Tail

The fee tail was largely abolished in the United States over 200 years ago. The principal architect of this reform was Thomas Jefferson, who feared that this estate would undermine democracy. He worried that fee tail would contribute to the development of a hereditary aristocracy (akin to the hated English aristocracy) that could control American political and social life.[15]

---

[15] Jefferson explained that the bill he proposed to abolish fee tail in Virginia was one of four measures: "forming a system by which every fibre would be eradicated of ancient or future aristocracy; and a foundation laid for a government truly republican. The repeal of the laws of entail would prevent the accumulation and perpetuation of wealth in select families, and preserve the soil of the country from being daily more and more absorbed in Mortmain." Thomas Jefferson, *Autobiography, 1743–1790, in* Thomas Jefferson: Writings 44 (Merrill D. Peterson ed., 1984).

Jefferson's utopia was a nation of small landowners. Ownership of land would empower each citizen with the self-sufficiency necessary to make independent political decisions, free from the pressure of a landed employer, creating a society founded on individual merit rather than ancestral status. Jefferson spearheaded a successful effort to convince the Virginia legislature to ban fee tail.

Eventually most other states also abolished fee tail.[16] Jeffersonian concerns played a role in this process,[17] as did the traditional concern for free alienation of land. Fee tail would limit the marketability of land, thus impairing American economic development. Suppose O owned fee tail in land suitable for a shipyard, but lacked the capital required to develop it. As a practical matter, O could not sell the land for shipyard use, because a buyer would receive only O's fee tail, which could end at any time; a prudent investor was unwilling to take this risk. Similarly, O could not finance the development of the shipyard with a loan secured by a mortgage on the land, because the mortgage would end whenever O died. In short, land held in fee tail was destined for economic limbo.

What happens if a modern grantor attempts to create fee tail? In almost every state, this contingency is addressed by statute. The majority of states interprets fee tail language as creating fee simple absolute in the first taker. Thus, if O conveys Greenacre "to S and the heirs of his body," S simply receives fee simple absolute.[18] A few states follow different views. In some, the fee tail is preserved for one generation, and is then converted to fee simple absolute in the issue of the first taker.[19] In other states, fee tail language creates a life estate in the first taker, followed by a vested remainder in fee simple absolute in the first taker's issue.

[D] Life Estate

[1] Characteristics

The *life estate* is a freehold estate whose duration is measured by the lives of one or more specified persons.[20] For example, a grant "to B for B's life" creates a life estate in B for as long as she lives. B, as the holder of the life estate, is called the *life tenant*. Alternatively, the duration of the

---

[16] In theory at least, fee tail may still be created in Delaware, Maine, Massachusetts, and Rhode Island. Yet as a practical matter, any fee tail owner in these states can avoid the entail easily. When a fee tail owner executes and delivers a deed that purports to convey fee simple, the grantee receives fee simple. An example is Caccamo v. Banning, 75 A.2d 222 (Del. Super. Ct. 1950), where the fee tail owner conveyed fee simple to a strawman, who reconveyed fee simple to her; the court held that this process eliminated the entail.

[17] *See, e.g.,* Robins Island Preservation Fund, Inc. v. Southold Dev. Corp., 959 F.2d 409 (2d Cir. 1992) (discussing New York's abolition of fee tail in historical context).

[18] What if the conveyance was "to S and the heirs of his body, and then to T"? Statutes in some states provide that such language gives S fee simple subject to an executory limitation and gives T an executory interest in fee simple (which becomes possessory if and when S dies without issue).

[19] *See, e.g.,* Long v. Long, 343 N.E.2d 100 (Ohio 1976).

[20] Restatement of Property § 18 (1936).

life estate may be measured by the life of a person other than the grantee (e.g., "to B for the life of C"); this is called a life estate *pur autre vie*.[21] The life estate is considered the smallest of the three freehold estates.

The life estate is most commonly encountered in the family gift. In the nineteenth and early twentieth centuries, life estates typically involved either the family home or the family farm. For example, suppose W owned a farm in 1920 and wanted both to support her aged sister S and to ultimately give the farm to W's grandchildren. W might devise a life estate in the farm to S, followed by a remainder in W's grandchildren. For a variety of reasons, creation of a legal life estate in land today is unwise and thus rare. The modern life estate is an equitable estate, usually created to facilitate a family gift in trust.

[2] Creation

After the Norman Conquest, the estates initially granted by the king to his supporters were for life terms only. Later, the holder of a fee simple could choose to create a life estate by using appropriate language in a deed or will. Under the formalistic English common law, a fee simple or fee tail could be created only by precise words in inheritance. Thus, any freehold estate created without such words of inheritance was deemed to be a life estate. A grant "to B," for example, created only a life estate in B.

Reversing the common law approach, modern American law presumes that every grant passes *all* of the grantor's estate, unless the grantor's contrary intention is clearly indicated. As a result, ambiguous language in a conveyance by a grantor holding fee simple (e.g., "to B") is judicially interpreted as transferring fee simple absolute.

An example is *White v. Brown,*[22] where the Tennessee Supreme Court construed a holographic will that provided: "I wish Evelyn White to have my home to live in and not to be sold."[23] Concluding that this sentence did not clearly state the intent of the testatrix, the court held that it devised a fee simple estate. Thus, today the holder of a fee simple estate can create a life estate only by using language that clearly reflects this intention (e.g., "to B for life" or "to B for his lifetime").[24]

Although life estates are usually created by an express grant or devise, they can sometimes arise by operation of law. For example, at common law a widow received "dower," a specialized type of life estate in certain lands owned by her deceased husband (*see* § 11.02[D][1]); similarly, in some states an attempt to create a fee tail will be construed as creating a life estate instead.

---

[21] "Pur autre vie" is old French for the phrase "for another life."

[22] 559 S.W.2d 938 (Tenn. 1977).

[23] White v. Brown, 559 S.W.2d 938 (Tenn. 1977) (emphasis in original).

[24] *See, e.g.,* Pigg v. Haley, 294 S.E.2d 851 (Va. 1982).

[3] Accompanying Future Interests

By definition, whenever a life estate is created a future interest also arises. If O, holding fee simple absolute in Greenacre, conveys "to A for life," he has granted A *less* than the sum of his property rights. O's resulting right to possession of Greenacre upon A's death is termed a *reversion* (*see* § 13.02[A]). But if O creates this future interest in a third person (e.g., "to A for life, and then to B and his heirs"), it is called a *remainder* (*see* § 14.03).

[4] Rights and Duties of Estate Owner

The life tenant is entitled to the use and enjoyment of the land, including any rents and profits it produces. But—like the fee tail owner—the life tenant cannot commit waste (*see* § 9.09). For example, if T has a life estate in the apple orchard known as Greenacre, she is entitled to harvest the apples or not to harvest them, as she chooses; but T cannot chop the trees down, for this would be considered waste.

Similarly, a life tenant has a restricted right of transfer. A life tenant may transfer what he or she has—possession of the land for the duration of the life estate—but nothing more. Thus, while a life tenant in theory might lease, mortgage, or even convey his or her interest, the land is bound by these transfers only for so long as the life estate endures; accordingly, as a practical matter, such transfers are difficult. Moreover, the normal life estate cannot be inherited or devised. In the example above, T's life estate ends when she dies. Suppose, however, that T holds a life estate pur autre vie, measured by the life of U. If T dies before U, T's life estate continues and may be transferred to others upon T's death.

The life tenant's right to sell his or her interest is often illusory because its value is uncertain and speculative. T's life estate in Greenacre, for example, may be virtually worthless (e.g., if T dies tomorrow) or quite valuable (e.g., if T lives for 50 more years). An interesting issue arises when the life tenant wishes to maximize the value of the interest by forcing a sale of the affected land over the objections of the remainderman. *Baker v. Weedon* [25] illustrates the problem. There the 73-year-old plaintiff was a life tenant in a Mississippi farm; the farm produced income of only $1,000 per year, too little for her to live on. But fee simple absolute in the farm was valued at $168,500. If the fee simple could be sold, and her life estate transferred to the sales proceeds, she would earn enough interest to support herself (e.g., over $8,000 per year assuming a 5% return). The remaindermen refused to join voluntarily in selling the fee simple because they expected that future construction of a nearby highway would double the land's value in a few years. Plaintiff sought a judicial decree that would (a) order sale of the fee simple absolute over the remaindermen's objections and (b) recognize her life estate in the proceeds. [26] Prior Mississippi

---

[25] 262 So. 2d 641 (Miss. 1972).

[26] *See also* United States v. 403.15 Acres of Land, 316 F. Supp. 655 (M.D. Tenn. 1970) (life tenant awarded income for life from entire condemnation award when federal government condemned land for reservoir project; court rejected remainderman's argument that life tenant should only receive the cash value of her life estate based upon actuarial table).

decisions had authorized such judicial sale only where necessary to preserve the estate, that is, if the property involved had deteriorated to the point that its income would not pay for required taxes and maintenance. But the *Baker* court embraced a new rule, holding that such a sale would be proper if "necessary for the best interest of all the parties."[27] The case was remanded to allow plaintiff the opportunity to prove that an immediate sale would serve the best interests of all.

Most states have enacted statutes in recent decades that expand judicial power to order the sale or other transfer of fee simple in this situation. There is quite a bit of state by state variation, but the most common approach echoes the *Baker* standard: sale will be decreed if it is "expedient."[28]

[5]   Evaluating the Life Estate

Today the legal life estate in real property has been eclipsed by a more effective tool—the trust (*see* Chapter 28). As *Baker v. Weedon*[29] illustrates, the legal life estate is relatively inflexible. Even if circumstances change dramatically, the future interest holder may have veto power over any alteration in the status quo. However, if an owner creates a life estate in trust (an "equitable life estate"), the trustee holds legal title and can accordingly take appropriate steps to protect all parties against changed circumstances, including selling trust assets. England abolished the legal life estate in land in 1925, and American states may ultimately follow this lead. In short, the legal life estate in land is headed toward extinction.

The life estate is commonly used in connection with personal property assets (e.g., stocks and bonds) held in trust. Thus, if O dies leaving a stock portfolio valued at $5,000,000, his will might create a testamentary trust for the benefit of his remaining family members. His wife W receives an equitable life estate in the stock portfolio, while his children C and D receive equitable vested remainders.[30]

§ 9.06   Freehold Estates: Absolute or Defeasible?

[A]   Basic Distinction

Each freehold estate is either *absolute* or *defeasible*. The distinction between the two categories turns on the answer to a simple question: how might the estate end?

Most estates are absolute, meaning that their duration is restricted only by the standard limitation that defines that category of estate. For example,

---

[27] Baker v. Weedon, 262 So. 2d 641, 644 (Miss. 1972).

[28] *See, e.g.,* N.Y. Real Prop. Acts. L. §§ 1602, 1604.

[29] 262 So. 2d 641 (Miss. 1972).

[30] The legal life estate retains some vitality in the context of personal property. For example, suppose O owns a rocking chair that has been in her family for decades and possesses special sentimental value. In order to control the chair's ultimate fate, she might bequeath a life estate in the chair to one family member, and a remainder to another.

the fee simple is defined as an estate that is potentially infinite, absent escheat. Thus, if O conveys Blueacre "to S and his heirs," S receives the standard type of fee simple, one which is potentially infinite and which will end (if at all) only by escheat; S owns fee simple absolute. Similarly, a life estate is defined as an estate whose duration is measured by the life of a person or persons. So if O conveys Greenacre "to D for life," D owns a life estate absolute. Its length—consistent with the basic definition—is measured by the life of a person.[31]

On the other hand, a defeasible estate is subject to a special provision—included in the language in the deed, trust, or will that creates the estate—that may end the estate prematurely if a particular future event occurs. Suppose O conveys Blueacre "to S and his heirs for so long as S refrains from smoking a cigar." S clearly owns a type of fee simple, yet it is clear that his estate will end if he smokes a cigar, long before any possible escheat. S holds a type of defeasible fee simple called fee simple determinable. Or O might convey Greenacre "to D for life, but if D ever smokes cigars, then to E and her heirs." Here D owns a form of life estate, but one which may end early; this is a fairly rare type of defeasible life estate, called a life estate subject to an executory limitation. Here, the estates of S and D may end prematurely, if either one smokes a cigar. Although the examples above assume a contingent future event (that is, one uncertain to occur), a defeasible estate will also be found where the stated event is virtually certain to occur, e.g., "to X until it next snows in Alaska."

The discussion of defeasible estates below focuses on the defeasible fee simple because—although defeasible estates are becoming an endangered species—the defeasible fee simple remains the most common type.

[B] Why Create Defeasible Estates?

Although widely used in the past, defeasible estates are rarely created today. The defeasible estate was once commonly utilized in conveyances for charitable purposes such as parks,[32] schools,[33] hospitals, orphanages, and the like. It provided leverage to ensure that the donor's intent was followed even after death. Suppose that D, holding fee simple absolute in Greenacre, wished to encourage the creation of a hospital by donating land for the hospital site. She could convey fee simple absolute in Greenacre to a non-profit hospital corporation. But this might allow the corporation to operate a hospital on the land for a few years, cease operations, and sell the land for another purpose. D could avoid this risk by conveying only a defeasible estate in Greenacre, such as "to Corporation for so long as Greenacre is used as a hospital." Under this granting language, if the hospital use ever ended, the Corporation's estate also ended. Logically, this threatened loss of title would induce a charitable donee to respect the donor's original intent.

---

[31] The "life estate absolute" is almost always abbreviated as "life estate."

[32] See, e.g., Ink v. City of Canton, 212 N.E.2d 574 (Ohio 1965).

[33] See, e.g., Mahrenholz v. County Bd. of School Trustees, 417 N.E.2d 138 (Ill. App. Ct. 1981).

Defeasible estates were also sometimes used to secure economic goals or to control the behavior of family members. If F, a farmer, wanted to ensure that his crops could be easily transported to market, he might grant a strip of his land to the railroad "for so long as used as a railroad."[34] Or if G, a strict teetotaler, hoped to persuade her son S never to drink alcohol, she might grant property to S "for so long as S never drinks alcohol."

The use of defeasible estates and related conditions to control the behavior of family members is controversial. Could parent P devise land to daughter D for so long as she remains married to H, follows certain religious practices, or pursues a specified career? Modern cases involving such conditions are scant.[35] The Restatement of Property generally provides that restrictions related to religion, personal habits, education, or occupation are valid;[36] but it limits the enforceability of restrictions concerning marriage, remarriage, divorce, or separation.[37]

[C]   Types of Defeasible Estates

[1]   Basic Distinctions

The three types of defeasible fee simple estates are:

  (1)   fee simple determinable;

  (2)   fee simple subject to a condition subsequent; and

  (3)   fee simple subject to an executory limitation.

Two basic distinctions are used in categorizing a defeasible fee: (a) who holds the future interest? and (b) is the defeasance language expressed in words of time or words of condition? Where the future interest is retained by the transferor (or his successors), the estate is fee simple determinable if words of time (e.g., "for so long as") are used, and fee simple subject to a condition subsequent if words of condition (e.g., "on condition that") are used. If the future interest is held by a transferee (that is, a person other than the transferor or his successors), the estate is a fee simple subject to an executory limitation where words of condition are used.

[2]   Fee Simple Determinable

The *fee simple determinable* automatically expires at a stated time, immediately giving the transferor the legal right to possession.[38]

---

[34] *Cf.* Nichols v. Haehn, 187 N.Y.S.2d 773, 775 (App. Div. 1959) (deed provided that land would revert to grantor "in case said Railway shall at any time be abandoned").

[35] *See, e.g., In re* Estate of Romero, 847 P.2d 319 (N.M. Ct. App. 1993) (if decedent intended to separate sons from mother by devise of home to sons for so long as mother did not live with them, then devise would violate public policy).

[36] Restatement (Second) of Property: Donative Transfers §§ 8.1–8.3 (1983).

[37] Restatement (Second) of Property: Donative Transfers §§ 6.1–7.2 (1983). *But see* Lewis v. Searles, 452 S.W.2d 153 (Mo. 1970) (upholding devise of property to niece "for so long as she remains single and unmarried").

[38] *See* Restatement of Property § 44 (1936).

Suppose W owns fee simple absolute in Silveracre and grants "to City for so long as Silveracre is used for a park." This conveyance creates a fee simple determinable estate in City. First, under this language W, the transferor, retained the future interest in Silveracre, called a *possibility of reverter*. Even though W's conveyance to the City does not expressly reserve any interest, her possibility of reverter arises as a matter of law simply because she did not convey her entire estate. Second, the defeasance language is expressed in words of time; the City's estate endures only so long as park use continues. Suppose City operates a park on the land for 10 years, and then builds a sewage treatment plant on the site. Once the park use ends, the City's estate expires according to its terms and the right to possession of Silveracre automatically reverts to W, all without any action on her part. W again holds fee simple absolute in Silveracre.

It is sometimes difficult to distinguish between fee simple determinable and fee simple subject to a condition subsequent. In general, the hallmark of a fee simple determinable is language of time or duration. [39] This estate is created by granting language indicating that a fee simple estate will continue only for the duration of a specified state of affairs such as "so long as," (e.g., "to City for so long as the land is used as a park"), "while," (e.g., "to City while the land is used as a park"), and "during," (e.g., "to City during the time the land is used as a park"). For example, in *Mahrenholz v. County Board of School Trustees*, [40] the grant of land to a school district with the restriction "this land to be used for school purposes only; otherwise to revert to Grantors herein" was held to create fee simple determinable. The appellate court reasoned that the term "only" indicated an intent to "give the land . . . only as long as it was needed and no longer." [41]

Where the granting language is so ambiguous that the above guidelines are unhelpful, most courts will construe the estate as fee simple subject to a condition subsequent in order to avoid forfeiture. [42] While the fee simple determinable causes automatic forfeiture when the stated event occurs, the fee simple subject to a condition subsequent presents only the risk of forfeiture. [43]

---

[39] *See, e.g.,* Mayor and City Council of Ocean City v. Taber, 367 A.2d 1233, 1236 (Md. 1977) (grant to federal government that provided "when the United States shall fail to use the said Life Saving Station, the land hereby conveyed for the purpose aforesaid, shall, without any legal proceedings, suit, or otherwise, revert to the said Trustees" held to create fee simple determinable).

[40] 417 N.E.2d 138 (Ill. App. Ct. 1981).

[41] Mahrenholz v. County Bd. of School Trustees, 417 N.E.2d 138, 142 (Ill. App. Ct. 1981).

[42] *See, e.g.,* Oldfield v. Stoeco Homes, Inc., 139 A.2d 291, 294 (N.J. 1958) (deed restriction that provided in part "a failure to comply with the covenants and conditions . . . will automatically cause title to all lands to revert to the City" held to create fee simple subject to condition subsequent).

[43] As the Pennsylvania Supreme Court further explained in Higbee Corp. v. Kennedy, 428 A.2d 592, 596–597 (Pa. 1981), the fee simple determinable "is more cumbersome upon the alienability of land than a fee simple subject to a condition subsequent."

[3] Fee Simple Subject to a Condition Subsequent

The *fee simple subject to a condition subsequent* is—as the name suggests—a fee simple where the granting words are followed by a limiting condition in favor of the transferor. The estate is accompanied by a future interest held by the transferor, most commonly called a *right of entry*.[44] The hallmark of this estate is that it does not automatically expire when the triggering condition occurs. Instead, once the condition occurs, the future interest holder has the power to take affirmative action to end the estate.[45] If the holder fails to exercise this option, the estate continues.

Suppose that W holds fee simple absolute in Silveracre and grants "to City, but if the land is not used as a park, W may re-enter and retake the premises." If City uses Silveracre as a park, but then 10 years later builds a sewage treatment plant there, the City's estate does not automatically end. Instead, W merely has a right to end the City's estate, which W may or may not choose to enforce. Until W acts, the City's estate continues.

While the fee simple determinable is characterized by words of time, the fee simple subject to a condition subsequent is characterized by words of event or condition. This estate is typically created by using phrases such as "on condition that" (e.g., "to City on condition that the land be used as a park"), "but if" (e.g., "to City but if the land is not used as a park, then . . ."), and "provided however" (e.g., "to City, provided however that the land shall be used as a park . . .").

Under the traditional English approach, once the stated condition occurred, the future interest holder could end the estate only by physically re-entering the land with accompanying witnesses. Today physical re-entry is no longer necessary in the United States; indeed, given the growing concern about the risk of violence stemming from self-help, this method should be deemed unacceptable in any event.[46] In some states, the future interest holder can end the estate simply by giving formal notice to the estate owner; other states require the future interest holder to file an ejectment or quiet title action against the estate owner.

[4] Fee Simple Subject to an Executory Limitation

The *fee simple subject to an executory limitation* is a fee simple estate that automatically expires when a stated event occurs (like fee simple determinable), but gives the right to possession to a transferee (unlike fee simple determinable).[47] This estate arose only after the Statute of Uses authorized executory interests in 1536.

Suppose O conveys Silveracre "to City, but if the land is not used as a park, then to Z and his heirs." Here the future interest owned by Z is an

---

[44] This future interest is sometimes also called a "power of termination" or "right of reentry."

[45] Forsgren v. Sollie, 659 P.2d 1068 (Utah 1983).

[46] *But see* Forsgren v. Sollie, 659 P.2d 1068 (Utah 1983) (grantor physically re-entered unimproved lot when grantee failed to perform conditions).

[47] Hall v. Hall, 604 S.W.2d 851, 854 (Tenn. 1980).

executory interest, which will automatically divest or "cut short" the City's estate if the park use ceases, without any affirmative act by Z. Because the future interest is held by Z (a transferee from O) rather than by O, the City's estate is a fee simple subject to an executory limitation.

What if O instead conveys Silveracre "to City for so long as the land is used as a park, and then to Z and his heirs"? Some authorities classify O's estate as fee simple determinable, but disagreement remains. Professor Roger Cunningham and others have suggested that this estate is more aptly described as a "fee simple determinable with an executory limitation."[48]

[5] Defeasible Life Estates

Defeasible life estates are permissible but exceedingly rare. For example, if O holds fee simple absolute in Greenacre, she could create any of the following estates: life estate determinable, life estate subject to a condition subsequent, or life estate subject to an executory limitation.

[6] Consequences of the Distinctions

The distinction between fee simple determinable and fee simple subject to a condition subsequent—however precise in theory—is becoming increasingly blurred. Historically, the distinction has produced three different legal impacts: (1) liability for rent; (2) commencement of the statute of limitations period for adverse possession; and (3) applicability of equitable defenses. Yet critics wonder whether grantors actually intend that these differing results follow from minor variations in granting language. Today there is a clear trend toward eliminating the distinction between the two estates, and treating both as fee simple subject to a condition subsequent.[49]

One traditional distinction is liability for rent. Once a fee simple determinable automatically expires, the former estate owner has no legal right to possession and is liable to the new owner for the fair rental value of the land. In contrast, if the land is held in fee simple subject to a condition subsequent, no rent liability attaches until the future interest holder takes affirmative action to end the estate. Suppose O grants a defeasible fee simple in Blueacre, a farm, to D and the triggering event is D's consumption of alcohol; D first drinks alcohol in 1999, but remains in possession of Blueacre until O brings suit in 2008. If D's estate was fee simple determinable, it ended in 1999, and D owes O rent for nine years; on the other hand, if D held fee simple subject to a condition subsequent, D owes no rent for his occupancy before O sues in 2008.

Another historic difference is when the statute of limitations for adverse possession commences. All states agree that once a fee simple determinable ends, continued possession by the former estate owner starts the adverse possession period; if D held fee simple determinable in the example above, he started adversely possessing Blueacre in 1999. But there is less logical consistency on the issue when a fee simple subject to a condition subsequent

---

[48] Roger A. Cunningham *et al.*, The Law of Property 58–59 (2d ed. 1993).

[49] *See, e.g.,* Cal. Civ. Code § 885.020 (abolishing fee simple determinable).

is involved. Seemingly, D's estate continues until O brings suit in 2008, so D's possession is not adverse until then; some states follow this view. But others hold—illogically—that the period begins running when the stated event occurs, here in 1999, regardless of whether the future interest holder chooses to terminate the estate.

Finally, equitable defenses such as waiver and estoppel are sometimes utilized to bar a future interest holder from terminating fee simple subject to a condition subsequent.[50] Because fee simple determinable ends automatically, such defenses are usually inapplicable.

[D] Rights and Duties of Estate Owner

The owner of a defeasible estate generally has virtually the same rights and duties as an owner of the parallel absolute estate, except that he or she cannot commit waste.[51] For example, absent a contrary condition in the grant or devise, one holding fee simple determinable is entitled to exclusive use and possession of the affected land, and has the full right to transfer the interest, just as if the holder owned fee simple absolute. Of course, any of these rights may be restricted by special conditions inserted by the transferor (e.g., "for so long as X refrains from picking the apples on the land" or "provided, however, that X allows neighbors to cross the land to reach the lake").

[E] Judicial Hostility Toward Defeasible Estates

American courts have been traditionally and understandably hostile toward defeasible estates.[52] In part, this attitude reflects the law's long-standing concern for the free alienation of land. Property held in a defeasible estate is often difficult to lease, mortgage, sell, or otherwise transfer because of the risk that title may be lost. Another reason for this hostility is judicial abhorrence of forfeiture. The termination of a defeasible fee is often seen as providing a windfall to the future interest holder (perhaps a distant relative of the original transferor), while imposing an inequitable loss on the estate owner.

Various judicial mechanisms are employed to limit the scope of defeasible estates. Most importantly, the granting language must indicate a clear intent to impose a condition on the estate. Words that merely recite the intent or purpose of the grantor do not limit the estate that is granted. For example, in *Wood v. Board of County Commissioners*,[53] a deed that recited

---

[50] *See, e.g.,* Storke v. Penn Mutual Ins. Co., 61 N.E.2d 552 (Ill. 1945) (plaintiffs waived right to terminate fee simple subject to condition subsequent because they were aware that stated event—sale of alcohol on property—had occurred but delayed for years in taking action). *But see* Martin v. City of Seattle, 728 P.2d 1091 (Wash. Ct. App. 1986) (plaintiffs who waited 71 years before seeking to terminate fee simple subject to condition subsequent had not waived right).

[51] *See* Restatement of Property §§ 193, 194 (1936).

[52] *See* Gerald Korngold, *For Unifying Servitudes and Defeasible Fees: Property Law's Functional Equivalents*, 66 Tex. L. Rev. 533 (1988).

[53] 759 P.2d 1250 (Wyo. 1988).

that the conveyance was "for the purpose of constructing and maintaining thereon a County Hospital"[54] was held to transfer fee simple absolute; the language did not restrict the fee simple granted, but only stated the grantor's purpose.[55] Similarly, words of covenant or promise (e.g., "and the grantee promises to use the land only for a hospital") merely create a contract obligation in the grantee, not a defeasible estate. In addition, where ambiguous language could be construed as creating either an absolute or a defeasible estate, courts uniformly follow a constructional preference for an absolute estate. Even where a defeasible estate clearly exists, courts tend to construe the conditional language narrowly, in order to avoid forfeiture.[56]

[F] The Lingering Demise of Defeasible Estates

The defeasible estates are slowly following the fee tail into extinction in a lingering death scene reminiscent of a tragic opera. Modern landowners rarely create new defeasible estates, preferring to convey fee simple absolute. In part, this shift reflects our changing culture; as a philosophical matter, landowners are less concerned with restricting the autonomy of future owners than were their nineteenth-century predecessors.

Moreover, as a practical matter, sophisticated landowners are increasingly aware of the constraints that a defeasible estate imposes on land. Land held in a defeasible estate is unlikely to be utilized for its highest and best use; potential buyers, lessees, and lenders, for example, are usually reluctant to invest in land when the owner's title might immediately end.

Finally, even if a new defeasible fee estate is created, statutes in many states indirectly facilitate its conversion to fee simple absolute, by restricting the duration and enforceability of the accompanying future interest (*see* § 13.05).

§ 9.07 Freehold Estates: Legal or Equitable?

Each estate and future interest discussed above could also be created in trust (*see* Chapter 28). O, holding fee simple absolute in Greenacre, might convey Greenacre "to T in trust for L for life, and then for R." This grant effectively splits the metaphorical bundle of rights in a different manner. T, the trustee, holds "legal" title to Greenacre, here fee simple absolute. But L and R, the beneficiaries, simultaneously hold "equitable" interests in Greenacre. S owns an equitable life estate and R holds an equitable vested remainder.

---

[54] Wood v. Board of County Comm'rs, 759 P.2d 1250, 1251–1252 (Wyo. 1988).

[55] *See also* Roberts v. Rhodes, 643 P.2d 116 (Kan. 1982).

[56] *See, e.g.,* Mahrenholz v. County Bd. of School Trustees, 544 N.E.2d 128 (Ill. App. Ct. 1989) (storage of desks and other equipment on land subject to determinable fee held use for "school purpose").

§ 9.08   Restrictions on Transfer: Rule Against Restraints on Alienation

[A]   The Importance of Free Alienation

One of the foundational precepts of the English property law system was that land should be freely transferable or "alienable." Accordingly, the law was extremely hostile to restraints on alienation—provisions in deeds or wills which purport to prohibit or restrict future transfers. Modern American law reflects similar antagonism.

Why should the legal system protect free alienation? Restraints on alienation are viewed as preventing the maximum utilization of land. Suppose O owns fee simple absolute in Greyacre, a perfect site for a new factory, but cannot transfer any interest because his deed contains an enforceable prohibition against transfer. Under these circumstances, O will probably be unable to secure financing to build and operate the factory because he cannot grant potential lenders a mortgage on Greyacre to secure the loan; O might be unwilling to invest his own money in improving Greyacre simply because he would never be able to recoup it through sale. Similarly, O cannot sell Greyacre to investors who already have sufficient capital for the factory project. If the restraint is valid, Greyacre remains devoted to a low-intensity use (e.g., agriculture) and society loses the benefits that the factory would produce.

Free alienation also serves two lesser policies. It protects the good faith expectations of creditors by allowing them to execute on property in order to satisfy the owner's unpaid debts. Finally, it prevents the undue concentration of wealth that—particularly in the young United States—was seen as a potential threat to democratic values.

[B]   Restraints on Fee Simple Estates

American courts uniformly hold that any total or "absolute" restraint on alienation of a fee simple estate (whether absolute or defeasible) is null and void, regardless of the form of the restraint.[57] Suppose O attempts to express a restraint in defeasible fee language, imposing a "forfeiture restraint." If O devises Greenacre "to B, but if B ever attempts to transfer Greenacre, then to C," a court would find the restraint void; thus, B owns fee simple absolute, and C receives no interest. A similar result follows if O imposes a "disabling restraint" by devising Greenacre "to B, however any transfer of Greenacre shall be void;" the restraint is invalid. Similarly, a "promissory restraint"—a promise by the grantee not to transfer the property—is generally held unenforceable.[58]

---

[57] *See, e.g.,* Mountain Brow Lodge No. 82, Independent Order of Odd Fellows v. Toscano, 64 Cal. Rptr. 816, 817 (Ct. App. 1967) (deed clause that provided property would revert to grantors "in the event of sale or transfer" held invalid restraint).

[58] An interesting issue arises if a grantor uses defeasible fee language that indirectly restrains alienation. For example, in Mountain Brow Lodge No. 82, Independent Order of Odd Fellows v. Toscano, 64 Cal. Rptr. 816, 817 (Ct. App. 1967), the grantors conveyed a fee simple

Suppose instead that O conveys Greenacre to B on condition that it "is never transferred to anyone other than C, D, or E" or "not transferred to anyone during the next 10 years." Such phrases impose only partial restraints on alienation. The law governing these limited restraints is somewhat unclear. For example, most courts will invalidate restraints that limit the number of transferees or prevent transfer for a specified duration.[59] But the Restatement (Second) of Property advocates a broader view; it suggests that a partial restraint that is reasonable given its purpose, nature, and duration should be upheld.[60]

[C] Restraints on Life Estates

The common law was substantially less concerned with restraints on alienation of the life estate, presumably because its limited duration already impairs marketability. The modern American rule is that forfeiture and promissory restraints on a life estate are valid, but—somewhat illogically—that disabling restraints are void.[61]

§ 9.09 Restriction on Use: Waste

[A] Waste in Context

Waste is the principal common law mechanism for resolving land use disputes where property rights are divided between persons holding present estates and future interests in the same land.[62] In general, absent a superseding agreement, the waste doctrine restrains the present estate owner from acting in a manner that unreasonably injures the affected land and thus reduces the value of the future interest. The law effectively presumes that the original grantor intended the estate holder to pass on possession of the land to the future interest holder in approximately the same condition as it was received.

Suppose L owns a life estate in Redacre, and R owns the ensuing vested remainder. L might prefer to exploit Redacre in a manner that maximizes his short term profit—for example, by extracting all the oil from Redacre—even if this causes long run damage to R's interest. As Judge Richard Posner

---

subject to a condition subsequent in a town lot to a fraternal lodge; the deed provided, inter alia, that the land would revert to the grantors "in the event the same fails to be used" by the lodge. When the lodge later sued, claiming a de facto restraint on alienation, the court upheld the restriction based on the historic common law refusal to extend the doctrine to mere use restraints.

[59] Similarly, a restraint that purports to preclude transfer based on the race, color, national origin, religion, or other personal characteristic of the transferee would—as a matter of public policy—be invalid. See, e.g., 42 U.S.C. § 3604(a) (residential property); Cal. Civ. Code § 53 (generally).

[60] Restatement (Second) of Property: Donative Transfers §§ 4.1, 4.2 (1983).

[61] Restatement (Second) of Property: Donative Transfers §§ 4.1–4.3 (1983).

[62] For an analysis of the development of the law of waste in the United States, see John G. Sprankling, *The Antiwilderness Bias in American Property Law*, 63 U. Chi. L. Rev. 519, 533–536 (1996).

observed, a life tenant in this situation has "an incentive to maximize not the value of the property, . . . but only the present value of the earnings stream obtainable during his expected lifetime."[63] Posner posits that various factors may prevent the life tenant and remainderman from negotiating a mutually-acceptable plan for using the land; he envisions waste as the law's solution to this stalemate.

Two principal types of waste are recognized today: affirmative waste and permissive waste. England and the young United States formerly recognized a third category, called ameliorative waste, under which any change in the character of the land was deemed actionable waste.[64] Converting forest into farm land was deemed waste, for example, even if this change increased the market value of the land. Nineteenth-century American courts abandoned this rule as inconsistent with the need for agrarian development of the nation's wilderness land.[65]

[B] Affirmative Waste

Affirmative waste (or *voluntary waste*) occurs when the voluntary acts of the present estate owner significantly reduce the value of the property. For example, if life tenant L wantonly destroys the valuable residence on the land, L will be liable to remainderman R in waste. Conversely, the demolition of obsolete and worthless improvements in order to permit the productive use of the land will not constitute waste, as explained in the classic *Melms v. Pabst Brewing Co.*[66] decision.

Does the life tenant commit waste by exploiting natural resources on the land such as minerals or timber? Most jurisdictions follow the traditional English rule regarding mining activities. If an open mine existed on the land when the present estate owner took possession, its operation may continue until the resource is totally depleted; this result is justified by the presumption that the original grantor intended to permit this ongoing use to continue. On the other hand, the present estate owner may not open a new mine, unless all affected future interest holders agree.[67] Similarly, American courts have relaxed the strict application of waste as applied to timber cutting. If the original owner engaged in commercial tree harvesting, by analogy to the "open mines" rule most courts will allow the life tenant to continue such cutting. Even absent such a history, American courts usually allow the life tenant to cut trees to the extent consistent with good husbandry, either to clear land for cultivation or to obtain firewood and building materials.

---

[63] Richard A. Posner, Economic Analysis of Law 72–73 (4th ed. 1992).

[64] *See, e.g.,* Brokaw v. Fairchild, 237 N.Y.S. 6 (Sup. Ct. 1929).

[65] *See, e.g.,* Melms v. Pabst Brewing Co., 79 N.W. 738 (Wis. 1899).

[66] 79 N.W. 738 (Wis. 1899) (life tenant's acts of demolishing valueless dwelling and grading lot surface down to street level to allow profitable business use of site were not waste).

[67] *Cf.* Nutter v. Stockton, 626 P.2d 861 (Okla. 1981) (where oil and gas lease executed by testator expired during life estate, life tenant could not execute new lease unless remainderman agreed).

[C] Permissive Waste

Permissive waste stems from inaction: the failure of the possessor to exercise reasonable care to protect the estate. Most permissive waste cases involve the life tenant who fails to repair a dwelling (e.g., fails to fix a leaky roof), resulting in substantial loss.[68] In addition, permissive waste will be found where the possessor fails to pay property taxes and assessments, mortgage payments, and related expenses necessary to preserve the estate for the future interest holder.

---

[68] *See, e.g.,* Moore v. Phillips, 627 P.2d 831 (Kan. Ct. App. 1981).

Chapter 10

CONCURRENT OWNERSHIP

SYNOPSIS

§ 10.01 The Nature of Concurrent Ownership

A present estate in real or personal property can be simultaneously owned by two or more persons, each holding the right to concurrent possession.[1] Three basic types of concurrent estates are generally recognized: the tenancy in common, the joint tenancy, and the tenancy by the entirety. Suppose O conveys fee simple absolute in Greenacre to A and B "as tenants in common." A and B now own the concurrent estate called tenancy in common; it provides them with equal rights to simultaneously use and enjoy all of Greenacre.

The rules governing concurrent estates attempt to reconcile three often-conflicting policies that underlie American property law: autonomy, efficiency, and equity. From the standpoint of the law and economics movement, communal ownership is inherently inefficient and does not maximize the productive use of property.[2] Judge Richard Posner asserts that cotenants such as A and B "are formally in much the same position as the inhabitants of a society that does not recognize property rights."[3] He observes, for example, that if A spends his own money to repair buildings on the common property, B will share in the enhanced value stemming from the repairs, but—despite the equities of the situation—has no obligation to compensate A. Ultimately, A can escape the cotenancy through partition, but at the expense of disregarding O's autonomy to dispose of his property as he wishes.

§ 10.02 Types of Concurrent Estates

[A] Tenancy in Common

[1] Characteristics

The simplest concurrent estate—and the most frequently encountered—is the *tenancy in common*. Each co-owner of this estate holds an undivided, fractional share in the entire parcel of land; and each is entitled to simultaneous possession and enjoyment of the whole parcel. This "unity of possession" is the hallmark of the tenancy in common.

Suppose again that A and B are tenants in common in fee simple absolute in Greenacre, a 100-acre farm; A holds a 75% undivided interest and B holds the remaining 25% interest. B is entitled to possession of all 100 acres, and so is A. Their respective fractional ownership shares are quite different,

---

[1] *See generally* Lawrence Berger, *An Analysis of the Economic Relations Between Cotenants,* 21 Ariz. L. Rev. 1015 (1979); N. William Hines, *Real Property Joint Tenancies: Law, Fact, and Fancy,* 51 Iowa L. Rev. 582 (1966), Evelyn A. Lewis, *Struggling with Quicksand: The Ins and Outs of Cotenant Possession Value Liability and a Call for Default Rule Reform,* 1994 Wis. L. Rev. 331; John V. Orth, *Tenancy by the Entirety: The Strange Career of the Common-Law Marital Estate,* 1997 B.Y.U. L. Rev. 35; Anne L. Spitzer, *Joint Tenancy with Right of Survivorship: A Legacy from Thirteenth Century England,* 16 Tex. Tech L. Rev. 629 (1985).

[2] *See* Robert C. Ellickson, *Property In Land,* 102 Yale L.J. 1315, 1338–1339 (1993).

[3] Richard A. Posner, Economic Analysis of Law 74 (4th ed. 1992).

but each has an equal right to possession of the whole parcel. Rather than viewing B, for instance, as effectively owning 25 acres, the law views B as owning an undivided share of the entire 100-acre tract. Notably, the other key unities required for a valid joint tenancy or tenancy by the entirety—time, title, and interest—are irrelevant to the tenancy in common. A and B can be tenants in common even if they acquired their interests at different times and by different instruments, and even though the fractional size of their shares is different.

Use of the tenancy in common has expanded in recent decades with the advent of the condominium (*see* Chapter 35). If K "owns" a condominium unit, she actually holds two related sets of rights. She owns title to her individual unit, which includes the air space within the unit (as bounded by the floor, ceiling, and common walls) and may also extend part way inside the exterior or common walls. In addition, a condominium owner such as K is normally also a tenant in common in the remaining parts of the building structure and in the underlying land.

Tenants in common do not have a right of survivorship, unlike joint tenants or tenants by the entirety. Thus, if A and B are tenants in common in Greenacre and A dies, A's tenancy in common interest will pass to his devisees or heirs, not to B.

[2] Creation

Today any conveyance or devise to two or more unmarried persons (e.g., "to A and B") is presumed to create a tenancy in common, absent clear language expressing an intent to create a joint tenancy.[4] This rule stems from state statutes that repudiate the traditional English preference for the joint tenancy. Under early English common law, a conveyance or devise[5] was presumed to create a joint tenancy (absent express language to the contrary), probably because its right of survivorship tended to vest ownership in one person, rather than in many; this process facilitated the collection of feudal services and incidents.

A tenancy in common may also arise involuntarily. The leading example is intestate succession. Suppose D, holding fee simple absolute in Blueacre, dies intestate and leaves three children—E, F, and G—as her only surviving relatives. Under these circumstances, the laws governing intestate succession will award each child a one-third interest in Blueacre as a tenant in common with the others. Similarly, a tenancy in common will arise when (a) severance ends a joint tenancy or (b) divorce ends a tenancy by the entirety.

---

[4] *See* Gagnon v. Pronovost, 71 A.2d 747 (N.H. 1949) (grant to A and B "and to the survivors of them" held to create a tenancy in common).

[5] The devise of an estate in land was possible in England only after 1540, when the Statute of Wills was enacted. 32 Hen. VIII, ch. 1 (1540).

[3] Transferability

A tenant in common has the right to sell, mortgage, lease, or otherwise transfer all or part of his interest without the consent of other co-tenants; and such a transfer does not end the tenancy in common.[6] Unlike the joint tenancy and tenancy by the entirety, the tenancy in common does not include a right of survivorship. Accordingly, a co-tenant may devise his interest or allow it to descend by intestate succession.

[B] Joint Tenancy

[1] Characteristics

The *joint tenancy* differs from the tenancy in common in that each joint tenant has a right of survivorship. Suppose C and D are joint tenants in fee simple absolute in Redacre. While C and D are both alive, each has an equal, undivided right to simultaneous possession and use of Redacre. But each has the right to sole ownership of Redacre if the other dies first. Thus, for example, if C dies, D now holds fee simple absolute in Redacre.

The right of survivorship stems from the common law's schizophrenic vision of a joint tenancy, expressed in archaic French as "per my et per tout."[7] Joint tenants were seen as both (a) a unit that owned the entire estate and (b) individuals who each owned an undivided fractional share (or *moiety*) in the estate. Since joint tenant D already owned the entire estate, C's death was not seen as creating any new rights in D. Rather, the death merely withdrew C's interest from the estate, leaving D as the only remaining owner.

What if D murders C? As a matter of public policy, the murderer cannot profit from the crime; the murder severs the joint tenancy. D receives only a one-half interest as a tenant in common, and the remaining interest passes to C's devises or heirs other than D.[8]

What if C and D die simultaneously, for example, in an auto accident? Here the joint tenancy is treated like a tenancy in common, with no right of survivorship. C and D are each deemed to own a half interest in the property that passes to their respective heirs or devises.[9]

[2] Creation

Consistent with its vision of joint tenants as a unit, English common law required four *unities* in order to create (and continue) a valid joint tenancy: time, title, interest, and possession. The joint tenants had to acquire title at the same *time*; they had to acquire *title* by the same deed or will, or by joint adverse possession; each *interest* had to be identical, meaning each

---

[6] *See* Kresha v. Kresha, 371 N.W.2d 280 (Neb. 1985) (tenant in common may lease his interest without cotenant's consent).

[7] Meaning, "by the share and by the whole."

[8] Unif. Probate Code § 2-803(c)(2); Duncan v. Vassaur, 550 P.2d 929 (Okla. 1979).

[9] Unif. Simultaneous Death Act § 3.

joint tenant owned the same fractional interest in the same estate; and each joint tenant had to have an equal right to *possession* of the entire parcel. For example, if O conveys a "one-half undivided share in Greenacre as a joint tenant" to E on Monday, and then conveys a similar interest to F on Tuesday, E and F are not joint tenants because the unities of time and title are missing; E and F acquired their interests at different times and by different deeds. Instead, E and F are tenants in common.

The modern standard for creating a joint tenancy differs markedly from the common law model. At common law, the joint tenancy was the law's "default" setting; absent clear contrary language, any concurrent estate was presumed to be a joint tenancy as long as the four unities were present. By contrast, today in most states a concurrent estate is considered a tenancy in common unless the intent to create another estate is clearly expressed.[10] The rationale for rejection of the English rule is straightforward. The original reason for favoring the joint tenancy ended with feudalism. Moreover, recognizing a right of survivorship in ambiguous cases may be inequitable, as where, for example, a merchant has extended credit in reliance on the deceased customer's apparent property rights.

Predictably, states vary widely on the phrasing that manifests the requisite intent to create a joint tenancy. In most jurisdictions, language such as "to E and F as joint tenants" or "to E and F as joint tenants with right of survivorship" will suffice.[11] On the other hand, phrases like "to E and F jointly" may be insufficient.

Moreover, some states have eroded the traditional unities requirement. For example, at common law an owner could not create a joint tenancy by conveying to herself and others, because the unities of time and title were absent. Of course, this requirement could be—and commonly was— circumvented by the use of a "straw man." A, owning fee simple absolute, would convey her entire interest to B, who would then convey to A and C as joint tenants with right of survivorship. A number of states now permit an owner to create a joint tenancy through a direct conveyance,[12] presumably because the common law bar could be routinely avoided through a sham transaction.

[3] Transferability

In contrast to the relatively free alienability of a tenancy in common interest, a joint tenancy interest is virtually inalienable. Due to the right of survivorship, a joint tenant's interest ends upon death, so the interest cannot be devised or descend by intestate succession. Similarly, any inter

---

[10] *See In re* Estate of Michael, 218 A.2d 338 (Pa. 1966). *But see In re* Estate of Vadney, 634 N.E.2d 976 (N.Y. 1994) (court reforms deed to add right of survivorship omitted by scrivener's error).

[11] *See* Palmer v. Flint, 161 A.2d 837 (Me. 1960) (conveyance to A and B "as joint tenants, and not as tenants in common, to them and their assigns and to the survivor, and the heirs and assigns of the survivor forever" created a joint tenancy).

[12] *See* Cal. Civ. Code § 683; Miller v. Riegler, 419 S.W.2d 599 (Ark. 1967) (joint tenancy in stocks). *But see* Hass v. Hass, 21 N.W.2d 398 (Wis. 1946).

vivos conveyance of a joint tenancy interest will break the unities of time and title, severing the joint tenancy; thus, the grantee receives merely a tenancy in common interest. The authorities are split as to whether a lease, mortgage, or other transfer of a lesser interest will sever a joint tenancy (*see* § 10.04[A][2]).

[4] Contemporary Relevance of the Joint Tenancy in Land

The joint tenancy in land has been extensively used in recent years as a tool to avoid the cost and delay of probate proceedings.[13] In particular, most married couples hold title to their family residences as joint tenants, presumably as a result of decades of well-intentioned (but simplistic) advice from real estate brokers and bank officers.[14]

Suppose H and W, a married couple about to purchase Greenacre jointly, want to ensure that the survivor obtains sole title. They could take title as tenants in common, and execute mirror-image wills that devise the interest of the first dying spouse to the surviving spouse. But if H now dies first, W's right to sole possession of Greenacre will not receive legal recognition until the probate of H's will is completed and H's 50% interest in Greenacre is distributed to W under judicial supervision; further, the inclusion of Greenacre in H's estate will increase the cost of the procedure. Instead, H and W might take title as joint tenants; when H eventually dies, W automatically becomes the sole owner without the need for H's interest to pass through probate.[15]

[5] Special Rules for Joint Bank Accounts

Bank accounts are often held in joint tenancy. One study discovered that 81% of all savings accounts reviewed were—at least in theory—jointly owned.[16] Yet even if the formal agreement with the bank appears to create a "joint account" or "joint and survivorship account," the account holders may not have intended the legal consequences that accompany a true joint tenancy. Depositor D might open a joint account with her son S so that S can handle her financial affairs; or D might plan to use the account as a will substitute, intending that S have no rights in the account proceeds until D's death.

Accordingly, the nature of a joint account turns on the intent of the parties, not the terms of the agreement with the bank. In applying this principle, most states follow two helpful presumptions contained in the

---

[13] For discussion of the benefits of joint tenancies, see Regis W. Campfield, *Estate Planning for Joint Tenancies*, 1974 Duke L.J. 669, 671–673.

[14] For example, one author noted that 85% of deeds recorded by married couples in California created joint tenancies. Nathaniel Sterling, *Joint Tenancy and Community Property in California*, 14 Pac. L.J. 927, 928 (1983).

[15] However, there is a risk in most states that one cotenant could defraud the other by secretly executing a severance deed. *See* § 10.04[A][1].

[16] N. William Hines, *Personal Property Joint Tenancies: More Law, Fact, and Fancy*, 54 Minn. L. Rev. 509, 574 (1970).

Uniform Probate Code. First, during the lifetime of the account holders, the amount on deposit is presumed to belong to each party in proportion to his or her contribution to the account, absent clear and convincing evidence of a contrary intent.[17] In effect, during life the account is treated like a tenancy in common, each party owning a fractional share based on actual contributions. Second, the amount remaining on deposit at the death of an account holder belongs to the surviving parties, again absent clear and convincing evidence of a different intent.[18] The law presumes the parties intended the right of survivorship that characterizes a joint tenancy.

[C] Tenancy by the Entirety

[1] Characteristics

The *tenancy by the entirety*—now abolished in most states—is a medieval relic.[19] Historically, the law viewed a husband and wife as a single legal unit controlled by the husband. Under this logic, a married couple could not hold title as tenants in common or joint tenants because a wife had no existence as a legal person. Thus, at common law, every conveyance or devise to a husband and wife was deemed to create a tenancy by the entirety that vested title in the spouses as a unit, without any individual shares.[20] A valid tenancy by the entirety required the four unities of time, title, interest, and possession, plus the fifth unity of a valid marriage.

Like the joint tenancy, the tenancy by the entirety provides a right of survivorship. But a tenancy by the entirety is a far more durable estate because it can be terminated[21] only by divorce of the couple, death of one spouse, or the agreement of both spouses. One spouse cannot unilaterally break the required unities and thereby transform the estate into a tenancy in common. However, if one spouse murders the other, the tenancy by the entirety is severed and the murderer cannot enforce the right of survivorship.[22]

Originally, this estate gave the husband exclusive possession of the land and the sole right to the rents and profits it produced.[23] The husband could transfer this possessory right to a third party over his wife's objection, but

---

[17] Unif. Probate Code § 6-103.

[18] Unif. Probate Code § 6-104. *Cf.* Wright v. Bloom, 635 N.E.2d 31 (Ohio 1994); Seman v. Lewis, 830 P.2d 1294 (Mont. 1992).

[19] *See generally* John V. Orth, *Tenancy by the Entirety: The Strange Career of the Common-Law Marital Estate,* 1997 B.Y.U. L. Rev. 35.

[20] Thus, they held "per tout et non per my," that is, "by the whole and not by shares."

[21] There is a split of authority on whether a tenancy by the entirety continues after the property is destroyed or sold. *See, e.g.,* Hawthorne v. Hawthorne, 192 N.E.2d 20 (N.Y. 1963) (estate did not attach to fire insurance proceeds after destruction of dwelling).

[22] Estate of Grund v. Grund, 648 N.E.2d 1182 (Ind. Ct. App. 1995).

[23] The common law view persisted with remarkable vigor, even in states such as Massachusetts. *See, e.g.,* D'Ercole v. D'Ercole, 407 F. Supp. 1377 (D. Mass. 1976) (state law giving husband sole control over family home owned in tenancy by the entirety did not constitute gender discrimination that violated the wife's rights to due process or equal protection).

could not defeat the wife's right of survivorship. In most jurisdictions, therefore, the husband's creditors could levy on property held in tenancy by the entirety to satisfy his debts. As one court admitted, "[i]t is possible that a wife might receive no benefits at all from land held by the entireties if she predeceases her husband."[24] The later Married Women's Property Acts largely redressed this imbalance by vesting control equally in both spouses.

[2] Creation

The tenancy by the entirety is recognized only in about twenty states. Many of these states still follow the common law presumption that any conveyance or devise to a married couple creates a tenancy by the entirety. In other jurisdictions that recognize the estate, however, the intent to create a tenancy by the entirety must be clearly expressed (e.g., "to A and B as tenants by the entirety").

Moreover, most jurisdictions still require the traditional five unities: time, title, interest, possession, and marriage. The principal exception to this rule permits one spouse to create a tenancy by the entirety by a direct conveyance to both spouses, even though the unities of time and title are absent. If W, married to H, holds fee simple absolute in Blueacre as her sole property, she can create a tenancy by the entirety by conveying "to W and H as tenants by the entirety."

What if a grantor attempts to create a tenancy by the entirety in two unmarried persons? Some states consider the resulting estate to be a joint tenancy, reasoning that it best approximates the grantor's intent. Other states apply the default standard, construing the estate as a tenancy in common.

[3] Transferability

The dominant characteristic of the estate is that neither spouse possesses a separate share; rather, the couple as a unit owns the entire estate. Thus, under traditional theory, the consent of both spouses was required to convey the estate. But, given his historical control, the husband could transfer his right of survivorship and the right to lifetime possession (including rights to future income), subject to the wife's right of survivorship.

However, the Married Women's Property Acts—adopted in all common law marital property states—have eliminated the husband's right of exclusive control. Under these statutes, either spouse has the power to manage and control marital property, including property held in tenancy by the entirety.[25]

---

[24] Dearman v. Bruns, 181 S.E.2d 809, 811 (N.C. Ct. App. 1971).

[25] Coraccio v. Lowell Five Cents Sav. Bank, 612 N.E.2d 650 (Mass. 1993) (husband can mortgage property).

[4] Rights of Creditors

[a] A Shield Against Creditors?

Does the modern tenancy by the entirety shield property from creditors' claims? As a potential source of debtor protection, the estate has enjoyed an undeserved reprieve from extinction in some states.

The legal muddle stems from judicial efforts to reconcile tenancy by the entirety theory with the provisions of the Married Women's Property Acts. The basic theme of these Acts is equality: each spouse owns, manages, and controls his or her separate property, which is subject to the claims of that spouse's creditors. For example, if H and W are married, H's wages (and all property acquired with those wages) are his separate property; H's creditors can levy on H's property, but not on W's property.

Before these reform statutes, the rights of creditors in tenancy by the entirety property were relatively clear. Because the husband controlled the property, creditors could levy on it to satisfy his debts; as a practical matter, the husband's debts were family debts, since the wife was deemed incompetent to contract. After the Married Women's Property Acts, however, states still recognizing the estate wrestled with a dilemma. If a wife is now entitled to the equal use and enjoyment of tenancy by the entirety property, how can that property be subject to the claims of her husband's creditors without her consent? Conversely, how can the wife's creditors levy on tenancy by the entirety property over the husband's objection? Most states resolve this dilemma by concluding that the creditor of an individual spouse cannot reach tenancy by the entirety property. Some states allow creditors to execute on the right of survivorship of the debtor spouse only,[26] while others permit creditors to sell the debtor spouse's interest subject to the non-debtor spouse's right of survivorship.

[b] Majority Approach: *Sawada v. Endo*

The Hawaii Supreme Court's decision in *Sawada v. Endo*[27] illustrates the majority view. There, the plaintiff Sawadas sued to cancel a fraudulent conveyance in order to collect on a personal injury judgment. Defendant Endo asserted that at the time of the conveyance, the property was held in tenancy by the entirety, and thus not subject to execution by creditors.

The court reasoned that the effect of the Married Women's Property Acts was to convert the tenancy by the entirety into a "unity of equals and not of unequals as at common law."[28] Accordingly, neither spouse owned a separate interest that could be conveyed to, or reached by, creditors. The court noted that this result protected the integrity of the family unit by ensuring that real property was available as housing and as security for educational and other expenses. Unfairness to creditors was avoided, the

---

[26] United States v. 1500 Lincoln Ave., 949 F.2d 73 (3d Cir. 1991); United States v. Certain Real Property Located at 2525 Leroy Lane, 910 F.2d 343 (6th Cir. 1990).

[27] 561 P.2d 1291 (Haw. 1977).

[28] Sawada v. Endo, 561 P.2d 1291, 1295 (Haw. 1977).

court observed, because they (a) were charged with notice of a spouse's limited estate in deciding whether to extend credit, or (b) never relied on the asset in the first place.

[c] Reflections on the *Sawada* Approach

The majority approach, as exemplified by *Sawada* may be criticized on several grounds.[29] Initially, one may ask whether state legislatures—bent on achieving gender equality between spouses—actually intended to curtail or frustrate creditors' rights. Certainly this result is not compelled by the common law tradition. Indeed, perhaps a more logical outcome would be to conclude that the equality resulting from Married Women's Property Acts subjects tenancy by the entirety property to claims of creditors against either spouse.[30]

The "family asset protection" rationale underpinning *Sawada* is overbroad. The majority rule insulates all property held in tenancy by the entirety from creditors, far beyond the amount required for family housing or support. For example, assume H and W hold title to a $5,000,000 beachfront estate and a $20,000,000 shopping center in tenancy by the entirety. Under the majority approach, neither asset can be reached by creditors. A more narrowly tailored doctrine—such as the homestead protection available in many states to insulate the ordinary family home from creditors—would be preferable.[31] In any event, why should certain property owners be exempt from creditors' claims, when wage earners too poor to own land are subject to wage garnishment for their debts?

Finally, the *Sawada* court may underestimate the impact on creditors. Victims of tortious conduct like the Sawadas obviously cannot protect themselves in advance by evaluating the creditworthiness of future tortfeasors. And to suggest that the Sawadas or other involuntary creditors cannot recover because the property "was not a basis of credit" (i.e., was not relied upon in deciding to extend credit) is disingenuous. The court seemingly vests tortfeasors with de facto immunity from suit as long as their assets are held in tenancy by the entirety.

[5] Requiem for the Tenancy by the Entirety?

The tenancy by the entirety is slowly withering away. Once the law finally acknowledged that married women were legally capable of owning property, the archaic rationale for the estate vanished. Most states have abolished the tenancy by the entirety and England—where the estate originated—banned it altogether in 1925.

---

[29] For an excellent pre-*Sawada* critique of the majority rule, see Richard G. Huber, *Creditors' Rights in Tenancies by the Entireties*, 1 B.C. Indus. & Com. L. Rev. 197, 205–207 (1959).

[30] *See* King v. Greene, 153 A.2d 49 (N.J. 1959) (sheriff's deed following execution sale against tenancy by the entirety property to satisfy wife's debt effectively conveyed, inter alia, wife's right of survivorship).

[31] The nature of any homestead protections varies widely among states. California, for example, provides exemptions ranging from $50,000 to $125,000, depending on age, income, disability, and other factors. Cal. Civ. Proc. Code § 704.730.

Certainly, the estate's new popularity as a debt avoidance device has temporarily arrested its decline in some states. But as the resultant creditor unfairness becomes more apparent, the demise will continue. In the interim, the patchwork of widely varying state approaches will undoubtedly provoke both confusion and injustice.

One interesting example is the problematic impact of this estate on the national battle against drug trafficking operations. Under federal law, property used to sell illegal drugs, or acquired with proceeds from such sales, is subject to civil forfeiture by government agencies; yet property owned by an "innocent" owner cannot be seized. [32] If property is held in joint tenancy or tenancy in common, the concurrent interest of the guilty spouse can be readily seized; the innocent spouse becomes either a cotenant with the government or receives half of the sales proceeds. But what if the property is held in tenancy by the entirety? Most courts conclude that only the survivorship right of the guilty spouse—whose value is speculative and uncertain—can be forfeited. [33] Accordingly, the innocent spouse is entitled to lifetime use of the property, together with a right of survivorship. This disparity may tend to encourage drug dealers to relocate to states that recognize the tenancy by the entirety.

§ 10.03 Rights and Duties of Cotenants

[A] Relationship Between Cotenants

The precise relationship between cotenants defies easy definition. [34] In some respects, the law treats them as relatively independent actors; for example, one cotenant cannot contract on behalf of other cotenants.

In other respects, the law seems to impose stringent duties. Cases and textbooks often recite that cotenants who receive their interests from a common source at the same time (e.g., from a single deed or will) owe fiduciary duties to each other; this universe would include all joint tenants and most tenants in common. Yet the assertion that a broad fiduciary relationship exists among most cotenants—like partners or trustees—is an overstatement. Most of the decisions making this claim arise in one situation: where a cotenant has acquired sole title to the cotenancy property through a foreclosure, tax sale, or other involuntary sale. [35] In that special-ized context, the acquiring cotenant is often deemed to hold title as a de

---

[32] 21 U.S.C. § 881.

[33] *See, e.g.,* United States v. Certain Real Property Located at 2525 Leroy Lane, 910 F.2d 343 (6th Cir. 1990).

[34] *See* Lawrence Berger, *An Analysis of the Economic Relations Between Cotenants,* 21 Ariz. L. Rev. 1015 (1979).

[35] Also, when a cotenant in possession attempts to claim sole title by adverse possession, many courts justify use of a more rigorous adverse possession standard by characterizing the cotenant as a fiduciary.

facto trustee for the benefit of the other cotenants, as long as they promptly pay their proportionate share of the acquisition price.[36]

However, most decisions hold that—unlike a fiduciary—a cotenant has little or no obligation to affirmatively safeguard the rights of other cotenants, e.g., by repairing a leaky roof or purchasing casualty insurance. Moreover, unlike a fiduciary, a cotenant is normally entitled to exclusive use of the cotenancy property without any duty to compensate other cotenants.

[B] Right to Possession

In theory, each cotenant has an equal right to possession and enjoyment of the whole property, regardless of the size of his or her fractional share.[37] Accordingly, under the majority rule, even a cotenant in exclusive possession of the property is not liable to the other cotenants for rent.[38] If A, B, and C are all tenants in common in Blueacre, and A holds sole possession of the land, in most jurisdictions A is not required to pay rent or other compensation to B or C.

Yet the basic precept that each cotenant has an equal right to possession is little more than a legal fiction. How can multiple cotenants each utilize the entire property simultaneously? Suppose again that A, B, and C are cotenants in Blueacre; A is standing on the property, occupying a particular square foot of land. In hyperbole that defies the laws of physics, the common law rule permits B and C to simultaneously occupy the same square foot of ground. Clearly, the respective possessory rights of A, B, and C conflict; three people cannot stand in the same place.[39]

The common law recognized one major exception to the rule that a cotenant had no duty to pay rent: ouster. *Ouster* occurs when a cotenant in possession refuses the request of another cotenant to share possession of the land.[40] For example, assume cotenant A holds sole possession of Blueacre; B appears at the front gate to Blueacre, and demands that A unlock the gate to allow him to enter and use the land; if A rejects this

---

[36] Laura v. Christian, 537 P.2d 1389 (N.M. 1975) (cotenant pays off mortgage obligation to avoid pending foreclosure sale); Massey v. Prothero, 664 P.2d 1176 (Utah 1983) (cotenant purchases at tax sale).

[37] Thus, if one cotenant leases his interest, the lessee is similarly entitled to an equal right to possession of the whole property. Schwartzbaugh v. Sampson, 54 P.2d 73 (Cal. Ct. App. 1936); Carr v. Deking, 765 P.2d 40 (Wash. Ct. App. 1988).

[38] *But see* Lerman v. Levine, 541 A.2d 523 (Conn. App. Ct. 1988) (applying minority rule that cotenant in possession is obligated to pay rent to other cotenant, even without ouster).

[39] Mastbaum v. Mastbaum, 9 A.2d 51, 55 (N.J. Ch. 1939) ("Two men cannot plow the same furrow.").

[40] Ouster is also established when a cotenant in exclusive possession of the common property claims to hold sole title to the property, adverse and hostile to the rights of other cotenants. In addition, some states recognize the special doctrine of "constructive ouster" in the context of divorce proceedings; when mutual antagonism makes it impracticable for spouses to share the family home while a divorce is pending, the spouse who leaves the home is entitled to partial rent from the remaining spouse. *See, e.g.,* Olivas v. Olivas, 780 P.2d 640 (N.M. Ct. App. 1989).

demand, he has ousted B. As an ousted cotenant, B is entitled to recover his pro rata share of Blueacre's fair rental value from A. On the other hand, if B simply demands that A pay him rent, no ouster occurs when A refuses because B has failed to demand shared possession.[41]

Professor Evelyn Lewis notes that the majority "no rent liability" rule originated in an agrarian age when property owners typically lived and worked on family farms.[42] The majority rule arguably made sense in that context because ordinary owners had an immediate economic use for cotenancy property; also, the rule tended to encourage the productive use of land. But today, Lewis argues, the rule imposes unjust economic burdens on cotenants who are unlikely to have a personal use for the cotenancy property. At a minimum, she suggests that a cotenant using cotenancy property as a personal residence should be required to pay rent under limited circumstances, e.g., when persons who are already living elsewhere acquire cotenancy interests by devise or intestate succession.

[C] Right to Rents and Profits

Each cotenant is entitled to a pro rata share of rents received from a third person for use of the land.[43] For example, if A, B, and C each own equal shares as tenants in common in Blueacre, and A receives $30,000 in rental income from X for use of the property, B and C are each entitled to $10,000 from A. If A refuses to pay, they may bring an *accounting* action against him to force payment.

Similarly, if a cotenant exploits natural resources on the cotenancy property such as minerals or timber, each cotenant is entitled to a pro rata share of the resulting net profits. In *White v. Smyth*,[44] a tenant in common holding a one-ninth interest mined and sold valuable rock asphalt from the property. When the other cotenants sued for compensation in an accounting action, the defendant asserted that he had removed less than one-ninth of the asphalt, and thus had only taken his fair share, just as he might have done through partition. The Texas Supreme Court ruled that the defendant could not effect a de facto partition through self-help and, accordingly, that each cotenant owned a share in the mined asphalt. The defendant was ordered to pay eight-ninths of his net profits to his cotenants.

[D] Liability for Mortgage and Tax Payments

As a general rule, all cotenants are obligated to pay their proportionate share of mortgage, tax, assessments, and other payments that could give rise to a lien against the property if unpaid.[45] Such payments are

---

[41] Spiller v. Mackereth, 334 So. 2d 859 (Ala. 1976).

[42] Evelyn A. Lewis, *Struggling with Quicksand: The Ins and Outs of Cotenant Possession Value Liability and a Call for Default Rule Reform*, 1994 Wis. L. Rev. 331.

[43] Goergen v. Maar, 153 N.Y.S.2d 826 (App. Div. 1956).

[44] 214 S.W.2d 967 (Tex. 1948).

[45] Laura v. Christian, 537 P.2d 1389 (N.M. 1975).

considered necessary to prevent the estate from being lost by foreclosure. If one cotenant pays more than a pro rata share, he or she may recover the excess in a *contribution* action.[46] For example, suppose K and L are tenants in common in Greenacre, each owning a one-half share. If Greenacre is subject to a mortgage requiring a payment of $2,000 per month, and K is forced to cover these costs for one year ($24,000) because L refuses to pay, K is entitled to recover half of his payments ($12,000) from L.[47]

However, in most states a special rule applies to the cotenant in sole possession of the property: the cotenant cannot recover for these payments unless they exceed the reasonable rental value of the property. Thus, if the fair rental value of Greenacre is $30,000 per year, and K held sole possession of Greenacre during the year, K cannot recover any part of his mortgage payments from L.

[E] Liability for Repair and Improvement Costs

Under the majority rule, a cotenant who pays for repairs or improvements to the common property is not entitled to contribution from the other cotenants, absent a prior agreement. Thus, if D, a joint tenant in a home known as Whiteacre, pays $15,000 to repair the leaky roof, he cannot sue his cotenants E and F to recover their $10,000 pro rata share. Why not? Cotenants exercising their business judgment may disagree over the necessity, character, extent, and cost of repairs and improvements.[48] If the law permitted contribution actions for such expenditures, courts might be forced to adjudicate multiple lawsuits between the same cotenants over comparatively minor disagreements, consuming undue time, energy, and money.

To break such stalemates, the law provides the remedy of *partition*. Any cotenant who cannot agree with another can permanently end the relationship. Upon partition, a cotenant like D will receive a credit for the excess cost of reasonable repairs he has borne.[49] Improvements are treated similarly; when partitioning the property, the court will either assign the improved portion of the property to the improving cotenant if feasible, or award that cotenant a credit for the added property value produced by the improvement.

---

[46] Alternatively, the cotenant may use the excess payment as a credit in an accounting or partition action. For example, if K has received $40,000 in rents from Greenacre, and L sues for an accounting, L will receive only $8,000 ($20,000, representing L's half share of the rents, less the $12,000 credit for payments K made on L's behalf).

[47] A cotenant's failure to pay his pro rata share is normally not considered an abandonment of his interest in the property. Cummings v. Anderson, 614 P.2d 1283 (Wash. 1980).

[48] Posner characterizes this relationship as an example of "the familiar bilateral-monopoly problem." Richard A. Posner, Economic Analysis of Law 74 (4th ed. 1992).

[49] Such repair costs may also be used as a credit in an accounting action brought against the cotenant.

[F]　Liability for Waste

In theory, a cotenant is liable for waste when he or she uses the common property in an unreasonable manner that causes permanent injury, under much the same standards that govern life tenants and other owners of present estates accompanied by future interests (*see* § 9.09). Yet the weight of authority treats certain acts by a cotenant that would normally constitute waste—such as extraction of minerals or cutting of timber—simply as sources of income (like rents from third parties) for which he must account to the other cotenants.[50] While such acts are often judicially characterized as "waste," the traditional penalties for waste are not imposed.

§ 10.04　Termination of Concurrent Estates

[A]　Severance of Joint Tenancy

[1]　Conveyance of Joint Tenant's Entire Interest

In general, a joint tenant has the absolute right to end or "sever" the joint tenancy without the consent (or sometimes even the knowledge) of the other cotenants.[51] The procedure is simple: the joint tenant merely conveys his interest to a third person.[52] For example, if A and B are joint tenants in Greenacre, and B conveys his estate to C, the unities of time and title are broken. This severs the joint tenancy, leaving A and C as tenants in common.

But can B convert the joint tenancy into a tenancy in common without losing his interest in Greenacre? The formal response of English law was "no." B could not convey his interest from himself (as a joint tenant) to himself (as a tenant in common) because the traditional ceremony of feoffment with livery of seisin required two participants; "one could not enfeoff oneself."[53] But indirectly, using one of those ingenious sleight-of-hand tricks that brought flexibility to the common law, the answer was "yes." In a prearranged, sham transaction, B simply conveyed his interest to C (an intermediary called a "straw man"), which severed the joint tenancy, and C conveyed the resulting tenancy in common interest back to B. Common law courts tolerated this fiction because it facilitated free alienation, and thus encouraged productive use of land. Because the interest was no longer burdened with a right of survivorship, it could be transferred more easily.

Although some states still require use of a "straw man," the modern trend is to allow a joint tenant to terminate the joint tenancy by conveying his

---

[50] *See, e.g.,* White v. Smyth, 214 S.W.2d 967 (Tex. 1948) (cotenant who removed rock asphalt required to account to other cotenants for his net profits).

[51] Robert W. Swenson & Ronan E. Degnan, *Severance of Joint Tenancies,* 38 Minn. L. Rev. 466 (1954).

[52] A joint tenancy may be severed when one joint tenant merely enters into a contract to sell his interest. Estate of Phillips v. Nyhus, 874 P.2d 154 (Wash. 1994).

[53] Riddle v. Harmon, 162 Cal. Rptr. 530, 533 (Ct. App. 1980).

interest directly to himself. The rationale for the traditional rule ended in 1677 when the Statute of Frauds effectively replaced livery of seisin with the deed. Moreover, as one court commented, "[c]ommon sense as well as legal efficiency dictate that a joint tenant should be able to accomplish directly what he or she could otherwise achieve indirectly by use of elaborate legal fictions."[54]

Yet the joint tenant's unilateral right to end the joint tenancy poses a hidden peril. As Professor Samuel Fetters observed, "one joint tenant, while secure in his own survivorship right, can defraud his cotenant of his survivorship right with impunity."[55] Assume that H and W take title to Redacre as joint tenants, but that unscrupulous H secretly executes a deed conveying his interest to B, his brother; H places the deed in his personal safe deposit box. If H dies first, the deed will be seen as having severed the joint tenancy during H's lifetime; thus W is a mere tenant in common with B. On the other hand, if W dies first, H simply destroys the hidden deed and acquires sole title to Redacre.[56]

What if A, B, and C are all joint tenants in Greenacre and C conveys her interest to D? D is a tenant in common because he does not share the unities of time and title with A and B. But C's conveyance does not affect the unities *between* A and B; thus, *as between themselves* A and B are still joint tenants. Greenacre is now held in a hybrid form of ownership: D owns a one-third interest as a tenant in common, while A and B each own a one-third interest as joint tenants.[57] Assuming A dies first, B and D will then be tenants in common, B owning a two-thirds interest and D retaining his one-third interest.

[2] Lease or Mortgage Executed by One Joint Tenant

When will a cotenant's transfer of less than her entire interest sever a joint tenancy? This issue arises in two main contexts: leases and mortgages.

It is unclear whether a joint tenancy is severed when one joint tenant leases the common property. "[T]he problem is like a comet in our law: though its existence in theory has been frequently recognized, its observed passages are few."[58] *Tenhet v. Boswell*,[59] an influential decision by the California Supreme Court, held that while a joint tenant had power to execute a valid lease, the lease did not effect a severance.[60] Thus, the lease

---

[54] Riddle v. Harmon, 162 Cal. Rptr. 530, 534 (Ct. App. 1980).

[55] Samuel M. Fetters, *An Invitation to Commit Fraud: Secret Destruction of Joint Tenant Survivorship Rights,* 55 Fordham L. Rev. 173, 175 (1986).

[56] *See* Crowther v. Mower, 876 P.2d 876 (Utah Ct. App. 1994) (joint tenant wife secretly conveyed her interest to child by a prior marriage). *But see* Cal. Civ. Code § 683.2 (allowing unilateral severance only if severing deed is recorded before grantor's death or shortly thereafter).

[57] Jackson v. O'Connell, 177 N.E.2d 194 (Ill. 1961).

[58] Tenhet v. Boswell, 554 P.2d 330, 334–335 (Cal. 1976).

[59] 554 P.2d 330 (Cal. 1976).

[60] *See* Swartzbaugh v. Sampson, 54 P.2d 73 (Cal. Ct. App. 1936).

was subject to the other cotenant's right of survivorship and ended when the lessor cotenant died. While the reasoning of the *Tenhet* court is somewhat circular, the decision seems to rest on the policy of protecting the good faith expectations of the nonleasing cotenant that her survivorship right will endure. Some decisions follow the *Tenhet* approach. Others conclude that a lease effects a permanent severance, because the unity of interest is lost; this result is presumably based on the policy of encouraging alienability by eliminating the survivorship right.

The law governing the effect of a mortgage on a joint tenancy, in contrast, is well developed. In states that follow the traditional view that a mortgage transfers legal title to the mortgagee, a mortgage executed by one cotenant effects a severance. This result is usually justified with the formalistic conclusion that the unities of time and title have been broken. As a policy matter, recognizing a severance protects the mortgagee (and thus presumably enhances the availability of credit) by ensuring that the mortgage will survive the death of the mortgagor joint tenant. Conversely, in states that follow the modern approach that a mortgage merely creates a lien, most courts find that no severance has occurred, again based on the formalistic rationale that the unities are intact.[61]

[3] Agreement Between Joint Tenants

A joint tenancy may be severed by agreement of all cotenants. The issue arises most commonly in divorce proceedings that result in a property settlement agreement. Does such an agreement sever a joint tenancy? Most courts appear to follow a presumption that a divorcing spouse does not intend to preserve any right of survivorship in the other spouse, and thus tend to interpret ambiguous agreements as terminating the joint tenancy.[62] However, an agreement between joint tenants that merely provides that one of them will occupy the common property does not effect a severance.

[B] Partition

The traditional "escape hatch" from the confines of cotenancy is partition. Any tenant in common or joint tenant may sue for judicial partition, which ends the cotenancy, distributes the property among the former cotenants as solely-owned property, and provides a final accounting among them. Absent a contrary agreement, each cotenant has a right to obtain partition—without proving any cause or reason—regardless of any inconvenience, burden, or damage to other cotenants.[63] Why? The conventional explanation is that free partition is central to the efficient use of land. If cotenants are stalemated by mutual disagreement about the future of their

---

[61] *See, e.g.,* Brant v. Hargrove, 632 P.2d 978 (Ariz. Ct. App. 1981); People v. Nogarr, 330 P.2d 858 (Cal. Ct. App. 1958); Harms v. Sprague, 473 N.E.2d 930 (Ill. 1984).

[62] Mann v. Bradley, 535 P.2d 213 (Colo. 1975) (agreement impliedly severed joint tenancy). *But see* Porter v. Porter, 472 So. 2d 630 (Ala. 1985) (divorce decree did not sever joint tenancy).

[63] *But see* Harris v. Crowder, 322 S.E.2d 854 (W. Va. 1984) (husband's creditors can reach his joint tenancy interest and force partition only if wife's rights are not prejudiced).

common property,[64] the land may not be developed for its most productive use. This perspective, which views all land as a relatively fungible commodity, ignores Professor Margaret Radin's concern for respecting the emotional attachment that many owners feel toward family residences and other "personhood" property.[65]

There are two basic types of partition: *partition in kind* and *partition by sale.* Partition in kind—the preferred technique—is a physical division of the property into separate parcels. If E, F, and G all own equal shares as tenants in common in Redacre, a 300-acre unimproved farm tract, a partition in kind would probably assign each one sole ownership of a 100-acre parcel. Of course, the value of the parcels might not be equal due to differences in soil quality, topography, access, or water availability; a court can equalize the distribution by ordering a money payment called *owelty.*

However, if physical division of the land is impossible, impracticable, or inequitable, a court may order partition by sale.[66] It is usually impracticable, for example, to divide a single-family home. Under this technique, the property is sold and the sales proceeds are divided among the cotenants according to their respective shares. Partition by sale typically forces poorer cotenants off their land simply because they cannot afford to bid successfully.[67]

The right to partition, while strongly favored in the law, is not absolute. An agreement to restrict partition will be upheld if the restraint on alienation it imposes is reasonable under the circumstances.[68] Moreover, statutes universally bar a condominium owner from obtaining partition; otherwise, any owner could effectively destroy a condominium project.

---

[64] Carr v. Deking, 765 P.2d 40 (Wash. Ct. App. 1988).

[65] Margaret J. Radin, *Property and Personhood,* 34 Stan. L. Rev. 957 (1982).

[66] Delfino v. Vealencis, 436 A.2d 27 (Conn. 1980).

[67] *See* John G. Casagrande, Jr., Note, *Acquiring Property Through Forced Partitioning Sales: Abuses and Remedies,* 27 B.C. L. Rev. 755 (1986).

[68] Michalski v. Michalski, 142 A.2d 645 (N.J. Super. Ct. App. Div. 1958).

Chapter 11

MARITAL PROPERTY

SYNOPSIS

§ 11.01   Gender and Marital Property

The historic foundation of American marital property law is gender bias. England's male-dominated society produced a body of common law that was overtly oriented in favor of men and against women. Broadly speaking, the law allowed men to exercise almost total control over marital property during the marriage, upon divorce, and at death. Most American states initially adopted this common law view.[1] Since then, piecemeal reforms have propelled this approach toward greater gender equality. Many critics contend that even this reformed common law approach is still profoundly flawed by gender inequality.

The principal alternative approach—adopted in eight states—is the community property system. Under this view, marriage is seen as an economic partnership between wife and husband, with each one having an equal interest in the resulting marital assets during marriage, upon divorce, and at death. The Uniform Marital Property Act, modeled on community property principles, may ultimately bridge the gap between these two approaches.

The movement toward a gender-neutral marital property law system is concerned more with practical economics than with abstract idealism. For example, under the traditional common law view, the spendthrift husband could waste family property, leaving his wife and children without financial support. Similarly, upon divorce the husband received the bulk of the family property, again endangering the financial security of his wife and children.[2] From the standpoint of utilitarian theory, it is desirable to craft a marital property system that ensures that family assets are available to support all family members.

§ 11.02   Traditional Common Law System

[A]   Gender Bias and the Common Law

Marital property presents the most striking example of gender bias found in the common law. Traditionally, as Blackstone summarized, "the husband and wife are one person in law: that is, the very being or legal existence of the woman is suspended during the marriage."[3] Upon marriage, a woman

---

[1] *See generally* Marylynn Salmon, Women and the Law of Property in Early America (1986).

[2] Even under modern marital property law, the financial condition of men tends to improve after divorce, while that of women tends to decline. Joan Williams, *Is Coverture Dead? Beyond a New Theory of Alimony*, 82 Geo. L.J. 2227 (1994).

[3] J.W. Ehrlich, Ehrlich's Blackstone 83 (1959). *See also* Dibble v. Hutton, 1 Day (Conn.) 221 (1804) (invalidating contract between husband and wife concerning sale of jointly owned land because under "the common law, the husband and wife are considered as one person in law, the existence of the wife being merged into that of the husband ").

lost her status as a legal person, and with it the right to control most of her own property. Under the doctrine of *coverture* she became a dependent (a "femme covert") entitled to her husband's protection and support, and obligated in return to provide domestic services for him. Women were viewed as physically, mentally, and morally inferior to men. Thus, the husband's legal power over his wife "resembled a guardianship of an incompetent."[4]

[B] Rights During Marriage

The husband obtained a life estate in all freehold lands that his wife held at the time of marriage or acquired later, called an estate jure uxoris. He was accordingly entitled to sole possession of these lands during the marriage and to receive all rents and profits that they produced. A wife could regain control over her lands only upon divorce or the husband's death. In addition, the personal property owned by the wife at marriage or acquired by her later became the husband's property, except for her clothing and jewelry. For example, if both H and W worked outside of the home, the earnings of both were owned by H.

[C] Rights Upon Divorce

When divorce occurred—which was relatively rare—property was divided between the spouses according to who held title. Whether the husband was still obligated to support the wife effectively hinged on whether the wife was at fault in causing the divorce, e.g., through infidelity. The blameless wife was entitled to continued support from the husband, called alimony. The blameworthy wife, in contrast, received no further support.

[D] Rights Upon Death

[1] Dower

Suppose A died, holding fee simple absolute in the family farm, and was survived only by his wife B and son C. Under the rules governing disposition of real property upon death, the farm would descend to C, not B; a widow was not considered an heir. C might support B thereafter, but such support was not assured (e.g., what if B was not C's mother, but rather A's second wife?). How could B survive?

The common law met this concern by giving the widow *dower*—a special life estate in one-third of her deceased husband's qualifying real property. During the marriage, the wife had a protected interest known as "inchoate dower" in all freehold lands in which the husband had an estate that could be inherited by the wife's issue. Thus, all fee simple estates and most fee tail estates[5] that the husband held at any time during the marriage were

---

[4] Jesse Dukeminier & James E. Krier, Property 324 (2d ed. 1988).

[5] If H held property in "fee tail special" (an estate that limited its descent to the children of a specified wife, say W1), then it would not be inheritable by the children of W2, H's second wife; W2 would have no dower rights in it.

subject to dower.[6] Without the wife's consent, the husband could not voluntarily transfer these interests to others, nor could creditors seize them to satisfy the husband's debts. Upon the husband's death, the widow's dower became "consummate" and one-third of the qualifying lands were set aside for her lifetime use. In theory, the widow could support herself by either leasing these lands to others or farming them herself.

Today dower is virtually obsolete.[7] Almost all states have abolished the doctrine in favor of more effective techniques for protecting the surviving widow. Even in its original form, the limitations of dower were clear. Unless the husband owned a qualifying estate in farm land or other income-producing real property, the widow might receive little practical benefit (e.g., imagine the widow holding a life estate in one-third of the family home). Over time, as family wealth increasingly took the form of stocks, bonds, cash, and other personal property—to which dower did not apply—the utility of the doctrine diminished.

[2] Curtesy

When a wife died before her husband, the common law provided the surviving husband with *curtesy*, the counterpart of dower. Curtesy was a special life estate the husband received in real property that his wife held in either fee simple or fee tail. While dower provided the wife with a life estate in only one-third of her husband's qualifying lands, curtesy gave the husband a life estate in all such lands held by his wife. Again unlike dower, curtesy arose only if the marriage produced issue capable of inheriting the wife's lands. Upon the birth of such issue, the husband received "curtesy initiate" in the wife's qualifying lands, which precluded his wife from transferring any interest in them without his consent. If his wife predeceased him, the husband acquired "curtesy consummate" upon her death. Like dower, curtesy has been abolished in almost all jurisdictions.

§ 11.03　Modern Common Law System

[A]　Statutory Reforms

The modern common law approach to marital property—which prevails in most states—bears little resemblance to its ancestor. Dramatically reshaped by two waves of statutory reforms, it increasingly resembles the community property system. At some point, the two systems will probably converge, creating uniform standards in all states.

---

[6] A prospective husband could not evade his future wife's dower rights by secretly conveying his property to another before the marriage; this might be considered a fraudulent conveyance in contemplation of marriage. *See* Strong v. Wood, 306 N.W.2d 737 (Iowa 1981).

[7] *See, e.g.,* Opinion of the Justices, 151 N.E.2d 475 (Mass. 1958).

[B] Rights During Marriage: Married Women's Property Acts

In the nineteenth century, reform legislation called the "Married Women's Property Acts" eroded much of the anachronistic, gender-based system that governed property rights during marriage.[8] Coverture was abolished; women were allowed to retain control of their property after marriage. Over time, all common law property states acknowledged the legal rights of married women to enter into contracts and to acquire and control property on terms generally equal to men. Accordingly, a spouse was not liable to creditors for non-marital debts incurred by the other spouse.[9] Professor Richard Chused has suggested that gender equality was not the exclusive impetus for these reforms; he notes that they were at least partly enacted to shield family property from the husband's creditors.[10]

Still, the result was a marital property system that—at least in theory—provides wife and husband with the legal opportunity to enjoy equal rights during marriage. The foundation of the reformed system is simple: property is owned by the spouse who acquires it. For example, consider rights to property that each spouse owns before marriage. If W already owns a farm worth $200,000 when she marries H, W retains complete control over this property after marriage. In the same manner, after marriage H continues to own the $100,000 stock portfolio that he previously owned. Similarly, each spouse owns whatever property he or she acquires during the marriage, absent a gift to the other spouse.

In practice, however, the promise of gender equality remains unfulfilled. Assume H and W are penniless when they marry. If H now begins earning wages from employment outside the home, these earnings—and all other assets purchased from them—are viewed as his property. W similarly has the legal right to own any wages she earns from outside employment. Yet during the nineteenth and twentieth centuries, married women were much less likely to work outside the home than were married men. Thus, if H works outside the home for 20 years, he "owns" his resulting wages and the assets they produce: the family home, car, furniture, bank account, and so forth. If W works only inside the home, the system assigns no monetary value to her labors; W owns nothing, unless H makes her a gift of his property. Under this model, H holds almost as much control over marital property as coverture formerly provided.

As married women increasingly work outside the home, this imbalance has lessened. Even for working women, however, inequality persists because husbands statistically earn more than wives.

---

[8] Richard H. Chused, *Married Women's Property Law: 1800–1850,* 71 Geo. L.J. 1359 (1983).

[9] For discussion of the impact of the Married Women's Property Acts on property held in tenancy by the entirety, *see* § 10.02[C][4].

[10] Richard H. Chused, *Married Women's Property Law: 1800–1850*, 71 Geo. L.J. 1359 (1983).

[C] Rights Upon Divorce: Equitable Distribution

[1] Toward Gender Equality

The late twentieth century brought revolutionary change to the law governing the property rights of divorcing spouses. In the 1970s, common law states began abandoning the traditional approach in favor of statutes requiring *equitable distribution*. Today all common law states follow this view, which—like the community property system—rests upon the foundation that marriage is an economic partnership.

Under this approach, the divorce court distributes property between wife and husband based on equitable principles after considering a variety of criteria relating to each spouse's needs, abilities, and circumstances.[11] Although these criteria vary considerably from state to state, most statutes direct the court to take into account factors such as:

(1) the income and property of each spouse at the time of marriage;

(2) the duration of the marriage;

(3) the age and health of each spouse;

(4) the income and property of each spouse when the divorce action begins;

(5) the occupation and vocational skills of each spouse;

(6) any antenuptial agreement;

(7) the special needs of each spouse;

(8) the contribution of each spouse to the marriage, in terms of both acquisition of assets and provision of household services;

(9) the dissipation of assets by each spouse during the marriage;[12]

(10) the opportunity of each spouse for future employment.

As courts apply these equitable distribution criteria, there is a clear trend toward equal distribution.[13] For example, statutes in some states presume that equal distribution is equitable, absent contrary criteria. Even without statutory guidance, many courts appear to utilize equal distribution as a starting point in determining an equitable result, by analogy to community property principles. Like all legal standards involving numerous criteria,

---

[11] Similarly, the court may temporarily alter the respective property rights of the spouses during the pendency of divorce proceedings. *See, e.g.,* Cote v. Cote, 599 A.2d 869 (Md. Ct. Spec. App. 1992) (court order restraining husband from entering family home due to danger of domestic violence against wife during divorce proceeding did not unconstitutionally "take" his rights in house; he received compensating benefit by not bearing cost of finding alternate housing for wife).

[12] *See, e.g.,* Gastineau v. Gastineau, 573 N.Y.S.2d 819 (Sup. Ct. 1991) (husband's breach of his contract as a professional football player was a dissipation of marital assets).

[13] Child support concerns may militate against equal distribution. *See, e.g., In re* Marriage of King, 700 P.2d 591 (Mont. 1985) (custodial parent properly awarded entire value of family home in lieu of child support from spouse, a professional gambler whose future income was uncertain).

the equitable distribution factors are difficult to apply in practice, leading some courts to adopt equal distribution as the easiest path.[14]

[2] Marital Property Defined

[a] General Principles

There are three different approaches to defining the "property" that is subject to equitable distribution.[15] In some states, the statute covers all property owned by either spouse, acquired at any time and from any source. A second group of states follows a somewhat more restrictive definition, limiting the scope of marital property to property acquired during marriage by either spouse from any source (including property obtained by gift, bequest, devise, or descent). Finally, a number of states apply equitable distribution only to property acquired from income earned during the marriage; this is essentially the same definition followed in community property states.

[b] Educational Degrees/Professional Licenses

Are educational degrees, professional licenses, or careers "property" that is subject to equitable distribution upon divorce? Beginning in the 1970s, as "no fault" divorce laws swept the nation, courts have struggled with this difficult issue.

[i] Majority Approach: Not Marital Property

Most jurisdictions refuse to recognize degrees, licenses, or the like as property.[16] An illustrative case is *In re Marriage of Graham*.[17] Anne Graham worked full-time as an airline stewardess for six years, financing the education of her husband Dennis Graham; Dennis obtained an undergraduate degree and a master's degree in business administration. Shortly thereafter, upon divorce, Anne petitioned the court for a share in the monetary value of Dennis's M.B.A. degree; the trial court awarded Anne $33,134, an amount equal to 40% of the statistically-anticipated future earnings attributable to the degree.[18]

---

[14] *But see* Painter v. Painter, 320 A.2d 484 (N.J. 1974) (upholding 80% award to husband, despite wife's argument that statute was unconstitutional as vague and uncertain).

[15] Many divorce cases pose the basic question of what is "property" in the first place. For example, does it extend to graduate degrees, professional licenses, goodwill, pension rights, or disability payments? *See, e.g.,* Morrison v. Morrison, 692 S.W.2d 601 (Ark. 1985) (disability retirement payments are marital property); Ciliberti v. Ciliberti, 542 A.2d 580 (Pa. Super. Ct. 1988) (true disability payments are not marital property).

[16] Interestingly, however, many courts hold that goodwill produced by a spouse's professional activities is marital property subject to judicial distribution. *But see* Prahinski v. Prahinski, 582 A.2d 784 (Md. 1990) (goodwill from husband's solo law practice was not marital property).

[17] 574 P.2d 75 (Colo. Ct. App. 1978). *See also* Todd v. Todd, 78 Cal. Rptr. 131 (Ct. App. 1969) (law degree not property).

[18] In concluding that Anne was entitled to a 40% share, the trial court assigned no importance to the housework she performed. It reasoned that she worked 40 hours per week, while Dennis studied 40 hours and worked 20 hours each week. Anne accordingly received a 40/100ths share.

The Colorado Supreme Court, however, concluded that an educational degree "is simply not encompassed even by the broad views of the concept of 'property.' "[19] In a widely-cited passage, the court reasoned that the degree had none of the traditional characteristics of property: it had no exchange value; was personal to the holder; could not be transferred to another; ended on the death of the holder and was not inheritable; and could not be assigned, sold, transferred, conveyed, or pledged. Rather, it was "simply an intellectual achievement that may potentially assist in the future acquisition of property."[20]

The court's formalistic approach to the definition of property—widely imitated by other courts—is troubling. For example, many types of property have no exchange value (e.g., old love letters); some property rights expire when the holder dies (e.g., a life estate); and often property rights cannot be transferred (e.g., a tenancy for years that is expressly not transferable).

Instead, the result in *Marriage of Graham* and similar decisions following the majority rule is better explained by two themes that lurk below the surface of the opinion. One theme revolves around whether human abilities should be considered property subject to private ownership. In part, the *Graham* court seems to suggest that Dennis's education (an "intellectual achievement") was attributable to the inherent abilities he possessed before marriage. For example, if Dennis still had two kidneys, while Anne had only one left, a court would not classify the extra kidney as marital property subject to equitable distribution, and the same rationale might be applied to an education. The other theme is the practical difficulty of appraising the value of an education. Statistics may have little relevance in the individual case. Dennis's future income will be influenced by a wide range of factors other than his education (e.g., his health, his interpersonal skills, his employer's solvency). Some courts express concern that any such valuation attempt is largely speculative.[21]

[ii] New York Approach: Marital Property

In contrast, it is well-settled in New York that educational degrees, professional licenses, and other career-enhancements are marital property subject to equitable distribution. The New York statute establishing the equitable distribution criteria directs the court to consider, among other things, the contribution of a spouse to "the career or career potential of the other party."[22] It further requires consideration of the contributions made to the acquisition of marital property by the spouse not holding title to it, including the "expenditures and contributions and services as a spouse, parent, wage earner and homemaker."[23]

The leading decision interpreting this standard is *O'Brien v. O'Brien*,[24] presenting facts strikingly similar to those in *Marriage of Graham*. The wife

---

[19] *In re* Marriage of Graham, 574 P.2d 75, 77 (Colo. Ct. App. 1978).

[20] *In re* Marriage of Graham, 574 P.2d 75, 77 (Colo. Ct. App. 1978).

[21] *See, e.g.,* O'Brien v. O'Brien, 489 N.E.2d 712 (N.Y. 1985) (Meyer, J., concurring).

[22] N.Y. Dom. Rel. Law § 236(B)(5)(d)(6).

[23] N.Y. Dom. Rel. Law § 236(B)(5)(d)(6).

[24] 489 N.E.2d 712 (N.Y. 1985).

worked as a teacher for nine years, allowing her husband to finish his undergraduate degree, graduate from medical school, and complete internship training. Two months after receiving his medical license, the husband initiated divorce proceedings. The trial court awarded the wife $188,800, representing 40% of the value of her husband's medical license.

The court had little difficulty affirming this result. It rejected plaintiff's plea—based on decisions like *Marriage of Graham*—that the license did not satisfy the traditional definition of property, reasoning that the applicable New York statute created a "new species of property" unknown at common law. The court observed that a working spouse often contributes substantial income and sacrifices personal educational, career, and childbearing opportunities, all to support the other spouse's pursuit of a professional degree that will ultimately benefit both. Consistent with the premise of equitable distribution that marriage is an economic partnership, it held that the medical license was the product of the parties' joint efforts, and thus marital property. As a secondary basis for its holding, the court noted that—even outside of the statute—a professional license is a "valuable property right" that, for example, cannot be revoked without due process of law.

Six years later, *Elkus v. Elkus*[25] extended *O'Brien* by holding that a plaintiff opera singer's career and celebrity status were marital property. The defendant husband sacrificed his own potential career in order to serve as his wife's voice coach and to care for their children, all of which increased the value of her career. Although plaintiff's successful career was primarily based on an "innate talent," the *Elkus* court reasoned that the appreciation in the value of her career due to the husband's efforts was marital property.

[iii] Alternative Approach: Reimbursement Alimony

Some states embrace a third approach, agreeing that graduate degrees and the like are not property, but awarding "reimbursement alimony" to compensate the supporting spouse for economic sacrifices made during the marriage.[26] Yet this remedy is quite limited. Usually only out-of-pocket contributions to educational expenses such as tuition can be recovered. Thus, for example, if W earned wages during the marriage, using $50,000 from her earnings to pay for H's medical school tuition, she will be able to recover $50,000 in alimony payments over time. But W's expenditures on rent, food, and other family needs will not be repaid. Moreover, if W worked only inside the family home and raised the couple's children, these non-monetary contributions will be ignored.

---

[25] 572 N.Y.S.2d 901 (App. Div. 1991).

[26] *In re* Marriage of Francis, 442 N.W.2d 59 (Iowa 1989); Mahoney v. Mahoney, 453 A.2d 527 (N.J. 1982); Hoak v. Hoak, 370 S.E.2d 473 (W. Va. 1988). *But see* Martinez v. Martinez, 818 P.2d 538 (Utah 1991) (reversing lower court's award of "equitable restitution" to wife for her contributions to husband's medical education).

[iv] Reflections on the "Degree Dilemma"

The legal scholarship exploring the "degree dilemma" emphasizes the unfairness to women generally if graduate degrees, licenses, and other forms of human capital are not treated as marital property.[27] Young families primarily invest in education or similar human capital, not tangible assets such as land or stocks, and most commonly this investment enhances the career potential of men, not women.[28] Thus, for example, a dissenting justice observed in *Marriage of Graham*: "As a matter of economic reality the most valuable asset acquired by either party during this six-year marriage was the husband's increased earning capacity."[29] The majority rule effectively assigns this asset to the professional spouse, who is usually the husband, to the detriment of the wife.

[D] Rights Upon Death: Elective Share

The *elective share* has replaced dower and curtesy in almost all common law property jurisdictions. The surviving spouse may elect to *either* (a) abide by the terms of the decedent spouse's will *or* (b) take a share (normally one-half or one-third) of all property the decedent owned at death. For example, suppose that H dies owning real and personal property valued at $1,000,000; his will bequeaths $50,000 in stocks to W, his widow, and gives the balance of his property to his cousin C. Under an elective share statute, W may either accept the $50,000 bequest or repudiate the will and receive an elective share, most likely $500,000.[30] Inter vivos gifts made by the decedent to the surviving spouse are normally not considered in this process; thus, for example, W would still receive her elective share even if H had given her $2,000,000 during his lifetime.[31]

Although the size of the elective share varies from state to state, there is a clear trend—presumably influenced by the community property system—toward a one-half share. The 1993 amendments to the Uniform Probate Code reflect this trend.[32] The Code formerly provided for a one-third share. As amended, the Code provides the surviving spouse with a share of the couple's combined assets, using a sliding scale based on the principle: "the longer the marriage, the larger the share." Thus, the surviving spouse who was married for 15 years or longer receives a one-half share, while one married for a shorter period receives less.[33]

---

[27] *See, e.g.,* Lenore J. Weitzman, *The Economics of Divorce: Social and Economic Consequences of Property, Alimony and Child Support Awards,* 28 UCLA L. Rev. 1181 (1981).

[28] Curtis J. Berger & Joan C. Williams, Property: Land Ownership and Use 468 (4th ed. 1997).

[29] 574 P.2d 75, 78 (Colo. 1978) (Carringan, J., dissenting).

[30] This example assumes that H left no debts outstanding at death. The elective share is usually computed based on the net estate remaining after creditors' claims are paid.

[31] *But see* Unif. Probate Code § 2-202(b) (providing that inter vivos gifts from decedent to surviving spouse are credited against the amount of the elective share).

[32] Unif. Probate Code § 2-202(a).

[33] Unif. Probate Code § 2-202(a). Similarly, the Uniform Marital Property Act provides the surviving spouse with a one-half share (*see* § 11.07).

Yet the elective share approach suffers from a major loophole that threatens to undermine its effectiveness: the inter vivos gift to a third party. Suppose that H gives all of his property to his cousin C, following the common law view that during life a spouse has complete control over his or her own property. One week later, H dies, leaving his wife W penniless. If we apply the standard rule that the elective share is computed based on the property the decedent owned at time of death, W receives nothing. How can these two seemingly inconsistent principles be reconciled? Judicial wrestling with this issue has produced a variety of compromise tests. Some states follow an "illusory transfer" standard, which allows the surviving spouse an elective share in property over which the decedent retained significant control (e.g., assets in a revocable trust, insurance policies).[34] Others focus on the scienter of the decedent, extending the elective share to property that the decedent transferred to a third party in order to defeat the survivor's elective share.[35] Ironically, for all their faults, the common law doctrines of dower and curtesy probably afforded better protection against inter vivos gifts; property subject to dower or curtesy could not be transferred without the consent of both spouses.

§ 11.04   Community Property System

[A]   Marriage As Partnership

The community property system is founded upon equality. It views marriage as an economic partnership between husband and wife in which the contributions of each spouse—whether outside or inside the home—are valued equally.

[B]   What Is Community Property?

[1]   General Principles

The broad outlines of the community property system are simple. In general, the earnings of either spouse during marriage—and all property acquired with those earnings—are deemed *community property*. Each spouse owns a one-half undivided interest in all community property. For example, suppose that after W and H marry, W works inside the home while H earns wages working in a bank; H's earnings during marriage are used to purchase a $200,000 house. The house is community property, with W and H each owning an undivided interest worth $100,000. In contrast to the approach of the Married Women's Property Acts, the identity of the spouse whose wages are used to purchase the house is irrelevant.

---

[34] *See, e.g.,* Newman v. Dore, 9 N.E.2d 966 (N.Y. 1937) (now superseded by statute in New York, but still followed in other states). *See also* Kerwin v. Donaghy, 59 N.E.2d 299 (Mass. 1945) (discussing rule).

[35] Knell v. Price, 550 A.2d 413 (Md. Ct. Spec. App. 1988) (upholding conveyance of remainder interest in home to decedent's nurse and companion because gift was not solely motivated by intent to deprive spouse of elective share; rather, decedent intended to reward grantee for care and companionship), *rev'd,* 569 A.2d 636 (1990).

But not all property is considered community property. Property that a spouse acquires before marriage, or acquires during marriage through gift, devise, bequest, or descent, is deemed *separate property*. Separate property is the sole property of the owner spouse who may use or transfer it freely, just as if the owner were unmarried. For example, suppose that W owns stocks worth $60,000 before she marries H and during the marriage H inherits family jewelry worth $40,000. The stocks and jewelry are the separate property of W and H, respectively.[36]

An unscrupulous spouse might attempt to disguise community property as separate property. Thus, property owned or possessed by either spouse during marriage is ordinarily presumed to be community property, regardless of who formally holds title. This presumption can be rebutted by evidence that the asset is separate property. For example, if O conveys fee simple absolute in Brownacre to H "as his sole and separate property" while H is married to W, the deed recital will be overcome by the presumption that Brownacre is now community property, unless H can prove its separate character.

Of course, spouses may alter or "transmute" the character of property by agreement; this is simply a specialized form of gift between spouses. Thus, H and W could agree to transmute community property (e.g., a sports car) into separate property.[37] Using the same process, they could convert separate property (e.g., stocks that W acquired before marriage) into community property.

[2] Assets Acquired with a Mixture of Community and Separate Property

Who owns property acquired with a combination of community and separate property? Suppose that during marriage H and W buy a house with a $200,000 cash payment that is a combination of community ($150,000) and separate ($50,000 owned by W) property. Virtually all community property states would agree that W owns a 25% interest in the home as her separate property and the remaining 75% interest is community property.

But what happens if the property is purchased with payments over time that start before marriage? Suppose, for example, that before marriage W purchases a $200,000 house, giving the seller S a $50,000 down payment and a promissory note for $150,000. Assume that H and W are now married and that H's earnings during marriage—community property—are used to make the loan payments to S. Who owns the house now?

---

[36] Are graduate degrees and professional licenses community property, separate property, or not property at all? Like most common law states (*see* § 11.03[C][2][b]), community property jurisdictions generally hold that degrees, licenses, and the like are not property. *See, e.g.,* Todd v. Todd, 78 Cal. Rptr. 131 (Ct. App. 1969) (law degree not community property). Similarly, some authorities conclude that nonvested pension rights are a mere expectancy, and thus not community property. *In re* Marriage of Brown, 544 P.2d 561 (Cal. 1976).

[37] *See, e.g., In re* Marriage of Lucas, 614 P.2d 258 (Cal. 1980) (community property motor home transmuted into wife's separate property by husband's gift).

The eight community property states differ in their approaches to this problem.[38] Some states follow a pro rata approach that reaches the same result as in the case of a lump sum payment: 25% is the wife's separate property, and 75% is community property.[39] Other states use an "inception of right" approach, under which the character of the asset is determined when the transaction begins; because W executed the purchase contact before marriage, the home would be her separate property. Finally, a few states employ a "time of vesting" rule that determines the character of the asset when title is transferred; the home would also be W's separate property under this view because she received title before the marriage.

[3]　Profits Received from Separate Property

Similar uncertainty surrounds a related issue: who owns profits or other income received during the marriage from separate property? In some states, all such income is considered community property. But most community property jurisdictions provide that income derived from separate property normally remains separate in character. One exception to the majority rule involves profits derived from a combination of capital and labor. Suppose, for example, that H devotes all of his time during marriage to managing his stock portfolio, which is separate property. Jurisdictions following the majority approach will typically treat H's stock profits as a mix of separate property (from the separate capital) and community property (from H's labor during marriage), and attempt to apportion them accordingly.[40]

[C]　Rights During Marriage

During marriage, the husband and wife have equal rights to use, manage, and otherwise control community property. For example, either spouse can sell community property, although some states require both spouses to consent to the sale of community real property. Gifts of community property pose a recurring problem. Some states allow either spouse to make reasonable gifts to third parties (e.g., small donations to charity) without consent of the other; other states prohibit all gifts unless both spouses consent.[41]

[D]　Rights Upon Divorce

Upon divorce, community property is divided between the spouses and separate property is retained by the owner spouse. Statutes in most states

---

[38] To complicate matters further, a state may use differing approaches depending on the nature of the asset; for example, insurance policies may be governed by one rule and pensions by another.

[39] See, e.g., In re Marriage of Lucas, 614 P.2d 285 (Cal. 1980).

[40] See, e.g., Beam v. Bank of Am., 490 P.2d 257 (Cal. 1971).

[41] But see Borelli v. Brusseau, 16 Cal. Rptr. 2d 16 (Ct. App. 1993) (even in California, a community property state, a wife owes a duty to support her husband; the wife's promise to care for her infirm husband in exchange for husband's promise to leave wife his separate property did not create an enforceable contract due to lack of consideration, because she owed a preexisting duty).

merely require an "equitable" division of community property based on consideration of various criteria. In a few states (notably California), courts are required to divide community property equally between the spouses, unless some special exception applies.[42]

[E] Rights Upon Death

Upon death, a spouse may transfer by will one-half of the community property and all of his or her separate property. Thus, if H and W own a community property home worth $400,000 and W owns $100,000 in separate property, at death W can transfer $300,000 ($200,000 in community property plus her $100,000 in separate property) to whomever she wishes.

Spouses holding assets as community property receive a special federal income tax benefit known as a "stepped up" basis when one spouse dies. Suppose H and W originally purchased their home for $150,000; if they sold it for $400,000 during the marriage, they would normally be obligated to pay federal income tax on the amount of gain they realize from the sale, here $250,000, absent any special exclusion. However, suppose W dies while they still own the home and devises her share to H. The home receives an adjusted tax basis of current fair market value, here $400,000; thus, if it is later sold for $400,000, no "gain" is realized and no federal income tax is due.

§ 11.05 Conflict Between the Systems: The Problem of Migrating Couples

What happens when both systems apply to a couple at different stages of their marriage? Suppose H and W live in a community property state where only H earns wages; all the property acquired with these earnings is community property. If H and W now move to a common law state where H dies, W enjoys the protection of both systems. She already has a half interest in the property brought to the new state; she now receives an elective share or intestate share in H's half.

But the transition from a common law jurisdiction to a community property jurisdiction may be problematic.[43] For example, in *Estate of Hanau v. Hanau*[44] a couple married and lived in Ohio for 25 years; only the husband worked outside the home. Under Ohio's common law property approach, the $500,000 in assets acquired from the husband's earnings were owned by the husband. The couple moved to Texas, a community property state; the husband soon died, bequeathing his estate to his daughter by a prior marriage. If the couple had remained in Ohio, the wife could have recovered an elective share of her husband's estate. However,

---

[42] *See, e.g.,* Cal. Fam. Code § 2550 (directing courts to "divide the community estate of the parties equally").

[43] *See also* Pacific Gamble Robinson Co. v. Lapp, 622 P.2d 850 (Wash. 1980) (creditor on non-marital debt incurred by husband while couple lived in common law state could recover against community property of couple after move to community property state).

[44] 730 S.W.2d 663 (Tex. 1987).

under the controlling Texas community property law, the entire estate was deemed the husband's separate property, which he could bequeath as he wished. [45]

§ 11.06 Attempts to Avoid the Systems: Premarital Agreements

An increasing number of couples enter into agreements before marriage that establish their property rights in the event of divorce. The common law was traditionally hostile to such premarital agreements on the basis that they tended to encourage divorce. Some courts still cling to this view, refusing to enforce such agreements on grounds of public policy.

The modern trend is to recognize the validity of premarital agreements. A majority of states have adopted the Uniform Premarital Agreement Act, [46] which provides that an agreement is generally enforceable unless (1) it was unconscionable when made and (2) the complaining spouse did not receive full financial disclosure from the other. Some states have adopted the Act with the modification that unconscionability or lack of full disclosure will invalidate the agreement, and several non-adopting states also appear to follow this approach.

§ 11.07 The Future of Marital Property Law?: Uniform Marital Property Act

The Uniform Marital Property Act may ultimately bridge the gap between the common law and community property systems. To date, however, the Act has received an unenthusiastic reception; it has been adopted only by Wisconsin. [47]

The Act dramatically alters property rights during the marriage, abandoning the "you earn it, you own it" approach of the Married Women's Property Acts. The Act essentially creates a community property system, although the phrase "community property" is delicately avoided. During the marriage, each spouse owns a present half-interest in all "marital property." Marital property consists of all earnings during marriage and the property acquired with those earnings. All property acquired before marriage, together with property acquired during marriage by gift, bequest, devise, or descent, is deemed separate property, not subject to the provisions of the Act.

For example, assume that when H and W are married, W owns stocks worth $100,000; during the first year of marriage, H earns $50,000 and receives a $10,000 painting by gift from his aunt. At this point in the marriage, both H and W own a $25,000 share in marital property; W owns

---

[45] California avoids this dilemma by treating separate property acquired with earnings in a common law state as "quasi-community property." Cal. Fam. Code §§ 63, 125, 2550.

[46] Unif. Premarital Agreement Act § 6, 9B U.L.A. 376.

[47] *See* Howard S. Erlanger & June M. Weisberger, *From Common Law Property to Community Property: Wisconsin's Marital Property Act Four Years Later*, 1990 Wis. L. Rev. 769.

the stocks as her separate property; and H owns the painting as his separate property.

The impact of the Act at divorce or death is relatively minor. Despite its stress on equal rights during marriage, it continues the equitable distribution approach to property rights upon divorce. Upon death each spouse may transfer one-half of the marital property, which is quite similar to the elective share system prevailing in common law states.

§ 11.08 Property Rights of Unmarried Couples

[A] Traditional Approach

The marital property law principles discussed above apply only to legally-married couples.[48] Most jurisdictions require a ceremonial marriage that is duly licensed and registered with the state, having long abolished the concept of "common law" marriage.[49] Under the traditional view, unmarried cohabitants cannot derive any property rights from their status as a couple. Suppose that A and B enter into an agreement to live together as an unmarried couple, sharing income and household duties equally. If A and B now separate, neither has any property rights against the other—despite their express contract—under the traditional approach.

Today this approach is followed only in a minority of states. Courts use a variety of bases to defend the historic rule. The repeal of statutes permitting common law marriage is widely viewed as evidence of legislative intent to confine the scope of marital property rights to ceremonial marriages. A second theme is that any cohabitation agreement is effectively a contract for prostitution, founded upon the illegal and immoral consideration of sexual services. Finally, some courts raise the broader concern that unmarried cohabitation tends to discourage marriage, and thus weakens "our family-based society."[50]

[B] The *Marvin v. Marvin* Revolution

The modern movement toward extending property rights to unmarried couples was sparked by the California Supreme Court's controversial "palimony" decision in *Marvin v. Marvin*.[51] Plaintiff Michelle Marvin alleged that she entered into an oral agreement with defendant Lee Marvin whereby (a) they would live together as husband and wife, (b) they would equally share their earnings and property, and (c) she would provide "services as a companion, homemaker, housekeeper and cook." Plaintiff

---

[48] Some states also protect "putative spouses," that is, couples who are not validly married, but who believe in good faith that they are.

[49] Some jurisdictions extend marital property rights to the "common law" marriage, i.e., the heterosexual couple who cohabit for a required period, holding themselves out as husband and wife.

[50] *See, e.g.,* Hewitt v. Hewitt, 394 N.E.2d 1204 (Ill. 1979).

[51] 557 P.2d 106 (Cal. 1976).

further asserted that she fully performed the agreement for six years, until defendant expelled her from his house. She sued for half of the $3.8 million that he had accumulated during their relationship.[52]

The court first held that plaintiff could maintain her express contract claim. It acknowledged that a contract between nonmarital partners would be unenforceable if it rested solely on the illegal consideration of sexual services; but it found other lawful consideration, e.g., the agreement to share earnings and property. As the court summarized: "[W]e base our opinion on the principle that adults who voluntarily live together and engage in sexual relations are nonetheless as competent as any other persons to contract respecting their earnings and property rights."[53]

The second strand of *Marvin* was more surprising: the court concluded that plaintiff might have enforceable property rights even without an express contract. It observed that unmarried cohabitants might have expectations that courts would "fairly apportion property accumulated through mutual effort," which should be protected in equity. Citing changing societal mores, the court concluded that moral considerations should not block this result. It also rejected concern about the stability of marriage, suggesting that unmarried cohabitation sometimes served as a trial period before marriage. Accordingly, it remanded the case to the trial court to determine whether the conduct of the parties demonstrated an implied contract, an implied agreement of partnership or joint venture, or a similar "tacit understanding," and whether principles of quantum meruit, constructive trust, or resulting trust might apply.

[C] Post-*Marvin* Decisions

In the wake of *Marvin*, the majority rule is that property rights may exist between unmarried cohabitants. In over 30 states, these rights stem from *Marvin* theories, most commonly express contract. In *Watts v. Watts*,[54] for example, on facts[55] even more compelling than those in *Marvin*, the Wisconsin Supreme Court held that a former cohabitant could sue in express contract and unjust enrichment, and utilize the constructive trust remedy.[56] And many other states still recognize common law marriage, which produces a similar result.[57]

---

[52] The case reached the court following the defendant's successful motion for judgment on the pleadings. Accordingly, the court treated plaintiff's allegations as true for purposes of the appeal.

[53] Marvin v. Marvin, 557 P.2d 106, 116 (Cal. 1976).

[54] 405 N.W.2d 303 (Wis. 1987).

[55] In *Watts*, the couple not only held themselves out as husband and wife generally, and entered into the type of agreement claimed in *Marvin*, but also produced two children who were given the defendant's surname; the couple also maintained joint tenancy bank accounts, filed joint income tax returns, and acquired real and personal property as husband and wife.

[56] *See also* Cook v. Cook, 691 P.2d 664 (Ariz. 1984) (holding that express contract between unmarried cohabitants would be enforceable).

[57] For a scholarly perspective on the issue, see William A. Reppy, Jr., *Property and Support Rights of Unmarried Cohabitants: A Proposal for Creating a New Legal Status*, 44 La. L. Rev. 1677 (1984).

[D] Gay and Lesbian Couples

Jurisdictions that recognize property rights between unmarried hetero-sexual couples have often extended this protection to gay and lesbian couples as well, particularly where an express contract is present.[58] However, the contours of debate are somewhat different. Legal scholars argue that the logic for recognizing rights for gay and lesbian couples is even stronger than that for heterosexual couples because the option of ceremonial marriage is unavailable.[59] Yet courts seem to accord less protection to gay and lesbian couples, more commonly relying on the theme of illicit consideration.

---

[58] *See, e.g.,* Crooke v. Gilden, 414 S.E.2d 645 (Ga. 1992) (express contract by lesbian couple); Ireland v. Flanagan, 627 P.2d 496 (Or. Ct. App. 1981) (same). *Cf.* Braschi v. Stahl Assoc. Co., 543 N.E.2d 49 (N.Y. 1989) (surviving member of gay couple may be "family member" of deceased member under rent control laws).

[59] *See, e.g.,* Kristin Bullock, Comment, *Applying* Marvin v. Marvin *to Same-Sex Couples: A Proposal for a Sex-Preference Neutral Cohabitation Contract Statute,* 25 U.C. Davis L. Rev. 1029 (1992).

Chapter 12

INTRODUCTION TO FUTURE INTERESTS

SYNOPSIS

§ 12.01 Future Interests in Context

The traditional English law governing future interests was an attempt to reconcile two competing goals: individual autonomy and overall social welfare.[1] Centuries of legal battle between these goals produced an intricate maze of rules that has confused generations of judges, lawyers, and law students. The common law allowed the creation of certain categories of future interests (*see* Chapters 13 and 14), but imposed somewhat different restrictions on each category. Broadly speaking, these restrictions were designed to ensure that land was not burdened with future interests for an unduly long period (*see* Chapter 14).

Accordingly, one crucial task is identifying the category into which a particular future interest falls. For example, is it a springing executory interest, a possibility of reverter, or something else? Complex rules govern the classification or "labeling" of future interests. After classification, the next question is how the restrictions apply to interests within the category. For example, the Rule Against Perpetuities applies to contingent remainders, but not to reversions. Many of these historic restrictions are now obsolete, and are being supplanted or modified by modern legislative reforms.

---

[1] For more detailed analysis of the law governing future interests, see generally Lewis M. Simes & Allan F. Smith, The Law of Future Interests (2d ed. 1956); *see also* Cornelius J. Moynihan, Introduction to the Law of Real Property 103–206 (2d ed. 1988).

§ 12.02 What Is a Future Interest?

Broadly speaking, a *future interest* is a right to receive possession of property at a future time. Professor Lewis Simes defined it more precisely as "an interest in land or other things in which the privilege of possession or of enjoyment is future and not present."[2] In other words, a future interest is a non-possessory interest that will—or may—become a possessory estate in the future. Despite its confusing name, a future interest is a presently-existing property right.

Suppose that O owns fee simple absolute in Greenacre; she wants her daughter D to have possession of Greenacre for D's life, and then wants her granddaughter G to receive fee simple absolute in the property. O can accomplish her goal in either of two ways. O could now convey a life estate in Greenacre to D, wait until D died, and *then* convey fee simple absolute to G. Under this first option, G has no rights in Greenacre at all until and unless O carries out her planned conveyance in the future. O may change her mind or die before this occurs. G has—at best—a hope or expectancy.

Alternatively, O could *now* convey to G a future interest—the right to receive possession of Greenacre after D's death. Under this second option, G now has a legally-enforceable right in Greenacre in the form of a future interest called a remainder. When D dies, G (or if G is then dead, her successors) will be entitled to possession of Greenacre, regardless of whether O dies or changes her mind in the interim. Until D dies, the practical utility of G's remainder is limited. Certainly G can sell or otherwise transfer her interest. Indeed, if Greenacre is a working gold mine and D is on the brink of death, G's remainder is quite valuable. And G may receive other minor benefits; for example, if D commits waste on the property, G can sue to enjoin D's conduct.

§ 12.03 Why Create a Future Interest?

[A] Family Support Motive

Future interests are most commonly encountered in family gifts—testamentary or inter vivos gifts of property to relatives. In effect, they are flexible estate planning tools that allow an owner to control the disposition of property even after death.

Suppose O owns fee simple absolute in Redacre, a farm; O's family consists of daughter D and grandson G. Assume that O's goal is to provide financial support to D and G after his own death. If O simply devises fee simple absolute in Redacre to D, D would be free to transfer her title to anyone before or upon her death. For example, if D gambled Redacre away during her life, she would be unable to devise it to G upon her death. O can avoid this risk by devising a life estate to D and a future interest to G; under this approach, D cannot eliminate or otherwise prejudice G's

---

[2] 1 Lewis M. Simes & Allan F. Smith, The Law of Future Interests § 1, at 2–3 (2d ed. 1956); *see also* Restatement of Property § 153 (1936) (defining future interest).

future right to Redacre. In this manner, O can ensure that his family-support goal is met, despite the risks of events that may occur after his death. Of course, a property owner like O might use future interests in a deed or a will to structure a gift in anticipation of many types of other events, such as the marriage, death, or birth of family members.

[B]　Charitable or Economic Motives

When future interests are found outside of the family setting, as was quite common in the nineteenth century, they typically serve either a charitable or economic motivation. Suppose that charitable O intends to donate Redacre to a local hospital group, and wants to ensure that it will be forever used as a hospital. To accomplish this goal, O might grant Redacre "only for so long as it is used as a hospital," retaining the future interest called a possibility of reverter. Or perhaps O has an economic goal—to ensure that the railroad runs by his farm, so that the wheat he grows can be easily sent to market. Under these circumstances, O might grant a strip of Redacre to the railroad "only for so long as it is used for railroad purposes." In either event, the grantee is motivated to carry out O's plan in order to avoid loss of title.[3]

§ 12.04　Types of Future Interests

[A]　Basic Categories

Five basic types of future interests are recognized:

   (1)　the *reversion*;

   (2)　the *possibility of reverter*;

   (3)　the *right of entry*;

   (4)　the *remainder*; and

   (5)　the *executory interest*.

Within each category, there may be further subdivisions; for example, there are four varieties of remainders. Table 2 below summarizes the universe of future interests.

The starting point for classifying a future interest is to determine the identity of the person who holds it: is the holder a transferor or a transferee? Suppose O, holding fee simple absolute in Greenacre, grants a life estate to L (e.g., "to L for life"). O is considered a *transferor* because she transferred an estate smaller than her own, while impliedly retaining a future interest (here, a reversion); once L's life estate ends, O or O's successors will be entitled to possession of Greenacre. The first three future interests

---

[3] Alternatively, the grantor might have both motivations. *See, e.g.,* Mahrenholz v. County Board of School Trustees, 417 N.E.2d 138 (Ill. App. Ct. 1981) (owner conveyed 1½ acre parcel to school board for school use, probably intending to both ensure nearby school for son and to benefit the school district).

above—the reversion, the possibility of reverter, and the right of entry—can be created only in a transferor and are discussed in Chapter 13.

Alternatively, suppose that by a single deed O grants a life estate in Greenacre to L and grants the future interest following the life estate (a type of remainder) to a third person, X; O might use deed language such as "to L for life, then to X." Here, X is considered a *transferee* because he receives his future interest from another person. The final two future interests mentioned above—the remainder and the executory interest—can be created only in a transferee and are discussed in Chapter 14.

TABLE 2: FUTURE INTERESTS

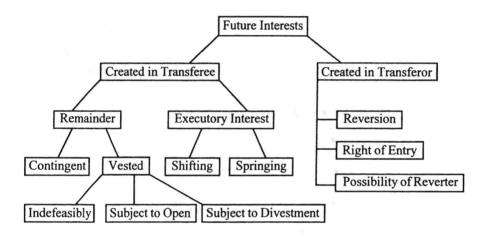

[B]　Subcategories of Future Interests

Future interests may be created in a variety of legal settings. For example, although the hypotheticals above concern real property, these future interests can also be created in personal property.[4] Indeed, today future interests are principally created in personal property such as stocks and bonds, not in land.

Similarly, future interests may be either legal or equitable. In the fact pattern above, O created a "legal" remainder in X. However, O could have created a remainder for X in trust (e.g., "to T in trust for the benefit of O for life, and then for the benefit of X") that would be an "equitable" remainder.

Finally, future interests may be either contingent or noncontingent. The legal remainder in X above is noncontingent, simply meaning that it is certain to become possessory upon L's death. However, O could grant a remainder that is contingent on future events, such as X attaining a certain age (e.g., "to L for life, and then to X if X reaches age 21"). This contingent

---

[4] *See, e.g.*, Gruen v. Gruen, 496 N.E.2d 869 (N.Y. 1986) (remainder created in painting).

remainder may never ripen into a possessory estate (e.g., if X dies at age 20).

[C]   A Future Interest in What Possessory Estate?

Each future interest will—or may—become a possessory estate. Thus, in classifying future interests it is conventional to identify both the type of future interest and the possessory estate linked to it. For example, if O grants Greenacre "to L for life, and then to X and his heirs," X's future interest is fully described as an *indefeasibly vested remainder in fee simple absolute*. It is the type of remainder called an *indefeasibly vested remainder*; and when the remainder ripens into a possessory estate, X will have *fee simple absolute*.

§ 12.05   Classifying Future Interests: An Overview

The classification of future interests is governed by elaborate and rather arcane rules, as discussed in Chapters 13 and 14. But classification in a general sense is relatively easy when a deed or will creates a present freehold estate that is followed by only *one* future interest, e.g., "to A for life, then to B and his heirs." In this situation, the identity of the first-created estate will determine the basic category of future interest that follows, as shown in Table 3 below.

TABLE 3: LINKING FREEHOLD ESTATES
AND FUTURE INTERESTS

	Future Interest	
Estate	**Created in Transferor**	**Created in Transferee**
Fee simple absolute	N/A	N/A
Fee simple determinable	Possibility of reverter	N/A
Fee simple subject to condition subsequent	Right of entry	N/A
Fee simple subject to executory limitation	N/A	Executory interest
Life estate absolute	Reversion	Remainder
Defeasible life estate	Reversion	Remainder or executory interest
Fee tail	Reversion	Remainder

The usefulness of Table 3 is limited. It may be necessary to determine the subcategory of future interest involved. Even though Table 3 reveals that B's interest is a remainder (because it follows an absolute life estate

and is held by a transferee), we must still assess which remainder subcategory it fits into. In addition, Table 3 provides little assistance when an
estate is followed by *multiple* future interests.

§ 12.06   Common Law Approach to Future Interests

[A]   Autonomy v. Marketability

Future interests present one of the clearest examples of the historic tension between individual autonomy and overall social welfare. On the one
hand, English landowners sought unfettered private property rights that
would allow them to transfer property by the use of future interests that
would survive the owner's death. On the other hand, mercantile and
commercial forces allied with the Crown demanded free marketability of
land. They insisted that future interests be limited, so that land could be
transferred for maximum societal benefit (*see* § 14.09).

For example, suppose O owns fee simple absolute in Blueacre, a farm
located on the Thames River near London. Agriculture is the natural use
of Blueacre, and O wants to protect his family against any ill-conceived
scheme to change the use. Thus, O devises Blueacre to his daughter D "only
for so long as Blueacre is used as a farm, and if Blueacre is not used as
farm, then to X and his heirs." One hundred years later, Blueacre and other
land fronting on the Thames is extremely valuable for dockyard use. Dockyard use would encourage trade, and thus benefit the English economy; but
Blueacre is much less valuable as farm land. If D's successors now try to
convert Blueacre into a dockyard, their title will end. Should the law respect
O's autonomy as a property owner by enforcing the "farm only" restriction
or should it ignore the restriction as inconsistent with the overall social
good? To what extent can the dead control the living?

[B]   The Common Law Compromise

In a broad sense, the common law governing future interests can be seen
as a grudging compromise between these competing factions. Over time,
property owners were given increasing latitude to create different types of
future interests, including interests held by transferees (entitled to less
judicial respect than those held by the original owner) and contingent
interests (which might never ripen into possession). This evolution culminated with the Statute of Uses, which first authorized the (seemingly
revolutionary) executory interest—a contingent, divesting future interest
held by a transferee.

At the same time, the law adopted various devices to limit the impact
of these interests on marketability. One device was to limit the transferability of such interests. Future interests that could not be freely transferred
were less likely to interfere with the marketability of the underlying estate.
Thus, for example, traditionally the possibility of reverter and the right of
entry could be transferred only by intestate succession, not by devise or

inter vivos conveyance. Another approach was to impose a time limit on how long a future interest could exist, as exemplified by the doctrine of the destructibility of contingent remainders. Probably the most famous device, however, was an effective ban on the creation of certain types of future interests, as seen in the Rule Against Perpetuities, the Rule in Shelley's Case, and the Doctrine of Worthier Title (*see* § 14.09).

§ 12.07   Modern Future Interest Legislation

Many jurisdictions have modified the common law approach to future interests through legislation. Two themes are evident in this reform effort. First, the complex and confusing categorization system is slowly being simplified, as legal commentators have long urged.[5] For example, some states have merged the executory interest into the remainder, treating both as a "remainder."[6] And the traditional common law restrictions on future interests such as the Rule in Shelley's Case, the Doctrine of Worthier Title, the destructibility of contingent remainders, and even the venerable Rule Against Perpetuities have been either abolished or greatly weakened (*see* §§ 14.09–14.14).

Second, legislation in a number of jurisdictions now effectively limits the duration of future interests, in a modern echo of the Rule Against Perpetuities. Statutes in some states provide that certain future interests simply lapse within a set period (usually 20 to 40 years), unless the holder records a notice of intent to preserve the interest under a "renewal" procedure afforded by the legislation (*see* § 13.05). And, under the "marketable title acts" (*see* § 25.08) in effect in many states, a record owner who has title stretching back for a specified period (usually 40 years) is deemed to have "marketable title," that is, title free of any encumbrances or other defects (including future interests) that are not reflected in documents recorded during the period. In effect, these marketable title acts invalidate most future interests and certain other claims to land title that were recorded before the statutory period began.

§ 12.08   Contemporary Relevance of Future Interests

The importance of future interests has been diminishing for decades. It is now extraordinarily rare to transfer a legal freehold estate in land other than fee simple absolute. Thus, legal future interests in real property are becoming uncommon.

Today future interests are still used as family estate planning tools, but principally for personal property held in trust. Over the last century, stocks, bonds, and other personal property have replaced land as the primary form of family wealth. Further, the trust has proven a much more effective estate planning device than the will or deed. Accordingly, equitable future interests are widely utilized.

---

[5] *See, e.g.*, Lawrence W. Waggoner, *Reformulating the Structure of Estates: A Proposal for Legislative Action*, 85 Harv. L. Rev. 729 (1972).

[6] *See, e.g.*, Cal. Civ. Code § 769; N.Y. Est. Powers & Trusts L. § 6-3.2.

As future interest usage shifted from real to personal property, the historic common law restrictions on future interests became increasingly anachronistic. Intended in large part to promote the marketability of land, these restraints have little or no application to personal property.

Chapter 13

FUTURE INTERESTS HELD BY THE TRANSFEROR

SYNOPSIS

§ 13.01　Three Future Interests

The common law traditionally classifies future interests according to the identity of the holder. Suppose O, owning fee simple absolute in Blueacre, conveys a life estate to A, retaining a future interest. Because O's future interest arose when O transferred the life estate to A, O is considered a *transferor*. A future interest can be created only through a deed, trust, or will; thus, only a grantor, settlor, or testator can be a transferor.

Three types of future interests may be created in a transferor: the reversion, the possibility of reverter, and the right of entry. These interests share a common theme: if one becomes possessory, the estate will belong to the transferor or his successors. In some contexts, the law accords more protection to future interests held by a transferor than to future interests given to a third party, or *transferee*. For example, the Rule Against Perpetuities does not apply to a transferor's future interests.

Modern law still tends to disfavor the possibility of reverter and the right of entry. Scholars have long argued that the arcane distinction between these two types of future interests should be abolished, and some courts have adopted this view.[1] More fundamentally, many states have severely

---

[1] *See, e.g.,* Verner F. Chaffin, *Reverters, Rights of Entry, and Executory Interests: Semantic Confusion and the Tying Up of Land,* 31 Fordham L. Rev. 303 (1962); Allison Dunham, *Possibility of Reverter and Powers of Termination—Fraternal or Identical Twins,* 20 U. Chi. L. Rev. 215 (1953).

curtailed the duration and enforceability of these interests through legislation. The law is slowly moving toward the abolition of both interests.[2]

§ 13.02 Types of Future Interests

[A] Reversion

When an owner conveys an estate deemed "smaller" than the estate he holds, he retains a future interest called a *reversion*. Assume O owns fee simple absolute in Brownacre and conveys a life estate to A. A's life estate is a "smaller" estate than O's fee simple absolute because a life estate has a shorter duration than a fee simple; accordingly O has failed to convey his entire estate. Even though the language of O's conveyance does not expressly reserve any future interest in O, it arises as a matter of law: O retains a reversion in fee simple absolute. Once A's life estate ends, O automatically receives fee simple absolute, without taking any action. Similarly, when a fee simple absolute owner conveys another estate that is smaller than fee simple (e.g., fee tail, term of years, or periodic tenancy), she retains a reversion. Fee simple determinable and fee simple subject to a condition subsequent are considered estates equal in quantum to fee simple absolute, and thus create different future interests in the transferor as discussed below.

Complexity arises when an owner creates a series of estates and other interests through a single conveyance, but the inquiry remains the same: has the owner conveyed his or her entire estate? Suppose O conveys Brownacre "to A for life, then to B for life, then to C for life, and then to D and his heirs if D passes the bar, and if D never passes the bar, then to E and his heirs if E passes the bar." O retains a reversion in fee simple absolute here because A, B, and C will all die and both D and E may never pass the bar, and thus O has not transferred his entire estate. If D and E do not pass the bar, Brownacre reverts to O (or, if O has died in the interim, to O's successors). It does not matter that O's reversion is contingent on future events; it is still considered a reversion.

The common law traditionally ranked the size or quantum of each estate, in descending order, as follows: fee simple, fee tail, life estate, and leasehold estates. Thus, for example, if L holding a life estate in Greenacre conveys a term of years tenancy to T, L automatically retains a reversion because L transferred less than her whole estate.

[B] Possibility of Reverter

When a transferor creates a fee simple determinable (*see* § 9.06[C][2]), the future interest retained is a *possibility of reverter*. For example, if O conveys Blueacre "to L for so long as the property is used as an orphanage,

---

[2] For a suggestion that defeasible estates be treated as a form of servitude, rather than as a true estate, see Gerald Korngold, *For Unifying Servitudes and Defeasible Fees: Property Law's Functional Equivalents*, 66 Tex. L. Rev. 533 (1988).

and then to me," she has expressly reserved a possibility of reverter. [3] Like the reversion, this future interest may also arise by operation of law merely because O has not conveyed away her entire interest; thus, if O conveys Blueacre "to L for so long as the property is used as an orphanage," O similarly retains a possibility of reverter. Under either example, once L stops using the property as an orphanage, his estate *automatically* ends without any action by O, leaving O with fee simple absolute. [4] L's occupancy of Blueacre thereafter will trigger the statutory period for adverse possession.

[C] Right of Entry

When a transferor creates a fee simple subject to a condition subsequent (*see* § 9.06[C][3]), the future interest retained is most commonly termed a *right of entry;* some authorities call this interest a *right of reentry* or *power of termination.* For example, if O conveys Blueacre "to L but if L fails to use the property as an orphanage, then O may re-enter and retake the premises," she has expressly retained a right of entry.

If L now converts Blueacre into a pornographic movie theater, however, O's right of entry is not automatically transformed into fee simple absolute. In this regard, the right of entry is fundamentally different from its close cousins, the remainder and the possibility of reverter. Holding a right of entry here, O must take affirmative action in order to end L's estate, most commonly by either giving L formal notice or bringing a quiet title action against L. Until and unless O acts, L's estate continues. Logically, then, the statute of limitations period for L to adversely possess against O should not commence until O elects to end L's estate, but the case law on point is divided.

§ 13.03 Transfer of Interest

Consistent with the common law insistence on free alienation of property rights, the reversion is freely transferable. If O holds a reversion in Blueacre, he may convey or devise it; if he dies intestate, it will descend to his heirs.

Yet future interests such as the possibility of reverter and right of entry—which may never become possessory—tend to impair the marketability of the affected land. If L's estate endures only so long as the land is used as an orphanage, for example, L may be unable to sell his rights. Moreover, because the Rule Against Perpetuities does not apply to such interests, they may cloud title for a long time. A paradox arises: should future interests that impair marketability of the underlying estate be freely marketable? The early common law answered this question with a clear "no" for the right

---

[3] *See, e.g.,* Mahrenholz v. County Board of School Trustees, 417 N.E.2d 138 (Ill. App. Ct. 1981).

[4] Modern courts tend to construe such forfeiture provisions narrowly, to avoid injustice. *See* § 9.06[E].

of entry.[5] It could be transferred only by intestate succession; thus, if O held a right of entry in Blueacre, he could not devise or convey it. The common law tended to impose the same restrictions on the possibility of reverter, although with less force, presumably because this interest seemed more like a reversion.

Today, in most jurisdictions, both the possibility of reverter and the right of entry are freely transferable; they can be conveyed, devised, and inherited.[6] Some jurisdictions still cling to the restrictive common law approach, but allow these interests to be "released," i.e., conveyed inter vivos to the holder of the defeasible estate.[7]

One final aspect of transferability merits mention. The transfer of a reversion, possibility of reverter, or right of entry by the transferor to a third party does not change the name of the affected future interest. Thus, if O first conveys Blueacre "to L for so long as the property is used as an orphanage," and later conveys his possibility of reverter to M, it remains a possibility of reverter even though it is now held by a third person.

§ 13.04 Other Rights of Interest Holder

[A] General Principles

During the period before a reversion, possibility of reverter, or right of entry becomes possessory, the rights of the holder are quite limited. The issue arises most commonly in two contexts: preventing waste and sharing in eminent domain proceeds.

[B] Preventing Waste

Suppose that O conveys Blueacre "to A for life," thereby retaining a reversion in fee simple absolute. If A now commits waste on Blueacre (for example, by starting a gold mining operation), O's rights as a reversion holder are clear; she can secure damages for past waste and enjoin future waste. On the other hand, if O merely holds a possibility of reverter or right of entry, her ability to prevent waste by A is almost nonexistent. Consistent with the common law's disdain for such tenuous and insubstantial interests, a special waste standard was recognized: the holder of such an interest could only enjoin actions that the prudent owner of a fee simple absolute estate would not have performed.[8] Under this standard, O cannot enjoin A's gold mining.

---

[5] 1 American Law of Property § 4.68, at 527–529 (A. James Casner ed., 1952).

[6] *See, e.g.,* City of Carthage v. United Missouri Bank of Kansas City, 873 S.W.2d 610 (Mo. Ct. App. 1994).

[7] *See, e.g.,* Mahrenholz v. County Board of School Trustees, 417 N.E.2d 138 (Ill. App. Ct. 1981).

[8] *See generally* Powell on Real Property ¶ 642[5] (Michael Allan Wolf ed., Matthew Bender). The policies underlying this rule have diminished relevance today. Just as the law increasingly acknowledges the rights of such future interest holders to share in condemnation proceeds, modern courts should empower them to prevent waste.

[C] Right to Eminent Domain Proceeds

Eminent domain decisions reflect a similar split. If the state condemns Blueacre in order to build an airport, O's reversion entitles her to a share of the eminent domain award; of course, the value of O's reversion, and thus the size of O's share, turns on the probable length of A's life. Conversely, under the traditional and (still majority) view, one holding a possibility of reverter or right of entry receives no share of eminent domain proceeds. Thus, if O conveys Blueacre "to A for so long as the property is used as an orphanage," and the state now condemns the property for an airport, A receives the entire eminent domain award. O's possibility of reverter is seen as too insubstantial and contingent to merit compensation. The Restatement of Property embraces this rule, except in the rare situation where the event that would terminate the defeasible estate will probably occur within a short period of time.[9]

The movement away from this harsh standard is highlighted by *Ink v. City of Canton.*[10] There, the descendants of Harry Ink conveyed property to Canton, Ohio in fee simple determinable for so long as the land was used as a public park. When the state later condemned most of "Ink Park" for a highway, the grantors' heirs argued that they should be compensated for the loss of their possibility of reverter. The Ohio Supreme Court agreed, reasoning that the eminent domain award represented the fair market value of the property for any use, which was presumably greater than the value of land restricted to park use only. Thus, the court held that the heirs were entitled to the difference between these two values.[11]

§ 13.05 Modern Reforms

Modern legislation in California, New York, and other states imposes severe restrictions on the possibility of reverter and the right of entry. This legislative hostility stems from two basic sources. One concern is fundamental fairness. Enforcement of these interests results in the forfeiture of the defeasible estate, often creating an unanticipated windfall for the interest holder. To paraphrase Oliver Wendell Holmes, the holder of the future interest may feel little or no "wrench" if it is restricted or even invalidated. A secondary concern is that such interests restrict the free alienation of the underlying estate.

These reform statutes usually follow the same basic pattern, though differing in details. First, such an interest will lapse within a specified period of time (usually 20 or 30 years) unless its holder files a notice of intent to preserve the interest; because few interest holders comply with this requirement, most interests will simply end. Second, even when the triggering event occurs that will make the interest possessory, it will not be enforced unless the court finds that the restriction on the fee estate

---

[9] Restatement of Property § 53 cmt. b, c (1936).

[10] 212 N.E.2d 574 (Ohio 1965).

[11] *See also* Leeco Gas & Oil Co. v. County of Nueces, 736 S.W.2d 629 (Tex. 1987) (following *Ink* approach).

substantially benefits the holder. Thus, if O's great-grandson R now holds the possibility of reverter attached to the fee simple determinable granted above to L "for so long as the property is used as an orphanage," R's interest will not become possessory unless R can establish that continuation of the orphanage restriction substantially benefits him. In most cases, the holder will be unable to meet this standard. Finally, many states impose relatively short statutes of limitations on actions to enforce the rights of the future interest holder. In Colorado, for example, suit must be brought within one year from the date of the triggering event.[12]

---

[12] Johnson v. City of Wheat Ridge, 532 P.2d 985 (Colo. Ct. App. 1975).

Chapter 14

FUTURE INTERESTS HELD BY THE TRANSFEREE

§ 14.01   An Intricate Common Law Maze

Suppose O, holding fee simple absolute in Blueacre, transfers a possessory estate to his daughter A and the accompanying future interest to his son B. Under the common law approach to classifying future interests, B is deemed a *transferee*—a third party who receives a future interest from the transferor.

The common law principles governing future interests held by transferees reflect the internal tensions of sixteenth-century English society, as discussed in Chapter 12. Landowners fought for the unfettered right to create future interests in their family members and other transferees, in order to control future events, perpetuate family wealth, and avoid taxation. Mercantile interests fought to limit such interests—particularly "contingent" interests—in order to encourage the productive use of land and thus maximize societal wealth. The Crown supported efforts to limit these future interests and thereby facilitate taxation. The intricate maze of rules and doctrines that resulted from this struggle may be broadly described as a compromise: future interests in transferees were permitted, but restricted. Contingent future interests were particularly restricted through doctrines such as the Rule Against Perpetuities, the Rule in Shelley's Case, the Doctrine of Worthier Title, and the destructibility of contingent remainders.

Precise classification of future interests was essential to the operation of this system, because different types of interests were restricted in different ways. The Doctrine of Worthier Title, for example, affected remainders but not executory interests. And the Rule Against Perpetuities might invalidate a contingent remainder, a vested remainder subject to open, or an executory interest, but not other interests.

Are these common law rules governing future interests in transferees still relevant today in the United States? The answer is a qualified "yes." Reform efforts in recent decades have somewhat simplified the traditional system, and this is the modern trend. The basic system for classifying future interests remains intact in most states, but the importance of precise classification is diminishing. Why? The law has largely abandoned the archaic restrictions imposed on future interests held by transferees. The Rule Against Perpetuities lingers, although most states have simplified it by statute. Ironically, England—the originator of our intricate common law system—abandoned it in the early twentieth century.

§ 14.02 Classifying Future Interests Held by the Transferee

The traditional common law recognizes only two broad categories of future interests that can be held by a transferee: the *remainder* and the *executory interest*. There are four types of remainders and two types of executory interests. Thus, if a transferee holds a future interest, it must be one of the following six types:

    (1)   indefeasibly vested remainder;

    (2)   vested remainder subject to divestment;

    (3)   vested remainder subject to open;

    (4)   contingent remainder;

    (5)   springing executory interest;

    (6)   shifting executory interest.

One of the confusing features of this system is that the identity of a transferee's future interest may *change* over time as events unfold. A future interest that is initially a vested remainder subject to open, for example, might become an indefeasibly vested remainder. Or a contingent remainder might be transformed into an executory interest. Other changes are similarly possible. Thus, one must constantly reassess whether a particular future interest still fits within its assigned label.

§ 14.03 Remainders

[A] Remainders in Context

Early English law barred the creation of a future interest in any transferee until a thirteenth-century breakthrough: judicial acceptance of the indefeasibly vested remainder. Suppose O conveyed Blueacre in 1290 "to A for life, then to B and his heirs." B held an indefeasibly vested remainder, that is, a future interest in an ascertainable transferee that was certain to become possessory upon the natural expiration of the prior estate, here A's life estate.

Yet the doctrine of seisin hindered any extension of the remainder beyond this point. The common law required that seisin be vested at all times in an identifiable person. A remainder could not be created in an unascertainable person or group, nor could a remainder be subject to any condition, because this created the risk that when the prior estate ended the future interest holder might be unascertainable; this would cause a gap in seisin. As the feudal system declined, the importance of seisin waned and landowners sought new methods of imposing future restrictions on their lands. The stage was set for the development of new future interests in transferees.

The sixteenth century brought revolutionary change. New types of remainders arose, including remainders held by unascertainable persons and remainders subject to a wide range of conditions. And the Statute of Uses effectively created an entirely different type of future interest: the executory interest. These new future interests injected a large dose of uncertainty into a relatively stable and predictable system.

[B] What Is a Remainder?

[1] Basic Definition

The formal definition of a remainder is simple to recite, but often difficult to apply.[1] A *remainder* is a future interest created in a transferee that is capable of becoming a possessory estate upon the natural termination of a prior estate created by the same instrument.[2] Any future interest in a

---

[1] For general discussion of remainders, see Percy Bordwell, *The Common-Law Scheme of Estates and the Remainder*, 34 Iowa L. Rev. 401 (1949); Jesse Dukeminier, *Contingent Remainders and Executory Interests: A Requiem for the Distinction*, 43 Minn. L. Rev. 13 (1958); Jesse Dukeminier, *The Uniform Probate Code Upends the Law of Remainders*, 94 Mich. L. Rev. 148 (1995); Edward C. Halbach, Jr., *Creditors' Rights in Future Interests*, 43 Minn. L. Rev. 217 (1958).

[2] *See generally* Restatement of Property § 156(1) (1936) (defining a remainder as "any future

possessory estate created in a transferee other than a remainder is an *executory interest* (*see* § 14.04).

This pithy definition of a remainder includes three components. First, the future interest must be *created in a transferee*, not retained by the transferor. Accordingly, an instrument that creates a future interest in the transferor (e.g., O's conveyance "to A for life" impliedly creates a future interest in O) does not create a remainder.

Second, both the remainder and a "prior" estate must be created by the *same instrument*, either a deed, trust, or will. Thus, for example, if an instrument merely creates a future interest (e.g., "to A if B ever smokes cigars"), it cannot be a remainder.

Finally, a remainder must be *capable of becoming a possessory estate when the prior estate naturally ends*. A remainder waits patiently for the prior estate to naturally terminate. It cannot "divest" or "cut short" the prior estate. Thus, a remainder can only follow a life estate (by far the most common estate associated with the remainder), a fee tail (where still recognized), or a term of years. Why? A fee simple estate—whether absolute or defeasible—has no natural termination point; it may endure indefinitely. So, for example, if a deed creates a future interest after a defeasible fee simple (e.g., "to A and his heirs, but if A ever smokes, then to B"), it cannot be a remainder. Rather, if A smokes, then B's future interest will "cut short" or "divest" A's estate to become a possessory estate. Thus, B has an executory interest.

There can be no time gap between the end of the prior estate and the point when the remainder becomes possessory. Suppose O conveys Blueacre "to A for life, and 10 minutes after A's death, to B and his heirs." B's interest is not "capable" of becoming a possessory estate at the very instant when A's life estate ends. So what happens? Here O effectively retained a reversion. When A dies, O acquires a fee simple estate, at least for 10 minutes. Because B's interest "cuts short" O's estate, B holds an executory interest.

[2] Application of Definition to Example

Suppose A conveys Blackacre "to B for life, and then to C and his heirs." B obviously receives a life estate under this conveyance. But what is C's interest? A series of logical steps provides the solution.

Because C does not have the right to present possession of Blackacre, he must hold some type of future interest. Further, this future interest was not created in the transferor (A), but rather in a transferee (C). Because C is a transferee, his interest must be either a remainder or an executory interest; these are the only two types of future interests that can be created in a transferee.

---

interest limited in favor of a transferee in such manner that it can become a present interest upon the expiration of all prior interests simultaneously created, and cannot divest any interest except an interest left in the transferor"). *But cf.* Abbott v. Holway, 72 Me. 298 (1881) (refusing to construe a deed to create a remainder in the grantee and a reserved life estate in the grantor where the deed expressly provided that it took effect only upon the grantor's death).

Now the remaining portions of our definition come into play. Is C's interest capable of becoming a possessory estate upon the natural termination of a prior estate created by the same instrument? Yes. B's life estate is a prior estate created by the same deed that created C's interest. The verb "conveys" connotes a transfer by deed, and the quoted language makes it clear that both were created by the same deed. Finally, C's future interest can become a present estate upon the natural termination of B's life estate. When B dies, his life estate ends, and C's future interest will automatically be transformed into a possessory estate: fee simple absolute. Thus, C holds a type of remainder—more precisely, an indefeasibly vested remainder in fee simple absolute.

[C] Types of Remainders

[1] Four Types

The common law distinguished between two basic categories of remainders: the *vested remainder* and the *contingent remainder*. It further divided the universe of vested remainders into three subcategories. Thus, there are only four types of remainders: [3]

    (1)   indefeasibly vested remainder (often loosely abbreviated as "vested remainder");

    (2)   vested remainder subject to divestment (sometimes called a "vested remainder subject to complete defeasance");

    (3)   vested remainder subject to open (sometimes called a "vested remainder subject to partial divestment"); and

    (4)   contingent remainder.

The traditional rules used to classify remainders depend heavily on the *exact* language of the devise or conveyance involved. For example, the wording differences between a contingent remainder and a vested remainder subject to divestment are often very slight. If O conveys "to S for life, then to T and his heirs if T survives S, and if not then to U and his heirs," T has a contingent remainder. But if O conveys "to S for life, then to T and his heirs, but if T does not survive S, then to U and his heirs," T holds a vested remainder subject to divestment.

[2] Vested Remainders

[a] In General

A vested remainder is a remainder that is (a) created in a living, ascertainable person and (b) not subject to any condition precedent (except

---

[3] In addition, a vested remainder could be *both* subject to open and subject to divestment. Suppose O conveys "to A for life, and then to the children of B and their heirs, but if any child of B fails to reach age 21, then that child's share shall go to the children of B who reach age 21 and the heirs of those children." At the time, B has one child, five-year-old C. C's vested remainder is subject to open (because later children of B might be born) and also subject to divestment (if C dies before age 21 and B has at least one other child who reaches age 21).

the natural termination of the prior estate).[4] John Chipman Gray's classic definition of the vested remainder expresses the same thought in slightly different language: a remainder is "vested if, at every moment during its continuance, it becomes a present estate, whenever and however the preceding freehold estates" terminate.[5] Any other remainder is, by definition, a contingent remainder.

All other things being equal, the common law favored the vesting of remainders.[6] Thus, courts traditionally construed an ambiguous remainder as vested, not contingent. Modern courts have eroded this rule of construction, to the point where it is probably no longer the majority view.[7]

[b] Indefeasibly Vested Remainder

The hallmark of the *indefeasibly vested remainder* is certainty: the identity of the holder is certain and the remainder is certain to become a possessory estate.[8] In other words, an indefeasibly vested remainder is a remainder in a presently identifiable person that is not subject to any condition or limitation.

For example, if A conveys Greenacre "to B for life, then to C and her heirs," C's remainder will someday become fee simple absolute. The holder of the interest is a known person, C. No future event can intervene to stop C's remainder from becoming an estate. B, being mortal, will inevitably die, and her life estate will terminate. C (or whoever then holds C's remainder) will own fee simple absolute in Greenacre. Why? The answer lies in the language of A's conveyance: A did not impose any condition or limitation on C's remainder. C's remainder is ready to become a present estate whenever B's life estate ends.

What if C dies before B? Or what if C never has any "heirs"? Under the language of A's conveyance, neither event has any effect on the remainder. If C dies before B, C's devisees or heirs take the remainder; and if C dies without devisees or heirs the remainder will escheat to the state. Note that A could have imposed a condition on the remainder (e.g., "to B for life, and then to C and her heirs if C is then alive") if she wished to do so.

Suppose A conveys Greenacre "to B for life, then to C for life, and then to D and his heirs." English common law classified C's interest as an indefeasible vested remainder for life. Yet, arguably C's remainder is not certain to become possessory, because C might die before B; this would nullify C's life estate. For this reason, some authorities—notably the

---

[4] *See generally* Kost v. Foster, 94 N.E.2d 302 (Ill. 1950) (discussing distinction between vested remainder and contingent remainder); *see also* Roland R. Foulke, *Vested and Contingent Remainders*, 15 Colum. L. Rev. 680 (1915); Edward H. Rabin, *The Law Favors the Vesting of Estates. Why?*, 65 Colum. L. Rev. 467 (1965).

[5] John C. Gray, The Rule Against Perpetuities § 9, at 6 (4th ed. 1942).

[6] *In re* Estate of Houston, 201 A.2d 592 (Pa. 1964).

[7] Browning v. Sacrison, 518 P.2d 656 (Or. 1974).

[8] *See* Restatement of Property § 157 cmt. f (1936) (defining the indefeasibly vested remainder).

Restatement of Property[9] —take the position that C merely has a vested remainder for life subject to complete divestment.

[c] Vested Remainder Subject to Divestment

The *vested remainder subject to divestment* is simply a vested remainder that is subject to a condition subsequent. In other words, the identity of the interest holder is certain and the remainder is certain to become a possessory estate, *unless* some specified event occurs. If the specified future event occurs, the remainder is extinguished. Assume A conveys Greenacre "to B for life, then to C and her heirs, but if C ever smokes a cigar during B's lifetime, then to D." C clearly has a type of vested remainder, because C is ascertainable and her interest is not subject to a condition precedent. C's remainder is immediately ready to become possessory whenever B's life estate ends. However, if C ever smokes a cigar during B's life, her remainder will be automatically terminated or *divested*. C holds a vested remainder subject to divestment.

The distinction between a *condition precedent* and a *condition subsequent* is critical in the classification of remainders. This is particularly true in distinguishing between the vested remainder subject to divestment, on the one hand, and the contingent remainder, on the other.

A condition precedent is an event (other than the natural termination of the prior estate) that, according to the creating language, must occur *before* the remainder can become a possessory estate. Suppose O devises Greenacre "to A for life and then, if B reaches age 21, to B and his heirs." The location of this age condition is crucial. Here the condition of B reaching 21 is intertwined with the language that makes the gift, and thus is a condition precedent to the gift. B's remainder here is not vested because it cannot "at every moment" become a present estate when the prior estate (A's life estate) ends. B's remainder is not ready to become a present estate *until* B reaches 21. B has a contingent remainder.

But suppose the devise reads "to A for life, and then to B and his heirs, but if B does not reach age 21, then to C and her heirs." In this second version, O's language first makes a completed gift to B, and then *adds on* a later (or *subsequent*) condition in another clause. This language would create a condition subsequent. Under the common law view, B's remainder is vested because it is fully able "at every moment" to become possessory when A's life estate ends *unless* B has not yet then reached 21. B has a vested remainder subject to divestment.

[d] Vested Remainder Subject to Open (or Subject to Partial Divestment)

The *vested remainder subject to open* is a vested remainder in one or more ascertainable members of a class that may be enlarged by the addition of presently unascertainable persons. The identity of the interest holder is certain and the remainder is certain to become a possessory estate; but the

---

[9] Restatement of Property § 157 (1936).

size of the holder's *share* in the estate is *uncertain*. If more interest holders are identified, the size of each share will diminish. This interest arises most commonly in gifts to classes described as a particular person's "children," "grandchildren," "great-grandchildren," or "issue."

Suppose A conveys Greenacre "to B for life, then to the children of C and their heirs." If at that time C has only one living child, D, then D has a vested remainder subject to open. D's remainder is vested because D is immediately ascertainable and her interest is not subject to a condition precedent. D's remainder cannot be entirely extinguished because it is not subject to any condition. However, the size of D's interest may shrink if additional "children of C" are born in the future. As long as C is still alive, the class of "children of C" is still "open," meaning that additional members may join the class. If C has additional children, each will receive a vested remainder subject to open. For example, if C has two more children (E and F) before his death, then each child (D, E, and F) will hold a one-third share in fee simple absolute in Greenacre upon B's death.

[3] Contingent Remainders

As its name suggests, the hallmark of the contingent remainder is an element of uncertainty or chance. A remainder is contingent if it is either: (a) subject to a condition precedent (other than the natural termination of the prior estate) or (b) created in an unascertainable person. Either way, it is not ready to become a possessory estate whenever the prior estate terminates. The vested remainder is like an open door, ready to allow its holder access to the present estate in an adjoining room. But the contingent remainder door is closed, unless and until the condition precedent is met or the holder is identified.

A remainder subject to a condition precedent is considered contingent because it is not ready to become a possessory estate *until* the event occurs. For example, suppose O devises Greenacre "to K for life, and then to L and his heirs if L reaches the age of 21." L is ascertainable. But if L is now 10, his remainder is subject to a condition precedent. An event must occur—L must reach age 21—*before* his remainder is eligible to become possessory upon K's death. This specified event may or may not occur; if L dies at age 11, for example, his remainder will automatically end and thus never become possessory. Ten-year-old L now holds a contingent remainder.

Similarly, a remainder created in an unascertainable person is deemed contingent, even if it is certain to become a possessory estate. Assume O devises Greenacre "to K for life, and then to K's heirs." It is impossible to determine who K's heirs are until K dies (*see* Chapter 28). A living person, after all, has no heirs. Because "K's heirs" are now unascertainable, "they" hold a contingent remainder.

[D] Examples of Remainders

The following illustrative conveyances and devises create remainders:

O conveys Greenacre "to A for life, then to B for life, then to C and her heirs." B holds an indefeasibly vested remainder for life, that is, in a life estate. C holds an indefeasibly vested remainder in fee simple absolute. Why? Both interests are remainders because both are capable of becoming possessory on the natural expiration of the prior life estate, without cutting that estate short. Both remainders are indefeasibly vested because (1) the holder of each is known (B and C, respectively) and (2) neither is subject to any condition or limitation.

O devises Greenacre "to A for life, and if B survives A, then to B and his heirs." B holds a contingent remainder in fee simple absolute. B's interest is capable of becoming possessory when A's life estate ends, and hence is a remainder. But B's remainder is subject to a condition precedent; B must first survive A before his remainder is ready to become a possessory estate. Thus, it is a contingent remainder.

O conveys Greenacre "to A for life, then to B and his heirs, but if B does not survive A, then to C and her heirs." B holds a vested remainder subject to divestment in fee simple absolute. B's remainder is vested because B is identifiable and no condition precedent must be met before the remainder takes effect, other than the natural expiration of A's life estate. But if a future event occurs (B dies before A), then B's remainder will be destroyed or divested. C's interest is not a remainder, but rather an executory interest in fee simple absolute.

O devises Greenacre "to A for life, then to the children of B who survive A and their heirs." Assuming A is alive, the class of "the children of B who survive A" have a contingent remainder in fee simple absolute. It is contingent because (a) the holders are presently unascertainable and (b) the interest of each holder is subject to a condition precedent (surviving A).

O conveys Greenacre "to A for life, then to A's children and their heirs." If A has a living child at the time of the conveyance, B, then B holds a vested remainder subject to open in fee simple absolute. The remainder is vested because B is identifiable and there is no condition precedent. However, assuming A is still alive, then additional children of A might be born and expand the class of "A's children," so the remainder is subject to open.

[E] Transformation into Other Future Interests

Events may automatically transform a remainder into another type of remainder or even into an executory interest. The classification of a remainder must be constantly reassessed in the light of developing events.

For example, events might transform a contingent remainder into a vested remainder. Suppose O devises Greenacre "to K for life, and then to L and his heirs if L reaches the age of 21." Assuming that L was 10 years old when the devise became effective, he held a contingent remainder because his interest was subject to a condition precedent. What happens if K is still alive when L reaches 21? Once this specified condition is fulfilled, the nature of L's remainder changes. No longer subject to the condition, his interest is now an indefeasibly vested remainder.

Similarly, a vested remainder subject to open might become an indefeasibly vested remainder. Assume O devises Greenacre "to K for life, then to L's children and their heirs." When O's will becomes effective, L is alive and has one living child, M. M holds a vested remainder subject to open. But if L now dies without having any additional children, M's interest becomes an indefeasibly vested remainder. Why? Here the "open" class of potential children of L "closes" when L dies;[10] after L is dead, he cannot have additional children. M is the only possible remainderman.

[F] Significance of the Contingent v. Vested Distinction

The distinction between the contingent remainder and the vested remainder—once critically important—has eroded in recent decades. There is a clear trend toward equating the contingent remainder and the vested remainder subject to divestment, which in turn suggests that the general distinction may similarly evaporate over time.

Traditionally, the contingent remainder received far less legal protection than the vested remainder. For example: (1) the contingent remainder could not be alienated, while the vested remainder was freely alienable; (2) the contingent remainder was "destructible," meaning that it was destroyed if it failed to vest before the termination of the prior estate, while the vested remainder survived; and (3) the contingent remainder might be invalidated by the Rule Against Perpetuities, while most vested remainders were immune from application of the Rule.[11]

Modern law increasingly accords the same protection to both types of remainders. For example: (1) both are freely alienable in most states (*see* § 14.07) and (2) with the demise of the destructibility doctrine, neither is destructible (*see* § 14.14). The main lingering difference in substance between the two is the Rule Against Perpetuities; the Rule still applies to contingent remainders, not vested remainders (*see* §§ 14.10, 14.11). However, because reform legislation has softened the common law version of the Rule in most jurisdictions, this difference is less significant than in the past.

---

[10] A class "closes" upon the first of two alternative events: (1) when no new members can be added to the class (e.g., a class defined as the "children of K" closes when K dies); or (2) under the "rule of convenience," when any class member is entitled to receive possession of his share and the prior estate ends.

[11] In addition, the holder of a vested remainder might receive possession sooner, under the principle of acceleration. Assume O devises Greenacre "to A for life, then to B and her heirs, but if B fails to graduate from law school, then to C and his heirs." If A dies while B is still in college, B's vested remainder subject to divestment allows her immediate possession of Greenacre. It "accelerates" into possession. What if O had devised Greenacre "to A for life, then to B and her heirs if B graduates from law school" and A dies while B is still in college? Here B holds a mere contingent remainder. She is not entitled to possession until the condition precedent (graduation from law school) is met.

§ 14.04 Executory Interests

[A] Executory Interests in Context

The lineage of the executory interest can be traced back to the use, a device which arose in thirteenth-century England. In this era, there was only one legal future interest that could be created in a transferee: the remainder. An owner could not create a future interest in a transferee that would cut short a present estate. Suppose O tried to convey Redacre "to B and his heirs, but if B inherits Greenacre, then to C and his heirs." C's interest is not a remainder, because it must divest or cut short B's estate; if C's interest did not exist, B's estate would continue in existence and descend to his heirs. Thus, C's interest was invalid at common law.

In this environment, creative medieval attorneys developed the *use*. Like the modern trust, the use separated the *legal title* to property from the *benefits* of holding title. Suppose now O conveys Redacre "to A and A's heirs, for the use of B and B's heirs, but if B inherits Greenacre, then to the use of C and C's heirs." A holds legal title, while the beneficial interests are split between B and C. Although the law courts would not recognize C's interest, it was enforceable in *equity*. If B inherited Greenacre, the equity courts would require A to honor his obligations to C, even though C's interest divests B's estate.

In practice, the use functioned as an early tax loophole: the beneficiary of the use did not hold legal title and thus was not obligated to provide feudal incidents to the lord. The use was so advantageous that, by the early 1500s, most English land was held in this manner. Confronting a financial crisis, King Henry VIII forced Parliament to enact the Statute of Uses, which took effect in 1536. This statute converted the use into a "legal" future interest—one recognized at common law and thus subject to the jurisdiction of the law courts—which accordingly made its holder liable for providing feudal incidents. The new interest was called an *executory interest*.

[B] What Is an Executory Interest?

An *executory interest* is a future interest created in a transferee that must "cut short" or "divest" another estate or interest in order to become a possessory estate.[12] It is more common to define the executory interest by comparing it to the remainder: an executory interest is any future interest created in a transferee other than a remainder (*see* § 14.03[B]).[13]

An executory interest may divest an estate, almost always a fee simple or a life estate. Assume O conveys Blackacre "to B and his heirs, but if C

---

[12] *See generally* Restatement of Property § 158 (1936); *see also* Percy Bordwell, *The Conversion of the Use into a Legal Interest*, 21 Iowa L. Rev. 1 (1935); John Makdisi, *The Vesting of Executory Interests*, 59 Tul. L. Rev. 366 (1984).

[13] *See, e.g.,* Capitol Fed. Sav. & Loan Ass'n v. Smith, 316 P.2d 252 (Colo. 1957) (invalidating racially-restrictive executory interest held by neighbors); Stoller v. Doyle, 100 N.E. 959 (Ill. 1913) (characterizing future interest as executory interest, not contingent remainder).

returns from France, then to C and her heirs." Under what circumstances can C's future interest become a possessory estate? B's defeasible fee simple estate has no natural termination point; it may potentially endure forever. In order to become a possessory estate, C's interest must cut short B's estate.

Due to a historical anomaly, the future interest following a determinable estate is also considered an executory interest. If O conveys Blackacre "to B and his heirs for so long as C remains in France, and then to C and his heirs," C's interest is deemed an executory interest even though it follows what might be described as the natural end of B's fee simple determinable.

Alternatively, an executory interest may divest a vested future interest. Suppose O conveys Blackacre "to A for life, then to B and his heirs, but if C returns from France, then to C and her heirs." B receives a vested remainder subject to divestment in fee simple absolute. In order for C's interest to become a possessory estate, it must divest B's remainder. Thus, C holds an executory interest. As a general rule, if one instrument creates (a) a vested remainder in fee simple in one transferee that is (b) followed by a second future interest in another transferee, the second interest is an executory interest.

[C] Types of Executory Interests

[1] The Basic Distinction

It is both traditional and convenient to distinguish between two categories of executory interests: the *shifting executory interest* and the *springing executory interest*. The difference between the two types hinges on the identity of the person whose estate or interest is divested. However, this distinction has no legal significance.

[2] Shifting Executory Interest

A shifting executory interest is simply one that divests another transferee. Assume O conveys Blackacre "to B and his heirs, but if C returns from France, to C and her heirs." C holds a shifting executory interest because it would cut short the fee simple estate held by B, another transferee.

[3] Springing Executory Interest

A springing executory interest, in contrast, is one that divests the transferor, following a gap in time during which no other transferee has the right to possession. Suppose O conveys Blackacre "to C and her heirs, if C returns from France." In order to become possessory, C's interest must "cut short" the estate held by O, the transferor. C has a springing executory interest.

[D] Examples of Executory Interests

The following illustrative conveyances and devises create executory interests.

O conveys Greenacre "to A and her heirs upon the birth of A's first child." A holds a springing executory interest in fee simple absolute. If a child of A is born, then A's interest will automatically become a possessory estate, which will divest or cut short O's prior estate.

O devises Greenacre "to A and her heirs, but if A becomes an attorney, then to B for life." B holds a shifting executory interest for life, that is, in a life estate. B's interest becomes possessory only if an event occurs (A becomes an attorney) that cuts short A's defeasible fee simple. Note that O retains a reversion following the expiration of B's life estate.

O conveys Greenacre "to A for life, then to B and his heirs, but if C gets married, then to C and her heirs." C holds a shifting executory interest in fee simple. C's interest becomes a possessory estate only if an event occurs (C gets married) that divests or cuts short B's interest.

O devises Greenacre "to A for life, then five years after her death, to B and his heirs." B holds a springing executory interest in fee simple absolute. B's interest is not capable of becoming possessory upon the expiration of A's life estate. The devise creates a gap—a five-year period that must expire before B's interest becomes possessory. During the gap, O holds title and thus in order to take, B must divest O's prior estate.

§ 14.05 Consequences of the Distinction Between Remainders and Executory Interests

At common law, the distinction between remainders and executory interests was quite important. Two examples illustrate the point. Contingent remainders were destroyed if they failed to vest when the prior freehold estate ended (*see* § 14.14), while executory interests remained intact. Similarly, the infamous Rule in Shelley's Case (*see* § 14.13) applied to remainders, but not to executory interests. Thus, the legal rights of an owner varied dramatically depending on how his or her interest was classified.

However, the legal significance of this distinction has melted away over the centuries with the demise of the destructibility of contingent remainders, the Rule in Shelley's Case and related doctrines.[14] In almost all jurisdictions, the contingent remainder holder and the executory interest holder have the same general rights and obligations. As the difference between vested and contingent remainders continues to erode (*see* § 14.03[F]), the distinction between remainders and executory interests will similarly dwindle.

The distinction between remainders and executory interests persists today in part as a customary method for labeling future interests. But there

---

[14] *See generally* Jesse Dukeminier, *Contingent Remainders and Executory Interests: A Requiem for the Distinction*, 43 Minn. L. Rev. 13 (1958).

is a trend toward eliminating even this usage. Statutes in California, New York, and certain other states have consolidated both types of interests into a single category, called a remainder.[15]

§ 14.06   Creation of Interests

Future interests may arise by implication in a transferor, but not in a transferee. Suppose O, owning Blueacre in fee simple absolute, conveys Blueacre "to A for life." Because O has failed to convey her entire interest, she retains a reversion. O's reversion arises by implication, not by language that expressly creates a reversion. It is not necessary for O to convey Blueacre "to A for life, and then to me." On the other hand, if O wishes to create a future interest in a transferee, she must do so by *express* language, e.g., "to A for life, then to B." Remainders and executory interests cannot arise by implication.

The only permissible birthplace for a remainder or executory interest in real property is either a will or a deed. These future interests cannot be created through the process of intestate succession; rather, they arise only from the voluntary decision of an owner. Moreover, this decision must be embodied in a written instrument—either a will or deed—pursuant to the Statute of Wills and Statute of Frauds, respectively. Remainders and executory interests in real property held in trust are governed by the same standards; the testamentary trust arises only through a will, while the Statute of Frauds requires a deed to transfer real property into an inter vivos trust.

The rules governing the creation of remainders and executory interests in personal property are somewhat more flexible. Of course, these interests can be created only through express language, not implication, and may arise in a will or deed. But—because the Statute of Frauds does not apply to personal property—such interests may be created orally (e.g., through an oral declaration of an inter vivos trust in personal property).

§ 14.07   Transfer of Interests

[A]   Toward Free Transferability

Remainders and executory interests may be freely transferred by devise, descent, or conveyance in most states. Only one obstacle impairs progress toward a uniform national rule of free transferability: the lingering insistence of some states that contingent remainders and executory interests may not be transferred by an inter vivos conveyance.

[B]   Vested Remainders

Under both traditional English common law and modern law, the vested remainder is freely transferable through devise, descent, or inter vivos

---

[15] Cal. Civ. Code § 769; N.Y. Est. Powers & Trusts Law § 6-3.2.

conveyance. Thus, if O conveys Blueacre "to A for life, then to B and her heirs," B has an unfettered right to transfer her vested remainder, just as if she held fee simple absolute. Suppose, however, O conveys Blueacre "to A for life, then to B for life, then to C and her heirs," and B dies before A. Once B dies, her vested remainder for life is extinguished, although it was fully transferable during her life.

[C] Contingent Remainders and Executory Interests

Contingent remainders and executory interests can—in general—be freely transferred by devise or descent. Assume O conveys Blueacre "to A for life, then to B and his heirs if C returns from Canada." B dies before C returns from Canada. B's contingent remainder will pass either by devise to his devisees or by descent to his heirs. On the other hand, conditions or limitations imposed on the interest by the transferor may preclude transfer. For example, if O conveys Blueacre "to A for life, then to B and his heirs if B survives A," B's contingent remainder is extinguished if B dies before A.

The more difficult problem is whether contingent remainders and executory interests can be transferred while the holder is still alive. The sixteenth-century English courts that first recognized these new interests viewed them as mere possibilities or expectancies, not presently existing legal rights. Moreover, English courts were generally hostile to these interests, in large part due to their potential to impair marketability of land title. Probably for both reasons, the rule developed that contingent remainders and executory interests were inalienable. As a logical corollary of the rule, creditors could not reach such interests to satisfy their claims against the holder. Predictably, over time, a series of exceptions eroded the prohibition on transfer. One holding a contingent remainder in real property could, for example, release it to the person in possession of the land; and the doctrine of estoppel by deed (*see* § 23.09) allowed sophisticated parties to circumvent the rule.

Under modern law, contingent remainders and executory interests are freely transferable in almost all states.[16] Although the law is clearly moving toward a uniform standard of free transferability, scattered traces of the common law ban remain. These remnants are typically encountered in older decisions in a handful of jurisdictions that have not recently considered the issue. For example, case law in some states permits inter vivos transfer of contingent future interests that are conditioned on an *event*, but prohibits the transfer of interests conditioned on the identity of a *person*. A few states still appear to follow the common law rule, as modified by the traditional exceptions.

---

[16] *See generally* Restatement of Property §§ 162, 163 (1936) (endorsing this approach).

§ 14.08 Other Rights of Interest Holders

[A] General Principles

The common law traditionally accorded greater protection to the holder of a vested remainder than to the owner of a contingent remainder or executory interest. Modern law still partially reflects this disparity as evidenced in two settings: remedies for waste and shares in eminent domain proceeds.

[B] Rights re Waste

Suppose O conveys Blueacre "to A for life, then to B and his heirs," and A subsequently commits waste by starting a gold mining operation on Blueacre. As the holder of an indefeasibly vested remainder, B's rights are adequate to protect his interest; he may recover compensatory damages for past waste and enjoin future waste. The law safeguards B's vested remainder because it is certain to become a possessory estate, and it is accordingly logical to limit A's conduct.

By contrast, little protection against waste is accorded to uncertain future interests, based on the rationale that they are less likely to become possessory estates. Thus, contingent remainders enjoy only minimal protection, while executory interests receive even less. Assume O conveys Blueacre "to A for life, then to B and his heirs if B survives A," and A starts mining gold on the land. English common law developed the rule, still followed today, that the holder of a contingent remainder cannot recover damages for waste committed by a life tenant. Thus, B cannot sue A for damages. Equity mitigated this harsh rule by allowing the contingent remainder holder to enjoin future waste, unless the remainder was highly unlikely to become possessory. Here, B could enjoin future mining by A.

But if B merely holds an executory interest, he has virtually no remedy against waste. Now suppose O conveys Blueacre "to A and her heirs, but if oil is discovered on the land, then to B and his heirs." At common law, the holder of a mere executory interest could not obtain damages for waste. Because modern courts still adhere to this principle, B cannot recover damages if A begins mining gold on the land. Equity did permit the holder of an executory interest to enjoin waste, but only under restrictive conditions: (a) there must be a reasonable possibility that the interest will become possessory; and (b) an injunction will issue only if a prudent owner of a fee simple estate would not have performed the actions at issue. B cannot establish either criterion here, and accordingly cannot enjoin A's mining.

[C] Right to Eminent Domain Proceeds

If the state uses its eminent domain power to take land, do future interest holders receive a share of the proceeds? The holder of a vested remainder certainly has this right. At one time, contingent remainders and executory interests were viewed as too insubstantial and tenuous to justify any share in eminent domain proceeds. Although this view may linger in some jurisdictions, most modern courts allow holders of such interests to share in an eminent domain award, unless the interest is highly unlikely to become possessory.

The traditional judicial reluctance here probably stems in part from the practical difficulties of valuing future interests that may never become possessory. One solution to this dilemma is simply to transfer the proceeds into a trust, which is administered according to the respective rights the parties originally held in the land. Under this approach, the estate holder receives all income from the trust until and unless the future interest becomes possessory; at this point, the trust ends and the principal is distributed to the future interest holder. The trust could also end if it becomes clear that the future interest can never become possessory, in which event the principal would be paid to the estate holder.

§ 14.09 Four Special Restrictions on Contingent Future Interests Held by Transferees

The evolution of the estates in land system in England culminated in a remarkable burst of sixteenth-century creativity. After steadfastly refusing to permit contingent future interests in transferees, the common law rapidly endorsed both the contingent remainder and the executory interest. Landowners could now create future interests to tie up their lands virtually forever, preserving family wealth from both taxation and the risks of an uncertain future.

Yet these new interests posed very real dangers. Land burdened with "uncertain" future interests was relatively inalienable. It was readily foreseeable that as the use of these contingent interests spread, the supply of freely alienable land would decrease. Consequently, land could not be devoted to its optimum productive uses. A sheep pasture suitable for use as a brickyard, for example, might be burdened by future interests held by unknown (and even unborn) persons; because the estate holder could not transfer fee simple absolute to the potential brickyard entrepreneur, the land would be locked into the less socially-valuable use of grazing. The resulting inalienability also tended to perpetuate the power and wealth of landowning families; land burdened with these interests was often unsuitable as security for debt—much like land held in fee tail—and thus was less likely to be lost to creditors than land held in fee simple absolute. If thousands of parcels like the sheep pasture were similarly rendered inalienable, England's expanding mercantile economy would suffer. At the same time, these new contingent interests had the practical effect of evading taxes—in the form of feudal incidents—which increasingly were owed directly to the Crown. Mercantile forces, the Crown, and other segments of English society accordingly sought limitations on these newly-authorized contingent interests.

In response, the common law recognized four doctrines designed to restrict contingent future interests held by transferees:

(1)   the Rule Against Perpetuities (*see* § 14.10),

(2)   the Doctrine of Worthier Title (*see* § 14.12),

(3)   the Rule in Shelley's Case (*see* § 14.13), and

(4)   the destructibility of contingent remainders (*see* § 14.14).

The overall result was a delicate compromise between individual property rights and overall social welfare: contingent future interests in transferees were allowed, but restricted. The new United States inherited this compromise system.

Today this intricate system has largely collapsed. The Doctrine of Worthier Title, the Rule in Shelley's Case, and the destructibility of contingent remainders are virtually obsolete in the United States.[17] Although the Rule Against Perpetuities lingers, modern reforms have diminished its impact.

What accounts for the demise of the common law approach? One major factor is enhanced twentieth-century concern for protecting the private property rights of landowners against legal doctrines that frustrate their intent. Another factor is found in the relative ease by which sophisticated attorneys could circumvent the traditional restrictions through drafting; this converted them from tools that protected the marketability of land into traps for the unwary drafter. A third factor is quite practical: legal future interests in land are rarely created today in transferees, so there is much less need to protect marketability. Modern future interests usually concern personal property. Future interests in land are almost always created in trust; since legal title to the trust property is held by the trustee, marketability is not impaired. Finally, the potential marketability problem is better addressed in most states by statutes that permit the creation of contingent future interests, but eliminate "stale" interests (*see* § 12.07).

§ 14.10   The Rule Against Perpetuities: At Common Law

[A]   The Rule In Context

[1]   A "Technicality-Ridden Legal Nightmare"?

The common law Rule Against Perpetuities (the "Rule") has perplexed generations of law students, attorneys, and judges.[18] Professor Leach, a leading authority on the Rule, once characterized it as a "technicality-ridden legal nightmare" and a "dangerous instrumentality in the hands of most members of the bar."[19] Indeed, in a controversial opinion, the

---

[17] Ironically, England abolished all three doctrines long ago by statute (Doctrine of Worthier Title: 1833; Rule in Shelley's Case: 1925; destructibility of contingent remainders: 1877).

[18] For scholarly analysis of the Rule, see Jesse Dukeminier, *A Modern Guide to Perpetuities*, 74 Cal. L. Rev. 1867 (1986); W. Barton Leach, *Perpetuities in a Nutshell*, 51 Harv. L. Rev. 638 (1938); W. Barton Leach, *Perpetuities in Perspective: Ending the Rule's Reign of Terror*, 65 Harv. L. Rev. 721 (1952). *See also* Frederic S. Schwartz, A Student's Guide to the Rule Against Perpetuities (1988).

[19] W. Barton Leach, *Perpetuities Legislation, Massachusetts Style*, 67 Harv. L. Rev. 1349, 1349 (1954).

California Supreme Court suggested that the Rule was so difficult to master that an attorney could not be held liable in malpractice for preparing a document that was invalidated by the Rule.[20] Due in part to these concerns, many states have adopted statutes that simplify the Rule (*see* § 14.11).

[2]   Statement of the Rule

The common law version of the Rule is easily stated: "No interest is good unless it must vest, if at all, not later than twenty-one years after some life in being at the creation of the interest."[21] Beneath the placid surface of this sentence, however, lurks confusing complexity. A five-step approach to the Rule (*see* [C], *below*) helps to grapple with this complexity.

The central core of the Rule is simple to understand: it is a *rule about time*. The Rule essentially imposes a time deadline on how long certain contingent future interests can exist. To comply with the Rule, it must be *logically provable* that within a specified period (equal to the length of one life plus 21 years) a covered interest will *either* "vest" (that is, change from a contingent interest to a vested interest or possessory estate) *or* "forever" fail to vest (that is, never vest after the period ends). Alternatively phrased, if there is any possibility—however remote—that a covered interest might remain contingent after this perpetuities period expires, the interest is void.

The Rule applies to legal or equitable interests created in real property or personal property. Although the discussion below focuses on legal interests in real property—the original concern of the Rule—such interests are becoming increasingly rare. An issue involving the Rule is more likely to arise today in connection with equitable interests in personal property (e.g., an equitable contingent remainder in a trust whose assets consist of stocks and bonds).

In applying the Rule, the only facts considered are those existing when the future interest becomes effective. We do not "wait-and-see" if a particular interest in fact does vest or forever fails to vest during the perpetuities period. Rather, to validate a covered interest it must be logically proven—based *only* on facts existing at the onset—that the interest will comply with the Rule.

An interest that violates the Rule is null and void when created, and thus is judicially stricken from the instrument.[22] Consider three examples. First, suppose O devises Blueacre "to A for life, then to the first child of A to reach age 30 and the heirs of that child." If A is alive and has no living child who is 30 or older when O's devise becomes effective, the interest in "the first child of A to reach age 30" is invalid under the common law Rule at the very minute the devise takes effect. With this interest invalidated, a court will construe the devise as if O had merely devised Blueacre "to A for life;" this leaves O with a reversion. Second, assume O conveys Blueacre "to A

---

[20] Lucas v. Hamm, 364 P.2d 685 (Cal. 1961).

[21] John C. Gray, The Rule Against Perpetuities § 201, at 191 (4th ed. 1942).

[22] *See, e.g.,* City of Klamath Falls v. Bell, 490 P.2d 515 (Or. Ct. App. 1971) (where executory interest was invalidated by Rule, grantor's successors retained possibility of reverter).

and his heirs for so long as used as an orphanage, then to B and his heirs;" the Rule would invalidate B's executory interest and the phrase "then to B and his heirs" would be stricken. This leaves O with a possibility of reverter. Finally, what if O conveys Blueacre "to A and his heirs, but if not used as an orphanage, then to B and his heirs"? When we strike the language creating the invalid gift to B ("but if not used as an orphanage, then to B and his heirs"), A is left with fee simple absolute.

[3]   The Dynamite Analogy

Consider an analogy that helps to explain the nature of the Rule. Suppose S interviews for a job with a mining company. F, the interviewer, explains that the company needs a new "Dynamite Remover." The company uses dynamite to open new mineral deposits in underground mine shafts. When blasting is planned, a dynamite charge is set underground, the mine is evacuated, and the explosives expert pushes a small plunger. Within the next five minutes, the dynamite charge usually explodes. If the charge fails to explode, the Dynamite Remover enters the mine and carries the dynamite back to the surface. Worried about risking his life, S inquires: "Can you prove to me—and I mean PROVE to me—that the dynamite will *either* definitely explode during the five-minute period *or* never explode thereafter"? Or S might ask the same question in a different way: "Is there any possibility that under any conditions, however unlikely, the dynamite *might* explode after the five-minute period ends, while I'm down there in the mine? If there is, I simply won't take the job!"

S's worry is similar to the basic concern of the Rule. Under the Rule, it must be logically proven at the beginning—not later—that a contingent interest (like the dynamite) will *either* definitely vest (explode) during the perpetuities period *or* forever fail to vest during the period (never thereafter explode). Alternatively phrased, the Rule is designed to invalidate certain contingent interests that *might vest* too late (after the perpetuities period ends) just as S fears a dynamite charge that *might explode* too late (after the five-minute period ends).

[B]   Rationale for the Rule

The Rule evolved in the seventeenth century as a limitation on gifts to family members of contingent future interests in land, most notably in the 1681 decision in the *Duke of Norfolk's Case*.[23] Its principal goal was to protect the marketability of real property, which in turn: (a) facilitated the productivity of land; and (b) contributed to the utilization of wealth by society in general, thus discouraging the long-term concentration of wealth in particular families.[24]

The Rule was seen as a rough balance between the respective interests of the dead and the living. Contingent future interests could be created in transferees, but only if they were guaranteed not to burden land for too

---

[23] Duke of Norfolk's Case, 22 Eng. Rep. 931 (Ch. 1681).

[24] *See, e.g.,* Wildenstein & Co., Inc. v. Wallis, 595 N.E.2d 828 (N.Y. 1992).

long. The resulting perpetuities period—one life plus 21 years—reflects this compromise. A landowner could provide for family members he knew personally (measured by any one "life") and for those in the next generation (defined as 21 years), but could not tie up land thereafter. As a device to protect marketability of land, however, the Rule suffered from a major loophole. It did not affect contingent future interests retained by the transferor—contingent reversions, possibilities of reverter, and rights of entry—all of which posed the same potential problems as contingent future interests held by transferees. Why not? The principal reason is found in historical chronology. The law governing future interests in transferors matured well before the Rule emerged in the seventeenth century; it was simply too late to subject these interests to the Rule.

The rationale for extending the Rule to encompass interests in personal property is less clear. By encouraging the transferability of money, stocks, bonds, and other forms of personal property, the Rule presumably facilitates commerce and permits the circulation of wealth in society.

[C] Five-Step Application of the Rule

[1] Summary of Approach

A five-step approach is helpful in applying the Rule:

(1)   determine if the Rule applies to the future interest at issue;

(2)   decide when the perpetuities period begins;

(3)   determine what must happen for the interest to vest or forever fail to vest;

(4)   identify the persons who can affect vesting; and

(5)   test each relevant life to determine if any one validates the interest.

[2] Does the Rule Apply to This Interest?

[a] Contingent Future Interests in Transferees

The Rule applies only to three types of future interests:

(1)   contingent remainders,[25]

(2)   vested remainders subject to open, and

---

[25] *See, e.g.,* Connecticut Bank & Trust Co. v. Brody, 392 A.2d 445 (Conn. 1978) (testator bequeathed assets in trust to his children for life, followed by a contingent remainder in his grandchildren for life, followed by a contingent remainder in his great-grandchildren; the class gift to the great-grandchildren was held invalid under the Rule because the interest of a potential after-born great-grandchild might vest too late, while the grandchildren's interest failed under the doctrine of infectious invalidity); North Carolina Nat'l Bank v. Norris, 203 S.E.2d 657 (N.C. Ct. App. 1974) (where testator devised life estate to children, contingent remainder for life to grandchildren, and contingent remainder to great-grandchildren, gift to great-grandchildren was held invalid under the Rule).

(3) "contingent" executory interests.[26]

On the other hand, the Rule does not apply to: (a) present estates, (b) future interests in a transferor (a reversion, possibility of reverter, or right of entry),[27] or (c) future interests in a transferee that are deemed "vested" (e.g., indefeasibly vested remainder) *except for* vested remainders subject to open.

The category of "contingent" executory interests requires explanation. Most executory interests are contingent, meaning that some uncertain event must occur *before* they can become possessory estates. For example, if O conveys Blueacre "to A and her heirs, but if any person ever goes to Jupiter, then to B and her heirs," B's executory interest is contingent; it will "vest," if at all, only when someone travels to Jupiter. However, some executory interests held by ascertained persons are *certain* to become possessory with the passage of time. If O conveys Blueacre "to A and her heirs 10 years from now," A's executory interest is certain to mature into a possessory estate; for purposes of the Rule, it is considered "vested."[28]

When applying the Rule, the whole instrument is not considered as a unit. Rather, each future interest is analyzed separately. For example, if a conveyance creates four future interests subject to the Rule, three might fail, while one might survive.

Consider the following hypothetical, which helps explain the five-step approach to the Rule outlined below. Suppose that on January 1, 2000, O devises Blueacre "to A for life, then to the first child of A to reach age 30 and the heirs of that child." Assume that A is alive on January 1, 2000, but has never had any children. A potential unborn person—"the first child of A to reach age 30"—receives a contingent remainder in fee simple absolute under this language. The remainder is contingent both because the person is unascertainable and a condition precedent must be met. In order for this interest to be valid under the Rule, it must be logically provable—based on facts known on January 1, 2000—that the interest will either definitely vest or forever fail to vest during the perpetuities period. If this cannot be shown, the interest is invalid.

[b] Options to Purchase and Preemptive Rights

The common law Rule also applies to a variety of commercial transactions. These include options to purchase[29] and, in most jurisdictions,

---

[26] *See, e.g.,* City of Klamath Falls v. Bell, 490 P.2d 515 (Or. Ct. App. 1971) (executory interest following defeasible estate held void under Rule); *see also* Fletcher v. Ferrill, 227 S.W.2d 448 (Ark. 1950).

[27] *See* Brown v. Independent Baptist Church, 91 N.E.2d 922 (Mass. 1950) (where will devised defeasible estate to church and accompanying future interest to other devisees, future interest was invalid under the Rule; thus, estate retained a possibility of reverter—not subject to the Rule—which passed to the same devisees under the residual clause of the will).

[28] *See, e.g., In re* Estate of Anderson, 541 So. 2d 423 (Miss. 1989).

[29] *See, e.g.,* The Symphony Space, Inc. v. Pergola Properties, Inc., 669 N.E.2d 799 (N.Y. 1996) (New York's statutory Rule Against Perpetuities applies to option to purchase); Central Delaware County Auth. v. Greyhound Corp., 588 A.2d 485 (Pa. 1991) (option to repurchase

preemptive rights or rights of first refusal. [30] The extension of the Rule to encompass such rights has been widely criticized as counterproductive, and there is a clear trend toward exempting commercial transactions. For example, the Uniform Statutory Rule Against Perpetuities (*see* § 14.11[D]) applies only to gifts, not commercial rights. [31]

[3]   When Does the Perpetuities Period Begin?

If the Rule applies, we next determine when the "perpetuities period" begins. The duration of the perpetuities period is *one life plus 21 years*. This period begins when the instrument that creates the interest becomes legally effective. Only a person who is living at this time can potentially be used as a "life" in this formula. Thus, we must know when the period begins in order to determine which lives can be used.

Different types of instruments become effective at different times. A will is effective when the testator dies. A deed is effective when it is delivered by the grantor. Because the example above (*see* [2], *above*) states that O "devises," the instrument involved is a will effective when O dies, on January 1, 2000. Thus, the perpetuities period for our hypothetical begins on that date.

The effective date of a trust is more troublesome. A testamentary trust (that is, one created under a will) takes effect when the settlor (the person creating the trust) dies because it is part of a will. On the other hand, an inter vivos trust (one created during the lifetime of the settlor) is effective for purposes of the Rule only when it becomes irrevocable, that is, *either* (1) when the settlor declares it to be irrevocable or (2) if no such declaration occurs, when the settlor dies.

[4]   What Must Happen for the Interest to Vest or Forever Fail to Vest?

[a]   Time of Vesting

We next determine what must happen in order for the interest to "vest," that is, to *change* from a contingent interest to a vested interest or estate, or to forever "fail" to vest. In other words, why is the interest contingent? It is crucial to understand that a future interest may become "vested" for purposes of the Rule, even though the holder is *not yet entitled to possession*

---

held void under Rule); United Virginia Bank/Citizens & Marine v. Union Oil Co. of California, 197 S.E.2d 174 (Va. 1973) (option to purchase held void under Rule). *But see* Texaco Ref. & Mktg., Inc. v. Samowitz, 570 A.2d 170 (Conn. 1990) (Rule does not apply to lessee's option to purchase leased premises).

[30] *But see* Cambridge Co. v. East Slope Inv. Corp., 700 P.2d 537 (Colo. 1985) (refusing to invalidate preemptive right under Rule because on facts of case it posed no threat to free alienation of condominium units involved).

[31] The draft Restatement (Third) of Property takes the position that the Rule does not apply to options and rights of first refusal for the purchase of land, or to other servitudes. Restatement (Third) of Property: Servitudes § 3.3 cmt. a (Tentative Draft No. 2, 1991).

of the land. The Rule concerns the *time of vesting,* not necessarily the *time of possession.*

A contingent remainder, by definition, is contingent because either one or more conditions precedent have not been met or because the remainder holder is unascertainable. Once the specified contingency is met, the contingent remainder will "vest," becoming an indefeasibly vested remainder. In our hypothetical (*see* [2], *above*), the contingent remainder in "the first child of A to reach age 30" is contingent for both reasons. A must have a child who reaches age 30 in order for the interest to vest. Until and unless this event occurs, the remainder will be contingent. On the other hand, if A dies without ever having had children, the interest will forever fail to vest, meaning that there is no possibility it may vest later. By definition, if A never has a child, it is impossible for any child of A to reach age 30.

A contingent executory interest is usually contingent upon the occurrence of a future event. Thus, it is considered contingent until the holder is entitled to possession of the land. Suppose, for example, that O devises Greenacre "to F and her heirs but if F ever cuts down a tree on Greenacre, to G and her heirs." The executory interest in G will vest only if and when G becomes entitled to possession of Greenacre. On the other hand, the interest will forever fail to vest once F dies. After F is dead, there is no possibility that she can cut down a tree!

[b] Special Rule for Class Gifts

Class gifts—that is, gifts to a class or group of persons—are governed by a special rule, dubbed the "all-or-nothing" rule: the interests of *all* class members must comply with the Rule in order for the interest of *any* class member to be valid. For example, if the interests of 99 members of a 100-person class comply with the Rule, but the interest of one member does not, the interests of all 100 members are invalid.

A vested remainder subject to open, again by definition, is "contingent" because all the members of the class cannot yet be identified. Suppose O devises Blueacre "to F for life, then to the children of G and his heirs." The class members described as "the children of G" cannot be ascertained until G dies; at this point, the class is said to "close" and the vested remainder subject to open becomes an indefeasibly vested remainder in G's children, thus "vesting" under the Rule.

The executory interest may also be the subject of a class gift (e.g., O conveys Blueacre "to my grandchildren who both survive my death and pass the bar"). In order for this interest to be valid, it must be proven that within the perpetuities period (a) the class will "close" and (b) the conditions precedent for each class member will either vest or forever fail to vest.

A class closes on the first of two alternative events: (1) when no new members can be added to the class (usually due to the death of an identified ancestor); or (2) under the "rule of convenience," when any class member is entitled to receive possession of his or her share and the prior estate ends.

[5] Who Are the "Relevant Lives"?

Because the length of the perpetuities period is equal to *one life plus 21 years*, it is crucial to identify the persons whose lives can be used in this formula. These persons who can potentially be used as yardsticks to measure the length of the period are called *relevant lives* or *lives in being*.

The relevant lives must be persons who are alive at the time the instrument becomes effective. In addition, a child in gestation at the time is considered a relevant life if later born alive. Almost always, the relevant lives are persons who can affect whatever has to happen for vesting to occur. These may include:

(1)   the holder of the interest;

(2)   the person creating the interest;

(3)   any person who can affect a condition precedent attached to the interest; and

(4)   any person who can affect the identity of the holder.

Of course, the transferor cannot frustrate the operation of the Rule by specifying an unduly large number of living persons as relevant lives (e.g., by incorporating all the names in a city telephone book).

Who are the relevant lives in the our hypothetical (*see* [2], *above*)? O and A are the only parties who are both (a) living on January 1, 2000, (the day the will becomes effective) and (b) arguably relevant to the interest in question. Thus, O and A are the only possible relevant lives here. For example, if A has a child, B, in 2002, B cannot be a relevant life; B was born too late.

[6] Does Any Relevant Life Validate the Interest?

Each relevant life is now tested to see if the interest will *necessarily vest or forever fail to vest* during a period equal to that person's life plus 21 years. In other words, we plug each relevant life into our formula to create a perpetuities period in a process of trial and error. We then attempt to logically prove that the interest will either vest or forever fail to vest during that person's life, at his death, or within 21 years after his death. The goal is to find one relevant life—called the *validating life* or *measuring life*— which will validate the interest. If we test five relevant lives and find that four do not validate, but one does, the interest is valid under the Rule. In applying the Rule, we do not "wait-and-see" if the interest actually vests or forever fails. Rather, we consider only the information available at the time the instrument becomes effective.

The ultimate goal of the Rule is to eliminate interests that *might* first vest too far in the future, thus clouding title to land. Thus, testing a relevant life is governed by a fantasy-like standard, called the "what-might-happen" rule. A party seeking to uphold the interest must meet a difficult standard: she must *prove* as a matter of logic that the interest *will definitely* vest or forever fail to vest during the period, regardless of any possible future events. Conversely, a party may invalidate the interest by meeting a very easy standard, one based on mere suggestion or imagination. If any future events *might occur, however improbable,* which would prevent the interest from necessarily vesting or forever failing to vest within the period, the life being tested will not validate the interest. *Alternatively phrased, if the creative legal mind can invent any possible scenario under which the interest might first vest after the perpetuities period expires—no matter how unlikely the scenario is—the interest is invalid.*

Consider our example (*see* [2], *above*) again. On January 1, 2000, O devises Blueacre "to A for life, then to the first child of A to reach age 30 and the heirs of that child." The person most likely to affect vesting is A, because part of the condition precedent is that he have a child. Test A first. Can we prove that during A's life, at his death, or within 21 years thereafter, a child of A will either reach age 30 (resulting in vesting) *or* no child of A will thereafter reach age 30 (making later vesting impossible)? No.

What might happen? Suppose that A's child B is born on January 1, 2002. B cannot serve as a relevant life; he was born too late. One day later, A is killed by a tidal wave (or a falling asteroid, a volcanic eruption, or the like). Suppose then that B reaches age 30 on January 1, 2032. At that point, B's interest "vests." But it vests too late. Here the perpetuities period based on A's life ended on January 2, 2023 (21 years after A died). Thus, it is *possible* that the interest in A's first child to reach age 30 *might* vest too late if A is the relevant life. So A's life cannot validate the interest. For similar reasons, O's life will not validate it. This contingent remainder is invalid under the Rule.

[D] Application of the Rule: Classic Examples

[1] The Fertile Octogenarian

Perhaps the most famous example of the "what-might-happen" principle is the so-called "fertile octogenarian" problem, illustrated in *Jee v. Audley.*[32] There, an eighteenth-century testator bequeathed 1,000 pounds "unto my niece Mary Hall and the issue of her body lawfully begotten, and to be begotten, and in default of such issue I give the said £1,000 to be equally divided between the daughters then living of my kinsman John Jee and his wife Elizabeth Jee." In an era when an English schoolmaster received only about £12 per year, the sum of £1,000 was a virtual fortune. Apparently concerned that Mary Hall might squander the bequest or flee to Paris, the four Jee daughters brought an action to compel Hall to post security to protect their rights. In defense, Hall argued that the daughters' future interest was invalid because it violated the Rule.

The court construed the bequest to create a fee simple estate in Hall (because fee tail could not be created in personal property), but subject to an executory interest in the Jee daughters "then living." The Rule applied because this executory interest was contingent on a future event: the

---

[32] 29 Eng. Rep. 1186 (Ch. 1787).

survival of at least one Jee daughter. Because the creating instrument was a will, it took effect upon the testator's death, when the following persons were alive: Hall, John and Elizabeth Jee (who were 70 years old), and four Jee daughters. Assume for purposes of illustration that the testator died in 1785.

What must happen in order for the Jee daughters' interest to either vest or forever fail to vest? In order for vesting to occur, (a) Hall's bloodline must expire and (b) *at that time,* there must be at least one living Jee daughter. In order for the interest to forever fail, all Jee daughters must die *before* Hall's bloodline ends. Because the court construed the bequest as a class gift, the interests of all Jee daughters had to be valid under the Rule in order for any interest to be valid.

Hall, the Jee parents, and the Jee daughters might all affect vesting, and are thus all relevant lives. Yet none of them will validate the interest because of the court's assumption that Mrs. Jee, a 70-year-old woman, *might* have another child, a fifth Jee daughter. Under the "what-might-happen" principle, this *might* cause the interest to vest too late. What might happen? Suppose one year after the will takes effect in 1785, Mrs. Jee has a fifth daughter, named A; on the same day, Hall has her first child, a son named B. Neither A nor B can be a relevant life because neither was alive (or in gestation) on the day the will took effect. Next, assume that one day later all the relevant lives (Hall, the Jee parents, and the original four Jee daughters) die due to plague (or an elephant stampede, a massive fire, or the like); A and B survive. In 1820, more than 21 years after the death of all the relevant lives, B dies without having had issue; A is still alive. At this instant, the Hall bloodline expires, and A's executory interest "vests," because A is now entitled to possession of the £1,000. Because the interest in the Jee daughters "then living" might remain contingent after the perpetuities period ends, it is deemed void at the onset.

The court might, of course, have tried to save the bequest to the Jee daughters by interpreting it as a gift to four specific daughters (not a class gift) or by refusing to assume that a 70-year-old woman could bear a child. However, illustrating the common law view that the Rule should be "remorselessly" applied, it refused to do so. Ironically, in light of recent developments in human reproductive technology, the possibility that a 70-year-old woman might give birth seems increasingly likely.

[2] The Unborn Spouse

A second classic perpetuities dilemma involves the unborn spouse, often dubbed the "unborn widow" problem. Suppose T devises Redacre "to A for life, then to A's widow for her life, then to A's issue then living and their heirs." When T's will becomes effective the following are all alive: A, B (A's wife), and C (the son of A and B). Is the interest in "A's issue then living" valid?

The Rule applies here because "A's issue then living" hold a contingent remainder; it is a remainder because it may become possessory as soon as the life estate in A's widow ends, but it is contingent because "A's issue then living" are currently unascertainable. The perpetuities period begins at T's death. In order for the interest to vest, A and A's widow must both die; at this time, we can ascertain the identities of "A's issue then living." So who are the lives in being who might validate the interest? Only A and C. B cannot be a life in being—and this is the central difficulty in the problem—because it is not certain she will be A's widow. After all, B might die many years later; and A might then marry D, a woman born after T's death who cannot qualify as a life in being.

Can we prove that the interest in "A's issue then living" will either vest or forever fail to vest within the perpetuities period? No. Consider a highly unlikely—but conceivable—series of events. Suppose T dies in 2000. B might die in 2025, and A might then marry D, a 20-year-old woman. C then dies one day after fathering his child, E, and A dies a week later. More than 21 years after the death of the only possible lives in being (A and C), say in 2050, D dies. At that time, the class of "A's issue then living" can be ascertained. If E is still alive, his contingent remainder will "vest." Because the interest in "A's issue then living" *might vest* more than 21 years after the death of A and C, the lives in being, it is void under the common law Rule Against Perpetuities.

[3]   The Slothful Executor

The "slothful executor" problem concerns the performance of a future administrative task by an executor, trustee, or other fiduciary.[33] Suppose T devises Redacre "to A for life, then to A's issue who are living upon final distribution of my estate and their heirs."

The Rule applies here because the class members ("A's issue who are living upon final distribution of my estate") cannot be ascertained, and thus their remainder is contingent. The perpetuities period began upon T's death. In order for the contingent remainder to vest, T's estate must be distributed at a time when A has living issue; the interest will forever fail if A has no issue, or no issue who survive that long. Here the only possible relevant lives are T and A.

Logically, it would seem that T or A should validate the interest. It seems obvious that T's estate will be distributed within 21 years after his death. However, under the "what-might-happen" rule, the interest is void. Why? One year after T's death, A might have a child, B; B is not a relevant life because she was born too late. Later, T's executor, E, and A both die. The replacement executor is F, who was born after T died, and is thus not a relevant life. F carelessly delays the handling of T's estate and, as a result, it is not distributed until 22 years after both A and E died. At this point, B's interest vests, too late to comply with the Rule.

---

[33] *See, e.g.,* Ryan v. Beshk, 170 N.E. 699 (Ill. 1930) (contingent remainder fails because it contemplates a future trust, and trustees might not be named for more than 21 years after the death of all relevant lives).

[E] Criticism of the Rule

In recent decades, the Rule has been vigorously attacked by its critics and staunchly defended by its supporters. In particular, the late 1970s witnessed a fierce and prolonged struggle among property law professors over the position that the Restatement (Second) of Property should adopt toward the Rule. This struggle culminated with the adoption of a Restatement section that substantially altered the traditional Rule, and effectively launched a national reform movement (*see* § 14.11).

Criticisms of the common law Rule are legion. First and foremost, it disregards the intent of the transferor and thereby frustrates the right to transfer property freely. The policy bases underlying the Rule are increasingly out of step with the enhanced modern concern for respecting owner autonomy.

Second, the Rule is often condemned as serving obsolete policies. The original goal of the Rule—to ensure the marketability of land—requires little protection today. Contingent legal future interests in land are now created only rarely, due to the strong modern preference to transfer fee simple absolute. The feudal fear that these interests would cause widespread inalienability ended long ago. One might argue that society derives benefit from ensuring that money, stocks, bonds, and other forms of personal property are not tied up for long periods by such interests and thus withdrawn from commerce. As a practical matter, however, most contingent future interests in personal property are equitable, not legal; and the trustee has a fiduciary duty to invest the trust assets productively, not to withhold them from the marketplace.

Finally, the Rule is increasingly unimportant because it can be circumvented by drafting. Virtually all interests can be insulated from the Rule through the insertion of a "savings clause." For example, a conveyance of Blueacre "to A for life, then to B and his heirs if anyone goes to Saturn" would be invalid under the Rule. Yet the addition of a few standard phrases will save the gift. The conveyance "to A for life, then to B and his heirs if anyone goes to Saturn, but if no one goes to Saturn within 21 years after the death of B, then the conveyance to B shall be null and void" is valid. Only the client who selects an incompetent attorney, the argument goes, is harmed by the Rule. Viewed in this light, the Rule is merely a trap for the unwary client, not a meaningful principle of law.

§ 14.11 The Rule Against Perpetuities: Modern Reforms

[A] Overview

Most states have modified the common law Rule Against Perpetuities through legislation, a process which began in the 1970s.[34] These reform

---

[34] The impetus for reform may be traced back, at least in part, to 1964, when England adopted legislation that substantially modified its Rule Against Perpetuities.

measures fall into two basic categories: (1) adopting a "wait-and-see" approach in lieu of the "what-might-happen" rule; and (2) permitting reformation to validate the interest where consistent with the transferor's intent. The widely-adopted Uniform Statutory Rule Against Perpetuities incorporates both approaches. A handful of states have enacted only piecemeal changes (e.g., overturning the presumption of fertility), while the common law Rule survives intact in others.

[B] Basic "Wait and See" Approach

Some states reacted to the perceived absurdity of the common law "what-might-happen" standard by adopting a simple reform called the "wait-and-see" test, either by statute or judicial decision.[35] Under this approach, the validity of an interest is not determined at the onset. Rather, the parties merely await future events. The interest is valid if it *actually* vests during the common law perpetuities period. It is invalid if it fails to vest during the period.

Consider again O's January 1, 2000, devise of Blueacre "to A for life, and then to the first child of A to reach age 30 and the heirs of that child" (*see* § 14.10[C][2][i]). Under the common law Rule, the contingent remainder in "the first child of A to reach age 30" would be invalid at the onset if A never had any children before the devise became effective. The "wait-and-see" approach, however, might well validate the remainder. For example, suppose A actually has a child, B, on January 1, 2002; A dies on B's 31st birthday, January 1, 2033. Here *in fact* A's life validates the interest. Within the perpetuities period (defined as A's life plus 21 years), B's interest "vested." On B's 30th birthday (while A was still alive), B met the condition precedent of reaching age 30; at that point, B's contingent remainder became an indefeasibly vested remainder and, for purposes of the Rule, then "vested."

The wait-and-see approach has proven extraordinarily controversial ever since its debut in a 1947 Pennsylvania statute.[36] The principal arguments in favor of the approach are that it (a) better implements the transferor's intent and (b) protects the transferor from the malpractice of an incompetent attorney who fails to draft a will or deed in conformity with the Rule. The validity of all contingent interests is measured by the same yardstick—what actually happens to the interest over time—regardless of the skill of the drafting attorney. In response, critics point out that this approach impairs the marketability of land and, more generally, keeps wealth out of the flow of commerce for decades. Under the common law Rule, the validity of any future interest can be determined at the onset. But under the wait-and-see approach, land and other forms of property may be tied up by

---

[35] *See, e.g.,* Hansen v. Stroecker, 699 P.2d 871 (Alaska 1985) (adopting wait-and-see approach); *In re* Estate of Anderson, 541 So. 2d 423 (Miss. 1989) (applying wait-and-see approach).

[36] *Compare* W. Barton Leach, *Perpetuities Legislation: Hail, Pennsylvania!*, 108 U. Pa. L. Rev. 1124 (1960) (supporting wait-and-see) *with* Lewis M. Simes, *Is the Rule Against Perpetuities Doomed? The "Wait and See" Doctrine*, 52 Mich. L. Rev. 179 (1953) (criticizing wait-and-see).

contingent future interests for 100 years or more while the parties simply "wait." Moreover, it is often practically difficult to identify the relevant lives to be used in the "wait-and-see" formula, absent litigation.

[C] Reformation or Cy Pres

Other states retain the common law Rule, but mitigate its impact by adding a new feature: a reformation or cy pres remedy. If an interest is invalidated by the Rule, a court may rewrite the language of the conveyance or devise to carry out the transferor's intent as closely as possible and thereby validate the interest.[37]

For example, returning to the hypothetical devise of Blueacre "to A for life, then to the first child of A to reach age 30 and the heirs of that child," a court following the cy pres approach would probably be empowered to reduce the age requirement to 21 if this would save the interest. Why? The court would reason that O's dominant intent was to benefit one of A's children who reached maturity, an intent which can be implemented only by reforming the conveyance. O's further intent to define maturity as age 30 is seen as subordinate to his overall goal, absent clear evidence to the contrary. In other words, if O were forced to choose between (a) allowing the interest to fail entirely or (b) reducing the age contingency to 21, the court presumes that O would prefer reformation.

The cy pres remedy has been applied to date in only a handful of decisions and its future impact is accordingly difficult to predict. The crucial question is whether it will effectively swallow the entire Rule. In other words, will courts *routinely* validate interests that would otherwise violate the Rule?

[D] Uniform Statutory Rule Against Perpetuities

The Uniform Statutory Rule Against Perpetuities (USRAP)[38] —now adopted by about half of the states—combines both reform approaches discussed above.[39] Notably, it applies only to gifts of contingent future interests; all commercial transactions (including options and rights of first refusal) are exempt.

Under USRAP, a covered interest is valid if *either:* (1) it meets the requirements of the common law Rule; *or* (2) using the wait-and-see

---

[37] *Cf.* Berry v. Union Nat'l Bank, 262 S.E.2d 766 (W. Va. 1980) (using doctrine of equitable modification to reform testamentary trust and thereby validate interest).

[38] Unif. Statutory Rule Against Perpetuities (amended 1990), 8B U.L.A. 321 (1993). For discussion of the Act, see Ira M. Bloom & Jesse Dukeminier, *Perpetuities Reformers Beware: The USRAP Tax Trap*, 25 Real Prop. Prob. & Tr. J. 203 (1990); John D. Moore, Comment, *The Uniform Statutory Rule Against Perpetuities: Taming the "Technicality-Ridden Legal Nightmare,"* 95 W. Va. L. Rev. 193 (1992); Lawrence W. Waggoner, *The Uniform Statutory Rule Against Perpetuities: The Rationale of the 90-Year Waiting Period*, 73 Cornell L. Rev. 157 (1988).

[39] The basic structure of the USRAP was derived from the earlier Restatement (Second) of Property: Donative Transfers (1976), which adopted both the wait-and-see approach and the cy pres remedy. For a chronicle of the furious debate surrounding the Restatement reforms, see Powell on Real Property § 75A.05 (Michael Allan Wolf ed., Matthew Bender).

approach, it *actually* "vests or terminates within 90 years after its creation." Thus, USRAP modifies the basic "wait-and-see" approach by using a fixed 90-year perpetuities period, instead of the classic period of one life plus 21 years, thus providing more certainty. The 90-year period was chosen as a rough approximation of the probable length of one life (about 70 years) plus 21 years.

Consider again O's January 1, 2000, devise of Blueacre "to A for life, then to the first child of A to reach age 30 and the heirs of that child." The contingent remainder in "the first child of A to reach age 30" does not comply with the common law Rule, as discussed above. However, the second prong of the USRAP test may save the interest. If A dies childless during the 90-year perpetuities period (from January 1, 2000, until January 1, 2090), the interest will terminate. If a child of A reaches age 30 during this same period, the interest will timely vest.

Alternatively, if a covered interest is invalidated, a court is empowered to reform the creating instrument "in the manner that most closely approximates the transferor's manifested plan of disposition and is within the 90 years" allowed for vesting. Thus, if it becomes clear that the contingent remainder in "the first child of A to reach age 30" might vest too late (e.g., if A dies in 2082, leaving a 20-year-old daughter), the court might well reform the conveyance by reducing the age contingency in order to accommodate O's likely intent.

[E] Future of the Rule Against Perpetuities

The common law Rule Against Perpetuities is slowly fading away. The national trend toward adoption of the USRAP will continue over time. The more provocative question is whether the USRAP or any version of the Rule will endure in the long run. A few states have already abolished the Rule, in whole or in part. If the reformation provisions of the USRAP are routinely used to validate otherwise invalid interests, the demise of the Rule Against Perpetuities will inevitably follow.

§ 14.12 The Doctrine of Worthier Title

O conveys Blueacre "to S for life, then to O's heirs." Under the common law Doctrine of Worthier Title, O's attempt to create a remainder in his heirs is invalid. Instead, as a matter of law O retains a reversion that becomes possessory when S's life estate terminates.

The Doctrine of Worthier Title is a medieval relic. The traditional version provided that if (a) an owner devised or conveyed real property to one party and (b) by the same instrument devised or conveyed the following remainder or executory interest to the owner's "heirs," then the owner retained a reversion and the "heirs" received nothing.[40] In effect, an owner could

---

[40] *See, e.g.,* Harris Trust & Sav. Bank v. Beach, 513 N.E.2d 833 (Ill. 1987) (refusing to apply doctrine of worthier title on facts of case); Braswell v. Braswell, 81 S.E.2d 560 (Va. 1954) (applying doctrine).

transfer property rights to heirs only through the "worthier" method of descent (that is, intestate succession), not by means of devise or conveyance. The doctrine was a rule of law that bound all parties, regardless of the owner's intent.

The doctrine originated as a tool to prevent landowners from avoiding the feudal incidents and, to a lesser extent, to protect free alienation. The incidents were owed only by tenants who acquired their estates through descent, not by those who took by conveyance or devise. If tenant O could convey or devise the family landholdings to his heirs, the heirs took the property free and clear of the incidents. At least initially, the doctrine was intended to plug this feudal tax loophole. After the demise of feudalism, English courts retained the doctrine because it encouraged the alienability of land. If Blueacre in the example above is burdened with a contingent remainder in the unascertainable heirs of O, it is impossible for O to convey clear title to the land, even after S's death. By eliminating such contingent interests, the doctrine facilitated the sale of fee simple absolute.

Today the doctrine is virtually—but not entirely—obsolete in the United States as a binding rule of law. For decades, there has been general agreement that the doctrine no longer applies to devises.[41] The extent to which the doctrine may still affect conveyances is less clear. Over three-quarters of the states have entirely abolished the doctrine in this context, either by statute or case law. In these jurisdictions, the rule may govern deeds or wills executed before the abolition occurred. Contemporary courts remain strongly focused on honoring the grantor's intent in this and other contexts, despite its impact on alienability. Abolition is the clear modern trend.

Perhaps ironically, the main lingering significance of the doctrine today stems from its revival by Judge Cardozo in 1919 as a rule of construction—an evidentiary presumption utilized to honor grantor intent.[42] Some jurisdictions apparently still presume that a grantor who (a) conveys a life estate in real or personal property to one party, and (b) then purports to convey a remainder or executory interest to his own heirs does not actually intend to convey anything to the heirs. In order to defeat this presumption, the heirs must provide evidence of the grantor's actual intention to benefit them. Because reported decisions involving the doctrine are extraordinarily rare, however, it is difficult to assess its vitality.

§ 14.13 The Rule in Shelley's Case

O conveys Blueacre "to S for life, then to the heirs of S." What interests arise? At common law—under the famous Rule in Shelley's Case[43]—such a conveyance effectively created fee simple in S, while the "heirs of S"

---

[41] *See, e.g.,* Restatement (Second) of Property: Donative Transfers § 30.2(2) (1987).

[42] *See* Doctor v. Hughes, 122 N.E. 221 (N.Y. 1919), where Judge Cardozo resurrected the doctrine, transforming it into a rule of construction and extending it to encompass both real and personal property.

[43] Wolfe v. Shelley, 76 Eng. Rep. 206 (1581).

received nothing. Much like the Doctrine of Worthier Title, the Rule in Shelley's Case transformed a remainder in the transferee's heirs into a remainder held by the transferee.[44]

The rule was simple. If a deed or will (a) created a life estate or fee tail in real property in one person (here S), and (b) also created a remainder in fee simple in that person's heirs (here the "heirs of S"), and (c) the estate and remainder were either both legal or both equitable, then the future interest belonged to that person, not the heirs.[45] S now owns all legal interests in Blueacre. Under the doctrine of merger, S's smaller interest (the life estate) would "merge" into his larger interest (the remainder in fee simple), giving S fee simple absolute. What if O conveys Blueacre "to S for life, then to T for life, then to the heirs of S"? Pursuant to the rule, S holds both a life estate and a remainder in fee simple absolute. No merger occurs in this example, however, because T holds an intervening interest.

The Rule in Shelley's Case was based on the same historic policies that supported the Doctrine of Worthier Title. Initially, the Rule prevented landowners from avoiding the feudal incidents. As the feudal system waned, the Rule was increasingly justified as a tool to help ensure the free alienability of real property, even though it frustrated the owner's intent.[46] Today the Rule is seen as an anachronism. As one judge lamented, "[t]hat rule is a relic, not of the horse and buggy days, but of the preceding stone cart and oxen days."[47]

The Rule in Shelley's Case has been abolished in all jurisdictions except Arkansas and Delaware. It may be confidently predicted that these holdout states will eventually follow the national trend.[48] Yet in many states the Rule still applies to instruments created before the effective date of abolition.

§ 14.14   The Destructibility of Contingent Remainders

O conveys Blueacre "to S for life, and then to T and his heirs if T reaches age 18." What happens if S dies two years later when T is merely age 17? At common law, T's interest would be extinguished because it failed to vest when S died. Thus, O or O's successors would own Blueacre in fee simple absolute, just as if O had merely conveyed "to S for life."

---

[44] In the era when bar examinations were oral, prospective attorneys were frequently asked, "What is the Rule in Shelley's Case?" As the story goes, one candidate responded, "Sir, the law is no respecter of persons. The rule in Shelley's case is the same as in every other case."

[45] *See, e.g.,* Evans v. Giles, 415 N.E.2d 354 (Ill. 1980) (discussing rule); Seymour v. Heubaum, 211 N.E.2d 897 (Ill. App. Ct. 1965) (applying rule to invalidate remainder); Society Nat'l Bank v. Jacobson, 560 N.E.2d 217 (Ohio 1990) (applying rule to invalidate remainder in personal property under trust agreement that became effective before Ohio abolished rule in 1941); Sybert v. Sybert, 254 S.W.2d 999 (Tex. 1953) (applying rule to invalidate remainder).

[46] *See, e.g.,* Jones v. Stone, 279 S.E.2d 13 (N.C. Ct. App. 1981) (discussing the effect of the rule on alienation).

[47] Sybert v. Sybert, 254 S.W.2d 999, 1001 (Tex. 1953) (Griffin, J., concurring).

[48] *See* John V. Orth, *Requiem for the Rule in Shelley's Case*, 67 N.C. L. Rev. 681 (1989).

common law doctrine of the destructibility of contingent remainders was straightforward.[49] A legal contingent remainder in real property was extinguished or "destroyed" if it failed to vest when the preceding freehold estate ended.[50] Why? In order to ensure the collection of feudal incidents, the rule developed that seisin must always be held by some person; a "gap" in seisin was impermissible. Thus, if the prior freehold estate ended before the remainder was ready to become possessory, the remainder was deemed destroyed and seisin shifted to the next interest. At the same time, the doctrine tended to protect the marketability of land, at least in theory, and this rationale survived after the demise of feudalism.

Yet—because courts ultimately held that it did not apply to executory interests—the doctrine could be circumvented through careful drafting. Instead of using a contingent remainder, the drafter could create an executory interest that had a similar impact. Similarly, the doctrine did not extend to equitable contingent remainders, so drafters could avoid it simply by creating interests in trust. Thus, the doctrine was less successful than anticipated in protecting marketability, leaving a hole which was partially plugged by the Rule Against Perpetuities.

Today, like the dinosaur, the doctrine is extinct in the United States. Almost all states have abolished it, by statute or decisional law. Although legal scholars debate the number of states in which the doctrine might persist (one? two? four?), the debate is largely academic. Over the last 30 years, American courts have simply not applied the doctrine.

---

[49] *See generally* Jesse Dukeminier, *Contingent Remainders and Executory Interests: A Requiem for the Distinction*, 43 Minn. L. Rev. 13 (1958); Samuel M. Fetters, *Destructibility of Contingent Remainders*, 21 Ark. L. Rev. 145 (1967).

[50] *See, e.g.,* Evans v. Giles, 415 N.E.2d 354 (Ill. 1980) (discussing doctrine); Abo Petroleum Corp. v. Amstutz, 600 P.2d 278 (N.M. 1979) (refusing to follow doctrine); *see generally* Samuel M. Fetters, *Destructibility of Contingent Remainders*, 21 Ark. L. Rev. 145 (1967).

Chapter 15

INTRODUCTION TO LANDLORD-TENANT LAW

§ 15.01 Landlord-Tenant Law in Context

American landlord-tenant law has undergone revolutionary change in recent decades.[1] Until these reforms began, landlord-tenant law was still based on English common law principles established during the post-feudal era. Under this approach, a lease was seen as the conveyance of a nonfreehold or "leasehold" estate; the landlord-tenant relationship was governed by property law principles that—unsurprisingly—heavily favored landlords. In the 1970s, however, courts began to reexamine these traditional rules in light of modern conditions, particularly the plight of the urban residential tenant. The result of this reexamination process has been a massive shift in the law toward enhanced protection for residential tenants. Courts increasingly view the residential lease as a contract, and thus subject to contract law doctrines premised on equitable principles. Commercial leases are still largely governed by traditional property rules, although even here some modernization has occurred.

Like all major transitions, the modern landlord-tenant "revolution" has produced complexity, confusion, and a certain amount of inconsistency in the law. Part of the common law foundation still endures, particularly the leasehold estate system. Yet another part of this foundation has been eroded away by a combination of (1) case law applying contract principles and (2) pro-tenant statutes. Because the pace of change differs from state to state, and from doctrine to doctrine, the law in one jurisdiction may vary widely from that of another. The overall trend, however, is clear: the rights of tenants are gradually expanding.

§ 15.02 What Is a Leasehold Estate?

The common law distinguished between two basic types of present estates: (1) freehold estates, discussed in Chapter 9; and (2) nonfreehold or "leasehold" estates, which are introduced in this chapter. Broadly speaking, laymen view the freehold estates as forms of "owning" land, while leasehold estates are seen merely as forms of "leasing" land. Over centuries, the branch of the law relating to freehold estates evolved quite differently from that governing leasehold estates. Yet both types of present estates share a common core: each entitles a holder to the *immediate possession of specific land.*[2]

In a technical sense, a leasehold estate is a legal interest that entitles the tenant to immediate possession of designated land, either for a fixed period of time (e.g., five years) or for as long as the tenant and landlord desire. Suppose L, holding fee simple absolute in Greenacre, leases the land

---

[1] *See generally* Curtis J. Berger, *Hard Leases Make Bad Law,* 74 Colum. L. Rev. 791 (1974); Mary A. Glendon, *The Transformation of American Landlord-Tenant Law,* 23 B.C. L. Rev. 503 (1982); John F. Hicks, *The Contractual Nature of Real Property Leases,* 24 Baylor L. Rev. 443 (1972); William M. McGovern, *The Historical Conception of a Lease for Years,* 23 UCLA L. Rev. 501 (1976); Edward H. Rabin, *The Revolution in Residential Landlord-Tenant Law: Causes and Consequences,* 69 Cornell L. Rev. 517 (1984).

[2] Restatement (Second) of Property: Landlord & Tenant § 1.2 (1977).

to T for a 25-year term. T now owns a leasehold estate known as a term of years. Because this estate has been carved out of L's conceptually larger fee simple absolute, L retains a future interest, a reversion.

Subject to limitations imposed by law or by the terms of the lease, a tenant such as T enjoys a wide range of rights. T is entitled to occupy and use Greenacre, including any crops or profits it produces, but cannot commit waste. T may exclude all other persons from the land, including L. Further, under some circumstances, T may transfer all or some of his rights in Greenacre to others.

§ 15.03　Leasehold Estate Distinguished from Nonpossessory Interests

[A]　Basic Distinction

A buys a ticket to see the new play at O's theater; B rents a room in O's hotel for one night; C, a farm worker, lives in a barracks provided by O as part of his compensation;[3] and D holds the perpetual right to walk across O's land. A, B, C, and D are all legally entitled to be present on land owned by O. But none of them owns a leasehold estate.

A, B, C, and D all have a mere *right to use* O's land for a limited purpose, subject to O's control. This falls far short of the *right of exclusive possession* necessary for a leasehold estate; for example, they could not exclude O from his land. The law recognizes a variety of nonpossessory interests that permit one to enter another's land. Here A, B, and C each have a *license* (a revocable privilege to enter land temporarily for a specific purpose; *see* § 32.13) while D holds an *easement* (a nonpossessory right to use land in a particular manner; *see* § 32.02).

[B]　Defining the Boundary Between Possession and Use

The boundary line between possession and use, however reassuring in theory, is often difficult to locate in practice. Suppose E is entitled to erect and maintain a billboard on F's land. Does E have possession of the land on which the billboard sits (and thus a leasehold estate) or merely the use of that land (and thus an easement or license)? Courts typically consider a variety of factors in such cases, including

　(1)　whether the party occupies a specific, distinct area,

　(2)　how much control the party has over the area, and

　(3)　whether the parties used lease-like terminology and provisions in defining their relationship.[4]

---

[3] *See, e.g.,* State v. Shack, 277 A.2d 369 (N.J. 1971) (farm worker housing); Vasquez v. Glassboro Service Ass'n, 415 A.2d 1156 (N.J. 1980) (same).

[4] *See, e.g.,* Friend v. Gem Int'l, Inc., 476 S.W.2d 134 (Mo. Ct. App. 1971) (A, who operated furniture department within department store owned by B, held to be tenant even though both A and B described the relationship as a license, because A occupied a "definite and specific area . . . to the exclusion of other merchants").

§ 15.04 Historical Evolution of Landlord-Tenant Law

[A] The Feudal Foundation

The lineage of modern American landlord-tenant law may be traced backward in time to the English feudal system. In the early feudal era, the lands of the nobility and gentry were cultivated by landless serfs under customary arrangements that differed little from slavery. The serf, tied to the land for life, provided as much labor as the lord demanded and, in return, received subsistence. It became common for the lord to assign serfs to work particular tracts of land, and the serfs were sometimes allowed to retain a share of the crops they produced. The lord was omnipotent, the serf powerless.

Over time, these feudal relationships evolved into the nonfreehold estates that form the foundation of landlord-tenant law (*see* § 15.05). This transition was accelerated by the Black Death, a widespread plague in the mid-1300s that so devastated the population that a labor shortage developed. With the feudal system waning, a landowner who wished to attract the labor necessary to keep his land under cultivation was forced to make concessions. A rudimentary lease emerged: the former serf was allowed to use a particular tract of land for an agreed-upon term in exchange for a fixed rent. The feudal lord-serf relationship gradually gave way to the medieval landlord-tenant relationship.

[B] The Paradigm Tenant: A Medieval Farmer

The early evolution of English landlord-tenant law was greatly affected by the economic and social context in which leases arose. During the era when this law developed, the lease was a *commercial* transaction—the lease of agricultural land for farming—not a *residential* arrangement. The identity and characteristics of the typical medieval tenant are important keys to understanding the general common law approach to leases.

The paradigm tenant was an enterprising farmer who lived in the rural, agrarian England of the Middle Ages.[5] His dominant interest was to obtain land to grow crops, raise stock, or pursue other agricultural endeavors. Although he might live on the farm, the residence or other structures were only of secondary importance. The tenant was a "jack-of-all-trades" who could easily keep the farm structures in good repair, without assistance from the landlord. If the structures were destroyed by fire or other natural disaster, the tenant could rebuild them himself, while continuing to farm the land. Finally, the tenant usually remained on the land for a long period (e.g., 21-year leases became popular in the 1300s).

The landlord in this classic scenario was an absentee owner or country "gentleman" whose social status precluded any manual labor. The landlord provided no services to the tenant, nor did the tenant expect any. Once the

---

[5] *See, e.g.,* Javins v. First Nat'l Realty Corp., 428 F.2d 1071 (D.C. Cir. 1970) (discussing attributes of medieval tenant farmer); Hilder v. St. Peter, 478 A.2d 202 (Vt. 1984) (same).

landlord transferred possession of the land, his only remaining role was passive: receiving rent.

[C] Common Law Approach: Lease As Conveyance

By 1500, the common law approach to the landlord-tenant relationship was well-developed, and molded to suit the paradigm farm lease. A lease was seen as the conveyance of an estate in land: the landlord transferred his right to possession of specific land to the tenant. Thus, the lease was governed by rather formalistic property law rules, not by contract law.[6] The medieval farm lease fit this conveyance model well. Consider the nature of a conveyance. Assume that O, holding fee simple absolute in Greenacre, conveys his entire estate to T. T now has the exclusive right to possession of Greenacre; O has no remaining right, title, or interest in the property, and thus no duty or obligation to T. The paradigm lease produced a similar effect. Suppose now that O transfers to T the exclusive right to possession of Greenacre for a fixed period of time—21 years. Once this transfer is completed, O owes no further duty or obligation toward T, except to refrain from interfering with T's use and enjoyment of the land during the lease period. T is free to farm or otherwise use Greenacre without interference from O for 21 years, absent waste.

The consequences of viewing the lease as a conveyance were profound. Under the early common law approach, for example:

(1)   the tenant had the sole duty to repair and maintain any structures on the premises, even if the structures were demolished by fire or other disaster;

(2)   the tenant was required to pay rent even if the structures were destroyed;

(3)   the tenant was required to continue the tenancy and pay rent even if the landlord breached any lease obligations he had undertaken (the tenant's sole remedy was to sue for damages, not end the lease); and

(4)   the landlord had no duty to mitigate damages if the tenant abandoned the premises.

Widespread residential leasing began in England in the 1500s and 1600s as urbanization increased. Courts routinely applied the standard landlord-tenant rules developed for agricultural leases to these new residential leases.

---

[6] *See generally* Hiram H. Lesar, *The Landlord-Tenant Relation in Perspective: From Status to Contract and Back in 900 Years?,* 9 U. Kan. L. Rev. 369 (1961); William M. McGovern, *The Historical Conception of a Lease for Years,* 23 UCLA L. Rev. 501 (1976).

§ 15.05 Categories of Leasehold Estates

[A] Four Categories

Four categories of leasehold estates were recognized at common law: the term of years tenancy, the periodic tenancy, the tenancy at will, and the tenancy at sufferance.[7] The main distinction between these estates stems from the answer to one question: when does the estate end? This common law classification system was quite rigid. Every leasehold had to be squeezed into one of the four permissible categories, even at the expense of logical consistency.

Modern law still recognizes these four basic categories. As a practical matter, however, today almost every tenancy is either a term of years or a periodic tenancy. The tenancy at will is rare, while the tenancy at sufferance results only from the tenant's wrongful failure to vacate after the lease ends.

A few jurisdictions—most notably New Jersey and the District of Columbia—have eroded these traditional categories by statues or ordinances that effectively create a fifth type of leasehold estate (see § 19.04[A][3]). They permit a tenant to remain in possession until the landlord has "good cause" for eviction, regardless of the original nature of the tenancy.[8]

[B] Term of Years Tenancy

[1] Nature of Estate

Almost all commercial leases (and some residential leases) utilize the *term of years* tenancy, sometimes called a *tenancy for years* or a *term for years*. The key characteristic of this estate is an advance agreement that it will continue for a designated period (e.g., five days, eight months, five years, or 99 years).[9] Thus, this tenancy lasts for a period of time that is either (a) fixed in advance (e.g., from July 1, 1995 to June 30, 2035), or (b) computed using a formula that is agreed to in advance (e.g., "for a term of 10 years after construction of the subject building is completed").[10] As the second example indicates, the lease term may *begin* upon the occurrence of a future event.

But what if the lease term *ends* upon the occurrence of a future event? Suppose L leases Greenacre to T for "25 years, so long as Greenacre is used as a farm." This creates a type of defeasible estate (see § 9.06): a term of years determinable. The beginning and ending dates of the maximum lease

---

[7] The remarkable decision of David Properties, Inc. v. Selk, 151 So. 2d 334 (Fla. Dist. Ct. App. 1963), involves all four categories.

[8] The landlord's right to terminate a tenancy may also be restricted by antidiscrimination legislation and by the doctrine of retaliatory eviction (see § 19.04[A]).

[9] Statutes in some states restrict the duration of a term of years tenancy. *See, e.g.,* Cal. Civ. Code § 717 (51-year maximum term for leases of agricultural land).

[10] Restatement (Second) of Property: Landlord & Tenant § 1.4 (1977).

term are fixed, even if the lease may end sooner due to an uncertain event. On the other hand, what if L leases Greenacre to T "for the balance of T's life"? Because the termination date is uncertain, most courts—following the traditional view—would not classify the resulting estate as a term of years.[11]

[2] Termination of Estate

The term of years automatically expires when the agreed period ends, without any notice of termination. For example, if L leases Greenacre to T "from 12:01 a.m. on January 1, 1999 until midnight on December 31, 2008," the lease automatically expires at midnight on December 31, 2008, without any need for T or L to notify the other.

In addition, most leases contain provisions that permit the landlord to terminate the tenancy upon the tenant's breach of specified lease terms or other circumstances, including non-payment of rent, waste, and illegal use of the premises.

[C] Periodic Tenancy

[1] Nature of Estate

The *periodic tenancy* lasts for an initial fixed period and then automatically continues for additional equal periods until either the landlord or tenant terminates the tenancy by giving advance notice.

The classic example of the periodic tenancy is the "month-to-month" residential lease. Suppose L and T enter into a month-to-month lease for an apartment, with the term to begin on January 1. The initial period of the lease is one month, January; but T's tenancy will automatically continue month after month until either L or T gives notice of termination. If neither gives notice, the tenancy will continue indefinitely. Although the month-to-month period is encountered most commonly, closely followed by the year-to-year tenancy sometimes used in agricultural leases, a period of any duration may be used.[12]

Complexity arises when the parties fail to reach a complete agreement. Suppose T leases Blueacre from L in return for "$800 per month in rent," but without any agreement about the term of the lease. American courts would uniformly construe this arrangement as a periodic, month-to-month tenancy (rather than, for example, a tenancy at will) based on the presumed intent of the parties.[13] But what if instead T leases Blueacre for "$9,600

---

[11] *See, e.g.,* Nitschke v. Doggett, 489 S.W.2d 335 (Tex. Civ. App. 1972), *vacated on other grounds,* 498 S.W.2d 339 (Tex. 1973); Garner v. Gerrish, 473 N.E.2d 223 (N.Y. 1984).

[12] *See, e.g.,* Lonergan v. Connecticut Food Store, Inc., 357 A.2d 910 (Conn. 1975) (commercial lease that provided that after expiration of initial five-year term, lease would be automatically extended "for a period of one year and thence from year to year, unless the Lessee shall give notice to the Lessor of termination" merely created a year-to-year periodic tenancy after the sixth year, which could be terminated by either party).

[13] *See* Restatement (Second) of Property: Landlord & Tenant § 1.5 cmt. d (1977); Wright v. Vickaryous, 598 P.2d 490 (Alaska 1979).

per year, payable $800 per month," again without an agreed termination date? Under the logic of the first example, this is a periodic tenancy, but is the period year-to-year or month-to-month? Most courts interpret such language as creating a year-to-year periodic tenancy,[14] although some would find a month-to-month tenancy if residential property is involved.[15]

A periodic tenancy may arise by implication based on the conduct of the parties, even in the absence of any express agreement. Suppose L permits T to move into Redacre, a house owned by L, without any agreement. T later gives L a $200 check for "rent" which L accepts and cashes, and this pattern continues each month. These actions create a periodic, month-to-month tenancy in T.[16] The same result follows if T takes occupancy of Redacre pursuant to an invalid term of years lease with L, but nonetheless pays rent monthly.

[2] Termination of Estate

[a] Common Law Requirements

At common law, either the landlord or the tenant could terminate the tenancy by delivering oral or written notice to the other. Each party had the unfettered right to end the tenancy for any reason or for no reason.

How far in advance must notice be given to terminate a periodic tenancy? At common law, termination of a year-to-year tenancy required six-months notice, while shorter tenancies required notice equal to the period involved (e.g., 30-days advance notice to terminate a month-to-month tenancy). Suppose T, a month-to-month tenant whose rent is due on the first day of each month, decides in June to end her tenancy. On June 15, she gives notice of termination; when will the tenancy end? At common law, notice terminated the tenancy on the last day of the fixed period, not in the middle of the period.[17] T's notice ends the tenancy on July 31, not July 15. Thus, even if T vacates the premises on July 15, she is still liable for rent through July 31.

[b] Statutory Modifications

The process for terminating a periodic tenancy is now governed by state statutes. The typical statute mandates that a particular form of written notice of termination be delivered to the other party in a designated manner.[18] Although the tenant's right to terminate the tenancy is still

---

[14] See Hill v. Turley, 710 P.2d 50 (Mont. 1985); Prescott v. Smits, 505 A.2d 1211 (Vt. 1985). See generally Restatement (Second) of Property: Landlord & Tenant § 1.5 cmt. d, illus. 3 (1977).

[15] See Unif. Residential Landlord & Tenant Act § 1.401(d), 7B U.L.A. 447 (absent definite term, tenancy is month-to-month).

[16] Cf. Crechale & Polles, Inc. v. Smith, 295 So. 2d 275 (Miss. 1974) (where landlord first elected to treat holdover tenant as trespasser, but then accepted monthly rent from tenant, a new periodic month-to-month tenancy arose).

[17] S.D.G. v. Inventory Control Co., 429 A.2d 394 (N.J. Super. Ct. App. Div. 1981).

[18] See Unif. Residential Landlord & Tenant Act § 4.301(b), 7B U.L.A. 500.

unfettered, various doctrines restrict the landlord's freedom to evict the tenant (*see* § 19.04).

There is considerable variation among the states on the timing of notice. Most states still follow the traditional standard, which requires 30-days notice for ending a month-to-month tenancy,[19] but periods in other states range from 7 days[20] to 60 days.[21] In some states, the timing of notice turns on the nature of the property involved (e.g., longer period for residential or agricultural land)[22] or the identity of the party giving the notice (e.g., longer period if landlord gives notice). Finally, most states have shortened the required notice for ending the year-to-year tenancy to two or three months.

A majority of states use the common law standard that the tenancy ends on the last day of the fixed period.[23] California[24] and certain other states allow a month-to-month tenancy to be ended any time after 30-days notice is given; thus if T gives notice on June 15, her tenancy expires on July 15, not July 31.

[D] Tenancy at Will

[1] Nature of Estate

The *tenancy at will* has no fixed duration and endures only so long as both the landlord and the tenant desire.[25] For example, at common law the estate ended immediately—without any advance notice—on the day the tenant abandoned the premises or the landlord delivered notice of termination. Given this fundamental insecurity, why would anyone voluntarily agree to create a tenancy at will?

Today most tenancies at will arise by implication, not from an express agreement. For example, if T occupies Redacre with L's consent, but without an agreement on the duration of the tenancy or the payment of rent, the court will find a tenancy at will. Why? Based on these facts, it is relatively clear L and T intended that T would have possession of Redacre as a tenant, and thus that some form of leasehold estate was intended; because the requirements for a term of years or periodic tenancy are not met, however, the relationship will be deemed a tenancy at will. In many jurisdictions, the same result follows where a tenant enters into possession either (a)

---

[19] *See, e.g.,* Cal. Civ. Code § 1946; Ohio Rev. Code Ann. § 5321.17.

[20] N.C. Gen. Stat. § 42-14.

[21] Del. Code Ann. tit. 25, § 5106. The Uniform Residential Landlord & Tenant Act requires 60-days notice to terminate a residential month-to-month tenancy, but this standard is largely ignored even by the minority of states that have adopted the Act. Unif. Residential Landlord & Tenant Act § 4.301(b), 7B U.L.A. 500.

[22] *See* Ariz. Rev. Stat. Ann. §§ 33-341, 33-1375 (10-day notice for commercial, 30-day notice for residential month-to-month tenant).

[23] S.D.G. v. Inventory Control Co., 429 A.2d 394 (N.J. Super. Ct. App. Div. 1981).

[24] Cal. Civ. Code § 1946.

[25] Restatement (Second) of Property: Landlord & Tenant § 1.6 (1977).

under an unenforceable lease (e.g., one that violates the Statute of Frauds),[26] or (b) before any lease has been negotiated.

Although agreements to establish a tenancy at will are seldom encountered, occasionally parties agree to create a leasehold estate that is terminable at the will of only one party, either landlord or tenant. Should this be construed as a tenancy at will or some other estate? The law governing this area is unsettled. What if the parties agree that a lease is terminable at the will of the landlord only? Although there is contrary authority, many courts imply a reciprocal right of termination in the tenant, and thus treat the estate as a tenancy at will.[27]

The more troublesome problem is posed by the agreement to create a leasehold estate that is terminable by the will of the tenant only. Suppose L and T agree that T may occupy the premises "for as long as he wants." Some courts would consider this a tenancy at will, under the logic described above. However, a substantial body of authority—including the first and second Restatements of Property[28]—would honor the clear intention of the parties by classifying the interest as a determinable life estate.[29] T is entitled to possession of the premises until his death or until he decides to terminate the lease, whichever comes first.

[2] Termination of Estate

At common law, a tenancy at will ended whenever the landlord or tenant chose. Any form of notice would terminate the tenancy immediately. In addition, even absent notice, any conduct by the landlord or tenant that demonstrated an intent to terminate the tenancy would suffice (e.g., abandonment by tenant, sale of the property by landlord, or death of either party).

Statutes in most states now regulate the termination of a tenancy at will. Many states provide that the tenancy can be ended only by advance notice, usually 30 days; this effectively converts the tenancy at will into a statutory form of periodic tenancy. Other states permit termination by advance notice, but also recognize that the conduct of the landlord or tenant may end the tenancy even without notice.

[E] Tenancy at Sufferance

[1] Nature of Estate

Most authorities agree that the *tenancy at sufferance* is not a true estate in land and does not create a landlord-tenant relationship. But it is a useful label to describe a peculiar form of occupancy somewhat akin to a leasehold estate.

---

[26] *Cf.* Martin v. Smith, 7 N.W.2d 481 (Minn. 1942) (unauthorized lease).

[27] Restatement (Second) of Property: Landlord & Tenant § 1.6 cmt. g (1977).

[28] Restatement of Property § 21 cmt. a (1936); Restatement (Second) of Property: Landlord & Tenant § 1.6 cmt. g (1977).

[29] *See, e.g.,* Garner v. Gerrish, 473 N.E.2d 223 (N.Y. 1984).

A tenancy at sufferance arises when a person in rightful possession of land—as a tenant or otherwise—wrongfully continues in possession after that right ends.[30] For example, suppose A, holding a term of years tenancy in Redacre that ends on December 31, remains in possession of Redacre on January 1 and thereafter. Her right to possession terminated on December 31, and thus her continued possession is wrongful. A is now a tenant at sufferance, one step above the level of a mere trespasser. Landlord B may either evict A or elect to renew her tenancy under the holdover tenant doctrine (*see* [3], *below*). A tenancy at sufferance also arises, for example, where a mortgagor retains possession after the mortgage is foreclosed, or a vendor remains in possession after conveying title to a vendee.

[2] Termination of Estate

Because the tenancy at sufferance is not an estate, no notice or other action by the landlord is required to terminate it. Instead, the landlord may evict the wrongful occupant at any time. In many states, the landlord can recover damages for the period of wrongful occupancy, measured either by fair rental value or prior rent.[31]

[3] Most Common Situation: The Holdover Tenant

A tenant who remains in possession of leased premises after the leasehold estate ends is considered a *holdover tenant*. This is the most common situation in which a tenancy at sufferance arises. At this point, the common law rule gives the landlord an option: in his sole discretion—and regardless of the tenant's wishes—the landlord may either (a) evict the tenant as a trespasser, or (b) hold the tenant to a new tenancy.[32]

What explains this remarkable rule? The most common justification is that the rule discourages a tenant from wrongfully holding over; faced with the risk of future rent liability the tenant will vacate the premises on time.[33] Thus, the incoming tenant can be assured that the premises will be available for occupancy when the new lease term begins. The rule also allows the landlord to receive compensation for the damage caused by the holdover when the new tenant who cannot take occupancy cancels the lease.

Legal scholars agree, however, that the rule often imposes a penalty far out of proportion to the tenant's offense or the landlord's damages. Why should a tenant be required to pay rent for years for unneeded premises simply because the tenant failed to vacate quickly enough? Moreover, the doctrine serves as a deterrent only if the tenant is aware of its existence; but the average tenant is unfamiliar with this principle. In light of these concerns, there is a modern tendency to curtail the holdover tenant doctrine. For example, if the tenant holds over for a very brief period (e.g.,

---

[30] *See, e.g.,* Crechale & Polles, Inc. v. Smith, 295 So. 2d 275 (Miss. 1974).

[31] *See, e.g.,* Mass. Gen. Laws ch. 186, § 3.

[32] *See, e.g.,* A.H. Fetting Mfg. Jewelry Co. v. Waltz, 152 A. 434 (Md. 1930); Crechale & Polles, Inc. v. Smith, 295 So. 2d 275 (Miss. 1974).

[33] Restatement (Second) of Property: Landlord & Tenant, ch. 14, tit. B, intro. note (1977).

several hours) or because of circumstances beyond the tenant's control (e.g., illness), most courts will not apply the doctrine.[34] And many jurisdictions have flatly abolished the rule, typically requiring instead that the holdover tenant pay a fixed amount to the landlord (e.g., three-months rent, treble damages, or double rent during the holdover period).[35]

Perhaps the most widespread reform involves the length of the new tenancy. At common law, the duration of the new tenancy was defined by the length of the original tenancy. Suppose, for example, that A leases Redacre from L for a five-year term; the lease ends on December 31, but A remains in possession of Redacre. At common law, L could unilaterally renew A's tenancy for another five-year term. Alternatively, if A was a periodic month-to-month tenant in Redacre, L could hold A over to a further one-month period. Today the maximum term for a holdover tenancy is *one year*, regardless of the original lease term.[36] Beyond this point of agreement, however, there is a split of authority as to when a shorter term or period is applicable. Suppose B leases Greenacre from C for a one-year term, with rent payable monthly, and then holds over after the year ends; C elects to hold B to a new tenancy. What is the nature of B's tenancy? Two issues arise: (1) is it a periodic tenancy or a term of years? and (2) is the term or period one year or one month? Most jurisdictions view B's tenancy as a periodic tenancy, some finding the relevant period to be one year (like the original lease term) and others concluding the period is one month (based on the interval for rent payment in the original lease).[37] In a minority of jurisdictions, B has a term of years tenancy, either for a fixed one-year term (like the original lease term) or for a one-month term (based on the rent payment interval).[38]

A surprising amount of litigation involves a question of mechanics: how does the landlord effectively exercise this option?[39] The landlord can expressly notify the tenant of his choice, but more commonly the landlord's decision is implied from conduct and other surrounding circumstances. Thus, landlord conduct that is inconsistent with an intent to treat the holdover tenant as a trespasser, such as demanding rent or accepting rent

---

[34] *See, e.g.,* Commonwealth Bldg. Corp. v. Hirschfield, 30 N.E.2d 790 (Ill. App. Ct. 1940) (no holdover occurred where tenants had removed most of their property but remained in apartment overnight after lease expired at midnight); *see also* Bockelmann v. Marynick, 788 S.W.2d 569 (Tex. 1990) (where one cotenant timely vacated premises, but other cotenant held over, new tenancy bound only cotenant who remained in possession).

[35] For example, the Uniform Residential Landlord & Tenant Act provides that the tenant who holds over willfully and in bad faith is liable for either three month's periodic rent or three times the landlord's actual damages, whichever is greater. Unif. Residential Landlord & Tenant Act § 4.301, 7B U.L.A. 500.

[36] Restatement (Second) of Property: Landlord & Tenant § 14.4 cmt. f (1977).

[37] Bransky v. Schmidt Motor Sales, Inc., 584 N.E.2d 892 (Ill. App. Ct. 1991); Moudry v. Parkos, 349 N.W.2d 387 (Neb. 1984).

[38] *See, e.g.,* Security Life & Accident Ins. Co. v. United States, 357 F.2d 145 (5th Cir. 1966).

[39] *See, e.g.,* Crechale & Polles, Inc. v. Smith, 295 So. 2d 275 (Miss. 1974) (letter from landlord demanding double rent if tenant held over construed as election to treat tenant as trespasser).

payments, normally indicates an intention to bind the tenant to a new tenancy.[40]

§ 15.06 Modern Revolution in Landlord-Tenant Law

[A] A Wave of Change

A tidal wave of change began sweeping over American landlord-tenant law in the 1960s.[41] These reforms were initially sparked by widespread concern over appallingly poor housing conditions. Common problems included leaky roofs, lack of heat, vermin infestations, lack of electricity, lead-based paint, nonfunctional toilets, and nonlocking doors. Social activists from the civil rights movement, the consumer movement, and even the anti-war effort united in a drive to provide adequate housing for the low-income tenant.

Three factors contributed to the nation's deteriorating housing. The housing codes and similar statutes intended to protect the residential tenant from health and safety risks were often ineffective due to weak enforcement. Further, because affordable rental housing was in short supply in many urban areas, the landlord had little market incentive to maintain the rental property in habitable condition. Finally, the traditional body of landlord-tenant law imposed no general repair duty on the landlord.

Over two decades—from roughly the late 1960s to the mid-1980s—the central doctrines of American landlord-tenant law were reevaluated and modernized by courts and legislatures. One prominent legal scholar quite correctly characterizes this process as a "revolution."[42] Although initially focused on housing conditions, the modernization effort soon expanded to encompass other concerns. Many traditional rules were overturned; others were substantially altered; a few remained untouched. The overall direction of the effort was clear: the rights of residential tenants were dramatically expanded.

The courts spearheaded this reform effort in most jurisdictions by developing case law that viewed the lease as a contract; they then applied contract law doctrines that afforded the tenant more protection than parallel property law rules.[43] Two related developments—the issuance of the Uniform Residential Landlord and Tenant Act ("URLTA") in 1972 and the Restatement (Second) of Property: Landlord and Tenant in 1977—further

---

[40] *But see* Crechale & Polles, Inc. v. Smith, 295 So. 2d 275 (Miss. 1974) (where landlord's letter manifested intent to treat holdover tenant as trespasser, landlord's later acceptance of rent created an entirely new periodic tenancy, not a tenancy based on the holdover tenant doctrine).

[41] *See generally* Mary A. Glendon, *The Transformation of American Landlord-Tenant Law,* 23 B.C. L. Rev. 503 (1982); Edward H. Rabin, *The Revolution in Residential Landlord-Tenant Law: Causes and Consequences,* 69 Cornell L. Rev. 517 (1984).

[42] Edward H. Rabin, *The Revolution in Residential Landlord-Tenant Law: Causes and Consequences,* 69 Cornell L. Rev. 517 (1984).

[43] *See* Javins v. First Nat'l Realty Corp., 428 F.2d 1071 (D.C. Cir. 1970).

accelerated the process. Roughly one-third of the states adopted the pro-tenant URLTA outright; others enacted reform legislation to modernize their laws, typically by endorsing and expanding the judicial effort.

[B] The New Paradigm Tenant: Poor Urban Resident

Long before the 1960s, the typical lease in the United States involved a residential tenancy. The traditional landlord-tenant rules—originally designed to govern the medieval farming lease—were ill-suited to the residential lease. The stage was set for a realignment of the respective duties of the landlord and tenant. As courts and legislatures began to craft a new approach in the 1960s, they were heavily affected by the identity and characteristics of the tenant most in need of assistance: the poor urban resident. Although clearly oversimplistic, this model continues to influence the evolution of the law.

The paradigm modern tenant is a poor, unsophisticated urban resident—usually a woman— whose dominant goal is shelter, not farm land.[44] Thus, her principal interest is in the structure on the land, not the soil itself. She seeks a "package of goods and services:"[45] habitable housing that includes adequate heat, light and ventilation, secure windows and doors, working plumbing facilities, proper sanitation, and proper maintenance. Unlike the medieval farmer, she lacks the skill necessary to repair defects in the prem-ises. Further, given the complexities of multi-unit buildings, she may lack the access necessary to fix defects; for example, while the medieval tenant might easily fix the fireplace in his simple hut, the modern tenant has no right of access to the central heating system of a 100-unit apartment complex. The paradigm tenant is unable to protect her interests by negotiat-ing an acceptable lease with her landlord because affordable rental housing is in short supply in many urban areas. Thus, the prospective tenant is typically presented with a "take-it-or-leave-it" form lease that waives any protection the law might ordinarily offer; and the continuing tenant is forced to tolerate substandard housing simply because no better housing is available on the market. Finally, the modern tenant is much more mobile than her medieval counterpart, and thus in need of greater protection.

The landlord in this scenario is a slumlord, who owns many apartment buildings in deplorable condition. His strategy is to "milk" his units by charging rents as high as the market will bear, while spending little or no money on repair and maintenance of his buildings.[46] The landlord ignores virtually all tenant complaints. Although he may sometimes promise to make repairs, the promise is rarely fulfilled. Even though his buildings will deteriorate in the long run, he receives a high short-term return on his investment.

---

[44] *See, e.g.,* Javins v. First Nat'l Realty Corp., 428 F.2d 1071 (D.C. Cir. 1970) (discussing characteristics of modern residential tenant).

[45] Javins v. First Nat'l Realty Corp., 428 F.2d 1071, 1074 (D.C. Cir. 1970).

[46] *See generally* Duncan Kennedy, *The Effect of the Warranty of Habitability on Low Income Housing: "Milking" and Class Violence,* 15 Fla. St. U. L. Rev. 485 (1987).

The impact of this new paradigm was profound. Courts and legislatures abandoned or drastically revised long-settled rules in order to accommodate the needs of the powerless low-income urban resident confronting the heartless slumlord. One can criticize this effort as overinclusive. Many residential landlord-tenant relationships differ sharply from this simple model. For example, the tenant might be sophisticated or wealthy; the landlord might be an elderly widow acting in good faith; or there might be a local surplus of affordable housing. In this sense, the new reforms undoubtedly benefit some tenants who need no special protection.

[C] The Lease in Transition: Conveyance, Contract, or Both?

Modern law reflects a clear trend toward treating the residential lease as a contract, not the conveyance of an estate in land.[47] As the District of Columbia Circuit concluded in the landmark decision of *Javins v. First National Realty Corp.*, "leases of urban dwelling units should be interpreted and construed like any other contract."[48]

The judicial rationale for using contract law to define the respective rights of landlords and tenants has two basic prongs. First, courts emphasize that the contract approach honors the legitimate expectations of the parties.[49] While the feudal lease was short and skeletal—like a conveyance—the modern residential lease appears to the average person to be a bilateral contract; it contains detailed covenants addressing a multitude of issues. Reasonable landlords and tenants should expect the lease to be governed by contract law, like any other contract.

Second, courts explain that the application of traditional property law rules to residential leases produces results that are inconsistent with contemporary values and standards.[50] Property law fails to accommodate the fundamental needs of the new paradigm tenant—the low-income urban resident. Under this view, the application of contract law principles is necessary to reform landlord-tenant law in light of modern conditions.

This judicial reappraisal of the lease has produced important consequences. Viewed as a conveyance, the lease is a one-time event; it imposes virtually no duty on the landlord. But once the lease is seen in contract terms, it is logical to treat the landlord-tenant relationship as one that imposes continuing duties on both parties. Moreover, while many property law doctrines still reflect the rigidity of medieval England, modern contract law has increasingly incorporated equitable principles. Under the modern approach to residential leases, for example:

---

[47] *See generally* Edward Chase & E. Hunter Taylor, Jr., *Landlord and Tenant: A Study in Property and Contract*, 30 Vill. L. Rev. 571 (1985); John F. Hicks, *The Contractual Nature of Real Property Leases*, 24 Baylor L. Rev. 443 (1972); Robert H. Kelley, *Any Reports of the Death of the Property Law Paradigm for Leases Have Been Greatly Exaggerated*, 41 Wayne L. Rev. 1563 (1995).

[48] 428 F.2d 1071, 1075 (D.C. Cir. 1970).

[49] *See, e.g.,* Teodori v. Warner, 415 A.2d 31 (Pa. 1980).

[50] Javins v. First Nat'l Realty Corp., 428 F.2d 1071 (D.C. Cir. 1970).

(1) the landlord is obligated to maintain the premises in habitable condition;[51]

(2) the tenant has no obligation to pay rent if structures crucial to the lease are destroyed;[52]

(3) the tenant may terminate the lease and stop paying rent if the landlord materially breaches any lease obligations;[53] and

(4) the landlord may be obligated to mitigate damages if the tenant abandons the premises.[54]

Is the modern residential lease a contract or a conveyance? Probably the best answer is "both." The nature of the residential lease is in transition. For some purposes (e.g., repair duty), courts tend to treat it as a contract; for other purposes (e.g., classification of estates), the property approach still lingers. The overall direction of the law's evolution is clear—the contract approach is gradually predominating—but the pace of reform varies from state to state. Even within a state, this piecemeal approach sometimes results in conflicting decisions. The bold assertion of the *Javins* court that residential leases should be interpreted and construed "like any other contract" remains an aspiration, not a reality.

In contrast, the commercial lease remains largely unaffected by the "landlord-tenant revolution." Most courts reason that the commercial tenant—like the medieval farmer—is sufficiently able to protect its own interests through the bargaining process.[55] This category of lease is still generally seen as a conveyance, governed by pro-landlord property rules. Yet the modern reform movement has produced a slight echo even here. There is a small but discernable trend toward revising some of the traditional rules to provide enhanced protection for the small-scale commercial tenant.

---

[51] Restatement (Second) of Property: Landlord & Tenant §§ 5.1–5.5 (1977).

[52] *See* Unif. Residential Landlord & Tenant Act § 4.106, 7B U.L.A. 487.

[53] Restatement (Second) of Property: Landlord & Tenant § 7.1 (1977).

[54] *See* Unif. Residential Landlord & Tenant Act § 4.203(c), 7B U.L.A. 495–496.

[55] *See, e.g.,* Lee v. Placer Title Co., 33 Cal. Rptr. 2d 572 (Ct. App. 1994); Rubin v. Dondysh, 588 N.Y.S.2d 504 (App. Term. 1991).

Chapter 16

CREATION OF THE TENANCY

SYNOPSIS

§ 16.01 The Lease

[A] The Lease in Context

The lease is the heart of the landlord-tenant relationship. It sets forth the agreed-upon terms that will govern the tenancy, including the amount of the rent, the duration of the tenancy, and the location of the leased premises.

Rules of law affect the lease in two basic ways. First, if the parties fail to reach agreement on a particular issue, the law will provide a utilitarian "default rule" to fill the gap. Most of the common law principles in the area were historically oriented toward this gap-filling function. Second, the law will supersede the parties' freedom of contract on particular issues when necessary to fulfill important public policies. Most of the major landlord-tenant developments since the 1960s fall into this latter category.[1]

Is the lease a contract or a conveyance? Modern landlord-tenant law is an evolving compromise between two competing bodies of law: traditional property law concepts and emerging contract law doctrines. At common law, the lease was exclusively seen as a conveyance, subject to property law. In recent decades, the lease has increasingly been viewed as a contract, governed by contract law. Today, the lease continues to be in transition, seen as part conveyance and part contract (*see* § 15.06), and thus subject to both bodies of law.[2]

[B] The Statute of Frauds

Almost all states have a Statute of Frauds that requires that a lease for a term of more than one year must be in writing. This requirement applies primarily to the term of years tenancy. Thus, for example, a lease for a five-year fixed term must be in writing, but an oral lease for a one-year term is enforceable. Suppose T and L enter into an oral month-to-month periodic tenancy, which continues for over a year without either party giving notice

---

[1] *See generally* Mary A. Glendon, *The Transformation of American Landlord-Tenant Law,* 23 B.C. L. Rev. 503 (1982); Edward H. Rabin, *The Revolution in Residential Landlord-Tenant Law: Causes and Consequences,* 69 Cornell L. Rev. 517 (1984).

[2] *See generally* John F. Hicks, *The Contractual Nature of Real Property Leases,* 24 Baylor L. Rev. 443 (1972); Robert H. Kelley, *Any Reports of the Death of the Property Law Paradigm for Leases Have Been Greatly Exaggerated,* 41 Wayne L. Rev. 1563 (1995). *See also* University Club v. Deakin, 106 N.E. 790 (Ill. 1914).

of termination. Is the lease now unenforceable? No, because the initial lease period was only 30 days, not long enough to trigger the Statute; the automatic continuation of the tenancy for more than a year is irrelevant.

To comply with the Statute of Frauds, the writing must set forth the basic lease terms: the parties, a description of the premises, the term, and the rent. The writing must also be signed. Some states only require the signature of the lessor; others demand the signatures of both parties; the largest group of states requires a signature by the party against whom enforcement of the lease is sought.

[C] Distinction Between Residential and Commercial Leases

Courts and legislatures have increasingly distinguished between residential leases and commercial leases. A residential lease is used in renting a home, typically an apartment, condominium, or single-family residence. A commercial lease involves renting property for any nonresidential purpose, such as a retail store, factory, church, or school.

Over the last thirty years, the branch of landlord-tenant law concerning residential leases has evolved quite differently from that governing commercial leases. The legal rights of residential tenants have been dramatically expanded by judicial decisions and statutes (see § 15.06), based in part on the perception that the ordinary tenant is unable to protect his or her interests in lease negotiations due to the superior bargaining power of the landlord. In the 1970s, as now, the typical prospective tenant was given a preprinted lease form on a "take-it-or-leave-it" basis; unsurprisingly, the landlord-drafted form was heavily biased in favor of the landlord. Due to the shortage of rental housing in many urban areas, the tenant was effectively forced to acquiesce to the landlord's terms without any opportunity for meaningful negotiation. Courts and legislatures intervened to redress this imbalance by making major changes in traditional landlord-tenant doctrines affecting residential tenants.

This perceived inequality in bargaining power also led many courts to interpret lease terms in favor of the residential tenant. In his landmark study, Professor Curtis Berger analyzed all residential landlord-tenant decisions reported in New York for a three-year period in the early 1970s.[3] He found that even though the lease forms involved were uniformly "stacked" in favor of the landlord side, landlords lost over 60% of the cases. He attributed this result to judicial "aversion to the standard form lease."[4]

In contrast, the traditional pro-landlord doctrines still largely govern commercial leases, with only slight momentum toward enhanced tenant protection. The law presumes that commercial tenants can adequately protect their interests through negotiation.

---

[3] Curtis J. Berger, *Hard Leases Make Bad Law,* 74 Colum. L. Rev. 791 (1974).

[4] Curtis J. Berger, *Hard Leases Make Bad Law*, 74 Colum. L. Rev. 791, 792 (1974).

§ 16.02 Selection of Tenants

[A] The Common Law Foundation

The common law did not restrict a landlord's freedom in selecting or evicting tenants. A landlord could refuse to rent for any reason or for no reason at all, consistent with an owner's traditional property right to exclude others from the land. Suppose A applied to rent an apartment owned by L. Under this owner-autonomy approach, L could arbitrarily reject A's application (e.g., because A is a woman, is left handed, or likes mystery novels). And, as a logical corollary to this approach, if L chose to rent to A, he could demand discriminatory rental terms (e.g., a $10 per month rent surcharge because A is a woman).

Today federal and state statutes prohibit certain types of discrimination in the rental or sale of real property. Except as supplanted by these statutes, the common law rule continues to apply to the selection of tenants. Thus, landlord L may not refuse to rent to applicant A due to race, gender, religion, national origin, or other discriminatory reasons. But he may still refuse to rent to A for *virtually* any reason (e.g., because A is left handed or likes mystery novels) or no reason at all. Of course, L's lack of a good faith reason for refusing A's application might suggest a discriminatory motive.

[B] Anti-Discrimination Legislation

[1] Fair Housing Act of 1968

[a] General Provisions

The principal federal statute affecting the landlord-tenant relationship is the Fair Housing Act,[5] part of the landmark Civil Rights Act of 1968. It currently[6] bars discrimination based on race,[7] color, religion, sex,[8] familial status,[9] national origin, or handicap[10] in connection with the sale or rental of a "dwelling."[11] Significantly, the Act does not prohibit discrimination based on marital status or sexual orientation.[12]

---

[5] 42 U.S.C. §§ 3601–3619.

[6] Later amendments supplemented the original Act by adding additional categories of proscribed discrimination: sex (1974); and familial status and handicap (1988).

[7] *See, e.g.*, United States v. Starrett City Assoc., 840 F.2d 1096 (2d Cir. 1988); Asbury v. Brougham, 866 F.2d 1276 (10th Cir. 1989); Jancik v. United States Dep't of Hous. & Urban Dev., 44 F.3d 553 (7th Cir. 1995); Huntington Branch, NAACP v. Town of Huntington, 844 F.2d 926 (2d Cir. 1988) (disparate impact).

[8] *See, e.g.*, Grieger v. Sheets, 689 F. Supp. 835 (N.D. Ill. 1988).

[9] *See, e.g.*, Jancik v. United States Dep't of Hous. & Urban Dev., 44 F.3d 553 (7th Cir. 1995); Soules v. United States Dep't of Hous. & Urban Dev., 967 F.2d 817 (2d Cir. 1992); Park Place Home Brokers v. P-K Mobile Home Park, 773 F. Supp. 46 (N.D. Ohio 1991).

[10] *See, e.g.*, Bronk v. Ineichen, 54 F.3d 425 (7th Cir. 1995).

[11] For a discussion of the purposes underlying the Fair Housing Act, see United States v. Starrett City Assocs., 840 F.2d 1096 (2d Cir. 1988).

[12] Some states prohibit discrimination on these bases. *See* § 16.02[B][3].

For example, the following actions violate the Act, if undertaken because of covered discrimination:

(a)   refusing to rent or sell;

(b)   refusing to negotiate for a rental or sale;

(c)   discriminating in the terms, conditions, facilities, or services involved in a rental or sale;

(d)   falsely representing that the property is not available for inspection, rental or sale; and

(e)   publishing any advertisement that indicates any preference or limitation on prospective tenants or buyers. [13]

The definition of "dwelling" extends to most types of housing. But two categories of property are exempted from almost all [14] of the Act: (a) a single-family residence rented or sold without the assistance of a real estate broker or salesperson; and (b) an owner-occupied building with four or less units. [15]

[b]   Proving Discrimination

The Act clearly applies to intentional discrimination. But what if discriminatory *intent* cannot be proven? Most courts agree that a plaintiff can establish a prima facie case under the Act by showing a discriminatory *effect*. The burden then shifts to the defendant to prove a good faith, legitimate reason for the conduct in question, such as a reasonable business purpose. [16] If such a reason is shown, the burden shifts back to the plaintiff to prove that reason was a pretext for discrimination.

There are two basic methods to demonstrate discriminatory effect. Under the *disparate impact* approach, statistical evidence is used to show that a particular defendant's policy or pattern of conduct has a disproportionate impact on persons in a protected category. For example, if landlord L rents to 75% of white applicants, but only 25% of African-American applicants, L's conduct produces a discriminatory effect based on race. Alternatively, the *disparate treatment* approach focuses on how an individual applicant is treated. Suppose L refuses to rent an apartment to A, a qualified African-American applicant, but then rents the same apartment to B, a later white applicant; [17] proof of this disparate treatment shifts the burden to L.

---

[13] 42 U.S.C. § 3604.

[14] The advertising prohibitions discussed above apply to all types of residential property. *See* 42 U.S.C. § 3603(b).

[15] 42 U.S.C. § 3603(b)(1).

[16] A defendant governmental entity (but not a private defendant) must also prove that its goal could not be achieved by a less discriminatory alternative.

[17] "Testers" are often used for this purpose. *See, e.g.,* Soules v. United States Dep't of Hous. & Urban Dev., 967 F.2d 817 (2d Cir. 1992).

[c] Discrimination Against Families with Children

Can a landlord refuse to rent to a family with children? The 1988 amendment which added familial status as a protected category under the Act has produced a wave of litigation. Two representative decisions illustrate how the Act is applied.

In *Soules v. United States Department of Housing and Urban Development*,[18] the Second Circuit upheld an administrative law judge's dismissal of claims under the Act. Plaintiff, mother of a 12-year-old daughter, responded to an ad for a three-bedroom apartment. Upon learning that plaintiff had a child, the rental agent asked the child's age. Plaintiff refused to answer, but asked the reason for the question. The agent replied that the downstairs apartment was occupied by an elderly couple who wanted to ensure that the occupants of the vacant upstairs unit did not make too much noise. The agent, who later testified plaintiff had "a very bad attitude," did not show the apartment to plaintiff, and indeed falsely represented that it was unavailable. The apartment was later rented to a single woman without children under 18.

The judge ruled that plaintiff had established a prima facie case of disparate treatment because: (1) plaintiff tried to rent an apartment for her family, which included a 12-year-old daughter; (2) the rental agent, aware of plaintiff's family status, refused to rent to her; and (3) the apartment was later rented to a person without children. On the other hand, the judge held that the agent had a legitimate business reason for asking the age of plaintiff's child: securing quiet neighbors for the existing tenants. This shifted the burden back to plaintiff to prove that the justification was a mere pretext for discrimination. Plaintiff was unable to meet this standard, largely because the agent had offered the same apartment to another family with children.

Suppose a landlord has a policy of refusing to rent a one-bedroom apartment to more than one person. Would the refusal to rent such an apartment to a mother and her five-year-old child constitute illegal discrimination under the Act? The Eighth Circuit's answer to this question in *United States v. Badgett*[19] was a resounding "yes." Although the one bedroom/one person standard was facially neutral, the court reasoned that it had a disparate impact on children, and thus established a prima facie case of discrimination. The only business justification offered for this policy—the shortage of parking spaces—was unreasonable. No rule prevented a one-bedroom resident from having more than one car; moreover, the policy ignored the reality that most children are legally unable to drive.

[d] Discrimination Based on Handicap

The definition of "handicap" includes a physical or mental impairment that substantially limits one or more of a person's substantial major life

---

[18] 967 F.2d 817 (2d Cir. 1992).

[19] 976 F.2d 1176 (8th Cir. 1992).

activities.[20] A wide range of conditions—including blindness, mental disability, AIDS, paralysis, and alcoholism—are considered handicaps under this standard.[21] A landlord cannot refuse to rent to a handicapped applicant, absent a reasonable business justification.

Perhaps anticipating reasons that some landlords might assert, the Act provides that failure to make "reasonable accommodations in rules, policies, practices, or services" that are "necessary" to allow a handicapped person equal opportunity for housing is also illegal.[22] In *Bronk v. Ineichen*,[23] for example, the Seventh Circuit commented that a deaf tenant's need for a trained "hearing dog" would presumably outweigh the economic and aesthetic concerns underlying the landlord's "no pets" policy, and thus mandate an exception to the policy as a reasonable accommodation.

[2] Civil Rights Act of 1866

The federal Civil Rights Act of 1866 prohibits discrimination based on race in the leasing or sale of any type of property.[24] Originally enacted after the Civil War, this Act was long interpreted as only barring discrimination by public entities. The Supreme Court's 1968 ruling in *Jones v. Alfred H. Mayer Co.*[25] that the Act bars discrimination by private persons as well has dramatically increased its scope.

The Act is broader than the Civil Rights Act of 1968 in one respect: it applies to all types of property, without any special exceptions for single-family homes or owner-occupied property. Conversely, the Act is narrower than the Civil Rights Act of 1968 in that it applies only to one type of discrimination—racial discrimination—and in that it does not cover advertising. In addition, it appears that the 1866 Act only bars intentional discrimination.

[3] State Legislation

State laws often provide enhanced protection against discrimination in residential leasing. Minnesota, California, and many other states, for example, prohibit discrimination based on marital status, which includes the refusal to rent to an unmarried couple.[26] A number of states also ban discrimination based on sexual orientation.[27]

---

[20] 42 U.S.C. § 3602(h).

[21] *See, e.g.*, Association for Advancement of the Mentally Handicapped, Inc. v. City of Elizabeth, 876 F. Supp. 614 (D.N.J. 1994) (zoning ordinance that restricted location of group homes for developmentally disabled persons was invalid under Fair Housing Act).

[22] 42 U.S.C. § 3604(f)(3)(B).

[23] 54 F.3d 425 (7th Cir. 1995).

[24] 42 U.S.C. § 1982; *see also* City of Memphis v. Greene, 451 U.S. 100 (1981).

[25] 392 U.S. 409 (1968).

[26] Smith v. Fair Employment & Hous. Comm'n, 913 P.2d 909 (Cal. 1996); *cf.* State v. French, 460 N.W.2d 2 (Minn. 1990).

[27] *See, e.g.*, Mass. Gen. Laws Ann. ch. 151B, § 4; *cf.* Poff v. Caro, 549 A.2d 900 (N.J. Super. Ct. Law Div. 1987); Braschi v. Stahl Assocs., 543 N.E.2d 49 (N.Y. 1989).

§ 16.03 Tenant's Duty to Pay Rent

[A] Role of the Lease

The tenant's duty to pay rent is usually governed by lease provisions that specify the amount and manner of payment. While residential leases typically provide for a fixed rent (e.g., $250 per month), many commercial leases provide that some or all rent is based on a percentage of the tenant's sales revenue (e.g., 5% of gross sales). But even absent an express agreement for the payment of rent, a person who possesses land with the owner's permission is generally liable for its fair rental value during occupancy. [28]

Traditionally, the rental amount and other related terms were seen as the product of private negotiation between landlord and tenant, and thus beyond the law's reach. In recent decades, however, some jurisdictions have enacted statutes that limit how much rent a landlord can charge; and many jurisdictions regulate security deposits.

[B] Rent Control

[1] Historical Context

Probably the most controversial product of the landlord-tenant "revolution" was the widespread enactment of local residential rent control ordinances in the 1970s. Rent control had been imposed as an emergency measure during World War I and World War II, but after the early 1950s only New York City retained such controls. During the 1970s, however, cities in California, Connecticut, New Jersey, New York, and elsewhere enacted ordinances that regulated residential rents, and most of these ordinances are still in effect. [29] Approximately 10% of all rental housing in the nation is now subject to rent control. Aside from a few isolated instances, rent control does not affect commercial properties. [30]

Most scholars explain these new rent control ordinances as a reaction to rent increases caused by inflationary pressures and housing shortages during the late 1960s and early 1970s. [31] As inflation diminished the real value of fixed rents, landlords significantly increased rents to stay even. Suppose landlord L charges $200 per month for an apartment, and the inflation rate is 10% per year; in order to receive the same effective return in the next year, L would have to compensate for inflation by raising rents by $20, to $220 per month. Another factor was the shortage of rental housing in many urban areas, which facilitated rent increases. Many urban

---

[28] *See, e.g.,* Unif. Residential Landlord & Tenant Act § 1.401(b), 7B U.L.A. 447.

[29] Indeed, the federal government imposed limited residential rent control from August 15, 1971 to January 12, 1973. The end of these restrictions increased pressure for local rent control ordinances.

[30] John J. Powers, Note, *New York Debates Commercial Rent Control: Designer Ice Cream Stores Versus the Corner Grocer,* 15 Fordham Urb. L.J. 657 (1987).

[31] *See, e.g.,* Edward H. Rabin, *The Revolution in Landlord-Tenant Law: Causes and Consequences,* 69 Cornell L. Rev. 517 (1984).

tenants—particularly those on fixed incomes—simply could not afford to pay increased rents. Some were evicted; others faced the threat of eviction. A tide of public outrage arose, fueled by well-publicized anecdotes of exorbitant rent increases, which contributed to the enactment of rent control ordinances.

[2] Provisions of Typical Ordinance

[a] Base Rent

Rent control ordinances vary widely in detail, but share a common core of relatively standard provisions. The typical ordinance establishes a *base rent* for each unit, usually the rent charged for the unit on a specified date before the ordinance was enacted (e.g., six months before passage). This rollback is intended to nullify any rent increases made in anticipation of future rent control.

[b] Rent Increases

Starting from this base rent, two types of rent increases are generally permitted: *automatic increases* for all units and *discretionary increases* for individual units. A typical ordinance automatically permits the landlord to charge an annual percentage increase in rent, usually tied to the rate of inflation as measured by the federal Consumer Price Index. In addition, the ordinance usually creates a rent control board or other administrative body that may allow a discretionary increase for a particular unit in response to a landlord's application, considering factors such as increases in operating and maintenance costs, landlord hardship, and the constitutional right to a reasonable rate of return. Similarly, the tenant can normally petition the board for a rent decrease based on discretionary factors (e.g., if the landlord decreases services). For example, suppose rent control is newly enacted in landlord L's city. The current monthly rent for L's Apartment 26 is $350, up from $300 two months earlier. Under the rollback provision, the new base rent for Apartment 26 is $300. One year later, L may raise the rent by the automatic 3% increase (the annual Consumer Price Index increase permitted by the ordinance) to $309. L may also apply to the local rent control board for a discretionary increase beyond this amount.

[c] Exemptions

The typical ordinance exempts some rental units. Units constructed after the ordinance are usually not subject to rent control. Some ordinances also exempt higher-priced or "luxury" units. Small owner-occupied buildings (e.g., 2–4 units) may also be excluded.

Perhaps the most important exemption frequently encountered is *vacancy decontrol*. Rent control ends when the tenant vacates the unit, so the landlord may charge the new tenant any price the market will bear. Once the new tenant takes possession, the rent control ordinance reattaches to the unit, and the agreed rent becomes the new base rent for computation of future increases.

[d] Eviction Control

An unscrupulous landlord might profit from evicting a tenant in a rent-controlled apartment. If the ordinance allows vacancy decontrol, the landlord could raise the rent to the market level. Even absent vacancy decontrol, a landlord might try to replace the existing tenant with a new tenant. The new tenant might be willing to pay an illegally high monthly rent or an initial "under the table" payment simply for being allowed to occupy the apartment. Or the new tenant might not be sophisticated enough to realize that the landlord is charging an illegally high rent.

To combat these potential abuses, the typical ordinance allows the landlord to evict only for a good faith reason, such as nonpayment of rent, serious tenant misbehavior, or the landlord's desire to reside in the unit.[32] The ordinance supersedes the parties' agreement about the duration of the lease. Suppose L and T enter into a periodic, month-to-month lease for Apartment 26. Once the ordinance is passed, T may still terminate the tenancy upon 30-days notice to L, but L can evict T only for good cause.

[e] Condominium Conversion Control

Alternatively, a landlord might seek to avoid rent control by converting the building into a condominium project, and selling individual units to home buyers.[33] Many states and cities restrict this process in order to preserve rental housing units by banning conversion, limiting the rate of conversion, or giving existing tenants preferential treatment in the event of sale (e.g., right of first refusal to purchase the unit).

[3] Policy Perspectives on Rent Control

[a] Is Rent Control Good Policy?

The question has generated vociferous debate among legal scholars, primarily at the level of broad theory. Surprisingly, the empirical evidence about the effects of rent control is both sparse and inconclusive. Rent control ordinances presumably restrict rent increases for residential tenants, but at what cost?

[b] Arguments Against Rent Control

The principal arguments against rent control are rooted in efficiency.[34] American economists generally agree in theory that rent control reduces

---

[32] *See, e.g.*, Braschi v. Stahl Assocs., 543 N.E.2d 49 (N.Y. 1989) (gay partner of decedent tenant could qualify as "family member," thus entitled to protection from eviction after tenant's death).

[33] Similarly, some ordinances also restrict the landlord's ability to convert his property to another use or to demolish the building.

[34] *See, e.g.*, Richard A. Epstein, *Rent Control and the Theory of Efficient Regulation*, 54 Brook. L. Rev. 741 (1988).

the quantity and quality of available housing.[35] They argue that as permissible rents fall below market levels, landlords seek to convert rental housing stock into owner-occupancy (e.g., condominiums, tenancy-in-common buildings, or cooperatives) or non-residential uses; further, investors tend to refrain from building new rental units due to fear of future rent control.[36] Under this view, the quality of housing also suffers because landlords tend to reduce maintenance expenditures and forego improvements. Even as the supply of quality rental housing falls, demand will increase (because lower rents allow more people to afford housing), exacerbating the housing shortage.

Moreover, even assuming that reducing rents for needy tenants is a desirable policy goal, many critics suggest that rent control is an inefficient subsidy mechanism. One scholar observes that empirical studies of mature rent control ordinances consistently find that "their benefits to tenants are much less than their costs to landlords,"[37] largely because they give current tenants an incentive to "overconsume" housing. For example, a New York City couple moving to the suburbs might retain an apartment for weekend use only because the rent-controlled price is so low. Further, the benefits of rent control are not targeted toward poor tenants; instead, middle and upper income tenants "receive the bulk of the benefits in the years immediately after the imposition of controls."[38] Another dimension concerns the impact of rent control on future tenants. Faced with multiple applicants for each unit, landlords will tend to select the affluent over the poor, in order to minimize the risk of default, thus further reducing housing opportunities for the poor. Would a cash payment directly to low-income tenants be a more efficient mechanism?

Another layer of opposition stems from libertarian theory. Government does not normally regulate the prices of consumer goods and services (e.g., food, medical care, clothing), absent emergency conditions. Some theorists, viewing rent control as a pure redistribution of income from landlords to tenants, ask why the property rights of landlords should be infringed in order to aid tenants.

[c] Arguments for Rent Control

Advocates of rent control assert that the "gloom and doom" predictions of theoretical economists about the supposed effects of rent control on housing quantity and quality are unsupported by convincing evidence. Their policy arguments in favor of rent control are mainly based on nonutilitarian grounds.

Supporters generally view rent control as a device to prevent excessive and unreasonable rents which would force existing poor tenants from their

---

[35] *See generally* Anthony Downs, Residential Rent Controls: An Evaluation (1988); Edgar O. Olsen, *Is Rent Control Good Social Policy?*, 67 Chi.-Kent L. Rev. 931 (1991).

[36] *See, e.g.*, Chicago Board of Realtors, Inc. v. City of Chicago, 819 F.2d 732 (7th Cir. 1987) (Posner, J., concurring).

[37] Edgar O. Olsen, *Is Rent Control Good Social Policy?*, 67 Chi.-Kent L. Rev. 931, 941 (1991).

[38] Edgar O. Olsen, *Is Rent Control Good Social Policy?*, 67 Chi.-Kent L. Rev. 931, 939 (1991).

homes. They argue that local housing shortages caused by governmental land use regulations and other factors have artificially inflated rent levels, permitting landlords to receive an exorbitant return. Under this view, rent control protects the needy tenant from the greedy landlord: the tenant pays a reasonable rent, while the landlord receives a reduced—but just—return.

Professor Margaret Radin, for example, defends residential rent control from the perspective of "personhood theory:"[39] it allows existing tenants to remain in their homes. She suggests that a tenant's right to remain is a form of "personal" property, that is, one inextricably intertwined with the tenant's identity as a person. Accordingly, it merits greater legal protection than an "ordinary market commodity." If this premise is adopted, then by definition a landlord has no right to insist on receiving fair market value, but must accept a below market return. Radin also justifies rent control under communitarian theory: by curbing the eviction of low-income tenants in general, rent control helps to preserve neighborhoods and communities.

[4] Constitutional Limits on Rent Control

[a] Is Rent Control Constitutional?

Rent control ordinances have been attacked under a variety of constitutional theories, in most instances without success.

[b] Substantive Due Process and Equal Protection

One line of decisions involves attacks based on substantive due process and equal protection under the Fourteenth Amendment. In *Pennell v. City of San Jose*,[40] the Supreme Court confirmed that rent control ordinances are subject to the same deferential standard of review traditionally accorded to economic legislation. Thus, a rent control ordinance will be upheld as long as it is rationally related to a legitimate governmental purpose.

This test is easily satisfied by virtually every rent control ordinance.[41] In *Pennell*, for example, the landlord challenged the San Jose rent control ordinance, which provided that "hardship" to the tenant[42] could be considered along with six other factors in determining the amount of an appropriate rent increase. The landlord argued that this provision served no purpose other than to transfer his property to poor tenants. The Court rejected this contention, observing that a legitimate and rational goal of rent control is "the protection of consumer welfare." Thus, protecting tenants from "burdensome rent increases"—the core concept underlying rent control—is a legitimate governmental purpose.

---

[39] Margaret J. Radin, *Residential Rent Control*, 15 Phil. & Pub. Aff. 350 (1986); *see also* John Cirace, *Housing Market Instability and Rent Stabilization*, 54 Brook. L. Rev. 1275 (1989).

[40] 485 U.S. 1 (1988).

[41] What if a rent control ordinance were enacted solely to alleviate an existing shortage of rental housing, but in fact exacerbated the shortage? Although the purpose would be legitimate, the ordinance might be deemed unconstitutional because it undercuts this purpose.

[42] The ordinance defined a "hardship" tenant to include a family of four with annual income up to $32,400.

[c] Regulatory Taking

A second decisional strand attacks rent control as a regulatory taking, in violation of the Fifth Amendment mandate that private property not be taken for public use without "just compensation." As the Supreme Court noted in *Pennell*, rent control per se is not a regulatory taking. Thus, even if a rent control ordinance significantly reduces a landlord's income, this is not considered a "taking" of property. At some point, a rent control ordinance might reduce the landlord's return to the point of denying "all economically beneficial or productive use" of the land, thus triggering the Court's regulatory takings threshold test as set forth in *Lucas v. South Carolina Coastal Council.*[43]

The *Pennell* majority refused to decide whether the San Jose "hardship" tenant provision violated the Takings Clause, explaining that the issue was premature because there was no evidence that the provision had ever been relied on to reduce an otherwise allowable rent increase. Dissenting, Justice Scalia would have found a regulatory taking. He argued that once a "reasonable" rent is established through use of the first six factors in the ordinance, the landlord could no longer be considered the cause of exorbitantly priced housing. Thus, to force the landlord to bear the burden of tenant poverty by further reducing rents would unfairly single out the landlord to solve a problem that should be borne by society at large. Just as a grocer cannot be required to sell food to the poor at a discount, in Scalia's view a landlord should not be required to reduce rent for needy tenants.

[C] Security Deposits

The security deposit is a standard component of the residential lease, innocuous in purpose but often abused in practice. When landlord L entrusts possession of his apartment unit to new tenant T, he confronts the possibility that T might someday vacate without notice, leaving the unit dirty and damaged and the rent unpaid. Thus, before the lease term begins, L will require T to pay a sum of money (usually equal to one or two month's rent) as security against these risks. In theory, the security deposit will be returned to T when the tenancy ends, if all rent is paid and the unit is clean and undamaged.

During the early 1970s, it became clear that some landlords were wrongfully and routinely refusing to return security deposits to former tenants. Tenants had no effective remedy to curtail this practice, since the amounts involved were typically too small to merit litigation.

In this atmosphere, over two-thirds of the states ultimately enacted statutes regulating residential security deposits. The primary goal of these statutes is to help the innocent tenant recover the deposit without litigation. Under a typical statute:

---

[43] 505 U.S. 1003 (1992). For a discussion of *Lucas*, see § 40.07.

(1)   the amount of the security deposit is limited;

(2)   the landlord must place the deposit in a trust account, without commingling, and pay interest on the deposit;

(3)   the types of permissible deductions from the deposit are specified (e.g., no deduction for ordinary "wear and tear");

(4)   the landlord must provide the tenant with a detailed list of any appropriate deductions from the deposit and refund the balance of the deposit within a fixed time period (e.g., two weeks) after the lease term ends; and

(5)   a statutory penalty (e.g., twice the amount wrongfully withheld) is imposed on the landlord for any violation.[44]

Such statues are viewed as remedial legislation intended to protect tenants' rights; accordingly, ambiguities in the statutory language are usually interpreted in the tenant's favor.[45]

The efficacy of these reform statutes is unclear. Almost every residential tenant has a security deposit "horror story" to recount, usually centered around a fact-intensive dispute about either the need for a deduction (e.g., "The carpet didn't need cleaning because I had already cleaned it.") or the extent of the deduction (e.g., "It wasn't necessary to paint the whole apartment just because of two small nail holes in one wall.").

§ 16.04 Landlord's Duty to Deliver Possession

[A]   The Issue

Suppose L leases Greenacre to T for a term of three years, beginning on July 1. T appears on July 1, only to find that Greenacre is occupied by a third party, X. What are T's rights?[46] The answer to this question hinges on X's status.

In all states, the landlord is obligated to deliver the legal right of possession to the tenant when the lease term begins; this obligation stems from an implied covenant in the lease. Thus, if X holds a legal right of possession because he leased Greenacre from L, L has violated his duty to T. L's act of leasing to X breached L's obligation to deliver legal possession to T. T may terminate the lease and recover damages from L.[47]

But what if X is a trespasser or holdover tenant, without any legal right to possession? Is L obligated to deliver physical possession of Greenacre to T or merely the legal right to possession? There is a sharp split of authority on this issue.

---

[44] See, e.g., Unif. Residential Landlord & Tenant Act § 2.101, 7B U.L.A. 453.

[45] See, e.g., Garcia v. Thong, 895 P.2d 226 (N.M. 1995).

[46] See generally Loraine P. O'Keefe, Duty of Landlord to Put Tenant into Possession, 15 Clev.-Marshall L. Rev. 387 (1966); Glen Weissenberger, The Landlord's Duty to Deliver Possession: The Overlooked Reform, 46 U. Cin. L. Rev. 937 (1977).

[47] The same result follows if T is precluded from taking possession because L is still occupying the premises.

[B] The "American" Rule

[1] Legal Right to Possession

Under the so-called "American" rule, the landlord is merely obligated to deliver the legal right to possession to the tenant when the lease term begins, absent a contrary provision in the lease.[48] Thus, the landlord has no duty to oust a trespasser or holdover tenant like X. Under this view, the tenant has no claim against the landlord. The tenant may of course bring suit against X to recover possession and damages. Ironically—given its name—the American rule is now a minority view in the United States.

[2] Policy Rationale

The traditional justifications for the rule reflect the nineteenth-century view that the landlord-tenant relationship is one of equality, an approach with waning relevance for the twenty-first century. One theme is freedom of contract. Courts stress that the landlord has not warranted against the wrongful acts of third parties. Indeed, since the landlord admittedly has no duty to oust a trespasser who takes possession even a day after the lease term begins, as the argument goes, it makes no sense to impose such a duty at the onset. A second theme is that the tenant has the same ability as the landlord—but greater incentive—to bring suit to recover possession.

A somewhat more modern concern is economic waste. Absent the American rule, might a landlord refuse to enter into a new lease until the prior tenant had already moved out? Suppose landlord O leases Blueacre, a residential condominium, to A for a one year term expiring on midnight on December 31. Without the protection of the American rule, O might wait until January 1 before leasing the property to new tenant B. But under normal circumstances a new tenant like B will not be ready to take possession of Blueacre for a month or so, perhaps not until February 1. Thus, Blueacre will remain vacant during January. Under the American rule, O might have been willing to sign a lease in November, allowing B to take possession on January 1. Thus, the American rule arguably facilitates full use of rental housing units and thereby tends to reduce rents.

[C] The "English" Rule

[1] Physical Possession

Today most states follow the confusingly-named "English" rule, which requires the landlord to deliver actual possession of the premises to the tenant when the lease term begins, in addition to the legal right to possession.[49] Under this view, the basis for the landlord's obligation is an implied covenant in the lease that the premises will be vacant when the term commences. Accordingly, under the hypothetical above, when T

---

[48] Hannan v. Dusch, 153 S.E. 824 (Va. 1930).

[49] *See, e.g.*, Adrian v. Rabinowitz, 186 A. 29 (N.J. 1936).

discovers X still in possession of Greenacre on July 1, he may either terminate his lease or recover damages from L.

[2] Policy Rationale

The policies underlying the English rule reflect the contemporary view that the landlord-tenant relationship is fundamentally unequal. As between the two, the landlord is seen as having a superior ability to ensure that the property is vacant when the lease term begins. The landlord is more likely to know whether the old tenant intends to hold over, and only the landlord has the legal right to evict the old tenant before the new lease term begins. In addition, the landlord is in a far better position to offer testimony to rebut any defenses that the holdover tenant might raise. Moreover, particularly where residential leasing is concerned, the landlord is typically both more sophisticated about the eviction process and better able to bear the costs involved.

In addition, the English rule best implements the actual (if unexpressed) intentions of the parties in most instances. The ordinary tenant and landlord presume that the tenant will receive actual possession when the lease term begins, not merely the right to bring a lawsuit.

§ 16.05   Tenant's Duty to Occupy

[A]   General Rule: No Duty to Occupy

Although a tenant has the right to possession, the prevailing American rule is that the tenant has no duty to take possession unless an express lease covenant so requires. Suppose T, a corporation owning a chain of popular gourmet supermarkets, executes a lease for space in L's aging shopping center, agreeing to pay $10,000 per month. Two months before the lease term begins, T discovers a much more desirable location in a new nearby shopping center owned by N, and executes a lease for space there. T is still obligated to pay rent to L. But, under the majority rule, T has no duty to occupy L's premises or operate a store there,[50] even though T's absence will impair the economic health of other stores in L's center that need the customers a popular supermarket would attract. Courts typically reason that the landlord could have protected itself by negotiating an express covenant.

[B]   Exception: Implied Covenant to Operate Business

But there is an exception to the general rule. An implied covenant to operate a business will commonly be found where all or most of the rent is computed as a percentage of the tenant's sales. Suppose that the lease in the gourmet supermarket hypothetical above obligates T to pay 8% of

---

[50] *Cf.* Slater v. Pearle Vision Center, Inc., 546 A.2d 676 (Pa. 1988) (discussing general rule). *But see* Columbia East Assocs. v. Bi-Lo, Inc., 386 S.E.2d 259 (S.C. Ct. App. 1989) (imposing duty to operate on similar facts).

its gross sales as rent to L, without any fixed minimum rent. Presumably both T and L intended that T would operate its store on the site when they agreed to this clause. Most courts would honor this presumed intent by interpreting the lease to find an implied covenant to operate.[51] Otherwise, a tenant could effectively prevent the landlord from receiving any rental income under the lease. However, no such covenant will be implied if a substantial minimum fixed rent is required in addition to percentage rent.[52]

---

[51] *See, e.g.*, College Block v. Atlantic Richfield Co., 254 Cal. Rptr. 179 (Ct. App. 1988).

[52] *See, e.g.*, Piggly Wiggly Southern, Inc. v. Heard, 405 S.E.2d 478 (Ga. 1991) (no covenant where annual base rent was $29,053.60, with percentage rent on sales exceeding $2,000,000 per year). *But see* Mercury Inv. Co. v. F.W. Woolworth Co., 706 P.2d 523 (Okla. 1985).

Chapter 17

CONDITION OF LEASED PREMISES

SYNOPSIS

§ 17.01 "Let the Tenant Beware"?

A defective roof beam in tenant T's rented house collapses, breaking T's arm. What are T's rights under these circumstances? Must landlord L repair the roof? If L refuses to do so, can T terminate the lease and move out, remain in possession without paying rent, or use another remedy? Is L liable in tort for T's broken arm?

The law governing these questions was radically transformed over the last 30 years.[1] At common law, the duty to maintain the condition of leased premises fell almost entirely on the tenant. The motto of the era was *caveat lessee*—let the tenant beware. Thus, if the above events occurred in seventeenth-century England, T probably would have no claim of any kind against L. However, the modern "revolution" in residential landlord-tenant law has swept away much of the common law system. The duty to maintain leased premises increasingly falls on the shoulders of the residential landlord. If this hypothetical were to occur today, T would probably enjoy the following rights: (1) L would be obligated to repair the roof; (2) if L failed to repair the roof after due notice, T could remain in possession and withhold rent, or select other remedies; and (3) L might be liable in negligence for T's personal injury.

What accounts for this dramatic change? The contemporary law governing residential landlords and tenants is a utilitarian response to the problem of substandard housing. During the nineteenth century, the combined forces of urbanization and rapid population growth helped to produce large slum areas in American cities, where housing conditions were both unhealthy and unsafe. This trend worsened as the twentieth century proceeded. The historic *caveat lessee* approach certainly contributed to this deterioration. The landlord had no legal duty to repair leased premises, while the tenant was often unable to make repairs. The 1960s brought new

---

[1] *See generally* Samuel B. Abbott, *Housing Policy, Housing Code, and Tenant Remedies: An Integration*, 56 B.U. L. Rev. 1 (1976); Roger A. Cunningham, *The New Implied and Statutory Warranties of Habitability in Residential Leases: From Contract to Status*, 16 Urb. L. Ann. 3 (1979); Edward H. Rabin, *The Revolution in Residential Landlord-Tenant Law: Causes and Consequences*, 69 Cornell L. Rev. 517 (1984).

societal concerns for the plight of low-income residents trapped in slum housing. Reflecting these concerns, courts—and later, legislatures—began to reevaluate and retool traditional landlord-tenant doctrines. This ongoing process has produced a set of new legal rules, expressly designed to upgrade the quality of rental housing.

Yet this tidal wave of change has had little impact on the law governing commercial leases. The rights and duties of commercial landlords and tenants are still largely governed by the traditional *caveat lessee* standard.

§ 17.02   The Common Law Foundation

[A]   Caveat Lessee

Suppose tenant T leases a farm from landlord L for a ten-year term in medieval England. After moving into the farm cottage, T discovers that the thatched roof contains a leak. Who is obligated to repair the leak? To help answer this question, one might examine the provisions of the T-L lease. There are three basic possibilities: (1) the lease is silent about the duty to repair; (2) it assigns the repair duty to the tenant; or (3) it assigns the repair duty to the landlord. Yet—*regardless of the terms of the lease*—the common law tilted heavily toward imposing the duty to repair on the tenant.

[B]   No Lease Provision on Repairs

In common law England, the lease was seen as a conveyance of land for a defined period, somewhat akin to the modern sale of land: the landlord transferred all of his rights in the land to the tenant for a specified term. Presumably, a prospective tenant could protect himself against defects by carefully inspecting the premises before entering into the lease. Beyond any obligations specified in the lease, the law imposed only two duties on the landlord: (1) to deliver exclusive possession of the land to the tenant; and (2) to refrain from interfering with the tenant's possession during the lease term.[2] Thus, if the lease was silent, the landlord had no obligation to repair the premises. There were a few narrow exceptions to this broad rule (*see* § 17.08[A][2]). For example, the landlord had a duty to repair under a short-term lease of furnished premises;[3] the landlord who fraudulently misrepresented the condition of the premises to the tenant was similarly liable; and the landlord aware of hidden or "latent" defects was obligated to disclose their existence. In general, however, the landlord was entitled to receive rent even if the premises fell into disrepair.

Where the lease contained no provision about repairs, the common law placed the burden squarely on the tenant through the doctrine of *permissive*

---

[2] Thus, the landlord made no warranty that the leased premises were suitable for the lessee's intended use. *See* Anderson Drive-In Theatre, Inc. v. Kirkpatrick, 110 N.E.2d 506 (Ind. Ct. App. 1953).

[3] *See, e.g.,* Ingalls v. Hobbs, 31 N.E. 286 (Mass. 1892) (finding landlord impliedly warranted that furnished house on short-term lease was fit for habitation).

waste. [4] Under this doctrine, a tenant was obligated to exercise reasonable care to protect the leased premises from injury. [5] Each tenant had a duty to effect any minor repairs that were necessary to maintain the condition of the premises. Accordingly, for example, our hypothetical tenant T would be obligated to fix the roof leak; otherwise, the leak might worsen and cause extensive water damage to the cottage. If T failed to make repairs, L could recover damages for the resulting injury to the cottage. On the other hand, the law did not require the tenant to effect major or permanent repairs, nor to remedy ordinary wear and tear. [6]

Commercial tenancies are largely governed by these common law principles, but they have little or no application to modern residential tenancies (*see* § 17.06).

[C] Lease Assigns Repair Duty to Tenant

Alternatively, the lease might expressly assign the repair duty to the tenant. Allocating the repair burden to the agricultural tenant made sense in the common law era. The medieval tenant farmer could easily make minor repairs to his simple dwelling; tenant T, for example, could quickly fix the leak in his thatched roof. Courts routinely enforced these clauses in all leases until the late twentieth century, when the birth of the implied warranty of habitability conferred new protection on the residential tenant (*see* § 17.06).

Commercial leases are still subject to the common law rule. In general, modern courts will enforce a lease provision that assigns the duty to repair to a commercial tenant. [7] Suppose commercial tenant T leases a grocery store building; the lease might obligate T to "maintain the premises in good repair." If the roof leaks, the plumbing fails, or a window breaks, T must undertake repairs.

However, general repair clauses in commercial leases sometimes present difficult questions of interpretation. Suppose that lightning ignites a fire that totally destroys T's building. Does T's duty to *repair* require him to *rebuild* the building? At common law, the tenant's repair covenant included the obligation to rebuild regardless of whether the tenant was at fault in causing the destruction. Today many jurisdictions reject the common law approach of automatic liability, and instead interpret the plain language of the lease in order to ascertain the parties' intent. [8] In most instances,

---

[4] Affirmative or voluntary waste occurs when the voluntary acts of the tenant significantly reduce the market value of the premises. *See* Sparkman v. Hardy, 78 So. 2d 584 (Miss. 1955) (tenant's alterations to premises did not cause permanent injury and thus did not constitute permissive waste); Rumiche Corp. v. Eisenreich, 352 N.E.2d 125 (N.Y. 1976) (same).

[5] *But see* Kennedy v. Kidd, 557 P.2d 467 (Okla. Ct. App. 1976) (holding duty to repair did not require tenant's estate to pay injuries to apartment caused by putrid odors from tenant's dead body).

[6] *See generally* Suydam v. Jackson, 54 N.Y. 450 (1873) (discussing common law rule).

[7] *See, e.g.,* Gehrke v. General Theatre Corp., 298 N.W.2d 773 (Neb. 1980).

[8] *See, e.g.,* Amoco Oil Co. v. Jones, 467 N.W.2d 357 (Minn. Ct. App. 1991).

courts conclude that a general repair clause was not intended to cover rebuilding.[9]

Suppose instead that a new city regulation requires that all grocery store buildings be retrofitted to withstand earthquakes. If T's lease requires that he both (a) keep the building in "good repair" and (b) "comply with all applicable statutes, ordinances, and regulations," who bears the burden of upgrading the building? The California Supreme Court addressed this issue in a pair of simultaneous decisions, *Brown v. Green*[10] and *Hadian v. Schwartz*.[11] The court endorsed a case-by-case approach, based on criteria that included the cost of the upgrade in relation to rent, the length of the lease term, which party benefited most from the upgrade, the likelihood that the parties contemplated the application of the particular law involved, and other factors. Under this approach, the court held that the *Brown* tenant was required to pay for the expenses of governmentally-mandated asbestos removal, while the *Hadian* landlord had the burden of paying the costs of governmentally-mandated earthquake retrofitting.

[D] Lease Assigns Repair Duty to Landlord

Even where the lease expressly assigned the repair burden to the landlord, the medieval tenant often had little effective recourse.[12] The common law viewed lease covenants as *independent* of each other, not *dependent* on each other. Even if the landlord breached the covenant to repair, the tenant was still obligated to perform the covenant to pay rent. The tenant's sole remedy was to sue the landlord for damages. The modern contract law concept that covenants are dependent on each other—such that a breach by one party excuses performance by the other party—was recognized only in one situation: actual eviction. If the landlord physically evicted a tenant, this allowed the tenant to terminate the lease and avoid liability for future rent.[13]

For example, suppose the L-T lease above obligated L to repair the cottage roof. L refuses to fix the leak, thus breaching the lease. At common law, this breach did not allow T to terminate the lease or to cease paying rent. T's only recourse was to sue L for damages, while remaining in possession of the farm, enduring the leaky roof, and paying full rent. In many cases, this right was purely illusory; tenants lacked access to attorneys, the money needed to finance litigation, and the willingness to sue.

---

[9] *See, e.g.,* Friedman v. Isenbruck, 244 P.2d 718 (Cal. Ct. App. 1952).

[10] 884 P.2d 55 (Cal. 1994).

[11] 884 P.2d 46 (Cal. 1994).

[12] *See also* Morris v. Durham, 443 S.W.2d 642 (Ky. Ct. App. 1969) (holding that repair clause does not obligate landlord to rebuild premises destroyed by fire).

[13] *Cf.* Smith v. McEnany, 48 N.E. 781 (Mass. 1897) (allowing tenant to suspend rent payments based on partial actual eviction where landlord built wall that occupied part of leased premises); Camatron Sewing Mach., Inc. v. F.M. Ring Assocs., Inc., 582 N.Y.S.2d 396 (App. Div. 1992) (holding landlord's plan to reduce size of leased premises as part of building renovations would constitute partial actual eviction).

Modern law provides more effective remedies when the landlord breaches the repair obligation. Under some circumstances, the doctrine of constructive eviction (*see* § 17.04) allows the commercial or residential tenant to vacate the premises, terminate the lease, and avoid future rent liability. And the implied warranty of habitability (*see* § 17.06) creates additional remedies for the residential tenant.

§ 17.03   The Problem of Substandard Housing

As the twentieth century dawned, the United States was undergoing a dramatic social and economic transformation. The dual pressures of technological change and population growth were molding a rural, agricultural society into an urban, industrial nation. As urbanization accelerated, the flaws in the historic *caveat lessee* approach became increasingly clear. Many urban residential landlords discovered that they could maximize profits by minimizing repairs, and thus refused to accept lease clauses that required them to repair. The common law assumption that residential tenants both could and would fill this vacuum by repairing their own dwellings proved disastrously false. Housing conditions in many urban areas were horrible, threatening the health and safety of residents. Diseases such as cholera, yellow fever, tuberculosis, and later polio were widespread; running water was rare; raw sewage was common; overcrowding was rampant; and filth was ubiquitous. In short, the common law system fostered slums, not decent housing.

During the early twentieth century, some cities responded to this crisis by enacting housing codes. The New York State Tenement House Law of 1901 established a comprehensive regulatory framework to improve the quality of rental housing. This became the model for similar housing codes across the nation. By the 1960s, housing codes were in place in almost all large cities and in thousands of other communities. The typical housing code of the era was a city ordinance that mandated that all dwellings have:

(1)   heat;

(2)   hot and cold water;

(3)   operable plumbing facilities;

(4)   adequate windows and ventilation;

(5)   no infestation of insects, vermin, or rodents;

(6)   safe electrical wiring;

(7)   a watertight roof; and

(8)   other features necessary to provide minimum living standards.

The owner of a dwelling that violated the ordinance could be fined or imprisoned.

Yet housing codes were weakly enforced, and thus ineffective. The system assumed that tenants would report violations, leading to inspection by a city official, and, if warranted, formal proceedings against the landlord. In general, however, tenants were reluctant to complain. A complaint might prompt governmental closure of the building, forcing the tenant to find replacement housing, a difficult task given the shortage of affordable housing in many areas. Alternatively, the landlord might raise the rent to finance required repairs or evict the tenant for complaining. Even if the landlord was successfully prosecuted, penalties were slight. One study calculated that the average fine for a housing code violation in New York City during 1965 was only *fifty cents*, while prison sentences were almost never imposed.[14] For the slumlord, it was cheaper to pay the fine than to repair the defect.

The 1960s brought a new approach to the problem of substandard housing: reforming the common law. Public interest attorneys representing poor urban tenants in litigation began asserting innovative legal arguments designed to overturn centuries of pro-landlord precedent. Efforts to expand the doctrine of constructive eviction (*see* § 17.04) were unavailing. But this campaign encountered temporary success with the birth of the illegal lease doctrine (*see* § 17.05), and final victory with the almost universal adoption of the implied warranty of habitability (*see* § 17.06).

§ 17.04 Constructive Eviction

[A] Nature of Doctrine

Suppose L leases Blueacre, a single-family residence, to T for a 20-year term; in the lease, L expressly agrees to maintain Blueacre "in good repair." A few days after T takes possession, rain leaking through the defective Blueacre roof leaves six inches of water inside the house. T temporarily moves into a motel. L refuses to fix the roof. L is clearly liable to T for breach of lease. But what is T's remedy?

At common law, a tenant like T had only one choice: remain in possession, continue to pay rent, and sue L for damages. The doctrine of *constructive eviction* offers T an alternative remedy. Under current law, a landlord's wrongful conduct that substantially interferes with the tenant's beneficial use and enjoyment of the leased premises is considered a constructive eviction. A tenant like T who has been constructively evicted may vacate the premises, terminate the lease, and be relieved of liability for future rent. Thus, constructive eviction does not impose a new duty on the landlord; rather, it provides the tenant with a new remedy for the landlord's breach of an existing duty.

The recent development of the implied warranty of habitability (*see* § 17.06) has reduced the importance of constructive eviction. Recognized in almost all states, the implied warranty generally offers broader protection for the residential tenant. Thus, absent unusual circumstances, constructive eviction has little application today in residential landlord-tenant disputes. This doctrine is now most commonly utilized in disputes involving commercial leases.

---

[14] Judah Gribetz & Frank D. Grad, *Housing Code Enforcement: Sanctions and Remedies*, 66 Colum. L. Rev. 1254, 1276 (1966).

[B]   Evolution of Doctrine

Early English law recognized that every lease contained an *implied covenant of quiet enjoyment*: a promise that the landlord (and those claiming under him) will not wrongfully interfere with the tenant's possession of the premises. Although the common law generally viewed lease covenants as independent, there was one major exception to this rule. The tenant's duty to pay rent was dependent on the landlord's performance of the covenant of quiet enjoyment. Thus, if a landlord breached the covenant by physically evicting his tenant, the tenant was excused from further rent liability.[15]

Suppose T leases a farm from L and performs all of his lease obligations. However, L wrongfully ejects T from the farm and retakes possession. This *actual* eviction of T breaches the implied covenant of quiet enjoyment in the L-T lease. Accordingly, T is not liable for future rent. The same result follows if T is evicted from the farm by someone claiming a right to possession received through L.

Yet even without physically evicting the tenant, a landlord's conduct might so substantially interfere with the tenant's possession as to constitute an eviction for all practical purposes. Suppose T leases a home from L; L immediately starts a huge bonfire on an adjacent lot, which continues to burn for months. As a result, nauseating smoke and fumes constantly pervade T's rented home, rendering it uninhabitable; after his complaints to L go unanswered, T eventually moves out. Is T liable for future rent? Rather than actual eviction, L's interference here amounts to a *constructive eviction*: L's wrongful conduct has effectively forced T to vacate the premises. Eventually, common law courts recognized that a constructive eviction breached the implied warranty of quiet enjoyment, thus excusing the tenant from payment of future rent.

[C]   Elements of Constructive Eviction

[1]   Overview

In general, constructive eviction occurs when wrongful conduct of the landlord substantially interferes with the tenant's use and enjoyment of the leased premises. Two key issues arise: (1) what is "wrongful conduct" by the landlord? and (2) what conduct "substantially interferes" with the tenant's use and enjoyment?

[2]   "Wrongful Conduct" of the Landlord

[a]   Acts and Omissions of Landlord

Almost any affirmative *act* by the landlord that seriously interferes with the tenant's enjoyment of the premises may meet this requirement. For

---

[15] *Cf.* Camatron Sewing Mach., Inc. v F.M. Ring Assocs., Inc., 582 N.Y.S.2d 396 (App. Div. 1992) (declaring that landlords' plan to occupy 46.5 square feet of tenant's premises would constitute a partial actual eviction).

instance, the early case of *Dyett v. Pendleton* [16] found constructive eviction where the landlord regularly brought "lewd women and prostitutes" into his home, causing such "noise and riotous proceedings" at night that the tenant who rented rooms there was forced to vacate. [17] Similarly, the landlord who engages in loud construction activities, repeatedly trespasses on the leased premises, or commits a nuisance may also trigger the doctrine.

The more troublesome issue is defining when the landlord's *failure to act* constitutes wrongful conduct. In general, an omission is deemed wrongful only when the landlord is under a duty to act. In most cases, the landlord's duty arises from an express clause in the lease, typically a provision that requires the landlord to repair the premises or to supply heat, water, and other utilities. [18] Suppose L leases an apartment unit to T for a five-year term; among other things, the lease obligates L to maintain the premises in good repair and to provide hot water. After taking possession, T learns that the apartment roof leaks badly, and only cold water is available. L's failure to comply with his lease obligations allows T to assert constructive eviction.

A wrongful omission also occurs when the landlord fails to comply with (1) a statutory duty concerning the leased premises (e.g., a statutory duty to provide heat) [19] or (2) the limited repair duties traditionally imposed on the common law landlord (e.g., duty to maintain common areas, duty to perform promised repairs) (*see* § 17.08[A][2]).

Beyond this point, the law's definition of actionable omissions is rather hazy. One of the more extreme cases on the issue is *Reste Realty Corp. v. Cooper*, [20] where the New Jersey Supreme Court suggested that "any act or omission of the landlord . . . which renders the premises substantially unsuitable for the purpose for which they are leased, or which seriously interferes with the beneficial enjoyment of the premises" constitutes constructive eviction of the tenant. [21] On the facts of the case, the landlord was clearly obligated by traditional common law principles (e.g., duties regarding common area, promised repairs, and latent defects) to remedy the defective condition, so the court's statement was dicta. [22] Yet it neatly frames the larger question: should *all* acts or omissions of the landlord that

---

[16] 8 Cow. 727 (N.Y. 1826).

[17] *See also* Phyfe v. Dale, 130 N.Y.S. 231 (App. Term. 1911) (finding constructive eviction on facts similar to *Dyett*).

[18] *Cf.* Automobile Supply Co. v. Scene-In-Action Corp., 172 N.E. 35 (Ill. 1930) (suggesting that landlord's breach of lease obligation to supply heat to rented office would constitute constructive eviction).

[19] *See* Unif. Residential Landlord & Tenant Act § 4.104, 7B U.L.A. 483 (providing constructive eviction remedy if, for example, landlord fails to provide heat, running water, hot water, or essential services).

[20] 251 A.2d 268 (N.J. 1969).

[21] Reste Realty Corp. v. Cooper, 251 A.2d 268, 274 (N.J. 1969).

[22] *See also* Petroleum Collections Inc. v. Swords, 122 Cal. Rptr. 114 (Ct. App. 1975) (observing that "any act or omission on the part of the landlord . . . which interferes with a tenant's right to use and enjoy the premises for the purposes contemplated by the tenancy" breaches the covenant of quiet enjoyment).

substantially interfere with the tenant's quiet enjoyment be deemed constructive eviction?

[b] Conduct of Third Parties

L leases an apartment to T1, and another to T2; the form lease used on each occasion provides that L may terminate the tenancy if the tenant "repeatedly causes loud noises that disturb other tenants." T2 routinely plays her stereo at maximum volume for several hours during the early morning when other tenants are trying to sleep; T1 complains to L, who takes no action. Has T1 been constructively evicted?

Under traditional law, the landlord is not responsible for the conduct of third parties that interferes with the tenant's quiet enjoyment, unless the landlord causes or consents to such conduct. Although there is still a split of authority on the point, the modern trend is to charge the landlord with responsibility if the landlord has the legal right to control the third party's conduct.[23] For example, in *Blackett v. Olanoff*[24] the Massachusetts Supreme Court found a constructive eviction on facts similar to those in the above hypothetical. Even though the offending tenant's conduct violated a noise limitation specified in the lease, the landlords took no action to enforce this provision. The court stressed that the landlords "had it within their control to correct the condition which caused the tenants to vacate their apartments."[25]

Suppose T leases retail space in L's shopping center to operate a fur salon which sells mink coats and similar products. Every weekend, animal rights activists enter the shopping center and stand on the parking lot in front of T's salon shouting anti-fur slogans; this conduct deters potential customers. If L ignores T's complaints, a constructive eviction may result under the modern rule. As the owner of the parking lot, L presumably has the legal right to control the conduct of the trespassing activists, even though they are not tenants; L could file a complaint with the police or initiate a civil action to restrict this behavior.[26]

[3] Conduct That "Substantially Interferes" with the Tenant's Use and Enjoyment of Leased Premises

[a] Defining Substantial Interference

The landlord's conduct must substantially interfere with the tenant's use and enjoyment of the premises. Minor interference (e.g., failure to fix a

---

[23] *See* Restatement (Second) of Property: Landlord & Tenant § 6.1 cmt. d (1977).

[24] 358 N.E.2d 817 (Mass. 1977).

[25] Blackett v. Olanoff, 358 N.E.2d 817, 819 (Mass. 1977). *But see* Louisiana Leasing Co. v. Sokolow, 266 N.Y.S.2d 447 (N.Y. City Civ. Ct. 1966) (rejecting landlord's petition to evict tenants for disturbing other tenants with noise).

[26] *But see* Net Realty Holding Trust v. Nelson, 358 A.2d 365 (Conn. Super. Ct. 1976) (rejecting tenant's constructive eviction claim based on landlord's failure to control trespassers onto tenant's premises in shopping center, where landlord employed adequate security guards to patrol center).

broken window) is insufficient.[27] The conduct must amount to such a major interference that a reasonable person would conclude a rented dwelling is uninhabitable (e.g., due to failure to supply heat to an apartment) or leased commercial premises are unusable for normal business (e.g., due to failure to eradicate rodent infestation in a day-care facility). The interference need not be permanent; nor need it totally prevent the tenant from occupying the premises. However, if the tenant is aware of the landlord's wrongful conduct when taking possession, the right to assert constructive eviction in the future is waived.

Reste Realty Corp. v. Cooper[28] illustrates the application of this standard. Defendant leased the basement floor of an office building for her jewelry firm; the offices were used for meetings and training of sales personnel. Whenever it rained, the offices were flooded by runoff from an adjacent driveway that left up to two inches of water on the floor; on these occasions, the offices could not be used as intended. Despite repeated promises, the landlord never fixed the problem. After another storm flooded the offices with five inches of water, defendant vacated the premises. The successor landlord sued two years later to recover unpaid rent, and defendant claimed constructive eviction. The New Jersey Supreme Court rejected the landlord's argument that permanent interference was required for constructive eviction. Because the flooding occurred "regularly upon rainstorms and is sufficiently serious in extent to amount to a substantial interference with use and enjoyment of the premises for the purpose of the lease, the test for constructive eviction has been met."[29]

[b] Partial Constructive Eviction

Suppose T leases two floors in an office building—the basement and the first floor—to house the executive offices for his grocery store chain. Every time it rains, the basement floor is flooded and hence unusable for its intended purpose. T vacates the basement, but continues to occupy the first floor. Can T claim constructive eviction?

An overwhelming majority of states hold that the tenant who remains in partial possession cannot claim constructive eviction. However, New York and a few other jurisdictions recognize *partial constructive eviction.*[30] Under this approach, when the landlord's wrongful conduct substantially interferes with the tenant's use and enjoyment of *part* of the leased premises, the tenant need only vacate that *part* in order to rely on constructive eviction. Thus, if T's offices are located in New York or a like-minded jurisdiction, T may assert partial constructive eviction.

---

[27] *See* Restatement (Second) of Property: Landlord & Tenant § 6.1 cmt. e (1977).

[28] 251 A.2d 268 (N.J. 1969).

[29] Reste Realty Corp. v. Cooper, 251 A.2d 268, 275 (N.J. 1969).

[30] *See, e.g.,* East Haven Assocs. v. Gurian, 313 N.Y.S.2d 927 (N.Y. City Civ. Ct. 1970) (unusable terrace in apartment); Minjak Co. v. Randolph, 528 N.Y.S.2d 554 (App. Div. 1988) (unusable loft space in apartment). *But see* Barash v. Pennsylvania Terminal Real Estate Corp., 256 N.E.2d 707 (N.Y. 1970) (finding no constructive eviction where landlord failed to supply air conditioning to office building on evenings and weekends).

[D] Remedies

[1] Terminate Lease and Sue for Damages

The tenant who is constructively evicted may vacate the premises and terminate the lease, thereby avoiding liability for future rent. In addition, the tenant may recover compensatory damages from the landlord. The tenant's general damages are equal to the amount by which the fair rental value of the premises exceeds the lease rent. Special damages (e.g., moving expenses, loss of fixtures) may also be available.

In order to use this remedy, the tenant must first take three steps:

(1) provide the landlord with notice of the interfering defect or condition;

(2) allow a reasonable period of time for the landlord to cure the problem; and

(3) vacate the premises within a reasonable period of time.[31]

There is an obvious tension between the second and third requirements. If the tenant waits too long for the landlord to fix the problem, this may constitute a waiver of the tenant's right to assert constructive eviction. Whether a particular delay is reasonable is a question of fact that turns on the circumstances of the individual case.[32] In most instances, a delay of three to four weeks is considered reasonable.

[2] Remain in Possession and Sue for Damages

Most jurisdictions allow the tenant to select an alternative remedy when the landlord breaches the implied covenant of quiet enjoyment: affirm the lease, remain in possession, and sue the landlord for damages.

[E] Limitations of Constructive Eviction Doctrine

As a practical matter, the constructive eviction doctrine provides little protection for the residential tenant in a tight housing market. Assume T is a periodic tenant in an urban area where housing is in short supply; L breaches her lease obligations to T by routinely failing to provide adequate heat. T regularly notifies L about the lack of heat, but the problem continues. In theory, T can now assert constructive eviction, terminate the lease, and vacate the apartment. But if T cannot find replacement housing, this remedy is illusory.

---

[31] *But see* Restatement (Second) of Property: Landlord & Tenant § 6.1 (1977) (providing that tenant can assert constructive eviction without vacating the premises).

[32] *Compare* Automobile Supply Co. v. Scene-In-Action Corp., 172 N.E. 35 (Ill. 1930) (holding tenant waived right by vacating three weeks after landlord failed to supply heat to rented office), *with* Reste Realty Corp. v. Cooper, 251 A.2d 268 (N.J. 1969) (finding no waiver where tenant vacated rented office nine months after landlord failed to fix flooding problem).

§ 17.05 Illegal Lease Doctrine

The landlord-tenant revolution of the 1960s produced innovative doctrines that began to erode the traditional approach to housing conditions. The illegal lease doctrine—announced in *Brown v. Southall Realty Co.* [33] in 1968—was the first step in this new direction. Although initially adopted by a number of states, the doctrine was soon supplanted by the implied warranty of habitability (*see* § 17.06).

Under the illegal lease doctrine, a lease of unsafe and unsanitary premises that violate the local housing code is deemed an illegal—and thus unenforceable—contract. The tenant can accordingly withhold rent and assert the illegality of the lease as a defense to the landlord's eventual eviction action based on nonpayment. Ultimately, the landlord may recover only the reasonable rental value of the premises in their defective condition.

The virtue of the illegal lease doctrine from the tenant's standpoint was simplicity: the tenant could simply withhold rent, without vacating the premises or bringing suit. However, three factors impaired the effectiveness of the doctrine. First, it generally applied only to defects existing when the tenancy began, not to defects developing later. Second, in many instances, the landlord was able to recover the entire rental balance because the agreed-upon rent already reflected the rental value of the premises in their defective condition; this provided landlords with little incentive to effect repairs. Finally, the landlord could retaliate by terminating the tenancy of any periodic tenant who withheld rent.

§ 17.06 The Implied Warranty of Habitability: New Common Law

[A] Nature of Implied Warranty

The implied warranty of habitability is undoubtedly the most important reform produced by the landlord-tenant revolution. [34] It effectively assigns the burden of repairing residential premises [35] to the landlord as a matter of law *regardless of the provisions of the lease.* Under this doctrine, each residential lease is deemed to contain an implied warranty that the landlord will deliver the premises in habitable condition, and maintain them in that condition during the lease term. If the landlord breaches the warranty, the tenant may choose one of several remedies, including the option of

---

[33] 237 A.2d 834 (D.C. 1968).

[34] *See generally* Roger A. Cunningham, *The New Implied and Statutory Warranties of Habitability in Residential Leases: From Contract to Status*, 16 Urb. L. Ann. 3 (1979); Charles J. Meyers, *The Covenant of Habitability and the American Law Institute*, 27 Stan. L. Rev. 879 (1975).

[35] Decisions in a few states extend the implied warranty of habitability to commercial property. *See, e.g.,* Davidow v. Inwood N. Prof'l Group—Phase I, 747 S.W.2d 373 (Tex. 1988); *cf.* Vermes v. American Dist. Tel. Co., 251 N.W.2d 101 (Minn. 1977) (holding landlord had duty to inform tenant of facts that might make premises unsuitable for tenant's proposed commercial use).

remaining in the premises and withholding rent until the defect is fixed. In most jurisdictions, the warranty cannot be waived.

The implied warranty was first created in a 1931 Minnesota decision.[36] But it attracted little attention until 1970, when it was adopted by the District of Columbia Circuit in the landmark decision of *Javins v. First National Realty Corp.*[37] *Javins* catapulted the warranty into national prominence, and it soon became the majority rule in the United States. In many states, the warranty was adopted through case law, as discussed in this section. In other states, it was established by legislation (*see* § 17.07).

[B] Policy Considerations

[1] Arguments for Implied Warranty

Javins and other modern courts justify the implied warranty as a utilitarian response to contemporary social and economic conditions.[38] The historic *caveat lessee* rule made sense when applied to the traditional paradigm tenant—the medieval farmer (*see* § 15.04[B]). But it is ill-suited to address the needs of the new paradigm tenant—the poor urban resident (*see* § 15.06[B]).

First, the medieval farmer was mainly interested in leasing agricultural land, not in obtaining shelter; and the farmer was quite capable of making any repairs that were needed. In contrast, the dominant goal of the typical modern tenant is to secure housing. The tenant seeks a "package of goods and services" including adequate heat, light, and ventilation, secure windows and doors, adequate plumbing facilities, etc. And today's tenant usually lacks the specialized skills needed to effect repairs to complex modern buildings. Thus, if the law allocates the repair burden to the modern tenant, defects are less likely to be repaired.

Second, while traditional law assumed an equal bargaining position between landlord and tenant, the typical modern tenant often cannot protect her interests through negotiation. Affordable housing is in short supply in many regions; and landlords usually offer only "take-it-or-leave-it" form leases without any meaningful opportunity to negotiate. Given this disparity in bargaining power, tenants are effectively forced to accept substandard housing. A variety of other, interrelated themes—including the enactment of housing codes, the movement toward treating the residential lease as a contract rather than a conveyance, and the growing societal belief that each person has a right to decent housing—also contributed to the rapid rise of the implied warranty.

---

[36] Delamater v. Foreman, 239 N.W. 148 (Minn. 1931); *see also* Lemle v. Breeden, 462 P.2d 470 (Haw. 1969) (adopting implied warranty).

[37] 428 F.2d 1071 (D.C. Cir. 1970).

[38] *See, e.g.,* Javins v. First Nat'l Realty Corp., 428 F.2d 1071 (D.C. Cir. 1970); Hilder v. St. Peter, 478 A.2d 202 (Vt. 1984).

[2] Arguments Against Implied Warranty

The principal argument against the implied warranty is that it reduces the quantity of affordable housing. Although empirical data is remarkably scant, law and economics scholars reason that:

    (1)   compliance with the warranty imposes extra costs on landlords;

    (2)   landlords will tend to pass these costs on to tenants through increased rents;

    (3)   some tenants will be unable to afford these higher rents; and

    (4)   therefore these tenants will be forced out of the housing market.

Suppose tenant T, who can only afford to pay $200 per month for housing, rents a substandard apartment for this amount; the apartment lacks hot water and electricity, but provides basic shelter. Forced by the implied warranty to correct these deficiencies, landlord L raises the rent to $250 per month; T cannot pay the higher rent, is evicted, and takes up residence in a cardboard box in a dark alley. If this scenario is at all realistic, it poses a clear policy dilemma: how should the law strike a balance between the quality and quantity of rental housing?

In fact, some empirical evidence suggests that the implied warranty has little impact on the quality or quantity of housing.[39] Many landlords apparently ignore the doctrine; and even tenants living in uninhabitable conditions who are aware of their rights rarely assert them.

[C] Scope of Implied Warranty

[1] Overview

What conditions breach the implied warranty of habitability? The basic yardstick is an objective test: the defects must be so serious that a reasonable person would find the premises uninhabitable. One or two minor defects that do not affect habitability, in contrast, are insufficient. To implement these rather vague principles, most states define the scope of the warranty by reference either to: (1) local housing codes; or (2) fitness for human habitation. Yet the precise scope of the warranty varies substantially from state to state.

Examples of conditions that, alone or in combination, are normally significant enough to violate the implied warranty include: broken windows;[40] defective door locks;[41] leaky roofs;[42] lead-based paint;[43] broken toilets,

---

[39] *See* Barbara Bezdek, *Silence in the Court: Participation and Subordination of Poor Tenants' Voices in Legal Process*, 20 Hofstra L. Rev. 533 (1992); Norman Krumholz, *Rent Withholding as an Aid to Housing Code Enforcement*, 25 J. Housing 242 (1968); Charles J. Meyers, *The Covenant of Habitability and the American Law Institute*, 27 Stan. L. Rev. 879 (1975).

[40] *See, e.g.,* Young v. Patukonis, 506 N.E.2d 1164 (Mass. App. Ct. 1987) (lead paint, cracked windows, missing window screens, stained ceiling, loose tiles, mice, ants, inadequate trash receptacles, inadequate door locks, missing balustrades on porches).

[41] *See, e.g.,* Rosier v. Brown, 601 N.Y.S.2d 554 (N.Y. City Civ. Ct. 1993) (broken smoke detectors, defective door lock, leaking waste line).

pipes, or other plumbing facilities;[44] defective wiring;[45] falling ceilings;[46] insect or rodent infestation;[47] lack of hot water;[48] excessive noise;[49] flooding;[50] sewage backup;[51] and poorly-maintained common areas.[52] However, the landlord need not maintain the premises in perfect condition. Isolated defects such as cosmetic wall cracks, inoperative Venetian blinds, torn wallpaper, peeling paint, or the presence of a few ants are too trivial to warrant relief. In addition, the landlord is not responsible for defects caused by the tenant.

[2] Compliance with Housing Code

Some states define the scope of the implied warranty by reference to the local housing code. Under this view, the landlord breaches the implied warranty only if the condition of the leased premises violates the code.[53] Most states in this group demand only substantial compliance with the code, not literal compliance.

For example, in the leading case of *Javins v. First National Realty Corp.*[54] the landlord brought a summary action to recover possession from several tenants who failed to pay rent. The tenants asserted: (1) their apartment building contained 1,500 violations of the local housing code; (2) the damages caused by these violations equaled the unpaid rent; and therefore (3) no rent was due. The District of Columbia Circuit held that the scope of the implied warranty of habitability was defined by the District's housing code: "We therefore hold that the Housing Regulations imply a warranty of habitability, measured by the standards which they set out, into leases of all housing that they cover."[55]

The main virtue of this approach is certainty: it is usually simple to determine whether a particular defect violates the housing code. Thus, in theory, the landlord knows the precise scope of his repair duty, and the tenant knows if the warranty is breached. Yet this approach may not provide adequate protection for the tenant; some localities have no housing codes at all, while others are quite skimpy.

---

[42] *See, e.g.,* Pugh v. Holmes, 405 A.2d 897 (Pa. 1979) (leaky roof, no hot water, leaking toilet and pipes, cockroach infestation, and hazardous floors and steps).

[43] *See, e.g.,* Young v. Patukonis, 506 N.E.2d 1164 (Mass. App. Ct. 1987).

[44] *See, e.g.,* Hilder v. St. Peter, 478 A.2d 202 (Vt. 1984) (defective toilet).

[45] *See, e.g.,* Solow v. Wellner, 569 N.Y.S.2d 882 (Civ. Ct. 1991).

[46] *See, e.g.,* Hilder v. St. Peter, 478 A.2d 202 (Vt. 1984).

[47] *See, e.g.,* Lemle v. Breeden, 462 P.2d 470 (Haw. 1969) (rats).

[48] *See, e.g.,* Wade v. Jobe, 818 P.2d 1006 (Utah 1991).

[49] *See, e.g.,* Wortman v. Solil Mgmt. Corp., 629 N.Y.S.2d 422 (App. Div. 1995).

[50] *See, e.g.,* Wade v. Jobe, 818 P.2d 1006 (Utah 1991) (flooding and sewage odor).

[51] *See, e.g.,* Miller v. Christian, 958 F.2d 1234 (3d Cir. 1992).

[52] *See, e.g.,* Tower West Assocs. v. Derevnuk, 450 N.Y.S.2d 947 (Civ. Ct. 1982).

[53] *See, e.g.,* Jack Spring, Inc. v. Little, 280 N.E.2d 208 (Ill. 1972); *see also* Restatement (Second) of Property: Landlord & Tenant § 5.5(1) (adopting standard based on "health, safety, and housing codes").

[54] 428 F.2d 1071 (D.C. Cir. 1970).

[55] Javins v. First Nat'l Realty Corp., 428 F.2d 1071, 1082 (D.C. Cir. 1970).

[3]　Fit for Human Habitation

In another group of states—probably a majority—the implied warranty mandates that leased premises must be "fit for human habitation," meet "bare living requirements," or comply with a similar standard, regardless of the housing code.[56] Thus, a landlord might breach the implied warranty even if the premises comply with the code. Even in these states, however, a material violation of the code is usually an important factor in applying the general standard.

The Vermont Supreme Court's decision in *Hilder v. St. Peter* [57] illustrates this approach. The tenant's apartment had a broken window, broken door lock, defective toilet, inoperable bathroom light, leaking water pipes, and falling plaster, all accompanied by the odor of raw sewage. Despite repeated promises, the landlord never fixed the defects; the tenant eventually moved out and sued for damages. Following the national trend, the court formally adopted the implied warranty of habitability: "[W]e now hold expressly that . . . an implied warranty exists in [a residential] lease . . . that the landlord will deliver over and maintain . . . premises that are safe, clean and fit for human habitation."[58] The court further held that the warranty covered all latent and patent defects in "essential facilities," that is, facilities that are vital to the use of the premises for residential purposes. Measured against these standards, the court held that the numerous defects violated the implied warranty.

In practice, the "fit for human habitation" standard is often difficult to apply. The *Hilder* court noted that the local housing code may provide a "starting point" for determining breach, but suggested that the key question was whether the defect has an impact on the health or safety of the tenant. For example, suppose the air conditioner in T's Arizona apartment is broken. Is the apartment "fit for human habitation"? Might one reasonably argue that an air conditioner in that location is an "essential facility"? Extreme heat may certainly affect a tenant's health and safety. On the other hand, millions of residents in southwestern states routinely live without air conditioning. And perhaps tenants like T could protect themselves without the landlord's assistance (e.g., by purchasing portable coolers). Is air conditioning a necessity or a luxury?

[D]　Procedure

In order to claim breach of the implied warranty, the tenant must first provide the landlord with notice of the defect, and then allow a reasonable time for repairs to be completed. The notice must be specific enough to inform the landlord about the nature of the defect. For example, a vague

---

[56] *See, e.g,* Green v. Superior Court, 517 P.2d 1168 (Cal. 1974); Marini v. Ireland, 265 A.2d 526 (N.J. 1970); Pugh v. Holmes, 405 A.2d 897 (Pa. 1979); Wade v. Jobe, 818 P.2d 1006 (Utah 1991); *see also* Unif. Residential Landlord & Tenant Act § 2.104, 7B U.L.A. 460 (requiring landlord to maintain premises, inter alia, "in a fit and habitable condition").

[57] 478 A.2d 202 (Vt. 1984).

[58] Hilder v. St. Peter, 478 A.2d 202, 208 (Vt. 1984).

complaint about "a big problem" is insufficient to trigger the landlord's repair duty. The length of the period that must be allowed for repair varies with the nature of the defect, its impact on habitability, and the complexity of the required work. If the only toilet in the apartment unit is inoperable, for instance, a period of one or two days will normally suffice. But if the entire roof must be replaced in order to correct minor leakage, a longer period will be allowed.

[E]   Remedies for Breach of Implied Warranty

[1]   Remain in Possession and Withhold Rent

If the landlord breaches the implied warranty, the tenant may remain in possession of the leased premises and stop paying rent. The landlord now faces a dilemma. In most jurisdictions, the landlord cannot successfully sue to evict this tenant for nonpayment of rent; breach of the implied warranty is a defense to a summary eviction action.[59] Nor can the landlord successfully sue the tenant for unpaid rent; breach of the warranty is also a defense to an action to collect back rent. Under the contract approach to leases, the tenant's duty to pay rent is dependent on the landlord's performance of his own duties, including the implied warranty. The landlord is not legally entitled to collect rent again until either the defective premises are repaired or a court determines that rent is due. Some jurisdictions require the tenant to deposit withheld rent payments in a special escrow account until the dispute is resolved through litigation.[60]

May the tenant withhold *all* rent for a *partial* breach of the implied warranty? Suppose landlord L neglects to repair two defects in tenant T's apartment (a broken front door lock and a leaky toilet) despite reasonable notice. If the lease requires T to pay $500 per month in rent, but L's breach of the implied warranty only reduces the rental value of the premises by $100 per month under the applicable damages test (*see* [3], *below*), can T withhold all rent? In almost all jurisdictions, the answer is "yes." Assume L now sues to evict T for nonpayment. The court will determine the amount of partial back rent owed, order the tenant to pay this sum, and deny the eviction request.[61] Without this protection against eviction, the rent withholding remedy would have little value. If a tenant could only withhold rent equal to the actual damages, the tenant who incorrectly estimated damages could still be evicted by the breaching landlord; the risk of eviction would deter tenants from using the remedy.

Rent withholding is usually the most effective remedy for breach of the implied warranty. From the tenant's perspective, it is an easily-understood form of self-help. Without initiating expensive litigation, the tenant can place economic pressure on the landlord to repair the premises. Indeed, the implied warranty gives the landlord a financial incentive to avoid rent withholding by maintaining leased premises in habitable condition.

---

[59] *See, e.g.,* Jack Spring, Inc. v. Little, 280 N.E.2d 208 (Ill. 1972).

[60] *See, e.g.,* King v. Moorehead, 495 S.W.2d 65 (Mo. Ct. App. 1973).

[61] *See, e.g.,* Pugh v. Holmes, 405 A.2d 897 (Pa. 1979).

[2] Remain in Possession and Use "Repair and Deduct" Remedy

A number of jurisdictions also allow the tenant to remain in possession, repair the defects, and then deduct the cost of repair from rental payments due to the landlord. If landlord L refuses to repair the broken toilet in tenant T's apartment, for example, T can pay a plumber $200 to fix the problem, and then deduct the $200 payment from the next month's rent payment. The repair and deduct remedy is typically subject to various restrictions that prevent abuse (e.g., the cost of repair must be reasonable in light of the rent amount due).[62]

[3] Remain in Possession and Sue for Damages

[a] Overview

Alternatively, if the landlord breaches the implied warranty, the tenant may remain in possession of the premises, continue paying rent, and sue the landlord for damages.[63] Under these circumstances, the tenant is entitled to receive reimbursement for excess rents paid. How should the tenant's damages be calculated? There is a three-way split of authority on the basic measure of damages. In addition, a few jurisdictions allow the tenant to recover punitive damages or emotional distress damages.[64]

[b] Measure of Damages

Difference between agreed rent and fair market value "as is": Some courts award the difference between the agreed rent and the fair market value of the premises in defective condition. For example, suppose T leases her apartment unit from L for $350 per month; during the tenancy the roof begins to leak, but L refuses to fix it. If the fair market value of the unit with a leaky roof is only $150 per month, then T is entitled to damages of $200 per month ($350 less $150). Yet this formula is clearly inadequate for dealing with defects that already exist when the tenancy begins. Suppose S leases an apartment unit with a leaky roof from L; aware of the problem S agrees to pay only $150 for the unit, its fair market value in defective condition. Under this formula, S recovers nothing.

Difference between fair market value "as warranted" and fair market value "as is": Other courts award the difference between the fair market value of the premises as warranted by the landlord and their fair market value in defective condition.[65] Assume now that S, fully aware that the apartment has a leaky roof, leases the apartment from L for the fair market value

---

[62] *See, e.g.,* Pugh v. Holmes, 405 A.2d 897 (Pa. 1979).

[63] Similarly, in a rent control jurisdiction the tenant may be able to petition for a reduction in rent if the landlord breaches the implied warranty. *See, e.g.,* Sterling v. Santa Monica Rent Control Bd., 214 Cal. Rptr. 71 (Ct. App. 1985).

[64] *See, e.g.,* Simon v. Solomon, 431 N.E.2d 556 (Mass. 1982) (approving emotional distress damages).

[65] *See, e.g.,* Hilder v. St. Peter, 478 A.2d 202 (Vt. 1984).

of the premises in defective condition—$150 per month. If L had provided the premises in the condition required by the implied warranty, their fair market value "as warranted" would be $375. Logically, T should recover damages of $225 per month ($375 less $150).

Percentage diminution in agreed rent: Finally, many courts lower the agreed rent by a percentage that reflects the tenant's loss of use.[66] Suppose again that T rents the apartment unit for $350 per month; but the leaky roof reduces the habitability of the unit by 50%. T recovers damages of $175 per month (50% of $350). One virtue of this formula is that it eliminates any need for the tenant to secure expert testimony on the issue of fair market value. Instead, this approach vests broad discretion in the trial court to determine the extent of diminished use.

[4] Terminate Lease and Sue for Damages

Finally, the tenant may elect to terminate the lease and sue the landlord for damages. The tenant's damages are measured by the formulas discussed above (*see* [3], *above*).

[F] Waiver of Implied Warranty

In most jurisdictions, any waiver of the implied warranty of habitability is invalid as against public policy.[67] As the District of Columbia Circuit explained in *Javins v. First National Realty Corp.*,[68] the implied warranty was adopted in part to compensate for the typical disparity in bargaining power between landlords and tenants; without adequate bargaining power, tenants cannot negotiate adequate housing conditions. If the implied warranty could be waived, presumably landlords would routinely compel tenants to waive this protection, thus frustrating the purpose of the law.

§ 17.07 The Statutory Warranty of Habitability

Statutes in more than 30 states now impose a warranty of habitability in residential leases.[69] Most of these statutes are based on the 1972 Uniform Residential Landlord and Tenant Act ("URLTA"). This statutory warranty largely parallels the implied warranty of habitability (*see* § 17.06). Only two differences merit special mention.

First, the scope of the URLTA warranty is quite broad. The residential landlord must comply with all building and housing codes; keep the

---

[66] *See, e.g.,* Wade v. Jobe, 818 P.2d 1006 (Utah 1991).

[67] *See, e.g.,* Knight v. Hallsthammar, 623 P.2d 268 (Cal. 1981); Hilder v. St. Peter, 478 A.2d 202 (Vt. 1984). *But see* Restatement (Second) of Property: Landlord & Tenant § 5.6 (1977) (suggesting that waiver may sometimes be appropriate).

[68] 428 F.2d 1071 (D.C. Cir. 1970).

[69] *See also* Billings v. Wilson, 493 N.E.2d 187 (Mass. 1986) (denying relief to tenant under state consumer protection act because landlord who rented one unit in owner-occupied duplex was not conducting "trade or commerce"); Haddad v. Gonzalez, 576 N.E.2d 658 (Mass. 1991) (authorizing recovery of emotional distress damages under state consumer protection act for landlord's breach of warranty).

premises in "a fit and habitable condition"; keep common areas in clean and safe condition; maintain all electrical, plumbing, sanitary, heating, ventilating, air conditioning, and other facilities in good working order; maintain appropriate trash receptacles; and supply running cold and hot water.[70]

Second, the URLTA allows the tenant to waive the warranty of habitability in certain circumstances. For example, the tenant who rents a single-family house may validly agree to shoulder responsibility for providing heat, water, and waste removal and for making various repairs, as long as the agreement is entered into in "good faith."[71] Additional restrictions are imposed on a waiver by a tenant living in any other type of rental unit; in particular, the tenant may not waive the landlord's duty to perform repair work that is necessary to comply with building or housing code provisions that materially affect health or safety.[72]

§ 17.08 Landlord Liability for Personal Injury

[A] Traditional Approach

[1] Landlord Immunity

At common law, the landlord was generally not liable for personal injury to tenants or others caused by dangerous conditions on leased premises,[73] even if the landlord was negligent. Most states still cling to this rule. Suppose, for example, that the roof of tenant T's rented home collapses due to a rotten beam that landlord L carelessly failed to discover. If the falling debris severs T's leg, landlord L is not liable. Why not?

The answer is found in the same agricultural lease model that justified the traditional rule that the landlord had no duty to repair the premises. The lease was seen as a conveyance by which the landlord transferred all control over the premises to the tenant; thus, the burden of keeping the premises safe shifted to the tenant. The principal object of the lease was land, not structures; the tenant possessed the ability to keep the property in good repair; and the tenant could fully inspect the premises before the lease began. Under these circumstances, only the tenant was liable if personal injury occurred on the premises.

[2] Exceptions

Predictably, the harshness of the landlord immunity rule slowly generated various equitable exceptions. These exceptions are united by a common

---

[70] Unif. Residential Landlord & Tenant Act § 2.104(a), 7B U.L.A. 460.

[71] Unif. Residential Landlord & Tenant Act § 2.104(c), 7B U.L.A. 460.

[72] Unif. Residential Landlord & Tenant Act § 2.104(d), 7B U.L.A. 460.

[73] See, e.g., Bowles v. Mahoney, 202 F.2d 320 (D.C. Cir. 1952); Borders v. Roseberry, 532 P.2d 1366 (Kan. 1975); see also Olin L. Browder, The Taming of a Duty—The Tort Liability of Landlords, 81 Mich. L. Rev. 99 (1982).

thread: each involves a situation where one of the assumptions underlying the rule (either ability to inspect or lack of landlord control) does not apply. Today many states recognize the following exceptions[74] to the traditional rule:[75]

Concealed latent defects: A landlord is liable for personal injury caused by a latent defect existing in the premises when the lease term began that was known to the landlord but concealed from the tenant. Suppose, for example, that landlord L knows that a roof beam is rotten, but fails to warn tenant T; if this defect later causes the roof to collapse, injuring T, L is liable.

Common area defects: A landlord is also liable for injury caused by the negligent failure to maintain the common area or other portions of the premises that the landlord controls. For instance, assume L neglects to repair a broken railing on the common area stairway of the apartment building; L is liable for T's resulting fall off the stairway.

Negligent repairs: A landlord who repairs the premises negligently is also liable for resulting injury. For example, assume L carelessly repairs the leaky roof over T's apartment unit; the leakage continues, making T's kitchen floor wet and slippery. L is liable if T slips and falls.

Breach of agreement to repair: A landlord who first agrees to repair the premises, but later breaches this agreement, is liable for personal injuries that result. Assume L agrees to repair T's leaky roof, but fails to perform his agreement; if T slips and falls on the resulting wet floor, L is liable for T's injuries.

Defects in premises leased for public use: A landlord who leases premises for public use is first obligated to conduct a reasonable inspection and to repair any defects. Suppose L leases his building for use as a public theater, without first carefully inspecting the roof. If the roof later leaks, causing a patron to slip and fall on the wet floor, L is liable.

[B] Modern Trends

The landlord's traditional immunity from personal injury liability is gradually collapsing. Over the last 30 years, many states have jettisoned the common law rule in favor of general principles of negligence liability. In Massachusetts, New York, Pennsylvania, Wisconsin and a number of other states, a residential landlord's liability is evaluated under the same "reasonable care" standard used in ordinary negligence litigation.[76] A

---

[74] Two other exceptions should be noted. First, some states apply ordinary negligence rules to determine liability for injuries arising from the short-term lease of a furnished dwelling. Second, under modern law, most states recognize that the landlord may be held liable in negligence for breach of a statutory or regulatory obligation to maintain and repair leased premises that results in personal injury.

[75] *See, e.g.,* Rollo v. City of Kansas City, 857 F. Supp. 1441 (D. Kan. 1994) (discussing exceptions to common law rule); Borders v. Roseberry, 532 P.2d 1366 (Kan. 1975) (same).

[76] *See, e.g.,* Newton v. Magill, 872 P.2d 1213 (Alaska 1994); Stephens v. Stearns, 678 P.2d 41 (Idaho 1984); Asper v. Haffley, 458 A.2d 1364 (Pa. Super. Ct. 1983); Williams v. Melby, 699 P.2d 723 (Utah 1985).

residential landlord in these states has a duty to use reasonable care under all relevant circumstances to prevent foreseeable harm.

This shift toward negligence liability parallels the evolution of the implied warranty of habitability. Courts note that the historic assumptions underlying the landlord immunity rule are inconsistent with modern economic and social conditions; this is the same basic argument used to justify the implied warranty. Further, if landlords are obligated to maintain leased premises in habitable condition to avoid severe inconvenience to tenants, *a fortiori* landlords should maintain the same premises in safe condition to avoid death or personal injury to those same tenants.[77]

The main obstacle toward imposing negligence liability on landlords is the question of control. If the landlord cannot control the leased premises, how can the landlord be held liable for dangerous conditions on those premises? Courts adopting the negligence approach stress that control is certainly relevant—but not determinative—in deciding whether the landlord exercised due care under all the circumstances.[78] For example, these courts usually impose a duty on the landlord to inspect for defects in the premises before possession is transferred to the tenant, that is, before the landlord loses control. Even while the tenant holds possession, the landlord may be liable if he knew or should have known of a particular defect from information provided by the tenant or others.

Should landlords be strictly liable for personal injury? California adopted—and later rejected—this standard. The pioneering case of *Becker v. IRM Corp.*[79] involved a tenant who slipped in the shower, shattered the shower door, and lacerated his arm on the sharp glass. The shower door was deemed defective because it was made from untempered glass, rather than tempered glass which would have substantially reduced the risk of serious injury. Analogizing to both (1) strict liability for defects in consumer products and (2) the implied warranty of habitability, the California Supreme Court held that a landlord engaged in the business of leasing dwellings was strictly liable for injuries resulting from a latent defect in the premises that existed when the lease began. However, ten years later the same court overruled *Becker*,[80] leaving Louisiana as the only state that still imposes strict liability on the landlord.[81]

---

[77] *See also* Crawford v. Buckner, 839 S.W.2d 754 (Tenn. 1992) (invalidating exculpatory clause in residential lease that barred recovery against landlord for negligence that injured tenant).

[78] *See, e.g.,* Sargent v. Ross, 308 A.2d 528 (N.H. 1973).

[79] 698 P.2d 116 (Cal. 1985).

[80] *See* Peterson v. Superior Court, 899 P.2d 905 (Cal. 1995) (overruling *Becker*).

[81] *See also* Ankiewicz v. Kinder, 563 N.E.2d 684 (Mass. 1990) (involving application of state statute that imposes strict liability on landlords for injuries suffered by children who ingest lead-based paint in rented dwellings).

[C] Special Problem: Landlord Liability for Criminal Attack

Traditionally, the landlord was not liable for personal injury to tenants or others caused by the criminal activities of third parties. For instance, if criminal C assaulted tenant T in the dark hallway of landlord L's apartment building, L was immune from liability even if his failure to fix defective lighting contributed to the attack. Why? A mixture of different policies supported this rule: the general precept that no person is obligated to protect another from criminal conduct; the notion that tenants control the leased premises and can thus protect themselves; the concern that assessing foreseeability of criminal conduct is difficult; the danger that imposing liability on landlords will increase rent levels; and the belief that the criminal's intentional conduct is a superseding cause of the harm.[82]

However, there is a growing trend toward holding landlords liable in negligence for third-party criminal conduct.[83] Most of the decisions imposing liability involve tenant injury caused by criminal attacks in common areas—parking lots, halls, stairways, and so forth.[84] The law historically held the landlord liable in tort for personal injuries arising from defects in negligently maintained common areas, largely because these areas were under the landlord's control. Using the same logic, modern courts increasingly require the landlord to exercise reasonable care to protect tenants against foreseeable criminal attacks in common areas. As between the landlord and the tenant, the landlord is in the best position to take the precautions necessary to protect the tenant from such attacks. Gate systems, video cameras, security guards, alarms, and other potential mechanisms to help safeguard tenants in common areas can only be implemented by the landlord.

§ 17.09 Fixtures

Suppose residential tenant T purchases a new chandelier and installs it in the dining room of her apartment. Five years later, T's tenancy ends. Can T take the chandelier with her?

The English common law on the point was simple: any chattel permanently affixed to the premises by the tenant was considered a *fixture*, and thus property of the landlord; it could not be removed by the tenant. The pro-commerce exception to this rule concerned fixtures installed by a tenant in order to carry on a trade or business (e.g., shelves attached to a bookstore wall). These "trade fixtures" remained the property of the tenant and accordingly could be removed before the tenancy ended. If not timely removed, however, they became property of the landlord.

---

[82] *Cf.* Feld v. Merriam, 485 A.2d 742 (Pa. 1984) (defending traditional rule).

[83] *See, e.g.,* Kline v. 1500 Mass. Ave. Apartment Corp., 439 F.2d 477 (D.C. Cir. 1970); Ann M. v. Pacific Plaza Shopping Ctr., 25 Cal. Rptr. 2d 137 (Cal. 1993); Walls v. Oxford Management Co., 633 A.2d 103 (N.H. 1993).

[84] *See, e.g.,*Trentacost v. Brussel, 412 A.2d 436 (N.J. 1980) (involving attack in apartment hallway).

Contemporary American law follows this basic pattern, but provides enhanced protection for tenants. Most important, in order for a chattel to become a fixture, the tenant must intend for it to become a permanent part of the premises. To test this intent, courts examine several objective criteria, which include the nature of the item, the method of attachment, and the purpose of attachment. In addition, American courts tend to interpret the trade fixtures exception broadly.[85] As a result of these combined developments, in most instances tenants are able to remove the chattels they have affixed to the premises.

---

[85] *See, e.g.*, Handler v. Horns, 65 A.2d 523 (N.J. 1949) (refrigeration compressors, machinery, ammonia tanks, piping, partitions fitted with refrigerator doors, and similar equipment installed to create cold storage rooms were trade fixtures).

Chapter 18

TRANSFER OF LEASEHOLD INTEREST

§ 18.01   Transfers in General

A, whose residential lease on Greenacre lasts for three more years, takes a new job hundreds of miles away. B, operating her bookstore under a 20-year commercial lease, wishes to sell her store in the middle of the lease term. C, the owner of a shopping center with 100 commercial tenants, plans to sell the center. A, B, and C all confront the same legal problem: the transfer of a leasehold interest.

Broadly speaking, both the tenant and the landlord are entitled to transfer all or part of their respective interests to third parties. Most modern leases, however, restrict the tenant's rights in this regard by providing that the landlord must consent to any transfer. What standards govern the landlord's consent? Heavily influenced by contract principles, the law in recent decades has moved toward requiring the landlord to act in a commercially reasonable manner unless the lease clearly specifies otherwise.

A tenant may transfer rights by either an *assignment* or a *sublease*.[1] The post-transfer rights and liabilities of the landlord, tenant, and transferee will differ substantially, depending on which method of transfer is used. The distinction between the two methods dates back to the feudal era. Although the original rationale for the distinction ended centuries ago, it persists today, more due to custom than to logic. Predictably, the law governing assignments and subleases is formalistic and—to the modern mind—somewhat antiquated.

§ 18.02 Distinguishing Between Assignment and Sublease

[A] The Issue

In legal theory, an assignment is the transfer of the tenant's existing lease to a third party. In contrast, a sublease is a wholly new lease between the original tenant and a third party. Despite this theoretical clarity, it is often difficult to decide which category a particular transfer falls into.

[B] Majority Test: All or Less Than All?

[1] Basic Test

The clear majority of states employs an objective (and rather mechanical) test in this situation, rooted in feudal principles. If the tenant transfers the right of possession for the *entire* remaining term of the lease, the transfer is an assignment.[2] However, if only *part* of the remaining term is transferred, a sublease arises. Suppose tenant A, who has 10 years remaining on his lease, transfers his entire lease term to B, except that A retains the right to occupy the premises on the last day of the term. Under the formalistic majority approach, the transfer is a sublease. Logically, the same result would follow if A merely kept the right of possession for the

---

[1] For a discussion of the historic roots of the distinction, see Jerome J. Curtis, Jr., *Assignments and Subleases: An Archaic Distinction*, 17 Pac. L.J. 1247 (1986).

[2] *See, e.g.,* Dayenian v. American Nat'l Bank & Trust Co., 414 N.E.2d 1199 (Ill. App. Ct. 1980) (assignment found where tenant transferred "the entire remainder of her estate and did not retain any reversionary interest" in an apartment unit); Ernst v. Conditt, 390 S.W.2d 703 (Tenn. Ct. App. 1964) (assignment resulted when tenant transferred "his entire interest in the property," without retaining any right to future possession); *see also* W.W. Ferrier, Jr., *Can There Be a Sublease for the Entire Unexpired Portion of a Term?*, 18 Cal. L. Rev. 1 (1929).

last minute or second of the term. The parties' actual intention is irrelevant under this view.

Like all "bright line" rules, the majority approach offers the benefit of predictability at the risk of individual injustice. Successor owners, creditors, and other interested persons can easily determine if a completed transfer is an assignment or sublease, without the delay and expense of ascertaining the parties' actual intent. Similarly, parties planning a transfer can readily structure the transaction (e.g., by determining who has the right to possession on the last day of the term) so that the law will uphold their intended method. However, because the majority rule may ignore the parties' actual intent, it presents the danger of inequity (*see* § 18.02[C]).

[2] Effect of Contingent Right of Reentry

One familiar problem is whether the tenant's reservation of a contingent right of reentry (or power of termination) creates a sublease. Suppose tenant T obtains a 10-year lease on landlord L's apple orchard; the lease requires that T maintain the apple trees in good condition. Two years later, T wishes to transfer his entire right of possession to X, who duly promises T that he (X) will care for the trees. Regardless of the form of transfer used, T will be liable to L if X fails to safeguard the trees. To minimize this liability, T might retain the right to terminate X's occupancy and retake possession of the orchard if X neglects his obligation.

Does a sublease result if T retains such a contingent right of reentry? Most jurisdictions still find an assignment in this situation, reasoning that such a right—which may indeed never be exercised—is too insubstantial an interest to trigger a sublease. Led by Massachusetts and Texas, a minority of states holds that this situation results in a sublease; these courts explain that the tenant has simply failed to transfer the *entire* right of possession. [3]

[3] Transfer of All Rights to Portion of Premises

What if the tenant transfers the *entire* right of possession to a *portion* of the leased premises (e.g., T transfers all of his rights in the south half of the apple orchard only)? Almost all courts consider this a partial assignment.

[C] Minority Test: Intent of Parties

A few courts rely on the intent of the parties to distinguish between assignment and sublease. Suppose T transfers the entire balance of his lease term to X. Under the majority test, this is clearly an assignment regardless of the parties' intent. Courts following the minority view, however, would ascertain whether T and X intended to create a new

---

[3] *See, e.g.,* Davis v. Vidal, 151 S.W. 290 (Tex. 1912) (sublease arose where tenant transferred entire remaining term of brewery lease, but retained right to reenter if transferee failed to pay rent).

landlord-tenant relationship between themselves (a sublease) or whether they intended that T's rights in the existing lease would merely be transferred to X (an assignment). Thus, under the minority approach it would be possible to transfer the entire lease term without subjecting the parties to the legal consequences of an assignment.[4]

The leading decision advocating the minority rule is *Jaber v. Miller*,[5] where an impassioned Arkansas Supreme Court rejected the majority approach as a meaningless relic of feudalism, inconsistent with the modern tendency to interpret documents in accordance with the intent of the parties. The court further warned that the majority rule imperiled the rights of unsophisticated parties: "[F]or the less skilled lawyer or for the layman the common law rule is simply a trap that leads to hardship and injustice by refusing to permit the parties to accomplish the result they seek."[6]

§ 18.03 Assignment

[A] The Assignment Triangle

Suppose landlord (or *lessor*) A leases Greenacre to tenant (or *lessee*) B in 1995 for a 10-year term; in 2000, B, as *assignor*, in turn assigns his entire remaining interest in the lease to C, the *assignee*. This assignment creates a triangle of relationships among A, B, and C. Each one enjoys rights against, and owes duties to, the other two parties.

When A leased to B in 1995, two separate and independent legal relationships arose between them: *privity of contract* and *privity of estate*. Privity of contract is simply the contract law label for the relationship between two parties who enter into a contract. Because the A-B lease can be viewed (at least in part) as a contract, it created privity of contract between A and B. Privity of estate, a property law concept, is somewhat more elusive.[7] As used here, privity of estate is essentially the property law label for the relationship between two parties to the conveyance of an estate in land. Because the A-B lease can be seen (again, in part) as a conveyance, it created privity of estate between A and B.

What happens when B assigns to C in 2000? The result is a equilateral triangle of legal connections, which generations of law professors have diagramed on blackboards:

Assignor/assignee (B/C): Privity of contract arises between assignor B and assignee C, because the B-C assignment agreement is a contract; B or C will be liable to the other if he breaches the terms of the agreement.

---

[4] The terminology used by the parties may not necessarily establish their intent. *See, e.g.,* Ernst v. Conditt, 390 S.W.2d 703 (Tenn. Ct. App. 1964) (concluding that the parties intended an assignment even though transfer documents, apparently drafted by an attorney, referred only to "subletting").

[5] 239 S.W.2d 760 (Ark. 1951).

[6] Jaber v. Miller, 239 S.W.2d 760, 764 (Ark. 1951).

[7] *See, e.g.,* Ernst v. Conditt, 390 S.W.2d 703, 706 (Tenn. Ct. App. 1964), where the court temporarily confuses the two types of privity.

Lessor/lessee (A/B): The prior privity of contract between lessor A and lessee B continues, unaffected by the assignment, because the A-B lease still exists; A or B will be liable to the other if the lease is breached. For example, B is still obligated to pay rent to A. Yet a dramatic change occurs in privity of estate. The assignment dissolves the prior privity of estate between A and B, because B has transferred his entire interest.

Lessor/assignee (A/C): The assignment creates new privity of estate between lessor A and assignee C, because C has obtained B's entire interest. In a very real sense, C has been substituted into B's place as the holder of B's nonfreehold estate. The privity of estate between A and C gives each the right to sue the other if certain covenants of the *original* lease are breached, as discussed below. This privity of estate will continue until the assignee reassigns his interest to another, the assignee vacates the premises, or the lease terminates.[8] In effect, the law imposes certain obligations on both lessor and assignee without their agreement. No privity of contract exists between A and C, unless C expressly agrees to assume the lessee's obligations under the original lease.[9]

[B] Rights and Duties of the Parties

Privity of estate confers rights and duties on both the assignee and the lessor. Each is obligated to perform those covenants of the original lease that "run with the land" as real covenants (*see* Chapter 33) or equitable servitudes (*see* Chapter 34). In order for a contract promise or "covenant" to bind the parties in this manner:

    (1)   the original parties to the lease must intend that successors be bound by the covenant;

    (2)   the covenant must "touch and concern" the land (meaning that it must affect the parties in their use or enjoyment of the land); and

    (3)   the assignee must have notice of the covenant before acquiring the interest.[10]

As a practical matter, most covenants in most leases "run with the land." Leases almost always contain standard language binding successor parties. And successors are usually charged with notice of the lease covenants, either because they prudently read the lease before agreeing to the transfer (and thus obtain actual notice) or because the lease is recorded (and provides constructive notice as a matter of law; *see* Chapter 25). The more troublesome element is "touch and concern." Modern courts generally hold

---

[8] A.D. Juilliard & Co., Inc. v. American Woolen Co., 32 A.2d 800 (R.I. 1943); *cf.* First Am. Nat'l Bank v. Chicken Sys. of Am., Inc., 616 S.W.2d 156 (Tenn. Ct. App. 1980) (where landlord relet premises after assignee abandoned, this terminated assignee's privity of estate, just as if assignee had reassigned the lease).

[9] First Am. Nat'l Bank v. Chicken Sys. of Am., Inc., 616 S.W.2d 156 (Tenn. Ct. App. 1980) (on facts of case, assignee did not actually assume lease).

[10] Privity is also required for a covenant to run at law, but is already present on the facts here.

that virtually all covenants found in a standard lease meet this test, including covenants to pay rent, perform repairs, furnish heat and other utilities, provide quiet enjoyment, pay taxes, utilize the leased premises for a particular purpose, provide parking space, or arbitrate disputes. On the other hand, there is widespread judicial disagreement on whether a few covenants sufficiently "touch and concern," such as covenants to return the tenant's security deposit, pay attorney's fees in litigation arising out of the lease, insure the premises for the landlord's benefit, or refrain from operating a competing business.

Consider a simple dispute. A leases to B, who then assigns to C. Who is liable if rent is not paid to A? Both B and C. B, the original lessee, is still liable for rent under privity of contract, simply because he agreed to pay rent in the lease. An assignment has no effect on the assignor's lease obligations to the original lessor, unless the lessor expressly agrees to release all rights against the assignor. In addition, C, the assignee, is liable under privity of estate for breach of the rent covenant in the original lease.[11] A may choose to sue either B or C. Of course, A cannot recover the same rent from both, for this would be a double recovery.

Complexity arises if both the assignee and assignor are liable for breach of the original lease covenants. Suppose the original A-B lease requires lessee B to regularly trim the trees on Greenacre, to preserve the lake view from A's adjacent home. B assigns his lease to C, who neglects to keep the trees trimmed; A sues B for this breach and collects $10,000 in damages. B may now sue C in indemnity to recover his $10,000 payment. Why? As between the assignor and the assignee, the law generally views the assignee as primarily liable for such breaches. This rule probably reflects the actual intention of the parties; moreover, the assignee, as the party in possession, is best situated to comply with lease covenants. The assignor is considered a guarantor or surety of the assignee's performance.

The assignee's reciprocal rights against the lessor under privity of estate should not be overlooked. Suppose lessor A covenants in the A-B lease to supply drinking water to Greenacre. After B assigns the lease to C, A fails to provide the promised water. C may sue A directly for damages or injunctive relief.

[C] Successive Assignments

Successive assignments pose interesting problems. Consider a variation on the rent liability hypothetical above. A leases to B, who assigns to C; C reassigns to D; no one pays rent to A. B is obviously liable under privity of contract. D is equally liable, because the C-D assignment created privity of estate between A and D. However, C is not liable; the C-D assignment terminated the privity of estate between A and C.[12] A different result follows if C had expressly assumed the obligations of the A-B lease. The

---

[11] *See, e.g.,* Ernst v. Conditt, 390 S.W.2d 703 (Tenn. Ct. App. 1964).

[12] A.D. Julliard & Co., v. American Woolen Co., 32 A.2d 800 (R.I. 1943); *cf.* First Am. Nat'l Bank v. Chicken Sys. of Am., Inc., 616 S.W.2d 156 (Tenn. Ct. App. 1980).

assumption would create privity of contract between A and C, and thus impose rent liability on C, despite the lack of privity of estate.

§ 18.04 Sublease

[A] Two Separate Landlord-Tenant Relationships

If landlord A leases Greenacre to B in 1995 for a 10-year term, the lease obviously creates a landlord-tenant relationship between A, as *lessor*, and B, as *lessee*. A and B have both privity of contract and privity of estate. Assume in 2000 B, as *sublessor*, subleases Greenacre for three years to C, as *sublessee*. This sublease creates a new landlord-tenant relationship between B and C, separate from the A-B relationship. B and C are now linked by both privity of contract and privity of estate.

A and B still are obligated to perform their duties under the original lease. The sublease has no effect on this prior relationship;[13] A and B still have both privity of contract and privity of estate between them. Thus, B is liable to A if the conduct of her sublessee C breaches the terms of the original lease (e.g., if C carelessly sets fire to a building on Greenacre). And the rights of B and C against each other are defined by the terms of their sublease, not by the original lease. As between themselves, B has the rights and duties of a lessor (e.g., the right to evict C), and C has the rights and duties of a lessee (e.g., the duty to pay rent). In short, two independent landlord-tenant relationships have arisen.

What legal connection exists between A and C? None, in theory. Because A and C are not linked by any contract, they do not have privity of contract between them. Similarly, because B did not transfer his entire interest to C—note that B retains a reversion in Greenacre (the right to possession for the final two years of the A-B lease)—privity of estate does not arise between A and C. As a practical matter, however, A and C are indirectly linked, as discussed below.

[B] Rights and Duties of the Parties

Suppose again that A leases to B, who in turn subleases to C. Who is liable if A receives no rental payments? Only B. As the lessee on the A-B lease, B is obligated to pay rent under both privity of estate and privity of contract. A has no legal relationship with C, and thus may not sue C for unpaid rent. As a general rule, a sublessee (C) is not obligated to pay rent to the original lessor (A) or to perform any other covenant of the original lease (the A-B lease). Predictably, however, this general rule is subject to several exceptions.

First, if the lessee's covenants in the original lease bind successors as equitable servitudes (*see* Chapter 34), the lessor will be able to enforce them against the sublessee. For example, if the original A-B lease required that

---

[13] This assumes, of course, that B had the right to sublease. *See* § 18.06.

Greenacre be used only for residential purposes, and the other equitable servitude requirements (intent to bind successors, "touch and concern," and notice to C) were met, A could enjoin any nonresidential use by C. The lack of privity between A and C is irrelevant here. Privity is not required in order for the burden of an equitable servitude to run to successors. Yet this exception does not allow the lessor to sue the sublessee for rent owed by the lessee/sublessor. Traditionally, money damages could be recovered against successors only for breach of a real covenant; however, privity is required for a real covenant to run at law (*see* Chapter 33) and no privity exists between the original lessor and a sublessee.

Second, the lessor may be able to sue under third-party beneficiary theory. As a matter of contract law, a contract made between two parties that is intended to benefit a third party may be enforced by that third party. Suppose that as part of the B-C sublease, C agrees to perform B's obligations under the A-B lease, including the agreement to pay rent to A. In most jurisdictions, A would be considered a third-party beneficiary of the B-C sublease; this special covenant in the sublease would create privity of contract between A and C.[14] Thus, if A received no rental payment, he could sue *either* B or C for compensation.

Finally, even if the sublessee is not legally obligated to perform the covenants of the original lease, there may be an economic incentive to do so. Why? Suppose B breaches his lease obligation to pay rent to A. This breach would allow A to terminate the A-B lease, which will automatically terminate the B-C sublease. A could then evict both B and C. Conceptually, a sublease is an estate that is carved out of a larger leasehold estate; if the original lease ends, the sublease ends. Thus, sublessee C might elect to pay A the delinquent rent owed by B, simply to avoid eviction, and reduce her sublease rent payments to B accordingly.

§ 18.05   Should the Assignment-Sublease Distinction Be Abolished?

Some scholars advocate that all transfers by lessees should be treated as assignments. Noting that the historic rationale for the assignment-sublease distinction became irrelevant centuries ago as feudalism waned, they argue that public policy supports its abolition.[15] First, as a matter of fundamental fairness, contract law provides that a transferee who accepts the benefits of a contract is impliedly bound to perform its obligations; why should contracts involving land—such as a lease—be excluded from this rule? Second, the sublease may pose a trap for the unwary, which

---

[14] *Cf.* Ernst v. Conditt, 390 S.W.2d 703 (Tenn. Ct. App. 1964) (although not discussed in opinion, language in transfer agreement included transferee's promise to "faithfully perform all conditions of the within lease [the original lease];" thus, even if the transfer was deemed a sublease, the transferee would still be liable to the landlord for rent under third-party beneficiary theory).

[15] *See, e.g.,* Jerome J. Curtis, Jr., *Assignments and Subleases: An Archaic Distinction,* 17 Pac. L.J. 1247 (1986); Walter B. Jaccard, *The Scope of Liability Between Landlord and Subtenant,* 16 Colum. J.L. & Soc. Probs. 365 (1981).

is inconsistent with the expectations of the parties. If A leases to B, and then B subleases to C, no legal relationship arises between A and C. Unless A and C are highly sophisticated parties, this result may be contrary to their actual intent. For example, A may reasonably—but incorrectly— expect that C is liable for the payment of rent.

The principal argument for retaining the distinction is freedom of contract: a sophisticated transferee should be able to determine the nature of the liability it wishes to incur. Just as a knowledgeable borrower may be able to negotiate a nonrecourse loan (i.e., a loan that imposes no personal liability for repayment on the borrower, but rather limits the lender's rights to foreclosure on its security), a transferee should have the option to avoid direct liability to the lessor, as long as the lessor has consented to subleasing.

§ 18.06   Tenant's Right to Assign or Sublease

[A]   Role of the Lease

Tenants are free to assign, sublease, or otherwise transfer their interests, absent an agreement to the contrary. Thus, if the lease between lessor A and lessee B is silent on the subject, B may assign or sublease to whomever he chooses, regardless of A's objection. This principle reflects the common law's traditional preference for the free alienation of interests in land (see § 8.04[C]). An exception to the general rule may arise if a special skill or ability of the original lessee is crucial to the lessor. Some courts imply a landlord consent requirement into even the silent lease where a percentage rental formula is used (reasoning that the lessor relied on the anticipated financial performance of the lessee)[16] or the rent includes personal services performed by the lessee.

The vast majority of leases, however, expressly restrict the tenant's right of transfer. Why? Among other reasons, the typical landlord insists on such a restriction to avoid an irresponsible or undesirable successor tenant. Suppose lessee B proposes to assign his retail store lease to C, a chronic bankrupt who has failed in every business he has ever attempted, or to D, a pyromaniac whose record includes 10 arson convictions. Under the common law rule, A cannot object to such assignments unless the lease contains a restrictive clause.[17]

The typical lease contains one of four different types of landlord consent clauses. The lease may flatly prohibit any transfer. More commonly, the

---

[16] But see Rowe v. Great Atlantic & Pacific Tea Co., Inc., 385 N.E.2d 566 (N.Y. 1978) (refusing to imply landlord consent requirement into lease with a partial percentage rental clause, where a substantial fixed monthly rent was also required and the parties were sophisticated negotiators).

[17] B admittedly has an economic incentive to avoid picking an improper assignee, because he will remain liable to A for performance of the lease covenants after the assignment. But this may not ensure sufficient protection for A. For example, B might assign the lease incident to the sale of his business to the assignee; if B gambles away the sales proceeds, he will be insolvent before A can recover from him.

lease permits transfer only upon the landlord's consent, and then: (1) provides the landlord can arbitrarily deny consent in its sole discretion; (2) requires that the landlord act reasonably in granting or denying consent; or (3) contains no standard for granting or denying consent. Clauses containing no standard—often called "silent consent clauses"—have sparked extensive controversy in recent years.

[B] Lease Prohibits Transfer

A lease clause that prohibits any transfer of the tenant's interest (e.g., by allowing the landlord to terminate the lease and reenter the premises if any transfer occurs) is enforceable in most jurisdictions.[18] While a complete prohibition on the transfer of a freehold estate would be an invalid restraint on alienation (*see* § 9.08[B]), this policy has less application to the nonfreehold estate, mainly due to the landlord's legitimate interest in safeguarding the reversionary interest. Because restraints on alienation are disfavored, however, courts interpret such clauses narrowly. For example, a ban on "assignment" does not preclude subletting. The Restatement suggests that absolute prohibition clauses are valid only if "freely negotiated"—that is, if the tenant has significant bargaining power in relation to the lease terms[19] —but this position has attracted little judicial support.

[C] Lease Allows Transfer if Landlord Consents

[1] Sole Discretion Clause

A lease may contain a "sole discretion clause," which gives the lessor discretion to approve or deny a transfer (e.g., "Lessor may withhold consent in his sole and absolute discretion."). Under this language, a lessor may refuse consent for *any reason whatsoever*—even an arbitrary, capricious, or unreasonable reason—or for *no reason at all*.[20] Suppose A leases to B pursuant to a lease containing a sole discretion clause. When B proposes to assign to C, A may deny consent because C drives a sports car, reads mystery novels, tells poor jokes, or for any other personal, subjective reason. Indeed, A is not obligated to provide any explanation for her decision. Federal and state anti-discrimination legislation provide the only substantial restriction on the landlord's discretion; A could not refuse consent, for example, based on C's race (*see* § 16.02[B]).

The sole discretion clause raises the same potential issues as an absolute prohibition. Despite occasional suggestions that an unreasonable denial might be challenged as an invalid restraint on alienation,[21] arbitrary

---

[18] *See, e.g.,* Cal. Civ. Code § 1995.230.

[19] Restatement (Second) of Property: Landlord & Tenant § 15.2 cmt. i (1977).

[20] *See generally* Susan E. Myster, *Protecting Landlord Control of Transfers: The Status of "Sole Discretion" Clauses in California Commercial Leases,* 35 Santa Clara L. Rev. 845 (1995).

[21] *See, e.g.,* Cohen v. Ratinoff, 195 Cal. Rptr. 84 (Ct. App. 1983); *cf.* Kendall v. Ernest Pestana, Inc., 709 P.2d 837 (Cal. 1985).

denials are routinely upheld. Similarly, the Restatement insistence that only "freely negotiated" sole discretion clauses are enforceable has—to date—fallen on deaf judicial ears.[22]

[2] Reasonableness Clause

Another variant is the lease clause that requires the lessor to act reasonably in approving or denying consent (*e.g.,* "Lessor shall not unreasonably withhold consent."). Under this standard, the lessor may deny consent only on an objective, commercially reasonable basis. As the Restatement notes, a denial "must be objectively sensible and of some significance and not based on mere caprice or whim or personal prejudice."[23] Thus, "[d]enying consent solely on the basis of personal taste, convenience or sensibility is not commercially reasonable."[24]

Reasonableness is a question of fact. In applying this standard, courts consider a number of factors, including:

(1)   the financial responsibility of the proposed transferee;

(2)   the nature of the new use proposed for the premises;

(3)   the suitability of the proposed use for the premises;

(4)   the legality of the use;

(5)   the need for alterations to the premises; and

(6)   whether the use will compete with the landlord's business or other existing tenants.[25]

For example, a landlord could legitimately refuse consent if the proposed use would create a fire hazard or require substantial alterations, or if the proposed transferee has a poor credit record or lacks sufficient business experience to operate successfully under a percentage lease. On the other hand, a landlord cannot deny consent based on dislike for the transferee, the transferee's marital status, the transferee's religious beliefs,[26] or other subjective reasons. Similarly, the landlord's desire to obtain a higher rent for the premises is not a valid basis for refusal. As the California Supreme Court explained in *Kendall v. Ernest Pestana, Inc.,*[27] this desire is unrelated to the legitimate reasons for the consent clause: to preserve the landlord's property and to ensure the performance of the lease covenants.[28]

---

[22] Restatement (Second) of Property: Landlord & Tenant § 15.2 (1977).

[23] Restatement (Second) of Property: Landlord & Tenant § 15.2 cmt. g (1977).

[24] Kendall v. Ernest Pestana, Inc., 709 P.2d 837, 845 (Cal. 1985).

[25] *See, e.g.,* Kendall v. Ernest Pestana, Inc., 709 P.2d 837 (Cal. 1985); Newman v. Hinky Dinky Omaha-Lincoln, Inc., 427 N.W.2d 50 (Neb. 1988).

[26] *See, e.g.,* American Book Co. v. Yeshiva Univ. Dev. Found., Inc., 297 N.Y.S.2d 156 (Sup. Ct. 1969) (landlord's religious objection to birth control was not a commercially reasonable basis for refusing consent for sublease to organization that advocated birth control).

[27] 709 P.2d 837 (Cal. 1985).

[28] Kendall v. Ernest Pestana, Inc., 709 P.2d 837 (Cal. 1985); Julian v. Christopher, 575 A.2d 735 (Md. 1990).

[3]   No Standard Specified: The Silent Consent Clause

[a]   The Classic Dilemma

One landlord consent scenario features prominently in recent decisions: the tenant's sale of a business operated on leased premises. Suppose A leases a retail store space to B for a 25-year term for a fixed rent of $1,000 per month. The only lease clause dealing with transfers vaguely states: "Landlord consent is required for any assignment or sublease." In other words, it requires landlord consent, but is silent on the standard for granting consent.

Over 10 years of hard work, B develops a profitable shoe store business, which she now wishes to sell (e.g., due to poor health; in order to retire; or to open a bigger shoe store elsewhere). B's store has value as an on-going business only if she can assign her lease to the buyer, and thereby transfer her goodwill (i.e., the continued willingness of customers to buy shoes at this location). Otherwise, B can only sell miscellaneous separate assets (e.g., her inventory of shoes, chairs and other equipment, accounts receivable, business name). B enters into a contract to sell her business (including an assignment of the remaining 15-year lease term) to C for $150,000.

A number of thorny issues might arise. Must A consent to the assignment? Can A require that B pay a premium (say 20% of the sales price) in return for consent? What if the fair rental value for the premises is now higher than the lease rent (e.g., $2,000 per month)? These and other issues all hinge on a single question: *if a commercial lease requires landlord consent but fails to specify a standard, should the sole discretion standard or the reasonableness standard govern?*

[b]   Traditional Rule

The traditional—and probably still the majority—approach applies the sole discretion standard in this situation. One historic rationale for this view is the intent of the parties: by giving the landlord the sole power to approve or deny any transfer—without express limitation on the scope of the power—the parties presumably intended to give the landlord total control and absolute control over the decision. Under this view, if the parties had intended a reasonableness limitation, they would have so specified in the lease. Slightly varying this theme, modern courts sometimes observe that parties to a commercial lease are presumed to know the traditional rule as a matter of custom and practice, and thus to have purposefully utilized a silent consent clause in order to invoke the sole discretion standard. [29] A secondary historic rationale focuses on the comparative

---

[29] *See, e.g.,* Dobyns v. South Carolina Dep't of Parks, Recreation & Tourism, 480 S.E.2d 81, 84 (S.C. 1997) ("The judicial function of a court of law is to enforce contracts as made by the parties and not to re-write or distort, under the guise of judicial construction, the terms of an unambiguous contract."). *But see* Julian v. Christopher, 575 A.2d 735 (Md. 1990) ("[T]enants might expect that a landlord's consent to a sublease or assignment [under a silent consent clause] would be governed by standards of reasonableness.").

importance of the property rights at stake; the landlord's interest in protecting land that will revert to him in fee simple absolute outweighs the tenant's transitory nonfreehold estate.

A more contemporary justification is the efficiency value of a "bright line" test. The reasonableness standard encourages litigation simply because parties may easily disagree on what is reasonable given the facts of any particular case; indeed, it is frequently impossible to predict the trial court's decision. [30] As an Idaho Supreme Court justice lamented, when dissenting from a majority decision adopting the reasonableness test: "[T]he effect of the decision is to potentially subject every denial of consent to litigation and approval by a judge." [31] The uncertainty produced by litigation may impair maximum productive use of the land (e.g., if the premises remain vacant or an older low-benefit use persists during the pendency of litigation) and cause needless expense and delay.

[c] Emerging Modern Rule

Over the last 20 years, an increasing number of jurisdictions have abandoned the traditional approach in favor of a reasonableness standard for commercial leases. [32] Most courts considering the issue in recent years have adopted this emerging minority view. [33]

The California Supreme Court's decision in *Kendall v. Ernest Pestana, Inc.* [34] illustrates this trend. There, A leased airplane hanger space to B. B in turn subleased to C under a 25-year sublease containing a silent consent clause. [35] B thereafter assigned the reversion on the sublease—including the sublessor's right to approve transfers by sublessee C—to Pestana. C operated an airplane maintenance business on the premises for

---

[30] For a discussion of the difficulty of applying the reasonableness standard, see Jacob L. Todres & Carl M. Lerner, *Assignment and Subletting of Leased Premises: The Unreasonable Withholding of Consent*, 5 Fordham Urb. L.J. 195 (1977).

[31] Funk v. Funk, 633 P.2d 586, 591 (Idaho 1981) (Bakes, C.J., dissenting).

[32] In contrast, residential leases are still governed by the traditional rule in virtually all jurisdictions. *See, e.g.,* Slavin v. Rent Control Board, 548 N.E.2d 1226 (Mass. 1990). The relationship between the residential landlord and tenant is seen as more personal than a commercial relationship; thus, as the argument goes, the landlord must have the flexibility of the sole discretion clause to adequately protect his or her interests. While this argument may have some merit for small owner-occupied buildings (e.g., a duplex), its blanket application to all residential properties makes little sense. Why is the relationship between a tenant in a 400-unit apartment complex and the corporate landlord any more personal than the link between Kendall and Pestana?

[33] *See, e.g.,* Kendall v. Ernest Pestana, Inc., 709 P.2d 837 (Cal. 1985); Julian v. Christopher, 575 A.2d 735 (Md. 1990); Newman v. Hinky Dinky Omaha-Lincoln, Inc., 427 N.W.2d 50 (Neb. 1988). *But see* 21 Merchants Row Corp. v. Merchants Row, Inc., 587 N.E.2d 788 (Mass. 1992) (retaining traditional rule).

[34] 709 P.2d 837 (Cal. 1985). *See also* Lynn Hayner, Note, *Assignment of Commercial Leases—The Reasonableness Standard and Withholding Consent: Kendall v. Ernest Pestana, Inc.,* 36 DePaul L. Rev. 285 (1987).

[35] Although the text at one point confusingly mentions that the silent consent clause was in the "lease," the clause was actually located in the sublease. Kendall v. Ernest Pestana, Inc., 709 P.2d 837, 840 n.5 (Cal. 1985).

11 years, and then contracted to sell his business to a buyer group including Kendall and others. But Pestana refused to consent to C's assignment of the sublease to the Kendall group unless it agreed to increased rent and "other more onerous terms." Pestana did not challenge the suitability of the Kendall group as a sublessee; indeed, the Kendall group's net worth was greater than C's own worth. Rather, Pestana relied on the traditional rule: a silent consent clause permits the landlord to arbitrarily deny consent.

The *Kendall* court, however, held that a commercial landlord may withhold consent under such a clause only if it has a "commercially reasonable objection" to the transferee or the proposed use. The decision rests on two separate bases—one drawn from property law and the other from contract law—reflecting the hybrid nature of the lease.

First, viewing the lease as a conveyance, the court relied on the property law rule restricting restraints on alienation. From the utilitarian perspective, this rule benefits society by ensuring, among other things, that land is devoted to its highest and best productive use (*see* § 9.08[A]). The court noted that there was already a shortage of commercial space in many places, suggesting the need for greater freedom of alienation. While the court conceded that the landlord's legitimate interests (preserving the property and ensuring performance of lease covenants) justified some restraint, it concluded that this goal could be met by allowing only commercially reasonable restrictions. In essence, the court adopted the minority rule as a compromise between two competing values: the social importance of unrestricted alienation and the landlord's personal interest in protecting his or her property rights.[36] Less dramatically perhaps, some courts have endorsed the minority rule by using the policy against restraints on alienation as a tool in lease interpretation: "If a clause in a lease is susceptible of two interpretations, public policy favors the interpretation least restrictive of the right to alienate freely."[37]

Second, the *Kendall* court reasoned that—viewing the lease as a contract—the implied covenant of good faith and fair dealing compelled the same outcome. Modern law recognizes that where a contract gives one party a discretionary power to affect the rights of the other, that discretion cannot be exercised arbitrarily; rather, the party must act in good faith and in accordance with accepted principles of fair dealing.[38] Moreover, the minority rule may reflect the actual intent of the typical landlord and tenant.[39]

---

[36] One might, of course, critique this analysis. If a total restraint on alienation of a leasehold estate is valid (*see* § 18.06[B]), how could a mere partial restraint be void?

[37] Julian v. Christopher, 575 A.2d 735, 739 (Md. 1990). *See also* Jon M. Laria, Note, Julian v. Christopher: *New Standards for Landlords' Consent to Assignment and Sublease*, 50 Md. L. Rev. 464 (1991).

[38] Kendall v. Ernest Pestana, Inc., 709 P.2d 837 (Cal. 1985); *see also* Newman v. Hinky Dinky Omaha-Lincoln, Inc., 427 N.W.2d 50 (Neb. 1988) (following *Kendall*).

[39] Kendall v. Ernest Pestana, Inc., 709 P.2d 837, 846 (Cal. 1985) (citing authority that "it must have been in the contemplation of the parties that the lessor be required to give some reason for withholding consent"); Julian v. Christopher, 575 A.2d 735, 738 (Md. 1990) ("Because most people act reasonably most of the time, tenants might expect that a landlord's consent to a sublease or assignment would be governed by standards of reasonableness.")

Although it has received little scholarly approbation,[40] the reasonableness standard is likely to become the majority rule. Arbitrary decision-making—however economically efficient it may be—is simply out of step with evolving standards of fairness and equity.

[D] Implied Waiver of Consent Requirement

Assume the lease between landlord A and tenant B expressly requires A's consent for any assignment of B's interest. B assigns to C with A's permission, and later C seeks to assign to D. Does A retain the right to object? The answer is somewhat unclear. In *Dumpor's Case*,[41] a sixteenth-century English court held that the landlord's consent to one assignment impliedly waived the right to object to future assignments; presumably this decision reflects the historic English policy in favor of free alienation.

Although most American courts ultimately adopted the same rule during the nineteenth century, there appears to be a trend in the opposite direction. Contemporary scholars uniformly condemn the doctrine.[42] It arguably disserves the goal of free alienation, since it discourages landlords from consenting to any transfer. Moreover, it is out of step with the modern concern for respecting the intent of the parties. It is difficult to assess the current status of the doctrine, however, because the issue rarely arises. Prudent draftsmen routinely circumvent the doctrine by including a lease clause to the effect that consent to one assignment does not eliminate the need for consent to future assignments.[43]

§ 18.07 Transfers by Landlord

[A] Landlord's Right to Transfer

The landlord's future interest in the premises—a reversion—is freely transferable to third parties, even over the objection of the tenant in virtually all cases. While a clause restricting the tenant's right to transfer is a standard feature in most leases, a parallel clause limiting the landlord's right is rare. Suppose A first leases Redacre to tenant B and then conveys his remaining interest to grantee C. The A-C conveyance does not nullify the earlier A-B lease. Rather, C takes title to Redacre burdened with the A-B lease, unless C can somehow qualify for protection as a bona fide purchaser under the recording acts.

---

[40] For example, see Professor Alex Johnson's thoughtful analysis of the *Kendall* rule from the standpoint of law and economics. Alex M. Johnson, Jr., *Correctly Interpreting Long-Term Leases Pursuant to Modern Contract Law: Toward a Theory of Relational Leases*, 74 Va. L. Rev. 751 (1988).

[41] 76 Eng. Rep. 1110 (K.B. 1578).

[42] *See, e.g.,* William G. Coskran, *Assignment and Sublease Restrictions: The Tribulations of Leasehold Transfers*, 22 Loy. L.A. L. Rev. 405, 552 (1989).

[43] *Cf.* Childs v. Warner Bros. Southern Theatres, Inc., 156 S.E. 923 (N.C. 1931).

[B] Rights and Duties of Parties

What impact does such a transfer have on the rights and duties of the parties? At common law, no rights and duties arose between the tenant (B) and the grantee (C) unless an *attornment* occurred. This feudal relic required the tenant to voluntarily acknowledge the grantee's status as landlord through an act such as the payment of rent.

Today attornment is no longer necessary in most states. Instead, the transfer itself automatically imposes rights and duties on the parties, in a fashion that mirrors an assignment of the tenant's interest (*see* § 18.03[A]). Once the landlord (A) transfers the reversion in Redacre, privity of estate arises between the tenant (B) and the grantee (C). This privity of estate gives both B and C the right to sue if the other breaches any of the covenants in the A-B lease that "run with the land" (*see* § 18.03[B]). Because A has transferred his entire interest, privity of estate no longer exists between A and B.

Chapter 19

TERMINATION OF THE TENANCY

SYNOPSIS

§ 19.01   The Struggle for Possession

Tenant A abandons her leased premises; landlord B terminates tenant C's lease in retaliation for his complaints to the local housing agency; and landlord D evicts tenant E at gunpoint. Each situation raises fundamental questions about the respective rights of landlord and tenant relating to termination of a tenancy.[1]

Just as the landing is the most dangerous portion of an airplane journey, disputes between landlord and tenant most frequently arise in connection with the ending of a tenancy. Part of the reason for this phenomenon turns on the different perspectives of the parties, a disparity most pronounced in the residential tenancy. The landlord typically views a leased apartment unit in economic terms; a vacant unit—or one occupied by a tenant in default on the rent—produces no income. The landlord's goal is to retake possession as soon as possible, so that the property can be leased to a rent-paying tenant, and investment income can be maximized. In contrast, the residential tenant sees the apartment unit in personal terms: as a private home, a refuge from the world. For the tenant, housing is a necessity, not an investment; even the *threat* of being forced from one's home—given the scarcity of affordable housing—may be devastating. Landlord-tenant law must reconcile these competing interests, protecting the tenant's possession when appropriate, and transferring possession to the landlord as necessary.

Two basic issues arise: (1) under what circumstances does a tenancy end? and (2) what procedure must the landlord follow in order to retake possession? The general evolution of the law over time on both issues is relatively clear, even if the details are sometimes murky. While the common law provided the residential landlord with broad discretion, the modern trend is to curtail these rights. Contemporary law increasingly protects the residential tenant's personal interest over the landlord's investment interest. Commercial tenancies, however, are still largely governed by the traditional pro-landlord rules.

§ 19.02   Surrender

The simplest method for terminating a tenancy in the middle of the lease term is an express surrender. Assume T leases a house from L for a term of five years, but wishes—two years later—to terminate the lease (e.g., in order to accept an out-of-state job). L may also be willing to end the lease early (e.g., because L can now relet the house for a higher rent). In these

---

[1] *See generally* Deborah H. Bell, *Providing Security of Tenure for Residential Tenants: Good Faith as a Limitation on the Landlord's Right to Terminate,* 19 Ga. L. Rev. 483 (1985); Thomas W. Earnhardt, *Peaceful Padlocking in a Perfect World: Commentary and Rebuttal,* 13 N.C. Cent. L.J. 195 (1982); Sarajane Love, *Landlord's Remedies When the Tenant Abandons: Property, Contract, and Leases,* 30 U. Kan. L. Rev. 533 (1982); Glen Weissenberger, *The Landlord's Duty to Mitigate Damages on the Tenant's Abandonment: A Survey of Old Law and New Trends,* 53 Temp. L.Q. 1 (1980); Randy G. Gerchick, Comment, *No Easy Way Out: Making the Summary Eviction Process a Fairer and More Efficient Alternative to Landlord Self-Help,* 41 UCLA L. Rev. 759 (1994); Geraldene Sherr, Note, *New Approach to Adjudicating Tenant's Abandonment of Premises,* 9 Cardozo L. Rev. 1811 (1988).

circumstances, T and L could mutually agree to terminate the lease, ending their respective rights and duties. In property terminology, T *surrenders* the premises, and L *accepts* the surrender. In most jurisdictions, the Statute of Frauds applies to an express surrender; in general, if the original lease had to be in writing, the surrender must also be in writing.

§ 19.03 Abandonment

[A] Abandonment in Context

It is crucial—and often difficult—to distinguish between abandonment and continued possession. Assume L suspects that T has abandoned the leased premises. If this assessment is correct, L may (among other rights) terminate the lease, reenter the premises, and retake possession. But if L's conclusion is wrong, the attempted reentry may be deemed forcible eviction,[2] subjecting L to liability for damages (*see* § 19.05[A]).

Assuming an abandonment has occurred, what are the landlord's rights? The common law offered the landlord a range of options in this situation, including the option of reletting the premises to mitigate the tenant's liability for future rent. Today the law is moving steadily toward restricting these traditional options. In an increasing number of jurisdictions, the landlord *must* mitigate damages, unless the lease is terminated altogether. The dominant issue in the area is: should mitigation be optional or mandatory?

[B] What Is Abandonment?

Abandonment occurs when the tenant:

(1) vacates the leased premises without justification;

(2) lacks the present intent to return; and

(3) defaults in the payment of rent.[3]

Because abandonment is a question of fact, a landlord may be uncertain as to whether this standard is met.[4]

The most common problem is ascertaining whether the tenant has vacated the property without a present intent to return. Suppose that midway through a ten-year lease for his wine store, T suddenly sells off most of his merchandise in a giant sale, fires his employees, places a "Closed" sign in the window, fails to pay the rent due on the first day of the month, and stops coming to the store. Two weeks later, L receives a postcard from Australia that reads: "Having a wonderful time. Wish you were here! Regards, T." L, peering through the store window, notices that the store

---

[2] *Cf.* Berg v. Wiley, 264 N.W.2d 145 (Minn. 1978) (landlord who wrongfully evicted tenant held liable for over $34,000 in damages, despite landlord's assertion that he believed tenant had abandoned the premises).

[3] Restatement (Second) of Property: Landlord & Tenant § 12.1 cmt. i (1977).

[4] *See generally* Geraldene Sherr, Note, *New Approach to Adjudicating Tenant's Abandonment of Premises,* 9 Cardozo L. Rev. 1811 (1988) (discussing application of standard).

is empty except for a few cases of wine. Has T abandoned? In resolving such cases, courts typically consider the tenant's statements, the nature and quantity of tenant property left behind, the duration of the tenant's absence, and related factors.[5]

[C] Rights of Landlord When Tenant Abandons

[1] Three Traditional Options

At common law, the landlord was free to choose among three remedies when a tenant abandoned the premises:

    (1)   leave the premises vacant and sue the tenant later for accrued rent;

    (2)   mitigate damages by reletting the premises to a new tenant, and then sue the original tenant for the unpaid balance; or

    (3)   terminate the lease.

This trio of options reflected the historic view that the lease was a conveyance, not a contract.

The landlord's choice among these options was based on self-interest. For example, if the abandoning tenant were solvent, and thus able to pay rent, the landlord would presumably select the first option. On the other hand, if the tenant were clearly insolvent, the landlord would minimize the loss by terminating the lease, retaking possession, and trying to lease the premises to a new tenant as quickly as possible.

The modern trend toward treating the lease as a contract has somewhat modified these options. There is a clear national trend toward requiring mitigation of damages if the landlord chooses not to terminate the lease.[6] Over time, this trend may entirely eliminate the first traditional option. Yet, this pro-tenant development is somewhat counterbalanced by a slight pro-landlord trend. If breach of lease is analyzed in contract terms, the landlord should be able to treat the tenant's abandonment as an anticipatory breach of contract. This would allow the landlord to both terminate the lease and sue the tenant for damages, a rule followed in many jurisdictions.

---

[5] *See, e.g.,* Berg v. Wiley, 264 N.W.2d 145 (Minn. 1978) (no abandonment found where defaulting tenant received notice to vacate from landlord, closed restaurant business, and fired employees, but left property on premises and engaged in remodeling work).

[6] *See generally* Sarajane Love, *Landlord's Remedies When the Tenant Abandons: Property, Contract, and Leases,* 30 U. Kan. L. Rev. 533 (1982); Glen Weissenberger, *The Landlord's Duty to Mitigate Damages on the Tenant's Abandonment: A Survey of Old Law and New Trends,* 53 Temple L.Q. 1 (1980).

[2]   Leave Premises Vacant and Sue Later for Rent

[a]   Common Law View

A landlord confronted with a tenant's abandonment could traditionally choose to leave the premises vacant and sue the tenant later for rent as it became due. Suppose T leases Greenacre from L for a five-year term, agreeing to pay $100 in rent each month; two years later, T abandons. Under this option, L would allow the land to remain vacant for the remaining three years of the lease term. L could sue T monthly as each separate rent installment became due. More realistically, once the lease term expired, L would sue T to recover the accrued rent of $3,600.

This option essentially continues the lease in full force, at least from the landlord's perspective. The landlord honors the tenant's exclusive right to possession of the premises for the full lease term, and receives the agreed rent for the entire term. This option similarly reflects the view that a lease is a conveyance. If L sold Greenacre to T, conveying fee simple absolute to him, T's decision not to live in Greenacre would be none of L's business. In the same manner, if T merely leased Greenacre for a five-year term, and then chose not to live there, the common law imposed no duty on L to mitigate damages by reletting the premises to another.

[b]   Modern Approach

The modern approach to this first option involves two opposing legal currents. On the one hand, many jurisdictions have expanded the landlord's rights—and thus encouraged use of the option—by enforcing "acceleration clauses."[7] The typical acceleration clause states that if the tenant abandons the leased premises, all future rents become immediately due and payable. Thus, under the hypothetical above, L could sue for the $3,600 in future rents as soon as T abandoned.

On the other hand, an increasing number of jurisdictions follow a wholly contrary view: abolishing this first option altogether.[8] In these jurisdictions, the landlord is required to either terminate the lease or mitigate damages by attempting to lease the premises to a new tenant. This trend is discussed below.

[3]   Mitigate Damages by Reletting Premises on Tenant's Behalf

[a]   Common Law View

The landlord's second traditional option was to continue the lease in effect, but relet the premises *on the tenant's behalf* in order to lessen or

---

[7] *See, e.g.,* Aurora Business Park Assoc. v. Albert, Inc., 548 N.W.2d 153 (Iowa 1996) (acceleration clause valid so long as it did not constitute a penalty). *See also* Restatement (Second) of Property: Landlord & Tenant § 12.1 cmt. k (1977).

[8] Unif. Residential Landlord & Tenant Act § 4.203(c), 7B U.L.A. 495.

mitigate the tenant's liability for rent. Suppose again that T abandons Greenacre three years before the lease ends. L could keep the L-T lease in effect, and—on T's behalf—lease Greenacre to X, a new tenant, for the balance of the lease term, applying the rent received from X to T's debt to L. T will owe $3,600 in rent over the next three years. Assuming X pays $95 in monthly rent, then X will pay $3,420 during this period. L will credit this $3,420 against the $3,600 owed by T, leaving T obligated only for an additional $180.

The existence of this second option leads to a practical question. Suppose T abandons, and L then relets the premises to a new tenant.[9] Did L indeed relet on the *tenant's* behalf (leaving T liable for any rent deficiency) or did L impliedly terminate the lease and relet on the *landlord's* behalf (eliminating T's rent liability)? The key is the intent of the landlord. But unless L notifies T about the reason for the reletting, a court may find difficulty distinguishing between the two situations. Under these circumstances, the court tries to ascertain the landlord's intent by examining how closely the new tenancy resembles the prior tenancy with respect to factors such as the length of the term, the nature of any alterations to the premises, and the rent amount.[10] For example, where the new tenancy is for a term longer than the remaining balance of the original tenant's lease, the landlord makes substantial alterations to the premises to suit the new tenant's needs, and the new rent is higher than the original rent, the reletting is on the landlord's behalf.

[b] Modern Approach

[i] Toward Mandatory Mitigation

In most jurisdictions, the residential or commercial landlord must now make a reasonable effort to mitigate the damages caused by a tenant's abandonment in order to recover the rent due under the lease.[11] The scope of this principle varies from state to state. While a majority of states require mitigation by all landlords, others apply the principle only to residential landlords. The overall trend, however, is clear. The number of jurisdictions adhering to the traditional no-mitigation rule continues to dwindle, despite its endorsement by the Restatement (Second) of Property.[12]

---

[9] *See, e.g.,* Mesilla Valley Mall Co. v. Crown Indus., 808 P.2d 633 (N.M. 1991) (where landlord reentered store space in shopping mall after tenant abandonment, and allowed a museum to occupy the space rent-free—thus attracting more customers to the shopping center—the original lease terminated).

[10] *But see* U.S. Nat'l Bank of Oregon v. Homeland, Inc., 631 P.2d 761 (Or. 1981) (reletting for a longer period and for a higher rent is not necessarily a termination of the original lease).

[11] *See* Austin Hill Country Realty, Inc. v. Palisades Plaza, Inc., 948 S.W.2d 293 (Tex. 1997) (observing that 42 states and the District of Columbia recognize that the landlord has a duty to mitigate in at least some situations); Reid v. Mutual of Omaha Ins. Co., 776 P.2d 896 (Utah 1989) (adopting rule); *see also* Unif. Residential Landlord & Tenant Act § 4.203(c), 7B U.L.A. 495 (requiring mitigation by residential landlords).

[12] Restatement (Second) of Property: Landlord & Tenant § 12.1 (1977).

In a jurisdiction following the modern trend, the landlord has an economic incentive to mitigate, but not a legal duty to do so. Suppose T leases L's house for one year, agreeing to pay $1,000 per month in rent; two months later, T abandons the property. If L takes reasonable steps to relet the house—even if his effort is unsuccessful—he is entitled to recover the full rental balance of $10,000. Assume that L is able to relet the house to new tenant X one month later, for $1,000 per month. The rent that L receives from X ($9,000) will be offset against the total rent owed by T ($10,000); this leaves T liable only for the difference ($1,000), plus reasonable leasing costs (e.g., $100 for advertising) that L has incurred. L receives a full recovery ($10,000). Suppose instead that L reasonably tries to relet the house, but cannot find a replacement tenant; T is still liable for the full rental balance of $10,000.

What if L does nothing at all to mitigate his damages? Here the law penalizes L for his failure: it reduces his rent recovery against T by the amount L could have obtained through mitigation. This reduction is usually measured by the fair rental value of the premises. Thus, if L *could have* obtained $9,000 in rents from a new tenant, T's $10,000 rent liability will be reduced by this sum, leaving T liable only for the $1,000 balance.

The modern trend toward mandatory mitigation is well-illustrated by the New Jersey Supreme Court's decision in *Sommer v. Kridel*.[13] Landlord Sommer leased an apartment unit in a large complex to tenant Kridel for a two-year term. At the time, Kridel was engaged to be married; he planned to live in the apartment with his new wife. But the wedding plans were canceled and, as a result, Kridel never occupied the apartment. He sent a letter to Sommer asking to be released from the lease. Instead of responding, Sommer exercised the common law landlord's first option: he allowed the unit to remain vacant for over a year without any effort to mitigate damages. When Sommer ultimately sued Kridel for accrued rent, Kridel asserted that the failure to mitigate barred recovery. Although finding a national split of authority on the issue, the court concluded that the trend in recent out-of-state cases appeared to be in favor of mandatory mitigation. Explaining that leases should be governed by the "more modern notions of fairness and equity" inherent in contract law, not "antiquated real property concepts," the court held that Sommer was obligated to mitigate his damages.[14] The policy rationale for mandatory mitigation—discussed only in general terms by the *Sommer* court—is evaluated in more detail below.

[ii] Policy Arguments on Mitigation

The utilitarian arguments in favor of mitigation focus on the waste of housing resources. The traditional rule motivates the landlord to keep the abandoning tenant's unit vacant. All other things being equal, a landlord would probably prefer receiving full rent for a vacant apartment than for an occupied apartment; an absent tenant, for example, imposes no wear

---

[13] 378 A.2d 767 (N.J. 1977).

[14] Sommer v. Kridel, 378 A.2d 767, 773 (N.J. 1977).

and tear on the unit. Thus, the traditional rule effectively removes tens of thousands of units from the market, decreasing the availability of rental housing.[15]

One might argue, of course, that the tenant can avoid this loss simply by assigning or subleasing, without any need for landlord mitigation. Yet the landlord is usually better situated to relet the unit than the abandoning tenant. Why? The landlord is in the business of renting units, and is thus more likely to be familiar with successful and cost-effective techniques. Indeed, the landlord may already have a marketing program in place that continually recruits new tenants; this program could easily be utilized to obtain a replacement tenant. Further, in many instances a tenant cannot assign or sublease because the remaining term of the lease is too short (e.g., only three months) to attract a replacement tenant. The landlord can overcome this practical difficulty by offering a lease term that is sufficiently long to attract tenants. In short, imposing the burden of reletting on the landlord is economically efficient. It maximizes the likelihood of success and minimizes the cost of the process.

Most standard arguments against mandatory mitigation rely on a rather rigid—and almost libertarian—vision of property rights.[16] If the lease is viewed strictly as a conveyance, the landlord need not be concerned with whether the tenant chooses to use the premises. And, having made a personal choice in the selection of the original tenant, the landlord should neither be forced to accept a replacement tenant nor be compelled to look for one. Rather, the landlord should be entitled to enforce the lease as written until and unless he voluntarily gives up his rights. Given the law's modern propensity to view the lease as a specialized form of contract, these arguments seem somewhat archaic.[17]

Perhaps a more persuasive justification for the traditional rule is the "lost sale." Suppose landlord L owns a two-unit apartment building; one unit ("unit A") is leased to T for $500 per month and the other ("unit B") is vacant. There is an excess supply of rental housing on the market, so finding new tenants is difficult. L has been seeking a new tenant for unit B for weeks, without success. T now abandons unit A. P, a prospective tenant, now approaches L. Assume L has no duty to mitigate. L shows P only unit B; P enters into a lease of unit B for $500 per month; and L is now entitled to a total of $1,000 per month in rents ($500 from T and $500 from P). Under the modern approach, however, L must show P both units in order to mitigate damages. If P now leases unit A for $500 per month, L must apply this rent to reduce the rent T owes. L is now entitled to only $500 per month in rents ($500 from P, and nothing from T), but still has a vacant unit.

---

[15] *See* Austin Hill Country Realty, Inc. v. Palisades Plaza, Inc., 948 S.W.2d 293 (Tex. 1997) (discussing rationale for mandatory mitigation).

[16] *See, e.g.,* Gruman v. Investors Diversified Servs., Inc., 78 N.W.2d 377 (Minn. 1956) (discussing reasons supporting traditional rule); Austin Hill Country Plaza, Inc. v. Palisades Plaza, Inc., 948 S.W.2d 293 (Tex. 1997) (same).

[17] *See also* Restatement (Second) of Property: Landlord & Tenant § 12.1 cmt. i (1977) (noting that abandonment of property is an invitation to vandalism that the law should discourage by requiring landlords to mitigate).

Under this scenario, mandatory mitigation both insulates the breaching T from liability and causes economic harm to L: a "lost sale." The sale is lost, of course, only if P would have leased unit B. While it is true that "each apartment may have unique qualities which make it attractive," as the New Jersey Supreme Court suggested in *Sommer v. Kridel*,[18] this rationale has no application to the typical large-scale apartment complex where the units are virtually identical. On the other hand, the "lost sale" objection has little weight if there is such demand for rental housing that a landlord can readily fill vacant units.

[iii]   Mechanics of Mitigation

Under the majority rule, a landlord must take reasonable steps to relet the premises to a new tenant on terms that will mitigate the original tenant's rent liability to the extent feasible.[19] This standard mandates a reasonable effort, not guaranteed success. No precise formula is used to measure the adequacy of the landlord's effort. In a broad sense, the landlord must make the same effort that any commercially reasonable landlord would undertake to rent any vacant unit.[20] Factors relevant to this inquiry include:

(1)   the extent to which the landlord advertised the unit for rent;

(2)   the extent to which the landlord offered or showed the unit to prospective tenants;

(3)   the remaining length of the original lease term;

(4)   the cost of preparing the property for a new tenant;

(5)   the market rent for comparable units; and

(6)   how far the terms of any replacement lease deviate from the terms of the original lease.

There is a wide split of authority concerning who has the burden of proof on reasonableness; some states place the burden on the landlord and others impose it on the tenant.[21]

One interesting cluster of issues revolves around the amount of rent demanded from the substitute tenant. For example, must the landlord relet the premises for *less* than the original rent if necessary to procure a new tenant? Some courts suggest that the landlord is not required to accept a reduced rent or a rent below market value, presumably because this might affect the amount of rent the landlord could charge for other units.[22] On

---

[18] 378 A.2d 767, 772 (N.J. 1977).

[19] *See, e.g.,* Austin Hill Country Realty, Inc. v. Palisades Plaza, Inc., 948 S.W.2d 293 (Tex. 1997) (duty to mitigate "requires the landlord to use objectively reasonable efforts to fill the premises when the tenant vacates in breach of the lease").

[20] *Cf.* Sommer v. Kridel, 378 A.2d 767 (N.J. 1977) (landlord should "treat the apartment in question as if it was one of his vacant stock").

[21] *See, e.g.,* Middagh v. Stanal Sound Ltd., 452 N.W.2d 260 (Neb. 1990) (burden on tenant); Portland General Electric v. Hershiser, Mitchell, Mowery & Davis, 738 P.2d 593 (Or. Ct. App. 1987) (burden on landlord).

[22] *See, e.g.,* Easterling v. Halter Marine, Inc., 470 So. 2d 221 (La. Ct. App. 1985).

the other hand, if the current fair rental value of the premises is less than the original tenant's lease rent, the landlord has no justification for refusing to accept the lower rent. But what if the landlord is able to relet the premises for *more* than the original rent? The situation arises only rarely. After all, if the premises can be relet at a higher rent, the landlord is likely to terminate the original lease and relet the premises for the landlord's own benefit. In the few mitigation cases where the issue arises, courts typically require the landlord to apply the "surplus" rents to cover any past rent defaults and leasing expenses; the logic of this approach suggests that once these obligations are satisfied, the balance of "surplus" rents should be paid to the original tenant.

[4] Terminate the Lease

[a] Common Law View

The final landlord option at common law was to terminate the lease. Under this option, the tenant's abandonment is deemed an *implied* offer of surrender. The landlord's acceptance of this offer terminates the lease, and ends the respective lease obligations of the parties (*see* § 19.02). The landlord is now free to retake possession of the premises, and lease them *on his own behalf* to a new tenant.

Suppose L elects to accept T's surrender of the Greenacre lease. L may now retake possession for his own benefit and either occupy Greenacre personally or lease it to a new tenant. T no longer has any rights in Greenacre and is not liable for future rent; of course, T is still liable for any unpaid rent that accrued before the lease ended. The common law did not allow damages for anticipatory breach of contract. Thus, a landlord like L who terminated a lease forfeited any claim to future damages from the tenant.

[b] Modern Approach

Just as at common law, a landlord may elect to treat the tenant's abandonment as an implied offer of surrender, accept the offer, and terminate the lease. But is the abandoning tenant liable for damages? A number of jurisdictions continue to follow the common law rule on the issue.

But in a majority of states, lease termination merely ends the tenant's liability for *rent* accruing in the future, not the tenant's liability for *damages*. Applying contract law principles, these jurisdictions view tenant abandonment as an anticipatory breach of contract.[23] Accordingly, they allow the landlord to terminate the lease, retake possession of the premises, and also sue the tenant for damages. Damages are typically measured by the difference, if any, between (a) the rent specified in the lease and (b) the fair rental value of the premises. For example, if T abandons the premises with three years remaining on her lease, the lease rent is $250 per month, and the fair rental value of the premises is $200 per month,

---

[23] *See, e.g.*, Sagamore Corp. v. Willcutt, 180 A. 464 (Conn. 1935).

T is liable for $1,800 ($50 per month for 36 months). More commonly, however, the rent agreed upon by the parties to a short-term lease accurately reflects the fair rental value of the premises, and accordingly the landlord's damages are zero. A more difficult situation arises if the tenant abandons in the middle of a long-term lease, e.g., where a 50-year lease term remains. Damages can be recovered for a reasonable period of time, but claims for later periods may be speculative (and thus unavailable) simply because it is difficult to predict fair rental value far into the future.

§ 19.04 Landlord's Right to Terminate Lease

[A] Periodic Tenancy

[1] In General

At common law, both the landlord and the tenant were completely free to terminate a periodic tenancy for any reason—or indeed, for no reason at all—simply by giving appropriate advance notice to the other party.[24] For example, L could end T's month-to-month tenancy because L disliked T's jokes or hated T's sports car. The rights of the contemporary tenant are still governed by this generous common law standard; T is free to end the tenancy by notice, without any reason.

For reasons of public policy, however, the landlord's parallel right to terminate the tenancy is increasingly restricted by modern law. In most jurisdictions, the landlord need not establish "good cause" in order to end a periodic tenancy. In this sense, the common law right endures; with advance notice, the landlord may terminate such a tenancy without any reason.[25] But termination undertaken for improper reasons—notably discrimination or retaliation—is illegal. L may not evict residential tenant T, for example, because of T's race, gender, or national origin (see § 16.02[B][1]). Similarly, in most states L may not evict T in retaliation for T's complaints concerning housing conditions or related issues.

In addition, the landlord has the right to terminate a periodic tenancy, even during its term, based on a material breach of the tenant's obligations under the same standards that apply to a term of years tenancy (see [B], below).

---

[24] *Cf.* Vasquez v. Glassboro Service Ass'n, Inc., 415 A.2d 1156 (N.J. 1980) (migrant farmworkers were not tenants, and thus not entitled to notice); Arbenz v. Exley, Watkins & Co., 50 S.E. 813 (W. Va. 1905) (notice from tenant technically insufficient to terminate periodic tenancy).

[25] *But see* Deborah H. Bell, *Providing Security of Tenure for Residential Tenants: Good Faith as a Limitation on the Landlord's Right to Terminate,* 19 Ga. L. Rev. 483 (1985) (arguing landlord should be able to evict residential tenant only for good faith reason).

[2] Retaliatory Eviction

[a] General Principles

The implied warranty of habitability and other reforms aimed at ensuring decent housing might, if left unprotected, be circumvented by evicting the periodic tenant. Suppose T, a month-to-month tenant, withholds rent because his landlord repeatedly refuses to fix the apartment's defective toilet. L fixes the toilet, and then promptly sends T a thirty-day notice terminating the tenancy. T's eviction rids L of a "troublemaker" who is likely to raise future complaints. Further, it sends a clear warning to L's other tenants that protest is dangerous. Especially if housing is in short supply, tenants in such an atmosphere would be unlikely to risk eviction by complaining. In order to close this potential loophole in the system, most jurisdictions now prohibit such *retaliatory eviction*.

The doctrine of retaliatory eviction originated in the 1969 decision of *Edwards v. Habib*.[26] After the tenant complained to local authorities about 40 sanitary code violations in her District of Columbia dwelling, the landlord served her with an eviction notice. In the summary eviction trial that ensued, the court concluded that evidence of the landlord's retaliatory intent was irrelevant, and directed a verdict for the landlord. The District of Columbia Circuit reversed, holding that a landlord was not free to evict a tenant in retaliation for housing complaints. The court's rationale focused on the congressional intent underlying two potentially conflicting federal statutes: the sanitary code and the general statutes permitting the eviction of tenants. The court reasoned that the enactment of the sanitary code reflected congressional concern to ensure safe and sanitary housing for "slum dwellers" in the District of Columbia, which suffered from a shortage of housing; this goal would be frustrated if tenants could be evicted in retaliation for reporting a violation. The two statutes could be harmonized, the court explained, if the eviction statutes were deemed inapplicable "where the court's aid is invoked to effect an eviction in retaliation for reporting housing code violations."[27]

In the wake of *Edwards,* some jurisdictions adopted the doctrine by judicial decision. However, a majority of jurisdictions—over 30 states— opted to provide statutory protection against retaliatory eviction. Most of these statutes are based on a provision of the Uniform Residential Landlord and Tenant Act.[28] As a general rule, the doctrine applies only to residential tenancies, but in a few states it may encompass commercial tenancies as well.[29]

---

[26] 397 F.2d 687 (D.C. Cir. 1968).

[27] Edwards v. Habib, 397 F.2d 687, 702 (D.C. Cir. 1968).

[28] Unif. Residential Landlord & Tenant Act § 5.101, 7B U.L.A. 503 (1972).

[29] *See, e.g.,* Windward Partners v. Delos Santos, 577 P.2d 326 (Haw. 1978).

[b] Scope of Doctrine

The scope of the retaliatory eviction doctrine varies broadly from state to state. The key variables are: (1) what tenant conduct is protected? and (2) what landlord conduct is prohibited?

The core activity protected under the doctrine is the tenant's exercise of rights to secure decent housing. Thus, covered tenant conduct typically includes complaints about housing conditions to the landlord or government agencies,[30] rent withholding for breach of the implied warranty of habitability, use of the repair-and-deduct remedy, and similar actions.[31] Beyond this core, the contours of protected activity are difficult to map. A number of jurisdictions extend protection to forming or joining a tenant's union or similar organization.[32] Some states apply the doctrine to conduct that has only a tenuous link—or no link—with concern for adequate housing (e.g., refusing to commit perjury at landlord's request, opposing the landlord's plan to develop the property, or reporting landlord's criminal behavior to police).[33] In theory, if the scope of the doctrine continues to expand, it could ultimately restrict the landlord's rights to the point where good cause is required for any eviction.

Despite its name, the retaliatory eviction doctrine prohibits types of retaliatory conduct other than eviction. A landlord may not raise rent or reduce services in retaliation for protected tenant conduct.[34] Otherwise, the landlord could easily circumvent any ban on eviction by the simple expedient of raising rent to an astronomical level or eliminating essential services. But a rent increase or service reduction that is applied uniformly to all tenants, without singling out particular tenants for discriminatory treatment, is unlikely to be considered retaliatory.

[c] Mechanics

How can a tenant prove that the landlord acted from a retaliatory motivation? If direct proof of landlord motivation were required, the doctrine would be relatively useless; the tenant would encounter great difficulty in trying to prove the landlord's state of mind.

Most jurisdictions overcome this obstacle through an evidentiary presumption: if the landlord takes a prohibited action within a certain period (usually 90 days to one year) after the tenant engages in protected conduct, the action is presumed to be retaliatory.[35] For example, if T complains that

---

[30] *See, e.g.,* Dickhut v. Norton, 173 N.W.2d 297 (Wis. 1970) (complaint to housing officials).

[31] *See, e.g.,* Robinson v. Diamond Hous. Corp., 463 F.2d 853 (D.C. Cir. 1972) (tenant's assertion of "illegal lease" theory to defeat landlord's earlier eviction action was protected conduct).

[32] *See, e.g.,* Hillview Assocs. v. Bloomquist, 440 N.W.2d 867 (Iowa 1989) (conduct of mobile home park tenants in forming tenants' association and making complaints about landlord's failure to maintain park was protected under Iowa law).

[33] *But see* Imperial Colliery Co. v. Fout, 373 S.E.2d 489 (W. Va. 1988) (eviction in retaliation for participating in labor strike not covered by doctrine).

[34] *See, e.g.,* Cal. Civ. Code § 1942.5.

[35] *See, e.g.,* Robinson v. Diamond Hous. Corp., 463 F.2d 853 (D.C. Cir. 1972) (approving use of presumption).

his apartment is infested by cockroaches and two days later L serves T with a notice ending his month-to-month tenancy, the eviction is presumed to be in retaliation for the complaint. Once the presumption arises, the burden shifts to the landlord to establish that the action was not motivated by retaliation. As a practical matter, this usually requires the landlord to demonstrate objective good cause for the action (e.g., the eviction notice was sent because the tenant routinely sold drugs on the premises).[36]

What if the landlord takes a prohibited action only after the specified period ends? Assume, for example, L serves T with a notice terminating his month-to-month tenancy 14 months after T complains about the cockroaches. T still has the right to assert retaliatory eviction, but can no longer utilize the presumption. In order to prevail, T must now prove L's intent was retaliatory. The time-limited presumption rests on the belief that—for most landlords—retaliatory motivation will dissipate over time as emotion ebbs and reason returns.

Another problem might be described as "mixed motivation." Does the doctrine apply to a landlord's action that stems from a blend of motives, part retaliatory and part non-retaliatory? The law on this issue is fragmented into a number of different approaches. The most widely accepted view, championed by the Restatement (Second) of Property, is that retaliation need only be the dominant purpose.[37] Under another approach, retaliation must be the landlord's sole motive;[38] at the opposite extreme, a third approach provides that any retaliatory motivation at all, however slight, triggers the doctrine.

The doctrine is principally used as a defense to a landlord's summary proceeding to recover possession of the premises. In some jurisdictions, it also provides a basis for obtaining either compensatory damages or an injunction against the landlord's wrongful conduct.

[3]　Good Cause Eviction

Two jurisdictions—New Jersey and the District of Columbia—follow the minority view that a residential landlord may evict a periodic tenant (or refuse to renew a term of years tenancy) only for "good cause."[39] This approach reflects a strong public policy in favor of protecting the family home against arbitrary landlord action. Suppose T enters into a month-to-month residential tenancy with L in one of these jurisdictions; L cannot evict T unless she can establish a legitimate reason (e.g., T fails to pay rent, intentionally injures the premises, engages in criminal behavior on the

---

[36] See, e.g., Robinson v. Diamond Hous. Corp., 463 F.2d 853 (D.C. Cir. 1972) (suggesting that landlord's financial inability to make required repairs could be basis for removing property from market, and thus evicting tenant); Hillview Assocs. v. Bloomquist, 440 N.W.2d 867 (Iowa 1989) (landlord proved non-retaliatory motivation by showing tenant shouted insults at landlord's agent and then physically attacked agent).

[37] Restatement (Second) of Property: Landlord & Tenant § 14.8 cmt. f (1977).

[38] See, e.g., Dickhut v. Norton, 173 N.W.2d 297 (Wis. 1970).

[39] D.C. Code Ann. § 45-2551; N.J. Stat. Ann. § 2A:18-61.1.

premises, or repeatedly causes unreasonably loud noises that disturb other tenants).

The good cause standard applies in two other contexts. First, tenants in public housing or federally-subsidized private housing are protected by federal laws that require just cause for eviction;[40] this rule is intended to safeguard the home against arbitrary governmental action. Second, local rent control ordinances impose a similar requirement, but for a different reason. Absent good cause eviction, landlords could minimize the effectiveness of a rent control ordinance by evicting low-rent tenants, and replacing them with tenants who are either unsophisticated about their rights or willing to pay an illegally high rent.

The good faith eviction standard effectively creates a new type of nonfreehold estate. Suppose L and T initially create a periodic, month-to-month tenancy in a jurisdiction following this standard. T is still free to terminate her lease for any reason or no reason, upon 30-days notice to L, as in a periodic tenancy. However, T has the right to remain in the leased premises for her lifetime, so long as she refrains from improper conduct; from this perspective, the estate resembles a tenancy at will.

[B] Term of Years Tenancy

Termination issues concerning the term of years tenancy arise in two contexts, each governed by different rules. The landlord might seek to end the lease in the middle of the term based on the tenant's breach. Alternatively, the landlord might refuse to renew or extend the lease beyond the agreed-upon term.

As a general rule, the early common law did not allow the landlord to terminate the lease due to the tenant's breach. Because lease covenants were seen as independent of each other (*see* § 17.02[D]), the landlord's remedy was to sue the tenant for damages, not end the tenancy.[41] English landlords quickly circumvented this rule by inserting "forfeiture clauses" into their leases; these clauses granted the landlord the right to terminate the lease upon the tenant's breach of a lease covenant.

Even absent a forfeiture clause, most jurisdictions now permit the landlord to terminate the tenancy if the tenant *materially* breaches any lease covenant. Examples of material breaches include: failure to pay rent; use of premises for an illegal purpose; unauthorized assignment; failure to insure the premises; and failure to keep the premises in good repair.[42] On the other hand, where the tenant's breach is relatively trivial or immaterial (e.g., a brief delay in paying rent), the landlord may only recover damages.[43]

---

[40] *See, e.g.,* 42 U.S.C. § 1437f(d)(1)(B).

[41] *See, e.g.,* Brown's Adm'r v. Bragg, 22 Ind. 122 (1864) (landlord could not terminate lease due to tenant's failure to pay rent).

[42] *Cf.* Medico-Dental Bldg. Co. v. Horton & Converse, 132 P.2d 457 (Cal. 1942) (landlord who covenanted to drug store tenant not to lease space in building to another drug store materially breached covenant by leasing to physician who operated pharmacy as part of his medical practice).

[43] *See, e.g.,* Foundation Dev. Corp. v. Loehmann's, Inc., 788 P.2d 1189 (Ariz. 1990) (two-day delay in payment of rent held immaterial).

Consistent with the maxim that equity abhors forfeiture, courts often stretch these rules to avoid terminating a long-term lease, by construing the tenant's duties narrowly or by finding the landlord waived the breach.

The landlord's traditional right to arbitrarily refuse to renew a term of years tenancy is no longer absolute. Most residential landlords, for example, cannot reject the tenant's renewal request for discriminatory reasons (*see* § 16.02[B][1]). Similarly, some courts hold that the landlord's refusal to renew a term of years tenancy constitutes retaliatory eviction, assuming the other elements of the doctrine are met.

§ 19.05 Self-Help Eviction

[A] The Common Law Foundation

Suppose T's lease terminates but T wrongfully remains in possession of the premises, ignoring L's pleas to vacate. How can L recover possession from T? At common law, the landlord had two options: (1) evict the tenant through judicial proceedings, which were usually prolonged and expensive; or (2) retake possession through "self-help," a quick and inexpensive method. While the English landlord who chose self-help could evict the tenant by force, he could not use more force than was reasonably necessary for this purpose. Under this standard, for example, L could presumably enter the premises in T's absence, remove T's possessions, and change the locks. On the other hand, if L hired a band of armed thugs to break down the door to the leased premises at midnight and throw T into the street, this would be seen as using excessive force, and thus unlawful.

Most jurisdictions in the United States still allow the landlord to recover possession through self-help. Within this group, however, there is a split of authority on what level of force is permitted. One cluster of states adheres to the traditional English rule: the landlord may use force to the extent reasonably necessary to evict a tenant. A second group follows a modified version: the landlord may retake possession only through "peaceable" methods.[44] The precise meaning of "peaceable" varies from state to state,[45] but in most states connotes an entry without threatened or actual force. For example, if L orders T out of the premises at gunpoint, the threat of force prevents the eviction from being considered peaceable, even though no actual violence erupted.

What is the tenant's remedy when the landlord uses improper force? Forcible entry and detainer statutes in many states permit the tenant to recover damages for wrongful eviction,[46] while some jurisdictions allow the

---

[44] *See* Restatement (Second) of Property: Landlord & Tenant § 14.1 statutory note (1977).

[45] *See, e.g.,* Spinks v. Taylor, 278 S.E.2d 501 (N.C. 1981) (padlocking apartment in tenant's absence was "peaceable").

[46] *See, e.g.,* Jordan v. Talbot, 361 P.2d 20 (Cal. 1961) (landlord who unlocked door of apartment and removed tenant's furniture to warehouse held liable for $6,500 for forcible entry, plus punitive damages); Berg v. Wiley, 264 N.W.2d 145 (Minn. 1978) (landlord who changed locks in tenant's absence held liable for $31,000 in lost profits, plus other damages). *See also* Luis J. DeGraffe, *The Historical Evolution of American Forcible Entry and Detainer Statutes,* 13 Seton Hall Legis. J. 129 (1990).

ejected tenant to sue in tort.[47]

[B] Criticism of Self-Help

To the modern eye, the self-help remedy is a feudal relic: an anachronism from an era when seemingly sacrosanct property rights were mechanically enforced regardless of the impact on human dignity. The case against self-help is dominated by three utilitarian arguments: (1) the risk of violence; (2) the possibility of unjustified eviction; and (3) the availability of an alternative remedy.[48]

The principal argument against self-help is the risk of violence.[49] It is readily foreseeable that violence may erupt when a landlord uses force to evict the tenant, potentially injuring the tenant, the landlord, or third parties.[50] Even the landlord's good faith belief that self-help will be peaceable may be mistaken. Suppose landlord L "knows" that his holdover tenant T has left the rented house and gone out of town on vacation for a week; L plans to enter the house and change the locks in T's absence. Two dangerous scenarios could occur. First, if L's information is wrong, T may still be in possession of the house. When L tries to enter, T may well defend his home; the potential for violence is even greater if T—unable to identify L in the sudden confusion—mistakes L for a burglar. Alternatively, even if L's information is correct and his initial occupation of the home is peaceable, violence may occur upon T's return.

A second concern is the possibility of unjustified eviction. A landlord may exercise self-help only if legally entitled to retake possession. Yet, in practice, the landlord becomes the judge of his or her own rights. Suppose T has the legal right to remain in the premises, but L (either aware of T's right or mistakenly believing T has no right) uses self-help to evict T. In theory, the law provides a safeguard against such landlord behavior: the tenant may sue for wrongful eviction. Yet, various barriers may render this remedy meaningless for most tenants, particularly poor residential tenants.[51] These barriers may include ignorance that a cause of action exists, the expense of litigation, the small amount of damages potentially

---

[47] *Cf.* Kobouroff v. Blake, 183 N.Y.S.2d 934 (N.Y. Mun. Ct. 1959) (landlord who peeked into tenant's apartment window and later padlocked the apartment was liable in damages for breach of warranty of quiet enjoyment).

[48] *See generally* Randy G. Gerchick, Comment, *No Easy Way Out: Making the Summary Eviction Process a Fairer and More Efficient Alternative to Landlord Self-Help,* 41 UCLA L. Rev. 759 (1994). *See also* Wheeler v. Thompson, D.C. Gen. Sess. L. & T. No. 103875-1 (December 1, 1969) (discussing rationale for abolition of self-help).

[49] *See, e.g.,* Berg v. Wiley, 264 N.W.2d 145 (Minn. 1978) (criticizing self-help remedy).

[50] *See generally* Thomas W. Earnhardt, *Peaceful Padlocking in a Perfect World: Commentary and Rebuttal,* 13 N.C. Cent. L.J. 195 (1982).

[51] *Cf.* Barbara Bezdek, *Silence in the Court: Participation and Subordination of Poor Tenants' Voices in Legal Process,* 20 Hofstra L. Rev. 533 (1992) (discussing practical barriers that poor tenants confront in litigation).

recoverable, inadequate access to attorneys, and a lack of confidence in the legal system.[52]

The final utilitarian strand focuses on the availability of an alternative remedy: summary eviction proceedings. At common law, the landlord's only judicial remedy was the slow process of ejectment (*see* § 19.06). In contrast, self-help was both inexpensive and quick. But today statutes in all states provide a simplified and expedited "mini-trial" procedure for recovering possession (*see* § 19.07). The availability of this procedure substantially undercuts the policy rationale that historically supported self-help.

[C]   The Demise of Self-Help

There is a clear movement toward abolishing the self-help remedy. Most courts that have had occasion to reconsider the common law rule in recent years have either abandoned it completely or narrowed it dramatically. In an ever-increasing number of states, the landlord's sole remedy is to evict the tenant through judicial process.[53]

Many jurisdictions have expressly jettisoned the self-help remedy by statute or case law.[54] The Minnesota Supreme Court joined this movement in the leading case of *Berg v. Wiley.*[55] The court explained that the modern trend was "founded on the recognition that the potential for violent breach of the peace inheres in any situation where a landlord attempts by his own means to remove a tenant who is claiming possession adversely to the landlord."[56] A number of states reach the same result by holding that the enactment of "forcible entry and detainer" statutes impliedly eliminated the self-help remedy.

Another approach is to redefine "peaceable" self-help. Suppose L enters the premises in T's absence by picking the locks, and then locks T out; no violence actually occurs. Traditionally such conduct was considered peaceable due to the absence of violence. Yet some modern courts —while supposedly following the common law rule—hold that self-help is not "peaceable" if the mere potential for violence exists. Under this view, L's conduct would be deemed wrongful due to the risk of violence.[57]

Suppose L, owning property in a jurisdiction that no longer permits self-help eviction, wishes to evict holdover tenant T. Can L avoid this ban by

---

[52] Personhood theory would supplement this argument by suggesting that concern for the tenant's personal interest in the family home should, under normal circumstances, outweigh the landlord's mere investment interest. *See* § 2.07.

[53] *See, e.g.,* Berg v. Wiley, 264 N.W.2d 145 (Minn. 1978). *But see* Restatement (Second) of Property: Landlord & Tenant § 14.2(1) (1977) (endorsing traditional rule).

[54] *See, e.g.,* Jordan v. Talbot, 361 P.2d 20 (Cal. 1961); Bass v. Boetel & Co., 217 N.W.2d 804 (Neb. 1974).

[55] 264 N.W.2d 145 (Minn. 1978).

[56] Berg v. Wiley, 264 N.W.2d 145, 151 (Minn. 1978).

[57] *See* Gulf Oil Corp. v. Smithey, 426 S.W.2d 262 (Tex. Civ. App. 1968); *see also* Berg v. Wiley, 264 N.W.2d 145 (Minn. 1978) (noting that such conduct would not be peaceable under the common law rule, but then rejecting the rule). *But see* Spinks v. Taylor, 278 S.E.2d 501 (N.C. 1981) (padlocking apartment in tenant's absence was "peaceable").

actions that do not involve entry into T's apartment unit, such as by cutting off T's electricity and water? No. Such provocative conduct presents virtually the same risk of violence as attempted entry. It would be considered a form of improper self-help.

With the demise of the common law rule, courts increasingly confront a new challenge: can the landlord and tenant agree in advance that the landlord may use self-help if the tenant wrongfully remains in possession? One might argue that the law should defer here to freedom of contract; presumably, the tenant received a rent discount in exchange for agreeing to allow self-help. On the other hand, such an agreement presents the same risk of violence and related concerns that triggered the demise of the common law rule. Almost universally, courts hold that these agreements are against public policy and thus void.

[D]   Constitutional Restrictions on Self-Help

The common law provided the landlord with a second self-help remedy, known as *distraint*: if the tenant defaulted in the payment of rent, the landlord could enter the leased premises, seize the tenant's personal property, and retain it until the rent was paid. Similarly, some states grant a landlord a statutory lien on the tenant's personal property to satisfy unpaid rent, together with the same right to seize tenant property to execute on the lien.[58] The constitutionality of this procedure is questionable. At least one federal court has rejected the procedure as a deprivation of property without prior notice and an opportunity for hearing, in violation of the Fourteenth Amendment's guarantee of procedural due process.[59] The issue is far from settled, however, because other courts have reached a contrary result, finding insufficient "state action" to trigger the Due Process Clause.[60]

§ 19.06   Ejectment

The common law landlord who opted for litigation over self-help could bring an ejectment action to recover possession from the breaching tenant. Yet ejectment was a frustratingly slow remedy. Courts treated an ejectment action like any other type of litigation. The tenant might remain in wrongful possession of the leased premises for months or even years, paying no rent, while the action dragged on. If the landlord ultimately recovered possession, and an accompanying judgment against the tenant for back rent, the tenant might well be insolvent. Understandably, landlords typically preferred the quick and inexpensive self-help remedy. Although ejectment is still available in theory, it has largely been supplanted by summary eviction proceedings.

---

[58] *See, e.g.,* Colo. Rev. Stat. § 38-20-102; Fla. Stat. Ann. § 713.691.

[59] *See* Hall v. Garson, 468 F.2d 845 (5th Cir. 1972).

[60] *See, e.g.,* Hitchcock v. Allison, 572 P.2d 982 (Okla. 1977).

§ 19.07 Summary Eviction Proceedings

[A] Procedural Overview

Statutes in all states now offer the landlord a special, expedited procedure for recovering possession from the breaching tenant. The procedure—usually termed *summary eviction* or *unlawful detainer*—is a type of accelerated and simplified litigation. It seeks to combine the strengths of self-help (quick and inexpensive eviction) with the virtues of judicial process (avoiding violence and unjustified eviction).

Summary eviction statutes follow the same basic pattern, although there are state-by-state variations on smaller points.[61] When a breach occurs (typically the tenant's failure to pay rent), the landlord may serve the tenant with a statutory notice that describes the nature of the breach and gives the tenant an opportunity to cure it; the tenant may avoid eviction by curing the breach within a short period (usually three to ten days). During this period, the tenant may vacate the premises, ending the lease. But if the notice period expires without tenant action, the landlord may file a lawsuit seeking summary eviction and serve the tenant with process.

Summary eviction actions are characterized by expedited timing and simplified procedures. The tenant has only a few days (usually two to five days) to respond to the complaint, instead of the 30-day period that is typical in most litigation. Pretrial discovery is often restricted or entirely unavailable. Statutes typically mandate an expedited trial of a summary eviction action; the trial may begin within days after the tenant's answer is filed, while months or even years may elapse before trial commences in an ordinary lawsuit.

The trial generally concerns only one issue: did the tenant breach a lease obligation? For decades, most states did not permit the tenant to raise any defense or counterclaim in such an action, consistent with the goal of providing a streamlined remedy. The modern "revolution" in landlord-tenant law has eroded this traditional rule. The residential tenant can defend a summary eviction action by proving a breach of the implied warranty of habitability in most jurisdictions or, in some, by establishing retaliatory eviction.[62]

The most important state-by-state variations include the delineation of which breaches trigger the remedy and what the landlord can recover. Some jurisdictions restrict the procedure to rent defaults, while others extend it to any tenant breach. In a relatively small number of jurisdictions the landlord can recover only possession, but most also allow the recovery of back rent.

Is summary eviction a quick and inexpensive remedy in practice? Isolated studies suggest that a sizable percentage of tenant-defendants (20-35%) fail

---

[61] *See, e.g.,* Lindsey v. Normet, 405 U.S. 56 (1972) (describing Oregon statute).

[62] *See* Edwards v. Habib, 397 F.2d 687 (D.C. Cir. 1968). *See also* Unif. Residential Landlord & Tenant Act § 4.105(a), 7B U.L.A. 485 (1972) (permitting tenant to raise defenses and counterclaims in summary eviction proceeding).

to file an answer, allowing the landlord to obtain a default judgment in as little as five to ten days after service of process, at minimal cost.[63] If the tenant contests the action, however, the summary eviction process may easily require two months or longer. Data on the cost of contested evictions are scant. One study sponsored by a landlord association concluded that eviction expenses (including attorneys fees, court costs, and uncollected rents) cost California landlords about $338 million annually, equal to 1% of gross revenue.[64]

[B] Constitutionality

The leading decision exploring the constitutionality of summary eviction is *Lindsey v. Normet,*[65] in which the Supreme Court largely upheld the Oregon procedure. The appellant-tenants principally argued that the statutory bar to raising defenses in the eviction action violated their rights to due process and equal protection. The Court fended off the due process attack, noting that the Oregon statute did not eliminate the tenants' claim, but merely restricted the forum in which it could be filed. The tenants were free to file a separate, non-summary lawsuit against the landlord if the claim could provide a basis for damages or other relief. The Court further rejected the tenants' equal protection argument, finding that the statute was reasonably related to the legitimate governmental purpose of achieving a rapid and peaceful settlement of landlord-tenant disputes. Significantly, it refused to accept appellants' argument that housing was a "fundamental right," which would have subjected the practice to more rigorous review.

Addressing the remaining issues, the Court upheld Oregon's requirement of an expedited trial in a summary eviction action. But it struck down Oregon's appeal bond standard—which forced the losing tenant to post a bond equal to *twice* the amount of the rent anticipated to accrue during the appeal—as a violation of equal protection.

---

[63] *See generally* Randy G. Gerchick, Comment, *No Easy Way Out: Making the Eviction Process a Fairer and More Efficient Alternative to Landlord Self-Help,* 41 UCLA L. Rev. 759, 794–795 (1994) (summarizing research).

[64] California Apartment Law Information Foundation, Unlawful Detainer Study (1991).

[65] 405 U.S. 56 (1972).

Chapter 20

THE SALES CONTRACT

SYNOPSIS

§ 20.01 Anatomy of a Sales Transaction

[A] Four Basic Stages

Millions of real property sales occur in the United States every year.[1] The vast bulk of these sales are relatively simple transactions involving *residential property*: single-family houses, condominiums, and other properties used as the owner's home. Transactions involving the sale of *commercial property*—office buildings, apartment complexes, farms, shopping centers, and the like—are typically more complex. Yet every real property sales transaction has four basic stages: (a) locating the buyer; (b) negotiating the contract; (c) preparing for the closing; and (d) closing the transaction.

Consider a hypothetical transaction. Suppose owner S wants to sell her house, Greenacre, for about $220,000. The key steps in S's sale are outlined below.

[B] Locating the Buyer

How can S find a buyer?[2] S selects real estate broker L to represent her in the transaction, and executes a written *listing agreement* that entitles

---

[1] *See generally* Michael Braunstein, *Structural Change and Inter-Professional Competitive Advantage: An Example Drawn from Real Estate Conveyancing*, 62 Mo. L. Rev. 241 (1997); Quintin Johnstone, *Land Transfers: Process and Processors*, 22 Val. U. L. Rev. 493 (1988); Anthony T. Kronman, *Specific Performance*, 45 U. Chi. L. Rev. 351 (1978); Joseph M. Perillo, *The Statute of Frauds in the Light of the Functions and Dysfunctions of Form*, 43 Fordham L. Rev. 39 (1974).

[2] The Fair Housing Act, 42 U.S.C. §§ 3601–3619, prohibits discrimination based on race,

L to a commission—probably 6% of the sales price—if he obtains a buyer willing to purchase Greenacre for $220,000 or another price acceptable to S (*see* § 20.03[C]). L, who is called the *listing broker,* now begins marketing the property. He places advertisements, holds "open houses," contacts other brokers, and otherwise tries to attract potential buyers. L may also provide information about S's house to the local *multiple listing service,* which will circulate it to all other brokers who are members of the service. Suppose C, another broker in the community, learns that Greenacre is available and calls it to the attention of her client B, who is looking for a new home. B tours Greenacre, likes it, and decides to make an offer. C, who is known as the *cooperating broker* or *selling broker,* will share in L's commission if the transaction closes.

[C] Negotiating the Contract

The transaction now moves into its second stage: contract negotiation. B makes an offer to purchase Greenacre for $200,000 by executing a written contract that satisfies the Statute of Frauds (*see* § 20.04[B]) and submitting it to S for signature; B also gives S a check for $2,000 as a good faith deposit. B might employ an attorney to draft the contract (*see* § 20.02). But instead, B will probably use a preprinted form contract originally prepared by an attorney, and broker C will help B to fill in the blanks on the form (*see* § 20.03).

Because B has not yet had the opportunity to investigate Greenacre thoroughly, he will be concerned about various issues, including the physical condition of the property (*see* Chapter 21), the availability of adequate financing (*see* Chapter 22), and the state of title (*see* Chapters 24–26). B will ensure that the contract contains various *conditions* that deal with these issues. For example, suppose B: (a) wants a licensed building contractor to confirm that Greenacre is structurally sound; (b) needs a $180,000 loan from a bank or other lender in order to purchase the property; and (c) wants to ensure that S holds valid title to Greenacre. The contract will provide that B is excused from performance if these conditions cannot be met (*see* §§ 20.06–20.07).

S might simply accept B's offer. But it is more likely that she will submit a counteroffer dealing with price and other issues. Attorneys might be involved in negotiating the transaction, but brokers L and C will probably undertake this role. Suppose S submits a written counteroffer that changes the selling price to $210,000 and B accepts. A valid contract has now been created.

---

color, religion, sex, familial status, national origin, or handicap by sellers, brokers, lenders, or others in connection with the sale of a home or other "dwelling." *See, e.g.,* Hobson v. George Humphreys, Inc., 563 F. Supp. 344 (W.D. Tenn. 1982). The Fair Housing Act is discussed in detail in connection with leases at § 16.02[B].

[D] Preparing for the Closing

During the third stage—sometimes called the *executory period* or *executory interval*—steps are taken to prepare for the closing, such as inspecting the property, negotiating financing, and evaluating title. For example, B's contractor will inspect Greenacre and provide a written report about her conclusions. State law might require that a professional inspect Greenacre for termite infestation or mandate that S, L, or C disclose to B information that adversely affects the value or desirability of Greenacre (*see* Chapter 21).

Assisted by C, B will apply to several banks or other institutional lenders for a $180,000 loan. Suppose that—after evaluating B's credit and appraising Greenacre—bank M agrees to make the loan on terms acceptable to B. M will insist that the loan be evidenced by a written *promissory note* signed by B and secured by a first priority *mortgage* that will encumber Greenacre at the closing (*see* Chapter 22).

Finally, B will evaluate the state of title to Greenacre. In many states, B's principal source of title assurance will be a *title insurance policy* issued at the closing (*see* § 26.04). Before closing, B will receive a *title report* or similar document that states (a) whether the insurer will insure title to Greenacre and (b) the terms and conditions of the policy; this document will usually identify one or more specific title defects (e.g., existing easements or CC&Rs) that the insurer is unwilling to cover. Alternatively, B might retain an attorney to provide a legal opinion on the state of title (*see* § 26.03).

[E] Closing the Transaction

The sales contract is fully and finally performed at the *closing*. In the eastern United States, an attorney often oversees the closing; in the West this function is usually performed by an *escrow agent* who follows written *escrow instructions* signed by the parties. At the closing, title is conveyed to the buyer, the purchase loan is made by the lender, the sales price is paid to the seller, the commission is distributed to the brokers, and various other tasks are performed.[3] Title is transferred by the seller's delivery of a *deed* (*see* Chapter 23) to the buyer.

Assuming all conditions are met, our hypothetical S-B transaction will successfully close. At the closing: (a) S will execute and deliver a deed conveying Greenacre to B; (b) M will loan $180,000 to B and B will give M the promissory note and the mortgage; (c) B will pay $210,000 ($180,000 from M's loan and $30,000 from B's savings) to S; and (d) S will pay the commission to L and C. The deed and mortgage will immediately be recorded (*see* Chapter 25), and B will receive a title insurance policy insuring his title to Greenacre (*see* Chapter 26).

---

[3] The Real Estate Settlement Procedures Act, 12 U.S.C. §§ 2601–2617, imposes detailed procedural requirements on almost all closings involving residential real property.

§ 20.02   Role of the Attorney

At one time, the attorney was the key professional in almost every sales transaction. His activities generally included:

   (1)   negotiating the deal;

   (2)   drafting the sales contract;

   (3)   evaluating title documents;

   (4)   issuing a title opinion;

   (5)   advising the client about zoning, tax, and other issues;

   (6)   negotiating the terms of financing;

   (7)   helping the client fulfill contract conditions;

   (8)   handling the closing; and

   (9)   negotiating or litigating any disputes that arose.

Attorneys usually still perform many of these functions in transactions involving commercial property. As a general rule, the more complex the transaction, the more likely an attorney is involved.

But the attorney's role in home sales is rapidly diminishing. As one observer concluded, attorneys "are involved only in about forty percent of residential transactions, and . . . their involvement is typically late and shallow."[4] For example, in California, Texas, and most western states, attorneys are usually not involved in home sales at all, unless a dispute arises. As discussed in the hypothetical S-B transaction (*see* § 20.01), the attorney's traditional tasks are divided among the brokers, the title insurance company, and the escrow agent. Even in the East, Midwest, and South—where the attorney is still sometimes involved in home sales—the role is typically limited to supervising the closing and resolving any disputes; attorneys rarely negotiate or draft contracts. The principal reason for this shift is the high cost of legal fees. In home sales transactions, brokers, title companies, and escrow agents generally provide adequate services for a lower price.

§ 20.03   Role of the Real Estate Broker

[A]   The Unauthorized Practice of Law?

The real estate broker has replaced the attorney as the key professional in home sales transactions. Except in a handful of states, the broker negotiates the deal, prepares the contract, handles the transaction until the closing, and—in some regions—supervises the closing. Do these actions constitute the unauthorized practice of law?

---

[4] Michael Braunstein, *Structural Change and Inter-Professional Competitive Advantage: An Example Drawn from Real Estate Conveyancing*, 62 Mo. L. Rev. 241, 241 (1997).

Most jurisdictions agree that the broker who merely fills in blanks on a standard, attorney-drafted form contract is not practicing law.[5] On the other hand, although the case law is scant, it seems that drafting a sales contract, advising a client about contract terms, or handling closings—as some brokers do—are traditional legal functions. In an influential decision, the New Jersey Supreme Court confirmed that brokers who handled home sale closings were engaged in the practice of law; but it refused to prohibit this conduct.[6] Because the procedure causes no "demonstrable harm to buyers or sellers, . . . saves money, and [was chosen by parties] of their own free will presumably with some knowledge of the risk, . . . the public interest will not be compromised by allowing the practice to continue."[7]

[B] Duties of Broker

Suppose owner S selects listing broker L to represent her in selling S's property. What duties does L owe to S? A real estate broker is a specialized type of *agent*. Like any agent, a broker owes a variety of fiduciary duties to the *principal*, including the duties of care, skill, diligence, loyalty, and good faith.[8] For example, a broker cannot disclose the principal's negotiation strategy to the opposing party in the transaction; nor can a broker accept a secret profit or "kickback" from the opposing party.

If L's marketing efforts attract cooperating broker C, whose client B enters into a contract to purchase S's property, what duties does L owe to B? At common law, the listing broker owed no duty to the buyer, except the obligation to avoid intentional fraud. Today, in some jurisdictions, a listing broker must disclose known defects in the property to the buyer.[9] On the other hand, the listing broker is not generally required to inspect the property in order to determine whether defects exist.[10]

Who is broker C's principal? One might assume that C is the agent of buyer B, her apparent client. Yet technically the cooperating broker is

---

[5] *See, e.g.,* Chicago Bar Ass'n v. Quinlan & Tyson, Inc., 214 N.E.2d 771 (Ill. 1966); State ex rel. Indiana State Bar Ass'n v. Indiana Real Estate Ass'n, 191 N.E.2d 711 (Ind. 1963); Cultum v. Heritage House Realtors, 694 P.2d 630 (Wash. 1985).

[6] *In re* Opinion No. 26 of the Committee on the Unauthorized Practice of Law, 654 A.2d 1344 (N.J. 1995).

[7] *In re* Opinion No. 26 of the Committee on the Unauthorized Practice of Law, 654 A.2d 1344, 1358 (N.J. 1995). *But see* State v. Buyers Service Co., 357 S.E.2d 15 (S.C. 1987) (prohibiting title company from handling real estate closings); Bowers v. Transamerica Title Ins. Co., 675 P.2d 193 (Wash. 1983) (holding title company liable in damages for failing to meet the standard of care required of an attorney conducting a closing).

[8] *See, e.g.,* Haymes v. Rogers, 222 P.2d 789 (Ariz. 1950) (listing broker cannot disclose to prospective buyer that seller will accept less than listing price for property).

[9] *See, e.g.,* Strawn v. Canuso, 657 A.2d 420 (N.J. 1995) (listing broker obligated to disclose presence of nearby hazardous waste dump site to home buyers).

[10] *See, e.g.,* Kubinsky v. Van Zandt Realtors, 811 S.W.2d 711 (Tex. Ct. App. 1991); Teter v. Old Colony Co., 441 S.E.2d 728 (W.Va. 1994); Thomson v. McGinnis, 465 S.E.2d 922 (W.Va. 1995). *But see* Easton v. Strassburger, 199 Cal. Rptr. 383 (Ct. App. 1984) (requiring listing broker to inspect residential property listed for sale and to disclose to buyers all material facts revealed by investigation); Cal. Civ. Code §§ 2079–2079.4 (codifying *Easton* rule).

usually deemed a subagent of the listing broker; this makes C an agent of the seller. In many instances, the cooperating broker is a *dual agent*, who—at least in theory—owes fiduciary duties to both the buyer and the seller. In the same manner, if there is only one broker in the transaction, he will probably be deemed a dual agent, even though this might not match the expectations of the parties. In an effort to combat this dilemma, some states have adopted legislation requiring brokers to disclose in advance which party or parties they represent.[11]

[C] Broker's Right to Commission

The broker's right to a commission is governed by the listing agreement. The listing agreement is a contract between the seller and the listing broker that authorizes the broker to procure a buyer for the property in return for a specified commission. There are three basic types of listing agreements: the *open listing,* the *exclusive agency listing,* and the *exclusive right to sell listing.* Under an open listing, the broker does not have any exclusive right to obtain a buyer; rather, it obligates the seller to pay a commission if the broker is the first person to procure a "ready, willing, and able buyer" for the property. The broker under an exclusive agency listing is designated as the only real estate broker authorized to procure buyers; thus, he is entitled to a commission if any broker produces a ready, willing, and able buyer, but not if the seller procures a buyer. Finally, under the exclusive right to sell listing, the broker receives a commission if anyone—including the seller—procures a ready, willing, and able buyer.

Suppose seller S enters into an exclusive right to sell listing with broker L; L produces B, a buyer who is ready, willing, and able to purchase the property. B and S enter into a sales contract, but B later refuses to perform. Is S obligated to pay a commission to L? Under the majority view, the commission is earned when the broker procures a buyer who is ready, willing, and able to purchase the property on terms acceptable to the seller, even if the buyer later fails to complete the purchase. This rule is patently unfair to the seller. The average seller reasonably expects to pay a commission only if the sale is completed. For this reason, an increasing number of courts hold that the broker is not entitled to a commission unless the sale is actually completed.[12] This rule is subject to one major exception: a commission is still owed if the sale fails due to a wrongful act of the seller.[13]

---

[11] *See, e.g.,* Cal. Civ. Code §§ 2079.13–2079.24.

[12] *See, e.g.,* Drake v. Hosley, 713 P.2d 1203 (Alaska 1986); Margaret H. Wayne Trust v. Lipsky, 846 P.2d 904 (Idaho 1993); Tristam's Landing, Inc. v. Wait, 327 N.E.2d 727 (Mass. 1975).

[13] *See, e.g.,* Dworak v. Michals, 320 N.W.2d 485 (Neb. 1982).

§ 20.04 Requirements for Valid Contract

[A] Basic Elements

All types of contracts must satisfy the same minimum requirements of offer, acceptance, consideration, reasonably certain terms, and so forth. Like any other contract, a real property sales contract must meet these requirements.[14] However, a contract for the sale of an estate or interest in real property is enforceable only if it is also evidenced by a writing whose terms satisfy the Statute of Frauds.[15]

What terms are required for a valid real property sales contract? The overlap between general contract law and the Statute of Frauds complicates the answer to this question. Courts dealing with the question often fail to distinguish between these two bodies of law, creating a certain amount of confusion. But the basic elements appear to be the same under both: the contract must adequately identify the parties, manifest the intent to buy and sell, describe the property, state the purchase price (usually), and contain any other material terms. Most of the law governing the answer to this question has developed under the Statute of Frauds, which is discussed in detail below.

[B] The Statute of Frauds

[1] The "Most Important Statute Ever Enacted"?

The Statute of Frauds was originally enacted in England in 1677[16] —as its name suggests—to prevent fraud and discourage perjury. Its provisions governing real property sales contracts were adopted (with slight variations) in all states except Louisiana, and became a fundamental part of American law. The Statute has always been controversial. One nineteenth-century author lauded it as "the most important statute ever enacted in either country [England or the United States], relating to civil affairs."[17] Yet critics have long argued that the Statute of Frauds does more harm than good, by effectively permitting the sophisticated to defraud the innocent. Partly due to this concern, courts have increasingly eroded away the rule by creating equitable exceptions.

[2] A Typical Statute of Frauds

A typical Statute of Frauds provides: "The following contracts are invalid, unless they, or some note or memorandum thereof, are in writing and

---

[14] *See, e.g.,* Phoenix Mut. Life Ins. Co. v. Shady Grove Plaza Ltd. Partnership, 734 F. Supp. 1181 (D. Md. 1990) (parties did not intend to be bound by sales contract); King v. Wenger, 549 P.2d 986 (Kan. 1976) (same).

[15] *See, e.g.,* King v. Wenger, 549 P.2d 986 (Kan. 1976); Hickey v. Green, 442 N.E.2d 37 (Mass. App. Ct. 1982); Schwinn v. Griffith, 303 N.W.2d 258 (Minn. 1981); Ward v. Mattuschek, 330 P.2d 971 (Mont. 1958); Cash v. Maddox, 220 S.E.2d 121 (S.C. 1975).

[16] Statute of Frauds, 29 Car. II, c. 3, § 4 (1677).

[17] Joel Bishop, The Doctrines of the Law of Contract 177 (1878).

subscribed by the party to be charged or by the party's agent: . . . (3) An agreement . . . for the sale of real property, or of an interest therein."[18] What does this rather vague language mean? As interpreted by case law, the Statute of Frauds imposes three requirements: (1) the *essential terms* of the sales contract (2) must be contained in a *memorandum or other writing* (3) that is *signed* by the party against whom enforcement is sought.[19] Each of these requirements is discussed below.

What happens if a sales contract violates the Statute of Frauds? The contract is deemed unenforceable, but not void. Compliance with the Statute is not required in order for the contract to be valid. The distinction between enforceability and validity is often significant. Suppose, for example, that B and S enter into an oral contract whereby B will purchase S's island for $500,000 in cash. When S later refuses to perform, B sues S for breach of contract. If S fails to raise the Statute of Frauds as a defense, it is deemed waived and B's lawsuit will succeed.

[3] Requirements for Enforceable Contract

[a] Essential Terms of Contract

Although the typical statute mandates that the "contract" be in writing, courts interpret this language to mean only that the "essential" or "material" terms must be in writing. What are the "essential" terms? In almost all transactions, there are only four essential terms. In general, the writing must:

(1) identify the parties,;

(2) include words showing an intent to buy or sell;

(3) specify the purchase price; and

(4) adequately describe the property.[20]

Most courts insist that the purchase price be specified if the parties have agreed on the amount. Even without such agreement, the contract is enforceable if the writing establishes a procedure for establishing the price in the future (e.g., through appraisal). Absent an agreed price or procedure, some courts will still enforce the contract by requiring the buyer to pay a reasonable price.[21] If the writing contains no provisions about financing terms, the buyer is obligated to pay the purchase price in cash.

The property description often causes difficulty.[22] The writing must be specific enough to identify the land with reasonable certainty, although a

---

[18] Cal. Civ. Code § 1624(a)(3).

[19] In most jurisdictions, however, an agreement to rescind a sales contract is not subject to the Statute of Frauds. *See, e.g.,* Niernberg v. Feld, 283 P.2d 640 (Colo. 1955).

[20] *See, e.g.,* Wiley v. Tom Howell & Assoc., 267 S.E.2d 816 (Ga. Ct. App. 1980) (price not specified); Estate of Younge v. Huysmans, 506 A.2d 282 (N.H. 1985) (all elements satisfied).

[21] *Cf.* Goodwest Rubber Corp. v. Munoz, 216 Cal. Rptr. 604 (Ct. App. 1985) (enforcing contract for sale at "fair market value").

[22] *See, e.g.,* Cash v. Maddox, 220 S.E.2d 121, 122 (S.C. 1975) (deposit check that referred to "15 acres in Pickens, S.C." did not describe property with sufficient certainty).

formal legal description (*see* § 23.04[A][2]) is not required. For example, a street address or community nickname (e.g., "Johnson's swamp") may suffice, because in each instance the land can be readily identified. On the other hand, if S owns 20 acres and contracts to sell "10 acres of my land," the description is too vague.

Beyond this point, the law is rather unpredictable. Depending on the surrounding circumstances, additional terms may be highly important to the parties, and thus be deemed "essential" terms that must be in writing. This is quite common in complex transactions involving commercial property, but fairly rare in home sales. Minor terms such as the time for closing, the type of deed to be used, or the identity of the escrow holder are seen as nonessential; and if the parties have failed to agree, the court will fill in such gaps with reasonable terms customarily used in similar transactions.[23]

[b]   Contained in Memorandum or Other Writing

The essential terms of the contract must be contained in a memorandum or other writing. Where the parties execute a written sales contract—as is customary—the contract itself serves as the required writing. A Statute of Frauds issue usually arises where the parties have entered into an oral agreement. Yet even an oral agreement will be enforceable if its essential terms are set forth in an adequate memorandum or other writing. The writing: (a) need not be intended by the parties as an agreement; (b) may be prepared after the agreement; (c) may consist of more than one document;[24] and (d) may be quite informal. Any document will suffice as long as it contains the essential terms and is properly signed. Thus, for example, a letter,[25] check,[26] informal note, escrow instruction, or even a civil pleading[27] may serve as the required writing.[28]

[c]   Signed by Party Against Whom Contract Is Enforced

The writing need not be signed by both buyer and seller. Rather, it must only be signed by the person *against whom* the contract is being enforced; this person is traditionally called the party "to be charged."[29] Suppose, for example, that B and S enter into an oral land sale contract; B then quickly writes down all the essential terms on the back of his business card and signs his name. The oral contract is enforceable by S against B, because

---

[23] *See* Powell on Real Property ¶ 880[1][d] (Michael Allan Wolf ed., Matthew Bender).

[24] *See, e.g.,* Ward v. Mattuschek, 330 P.2d 971 (Mont. 1958).

[25] *See, e.g.,* Estate of Younge v. Huysmans, 506 A.2d 282 (N.H. 1985).

[26] *Cf.* Hickey v. Green, 442 N.E.2d 37 (Mass. App. Ct. 1982) (court notes that deposit check endorsed by plaintiffs in connection with sale of their property to a third person—not party to case—was probably sufficient to satisfy Statute of Frauds).

[27] *See, e.g.,* Timberlake v. Heflin, 379 S.E.2d 149 (W.Va. 1989) (wife's complaint for divorce deemed sufficient memorandum of prior oral agreement).

[28] *See* Powell on Real Property ¶ 880[1][c] (Michael Allan Wolf ed., Matthew Bender).

[29] *Cf.* Ward v. Mattuschek, 330 P.2d 971 (Mont. 1958) (discussing rule).

B signed the writing. On the other hand, B cannot enforce the contract against S because S did not sign. Alternatively, the writing may be signed by an agent of the party to be charged. Statutes in many states mandate that the authority of such an agent must itself be in writing and signed by the principal.[30]

A formal signature is not generally required. For example, in most jurisdictions a party's initials or nickname will satisfy the requirement.[31]

[4] Exceptions to Statute of Frauds

[a] Overview

Rigid application of the Statute of Frauds may produce harsh results. Suppose S and B enter into an oral contract whereby B agrees to purchase S's house Greenacre for $100,000 in three months. When B asks that the contract be reduced to writing, S replies: "Don't worry about it! I'm a man of my word." In reliance on the deal, B immediately (a) pays a $20,000 down payment to S, (b) hurriedly sells his current home Redacre for $10,000 less than its fair market value, and (c) moves into Greenacre to fix up the property. Over the ensuing weeks, B invests $50,000 to improve Greenacre. With Greenacre in pristine condition, S now enters into a written contract to sell the property to X for $200,000, its current market value. When B protests, S replies: "Sure, we had a deal, but it was only oral! Sorry."

Under the literal language of the Statute of Frauds, the B-S contract is unenforceable. This result imposes an inequitable loss on B, the innocent party. B will recover only his $20,000 down payment and $50,000 in out-of-pocket expenses. In the same manner, this outcome confers an unfair advantage on S, the breaching party. S will receive $200,000 from X, pay $50,000 to B, and recover a net purchase price of $150,000 instead of the $100,000 he originally agreed to accept from B.

Confronted with similar sad sagas, courts gradually created two equitable exceptions to the Statute of Frauds which substantially soften its impact: *part performance* and *equitable estoppel*. These exceptions apply where a buyer or seller seeks specific performance of the sales contract, not in an action for damages.

[b] Part Performance

Courts consider three potential actions of the buyer in determining whether the part performance exception is satisfied: (1) taking possession of the property; (2) paying all or part of the purchase price; and (3) making improvements to the property.[32] If all three actions are present—as in the

---

[30] *See, e.g.,* King v. Wenger, 549 P.2d 986 (Kan. 1976) (statute required written authority for agents of all parties). *But see* Schwinn v. Griffith, 303 N.W.2d 258 (Minn. 1981) (auctioneer had inherent authority as agent of successful bidder to sign memorandum).

[31] *See* Powell on Real Property ¶ 880[1][e][i] (Michael Allan Wolf ed., Matthew Bender).

[32] *See* Burns v. McCormick, 135 N.E. 273 (N.Y. 1922) (oral promise to devise home in return for lifetime care was not enforceable under the part performance exception).

S-B hypothetical above—part performance is clearly established in virtually all states. Courts generally find part performance where only two of the specified actions occur, though they differ widely on which two are necessary.[33] One common formula requires that the buyer *both* (a) take possession of the property *and either* (b) pay part or all of the purchase price *or* (c) make improvements to the property. Conversely, some jurisdictions demand payment *plus either* possession *or* improvements. If part performance is established, either the buyer or the seller may seek specific performance.[34]

What explains the part performance exception? The "evidentiary theory" views the buyer's actions as evidence of an oral contract to purchase the property; after all, a reasonable person would not have performed such acts unless such a contract existed. As Justice Cardozo summarized in a famous phrase, the buyer's acts must be "unequivocally referable to a contract for the sale of land."[35] Alternatively, the more modern "estoppel" or "reliance" theory explains the part performance exception as necessary to avoid serious or irreparable injury to a party who has substantially changed his position in reasonable reliance on the oral contract.[36] This rationale overlaps substantially with the separate estoppel exception (*see* [c], *below*), and some courts seem to blend the two exceptions together.

[c] Equitable Estoppel

The modern status of the equitable estoppel exception is rather puzzling. The few jurisdictions that refuse to recognize part performance have long accepted estoppel as an exception to the Statute of Frauds. Estoppel is applicable where (a) one party has been induced by the other to substantially change position in justifiable reliance on an oral contract and (b) serious or irreparable injury would result from refusing specific performance of the contract.

More recently—influenced by the Restatement (Second) of Contracts—a growing number of courts have enforced oral agreements under an estoppel-based standard, while claiming to apply the part performance exception. The confusion stems from Restatement section 129, which blurs together the part performance and estoppel exceptions. It permits the enforcement of a land purchase agreement if "the party seeking enforcement, in reasonable reliance on the contract and on the continuing assent of the party against whom enforcement is sought, has so changed his position that injustice can be avoided only by specific enforcement."[37] Comment d makes it clear that possession, payment, and improvement—the traditional hallmarks of part performance—are not required where the contract "is admitted or is clearly proved."[38] Instead, any substantial act of reasonable

---

[33] *See, e.g.,* Roundy v. Waner, 570 P.2d 862 (Idaho 1977); Shaughnessy v. Eidsmo, 23 N.W.2d 362 (Minn. 1946).

[34] *See* Powell on Real Property ¶ 880[2][c] (Michael Allan Wolf ed., Matthew Bender).

[35] Burns v. McCormick, 135 N.E. 273, 274 (N.Y. 1922).

[36] *See, e.g.,* Hickey v. Green, 442 N.E.2d 37 (Mass. App. Ct. 1982).

[37] Restatement (Second) of Contracts § 129 (1981).

[38] Restatement (Second) of Contracts § 129 cmt. d (1981).

reliance (e.g., selling other property, rejecting other offers, or providing personal care services) will justify enforcement of the contract.[39]

Hickey v. Green[40] illustrates the doctrine. In reliance on an oral agreement to purchase Green's lot as a future homesite, the Hickeys entered into a binding contract to sell their existing home to a third party. After receiving a better offer, Green breached. When the Hickeys sued for specific performance, Green did not deny the oral contract; she simply asserted the Statute of Frauds defense. Citing Restatement section 129, the court held that the Hickeys had reasonably relied on the contract by agreeing to sell their own home; thus, "principles of equitable estoppel" required enforcement of the contract.[41]

[5] Policy Rationale for Statute of Frauds

At least in theory, the Statute of Frauds serves three related purposes in the land sales context. These are sometimes described as the *evidentiary, cautionary* and *channeling functions.*[42] The Statute was originally enacted to serve the evidentiary function, and this remains its primary mission. Compliance with the Statute ensures clear evidence about the existence and key terms of the contract, thus avoiding the pitfalls of perjury and faulty memory; this minimizes the need for litigation and helps to ensure a correct result if litigation does occur. Scholars suggest that the Statute also has a cautionary function; it requires a formal ceremony—the signing of a written document—which helps to caution the parties that they are entering into an important relationship. Finally, the Statute provides a simple mechanism for distinguishing between mere negotiations (oral) and an enforceable contract (written), and thereby allows the parties to express their intent in a legally effective manner; this is called the channeling function.

Critics suggest that judicial interpretation has so eroded the Statute of Frauds that it no longer serves these functions in any meaningful way—if indeed it ever did.[43] After all, a few words, numbers, and initials scrawled on a scrap of paper may constitute a sufficient memorandum of a real property sales contract, even though such an informal event is unlikely to serve the evidentiary, cautionary, or channeling functions very well. Moreover, the judicially-created exceptions have carved out huge loopholes in the Statute, significantly reducing its scope.

---

[39] *But see* Burns v. McCormick, 135 N.E. 273 (N.Y. 1922) (refusing to apply part performance exception to enforce oral promise to devise home in exchange for lifetime care).

[40] 442 N.E.2d 37 (Mass. App. Ct. 1982).

[41] Hickey v. Green, 442 N.E.2d 37, 40 (Mass. App. Ct. 1982).

[42] *See generally* Joseph M. Perillo, *The Statute of Frauds in the Light of the Functions and Dysfunctions of Form,* 43 Fordham L. Rev. 39 (1974).

[43] *See, e.g.,* Michael Braunstein, *Remedy, Reason, and the Statute of Frauds: A Critical Economic Analysis,* 1989 Utah L. Rev. 383.

§ 20.05 A Typical Sales Contract

In most home sale transactions, the contract is a preprinted standard form. Because sales transactions are primarily governed by state law, these form contracts differ somewhat from state to state, and indeed, from region to region. The typical form is prepared by the local board of realtors, and—predictably—includes provisions that strongly protect the broker's right to a commission.

The buyer and seller usually focus on the price and other economic terms of the deal. The typical form contract contains appropriate blank spaces where the broker can insert these terms, along with the names of the parties and a description of the property. But the parties usually pay less attention to the non-economic terms of the form contract. These terms are typically buried in long paragraphs of small print, difficult to read and to understand, which tends to discourage amendments or revisions.

These non-economic terms fall into four basic categories:

(1) title, financing, inspection, and other contingencies that must be satisfied before the buyer is obligated to purchase (*see* §§ 20.06–20.07);

(2) provisions governing the mechanics of the closing (e.g., time and place, type of deed, prorations of income and expenses, payment of commission) (*see* § 20.08);

(3) provisions dealing with breach of the contract (e.g., liquidated damages clause, attorney's fees clause) (*see* § 20.09); and

(4) miscellaneous "boilerplate" provisions (e.g., integration clause).

§ 20.06 Contract Provisions on Title

[A] Purchase of Title

Suppose B agrees to purchase Blackacre, a house situated on 20 forested acres, from S. What is B buying? S and B would probably characterize the transaction as the purchase of "land." But in reality, B is buying *title to the land,* not the *land* itself. There is an obvious risk that S's title to Blackacre may be somehow defective. S might not own the estate (presumably fee simple absolute) that she purports to be selling; she might own a lesser estate (e.g., a life estate) or no estate at all. And even if S does own the correct estate, it might be burdened with liens, easements, or other encumbrances that affect the value or desirability of the land.

The prudent buyer will negotiate an express contract provision that specifies the quality of title that the seller must deliver. If the sales contract is silent on the issue, the law provides a "default standard:" an implied covenant that the seller must deliver *marketable title.* Thus, if the buyer discovers *before* the purchase is consummated that the seller cannot convey the required title, he may rescind the contract or use other remedies. Yet these express and implied title provisions in the contract expire when the transaction closes, under the doctrine of *merger*. [44] Accordingly, if the buyer discovers title defects *after* the purchase is consummated, he must rely on covenants of title in the deed or other sources of title assurance (*see* Chapter 26).

[B] Implied Covenant of Marketable Title

[1] General Rule

If the contract is silent about the quality of title that the seller must deliver, the law fills in the gap by requiring *marketable title*; this standard is sometimes also called *merchantable title*. The seller's obligation to provide marketable title is viewed as both an implied condition and an implied covenant. Thus, if the seller cannot deliver such title, the condition fails (excusing the buyer from all duties under the contract) and the covenant is breached (allowing the buyer to sue the seller for breach).

The marketable title doctrine is a compromise between two extreme alternatives. If the buyer foolishly fails to demand an express title covenant, the law might simply allow the buyer to live with the bargain he struck: a contract to purchase whatever title the seller has, if any. A seller with seriously defective title could still enforce the contract. The law rejects this extreme position in order to honor the buyer's good faith expectation that the seller holds adequate title, and thereby protect the buyer from unfair surprise. Yet the doctrine does not demand that the seller deliver perfect title. In the real world, perfect title is extraordinarily rare. Virtually every title has at least a few minor blemishes or warts—insignificant defects which are highly unlikely to cause difficulty.

[2] What Is Marketable Title?

A precise definition of "marketable title" is surprisingly elusive. Different courts use widely differing language in attempting to describe the doctrine. Yet all definitions share the same basic idea: it is title "free from reasonable doubt, but not from every doubt."[45] So what is title "free from reasonable doubt?" Two clear rules govern the easy cases. First, title is unmarketable if the seller does not own the estate he or she purports to be selling (*see* [3], *below*). Second, title is generally unmarketable if it is subject to any lien, easement, or other encumbrance (*see* [4], *below*).

Beyond this point, what is the acceptable degree of "doubt" in marginal cases? In trying to distinguish between trivial doubt and significant doubt, judicial definitions usually focus on the quality of title that a reasonable

---

[44] Under the doctrine of merger, the seller's covenants in the sales contract concerning the state of title, the amount of land being conveyed, and occasionally other matters are said to be "merged" into the deed and thereby extinguished, unless they are expressly set forth in the deed. On the other hand, contract promises that would not normally be contained in a deed (e.g., the seller's warranty that home is in "good condition") are seen as collateral promises that continue to exist after the deed is delivered. *See, e.g.,* Mallin v. Good, 417 N.E.2d 858 (Ill. App. Ct. 1981).

[45] Norwegian Evangelical Free Church v. Milhauser, 169 N.E. 134, 135 (N.Y. 1929).

buyer would accept. Thus, one court explained that marketable title was "title that a prudent person with full knowledge of all the facts and legal consequences would be willing to accept,"[46] while another described it as "a title not subject to such reasonable doubt as would create a just apprehension of its validity in the mind of a reasonable, prudent and intelligent person, one which such persons, guided by competent legal advice, would be willing to take and for which they would pay fair value."[47] A second theme in most definitions concerns the risk of future litigation. If "it is reasonably probable that the purchaser would be exposed to litigation not of a frivolous nature concerning the title,"[48] then title is unmarketable. In practice, these vague, fact-specific definitions provide little guidance to parties, attorneys, and courts.

[3] Seller Lacks Title

Title is unmarketable if the seller clearly does not own the estate he or she purports to be selling. Consider again S's proposed sale of fee simple absolute in Blackacre to B (see [A], above). At the close of escrow, title is unmarketable if—for example—(a) S merely owns a life estate in Blackacre or (b) S owns fee simple absolute only in part of Blackacre.[49]

However, most cases are not so simple. More typically, the seller appears to hold valid title, but there is a small chance that that title may be defective. For example, suppose that S claims title to Blackacre based on adverse possession, but has not obtained a judgment quieting title in her favor. A number of states hold that title by adverse possession is marketable where the seller proves there is no real possibility that the record owner will ever succeed in regaining title.[50] The problem with this approach is that the decision does not bind a key non-party: the record owner. The buyer always confronts the risk that he might lose if the record owner eventually sues to quiet title. For this reason, a few jurisdictions hold that title derived from adverse possession is not marketable until it is confirmed by a successful quiet title action.[51]

As its name suggests, the doctrine of marketable title concerns only the quality of the seller's title to land, not the physical condition or value of the land. For example, if the buyer discovers that the land is located in an earthquake zone, subject to flooding, covered with hazardous wastes,[52] or dangerously close to a nuclear reactor, title is still marketable. "One can

---

[46] King v. Knibb, 447 A.2d 1143, 1145 (R.I. 1982).

[47] Seligman v. First Nat'l Invs., Inc., 540 N.E.2d 1057, 1060 (Ill. App. Ct. 1989).

[48] Keown v. West Jersey Title & Guaranty Co., 390 A.2d 715, 717 (N.J. 1978).

[49] See, e.g., Tri-State Hotel Co. v. Sphinx Invest. Co., 510 P.2d 1223 (Kan. 1973) (title held unmarketable where seller did not hold title to small sliver of land within tract to be conveyed).

[50] See, e.g., Conklin v. Davi, 388 A.2d 598 (N.J. 1978).

[51] See Powell on Real Property ¶ 881[6][d][ii] (Michael Allan Wolf ed., Matthew Bender).

[52] Cf. Lick Mill Apartments v. Chicago Title Ins. Co., 283 Cal. Rptr. 231 (Ct. App. 1991) (presence of hazardous substances did not render title unmarketable for purposes of title insurance coverage).

hold perfect title to land that is valueless; one can have marketable title to land while the land itself is unmarketable."[53]

[4]　Seller's Title Is Subject to Encumbrance

[a]　Generally

As a general rule, title is unmarketable if the seller's title is subject to any *encumbrance*. An encumbrance is a right or interest in land—other than a present freehold estate or future interest therein—that reduces the value or restricts the use of the land. Mortgages, easements, covenants, leases, tax liens, encroachments,[54] options, judgment liens, mechanic's liens, and water rights are all examples of encumbrances. Suppose now that S holds fee simple absolute in Blackacre (*see* [A], *above*), but her title is burdened by an easement that allows G to cross Blackacre; S's title is unmarketable. Or suppose S's title is subject to a set of recorded covenants in favor of H; again, S presumably holds unmarketable title. What if Blackacre lacks access to a public road? Most courts would find S's title to be unmarketable, reasoning that litigation may be required to obtain an easement.

On the other hand, an insignificant blemish does not render title unmarketable. For example, suppose 25 years ago, S leased Blackacre to J for a 15 year term; a "memorandum of lease"—which merely recites the existence of the lease—was later recorded. Even though the lease lapsed 10 years ago, the memorandum of lease still appears in the public records. But because the S-J lease has no effect today, the memorandum of lease is a legal nullity and title is marketable.[55]

[b]　Effect of Land Use Regulations

All jurisdictions agree that the mere *existence* of zoning, building, and other land use regulations does not make title unmarketable.[56] Why not? A cluster of reasons supports this rule. Most importantly, the law is not an encumbrance under the standard definition of the term. In addition, the normal buyer intends to use the land as it has been used in the past; if B purchases Blackacre, he presumably intends to use it as a residence, just as S did. If Blackacre is currently zoned for residential use, the existence of the zoning ordinance has little or no impact on a buyer like B. Moreover, a buyer should reasonably expect the land to be subject to land use regulations, because they affect virtually all parcels to some degree. Hence,

---

[53] Hocking v. Title Ins. & Trust Co., 234 P.2d 625, 629 (Cal. 1951).

[54] *See, e.g.,* Bethurem v. Hammett, 736 P.2d 1128 (Wyo. 1987).

[55] *Cf.* G/GM Real Estate Corp. v. Susse Chalet Motor Lodge, 575 N.E.2d 141 (Ohio 1991) (improperly recorded memorandum of lease intended to give notice of lease that had lapsed did not render title unmarketable).

[56] *See, e.g.,* Voorheesville Rod & Gun Club v. E.W. Tompkins Co., 626 N.E.2d 917 (N.Y. 1993). *But see, e.g.,* Create 21 Chuo, Inc. v. Southwest Slopes, Inc., 918 P.2d 1168 (Haw. Ct. App. 1996) (state law that protected archeological site held encumbrance that rendered title unmarketable).

the buyer who intends to devote the land to a new use will investigate the governing law in advance, without any need for the special protection afforded by the marketable title doctrine. The risk of title uncertainty or future litigation is remote.

Most courts hold that the *violation* of a zoning ordinance *does* render title unmarketable.[57] Suppose, for example, that the Blackacre house is set only 20 feet back from the road, while the local ordinance requires a setback of 25 feet. S's title to Blackacre is unmarketable under these conditions. If B purchased the land, he would be subject to the risk of civil or criminal litigation; the local zoning authority might compel him to move the house or to pay a fine. Although a buyer should expect the existence of zoning ordinances, he or she would not reasonably expect that the property currently violates the law. The violation of a law is not an "encumbrance" in the traditional sense of the term, but courts have extended the scope of the marketable title doctrine to protect the unwary buyer.

However, the majority view is that the violation of a building code does not make title unmarketable.[58] The rationale for this rule is not well defined. Logically, if the construction of the Blackacre house violated the building code (e.g., by lack of adequate fire walls), buyer B would be subject to the risk of enforcement litigation after purchase, just as if the house's location violated the zoning ordinance. What accounts for the rule? Part of the answer lies in the common law's reluctance to hold the seller liable for defects in the physical condition of the property. Under the doctrine of caveat emptor (*see* § 21.01), a seller had no duty to inform the prospective buyer about defects in the premises. If a building code violation rendered title unmarketable, this would mean that the seller effectively warranted the condition of the property, thus undercutting the caveat emptor doctrine. In addition, building code defects are generally more difficult to discover than zoning violations. Owner S might easily learn about the zoning violation by measuring the distance between her house and the street; but she is unlikely to cut inside the house walls to evaluate their fire resistance.

[c] Effect of Visible Encumbrances

Suppose that a paved lane crosses through the middle of Blackacre, connecting the public road to property owned by E; B observes E driving his car along the lane before agreeing to purchase Blackacre. Can B now rescind the contract on the basis that E holds an easement that renders title unmarketable? Many courts hold that visible easements for roads, power lines, sewer pipes, or other utilities do not affect marketability.[59] If a buyer knows or reasonably should have known that an easement exists, and enters into a purchase contract that fails to mention the easement, he or she presumably agreed to accept title subject to the easement.

---

[57] *See, e.g.,* Lohmeyer v. Bower, 227 P.2d 102 (Kan. 1951) (violation of zoning ordinance requirement that house be at least three feet from lot line rendered title unmarketable).

[58] *Cf.* Frimberger v. Anzellotti, 594 A.2d 1029 (Conn. Ct. App. 1991) (illegal construction of bulkhead and filling of tidal wetlands did not constitute encumbrance for purpose of deed covenant against encumbrances).

[59] *See* Powell on Real Property ¶ 881[6][d][iii] (Michael Allan Wolf ed., Matthew Bender).

[C] Express Title Covenant

The prudent buyer will negotiate an express contract provision concerning title.[60] Most commonly, contracts specify that the seller will deliver *marketable title* (*see* [B], *above*); vague phrases such as "good title" or "clear title" are usually construed to mean marketable title as well. Another approach is to require *insurable title*;[61] this standard is met if a title company is willing to issue a policy insuring the buyer's title. This standard may not offer enough protection to the buyer because (a) all title policies contain extensive exceptions and (b) a title company may be willing to take the business risk of insuring a title that a reasonable buyer would not accept. Or the contract could require *record title*; this merely requires proof that the recorded chain of title shows the seller as holding title to the property, and does not guard against off-record defects (e.g., adverse possession) or encumbrances on title. Finally, the contract might simply contain a *buyer approval clause* (e.g., "title must be satisfactory to the buyer"); after reviewing the status of title shown by a title opinion or preliminary title report, the buyer must act reasonably in approving or disapproving title. Of course, two or more of these standards could be combined; for example, a contract could require "marketable and insurable title."[62]

Suppose S knows that her title to Blackacre is encumbered by (a) an easement for a future road held by City and (b) a short-term lease held by L. How can S possibly agree to deliver marketable title, or insurable title, or any other particular quality of title? The answer is that S and B can exclude certain known defects from the scope of the title clause. For example, the S-B contract could obligate S to deliver "marketable title except for (a) a road easement held by City and (b) a lease held by L."

What if the S-B contract requires S to deliver "marketable title except for easements and restrictive covenants of record"? Title clauses like this one which waive broad categories of potential defects may be a recipe for disaster: the buyer has agreed to take title even if major problems are later discovered. For example, under this language B is obligated to perform the contract even if investigation reveals that (a) the state holds a recorded easement to build a ten-lane freeway through Blackacre or (b) a recorded covenant requires that all of Blackacre (other than the house site) be devoted "only to forest use in perpetuity."[63] However, suppose instead that B learns that Blackacre is burdened by a recorded covenant that mandates that any house on the property be two stories in height; if the existing Blackacre house is only one story high, and thus violates the covenant, S's title is unmarketable.[64] B consented to the existence of recorded covenants, not to their violation.

---

60 *But see* Wallach v. Riverside Bank, 100 N.E. 50 (N.Y. 1912) (buyer's agreement to accept quitclaim deed did not waive seller's duty to deliver marketable title).

61 *Cf.* Laba v. Carey, 277 N.E.2d 641 (N.Y. 1971).

62 *See, e.g.,* Conklin v. Davi, 388 A.2d 598 (N.J. 1978).

63 *Cf.* Laba v. Carey, 277 N.E.2d 641, 642 (N.Y. 1971) (buyers who agreed to take title subject to "[c]ovenants, restrictions, utility agreement and easement of record, if any" could not refuse to perform after later discovering recorded easement and recorded covenant).

64 *Cf.* Lohmeyer v. Bower, 227 P.2d 102 (Kan. 1951) (violation of covenant requiring two-story house rendered title unmarketable).

[D] Breach of Title Covenant

The seller is obligated to deliver marketable title (or such other title as is specified in the contract) at the time of closing. [65] The buyer who learns of title defects before the closing must notify the seller and allow a reasonable opportunity for the seller to cure the defects. [66] For example, if the seller's title is encumbered by a mortgage, the seller can eliminate this defect simply by repaying the underlying debt and obtaining a release from the mortgagee. It is fairly common for mortgages and other liens to be paid at the closing.

If the seller fails to deliver the required title at closing, (a) the buyer is excused from performing the contract and (b) the seller is liable for breach of contract. The buyer now enjoys a choice of remedies. She may seek specific performance of the contract with an abatement; she may rescind the contact, recover the down payment, and obtain other restitution; or she may sue the seller for damages [67] (see § 20.09).

§ 20.07 Contract Provisions on Financing

[A] Negotiating the Condition

The buyer is rarely willing or able to pay the entire purchase price in cash. Accordingly, he will try to ensure that the contract protects his ability to obtain adequate financing. Suppose B wishes to purchase S's property Redacre for $200,000, but has only $20,000 in cash. B and S might negotiate a contract that provides: (a) B will pay S a $20,000 cash down payment; and (b) B will give S a promissory note for the $180,000 balance, secured by a first-priority mortgage on Redacre.

Alternatively, B might choose to obtain the balance of the purchase price through a loan from a bank, savings and loan association, or other institutional lender. B will wish to insert a financing condition into the B-S contract, to ensure that he is not obligated to purchase if he cannot obtain a suitable loan. A sample clause might provide: "This contract is contingent on B obtaining a commitment from a bank or other institutional lender within 30 days for a new first-priority loan in the amount of $180,000, payable monthly at approximately $1,321 at a fixed interest rate not to exceed 8%, all due 30 years after origination." If B cannot obtain such a loan, he is excused from performing the contract. [68]

---

[65] See Luette v. Bank of Italy Nat. Trust & Sav. Ass'n, 42 F.2d 9 (9th Cir. 1930) (vendor's lack of title long before closing did not entitle vendee to rescind installment land contract).

[66] This may extend the closing date for a reasonable period, particularly if the contract contains no provision that time is of the essence (see § 20.08[B]).

[67] See, e.g., Warner v. Denis, 933 P.2d 1372 (Haw. Ct. App. 1997).

[68] But see Bruyere v. Jade Realty Corp., 375 A.2d 600 (N.H. 1977) (where buyers obtained adequate financing commitment, but later decided to divorce, leading to lender's cancellation of commitment, buyers were still obligated to perform contract).

[B] Vague and Indefinite Language

Financing conditions are a fertile source of litigation. One frequent issue is whether the language of the financing condition is so vague and indefinite that the entire contract is unenforceable. Suppose, for example, that the entire financing clause in the B-S contract reads: "Subject to B obtaining the proper amount of financing."[69] What loan amount, interest rate, or payment schedule is appropriate? Where the parties adopt a vague clause, they have effectively failed to reach agreement on material terms of the contract. Modern courts are increasingly willing to fill in the gaps with "reasonable" terms—if possible—based on the circumstances of the transaction, local custom, or the expectations of the parties.[70] If this cannot be done, however, the contract is deemed illusory, and hence unenforceable.[71]

[C] Sufficiency of Buyer's Effort to Obtain Loan

Another common issue is whether the buyer made a sufficient effort to obtain the contemplated loan. This scenario might arise when the buyer—unable to obtain a loan—sues the seller to recover the deposit. The seller then defends the action by claiming that the buyer's activities were insufficient. Courts generally hold that a buyer must make a reasonable effort to satisfy the financing condition.[72] The precise phrasing of this implied covenant differs from state to state; "good faith" or "reasonable diligence" express the same theme.[73] The buyer's failure to make the required effort is treated as a breach of contract. Lurking beneath the surface here is judicial concern that the buyer—having changed her mind about purchasing the property—is trying to invalidate the contract. If the law imposed no duty, a buyer could always escape the contract by the simple expedient of failing to seek a loan.

The adequacy of the buyer's effort to obtain financing is a question of fact. In one illustrative decision, the buyer applied only to one lender, and then canceled her application a few days later; when she sued the seller to retrieve her deposit, the court found this minimal effort to be insufficient.[74] Decisions vary widely on whether an application to only one lender is sufficient. On the other hand, the buyer who diligently but unsuccessfully applies to two or more lenders has probably met this burden.[75]

---

[69] *Cf.* Gerruth Realty Co. v. Pire, 115 N.W.2d 557, 558 (Wis. 1962) (contract that was "contingent on the purchaser obtaining the proper amount of financing" was too indefinite to enforce).

[70] *See, e.g.,* Smith v. Vernon, 286 N.E.2d 99 (Ill. App. Ct. 1972) (where condition failed to specify loan amount, local business practice and custom should determine reasonable amount).

[71] *See, e.g.,* Homler v. Malas, 494 S.E.2d 18 (Ga. Ct. App. 1997) (condition too vague and indefinite); Gerruth Realty Co. v. Pire, 115 N.W.2d 557 (Wis. 1962) (same).

[72] *See, e.g.,* Smith v. Vernon, 286 N.E.2d 99 (Ill. App. Ct. 1972) (plaintiff-buyers failed to prove they made a reasonable effort to obtain a mortgage, and could not recover deposit).

[73] *See, e.g.,* Liuzza v. Panzer, 333 So. 2d 689 (La. App. Ct. 1976) (buyer who submitted one unsuccessful loan application did not make "good faith" effort); Lynch v. Andrew, 481 N.E.2d 1383 (Mass. App. Ct. 1985) (buyers failed to exert reasonable "diligence" by refusing to agree to lender's requirements).

[74] Bushmiller v. Schiller, 368 A.2d 1044 (Md. Ct. Spec. App. 1977).

[75] *But see* Fry v. George Elkins Co., 327 P.2d 905 (Cal. Ct. App. 1958) (buyer who unsuccessfully submitted loan applications to two lenders failed to act in good faith).

§ 20.08 Closing the Transaction

[A] Tender of Performance

Suppose S and B enter into a valid contract whereby B agrees to purchase S's property, with the closing set for July 1. S appears at the closing on July 1, but B fails to show up.[76] What are S's rights? In general, the seller's obligation to deliver the deed and the buyer's obligation to pay the purchase price are concurrent conditions. This means that the performance of each party is a condition to the performance of the other party. Until S performs—or *tenders* performance—B is not obligated to perform and thus has not yet breached the contract.[77] Of course, S could put B in breach by actually delivering the deed to B, but this approach carries unacceptable risk. Instead, S need only "tender" or offer performance. If S is (a) able to deliver title as required by the contract and (b) clearly offers to deliver such title, this constitutes a "tender."[78]

[B] Time for Performance

Suppose that when B fails to appear at the July 1 closing, S immediately sends B a hand-delivered letter tendering performance. The rights of the parties now turn on whether "time is of the essence" under the contract. Time may be deemed of the essence either because the contract includes an express provision (e.g., "Time is of the essence in this Agreement") or because the circumstances of the transaction demonstrate that the parties so intended. If time is of the essence, the parties must perform at the time specified in the agreement.[79] Here, B is now in breach and cannot enforce the contract against S; S has a variety of remedies against B (*see* § 20.09).

Conversely, if time is not of the essence, a party can still obtain specific performance of the contract if he performs or tenders performance within a reasonable time.[80] For example, if B performs on July 2, the next day, he can presumably still secure specific performance; however, B is liable to S for any actual damages caused by the delay (e.g, loss of interest on the sales price).

---

[76] What happens if B died before the closing? The contract is still valid. Under the doctrine of equitable conversion, B's heirs or devisees are entitled to the property and his estate is liable for the purchase price. *See* Powell on Real Property ¶ 881[1][a] (Michael Allan Wolf ed., Matthew Bender).

[77] *Cf.* Century 21 All Western Real Estate & Inv., Inc. v. Webb, 645 P.2d 52 (Utah 1982) (buyers' specific performance action dismissed because buyers failed to tender).

[78] Tender is excused under limited circumstances, e.g., if the other party has previously repudiated the contract or if it is impossible for the other party to perform. *See, e.g.,* Cohen v. Kranz, 189 N.E.2d 473 (N.Y. 1963) (buyer's anticipatory breach of contract excused seller's tender).

[79] *See, e.g.,* Doctorman v. Schroeder, 114 A. 810 (N.J. 1921) (recognizing rule, but finding waiver on facts).

[80] *See, e.g.,* Kasten Constr. Co. v. Maple Ridge Constr. Co., 226 A.2d 341 (Md. 1967) (allowing specific performance despite delay); Century 21 All Western Real Estate & Inv., Inc. v. Webb, 645 P.2d 52 (Utah 1982) (recognizing rule).

§ 20.09   Remedies for Breach of Contract

[A]   Specific Performance

[1]   General Requirements

A specific performance decree mandates that the breaching party perform the sales contract.[81] For example, if the seller unjustifiably refuses to perform, the court will order the seller to convey title to the buyer, contingent upon the seller's receipt of the sales price. Specific performance is usually the best remedy for breach of a land sale contract because it gives the non-breaching party exactly what he or she bargained for.

Because specific performance is an equitable remedy, it is not always available. One limitation is that specific performance will be awarded only if the usual remedy of money damages is inadequate; as discussed below, this standard is always met when the buyer seeks specific performance, and usually met when the seller seeks such relief. In addition, the court has broad equitable discretion in deciding whether to grant specific performance; for example, if this remedy would cause unusual hardship to the breaching party, the court may refuse to compel performance and only award damages. Finally, laches,[82] unclean hands, and the other usual equitable defenses may preclude the remedy.

When a title defect prevents the seller from conveying title as required, the buyer may compel specific performance of the contract with an *abatement* —that is, a reduction—of the purchase price. This tool is particularly useful when the title problem can be easily quantified. For example, if the seller contracts to sell ten acres, but can only deliver title to nine acres, the buyer can presumably obtain specific performance of the nine acres in exchange for only 90% of the contract price. Similarly, in one case the seller contracted to convey full title to a condominium unit, but was unable to do so because he only owned a one-half interest as a cotenant with his estranged wife, who refused to convey her interest; the court ordered the seller to convey his half interest, and abated half of the purchase price.[83]

[2]   Inadequacy of Money Damages

Why are money damages an inadequate remedy for breach of a real property sales contract? When the buyer seeks specific performance, the conventional answer to this question is straightforward. Early English courts adopted the view that each parcel of land is "unique" as a matter of law. Under this approach, the location, size, amenities, appearance, condition, and other qualities of a particular parcel at issue cannot possibly be duplicated. If the buyer was awarded money damages, he could never purchase an identical replacement parcel. Hence, the rule arose that

---

[81] *See* Anthony T. Kronman, *Specific Performance,* 45 U. Chi. L. Rev. 351 (1978).

[82] *See, e.g.,* Estate of Younge v. Huysmans, 506 A.2d 282 (N.H. 1985) (specific performance refused due to laches).

[83] Sanders v. Knapp, 674 P.2d 385 (Colo. Ct. App. 1983).

damages could never be adequate to compensate for the seller's refusal to convey title.

The logic of this blanket rule is questionable today. While each rural parcel in medieval England may indeed have been unique, the same cannot realistically be said for many modern parcels. For example, unit 10C—on the tenth floor of a hypothetical condominium development—may be identical to adjacent unit 10D for all practical purposes. However, courts still uniformly follow the traditional rule, without examining whether the particular property is in fact unique.[84] Thus, for example, a buyer can compel specific performance of a contract to purchase unit 10C, even though unit 10D is available for purchase at the same price.

As a general rule, damages are also deemed an inadequate remedy when the seller seeks specific performance. But why? The answer to this question is somewhat elusive. Suppose the fair market value of S's property Brownacre is $90,000; S enters into a contract to sell Brownacre to B for $100,000, and B breaches. If S obtains specific performance, he recovers the $100,000 sales price from B. If S is limited to damages, he still obtains $100,000 in value: (a) $10,000 in damages from B (the difference between contract price and fair market value) and (b) title to Brownacre, worth $90,000. So why is the damages remedy inadequate for a seller like S? The leading justification is that the seller may encounter problems in proving damages with reasonable certainty, because the fair market value of land is difficult to determine. Alternatively, the seller may have trouble reselling the land quickly, and thus lose the opportunity to invest the sale proceeds productively.

Both rationales collapse under scrutiny. Courts routinely use expert appraisal testimony to value real property for a variety of purposes (e.g., eminent domain actions), and most parcels can be resold within a short time. As evidenced by the New Jersey decision of *Centex Homes Corp. v. Boag*,[85] there is a slight modern trend toward abandoning the automatic rule that damages are an inadequate remedy for the seller. On the facts of *Centex Homes,* the court found that the damages sustained by the seller—a condominium developer—could be easily measured and thus the damages remedy was adequate.

[B] Damages

[1] Loss of Bargain Damages

The basic measure of damages for breach of a real property sales contract is the difference between the contract price and the fair market value of the property at the time of the breach.[86] For example, suppose B enters

---

[84] *See, e.g.,* Giannini v. First Nat'l Bank of Des Plaines, 483 N.E.2d 924 (Ill. App. Ct. 1985); Pruitt v. Graziano, 521 A.2d 1313 (N.J. Super. Ct. App. Div. 1987). *But cf.* Centex Homes Corp. v. Boag, 320 A.2d 194 (N.J. Ch. 1974) (criticizing rule in dicta).

[85] 320 A.2d 194 (N.J. Ch. 1974).

[86] *See, e.g.,* Donovan v. Bachstadt, 453 A.2d 160 (N.J. 1982) (applying general rule to reject buyers' claim to measure loss of bargain damages based on interest rate differential).

into a contract to purchase Blueacre from S for $500,000, and then breaches two months later when the value of the property has fallen to $460,000. Under the general rule, B is liable to S for $40,000 in damages. Conversely, if the market value of Blueacre is $500,000 on the date of B's breach, S is not entitled to damages under this standard.

About half the states recognize an exception to this standard where the buyer sues the seller for breach. In these jurisdictions, under the so-called "English rule," the seller is not liable for loss of bargain damages if the breach was caused by good faith inability to convey marketable title; rather, the buyer only recovers any payments made to the seller, plus incidental damages.[87] Assume, for example, that O conveys Greenacre to B, who fails to record his deed or take possession; O then purports to convey Greenacre as a gift to C. C, unaware of the O-B deed, contracts to sell Greenacre to D in good faith. B now records. As between B and C, B owns Greenacre because his interest was acquired first in time, while C, as a donee, cannot qualify for protection as a bona fide purchaser (see Chapter 24). Under the good faith limitation rule, C is not liable to D for loss of bargain damages. The seller who knows or reasonably should know about the title defect at the time he enters into the contract is deemed to act in bad faith and receives no protection under this rule. Similarly, if the seller breaches for reasons *other than* inability to deliver good title, good faith is irrelevant; the buyer may recover normal benefit of the bargain damages.[88]

The original rationale for the good faith limitation—the difficulty in ascertaining land title in eighteenth-century England—no longer exists. The comprehensive recording system in the United States makes it relatively easy for a landowner to confirm the validity of his or her title before entering into a sales contract, at least in most instances.[89] As a result, modern decisions reveal a growing trend toward the so-called "American rule," which allows the buyer to recover full loss of bargain damages regardless of the seller's good faith.[90]

[2] Incidental and Consequential Damages

Particularly when full loss of bargain damages are not available, the non-breaching party may receive *incidental damages*—compensation for the out-of-pocket expenses incurred in reliance on the contract. For example, the buyer can recover the costs of property inspections, escrow fees, title examination expenses, and attorney's fees.

Where the breach causes a special, foreseeable loss to the non-breaching party, *consequential damages* may also be available. The issue arises most frequently when the non-breaching buyer seeks to recover profits that would have been made from the property if the seller had fully performed,

---

[87] *See, e.g.,* Kramer v. Mobley, 216 S.W.2d 930 (Ky. Ct. App. 1949) (following English rule).

[88] *See, e.g.,* Beard v. S/E Joint Venture, 581 A.2d 1275 (Md. 1990).

[89] For example, even the most careful search of record title would not reveal B's prior, unrecorded deed, which prevails over C's later interest.

[90] *See, e.g.,* Donovan v. Bachstadt, 453 A.2d 160 (N.J. 1982) (repudiating English rule, adopting American rule); Smith v. Warr, 564 P.2d 771 (Utah 1977) (adopting American rule).

e.g., from continued operation of an existing business. Lost profits are awarded only if they can be proven with reasonable certainty. And most courts refuse to award them at all if the buyer obtains full loss of bargain damages.

[3] Liquidated Damages

The parties may supersede the usual rules governing damages by including a *liquidated damages clause* in the sales contract. As its name suggests, a liquidated damages clause specifies or "liquidates" the amount of damages due if the contract is breached. Liquidated damage clauses offer the benefit of certainty, because each party knows its maximum exposure for breach and can plan accordingly; they also serve to minimize litigation by eliminating the need for proof of damages.

The liquidated damages clause is most commonly used to deal with the buyer's breach of a home sale contract.[91] Suppose S and B enter into a contract by which B agrees to purchase S's house Whiteacre for $200,000; B immediately pays the $10,000 deposit required under the contract, and agrees to pay the balance at the closing. The contract provides: "If the Buyer fails to perform his obligations hereunder, the Seller shall retain the Buyer's deposit as liquidated damages." If B breaches, can S rely on this clause to keep the $10,000 deposit?

Under the majority approach, a liquidated damages clause is valid if (a) future damages are difficult or impossible to determine in advance and (b) at the time the contract was signed, the specified amount of liquidated damages was a reasonable estimate of the future damages. The tension between these two criteria is obvious. If future damages are "impossible" to determine when the contract is signed, how can the estimate be "reasonable"? As a practical matter, courts largely seem to ignore the first element, and focus heavily on the second element—the reasonableness of the estimate.[92] Even here, the modern trend is to consider the reasonableness of the estimate in comparison to the actual damages incurred.[93] For example, suppose that S immediately resells Whiteacre to X for $250,000; on these facts, S has suffered no loss from B's breach, but rather has made a $50,000 profit. Can S still keep B's $10,000 deposit? Even if $10,000 was a reasonable estimate when the contract was signed, some courts will refuse to enforce the liquidated damages clause here because it has no relationship to the seller's actual damages and thus constitutes a penalty.[94]

---

[91] *See, e.g.,* Lynch v. Andrew, 481 N.E.2d 1383 (Mass. App. Ct. 1985); Mahoney v. Tingley, 529 P.2d 1068 (Wash. 1975).

[92] *See, e.g.,* Wallace Real Estate Inv. v. Groves, 881 P.2d 1010 (Wash. 1994).

[93] *See* Restatement (Second) of Contracts § 356 (1981).

[94] *Cf.* Colonial at Lynnfield, Inc. v. Sloan, 870 F.2d 761 (1st Cir. 1989) (refusing to enforce $200,000 liquidated damages clause against buyer where seller made a $251,000 profit by reselling after the buyer's breach).

[C] Rescission and Restitution

Alternatively, the non-breaching party may rescind the contract and obtain restitution. *Rescission* cancels the contact, so that it has no further legal force or effect; the non-breaching party is excused from further performance. The law now restores the parties to the positions they held before the contract was created—just as if no contract had ever been formed—by requiring each to return the performance of the other; this process is called *restitution*. Suppose K agrees to purchase L's property Brownacre for $300,000, and gives L a $15,000 down payment; L allows K to take possession of Brownacre before the closing. Two months later, L breaches and K rescinds the contract. Under the restitution remedy, L must return the $15,000 deposit to K and K must pay L the fair rental value of Brownacre for two months.

Chapter 21

CONDITION OF THE PROPERTY

§ 21.01　"Let the Buyer Beware"?

Suppose B contracts to purchase a home from S for $200,000. S is aware that the home is perched over a huge underground cavern, but withholds this information from B. The day after escrow closes, the earth gives way and the home tumbles into the cavern, a total loss. What are B's rights?

The common law afforded the buyer of real property virtually no remedy for defective conditions, whether discovered before or after the close of escrow. The law presumed that a buyer could conduct a pre-purchase investigation and protect his rights by negotiating an express warranty or other contract terms. *Caveat emptor*—in Latin, "let the buyer beware"— summarized the law's approach. Under this approach, B has no remedy

327

against S. Although the conduct of S may be morally or ethically reprehensible, S had no legal duty to inform B about the probable collapse of the house.

Over the last 50 years, the law has moved steadily away from caveat emptor, driven by the same consumer-oriented currents that brought revolutionary change to the traditional rules governing landlord-tenant law and product liability. There is a clear national trend toward holding sellers, brokers, and in some instances builders responsible to buyers for significant defects in homes and other residential property. Similarly, a growing minority of jurisdictions requires that the seller bear the loss caused by fire, flood or other injury to the property that occurs after execution of the contract but before close of escrow.

§ 21.02 Seller's Duty to Disclose Defects

[A] Common Law Approach

Under caveat emptor, the seller of real property had no duty to disclose latent defects to the buyer absent unusual circumstances (e.g., a fiduciary relationship between seller and buyer). Like S in the cavern hypothetical, the common law seller was permitted to remain silent, even if aware of facts that would be crucial to any reasonable buyer. Some states still cling to this view. In the common law tradition, these states distinguish sharply between inaction ("nonfeasance") and wrongful action ("misfeasance"). Thus, the seller can remain silent, but cannot mislead the buyer by words or conduct.

The seller cannot intentionally misrepresent facts about the property to induce the buyer to buy; this is fraud. A fraudulent misrepresentation is

(1)   a false statement of material fact made by the seller to the buyer,

(2)   known to the seller to be false,

(3)   made with the intent to induce the buyer to purchase,

(4)   which the buyer justifiably relies on in deciding to purchase,

(5)   to the buyer's detriment or loss.

Suppose that before the cavern house purchase, S had said to B: "Don't ever worry about this house! It's built on solid rock." This statement would probably meet the elements of misrepresentation, allowing B to either rescind the purchase contract or recover damages from S. The line between statements of fact and expressions of opinion or standard sales "puffery" is often hard to draw. What if S had merely said "This is a great house" or "You're getting a very good deal!"?[1]

Suppose instead that before B inspects the home, S fills in a few foundation cracks caused by the cavern and covers these patched areas with fresh paint. S says nothing at all to B about the house. Does B have any

---

[1] *See, e.g.*, Lyons v. McDonald, 501 N.E.2d 1079 (Ind. Ct. App. 1986) (seller, aware his house was infested with termites, committed fraud when he told the buyer that he was not aware of any "particular problems" with the house).

recourse against S when the house collapses? The common law imposed liability for fraudulent concealment or suppression of facts. S's act of concealing the cracks would be seen as the equivalent of an affirmative misrepresentation.

[B] Modern Trend Toward Requiring Disclosure

[1] General Principles

Today most states require the seller of residential property to disclose known latent defects to the buyer under certain conditions.[2] If the seller breaches this duty, the buyer can either rescind the contract or recover compensatory damages.

There is broad agreement on the basic disclosure standard, although states vary somewhat on detail. In general, a seller of residential property who knows of a hidden or "latent" defect in the property that substantially affects the value or desirability of the property must disclose it to the buyer. In California, for example, a seller who "knows of facts materially affecting the value or desirability of the property which are known or accessible only to him and also knows that such facts are not known to, or within the reach of the diligent attention and observation of the buyer" has a duty to disclose them to the buyer.[3] In addition to this emerging common law duty, statutes in many states require the seller of residential property to provide the buyer with a written disclosure form listing certain types of defects.[4] However, most jurisdictions still follow the rule of caveat emptor for commercial property transactions.[5]

Johnson v. Davis[6] illustrates the national trend. The Johnsons, fully aware that the roof on their Florida home leaked badly, agreed to sell it to the Davises without disclosing the problem. Shortly after the Davises paid the $31,000 deposit required by the contract, they inspected the home again, only to find rain water "gushing" in through the ceiling and around the windows. When the Davises sued the Johnsons to recover their deposit, the Johnsons asserted the traditional Florida rule of caveat emptor. The Florida Supreme Court—observing that cases following caveat emptor were "not in tune with the times and do not conform with current notions of justice, equity and fair dealing"[7] —jettisoned the old rule. Following the

---

[2] *But see* Alan M. Weinberger, *Let the Buyer Be Well Informed?—Doubting the Demise of Caveat Emptor*, 55 Md. L. Rev. 387 (1996).

[3] Lingsch v. Savage, 29 Cal. Rptr. 201, 204 (Ct. App. 1963); *see also* Johnson v. Davis, 480 So. 2d 625 (Fla. 1985) (following California standard).

[4] *See generally* Robert M. Washburn, *Residential Real Estate Condition Disclosure Legislation*, 44 De Paul L. Rev. 381 (1995).

[5] *But see* Lingsch v. Savage, 29 Cal. Rptr. 201 (Ct. App. 1963) (disclosure required in sale of apartment complex). *See generally* Kathleen M. Tomcho, Note, *Commercial Real Estate Buyer Beware: Sellers May Have the Right to Remain Silent*, 70 S. Cal. L. Rev. 1571 (1997).

[6] 480 So. 2d 625 (Fla. 1985).

[7] Johnson v. Davis, 480 So. 2d 625, 628 (Fla. 1985).

California formulation of the disclosure duty, it held that the Johnsons were obligated to disclose the leaky roof to the Davises before the contract was signed. Thus, the Davises were entitled to rescind the contract and recover their deposit.

[2] Why Require Disclosure?

Most of the landmark decisions abandoning caveat emptor—like *Johnson v. Davis*—are remarkably laconic about the underlying policy rationale. Exactly what are "current notions of justice, equity and fair dealing"? The policy debate surrounding the issue is more complex than the phrase suggests.

Consider an analogy. F, a widget manufacturer, sells 100,000 widgets to G at a price of $50.00 each. Before entering into the contract, F is fully aware that the market price of widgets is about to fall sharply (because F is about to open a new widget factory that will glut the market) but fails to inform G. We might say that F made a "good business deal," while G made a mistake. This is a pattern in many business transactions. One side, armed with superior information, is able to strike a superior bargain. Should the law intervene to require business entities like F to disclose advantageous bargaining information before a contract is reached?

If not, libertarian theorists would argue, why should real property transactions be treated differently? The buyer may demand the opportunity to inspect the land, using whatever experts he thinks appropriate, and may protect against uncertainty by insisting that the seller provide an express warranty as to the condition of the property. Because of the number of properties available, the seller is unlikely to own enough properties so as to exercise market control. The buyer and seller are free to negotiate an arms-length sales contract. Moreover, if the law requires seller disclosure, would it logically impose a parallel disclosure duty on buyers? For example, if the geologist buyer knows the property is situated over an oil deposit, must he disclose this information to the seller before entering into the contract?

So why require disclosure? A variety of policy strands underlie the emerging majority rule. Law and economics scholars focus on the parties' comparative access to information concerning the defect. The seller already knows about the defect. Yet unless the law mandates seller disclosure, the prudent buyer will be forced either to (1) pay for an expert inspection, or (2) negotiate for the seller to provide an express warranty on the home's condition,[8] both of which impose unnecessary transaction costs on the buyer. As Judge Posner observes, the disclosure duty saves "the expense of the self-protective measures that buyers would have to take if there were no legal remedies."[9] Moreover, in some instances, (1) the buyer reasonably

---

[8] Even the buyer who believes he has successfully negotiated for an express warranty may ultimately receive little protection. *See, e.g.,* P.B.R. Enters. v. Perren, 253 S.E.2d 765 (Ga. 1979) (oral warranty lost through merger); Garriffa v. Taylor, 675 P.2d 1284 (Wyo. 1984) (seller's oral statements regarding septic system held mere expression of opinion, not a warranty).

[9] Richard A. Posner, Economic Analysis of Law 110 (4th ed. 1992).

believes that the seller will disclose known defects (presumably equating nondisclosure with the moral equivalent of lying), or (2) the defect is so well-concealed that it cannot be discovered through inspection.

The unique nature of the family home—as opposed to other types of property—is also relevant in the policy calculus. A home is the biggest investment that most families will ever make. Moreover, perhaps reflecting the personhood perspective to some degree, the law has increasingly recognized the social value of affording enhanced protection for the family* home.

[3]   What Must Be Disclosed?

[a]   Material Defects Generally

The principal challenge in applying the standard is determining whether a particular defect is significant enough to require disclosure. The line is easy enough to draw in the abstract: the seller need disclose only significant or material defects, not those that are minor or trivial. Most states use an objective standard to assess materiality; some require disclosure if a reasonable person would consider the defect an important factor in the decision to purchase, and others mandate disclosure if the defect has a significant effect on the property's market value. A few jurisdictions appear to utilize a subjective standard, requiring disclosure if the defect would be material to the particular buyer. In practice, these standards are often difficult to apply, especially in marginal cases.

[b]   Physical or Legal Defects

The paradigm nondisclosure case involves a latent physical defect in the house or lot, such as a leaky roof, crumbling foundation, termite-damaged structure, or sliding hillside lot.[10] Physical defects of this magnitude are universally seen as material. A number of states also compel disclosure of zoning violations, building code violations, and other legal conditions affecting the use or enjoyment of the property.

[c]   Off-Site Conditions

Off-site conditions that may affect the property pose a particular problem. For example, if the property adjoins a toxic waste dump, presumably the potential for future injury is sufficiently real to require disclosure; but what if the dump is five blocks away or two miles away?[11] Similar dilemmas are posed if the house is, for example, near an airport, in an earthquake zone, near a local "crack house," in a high-crime area, near a nuclear power plant,

---

[10] See, e.g., Tusch Enters. v. Coffin, 740 P.2d 1022 (Idaho 1987) (seller failed to disclose that duplexes were built on uncompacted "fill soil," and thus that foundation problems were likely).

[11] See Serena M. Williams, *When Daylight Reveals Neighborhood Nightmares: The Duty of Builders and Developers to Disclose Off-Site Environmental Conditions*, 12 J. Nat. Resources & Envtl. L. 1 (1997).

or across the street from noisy neighbors.[12] These are difficult, fact-intensive cases, which usually hinge on factors such as the proximity of the condition, the magnitude of the risk it presents, and the gravity of the threatened harm.

[d] "Psychologically Impacted" Property

[i] The Issue

Suppose a former resident contracted AIDS or a mass murder occurred in the home.[13] Must a seller disclose such "intangible" or psychological factors, which might stigmatize a particular house?[14]

[ii] *Stambovsky v. Ackley*

The leading case on point is *Stambovsky v. Ackley*,[15] where the buyer sought to rescind the contract for the purchase of a New York house due to the seller's failure to disclose that the house had a reputation for being haunted by ghosts. The plaintiff-buyer alleged that the seller had created the reputation by publicizing her sightings of "spectral apparitions" to Reader's Digest and local newspapers, and that this stigma greatly reduced the market value of the property. Because New York still followed caveat emptor, however, the trial court dismissed the complaint. In an amusing, tongue-in-cheek decision, the New York appellate court reversed, holding that on these facts the seller was obligated to disclose.

The *Stambovsky* court's apparent rationale is somewhat strained. At least superficially, it reached its result by distinguishing prior New York caveat emptor cases on the basis that the buyers' prudent inspection might have revealed the defects, whereas in *Stambovsky* "the most meticulous inspection and search would not reveal the presence of poltergeists at the premises or unearth the property's ghoulish reputation in the community."[16] Yet this is an obvious overstatement. Although the court humorously muddled the issue, plaintiff was seeking to rescind based on the house's reputation for being haunted, not because the house was actually haunted. This "ghoulish reputation" was in fact easily discoverable by the simple expedient of asking any neighbor about the house in general terms, e.g. "Is there anything special I should know about that house?" More fundamentally, the result in *Stambovsky* stems from the same policy factors that have fueled the national movement away from caveat emptor. The court refers to these policies only obliquely, noting that "fairness and common sense" compel an exception to caveat emptor.

---

[12] *See, e.g.*, Alexander v. McKnight, 9 Cal. Rptr. 2d 453 (Ct. App. 1992) (obnoxious neighbors).

[13] *See, e.g.*, Reed v. King, 193 Cal. Rptr. 130 (Ct. App. 1983) (seller had duty to disclose that mass murder had occurred in house ten years earlier).

[14] *See generally* Paula C. Murray, *AIDS, Ghosts, Murder: Must Real Estate Brokers and Sellers Disclose?*, 27 Wake Forest L. Rev. 689 (1992).

[15] 572 N.Y.S.2d 672 (App. Div. 1991).

[16] Stambovsky v. Ackley, 572 N.Y.S.2d 672, 676 (App. Div. 1991).

[iii] Reflections on *Stambovsky v. Ackley*

At bottom, *Stambovsky* is a transitional case, a stepping stone for future New York courts between caveat emptor and the modern disclosure standard. Consider the new test that the case offers: "Where a condition which has been created by the seller materially impairs the value of the contract and is peculiarly within the knowledge of the seller or unlikely to be discovered by a prudent purchaser exercising due care with respect to the subject transaction," the seller's nondisclosure allows the buyer to rescind.[17] This is reasonably close to the national standard except for the odd requirement (clearly linked to the facts of *Stambovsky*) that the seller must have created the condition. After *Stambovsky*, how would a New York court resolve the cavern hypothetical which began this section? Logically, the court would hold that the cavern home seller had no duty to disclose, because he did not create the cavern. Such an unusual distinction seems unlikely to endure in the long run.

Decisions that allow rescission based on nondisclosure of an intangible defect threaten one of the enduring policy themes underlying America property law: protecting the stability of land title. As *Stambovsky* illustrates, courts often attempt to mitigate the impact of rescission in such instances by requiring proof that the stigmatizing defect in fact reduces the property's market value. In a broad sense, a reduction in market value can reflect a public consensus that the particular defect is material.

[iv] Statutory Restrictions on Duty to Disclose Intangible Defects

The judicial movement toward requiring disclosure of such intangible defects has sparked restrictive legislation in many states. The typical statute provides that matters such as the following need not be disclosed by the seller: (1) a past occupant of the property was infected with HIV or contracted AIDS; and (2) the property was the site of a homicide or suicide.[18]

[4] Waiver of Duty

Can the parties expressly agree to relieve the seller of the common law disclosure obligation? A clear, specific waiver will be enforced in most jurisdictions. The law is less clear on the effect of the simple "as is" clause, yet some courts will find a waiver here as well. Consistent with libertarian theory, an express waiver presumably indicates that the buyer has (1) consciously considered the risk of unknown defects and (2) reduced the purchase price to compensate for these unknown risks. Yet even such a knowing waiver undercuts the utilitarian policies that support the disclosure duty. Statutes in three states—Maryland, Oregon, and Virginia—expressly allow a home seller to choose between two methods of sale: (1)

---

[17] Stambovsky v. Ackley, 572 N.Y.S.2d 672, 676 (App. Div. 1991).

[18] *See, e.g.*, Mo. Ann. Stat. § 442.600.

providing a written disclosure of defects or (2) disclaiming liability for any defects and selling the home on an "as is" basis.[19]

[C] Special Rules for Disclosure of Hazardous Substance Contamination

Federal law mandates disclosure of hazardous substance contamination in two special situations. A seller of residential property constructed before 1978 who is aware his property contains lead-based paint must so inform the buyer and provide the buyer with a "lead hazard information pamphlet" issued by the federal government.[20]

The Comprehensive Environmental Response, Compensation, and Liability Act of 1980[21] ("CERCLA") or "Superfund" law may have a similar impact on the owner of property known to be contaminated with a hazardous substance. An owner who innocently purchases contaminated property, without actual knowledge of the contamination or any reason to know about it after conducting a diligent, pre-purchase investigation, will qualify for the "innocent purchaser" defense if he later discovers that the land is contaminated, and, accordingly, will not be held strictly liable for cleanup costs. However, the innocent owner will lose the protection of this defense if he sells the property without fully informing the buyer about the known contamination.

§ 21.03 Broker's Duty to Disclose Defects

Under basic principles of agency law, the real estate broker representing the buyer has long been required to disclose known defects or other material facts. The buyer's broker, as an agent, owes a fiduciary duty to his principal, the buyer, which includes the obligation of full disclosure. However, under the caveat emptor regime, the seller's agent—like the seller—was not obligated to disclose.

The trend toward mandating disclosure by the seller has produced a similar (if slower) movement toward imposing the same disclosure duty on the seller's agent. California has even gone so far as to require the seller's agent to conduct a visual inspection of the property and to report to the buyer any defects that are discovered.[22] In effect, this provides the buyer with a cause of action for negligent nondisclosure if the seller's agent breaches his duty. The vast majority of states, however, still follows the traditional rule, which imposes no such inspection duty.[23]

---

[19] See, e.g., Md. Code Ann., Real Prop. § 10-702.

[20] Residential Lead-Based Paint Hazard Reduction Act, 42 U.S.C. §§ 4851–4856.

[21] 42 U.S.C. §§ 9601–9675.

[22] Easton v. Strassburger, 199 Cal. Rptr. 383 (Ct. App. 1984); see also Cal. Civ. Code §§ 2079–2979.5 (codifying Easton standard); see also Note, Imposing Tort Liability on Real Estate Brokers Selling Defective Housing, 99 Harv. L. Rev. 1861 (1986).

[23] See, e.g., Kubinsky v. Van Zandt Realtors, 811 S.W.2d 711 (Tex. Ct. App. 1991) (seller's broker not liable to buyer for failing to inspect home); Thomson v. McGinnis, 465 S.E.2d 922 (W.Va. 1995) (seller's broker owed buyer no duty to investigate condition of home, but broker who volunteered to secure expert inspection of home for benefit of buyer could be liable for negligently selecting inspector).

§ 21.04   Builder's Implied Warranty of Quality

[A]   The Warranty in Context

At common law, the builder who constructed a new home and then sold it to a buyer was shielded from liability by caveat emptor, even if the home was negligently constructed. Only the rare buyer protected by an express warranty in the sales contract had any legal recourse against the builder.

Over the last 30 years, however, a clear majority of states has repudiated this rule.[24] Most jurisdictions now hold that—as a matter of law—an implied warranty accompanies the sale of a new home by a builder, developer, or other "merchant" of housing.[25] The warranty is typically termed the implied warranty of quality, implied warranty of fitness, or implied warranty of habitability. Yet, however denominated, the basic protection afforded by the warranty is generally the same in each state: the builder impliedly warrants that the house has been constructed in a workmanlike manner and is fit for human habitation. In most states, the implied warranty does not impose strict liability on the builder, and thus does not guarantee that the home is free from all defects. Rather, it allows the buyer to recover if the builder failed to exercise the standard of skill and care customarily exercised by professional builders. Although some courts find that even minor problems breach the implied warranty, a majority of courts—aware that virtually every new house contains a few imperfections—extends the warranty only to significant defects.[26] Most courts also apply the warranty only to latent or hidden defects, not to obvious defects that an inspection would easily reveal.[27]

The rapid development of the implied warranty undoubtedly reflects the growing view that a new home is merely a specialized type of product.[28]

---

[24] In contrast, efforts by home buyers to impose liability for defects on the bank or other lender who financed the construction project have been almost always unsuccessful. *See, e.g.,* Parker v. Columbia Bank, 604 A.2d 521 (Md. Ct. Spec. App. 1992) (bank that made construction loan owed no duty of care to borrowers regarding quality of construction, and thus was not liable for fraudulent concealment, negligent misrepresentation, negligence, or breach of fiduciary duty). One of the rare exceptions is Connor v. Great Western Savs. & Loan Ass'n, 447 P.2d 609 (Cal. 1968).

[25] *See generally* Paul G. Haskell, *The Case for an Implied Warranty of Quality in Sales of Real Property,* 53 Geo. L.J. 633 (1965); Jeff Sovern, *Toward a Theory of Warranties in Sales of New Homes: Housing the Implied Warranty Advocates, Law and Economics Mavens, and Consumer Psychologists Under One Roof,* 1993 Wis. L. Rev. 13; Robert T. Strickland, Note, *Implied Warranties in New Home Sales—Is the Seller Defenseless?,* 35 S.C. L. Rev. 469 (1984). *See also, e.g.,* Evans v. J. Stiles, Inc., 689 S.W.2d 399 (Tex. 1985).

[26] For example, in Petersen v. Hubschman Constr. Co., Inc., 389 N.E.2d 1154 (Ill. 1979), the Illinois Supreme Court held that the implied warranty of habitability is breached when a home contains latent defects that interfere with the buyers' legitimate expectation that the home will be reasonably suited for its intended use.

[27] Although the implied warranty stems from judicial action in most states, certain states have imposed the requirement by statute. *See, e.g.,* N.Y. Gen. Bus. Law §§ 777–777b.

[28] Significantly, the warranty is implied only in sales of new homes by professional builders, developers, and other "merchants." *See* Gaito v. Auman, 327 S.E.2d 870 (N.C. 1985) (where home built four years earlier had been occupied for total of eight months prior to sale, the

Just as the adoption of the Uniform Commercial Code abolished caveat emptor in the sale of goods, courts increasingly see little reason to retain the rule in the context of new homes.[29] Even as expanded duties are imposed on the manufacturer of goods, the same policies support finding an implied warranty by the manufacturer of new housing:

(1)   the buyer's prepurchase investigation is unlikely to reveal the defect both because the buyer lacks sufficient expertise and because many defects will not become apparent for years;

(2)   the buyer reasonably expects that the builder will construct a suitable home;

(3)   the builder's expertise allows him to avoid defects through careful construction; and

(4)   the builder has the ability to spread any loss by increasing prices to the public.

Moreover, two factors unique to the family home buttress the implied warranty: (1) the home is the biggest investment that most families will make; and (2) from the personhood perspective, the family home merits special protection. Because the purchase of commercial property does not trigger these policy concerns in most instances, the implied warranty does not extend to such transactions.[30]

Suppose B purchases a new home from builder S pursuant to a contract that provides that "Purchaser hereby waives and disclaims all implied warranties of any kind or nature whatsoever." Two months after B takes title to her new home, the roof collapses. Can B sue notwithstanding the disclaimer? Scholars argue that the public policies that support the implied warranty in the first instance should equally prevent its disclaimer.[31] Yet courts appear to enforce disclaimers that are clear and unambiguous, while largely ignoring "boilerplate" disclaimer clauses.[32]

---

initial purchasers could still sue for breach of implied warranty of habitability); Frickel v. Sunnyside Enters., Inc., 725 P.2d 422 (Wash. 1986) (implied warranty of habitability did not apply to later sale of 40-unit apartment complex that builder initially constructed and operated for investment purposes). In most jurisdictions the warranty is inapplicable to the resale of a used home by an ordinary seller. *See also* Vetor v. Shockey, 414 N.E.2d 575 (Ind. Ct. App. 1980).

[29] For a useful discussion of the policies underlying judicial recognition of the implied warranty, see Petersen v. Hubschman Constr. Co., Inc., 389 N.E.2d 1154 (Ill. 1979).

[30] Frona M. Powell & Jane P. Mallor, *The Case for an Implied Warranty of Quality in Sales of Commercial Real Estate*, 68 Wash. U. L.Q. 305 (1990). *But see* Tusch Enters. v. Coffin, 740 P.2d 1022 (Idaho 1987) (applying implied warranty where buyer purchased three duplexes as an investment).

[31] *See, e.g.,* Frona M. Powell, *Disclaimers of Implied Warranty in the Sale of New Homes*, 34 Vill. L. Rev. 1123 (1989); Roy R. Anderson, *Disclaiming the Implied Warranties of Habitability and Good Workmanship in the Sale of New Houses: The Supreme Court of Texas and the Duty to Read the Contracts You Sign*, 15 Tex. Tech L. Rev. 517 (1984).

[32] *See, e.g.,* Tusch Enters. v. Coffin, 740 P.2d 1022 (Idaho 1987) (disclaimer must be "clear and unambiguous"); Tyus v. Resta, 476 A.2d 427 (Pa. 1984) (implied warranties may be "limited or disclaimed only by clear and unambiguous language"). *But see* G-W-L, Inc. v. Robichaux, 643 S.W.2d 392 (Tex. 1982) (boilerplate integration clause that included disclaimer of any "warranties, express or implied" held sufficient).

[B] Rights of Successor Owners

One major unsettled issue is whether the implied warranty extends to successor owners. Suppose A purchases a new home from builder-developer D in 2000, and A resells to B. If the home foundation later crumbles, can B sue D based on the implied warranty?

The issue reveals widespread judicial disagreement about the theoretical basis for the implied warranty. Some courts reason that it is founded on tort concepts; others conclude that it is based on contract; and still others echo Dean Prosser's view that it is "a freak hybrid born of the illicit intercourse of tort and contract."[33] Courts that justify the implied warranty under contract law often refuse to extend the warranty to a subsequent purchaser (like B) who lacks privity of contract with the builder (here D).[34]

The current trend, however, is to recognize that a subsequent purchaser may sue the builder[35] under the implied warranty,[36] based on the same public policies that apply to the initial purchaser. "[T]he contractor should not be relieved of liability for unworkmanlike construction simply because of the fortuity that the property on which he did the construction has changed hands."[37] Further, barring the subsequent buyer's recovery might encourage sham first sales to shield builders from liability. The main counterweight to these policy arguments is the burden of perpetual liability. If the builder is liable to subsequent purchasers, will he be liable forever? Courts usually deal with this concern by holding that the builder is liable only for a "reasonable" period.

§ 21.05 Risk of Loss Before Conveyance

[A] Equitable Conversion

Suppose that on July 1, S and B enter into a contract for the sale and purchase of Greenacre—a single-family home—with escrow to close on July 31. The contract is silent on risk of loss. On July 4, an errant firecracker set off by an unknown person sparks a fire that destroys the Greenacre house. Is B still obligated to purchase?

Perhaps incredibly, in most states the answer is "yes." Under the common law doctrine of *equitable conversion*, the buyer is deemed the equitable owner of the land until close of escrow unless the contract specifies otherwise.[38] It is an ancient maxim that "equity regards as done that which

---

[33] William L. Prosser, *The Assault Upon the Citadel*, 69 Yale L.J. 1099, 1126 (1960).

[34] *See, e.g.,* Oates v. Jag, Inc., 333 S.E.2d 222 (N.C. 1985) (subsequent purchaser allowed to sue in negligence, but not on implied warranty).

[35] *Cf.* Tusch Enters. v. Coffin, 740 P.2d 1022 (Idaho 1987) (allowing buyer who purchased from developer to sue original builder under implied warranty despite lack of privity).

[36] Richards v. Powercraft Homes, Inc., 678 P.2d 427 (Ariz. 1984); Lempke v. Dagenais, 547 A.2d 290 (N.H. 1988).

[37] Lempke v. Dagenais, 547 A.2d 290, 294 (N.H. 1988), *quoting* Aronsohn v. Mandara, 184 A.2d 675, 689 (N.J. 1984).

[38] *See, e.g.,* Ross v. Bumstead, 173 P.2d 765 (Ariz. 1946) (after fire destroyed packing plant

ought to be done." Thus, English courts developed the rule that once a sales contract was signed, the buyer was considered the owner in equity, while the seller merely retained a right to receive the purchase price.[39] The later injury or destruction of the property by fire, flood, hurricane, earthquake or other disaster after the contract date was irrelevant to the parties' obligations. Courts have extended the doctrine to include post-contract zoning amendments, eminent domain proceedings, and similar developments affecting the legal status of the property.[40]

Modern scholars uniformly condemn equitable conversion.[41] It is fundamentally inconsistent with the expectations of the ordinary buyer and seller. Moreover, because the seller usually retains possession until close of escrow, he is better situated to protect the property. Law and economics scholars would undoubtedly note the "moral hazard" issue posed by the rule; already entitled to receive the sales proceeds, the seller has little incentive to preserve the property from injury. Finally, in most instances the seller still has casualty insurance on the property until close of escrow, and thus may not need the protection that the rule affords, while the buyer rarely insures before the closing.

Why is this seemingly inequitable doctrine still the majority rule? Two factors obscure the need for reform. First, virtually all sales contracts contain a "risk of loss" clause, which expressly assigns the risk of loss in the event the property is damaged or destroyed before the close of escrow. Such clauses typically provide that the risk of loss remains with the seller until escrow closes. Thus, the use of equitable conversion as a "gap-filling" rule is comparatively rare. Second, courts have often mitigated the harshness of the rule in the standard situation where only the seller has insured the property. In theory, equitable conversion would allow the seller to receive both the purchase price and the insurance proceeds, a double recovery. Most courts, however, will impose a constructive trust on the policy proceeds, requiring the seller to apply them for the benefit of the buyer.[42]

---

and warehouse on property, buyer held liable for damages when he refused to perform); Bleckley v. Langston, 143 S.E.2d 671 (Ga. Ct. App. 1965) (buyers still liable to perform contract after fire destroyed pecan orchard on land).

[39] Thus, in a related application of equitable conversion, some courts hold that the vendor's interest in property subject to an installment land contract is personal property, not real property to which a judgment lien could attach. *See, e.g.,* Cannefax v. Clement, 818 P.2d 546 (Utah 1991).

[40] DiDonato v. Reliance Standard Life Ins. Co., 249 A.2d 327 (Pa. 1969) (buyer bears risk of zoning change under equitable conversion). *But see* Clay v. Landreth, 45 S.E.2d 875 (Va. 1948) (refusing to apply equitable conversion in seller's specific performance action where property was rezoned before close of escrow to bar the buyer's intended use).

[41] *See, e.g.,* George R. Nock et al., *Equitable Conversion in Washington: The Doctrine That Dares Not Speak Its Name,* 1 U. Puget Sound L. Rev. 121 (1977).

[42] *See, e.g.,* Holscher v. James, 860 P.2d 646 (Idaho 1993); Gilles v. Sprout, 196 N.W.2d 612 (Minn. 1972). *See also* Skelly Oil Co. v. Ashmore, 365 S.W.2d 582 (Mo. 1963) (affirming judgment requiring seller to apply fire insurance proceeds to purchase price where buyer sought specific performance of sales contract). *But see* Raplee v. Piper, 143 N.E.2d 919 (N.Y. 1957) (observing that only proceeds from insurance purchased by the buyer need be applied to the purchase price).

[B] Alternative Approaches to the Risk of Loss Dilemma

There is a clear trend away from equitable conversion. The most widely-accepted alternative is the Uniform Vendor & Purchaser Risk Act, adopted in New York, California and ten other states.[43] Under the Act, the risk of loss due to physical destruction or eminent domain remains with the seller until either possession or title is transferred to the buyer. For example, if the Act applies to the Greenacre hypothetical above, the fire renders the contract unenforceable, and B may recover any monies already paid to S. Another group of states reaches much the same result under the "Massachusetts Rule." These states recognize an implied condition that the contract will not be binding if (a) the building is destroyed or significantly damaged and (b) the terms of the contract demonstrate that the building was an important part of the subject matter of the contract.[44]

---

[43] Unif. Vendor & Purchaser Risk Act, 14 U.L.A. 471; *cf.* Lucenti v. Cayuga Apartments, Inc., 399 N.E.2d 918 (N.Y. 1979) (allowing buyer to seek specific performance with an abatement in purchase price after fire destroyed one of two buildings on property).

[44] *See, e.g.,* Skelly Oil Co. v. Ashmore, 365 S.W.2d 582 (Mo. 1963) (endorsing the Massachusetts rule in case where grocery store building was destroyed by fire); *see also* Sanford v. Breidenbach, 173 N.E.2d 702 (Ohio Ct. App. 1960) (adopting similar rule).

Chapter 22

THE MORTGAGE

SYNOPSIS

§ 22.01   The Role of Security for Debt

Modern American society is founded on the availability of credit. Virtually all large transactions—such as the purchase of a family home, the development of a new shopping center, or the expansion of a profitable factory—are financed with borrowed money. The lender in such a transaction will demand that the borrower post security for the loan. Most commonly, this security takes the form of a mortgage, deed of trust, installment land contract, or similar device that encumbers real property.[1]

Why do lenders insist on security? Suppose B borrows $1 million from L—without security—in order to purchase Blueacre. B signs a promissory note agreeing to repay the loan, with interest, in five years, and then uses the money to buy Blueacre. Consider the difficulties that L might encounter in collecting the loan. B might lose Blueacre in a wild poker game and file bankruptcy, leaving L and other creditors unpaid. Or B might sell Blueacre quickly and flee with the proceeds to a remote country that will not extradite him to the United States. The lender holding a mortgage, however, avoids these risks. If the loan is not repaid as promised, the lender forecloses on the mortgage, sells the land, and uses the sales proceeds to pay off the debt.

The law governing mortgages and related security devices is primarily oriented toward dual utilitarian goals: shielding the borrower against unfair or inequitable treatment by the lender, while ensuring an adequate supply of credit. If mortgage law were skewed toward complete borrower protection, interest rates would rise dramatically and credit would be less available. Conversely, under a pure free-market approach, the lender could dictate virtually any terms and the borrower might receive harsh treatment.

In seeking to strike an appropriate balance between the competing interests of lenders and borrowers, the law has become both complex and technical. Today, this area is governed by a bewildering combination of case law and state statutes, differing widely from state to state, with only limited federal involvement. The recently-adopted Restatement (Third) of Property: Mortgages[2] may help bring uniformity to this legal patchwork.

§ 22.02 What Is a Mortgage?

A *mortgage* is the conveyance of an interest in real property as security for performance of an obligation.[3] The obligation is almost always a loan of money evidenced by a *promissory note*. In general, if the borrower (the *mortgagor*) fails to make the payments required by the note or otherwise defaults on the obligation, the lender (the *mortgagee*) may cause the secured property to be sold and apply the sales proceeds to satisfy the unpaid debt. This process is called *foreclosure*.

---

[1] *See generally* Lawrence Berger, *Solving the Problem of Abusive Mortgage Foreclosure Sales,* 66 Neb. L. Rev. 373 (1987); Eric T. Freyfogle, *Vagueness and the Rule of Law: Reconsidering Installment Land Contract Forfeitures,* 1988 Duke L.J. 609; Grant S. Nelson & Dale A. Whitman, *The Installment Land Contract—A National Viewpoint,* 1977 BYU L. Rev. 541; Michael H. Schill, *An Economic Analysis of Mortgagor Protection Laws,* 77 Va. L. Rev. 489 (1991).

[2] Restatement (Third) of Property: Mortgages (1997).

[3] Restatement (Third) of Property: Mortgages § 1.1 (1997).

This pithy definition of the mortgage, however, masks conceptual complexity. There are three separate theories concerning the nature of the mortgage. About two-thirds of the states follow the *lien theory*. Under this prevailing view, the mortgage is seen as a mere lien on the secured property. Thus, the mortgagee merely holds a security interest, not title; the mortgagee is entitled to foreclose on the property if a default occurs, but is not entitled to possession before foreclosure.[4] Some states cling to the common law concept that the mortgage is the transfer of title to the mortgagee until the debt is repaid.[5] In these *title theory* states, the mortgagee has the theoretical right to take possession of the secured property—and thus obtain its rents and profits—without foreclosure. In practice, however, this right is rarely exercised until a default has occurred. Finally, a few states follow the *intermediate theory*, under which the mortgagee is entitled to possession of the property only upon the mortgagor's default but before foreclosure is completed.

§ 22.03 Evolution of the Mortgage

The lineage of the modern mortgage[6] may be traced to fourteenth-century England. The medieval English mortgage took the form of a conveyance of fee simple subject to a condition subsequent. B, the mortgagor, transferred title to his property to L, the mortgagee, subject to the condition that if B repaid the loan on a specified day (called the *law day*), L would transfer title back to B. If B failed to repay the entire loan precisely on time, his interest in the property automatically ended, leaving L with fee simple absolute. Even though L was entitled to possession of the property during the loan period, he would customarily allow B to retain possession.

This rigid system sometimes produced harsh results. A minor or technical error in the mortgagor's performance—such as a payment that was a few days late—would result in forfeiture of the property. And the mortgagor who failed to perform because of fraud, duress, or excusable mistake also lost the land. As a result, defaulting mortgagors began to petition the King's Chancellor for redress. If fairness and equity warranted, the Chancellor ordered the mortgagee to reconvey the property after receiving full payment. By the seventeenth century, the Chancellor's court (or chancery court) routinely allowed the mortgagor to recover or *redeem* the property if the entire loan was repaid within a reasonable period after the due date, regardless of the reason for late payment. This right became known as the mortgagor's *equity of redemption*.

The equity of redemption placed the mortgagee in a dilemma. Every defaulting mortgagor might someday seek to redeem, and thereby nullify the mortgagee's title to the land. How long would this danger last? The solution to the mortgagee's difficulty was the foreclosure action. A concerned mortgagee could petition the chancery court to end or *foreclose* the

---

[4] *See also* Restatement (Third) of Property: Mortgages § 4.1(a) (1997) (adopting lien theory).

[5] *See* Powell on Real Property § 37.03 (Michael Allan Wolf ed., Matthew Bender).

[6] The term "mortgage" literally means "dead pledge" in Norman French, which reflected the nature of the twelfth-century mortgage.

mortgagor's equity of redemption. The court would establish a final date for payment of the loan; if the mortgagor failed to meet this deadline, the equity of redemption ended. Later transplanted to the United States, this proceeding was called *strict foreclosure.*

Strict foreclosure was inequitable to the mortgagor when the value of the security exceeded the debt. Suppose, for example, that mortgagor B borrowed $100 from mortgagee L, secured by a mortgage on land worth $1,000, and then defaulted. Strict foreclosure allowed L to retain the entire parcel, worth 10 times the debt. During the nineteenth century, most states adopted legislation that imposed a new requirement on the mortgagee seeking a judgment to foreclose the equity of redemption. Under court supervision, the foreclosing mortgagee was forced to sell the property at a public auction, and distribute any surplus sales proceeds to junior lienholders and the mortgagor. This process became known as *judicial foreclosure.*

The nineteenth century brought another milestone in mortgage history— the evolution of the *power of sale mortgage* (also called the *mortgage with power of sale*). Originating in the efforts of English mortgagees to avoid chancery court, it quickly spread to the United States. The power of sale mortgage contains express provisions by which the mortgagor consents to foreclosure of the equity of redemption by a public auction sale, but without any judicial involvement. This method is called *power of sale foreclosure.*

§ 22.04 Creation of a Mortgage

[A] The Loan Process

The average loan transaction is relatively straightforward. B, a prospective borrower completes a written loan application and supplies it to L, the prospective lender. L reviews the loan application, investigates B's financial condition, and commissions an appraisal of the property offered as security. If L wishes to make the loan, L will probably issue a *loan commitment* to B that states the terms and conditions L will require. The loan commitment is usually viewed as an acceptance of the borrower's offer (embodied in the loan application), and accordingly creates an enforceable contract that binds both parties to the loan transaction.

The loan process is increasingly regulated by federal laws that govern banks, savings and loan associations, and other institutional lenders. The federal Truth-In-Lending Act,[7] for example, requires extensive disclosure to the prospective residential borrower concerning the true costs associated with the loan. Further, the federal Fair Housing Act[8] bars lenders from discriminating in the financing of residential real property based on race, color, religion, sex, familial status, national origin, or handicap (*see* § 16.02[B]). Still, the widespread practice of *redlining* effectively discriminates against racial and ethnic minorities. Redlining is the denial of

---

[7] Truth-In-Lending Act, 15 U.S.C. §§ 1601–1693r.

[8] Fair Housing Act, 42 U.S.C. §§ 3601–3619.

mortgage financing because the property involved is located in a older, low-income neighborhood. Rather than considering each application on its individual merits, some lenders follow a blanket policy of refusing to make any loans—or, alternatively, imposing more onerous loan terms—in regions perceived as particularly risky. The plethora of federal and state statutes expressly enacted to eliminate redlining has reduced but not eliminated the problem.[9]

[B] Execution Formalities

The mortgage is viewed as the transfer of an interest in real property. Thus, the formalities required for an effective deed (*see* § 23.04) also apply to mortgages in most states. Although some states impose additional requirements, at a minimum: (a) the material provisions of the mortgage (names of parties, description of secured property, words manifesting intent to use property as security, etc.) must be set forth in a written document executed by the mortgagor; and (b) the mortgage must be delivered to the mortgagee.

Until recently, there was little standardization of mortgage forms. Lenders in different localities tended to use different forms. But today almost all residential loans made by institutional lenders utilize standard mortgage forms jointly developed by two federal agencies, the Federal National Mortgage Association (FNMA) and the Federal Home Loan Mortgage Corporation (FHLMC). Why? Mortgage loans are typically created by local lenders who then sell these loans to FNMA, FHLMC, and others—in what is called the *secondary market*—in order to obtain capital to make additional loans. Because these agencies will only purchase loans made with their forms, the use of the FNMA/FHLMC mortgage forms has become standard industry practice. In contrast, the commercial mortgage is still often individually drafted to suit the particular transaction.

An unrecorded mortgage is fully valid and binding. However, it is customary to record the mortgage in order to provide notice to the world of the mortgagee's interest, and thus preclude later purchasers, mortgagees, and others from claiming that their interests take priority.

[C] Priority

A single property may be encumbered by multiple mortgages and other liens. Suppose, for example, that B's property Greenacre is subject to three mortgages, securing a total indebtedness of $350,000. Assume that Greenacre is sold at foreclosure for $250,000, its fair market value. Who receives the proceeds? The answer turns on the respective *priority* of each mortgage, which is largely governed by the general rules concerning land title (*see* Chapter 24). Assuming that the first-priority mortgage (or *first mortgage*) was foreclosed, it is paid first, the second-priority mortgage (or *second mortgage*) is paid next, and so forth. Thus, if the first mortgage on

---

[9] *See* Powell on Real Property § 37.11 (Michael Allan Wolf ed., Matthew Bender).

Greenacre secures a $240,000 debt, it is paid in full from the sale proceeds. If the second mortgage secures a $50,000 debt, its holder will receive only $10,000 from the sale proceeds. And the mortgagee holding the third mortgage will receive nothing from the sale. Junior mortgages, in short, are substantially more risky than a first mortgage. For this reason, they normally command a somewhat higher interest rate.

A special rule governs the priority of the "purchase money" mortgage. Suppose that G contracts to purchase H's property Blueacre for $100,000, paying $10,000 in cash and the balance in the form of a $90,000 promissory note secured by a first mortgage on Blueacre. J holds a judgment lien, which already encumbers all of G's real property, and which will also attach to Blueacre when G receives title. Once escrow closes on the G-H transaction, which lien has priority—H's mortgage or J's judgment lien? As a general rule, a purchase money mortgage takes priority over all liens that attach to the property through the buyer-mortgagor. Because J's judgment lien here arises out of G's actions, it is junior in priority to H's purchase money mortgage. Although the issue arises most commonly with judgment liens, dower and homestead claims are also included within the scope of the rule.

§ 22.05   The Secured Obligation

[A]   Role of the Obligation

The mortgage is a legal nullity unless it secures an obligation. In a very real sense, the mortgage merely provides a remedy to compel performance of the obligation. Suppose L holds a mortgage on Blackacre to secure B's repayment of a $100,000 promissory note. If B fails to pay as required by the note, L may foreclose her mortgage, sell Blackacre at auction, and use the foreclosure sale proceeds to pay the $100,000 debt. What if L merely holds a mortgage on Blackacre that does not secure any obligation (e.g., because the promissory note it once secured has been repaid)? Under these circumstances, L's mortgage has no legal force or effect.

Most commonly, the mortgage secures repayment of a loan evidenced by a written *promissory note*.[10] The $100,000 note that B executed in favor of L presumably provides that B will make monthly payments to L until the debt is fully repaid. The note (or the mortgage itself) would typically impose related obligations on B that are designed to preserve the security, such as the duty to insure the property against casualty loss, to avoid waste, and so forth. L may foreclose if B fails to perform any of the specified obligations.

---

[10] Although the Statute of Frauds mandates that a mortgage be evidenced by a writing, in most states the mortgage could secure an oral debt. *See* Powell on Real Property § 37.12 (Michael Allan Wolf ed., Matthew Bender).

[B] The Promissory Note

[1] A Specialized Contract

The promissory note is simply a specialized form of contract between the lender and the borrower. The note—usually a standardized FNMA/FHLMC form in simple residential transactions—identifies the borrower and lender, contains the borrower's promise to repay the loan on stated terms and conditions, recites that its repayment is secured by a mortgage or deed of trust, and is signed by the borrower. Beyond these basic provisions, the note contains four key components: (a) the amount; (b) the interest rate; (c) the term; and (d) the amortization schedule.

[2] Key Components

[a] Amount

The amount of the loan is usually limited by the applicable *loan-to-value ratio*. Banks, savings and loan associations, and other institutional lenders subject to federal and state regulation may loan up to a certain percentage of the appraised value of the secured property. If the appraised value of Blackacre is $200,000 and regulations allow up to a 90% loan-to-value ratio for this type of loan, the maximum amount that Bank L can loan on the security of Blackacre is $180,000 (90% of $200,000).

[b] Interest Rate

The interest rate may be either a fixed rate (which remains the same during the entire life of the loan) or an adjustable rate (which varies over the life of the loan). In an adjustable rate mortgage, the interest rate is equal to (a) a specified external index rate that fluctuates according to market conditions (e.g., the federal reserve discount rate) *plus* (b) a fixed margin (usually about 2%). For example, if the index rate is 5.5% during a particular month, and the margin is 2%, then during that month the interest rate on the loan is 7.5%; if the index rate drops to 5% by the next month, that month's loan interest rate is 7%.

Can a lender charge the highest interest rate that the borrower is willing to pay? In the early medieval period, the Roman Catholic Church considered the charging of any interest to be a mortal sin. Over time, this tradition led to the widespread passage of state *usury* laws, which place a legal ceiling on the interest rate a lender may receive. In California, for instance, an ordinary lender could legally charge only 10% for many years, even though the borrower would have willingly paid more. The apparent modern purpose of the usury laws is to prevent "loan-shark" lenders from taking unfair advantage of vulnerable borrowers. Almost by definition, however, these laws restrict the supply of available credit. Unsurprisingly, the usury laws are riddled with exclusions and exemptions. For example, secured loans exempt from these laws in most jurisdictions include: (a) loans to corporations; and (b) loans that the seller of land extends to the buyer to help finance the purchase, so-called "purchase money" loans. And—as the result of federal preemption—almost all loans secured by first-priority mortgages on residential property that are made by banks, savings and loans associations, and other institutional lenders are entirely exempt from state usury laws. Accordingly, the usury laws are relatively ineffective today.

[c] Term

The typical residential loan has a term of 25 or 30 years. This simply means that the entire loan amount plus interest must be repaid within the term, according to the agreed-upon amortization schedule (*see* [d], *below*). Modern borrower-lender disputes involving the term of the loan usually arise in one of two contexts: (1) prepayment of the loan; or (2) sale of the secured property.

Suppose B obtains a secured loan for $200,000 from Bank L, payable over a 30-year term, at a fixed interest rate of 8%. Two years later, prevailing interest rates fall to 6%. B wishes to *refinance* the property (here, to replace her 8% loan with a 6% loan). Can B repay her above-market 8% loan in advance of the due date? There is no common law right to prepay a loan. However, promissory notes often contain a *prepayment clause,* which permits the borrower to prepay the loan in return for payment of a monetary penalty (e.g., six months interest on the amount prepaid) or which precludes prepayment for a specified period (e.g., the first seven years of the term).[11] Such prepayment clauses are generally enforced, unless they constitute an unreasonable restraint on alienation[12] or impose an unconscionable penalty.

Alternatively, suppose that prevailing interest rates have risen to 10%; B now hopes to sell her property and pass on the benefit of her below-market 8% loan to the buyer.[13] But B's promissory note probably contains a *due-on-sale clause* that prevents this result. The standard due-on-sale clause provides that the lender may demand repayment of the entire loan if the mortgaged property is sold or otherwise transferred. During the 1970s, a few outraged borrowers were successfully able to attack the due-on-sale clause as an invalid restraint on alienation.[14] Since 1982, however, state court rulings on the issue have been preempted by federal law that validates the due-on-sale clause in almost all loans.[15]

---

[11] *See generally* Frank S. Alexander, *Mortgage Prepayment: The Trial of Common Sense,* 72 Cornell L. Rev. 288 (1987).

[12] *See, e.g.,* McCausland v. Bankers Life Ins. Co., 757 P.2d 941 (Wash. 1988) (prohibition on prepayment of a commercial loan for seven years was not unreasonable restraint on alienation).

[13] Alternatively, absent an enforceable due-on-sale clause, B could enjoy the benefits of this interest rate differential by using a *wrap-around mortgage.* Suppose B agrees to sell to N for $250,000, in return for $20,000 in cash and a $230,000 promissory note at 10%, secured by a wrap-around mortgage on the property. B keeps the old 8% loan in place, and makes all required payments. For an illustration of the wrap-around mortgage in practice, see Schrader v. Benton, 635 P.2d 562 (Haw. App. 1981).

[14] The leading case on point is Wellenkamp v. Bank of Am., 582 P.2d 970 (Cal. 1978).

[15] *See, e.g.,* McCausland v. Bankers Life Ins. Co., 757 P.2d 941 (Wash. 1988) (finding that federal law validating due-on-sale clauses preempted prior Washington state law).

[d] Amortization Schedule

The amortization schedule specifies the method by which the borrower repays the loan; it sets forth the amount and due date for each loan payment. Most fixed-rate residential loans are fully-amortized, requiring a fixed monthly payment over the entire term (e.g., $734 per month). The payment amount is established so that the entire loan balance will be repaid when the final payment is made. A payment of $734 per month over a 30-year term, for instance, will fully repay an 8% loan of $100,000. Other loans (e.g., certain commercial loans or second-priority mortgage loans on residential property) are not fully-amortized and, accordingly, one or more balloon payments are required to pay the loan balance.

§ 22.06   Foreclosure of Mortgage

[A] Foreclosure in Context

Two methods of foreclosure are commonly used in the United States. *Judicial foreclosure* is available in all jurisdictions, and is the dominant method in about half of the states. The other principal method is *foreclosure by power of sale*, which predominates in the remaining states.[16] The common law remedy of strict foreclosure is still permitted in only two states.[17]

The broad outline of the foreclosure process is similar for both judicial foreclosure and foreclosure by power of sale, despite the very real differences between them. Five points of similarity can be identified in most jurisdictions. First, the mortgagor receives written notice that foreclosure is beginning, and thus has the opportunity either to pay off the debt or to contest the foreclosure through litigation. Second, the mortgagor retains the right to *redeem* the property by repaying the entire debt until the end of the process, when the equity of redemption is eliminated. Third, the foreclosure process culminates in a public sale, where the property is sold at auction to the highest bidder, usually the mortgagee. Fourth, any surplus sales proceeds are paid to junior lienholders or the mortgagor. Suppose, for example, that the sale brings $200,000 in proceeds, while the unpaid debt and sales expenses total only $50,000; the extra $150,000 is distributed to junior lienholders to the extent necessary to satisfy their liens, and any remaining surplus goes to the mortgagor. Finally, if the sale fails to produce enough money to satisfy the debt, the mortgagor may be liable for a *deficiency judgment*. Suppose now that the sale brings in only $50,000, while the unpaid debt and expenses of sale total $200,000. In many states, the mortgagee can obtain a judgment against the mortgagor for the remaining $150,000, which can be satisfied through levy on the mortgagor's other assets; some states restrict the mortgagee's ability to secure a deficiency judgment (*see* § 22.07[B]).

---

[16] *See* Powell on Real Property § 37.42 (Michael Allan Wolf ed., Matthew Bender).

[17] *See* Dieffenbach v. Attorney General, 604 F.2d 187 (2d Cir. 1979) (upholding constitutionality of Vermont's strict foreclosure laws).

[B] Judicial Foreclosure

Judicial foreclosure is a specialized type of litigation. It may be a slow, expensive, and complex process. For this reason, mortgagees usually prefer the quick, cheap, and simple process of foreclosure by power of sale if it is available in the jurisdiction.

The mortgagee, as plaintiff, begins the judicial foreclosure process by filing a complaint against the mortgagor, junior lienholders, and other persons holding interests in the property that are subordinate to the mortgage. The complaint alleges that a default has occurred in the obligation secured by the mortgage (usually the mortgagor's failure to make required payments) and requests that the mortgage be foreclosed in a court-supervised sale. After service of process is completed, the mortgagor and other defendants have an opportunity to answer the complaint and raise any appropriate objections to foreclosure (e.g., no mortgage exists or no default exists). In the vast majority of proceedings, no answer is filed and the plaintiff-mortgagee obtains a judgment by default. Otherwise, a hearing is conducted to determine whether foreclosure is justified.

The successful mortgagee receives a judgment that states the amount due on the mortgage, directs the property to be sold at public auction within a specified period if the debt is not paid, and establishes the terms of the sale. Notice of the pending sale is given to the public, usually through newspaper advertisements. In most jurisdictions, the mortgagor is entitled to pay off the entire debt and thus redeem the property until late in the process (usually either until the sale or until judicial confirmation of the sale).

The sale is held in a public location (e.g., the courthouse steps) during normal business hours and is usually conducted by a court-appointed official (e.g., the sheriff). The mortgagor, mortgagee, and any member of the public may bid at the sale. The mortgagee, however, enjoys an important advantage in the process: it can bid without cash, using instead the unpaid loan balance owed to it. In general, all other bidders—including the mortgagor—can bid only in cash. As a practical matter, the mortgagee is usually the only bidder, and thus the successful bidder, at the sale.[18]

The final step is judicial confirmation of the sale. In theory at least, the court has the discretion to refuse confirmation if necessary to protect the mortgagor's legitimate interests. Despite this power, confirmation is routinely granted absent evidence that the sale was conducted in an unfair or inequitable manner. Statutes in a few jurisdictions impose a minimum sale price requirement (e.g., two-thirds of appraised value), but in most states the mere inadequacy of the sales price is not a basis for refusing confirmation. Upon confirmation, the responsible official executes and

---

[18] Of course, the mortgagee who purchases at the sale may incur liability for the cleanup of any hazardous substances on the property, pursuant to the Comprehensive Environmental Response, Compensation, and Liability Act, 42 U.S.C. §§ 9601–9675. *Cf.* United States v. Maryland Bank & Trust Co., 632 F. Supp. 573 (D. Md. 1986) (imposing cleanup liability on foreclosing mortgagee based on law prior to mortgagee-protective amendments adopted in 1996).

delivers the deed to the highest bidder. If bid proceeds remain after the debt and sales expenses are paid, the court determines how the surplus is allocated. Conversely, if the bid price is insufficient to pay the debt and expenses, the court in many jurisdictions instead issues a deficiency judgment in favor of the mortgagee.

[C]　Power of Sale Foreclosure

The power of sale foreclosure is a purely private procedure, without judicial involvement or approval. While judicial foreclosure is a remedy provided by statute, the power of sale foreclosure arises from contract. It is permitted only when authorized by the express terms of the mortgage. This lack of judicial involvement creates the potential for abuse. Without judicial oversight, what prevents the mortgagee from taking unfair advantage of the mortgagor? States that allow power of sale foreclosure usually provide statutory safeguards for the mortgagor.

One safeguard is adequate advance notice to the mortgagor. If foreclosure is unjustified (e.g., if no default has occurred), the alerted mortgagor can file suit to enjoin any sale. Alternatively, he can avoid foreclosure by paying the debt or selling the property. The notice requirements for a power of sale foreclosure vary widely. In a typical state, the process begins when the mortgagee provides a written notice of intent to foreclose to the mortgagor and other affected parties.[19] State law may require that the notice be personally delivered, printed in a local newspaper, or both. After a fixed period of time (e.g., five weeks) elapses, the mortgagee provides a second notice, which announces the date, time, and place of the sale. In some states, these two forms of notice are combined into a single document.

The sale itself is conducted by the mortgagee or a designated official (e.g., sheriff) in a public location, and follows a format similar to the judicial foreclosure sale. As a general rule, anyone may bid, but all bidders other than the mortgagee can bid only with cash. The property is sold to the highest bidder, which is normally the mortgagee. Judicial confirmation is not required. Rather, the sale is complete—and the mortgagor's equity of redemption ends—when the bidding is over.

Only in exceptional circumstances can the mortgagor challenge the validity of a completed sale. Assume L forecloses on B's $200,000 home to collect on a $50,000 debt; L, the only bidder, purchases the property with a $5,000 bid. Does B have any recourse? Most states allow the mortgagor to bring suit to cancel the sale only where the bid price is so grossly inadequate as to "shock the conscience" of the court[20] or if fraudulent or unconscionable conduct has occurred. Here, L's purchase price is probably small enough to invalidate the sale. The vast majority of foreclosure sales, however, are immune from attack under this standard.

---

[19] *See* N.Y. Real Prop. Acts. Law §§ 1402, 1403.

[20] *See, e.g.,* Central Fin. Servs., Inc. v. Spears, 425 So. 2d 403 (Miss. 1983) (sale set aside based on price inadequacy where mortgagee purchased property with bid of $1,458.86, and sold property 12 days later for $4,000).

A few states have gone much farther, imposing a duty on the mortgagee to obtain a fair and reasonable price under the circumstances.[21] This "good faith" standard may require, for example, that the mortgagee exert diligent efforts to attract third party bidders, or adjourn the sale if a fair price is not offered. The goal is to increase bid prices, and thereby shield the mortgagor from the forfeiture of equity and the imposition of a deficiency judgment.

Yet critics suggest that the uncertainty produced by the good faith standard may actually produce lower bid prices. Under the traditional "shock the conscience" standard, the bidder has reasonable assurance that the sale is unlikely to be later nullified by a court, and thus may bid with confidence. If the good faith standard applies, however, critics argue that a bidder may bid less simply to compensate for the risk that the sale might later be set aside. Perhaps a more compelling argument against the good faith standard lies in its potential to increase overall interest rates charged to mortgagors. If a sale is adjourned, loan repayment is delayed, and the mortgagee loses the interest that could have been earned by making a new loan immediately to a replacement borrower. Further, the mortgagee who must try to conduct a sale on two, three, or more occasions before obtaining an adequate bid will incur higher advertising and administrative costs. Under the good faith standard, the extra costs caused by defaulting mortgagors will be passed along to all mortgagors in the form of higher interest rates.

§ 22.07 Special Mortgagor Protection Laws

[A] Potential for Abuse

The mortgagor-mortgagee relationship is inherently unequal. Particularly in an era of economic recession—as the depression of the 1930s evidenced—the mortgagee may be able to gain an unfair advantage over the mortgagor through the foreclosure process. The image of the foreclosing mortgagee as villain still lingers in popular culture. Many states have accordingly intervened to provide special statutory protection for the mortgagor. These statutes focus on cushioning the homeowner, farmer, or other small-scale owner from the effects of an economic downturn, when employment is scarce and property values are artificially depressed.

[B] Anti-Deficiency Legislation

Legislation in some states restricts the mortgagee's ability to secure a deficiency judgment after foreclosure. An example illustrates the rationale for this intervention. Suppose B is unable to repay a $100,000 loan owed to L and secured by a mortgage on B's property Greenacre. Upon foreclosure, L is the only bidder and acquires Greenacre for a bid price of $20,000. Under traditional law, L is now entitled to receive a deficiency judgment

---

[21] See, e.g., Murphy v. Fin. Dev. Corp., 495 A.2d 1245 (N.H. 1985).

of $80,000, which it can satisfy by executing on B's other property. But what if the fair market value of Greenacre at the time of sale was $120,000? If so, L has received $200,000 (the $120,000 value of Greenacre plus the $80,000 judgment) in payment of a $100,000 loan, and B has been unfairly penalized.

The most common response to this dilemma is *fair value* legislation. Such statutes limit the amount of the mortgagee's deficiency judgment to the difference between (a) the unpaid loan balance and (b) the fair market value of the property.[22] Applied to the above example, the fair value limitation would permit a deficiency judgment of zero, because the property's fair market value at the time of foreclosure ($120,000) exceeds the unpaid balance ($80,000).

Ten states—mainly in the West—completely bar deficiency judgments in certain situations.[23] Within this group, some preclude such judgments after any power of sale foreclosure, apparently concerned about abuses that may occur in the absence of judicial supervision. Others prohibit deficiency judgments on purchase money mortgages, regardless of the foreclosure method involved; this reflects a policy judgment in favor of encouraging home ownership by restricting the mortgagor's personal liability.[24]

[C] Statutory Redemption

Approximately half of the states allow the mortgagor to redeem the property after foreclosure in a process called *statutory redemption*.[25] In these jurisdictions, the mortgagor may regain title by paying a set amount (typically the foreclosure sale price plus other expenses) to the successful bidder within a specific period (normally ranging from 6 to 24 months). During the redemption period, the mortgagor remains in possession of the property. If the mortgagor fails to redeem, any junior lienholder may redeem instead.

Scholars debate whether statutory redemption serves its intended purpose of protecting the mortgagor.[26] In theory, the doctrine helps to prevent underbidding at the foreclosure sale, thereby preserving the mortgagor's equity. Suppose M's home Redacre is worth $100,000; the home is encumbered by a $90,000 mortgage, so M has an equity of $10,000. M defaults on his mortgage and bidder B attends the resulting foreclosure sale.

---

[22] *See, e.g.,* Cal. Civ. Proc. Code § 580(a); N.Y. Real Prop. Acts. Law § 1371.

[23] *See, e.g.,* First State Bank v. Chunkapura, 734 P.2d 1203 (Mont. 1987) (no deficiency judgment following foreclosure of deed of trust on small parcel). *But see* Mid-Kansas Federal Savings & Loan Ass'n v. Dynamic Dev. Corp., 804 P.2d 1310 (Ariz. 1991) (Arizona law barring deficiency judgment after nonjudicial sale of property used as one-family dwelling did not apply to commercial developer of subdivision whose "spec" homes were still under construction).

[24] *See, e.g.,* Cal. Civ. Proc. Code § 580(b).

[25] *See* Powell on Real Property § 37.46 (Michael Allan Wolf ed., Matthew Bender).

[26] *Compare* Michael H. Schill, *An Economic Analysis of Mortgagor Protection Laws*, 77 Va. L. Rev. 489 (1991) (suggesting that statutory redemption promotes efficiency) *with* George M. Platt, *Deficiency Judgments in Oregon Loans Secured by Land: Growing Disparity Among Functional Equivalents*, 23 Willamette L. Rev. 37 (1987) (criticizing doctrine as inefficient).

Advocates of statutory redemption argue that B now has an incentive to bid a high price in order to preclude M from redeeming. If B bids $99,000, for example, the mortgage is repaid in full and M receives the remaining proceeds after deducting the costs of sale. Because M has recovered most of his equity, he is unlikely to exercise his right of statutory redemption.

Critics suggest that in reality, however, statutory redemption encourages underbidding, which injures the mortgagor. Why? Consider the viewpoint of B, the foreclosure sale bidder. Although B must pay the bid price immediately, he cannot take possession until the lengthy redemption period ends. Moreover, B will be justifiably concerned that M may not maintain the property in good condition. M might be tempted out of spite to damage or even destroy the improvements on the property; and M is probably insolvent, which will preclude B from recovering compensatory damages from him. Finally, if M eventually does repurchase the property, B may suffer a net loss caused by an interest rate differential; while B will receive back the sales price he paid plus interest, the interest rate set by state statute is often below the market interest rate. Because of these risks, bidders like B are reluctant to offer a fair market value bid at the sale. Do mortgagors or junior lienors respond to the resulting low sale prices by redeeming, as the theory underlying the doctrine predicts? No! In practice, post-sale redemption is fairly rare.[27]

[D] Cost of Mortgagor Protection Laws

The utilitarian value of mortgagor protection laws is hotly debated. Some scholars conclude that such laws simply increase the average interest rate paid by all borrowers.[28] In effect, they argue, lenders pass on the added cost of these protections to borrowers in general, and thus responsible borrowers end up subsidizing irresponsible borrowers. Other commentators— viewing these statutory protections as a form of insurance against catastrophic loss—maintain that they are economically desirable.[29]

§ 22.08 An Alternative Financing Device: The Installment Land Contract

[A] Nature of Installment Land Contract

The installment land contract is frequently used as an alternative to the mortgage. Under such a contract, the buyer (or *vendee*) agrees to pay the purchase price in installments to the seller (or *vendor*) over a period of years

---

[27] *See* Patrick B. Bauer, *Statutory Redemption Reconsidered: The Operation of Iowa's Redemption Statute in Two Counties Between 1881 and 1980*, 70 Iowa L. Rev. 343 (1985) (discussing empirical studies of redemption rates ranging between 1% and 18%).

[28] *See, e.g.,* Mark Meador, *The Effects of Mortgage Laws on Home Mortgage Rates*, 34 J. Econ. & Bus. 143 (1982) (concluding that anti-deficiency protection and statutory redemption together increase average interest rates by .31%).

[29] *See, e.g.,* Michael H. Schill, *An Economic Analysis of Mortgagor Protection Laws*, 77 Va. L. Rev. 489 (1991).

(sometimes up to 20 or more years). The contract provides that the vendor retains title to the property until all payments are made, at which time the vendor is required to transfer title to the vendee. The vendee usually receives possession of the property during the contract period. The contract typically provides that in the event of any default by the vendee, the vendor may cancel the contract, retake possession of the land, and retain all installments paid by the vendee, without any foreclosure sale or judicial action.

The parallel to the mortgage is clear. The vendee is the equivalent of the mortgagor, while the vendor is the counterpart of the mortgagee. The vendor retains title if the vendee fails to perform, which is similar to the mortgagee's right to foreclose (and thus obtain title) if the mortgagor defaults.

[B] Impact of Vendee's Breach

American courts traditionally viewed the installment land contract simply as a variety of contract. Accordingly, they routinely enforced the standard clauses providing for forfeiture upon the vendee's default.[30] Suppose that in 1950, vendee E entered into an installment land contract to purchase a 100-acre forest tract from vendor R, promising to pay R $1,000 each month for 20 years. Struck by a lengthy illness in 1960, E lost his job and missed one payment. R then unilaterally canceled the contract, retaining both title to the land and the $120,000 that E had already paid. Relying on freedom of contract rhetoric, courts were unwilling to shelter E and other defaulting vendees from the forfeiture provisions to which they had originally assented. And because the installment land contract was—in form at least—not a mortgage, the broad range of safeguards available to the mortgagor (including the right of redemption, foreclosure protections, and the right to receive excess foreclosure sale proceeds) did not protect the vendee.

Modern courts are far more sympathetic to the plight of the defaulting vendee.[31] Particularly where the vendee has already paid a substantial part of the purchase price, forfeiture seems inconsistent with contemporary standards of fairness and equity. Another factor is the average vendee's lack of legal sophistication. One major use of installment land contracts has been to finance the purchase of housing by low-income families who are unable to qualify for bank loans or other standard financing. These relatively unsophisticated vendees are particularly vulnerable to the risk of forfeiture.

Today there is a clear trend toward treating the installment land contract as a mortgage, and, accordingly, extending the mortgagor's protections to

---

[30] *See, e.g.,* Stonebraker v. Zinn, 286 S.E.2d 911 (W. Va. 1982) (enforcing forfeiture clause despite vendees' argument that clause was an unenforceable penalty rather than a true liquidated damages provision).

[31] *See generally* Eric T. Freyfogle, *Vagueness and the Rule of Law: Reconsidering Installment Land Contract Forfeitures,* 1988 Duke L.J. 609 (discussing modern approach to forfeiture provisions).

the vendee. Courts in Indiana[32] and New York[33] spearheaded this effort by expressly holding that the installment land contract will be equated with the mortgage, at least where the vendee has paid a substantial part of the purchase price before default.[34] Where the vendee has merely paid a minimal sum, or abandons the property after default, forfeiture provisions can seemingly still be enforced even in these states. A small but growing number of jurisdictions have adopted statutes that require the installment land contract to be foreclosed under the general provisions governing mortgages.[35] The Restatement (Third) of Property: Mortgages adopts this position as well.[36]

In many jurisdictions, the movement toward mortgage-equivalence is more gradual. Some states, for example, provide the defaulting vendee with a right of redemption, especially if a substantial portion of the purchase price has been paid.[37] The vendee effectively receives one last chance to pay off the entire remaining balance of the contract price. Others extend the remedy of restitution to the vendee; after default, the vendee receives back the difference between: (a) the total amount of installment payments made to the vendor; and (b) the compensatory damages suffered by the vendor due to the breach, plus the fair rental value of the property during the period of the vendee's occupancy.[38]

[C] Evaluating the Installment Land Contract

The installment land contract is a legal dinosaur, destined to be superseded by the modern mortgage with power of sale. As a financing device, the installment land contract offers no real advantages over the mortgage, yet subjects both parties to unnecessary risk and uncertainty.

From the vendee's viewpoint, there are two main dangers. If the vendee defaults, he will probably receive less protection than a mortgagor, depending on the jurisdiction. In extreme instances, the forfeiture provisions of the contract might be enforced. The vendor's other creditors present a different risk. Depending on state law—and whether the contract is timely recorded—the vendee's interest may be junior in priority to mortgages and other post-contract encumbrances placed on the property by the vendor.

The vendor's principal problem is the legal uncertainty surrounding the installment land contract. In most jurisdictions, litigation may be required in order to ascertain the respective rights and duties of the parties upon the vendee's default, and to clear record title so that the vendor can resell the property.

---

[32] Skendzel v. Marshall, 301 N.E.2d 641 (Ind. 1973).

[33] Bean v. Walker, 464 N.Y.S.2d 895 (App. Div. 1983).

[34] See also Sebastian v. Floyd, 585 S.W.2d 381 (Ky. 1979) (treating all installment land contracts like mortgages, regardless of amount paid by vendee).

[35] See, e.g., Okla. Stat. Ann. tit. 16 § 11A.

[36] Restatement (Third) of Property: Mortgages § 3.4 (1997).

[37] See, e.g., Petersen v. Hartell, 707 P.2d 232 (Cal. 1985).

[38] See, e.g., Union Bond & Trust Co. v. Blue Creek Redwood Co., 128 F. Supp. 709 (N.D. Cal. 1955), aff'd, 243 F.2d 476 (9th Cir. 1957).

§ 22.09 Other Financing Devices

[A] Deed of Trust

Another financing device—particularly popular in states allowing power of sale foreclosure—is the *deed of trust*. While the mortgage involves two parties (mortgagor and mortgagee), the deed of trust creates a three-party relationship (trustor, trustee, and beneficiary). Historically, the deed of trust was seen as the conveyance of title to the secured property in trust. The borrower (the *trustor*) executed a written instrument conveying legal title to a neutral third party (the *trustee*), as security for an obligation owed to the lender (the *beneficiary*). If the trustor duly repaid the loan, the trustee would *reconvey* title. On the other hand, if the trustor defaulted on the debt, the trustee would conduct an auction sale of the property; after the sale, the trustee would repay the beneficiary and affected creditors and distribute any remaining sales proceeds to the trustor.

What accounts for the widespread use of the deed of trust? Before the birth of the power of sale mortgage, it was the only financing device that could be foreclosed through a quick and inexpensive nonjudicial sale. Further, the deed of trust was thought to be exempt from various debtor protection statutes enacted to regulate mortgages. Over the decades, however, the gap between the mortgage and the deed of trust has been virtually eliminated by statutes and judicial decisions. The deed of trust persists largely due to custom.

Today the deed of trust is effectively the same as a power of sale mortgage. Although the outdated terminology is still utilized, the modern deed of trust is not deemed to create a true trust and the trustee is not bound by the obligations of a true trustee.[39] In lien theory states, the deed of trust—like the mortgage—merely transfers a lien to the beneficiary. It may be foreclosed through judicial foreclosure or through a private nonjudicial sale conducted by the trustee.

[B] Equitable Mortgage

Suppose O—burdened with a poor credit record—asks his acquaintance S for a $100,000 personal loan, offering his home Blueacre as security. S is willing to make the loan, but only if O is willing to pay a usurious (and hence illegal) interest rate of 50% per year. To avoid the usury laws, S disguises the transaction as a sale. O conveys Blueacre to S for $100,000, receiving in return an option to repurchase the property one year later for $150,000 (the $100,000 loan amount, plus $50,000 in interest). If O cannot raise the funds necessary to exercise his option, what remedy does he have?

Courts of equity developed the *equitable mortgage* doctrine to resolve such situations. If the parties actually intend a deed, lease, or other instrument

---

[39] Monterey S.P. Partnership v. W.L. Bangham, Inc., 777 P.2d 623 (Cal. 1989) ("Just as a panda is not a true bear, a trustee of a deed of trust is not a true trustee. . . . Regrettably, it appears to be too late in the development of our vocabulary to rename deeds of trust.").

to be security for debt, courts will treat it as a mortgage, regardless of the form of the transaction.[40] Equity, after all, traditionally looks through form to substance. Thus, in the above example, O can eliminate S's security interest in Blueacre by repaying the loan principal and whatever interest is legally due under the state's usury law.

---

[40] *See, e.g.,* Koenig v. Van Reken, 279 N.W.2d 590 (Mich. Ct. App. 1979) (where plaintiff seeking to avoid foreclosure transferred title to grantee who paid no value, but gave plaintiff a lease-option that allowed her to repurchase property in future, transaction was deemed an equitable mortgage). *But see* Duvall v. Laws, Swain, & Murdoch, P.A., 797 S.W.2d 474 (Ark. App. 1990) (transaction between attorney and client, by which client conveyed mineral rights to attorney for professional fees and retained option to repurchase, was not equitable mortgage).

Chapter 23

THE DEED

§ 23.01 The Deed in Context

The deed is the basic document used to transfer an estate or other interest in land during the owner's lifetime. Suppose S owns Greenacre and wishes to transfer her title to B. S, the *grantor*, will use a deed to convey title to B, the *grantee*. Of course, title can be transferred by other methods, such as through adverse possession (*see* Chapter 27), by a will effective upon the owner's death (*see* Chapter 28), or through an eminent domain lawsuit (*see* Chapter 39). But the deed is routinely utilized to transfer title in virtually every real property sale or gift transaction other than testamentary gifts. Millions of deeds are executed and delivered each year in the United States.

The law governing deeds is reasonably well-settled, attracting little scholarly attention.[1] One theme dominates the subject: what are the requirements for a valid deed? The long-term trend in this area is simplification. For example, while the deed in common law England was an intricate, painstakingly drafted document, the modern American deed is typically a short standard form.[2] Similarly, while disputes still sometimes arise on questions such as the adequacy of the deed's property description or whether the deed was "delivered"—particularly in family gift transactions—they are becoming increasingly rare.

Perhaps the most difficult problem is to resolve the competing title claims of two "innocent" parties: the original owner who never intended to transfer title and the later purchaser who bought the land without knowledge of any title defects. The central question here is whether "invisible" deed defects (such as forgery or lack of delivery) may be asserted against an innocent purchaser. Should the law respect the existing property rights of the true owner or protect the reasonable expectations of the innocent later buyer? The answer to this inquiry reveals much about the policies underlying American property law.

§ 23.02 Evolution of the Deed

In feudal England, a fee simple estate in land was transferred through an elaborate ritual known as *feoffment with livery of seisin*, which faintly resembles the modern marriage ceremony. The *feoffor* (transferor), *feoffee* (transferee), and their witnesses assembled together on the affected land. The feoffor orally declared that he was transferring title to the feoffee, and gave the feoffee a branch, twig, stone, clod of earth, or other token that represented ownership of the land. No deed or other document was used in the process. In an era when most members of society were illiterate, this ritual was an effective method of providing proof of the transfer if any title dispute later arose. The parties and witnesses would long remember such a dramatic event, and could testify accordingly. Less important interests in land—for example, nonfreehold estates and easements—were transferred through a written instrument known as a *grant*, which was informally handed to the recipient.

---

[1] For a sampling of scholarship in the area, see Allison Dunham, *Merger by Deed—Was It Ever Automatic?*, 10 Ga. L. Rev. 419 (1976); Marion E. James, Note, *The Issue of Delivery Raised by "Dispositive" Conveyances*, 18 Drake L. Rev. 67 (1968).

[2] To minimize the risk of dispute, most states have adopted legislation approving the use of short statutory deed forms.

As feudalism waned, the traditional ritual became increasingly anachronistic, particularly given the convenience of employing a simple document to transfer title and the widespread use of written records. Under the Statute of Uses in 1536, it became possible to convey a fee simple estate by means of a written instrument—most notably the "bargain and sale" deed—without livery of seisin.[3] For more than a century, an English landowner could transfer title through either method. The deed finally emerged victorious from this rivalry in 1677, when the Statute of Frauds mandated that every conveyance of an interest in land must be in writing. Thus, the body of English property law inherited by the new United States recognized only one method for conveying land title: the deed.

§ 23.03   Types of Deeds

[A]   Three Basic Types

Three types of deeds are commonly used in the United States: the *general warranty deed*, the *special warranty deed,* and the *quitclaim deed.* The main difference among them is the extent to which the grantor warrants the quality of title. Although the parties are free to negotiate which type of deed will be used, it is customary in about two-thirds of the states to employ general warranty deeds; special warranty deeds are the norm in a few states; and both types are utilized in the remaining states.

[B]   General Warranty Deed

A general warranty deed provides the most title protection. It contains[4] six specific covenants of title that warrant against any defect in the grantor's title (*see* § 26.02). For example, in the *covenant against encumbrances*, the grantor warrants that there are no mortgages, easements, liens, or other encumbrances on the property as of the time the deed is delivered. If one of these title covenants is breached, the grantor is liable in damages. The prudent grantee who is paying full fair market value for the property—and thereby assuming the grantor's title is near perfect—will demand a general warranty deed. If the purchase price has been reduced to compensate for a known title defect (e.g., an easement for sewer pipes under the land), a general warranty deed can still be used, with a specially-drafted provision that the title covenants do not extend to the particular defect.

---

[3] *See generally* French v. French, 3 N.H. 234 (1825).

[4] The title covenants may not actually be written on the deed. Most states have adopted some type of statutory "short form" deed; the use of this form automatically incorporates certain specified statutory warranties. For example, in Michigan a deed that merely includes the phrase "conveys and warrants" is considered a general warranty deed. Mich. Comp. Laws Ann. § 565.151.

[C] Special Warranty Deed

The special warranty deed usually contains[5] the same six title covenants found in the general warranty deed, but applies them only to defects caused by the *acts or omissions of the grantor* (*see* § 26.02). Suppose S conveys title to B pursuant to a special warranty deed. B soon discovers that the property is burdened with an easement that allows sewer pipes to cross under the land. If S created the easement, she is liable for breach of the covenant against encumbrances. But the special warranty deed affords no protection against the *acts or omissions of third parties*. So if the easement was granted by an owner who held title to the property before S, B has no recourse under the deed covenants. Similarly, in effect, the seller using a special warranty deed does not even warrant that he owns the property.

Why would a prudent buyer accept such inadequate protection? Local custom plays a role here, but the dominant reason is probably the availability of a superior form of title protection: title insurance. In some states where title insurance is common—notably California and Pennsylvania—the special warranty deed is used in most sales transactions. In practice, even the general warranty deed may afford only limited title protection (*see* § 26.02).

[D] Quitclaim Deed

The quitclaim deed contains no title covenants. By its use, the grantor does not warrant that he owns the property or—if he has any title—that his title is good. A quitclaim deed merely conveys whatever right, title, or interest the grantor *may have* in the property. So why would a buyer ever accept a quitclaim deed? One common use is to release a doubtful title claim. Suppose A has undeniably fulfilled all legal requirements to adversely possess O's property Greenacre. A could perfect her title to Greenacre by bringing a quiet title action against O. But A can avoid the cost and delay of litigation by simply asking O to convey title to her. O will be unwilling to warrant title, but should reasonably be willing to quitclaim any theoretical interest he retains. Or assume B is about to purchase land in a community property state that is believed to be the separate property of seller H, a married man; to preclude any later claim that the land was community property, B may insist that H's wife, W, execute a quitclaim deed in favor of B. The quitclaim deed is also used to transfer title following an involuntary sale of property (e.g., a foreclosure sale on a judgment or tax lien).

---

[5] Title covenants may be incorporated by reference where a statutory deed form is used. For example, in California a deed containing the term "grant" is considered a special warranty deed. Cal. Civ. Code § 1113.

§ 23.04 Requirements for Valid Deed

[A] Essential Deed Components

[1] General Principles

The basic requirements for a valid deed are simple and noncontroversial. In general, a deed must

    (1)   be in writing,

    (2)   be signed by the grantor,

    (3)   identify the grantor and grantee,

    (4)   contain words of conveyance, and

    (5)   describe the property.

The first four elements are discussed below, while the property description element is discussed separately in [2], *below*. Some states impose additional requirements by statute (*see* [3], *below*).

The first two elements stem from the Statute of Frauds. In general, a conveyance of any interest in real property must be memorialized in a writing that is signed by the grantor. No particular form of deed is required, although statutes in many states authorize a "short form" of deed that parties may voluntarily choose to use. Even a letter or other informal document may meet the Statute of Frauds requirement.[6] The standard exceptions to the Statute of Frauds, notably part performance and estoppel, may obviate the need for a writing (*see* § 20.04[B][4][a]).

The third requirement—identification of the grantor and grantee—is rarely problematic. But what if the grantor executes and delivers a deed that leaves the name of the grantee blank? If the grantor expressly or impliedly authorizes the recipient of the deed to insert the name of the ultimate grantee, most courts find the deed valid *after* the name is added.[7] Until that point, the deed is considered void.

The fourth requirement—words of conveyance—is straightforward. The law does not require use of technical language. Any words indicating the grantor's intention to immediately convey title (e.g., "grant," "convey," "transfer," or "give") will suffice.[8]

---

[6] *See, e.g.,* Metzger v. Miller, 291 F. 780 (N.D. Cal. 1923) (mother's letters to son were a valid deed).

[7] *See, e.g.,* Womack v. Stegner, 293 S.W.2d 124 (Tex. Ct. Civ. App. 1956).

[8] *See, e.g.,* Harris v. Strawbridge, 330 S.W.2d 911 (Tex. Ct. Civ. App. 1959) (language of habendum clause construed as words of grant). *But see In re* O'Neill's Will, 185 N.Y.S.2d 393 (App. Div. 1959) (letter that stated claimants "are welcome to live as long as they wish in the . . . house—as long as they wish" did not create a life estate).

[2] Description of Land

[a] Methods of Describing Land

A deed must identify the land to be conveyed in sufficient detail that it can be distinguished from all other parcels. At common law, this requirement was strictly enforced; for example, a conveyance of land described as "the Jones farm" was inadequate because the property could not be located by using only the deed language. Modern courts are somewhat more willing to admit extrinsic evidence to clarify an ambiguous description. But the traditional insistence that the deed must contain a complete description retains much vitality.[9]

A property description is essentially a method of locating the boundary lines of a parcel of land on the surface of the earth. Three methods of describing land are commonly used in the United States: (1) metes and bounds; (2) government survey; and (3) plat or subdivision map. The recent development of global positioning systems that can precisely locate any point on the earth's surface allows a parcel to be identified by latitude and longitude, which may well replace these traditional systems.

[b] Metes and Bounds

The most rudimentary method is the metes and bounds description. Adopted by the original 13 colonies before American independence, it is still the dominant technique used in eastern states and is used to some extent in all states.

A metes and bounds description begins at an identifiable geographic location or "point of beginning" on the boundary of the parcel. It then proceeds to describe each boundary line in sequence, until the last boundary line returns to the point of beginning, and thus creates a closed geometric figure. An early metes and bounds description might begin: "Beginning at the big pine tree 2 miles north of Smith's farm, thence approximately 500 feet north to the creek, thence northeasterly along the creek approximately 800 feet, etc." Over time, using natural features of the land such as trees and watercourses to establish boundaries proved unreliable: the tree could die and the stream could change its course. Modern metes and bounds descriptions are much more precise, usually beginning at identifiable manmade monuments, and then proceeding to describe each boundary line with a *course* (a statement of direction in degrees) and a *distance* (e.g., "thence South 41 degrees 32 minutes East 112.6 feet") until the boundary line returns to the point of beginning.

What if the metes and bounds description is internally inconsistent due to human error, destruction of monuments, or the like? Over time, courts have developed a priority list for choosing between inconsistent components of a description, from most reliable to least reliable:

---

[9] *See, e.g.,* Bowlin v. Keifer, 440 S.W.2d 232 (Ark. 1969) (instrument that contained no property description was not an effective deed); Grand Lodge v. City of Thomasville, 172 S.E.2d 612 (Ga. 1970) (deed held void because land description was indefinite).

    (a)   natural monuments,

    (b)   artificial monuments,

    (c)   adjacent tracts or boundaries,

    (d)   courses or directions,

    (e)   distance,

    (f)   quantity or area, and

    (g)   place names.[10]

For example, if the courses and distances in a metes and bounds description enclose a 50-acre tract, this will prevail over the description of the parcel as containing "65 acres."[11]

[c] Government Survey

Hoping to encourage western settlement and well aware of the inadequacies of the metes and bounds system, Thomas Jefferson spearheaded the adoption of a government survey program in 1785. Virtually all land added to the United States thereafter—excluding Texas—was surveyed by the federal government. Most land in the United States can be described by reference to these surveys.[12] This method is routinely used to describe large tracts of land, typically rural or agricultural parcels.

The government survey system (or "rectangular system") is essentially a series of rectangles. The system is based on a national network of survey lines: *principal meridian lines* (which run north-south) and *base lines* (which run east-west). Using the locations where these lines intersect as starting points, land was divided into square tracts called *townships*, each measuring six miles by six miles, and containing 36 square miles. Each township was further subdivided into 36 square tracts called *sections*, each containing one square mile. Almost any square mile in the nation can be identified by ready reference to this system. For example, "Section 10, Township 3 South, Range 4 West, Michigan Meridian" refers to only one particular square mile. Because each section contains 640 acres, portions of a section can be described with equal ease.[13] The "southwest quarter of the northwest quarter of Section 10, Township 3 South, Range 4 West, Michigan Meridian" designates only one 40-acre parcel. A metes and bounds description can be combined with a government survey description to identify an irregularly-shaped parcel.

---

    10 *See, e.g.,* Theriault v. Murray, 588 A.2d 720 (Me. 1991) (stakes are monuments that prevail over courses and distances); Doman v. Brogan, 592 A.2d 104 (Pa. 1991) (monument prevails over distance). *But see* Pritchard v. Rebori, 186 S.W. 121 (Tenn. 1916) (based on extrinsic evidence of parties' intent, course and distance prevail over adjacent boundary).

    11 *Cf.* Parr v. Worley, 599 P.2d 382 (N.M. 1979) (center of highway, as monument, prevailed over acreage statement in deed).

    12 The principal exceptions are the Atlantic states and Kentucky, Maine, Tennessee, Texas, West Virginia, and Vermont.

    13 *See, e.g.,* Bybee v. Hageman, 66 Ill. 519 (1873) (using government survey to describe 1½ acre parcel).

[d] Plat or Subdivision Map

Today a plat or "subdivision map" description is used in conveying most urban and suburban land, particularly in residential subdivisions. A plat is simply a map depicting the lots in a new subdivision, usually prepared by a surveyor employed by the subdivider. The plat depicts the location and dimensions of each lot, together with planned streets and other improvements. Each lot in the subdivision is assigned a particular number. The plat also includes information that allows the subdivision as a whole to be located, usually by reference to an external monument or the government survey system.

Once the plat is approved by the local planning commission or other responsible government agency, it is recorded in the official land records. Thereafter, each lot can be conveyed using a brief description that incorporates the plat by reference.[14] For example, a deed could simply specify: "Lot 26, as shown on that certain Plat recorded in Book 212, Page 36, Records of Golden County, Colorado."

[3] Nonessential Deed Components

Consideration is necessary for a valid contract, but not for a valid deed.[15] Gifts of real property, such as gifts among family members or gifts to charity, are quite common. A deed delivered to a donee is equally effective as one delivered to a purchaser. However, the absence of consideration may have other legal consequences, notably: (1) a donee does not share the title protection accorded to the bona fide purchaser (*see* § 24.04[C]); and (2) the measure of damages for breach of the grantor's title covenants will probably be zero (*see* § 26.02[D]). Accordingly, if consideration was paid, this fact is customarily recited in the deed. While not conclusive on the point, such a recital creates a presumption that consideration was paid.

Recordation of a deed is irrelevant to its validity. An unrecorded deed is fully effective and binding. It is customary, however, to record the deed in order to give notice to the world of the grantee's title, and thereby preclude adverse title claims by bona fide purchasers (*see* § 23.06).

Acknowledgment by a notary public is routine and usually required in order to record a deed, but is not necessary for validity (*see* § 25.04[A]).

Witnesses to the execution of the deed are also unnecessary, except in a few states. In contrast, witnesses to the testator's signature are generally required for a valid will.

A *seal* is required only in a handful of states. The old adage that a deed must be "signed, sealed, and delivered" is archaic. When illiteracy prevailed,

---

[14] Because lots created by a plat may be irregularly shaped, confusion may arise when later attempts are made to divide them further. *See, e.g.,* Walters v. Tucker, 281 S.W.2d 843 (Mo. 1955).

[15] Chase Fed. Sav. & Loan Ass'n v. Schreiber, 479 So. 2d 90 (Fla. 1985) (following general rule, despite dissent's plea that allowing gift deeds among non-relatives "provides a means to protect title to real property for gigolos, mistresses, and con artists").

the grantor's personal seal served to help identify the grantor and thus to authenticate the deed.

[B] Delivery

[1] General Principles

A deed is not effective until it is "delivered." An undelivered deed is void and passes no title to the grantee or his successors even if they are bona fide purchasers. In order to deliver a deed, the grantor must manifest by words or actions an intent that the deed be immediately effective to transfer an interest in land to the grantee.[16] The typical grantor delivers a deed through the act of physically handing it to the grantee, with words indicating the grantor's intent to transfer the interest immediately. Indeed, it is not a coincidence that this common form of delivery closely resembles the ancient ceremony of feoffment with livery of seisin.

Yet delivery may be found in cases that are far less clear than this usual pattern. It is important to understand that either words or actions may suffice to evidence the grantor's intent. As Lord Coke observed in a famous dictum: "As a deed may be delivered to the party without words, so may a deed be delivered by words without any act of delivery." Consider an example of manual delivery without words. Suppose O enters into a contract to sell Blueacre to B for $500,000; on the day selected for the transfer of title, B hands O a cashier's check for $500,000 and O silently hands B the deed to Blueacre. Despite O's silence, all courts would find delivery here, given the factual circumstances surrounding O's act of physically handing over the deed.[17] Delivery by words alone is also possible. Suppose O executes a deed conveying Blueacre to B, but learns that B is on vacation in Alaska when he attempts to hand over the deed to B. O reaches B by telephone, saying: "Congratulations! You're the new owner of Blueacre. I just conveyed it to you!"

Delivery issues mainly arise in the context of family gifts.[18] In the routine sales transaction, there is no doubt of the grantor's intent and the escrow agent, attorney or other professional supervising the transaction can easily ensure that a valid delivery occurs. But these safeguards are sometimes absent in a gift transaction. The most common delivery problems are presented by the grantor who manifests an intent to retain some control over the deed or the property itself after execution of the deed. Is this an immediately effective transfer of title to the grantee (and thus a valid

---

[16] *See, e.g.,* Pipes v. Sevier, 694 S.W.2d 918, 926 (Mo. Ct. App. 1985) (grantor must part "with the instrument with the intention to relinquish all dominion and control over it so as to make the deed a presently effective and operative conveyance of title to the land").

[17] But delivery does not necessarily occur when the grantor hands the deed to the grantee. *See, e.g.,* Martinez v. Martinez, 678 P.2d 1163 (N.M. 1984) (no delivery occurred where grantors gave deed to grantees with instructions to place deed in escrow until mortgage was paid, but grantees recorded deed instead).

[18] *See, e.g.,* Capozzella v. Capozzella, 196 S.E.2d 67 (Va. 1973).

delivery) or a disguised substitute for a will (and thus an ineffective delivery)? The question often surfaces in title litigation between the grantee and the residual devisees under the grantor's will. If the grantor intends the deed to take effect only upon death, no delivery has occurred; thus, the deed is a nullity, and the property is legally part of the grantor's estate, where it will be distributed according to the will.[19] Some courts find valid delivery by construing the deed as an immediate transfer of a future interest that merely becomes possessory upon the grantor's death.

Once a deed is validly delivered, title vests in the grantee. Suppose O duly delivers a deed conveying Blueacre to G, but then changes his mind and demands that G return the deed to him, which G does. Or suppose that G burns the deed at O's request, in order to undo the conveyance. In both instances, G still owns Blueacre. Once delivery has occurred, the fate of the deed document is irrelevant. In order to transfer title back, G must execute and deliver a new deed to O.

[2] Why Require Delivery?

In theory, delivery serves essentially the same evidentiary and cautionary functions that underlie the Statute of Frauds (*see* § 20.04[B][5]). The ceremony of delivery in the presence of witnesses might facilitate testimonial evidence of the conveyance, which minimizes the risk of later dispute. Yet because a valid delivery can occur without any witnesses, the requirement often fails to provide such evidence. Similarly, the requirement might help impress the grantor with the significance of his actions, like the Statute of Frauds requirement that the grantor execute the deed, thus safeguarding against the accidental or inadvertent loss of title. Unless the owner demonstrably intends to make an immediately effective conveyance, the deed is ineffective. Suppose, for example, that O executes a deed conveying his land Redacre to his favorite niece A, intending to deliver the deed to A as a present for her birthday; but two days before her birthday, A dies, leaving all her property to her odious husband B. If a deed was effective upon execution, without a delivery requirement, then B would own Redacre, a result contrary to O's intent. Yet perhaps O's execution of the deed should have alerted him to the legal significance of his conduct. In short, if the delivery requirement is aimed at goals already fulfilled by the Statute of Frauds, its benefit is quite limited.

Does the cost of the delivery rule outweigh its benefit? In some respects, the doctrine is quite inconsistent with the law's overall concern for ensuring the stability of land title through the use of clear, "bright line" rules. It poses a particular danger for future purchasers in the chain of title. Suppose O executes a deed conveying Blueacre to R, but intentionally fails to deliver it; R obtains the deed, records it, and conveys to S; S conveys to T. In most jurisdictions, O still holds title, even if T is a bona fide purchaser. How can later buyers like T reasonably be expected to know that the O-R deed was invalid? As between O and T, two innocent parties, it might make more

---

[19] *See, e.g.,* Rosengrant v. Rosengrant, 629 P.2d 800 (Okla. Ct. App. 1981) (no delivery occurred where grantors did not intend deed to take effect until their death).

sense to place the loss of title on O, who was best situated to prevent the loss in the first place, by analogy to the rule governing deeds induced by fraud (*see* § 23.08[A]). If the grantor's carelessness allowed the deed to be placed into the stream of commerce, why shouldn't downstream purchasers be protected? In operation, this rule is rarely as draconian as it might appear, because (1) the disappointed purchaser will recoup the loss through title insurance or deed warranties, or (2) the culpably negligent grantor will be deemed estopped from challenging the bona fide purchaser's title.

[3] Presumptions

Delivery is a question of fact. The typical delivery dispute involves intricate and often conflicting evidence about the grantor's intent. Courts have developed a set of rebuttable presumptions to resolve these difficult cases. In most states, delivery will be presumed if (1) the deed is recorded, or (2) the grantee has physical possession of the deed. [20] Suppose O executes a deed in favor of his nephew N. N ultimately obtains physical possession of the deed and records it. If O now brings suit to cancel the deed based on nondelivery, he will confront a judicial presumption that delivery occurred. O can overcome this presumption with affirmative evidence demonstrating a lack of delivery (e.g., if N stole the deed from O's office). [21]

[4] "Deed in a Box" Cases

The most persistently troublesome (and inconsistent) delivery cases involve the "deed in a box." Suppose O executes a deed conveying Brownacre to B, and places it in a safe deposit box (or other locked box) where it is discovered after O's death. So far, courts all agree that O has not manifested the requisite intent for delivery. [22] But the addition of even a single fact to this basic scenario may bring uncertainty. For example, suppose O gives B a key to the safe deposit box; this might be seen as a symbolic act that gives B control and dominion over the deed. [23] Or what if B is O's wife? Courts are more likely to find delivery where the grantee is a close relative, on the theory that the conveyance is consistent with prudent estate planning. Or suppose O announces to his family while signing the deed: "I want B to own Brownacre." Such a public statement is usually viewed as strong evidence of delivery. [24] Predicting the outcome of these fact-specific cases is extraordinarily difficult.

---

[20] LeMehaute v. LeMehaute, 585 S.W.2d 276 (Mo. Ct. App. 1979); *see also* Sweeney v. Sweeney, 11 A.2d 806 (Conn. 1940).

[21] *See, e.g.,* Lenhart v. Desmond, 705 P.2d 338 (Wyo. 1985) (grantor overcame presumption of delivery by showing that grantee had taken deed from safe deposit box without his knowledge or consent).

[22] *See, e.g.,* Williams v. Cole, 760 S.W.2d 944 (Mo. Ct. App. 1988); Wiggill v. Cheney, 597 P.2d 1351 (Utah 1979).

[23] *See, e.g.,* Kresser v. Peterson, 675 P.2d 1193 (Utah 1984) (delivery valid where, inter alia, grantees were cotenants in safe deposit box).

[24] *See, e.g.,* Kresser v. Peterson, 675 P.2d 1193, 1194 (Utah 1984) (at time of signing deed, grantor stated that she intended her sons to have the property).

[5] Conditional Delivery to Grantee

Suppose O executes a deed conveying title to Greenacre to G "effective when G reaches the age of 25"; O then hands the deed to G, his 22 year old daughter. Has a valid delivery occurred? Most jurisdictions still follow the common law view that a grantor may not condition delivery to the grantee. Yet there is a split of authority on how this rule is applied. Some courts hold that any condition prevents a valid delivery; they reason that delivery requires that the grantor intend an immediate transfer of title, not a transfer that becomes effective at some later date when the condition is fulfilled.[25] Under this view—which closely tracks the logic of the common law rule—the grantee receives nothing at all.[26]

Surprisingly, a majority of courts deals with this situation by ignoring the condition and vesting absolute title in the grantee. As one court summarized: "Conditional delivery to a grantee vests absolute title in the latter."[27] Why? The majority rule reflects the law's historic concern to protect the certainty of land title. If the identity of the owner hinges on whether a condition has been fulfilled, it may be difficult to ascertain who holds title. Given this uncertainty, title claimants will be reluctant to invest their time and resources in enhancing the productive value of the land, and lenders will be unwilling to extend credit based on such doubtful collateral.[28]

Despite the rule against conditional delivery, the creative grantor can accomplish the same result in most instances by unconditionally delivering a conditional future interest. Consider the phrasing in the example above: "effective when G reaches the age of 25." Depending on the surrounding facts, this same language might alternatively be construed as an immediate transfer of an executory interest to G, which merely becomes possessory in the future. If so, a valid delivery of a future interest has occurred. The key—and perhaps artificial—distinction turns on when the grantor intends the deed to be effective: now or later?

Disputes arising from conditional delivery to the grantee arise most commonly in connection with a "death condition." Suppose O conveys Greenacre "to G effective upon my death." Despite the general rule discussed above, in this special context many courts find that no delivery has occurred, reasoning that O did not intend her deed to be immediately effective. Other courts construe this situation as an immediate transfer of a future interest to G, which merely becomes possessory upon O's death, and

---

[25] *See, e.g.,* Martinez v. Martinez, 678 P.2d 1163 (N.M. 1984) (no delivery occurred where grantors handed deed to grantees with instructions to place deed in escrow until mortgage on property was paid, but grantees instead recorded deed).

[26] *But see* Chillemi v. Chillemi, 78 A.2d 750 (Md. 1951) (permitting conditional delivery to grantee, but finding that condition was not met, so title did not pass).

[27] Sweeney v. Sweeney, 11 A.2d 806 (Conn. 1940) (oral condition—that deed would take effect only if grantor died before grantee—held invalid).

[28] *See also* Sweeney v. Sweeney, 11 A.2d 806, 808 (Conn. 1940) ("The safety of real estate titles is considered more important than the unfortunate results which may follow the application of the rule in a few individual instances. To relax it would open the door wide to fraud and the fabrication of evidence.").

thus find valid delivery. Of course, O could avoid this difficulty by expressly conveying only a vested remainder to G, and reserving a life estate in himself.

What if the grantor reserves a right to revoke the deed? O could convey Greenacre "to G, but in O's sole and absolute discretion O can revoke and cancel this deed at any time." Arguably, G receives an immediate transfer of an unusual fee simple subject to a condition subsequent in Greenacre: G enjoys fee simple in Greenacre until and unless O changes her mind. Of course, O could change her mind as long as she lives; thus some courts find no delivery, on the rationale that G has not effectively received any interest at all until O dies without changing her mind. Probably the majority of courts—albeit reluctantly—finds a valid delivery under these circumstances.[29] These courts usually rely on the formalistic argument that a grantee like G has received an immediate interest, even if it is speculative and uncertain. The better explanation for this outcome focuses on the policies underlying the delivery requirement. If the grantor executes a deed that includes written conditions and manually delivers it to the grantee, the evidentiary and cautionary policies that the requirement is intended to serve are both met. The grantor is fully aware she is performing a legally binding act, while the deed and the surrounding circumstances clearly evidence the grantor's intent. With the modern acceptance of revocable will substitutes such as inter vivos trusts, life insurance policies, and joint tenancy bank accounts, courts are increasingly reluctant to invalidate the revocable deed.

[6] Delivery to Third Party

[a] Sale Escrow

In many real property sales transactions, the deed is conditionally delivered to an escrow agent with instructions that it be delivered to the grantee when the contract conditions are met. Although a deed cannot be conditionally delivered directly to a grantee, it may be conditionally delivered to a third party. The escrow agent is essentially a neutral third party who is retained to facilitate the transaction, usually an attorney, title insurance company, escrow company, or financial institution.

Suppose O contracts to sell fee simple absolute in Redacre to B for $500,000. O executes and delivers his deed to an escrow agent with instructions that it be delivered to B once B's payment is received in escrow. B deposits the sales price into escrow with parallel instructions. When all conditions of the parties' instructions are met, the deed is delivered and title passes; the escrow agent disburses the deed to B and the sales price to O.[30]

When is delivery through escrow effective? Assume O delivers his deed into escrow on January 1, but all conditions of the parties' instructions are

---

[29] *See, e.g.,* St. Louis County Nat'l Bank v. Fielder, 260 S.W.2d 483 (Mo. 1953).

[30] *Cf.* Ferguson v. Caspar, 359 A.2d 17 (D.C. 1976) (buyers breached their contractual duty by imposing additional conditions to payment).

not met until March 1; the escrow agent delivers the deed to B on March 1. Here a curious legal fiction arises. Once the conditions of delivery are fulfilled, and delivery occurs, the effective date of the delivery is said to "relate back" to the original deposit into escrow if required to prevent injustice. Under this relation back doctrine, the law deems that O's deed was delivered to B on January 1, not March 1. The effective date of delivery is often important. For example, if O's creditor attempts to impose a $300,000 judgment lien on Redacre on February 1, the lien has no effect on Redacre or on B's rights if the doctrine applies. The doctrine operates in a similar fashion where the grantor dies or becomes incompetent after delivering the deed into escrow.

The rare escrow agent who violates instructions by giving the deed to the buyer before all conditions are met creates an unfortunate mess. In one celebrated decision,[31] the seller gave an executed deed to the buyer's real estate broker, to hold as an escrow agent pending the seller's inspection of an apartment building that the buyer proposed to trade for the seller's property. Before this condition was met, the buyer obtained possession of the deed, recorded it, and resold the property to an innocent purchaser for value. Citing the standard rule that any delivery of a deed from escrow before conditions are fulfilled is void, the court noted—quite properly—that the deed was ineffective as between the seller and buyer. Yet, with little further analysis, the court mechanically applied this same principle to nullify the deed as between the original owner and the innocent purchaser for value. Most American courts still follow this view, except where the grantor was clearly negligent in selecting the escrow holder or unduly delayed in asserting his claim. However, scholars argue strongly that the innocent purchaser should always be protected in this situation, relying on the familiar adage that when a loss must fall on one of two innocent parties, it should fall on the party who best could have prevented the loss.[32] Under this reasoning, the original owner—who participated in selecting the culpable escrow agent—should bear the loss.

[b] "Death Escrow"

Can delivery to a third party be conditioned on the grantor's death? Suppose (a) O executes a deed conveying title to her property Blueacre to G, (b) hands the deed to T, and (c) tells T to deliver the deed to G when O dies. Has the O-G deed been delivered? There is widespread judicial agreement that the answer turns on O's ability to retrieve the deed from T. If the grantor can recover the deed from the third party (e.g., if the third party is an agent of the grantor), most courts reason that this is sufficient retained control to preclude delivery.

This rule may produce harsh results. In one case, for example, an elderly, childless couple executed a deed conveying their family farm to a nephew and announced that they wanted him to have "the place."[33] The

---

[31] Clevenger v. Moore, 259 P. 219 (Okla. 1927).

[32] John Mann, *Escrows—Their Use and Value*, 1949 U. Ill. L.F. 398.

[33] Rosengrant v. Rosengrant, 629 P.2d 800 (Okla. Ct. App. 1981).

grantor-couple asked the nephew to leave the deed at their bank until they died; and the banker assured the nephew that he would put the deed in an envelope and keep it in the vault until the nephew called for it. After the couple died, the deed was discovered in the bank vault inside an envelope that a bank employee—without the knowledge of the parties—had labeled with the names of *both* the grantee and one grantor. Because the bank's standard practice would have allowed the grantors to retrieve such an envelope and thus revoke the deed—even though the grantors were apparently unaware of this—the court found no delivery had occurred. Results like this that frustrate a grantor's clear and unambiguous intent have prompted strong criticism of the ban on revocable escrows. The grantor-couple could have achieved their objective here by simply transferring title to the property into a revocable trust and naming the nephew as its sole beneficiary; indeed, a prudent attorney would have recommended this procedure. Given the modern acceptance of revocable trusts as an estate planning device, scholars suggest that revocable "death escrows" should similarly be permitted.

On the other hand, the irrevocable death escrow is usually held valid. When the grantor delivers a deed to a third party with instructions to deliver it to the grantee upon the grantor's death—without retaining any power to retrieve the deed—the delivery requirement is satisfied.[34] A judicial fiction is employed to mute the logical inconsistency of this result with the common law standard. In most states, although the deed appears on its face to convey fee simple absolute, it is construed to *immediately* convey a future interest to the grantee, which becomes possessory when the grantor dies.

[C] Acceptance

In theory, the grantee must accept the deed in order for a conveyance to be effective. Yet, in practice, acceptance is rarely important. The law presumes that a grantee will accept a beneficial conveyance. On the other hand, suppose O conveys Greyacre (a toxic waste dump) to G without G's knowledge, hoping to avoid statutory liability for cleanup costs (*see* § 29.08). The acceptance element allows G to disclaim the conveyance, and thus avoid the cleanup liability that may accompany title. A disclaimer must be made within a reasonable period of time after the grantee becomes aware of the conveyance.

§ 23.05 Interpretation of Deeds

The ambiguous deed poses a special problem. The central rule in deed interpretation is to follow the intent of the parties.[35] Initially, a court will

---

[34] *See, e.g.,* Pipes v. Sevier, 694 S.W.2d 918, 921 (Mo. Ct. App. 1985) (grantor gave deeds to her attorney with instructions to deliver them after she died, aware that she "could not thereafter cancel the deeds or change my mind").

[35] *See, e.g.,* Grayson v. Holloway, 313 S.W.2d 555 (Tenn. 1958) (rejecting common law rule that granting clause in deed prevails over inconsistent habendum clause, in favor of modern rule that interprets deeds in accordance with intent of parties).

attempt to ascertain this intent from the "four corners" of the deed itself, considering all of its provisions. If the ambiguity remains, extrinsic evidence (e.g., statements and conduct of the grantor and grantee) will be examined.

The classic scenario involves a deed that is so ambiguous that the parties dispute the nature of the estate or interest it conveys, as where a deed could be interpreted as conveying either fee simple absolute or an easement. If the basic rules above fail to resolve the problem, courts usually presume that the grantor intended to convey his entire interest in the property, not merely a portion.[36] This rule of construction serves to minimize quiet title suits and to prevent fragmentation of property ownership.

§ 23.06 Recordation of Deeds

Virtually all deeds are "recorded." The mechanics of recording are simple. The grantor must execute the deed in the presence of a notary public or similar official; the notary will then sign an acknowledgment form attesting under penalty of perjury that the grantor in fact executed the deed. Once a deed has become effective through delivery, the grantee (or the grantee's agent) presents the original deed to the recorder's office or similar agency and pays a small fee. A clerk stamps an identification number on the deed, places a copy of the deed (often on microfilm or microfiche) into the official land records, lists information about the deed in various public indices so that it can be located by title searchers, and returns the original deed to the grantee.

Why are deeds recorded? Recordation is not required for a deed to be valid. An unrecorded deed is fully effective. Yet the prudent grantee will immediately record his deed in order to protect his title against later claimants. As discussed in more detail in Chapter 24, under some circumstances the law will vest title in a *bona fide purchaser*—a later purchaser for value who has no notice or knowledge of previously-created interests. Recording a deed gives "notice to the world" of the grantee's title, and effectively eliminates this risk.

§ 23.07 Effect of Forgery

A forged deed is completely *void*.[37] It conveys nothing to the grantee or any subsequent grantee in the chain of title, including any later bona fide purchaser. Assume F forges a deed that purports to convey fee simple absolute in Whiteacre from its true owner, O, to F, and duly records the deed. After confirming through a title search that F holds record title, innocent buyer B—unaware of the forgery—purchases F's interest for $300,000 and F conveys title to B. Even though B paid fair market value,

---

[36] *See, e.g.,* First Nat'l Bank v. Townsend, 555 P.2d 477 (Or. Ct. App. 1976) (applying presumption, court construes deed as conveying fee simple absolute, not merely timber and mineral rights).

[37] *See* Martin v. Carter, 400 A.2d 326 (D.C. 1979) (where true owner of property gave prompt notice after learning that forgery had occurred and sued to quiet title four months later, laches did not bar action).

and had no notice of O's continued claim to the property—the hallmarks which protect the bona fide purchaser—B has no interest at all in Whiteacre. The forged O-F deed is void, and hence the F-B deed is similarly void.

Why is a forged deed void even as to an innocent purchaser? A contrary rule might well tend to encourage forgery, as innocent buyers became less careful or as forgers collusively transferred title to "innocent" conspirators. Further, as between the true owner and the later purchaser, the purchaser is in a somewhat better position to protect himself through careful inquiry and inspection if only because (unlike the true owner) the purchaser is aware that a sales transaction is underway. In any event, standard title insurance policies protect the insured purchaser against forgery, so most purchasers will suffer little or no loss.

§ 23.08 Effect of Fraud

[A] Fraud in the Inducement

F offers to trade his ancient and valuable vase to O, in exchange for title to O's vacation cabin known as Greenacre; O accepts. O executes and delivers a deed conveying title to F, and F hands O the vase together with a bill of sale. Three days later, O takes his vase to an appraiser, who informs him that it is merely a modern reproduction, worth almost nothing. It is well-settled that a deed induced by the grantee's fraud is *voidable* in an action brought by the true owner against the grantee. Thus, O could sue F to rescind the transaction and recover title.

But what if F conveys Greenacre to innocent purchaser B one day after F acquires title? Under these circumstances, B prevails over O. When one of two innocent parties must incur a loss due to a third party's fraud, courts usually allocate the loss to the party who was in the best position to avoid the loss in the first place.[38] Here, O knew he was conveying title to his land; he could have discovered F's fraud through prudent pre-purchase investigation, such as by demanding an appraisal of the vase before the conveyance occurred. B, on the other hand, had no opportunity to know that the deed was induced by fraud, and has the normal equities associated with any bona fide purchaser (*see* § 24.03).

[B] Fraud in the Inception

A different result flows from fraud in the inception, where fraud prevents the grantor from knowing that he is executing a deed. Suppose F knocks on widow O's door, pretending to sell magazine subscriptions. When elderly

---

[38] *See, e.g.,* McCoy v. Love, 382 So. 2d 647, 649 (Fla. 1979) (illiterate, elderly owner executed deed in reliance on buyer's false representation that it conveyed only part of her property, when in reality it conveyed all; because the "law charged her with the responsibility of informing herself as to the legal effect of the document she was signing," subsequent parties would hold title if they were bona fide purchasers).

O agrees to subscribe, F tells her she is signing a subscription form, but F takes care to ensure that O's signature is actually placed on the bottom of a deed protruding below the subscription form. In this situation, many courts hold that a deed procured by fraud in the inception is *void* for all purposes, and treat it like a forged deed, particularly if the grantor is elderly, infirm, or unsophisticated. [39] On the other hand, where the grantor is capable of protecting his own interests, a court is more likely to conclude that his conduct was negligent and estop him from challenging the rights of a later bona fide purchaser.

§ 23.09   Estoppel by Deed

Suppose O conveys title to Redacre to G, using a warranty deed. At the time, O does not own title to Redacre but G is unaware of this fact. One month later, O acquires title to Redacre. What happens? Under the doctrine of estoppel by deed, G owns Redacre. The doctrine applies when a grantor uses a warranty deed to purportedly convey title to land he does not own to an innocent grantee. If the grantor later acquires title to the land, it automatically passes to the grantee. [40] Why? In equity, the grantor is estopped to claim title that is superior to that of his grantee. Moreover, the grantee could bring suit against the grantor for breach of deed warranties in any event, so the doctrine shortcuts the process.

---

[39] *See, e.g.,* Hauck v. Crawford, 62 N.W.2d 92 (S.D. 1953) (where grantor believed he was signing a mineral lease but was actually signing a mineral deed, deed was void as to grantee).

[40] *See, e.g.,* Schwenn v. Kaye, 202 Cal. Rptr. 374 (Ct. App. 1984) (grantor purported to convey fee simple absolute to grantees via warranty deed, even though grantor did not own all mineral rights in the property; when grantor later received certain oil and gas rights in the land, they automatically passed to grantees).

Chapter 24

FUNDAMENTALS OF LAND TITLE

SYNOPSIS

§ 24.01 The Problem of Conflicting Title Claims

How does the law resolve conflicting title claims?[1] Suppose O first conveys fee simple absolute in Redacre to A, and a month later conveys the same estate to B. Who owns title to Redacre? Or suppose L grants an easement burdening Greenacre to C, and then transfers title to Greenacre to D. Does D take title subject to C's easement?

Title disputes commonly arise in three situations. First, two or more claimants may dispute who holds the present possessory estate in a particular tract of land; in the above hypothetical, both A and B claim to hold fee simple absolute in Redacre. Second, a title dispute may arise between the holder of the present possessory estate and someone claiming a nonpossessory interest (e.g., a lien, easement, or covenant) in the same land; in the above hypothetical, D might claim that his title to Greenacre is unaffected by C's easement, while C might insist that his easement still burdens Greenacre. Finally, two or more holders of nonpossessory interests may dispute their respective priority. Assume, for example, that Blueacre is only worth $40,000, but is burdened by two mortgages: a $30,000 mortgage held by E, and a $25,000 mortgage held by F. If a foreclosure sale occurs, whose mortgage is paid off first?

American property law uses the same principles to resolve all types of conflicting title claims. In a nutshell, the system consists of *one general rule* and *two exceptions to the rule.* The traditional common law rule is that the person whose interest is first delivered prevails over anyone who acquires an interest later (*see* § 24.02). All states have modified this general rule through legislation known as *recording acts.* The recording acts in almost all states create a major exception to the general rule: in a title dispute between a first-in-time claimant and a later *bona fide purchaser for value,* the bona fide purchaser prevails (*see* § 24.03). The general rule is usually subject to a second, minor exception called the *shelter rule*: one who acquires an interest from a bona fide purchaser also prevails over a first-in-time claimant (*see* § 24.07).

The law in this area is a compromise between two goals. On the one hand, it seeks to provide security and stability by respecting the property rights of current owners; the general first-in-time rule reflects this goal. On the other hand, the law also seeks to facilitate the transfer of property rights to new owners. Accordingly, virtually all states protect the later buyer who innocently paid value without any notice of prior claims. Absent this special protection, the purchase of interests in land would be extraordinarily risky, and buyers would be less willing to buy (*see* § 24.09).

---

[1] *See generally* Corwin W. Johnson, *Purpose and Scope of Recording Statutes,* 47 Iowa L. Rev. 231 (1962); Taylor Mattis, *Recording Acts: Anachronistic Reliance,* 25 Real Prop. Prob. & Trust J. 17 (1990); Francis S. Philbrick, *Limits of Record Search and Therefore of Notice,* 93 U. Pa. L. Rev. 125 (1944).

§ 24.02 General Rule: First in Time Prevails

Suppose O conveys fee simple absolute in Redacre to A, and later conveys the same estate to B. Who owns Redacre, A or B? The common law used a first-in-time rule to resolve this title conflict: the person whose interest is first delivered prevails.[2] For example, if A's deed was delivered on Monday, and B's deed was delivered a day later on Tuesday, then—all other things being equal—A owns Redacre. Whether A paid value for Redacre or received it as a gift is irrelevant; the first-in-time rule protects purchasers and donees alike.

Conflicts between possessory estates and nonpossessory interests are resolved in the same fashion. For example, if L grants an easement burdening Greenacre to C, and later conveys fee simple absolute in Greenacre to D, C's easement is first in time. Thus, although L's conveyance to D is valid, D takes title to Greenacre burdened by the easement. Conversely, if L conveys fee simple absolute in Greenacre to D, and thereafter grants an easement to C, D's deed is first in time under the basic rule. Accordingly, D takes title to Greenacre free and clear of the easement; C has no interest in Greenacre.

This traditional first-in-time rule is still a starting point for resolving title conflicts. But its significance has been greatly reduced by legislation. The recording acts adopted in most states carve out two exceptions to the basic first-in-time rule.

§ 24.03 First Exception to General Rule: Subsequent Bona Fide Purchaser Prevails

[A] Nature of the Exception

Almost all states recognize a major exception to the first-in-time rule: the *bona fide purchaser* doctrine. In general, a bona fide purchaser is one who purchases an interest in land for valuable consideration without notice of an interest already held by a third party. In a title dispute between a first-in-time owner and a later bona fide purchaser, the bona fide purchaser prevails.[3]

Suppose O conveys title to Blueacre to A, who fails to record his deed or take possession of the land. A few days later, B approaches O about buying Blueacre. O expresses interest in selling the land and fails to disclose his prior conveyance to A. B searches record title and inspects Blueacre, without detecting any adverse title claim. At close of escrow, (1) B pays O for the land, (2) O conveys title to B, and (3) B records her deed. B takes possession of Blueacre. Two weeks later, B first learns about the unrecorded O-A deed. Who owns Blueacre? In all states, B is the owner.

---

[2] The equity courts recognized one main exception to this rule: the later bona fide purchaser of a legal interest prevailed over one holding a prior equitable title.

[3] *But see* Mugaas v. Smith, 206 P.2d 332 (Wash. 1949) (holding that record owner's conveyance of title to bona fide purchaser did not extinguish title held by adverse possessor).

B, the subsequent bona fide purchaser, prevails over A, the first-in-time owner.[4]

The recording act in each state defines the precise requirements for bona fide purchaser status. Although the statutory language varies widely from state to state, there are three basic types of recording acts: notice; race-notice; and race. Roughly half of the states are *notice* jurisdictions, which use the general bona fide purchaser definition described above (*see* § 24.04). And about half of the states are *race-notice* jurisdictions, which add the requirement that the bona fide purchaser must also be the first to record (*see* § 24.05).[5] Finally, two states are *race* jurisdictions, which do not recognize the bona fide purchaser exception at all (*see* § 24.08).

[B] Relativity of Title

At this point, a reader considering the above hypothetical might mentally protest: "But O first conveyed Blueacre to A. He had nothing left to transfer to B. So how can B be the owner?" The short answer to this question is that property rights are defined by law, not by the intentions of private parties. Property rights exist only to the extent that they are recognized by our legal system. The law may choose to recognize different persons as the "owner" of the same property, depending on the circumstances. A basic precept of American property law is that title is *relative*, not absolute (*see* § 4.05[C]).

In the above hypothetical, the O-A deed is fully effective *as between O and A*. In any title contest between O and A, the law will recognize A as the owner of Blueacre. However, *as between A and B*, the law chooses to recognize B as the owner of Blueacre for various policy reasons (*see* § 24.09). After all, A carelessly failed to record his deed or otherwise warn later buyers, while B is an innocent party who paid value for the land. As between negligent A and diligent B, the law vests title in B.

§ 24.04 Who Is a Bona Fide Purchaser?: Notice Jurisdictions

[A] A Subsequent Purchaser for Value Without Notice of the Prior Interest

In notice jurisdictions, a bona fide purchaser is a subsequent purchaser who pays valuable consideration for an interest in real property, without any notice of an interest that a third party already holds in the land. The definition has three key parts:

    (1)   a subsequent purchaser,

---

[4] *See* Powell on Real Property, Ch. 82 (Michael Allan Wolf ed., Matthew Bender). *Cf.* Earle v. Fiske, 103 Mass. 491 (1870) (bona fide purchaser prevailed over claimants holding earlier unrecorded deed).

[5] *See, e.g.,* Messersmith v. Smith, 60 N.W.2d 276 (N.D. 1953).

(2)   for value,

(3)   without notice of the prior interest.

[B]   "A Subsequent Purchaser"

In ordinary usage, nonlawyers equate "purchaser" with someone who acquires "ownership" of land. But the recording acts use the term in a broader sense: a *purchaser* is almost any person who acquires any interest in land. Of course, someone who obtains fee simple or another freehold estate is considered a purchaser. The term also encompasses any person who acquires an easement, lease, lien, mineral interest, mortgage, restrictive covenant, or other possessory or nonpossessory interest.[6]

It is important to understand that only a *subsequent* purchaser requires the shelter of the recording acts. A *prior* purchaser is first-in-time, and accordingly protected under the common law rule unless there is a *subsequent* bona fide purchaser.

[C]   "For Value"

[1]   Defining Value

In order to qualify for bona fide purchaser status, the purchaser must pay *value*. The recording acts seek to protect the reasonable expectations of persons who make economic investments in good faith reliance on the state of record title, not those who merely receive gifts. Thus, donees, devisees, and heirs are not purchasers for value.

How much must a grantee pay to be considered a purchaser for value? It is clear that the grantee need not pay full market value. And almost all courts agree that a grantee must pay more than mere nominal value.[7] Between these two extremes, however, the law is remarkably unclear. Some courts require a "substantial" amount in relation to market value;[8] others simply insist that the purchase price cannot be "grossly inadequate"; and still others merely require an amount that is greater than nominal consideration.[9]

Assume, for example, that B is about to purchase fee simple absolute in Greenacre, an apple orchard worth $300,000. In order to qualify as a purchaser for value, B need not pay $300,000 or any amount even close to this sum. On the other hand, a nominal payment of $1.00 or $5.00 is

---

[6] A person who pays value in good faith for a mortgage or other lien is commonly called a *bona fide encumbrancer*, but is governed by the same principles that affect bona fide purchasers.

[7] *See, e.g.,* Hood v. Webster, 2 N.E.2d 43 (N.Y. 1936) (finding deed recital of $1.00 "and other good and valuable consideration" was inadequate). *But see* Strong v. Whybark, 102 S.W. 698 (Mo. 1907) (finding $5.00 adequate).

[8] *See, e.g.,* Anderson v. Anderson, 435 N.W.2d 687 (N.D. 1989).

[9] *See, e.g.,* Horton v. Kyburz, 346 P.2d 399 (Cal. 1959) (holding that installation of fences, wells, and other improvements was more than mere nominal consideration and thus adequate).

insufficient in most jurisdictions. Presumably, even $50,000 or $10,000 constitutes "value." But what about $1,000 or $500? Only a vague guideline can be offered: the smaller the purchase price, the greater the risk that it will be held inadequate.

The confusion in this area probably stems from two sources. First, courts are attempting to distinguish between the purchaser who negotiated a bargain price, on the one hand, and the donee, on the other. The buyer who pays $100 for property worth $300,000, for example, seems more like a donee than a true purchaser for value, and does not merit protection under the recording laws. In many instances, the line between "bargain purchaser" and "donee who paid token consideration" requires a case-by-case adjudication. Second, courts are aware that the effective operation of the recording system requires both certainty and low administrative costs. The system cannot function if litigation is commonly necessary to determine a party's status as a bona fide purchaser. Accordingly, there is a clear judicial tendency to find that even very low amounts of consideration—such as $5,000 for a $300,000 property—constitute "value."

[2] Debt As Value

In general, the mortgagee or other creditor who makes a loan and receives an interest in real property to secure repayment of the debt is considered a purchaser for value. Thus, if O borrows $1,000 from L, and in return gives L a promissory note for $1,000 secured by a mortgage on O's property Blueacre, L is protected by the recording acts.

There are two main exceptions to this rule. In most states, a pre-existing debt is not seen as value.[10] Suppose O borrows $1,000 from L and in return gives L an unsecured promissory note for $1,000. Six month later, L demands that O provide a mortgage on Blueacre to secure the debt, without giving O any new value; O complies. Under these circumstances, L is not a purchaser for value. The same logic applies to the creditor who obtains a judgment lien.[11] Suppose O injures P in a traffic accident; P sues O for personal injury and obtains a $10,000 judgment. P records his judgment, creating a judgment lien that encumbers O's property Blueacre. In most states, P is not considered a purchaser for value because he gave no new value in return for his lien. Thus, P is not protected by the recording acts.[12]

[3] Notice After Partial Payment

On May 1, B contracts to purchase title to Redacre from O for $100,000; B gives O a down payment of $20,000 and agrees to pay the balance on

---

[10] *See, e.g.,* Gabel v. Drewrys Ltd., U.S.A., 68 So. 2d 372 (Fla. 1953).

[11] *See generally* Dan S. Shechter, *Judicial Lien Creditors Versus Prior Unrecorded Transferees of Real Property: Rethinking the Goals of the Recording System and Their Consequences,* 62 S. Cal. L. Rev. 105 (1988).

[12] *But see* Osin v. Johnson, 243 F.2d 653 (D.C. Cir. 1957) (holding that judgment creditor who could show reliance on record title should be treated as a purchaser for value); Rowe v. Schultz, 642 P.2d 881 (Ariz. Ct. App. 1982) (protecting judgment creditor as bona fide purchaser).

August 1. On May 15, B learns that O had previously conveyed Redacre to S on April 1. What are B's rights in Redacre?

In most jurisdictions, the buyer who receives actual notice of a prior interest after paying part of the purchase price is considered a bona fide purchaser *pro tanto*: payments made before notice are protected, but not later payments.[13] Here, B is a bona fide purchaser to the extent of her $20,000 down payment. In litigation between B and S, a court would have discretion to protect B in any one of three methods: (1) award all of Redacre to S, but require S to repay B's $20,000 down payment; (2) award a one-fifth interest in Redacre to B; or (3) allow B to obtain full title to Redacre by paying the $80,000 balance to S. A more difficult situation arises if the buyer is merely charged with record notice. Suppose that S records his deed from O on May 15, but B never actually learns about S's interest until August 2, after B has paid O in full. Under these circumstances, many courts hold that the buyer is a bona fide purchaser as to the entire purchase price, while others merely protect the buyer *pro tanto*.

In one illustrative case, the buyers paid $350,000 in advance, received a deed from the seller, and paid the $1,950,000 balance of the purchase price a year later. A third party, who had recorded a lis pendens before the buyers made this final payment, then claimed title to the land. The court found that the buyers were bona fide purchasers as to the entire purchase price, noting that otherwise a buyer who already held title would have to undertake a title search before making each later payment; "[s]uch an obviously absurd result is fundamentally contrary to the whole purpose of the recording statutes."[14]

[D] "Without Notice of the Prior Interest"

A notice statute protects the subsequent purchaser for value who has *no notice* of the prior interest. The purchaser's knowledge is measured when the deed or other instrument is delivered, not later. As discussed below (*see* § 24.06), a purchaser might receive notice in four different ways:

(1)   actual notice,

(2)   record notice,

(3)   inquiry notice, and

(4)   imputed notice.

Suppose O conveys fee simple absolute in Blueacre to A. Two weeks later, on May 1, O conveys the same estate to B in exchange for valuable consideration. The next day, May 2, B receives a phone call from A, in which A informs B about the O-A deed. On May 3, B records the O-B deed. Who owns Blueacre? A is first-in-time, so B can prevail only if B is a bona fide purchaser. In notice jurisdictions, the key question is: did the subsequent purchaser for value have notice of the prior interest? As applied to these

---

[13] *See* Daniels v. Anderson, 642 N.E.2d 128 (Ill. 1994).

[14] Lewis v. Superior Court, 37 Cal. Rptr. 2d 63, 81 (Ct. App. 1994). *But see* Alexander v. Andrews, 64 S.E.2d 487 (W. Va. 1951) (contra).

facts, we would ask: did B have notice of A's interest on May 1 (the day when B obtained delivery of the O-B deed)? No! The fact that B received actual notice on May 2—after the O-B deed was delivered—is irrelevant.

[E] Application of Rule

Consider a hypothetical. O, holding fee simple absolute in Greenacre, conveys a road easement to A on June 1; A fails to record his easement deed. On July 1, O encumbers the property with a mortgage in favor of B; B records on the same day. Finally, on August 1, O conveys fee simple absolute in Greenacre to C, a purchaser for value. In a notice jurisdiction, who holds what interest in Greenacre?

Suppose B forecloses on his mortgage and purchases Greenacre at the foreclosure sale. Does B take title with A's easement in place? A's interest is first in time, so B can prevail only if he qualifies for bona fide purchaser status. Thus, the question becomes: did B have notice of A's easement when the mortgage was delivered? On these facts, the answer appears to be "no." Because A's easement deed was never recorded, B is not charged with record notice; and B had no actual notice. Perhaps A used the easement in such an obvious and frequent manner that B is charged with inquiry notice. Otherwise, B qualifies for bona fide purchaser status and takes title free and clear of A's easement.

But what about O's deed to C? As between B and C, B's interest is first in time, so C can prevail only if she qualifies for bona fide purchaser status. C is a subsequent purchaser for value. However, B's mortgage was recorded before C acquired her interest. This record notice bars C from protection as a bona fide purchaser. Accordingly, B owns fee simple absolute in Greenacre after the foreclosure.

§ 24.05　Who Is a Bona Fide Purchaser?: Race-Notice Jurisdictions

[A] A Subsequent Purchaser for Value Without Notice of the Prior Interest Who Records First

In a race-notice jurisdiction, a bona fide purchaser is a subsequent purchaser for value without notice of the prior interest who records his or her interest first. The first three elements are the same ones required in a notice jurisdiction: *a subsequent purchaser . . . for value . . . without notice of the prior interest (see § 24.04).*[15] Thus, race-notice jurisdictions merely add on a fourth requirement: the subsequent purchaser must be the first one to record.[16]

---

[15] *But see* Eastwood v. Shedd, 442 P.2d 423 (Colo. 1968) (interpreting Colorado statute to protect subsequent donee).

[16] *See, e.g.,* Simmons v. Stum, 101 Ill. 454 (1882) (holding prior mortgage had priority over later unrecorded deed); Gregerson v. Jensen, 669 P.2d 396 (Utah 1983) (holding prior grantee under unrecorded deed took property free and clear of claims based on later unrecorded contract).

[B] Application of Rule

Assume O, holding title to Redacre, conveys the mineral rights to D on June 1; D fails to record the mineral deed. On July 1, O executes a lease in favor of E, who fails to record his lease or take possession of Redacre. On July 15, D records. Finally, on August 1, O conveys title to Redacre to F, a purchaser for value, who records. E then records. In a race-notice jurisdiction, who holds what interest in Redacre?

On these facts, D prevails over E. D is first-in-time, while E cannot qualify for bona fide purchaser protection because D recorded first. F also prevails over E. As between E and F, E was first in time, but here F is a bona fide purchaser for value who recorded before E did. Accordingly, E has no remaining interest in Redacre.

What about the respective rights of D and F? As between the two, D was first-in-time. Thus, F can prevail only if he both (1) is a bona fide purchaser for value and (2) recorded first. F is a purchaser for value. However, D recorded on July 15, before F obtained his interest on August 1. F accordingly had record notice of D's mineral deed, and cannot be a bona fide purchaser; in any event, D recorded before F did. Thus, F holds title to Redacre subject to D's mineral deed.

§ 24.06 What Constitutes Notice?

[A] Sources of Notice

The law recognizes four different types of notice:

    (1)   actual notice,

    (2)   record notice,

    (3)   inquiry notice, and

    (4)   imputed notice.

A later purchaser who is charged with notice from any one of these sources cannot qualify for protection as a bona fide purchaser.

[B] Actual Notice

Actual notice simply means knowledge of the prior interest. A person who knows that a prior interest exists has actual notice. Suppose O first conveys Redacre to A; O then tells B, "I just conveyed Redacre to A." B now has actual notice of A's interest in Redacre. If B foolishly proceeds to purchase Redacre from O, B will not qualify for bona fide purchaser status in a later title dispute with A. A subsequent purchaser might obtain actual notice through any method of written, oral, or nonverbal communication (e.g., deed, letter, newspaper, phone call, radio broadcast, e-mail, personal conversation, or sign language) or by personal observation.

[C] Record Notice (aka Constructive Notice)

Record notice (sometimes called *constructive notice*) means notice of any prior interest that would be revealed by an appropriate search of the public records affecting land title. A subsequent purchaser is charged with notice of such a prior interest, even if he or she never conducts a title search. Assume O conveys Greenacre to C, who promptly records his deed. Two months later, without first searching the public records, D purchases title to Greenacre from O. D could have found the recorded O-C deed in the public records. D has record notice of C's interest and cannot qualify for protection as a bona fide purchaser.

Which public records impart record notice? Deeds, mortgages, liens, easements, and other documents appropriately recorded in the local land records office provide record notice, under a complex maze of rules described in detail in Chapter 25. In addition, certain public records maintained by agencies other than the land records office (e.g., court files and property tax records) impart notice in many jurisdictions.

[D] Inquiry Notice

[1] Defined

Inquiry notice is based on the purchaser's duty to investigate suspicious circumstances. If a purchaser has actual notice of facts that would cause a reasonable person to inquire further, he is *deemed* to know the additional facts that inquiry would uncover *whether he inquired or not.*[17] The purchaser who performs the required investigation will receive actual notice. Thus, inquiry notice usually arises when the purchaser fails to investigate suspicious circumstances. Of course, if prudent investigation would not have revealed a fact, the purchaser is not charged with notice of that fact.

Inquiry notice issues arise most commonly in two situations: (1) notice from possession of land; and (2) notice from a reference in a recorded document. Traditionally, courts found inquiry notice in a third situation: notice from a quitclaim deed. Any conveyance by a quitclaim deed was considered inherently suspicious, giving inquiry notice of all unrecorded interests to the grantee and successors in the chain of title. Most jurisdictions have either abandoned or restricted this rule.

[2] Notice from Possession of Land

[a] General Principles

In most states, the purchaser is obligated to make a reasonable inspection of the land before purchase. And if a person other than the grantor is in possession, the purchaser is usually obligated to inquire about the

---

[17] *See, e.g., In re* Weisman, 5 F.3d 417 (9th Cir. 1993) (charging bankruptcy trustee with inquiry notice); Horton v. Kyburz, 346 P.2d 399 (Cal. 1959) (finding no basis for inquiry notice on facts).

possessor's rights.[18] Why? Possession by a stranger is suspicious. The possessor might be a friend or relative of the grantor, or perhaps a trespasser. But the possessor might hold an unrecorded interest in the land. As one court summarized, "[p]ossession of land by one under claim of title is notice to the world of such claim."[19]

Suppose B purchases Blueacre from O, its record owner, at a time when X is in possession. Possession by X is inconsistent with record title. If B neglects to inspect the land at purchase, and thus fails to discover X's possession, he is charged with inquiry notice of any interest X may hold in Blueacre (e.g., an unrecorded deed or contract to purchase). If B does inspect the land, but neglects to inquire about X's status, he is similarly charged with inquiry notice.

Conversely, assume that O and X are sharing possession of Blueacre; X is O's daughter. Under these circumstances, B is not obligated to inquire. B may reasonably assume that X will vacate Blueacre along with O when the sale is complete.

[b] Tenants in Possession

Inquiry notice issues frequently arise when a tenant is in possession of the property. Suppose L plans to sell her 100-unit apartment complex to B; one of L's tenants is T, who rents unit #23. L gives B copies of the leases for all units, including T's lease. Each lease is a standard form document providing for a five-year term. Must B inquire further? In most jurisdictions, the answer is "yes." The purchaser is charged with inquiry notice of the rights of tenants in possession, whether or not they are reflected in written leases. Thus, a purchaser like B has a duty to question T and all other tenants about their interests in the property.[20] For example, it is possible that T has entered into a new 50-year lease with L at a bargain rent, which L concealed from B; or perhaps T holds an unrecorded right of first refusal to purchase the apartment complex. This rule imposes an enormous (and expensive) burden on purchasers of multi-unit buildings.

What if the tenant's lease is recorded? Some courts hold—quite appropriately—that if the tenant's possession is consistent with a recorded lease, the purchaser has no duty to inquire further. A fundamental precept of the recording acts is that a purchaser is entitled to rely on recorded documents. For example, if the tenant's recorded lease is merely a standard term of years lease, the purchaser is not charged with inquiry notice of the tenant's unrecorded option to purchase the property.[21]

---

[18] See, e.g., Waldorff Ins. & Bonding, Inc. v. Eglin Nat'l Bank, 453 So. 2d 1383 (Fla. Dist. Ct. App. 1984) (holding that occupancy of condominium unit gave inquiry notice of occupant's unrecorded purchase contract).

[19] Russell v. Scarborough, 124 So. 648, 648 (Miss. 1929).

[20] See, e.g., Cohen v. Thomas & Son Transfer Line, Inc., 586 P.2d 39 (Colo. 1978); Martinique Realty Corp. v. Hull, 166 A.2d 803 (N.J. Super. Ct. App. Div. 1960).

[21] See, e.g., Gates Rubber Co. v. Ulman, 262 Cal. Rptr. 630 (Ct. App. 1989).

[c] Acts Constituting Possession

There is little judicial agreement about the acts that constitute sufficient possession to put a purchaser on inquiry notice. Many courts seem to analogize to the law of adverse possession by requiring conduct that is visible, open, notorious, exclusive, and so forth. For example, *Wineberg v. Moore* [22] involved competing title claims to an 880-acre tract of forest land, mainly suitable for growing timber, hunting, and fishing. One Barker, the original owner, first conveyed title to Wineberg, who failed to record. However, Wineberg (1) posted several "no trespassing" signs bearing his name; (2) occupied the cabin on the land occasionally for recreation; and (3) left items of personal property in the cabin that could be identified as his. When Barker later transferred interests in the land to two other parties, the court held that Wineberg's actions were enough to place the later purchasers on inquiry notice. [23]

At the other extreme, some courts hold that even minor and inconspicuous acts—which realistically would not afford notice—are enough to place a purchaser on inquiry. [24] The leading case is *Miller v. Green*. [25] After purchasing a 63-acre farm from Green, Miller plowed two acres and hauled a pile of manure to the land. Green later sold the farm to other buyers. Upon inspection, the buyers would have seen the plowed ground and the manure pile. These facts were held sufficient to afford inquiry notice. Why? Why shouldn't the later purchasers reasonably assume that Green or her agents had performed these acts?

[3] Notice from Reference in Recorded Document

In most states, a reference in a recorded document to an unrecorded document is sufficient to give inquiry notice. [26] For example, in *Harper v. Paradise* [27] a recorded 1928 deed recited that it was made to "take the place of" a 1922 deed that had been "lost or destroyed and cannot be found." [28] In fact, the provisions of the 1928 deed differed significantly from those of the original deed. The Georgia Supreme Court held that later purchasers for value were on inquiry notice of the contents of the 1922 deed.

---

[22] 194 F. Supp. 12 (N.D. Cal. 1961).

[23] *See also* Bank of Mississippi v. Hollingsworth, 609 So. 2d 422 (Miss. 1992) (holding that fencing of land by first buyer placed later lender on inquiry notice).

[24] *See generally* John G. Sprankling, *The Antiwilderness Bias in American Property Law*, 63 U. Chi. L. Rev. 519, 540–544, 574–577 (1996).

[25] 58 N.W.2d 704 (Wis. 1953).

[26] *See, e.g.,* Jefferson County v. Mosley, 226 So. 2d 652 (Ala. 1969) (holding later purchaser was on notice of unrecorded right-of-way referenced in deed); Guerin v. Sunburst Oil & Gas Co., 218 P. 949 (Mont. 1923) (holding later purchaser was on notice of unrecorded oil and gas lease referenced in recorded option).

[27] 210 S.E.2d 710 (Ga. 1974).

[28] Harper v. Paradise, 210 S.E.2d 710, 711–712 (Ga. 1974).

[E]   Imputed Notice

Imputed notice arises from a special relationship between two or more persons; if one has actual knowledge of a fact, the others are also deemed to know the fact. For example, in some situations an agent's knowledge is imputed to the principal, just as the knowledge of one general partner is imputed to the other partners.

§ 24.07   Second Exception to General Rule: The "Shelter Rule"

Under the *shelter rule*, a grantee from a bona fide purchaser is protected as a bona fide purchaser, even though the grantee would not otherwise qualify for this status.[29] In effect, a bona fide purchaser transfers this protected status to later grantees. The shelter rule is necessary to make bona fide purchaser protection meaningful. Without it, a bona fide purchaser might well be unable to sell the property.

Assume O first conveys fee simple absolute in Greenacre to A, and later conveys the same estate to B, a bona fide purchaser for value who records first. In all jurisdictions, B owns Greenacre. When B lists Greenacre for sale ten years later, A stands outside waving a huge banner that reads: "I obtained title to Greenacre before B did. I'm the real owner!" Prospective buyer C sees A's banner, and thereby obtains actual notice of A's prior interest. In a notice or race-notice jurisdiction, C and other potential buyers who see A's banner cannot qualify for bona fide purchaser status on their own. A's conduct might well prevent B from selling Greenacre—and thus recovering his economic investment in the property—unless B can pass on his protected status to his ultimate buyer. The shelter rule allows B to transfer his bona fide purchaser protection to later grantees.

§ 24.08   Special Rule for Race Jurisdictions: First Purchaser for Value to Record Prevails

Under a race recording statute, the first purchaser for value to *record* prevails. Suppose O conveys title in Blueacre to buyer A on Monday, and then to buyer B on Tuesday. If buyer B records her deed first, the law recognizes her as the owner of Blueacre. Conversely, if buyer A records first, he holds title. Priority is determined simply by which purchaser wins the "race" to the recorder's office. Thus, the race approach is a variant on the common law first-in-time rule. Race jurisdictions afford no special protection to the donee or other interest holder who fails to pay value. For example, assume O first conveys title to Blueacre to buyer C, and then conveys the same estate to donee D as a gift. Even if D records before C, C still owns Blueacre.

Notice is irrelevant in a race jurisdiction. Suppose that O conveys title to Blueacre to buyer A on Monday, and A fails to timely record. When B

---

[29] *See, e.g.,* Hatcher v. Hall, 292 S.W.2d 619 (Mo. Ct. App. 1956).

inquires about buying the land on Tuesday, O fully informs her about A's prior interest. Despite this actual notice, B proceeds to purchase Blueacre from O; O conveys title to Blueacre to B on Tuesday afternoon. If B records before A, B is deemed the owner of Blueacre.

The importance of the race approach is dwindling. Only two states— Louisiana and North Carolina—still apply the race approach to all transactions.[30] A handful of other states use this approach only for mortgages or deeds of trust.[31]

§ 24.09   Why Protect the Bona Fide Purchaser?

The first American recording acts were simple race statutes. Yet today almost all states extend special protection to the bona fide purchaser. And the handful of lingering race statutes seems destined for extinction. Why?

One reason is that the bona fide purchaser doctrine prevents fraud and quasi-criminal conduct, while a race statute allows the sophisticated to plunder the naive. Suppose O first conveys title to Greenacre to N for $10,000; O immediately conveys the same estate to his henchman S, who takes care to record the O-S deed before N does. O vanishes; S owns Greenacre; and N loses $10,000. O and S later split their ill-gotten gains.

A second theme might loosely be described as comparative negligence. When one of two innocent people must suffer a loss, the law usually allocates that loss to the person who had the best opportunity to avoid the problem in the first place. Suppose O first conveys title to Redacre to N, who carelessly fails to record his deed; one year later, O then conveys the same estate to P, who performs a careful title search before completing the transaction and recording his deed. N then records. As between N and P, who should suffer the loss of title? Prudent P did everything reasonably possible to avoid the loss. Negligent N, in contrast, could have prevented the loss by the cheap and simple expedient of recording his deed promptly. As law and economics theorists might explain it, allocating the risk of loss to the first-in-time buyer is economically efficient because he or she can avoid the loss at the cheapest cost.

A third rationale is that the notice variant of the bona fide purchaser doctrine encourages the commercial transfer of land, which in turn tends to allocate land to its most productive use. Suppose S owns a sheep pasture suitable for use as a factory site. In a race jurisdiction, prospective buyer B may be unwilling to take the risk of buying S's property. B might pay S $100,000 for title to the land at 9:00 a.m. on Monday, only to learn later that P had purchased the same land from S on Sunday and recorded his deed at 9:01 a.m. on Monday. P prevails over B in a race jurisdiction because P's deed was recorded first. Conversely, in a notice jurisdiction, B is a bona fide purchaser and prevails over P; when B acquired her interest at 9:00 a.m. on Monday, she had no notice of S's prior deed. All other things being

---

[30] *See* Powell on Real Property § 82.02[1] (Michael Allan Wolf ed., Matthew Bender).

[31] *See* Powell on Real Property § 82.02[1] (Michael Allan Wolf ed., Matthew Bender).

equal, as the argument goes, the bona fide purchaser doctrine shelters the prudent investor from unknown adverse claims, and thereby encourages socially-beneficial investment.

The principal criticism of the bona fide purchaser doctrine comes from the law and economics movement. A central precept of law and economics is that transaction costs impair the free transfer of property rights, and thus undercut efficiency (*see* § 2.05[A]). Bona fide purchaser protection certainly increases transaction costs. To qualify, a buyer must diligently search record title, carefully inspect the property, and investigate any suspicious circumstances; all three steps consume time and money. Yet even a thorough pre-purchase inquiry cannot guarantee the buyer's title. Adverse title claimants may argue in later litigation that the buyer's inquiry was insufficient. The buyer who defeats this argument still suffers the expense and inconvenience of litigation, while the unsuccessful buyer loses title entirely. Law and economics theorists suggest that the race approach offers a "bright line" standard that reduces transaction costs.

A related argument is that the bona fide purchaser doctrine tends to undercut certainty of title. The new buyer's title is subject to potential challenge by prior adverse claimants. For example, suppose B purchases a farm from O. Adverse claimant A might later assert that B should be charged with inquiry notice of A's prior interest merely because A placed a haystack on the farm before B purchased. Because notice is always a question of fact, it is possible—though unlikely—that A might prevail. In any event, litigation would be required to resolve the dispute. Thus, as the argument goes, buyers like B may be less willing to invest in improving their lands. Why should B invest $1 million to build a new factory on the land, for example, if he may someday lose title? In contrast, a race statute provides a "bright line" test to determine who hold title: the first purchaser to record prevails. This standard arguably enhances the confidence of buyers to invest in socially-beneficial improvements.

Chapter 25

THE RECORDING SYSTEM

§ 25.01 The Recording System in Context

O owns Greenacre, a ranch worth $500,000. What prevents O from defrauding buyers by "selling" Greenacre two or more times? Consider the following scenario. O conveys title to A in exchange for $500,000; two days later O conveys title to B for the same price; finally, a week later, O conveys title to C for the same price. O pockets $1,500,000 and flees to a foreign paradise. While possible in theory, this scenario is highly unlikely in practice, thanks primarily to the recording system.[1]

In concept, the recording system is simple. Deeds, mortgages, CC&Rs, judgments, and other documents affecting title to real property may be brought to a government office and placed in the public record for the world to see. As discussed in Chapter 24, the recording acts in 48 states generally provide that a later purchaser is charged with constructive notice[2] of the recorded prior interest—*even if he or she fails to search the records*—and accordingly cannot qualify for protection as a bona fide purchaser (*see* § 24.03). In the two remaining states, the later purchaser loses if he or she fails to record first as required by statute (*see* § 24.08).

Yet the recording system is confusingly complex in practice. The difficulty can be summarized in a sentence: *not all recorded documents give constructive notice.*[3] The rules governing which documents do provide notice—and which do not—are quite intricate. In large part, this law developed in reaction to the difficulty of searching voluminous paper records before the development of computers. Title documents that can be discovered only by unusually burdensome search methods do not provide notice in most jurisdictions.

§ 25.02   Purposes of the Recording System

The recording system serves two basic purposes. First, it *protects existing owners* from losing their property to later purchasers. For example, if A immediately recorded her deed from O in the above scenario, both B and C would be charged with notice of the O-A deed in a notice or race-notice jurisdiction. Because neither B nor C is a bona fide purchaser, A—the first-in-time owner—holds title to Greenacre (*see* § 24.02). A also prevails in a race jurisdiction because she recorded first. The title protection arising from the recording system encourages owners like A to undertake the investment necessary to maximize the productivity of their lands, and serves other utilitarian goals.

Second, the recording system *protects new buyers.* A prudent buyer can commission a search of the public records before completing the purchase and thereby determine whether the seller is able to convey clear title. For example, if B hires an attorney to examine title to Greenacre, the attorney will quickly discover the recorded O-A deed and advise B not to proceed with the transaction. On the other hand if the O-A deed was never recorded, B's title search will not uncover any adverse claim to Greenacre. B can now

---

[1] *See generally* Harry M. Cross, *The Record "Chain of Title" Hypocrisy,* 57 Colum. L. Rev. 787 (1957); Corwin W. Johnson, *Purpose and Scope of the Recording Statutes,* 47 Iowa L. Rev. 231 (1962); Taylor Mattis, *Recording Acts: Anachronistic Reliance,* 25 Real Prop., Prob. & Trust J. 17 (1990); Francis S. Philbrick, *Limits of Record Search and Therefore of Notice,* 93 U. Pa. L. Rev. 125 (1944).

[2] This type of notice is sometimes also called "record notice" (*see* § 24.06[C]). To avoid semantic confusion, this chapter refers to it only as "constructive notice."

[3] *See, e.g.,* Luthi v. Evans, 576 P.2d 1064 (Kan. 1978); Messersmith v. Smith, 60 N.W.2d 276 (N.D. 1953).

proceed to buy the land as a bona fide purchaser, secure in the knowledge that the law will protect her title against any unknown prior interests.[4] In this manner, the recording system gives buyers the confidence necessary to invest.

§ 25.03   Anatomy of the Recording System

The recording system functions much like a specialized library. Imagine that almost anyone can write a book and place it on the library shelves, without any investigation by librarian L to determine if the book is accurate. Because the library contains so many books, L maintains a written catalogue or index that lists each one. Now suppose that student S wants to conduct research to answer a particular question. S consults the library catalogue, locates the books that appear relevant, examines these books, evaluates their accuracy, and ascertains the answer to her question, all without any assistance from L.

Like our hypothetical librarian, government officials have very little control over which documents are recorded. A clerk briefly examines the form of documents submitted for recording (see § 25.04[A]) but does not investigate their validity or accuracy. Did the grantor ever own title to the property? Did the grantor intend to deliver the deed? Did the grantee forge the grantor's signature? Is the property description correct? Government makes no effort to answer substantive questions like these; rather, it functions as a passive custodian. Inevitably, some recorded documents are ineffective or inaccurate.

Much like our hypothetical student, a title searcher must:

(1)   examine official indexes to discover the documents that affect the parcel at issue,[5]

(2)   read the relevant documents, and

(3)   *independently* evaluate their legal significance to determine the state of title (see § 25.05).

The government makes no representations about title. Instead, it leaves the process of determining title exclusively to private searchers.[6]

It is important to understand that the recording system extends to *all* interests in real property, not merely freehold estates. Thus, a person holding a recorded easement, mortgage, or other interest receives the same protection against later claims as the person holding record title. In the same fashion, a person who is planning to acquire an easement, mortgage, or other interest is charged with constructive notice of previously-recorded

---

[4] Yet even if a title search reveals no adverse interest, a buyer may still be subject to various prior unrecorded interests that arise as a matter of law (e.g., dower rights or title based on adverse possession).

[5] *See, e.g.,* Luthi v. Evans, 576 P.2d 1064 (Kan. 1978) (searcher could not discover assignment of lease in index due to inadequate property description).

[6] A handful of jurisdictions utilize a registration system, under which government does determine the state of title. *See* § 26.05.

documents, and thus must undertake the same title search as someone planning to purchase title.

§ 25.04   Procedure for Recording Documents

[A]   Mechanics of Recording

Suppose O conveys title to Blueacre to A. What steps must A take in order to record the O-A deed?

In order to qualify for recordation, a deed or other title document need only satisfy a few minimal requirements. First and foremost, virtually all states require that the document be acknowledged before a notary public or similar official. An acknowledgment is a declaration (1) by the grantor that he actually signed the deed or other document or (2) by a witness that he saw the grantor sign it. The acknowledgment is evidenced by a written certificate of acknowledgment, duly executed by the notary and physically attached to the deed. A second basic requirement is that the document must—at least loosely—take the form of a type of document that affects the title to or possession of real property, and, accordingly, is authorized to be recorded under state law (e.g., a deed, mortgage, or judgment). For example, a newspaper or theater ticket does not qualify for recording. Some jurisdictions impose additional requirements, such as affixing a seal or paying a transfer tax.

The actual recording process is quite simple. A presents the original deed to a clerk in the appropriate county agency (usually called the *recorder*) and pays a small fee. The clerk stamps the date and exact time of receipt onto the deed, together with its assigned document number. For example, if A's deed is the 10,347th document recorded in that county during 2000, it probably bears the document number "2000-10,347." The clerk provides A with a photocopy of the stamped deed, and retains the original deed temporarily. A copy of the deed is then placed in the official county records and the deed is "indexed," as described in [B], *below*. After processing, the original deed is returned to A by mail.

[B]   Filing and Indexing

After a document is accepted for recording, it is entered into the county land records and noted in the appropriate index. Consider the hypothetical O-A deed again. Once grantee A leaves the recorder's office, a photocopy of the O-A deed is placed in the official records. The traditional method is to insert title documents into bound volumes (often called *deed books*) in the sequence of their recording. For example, if the most recently recorded document was placed on page 123 of book 86, then the photocopy of the O-A deed will be placed on page 124 of the same book; the original deed will be stamped to indicate that it was recorded at "Book 86, Page 124." Today many recorder's offices store new title documents on microfilm rolls or microfiche. Despite the advent of the computer age, only a handful of offices utilize computerized data bases. Thus, the heart of an average recorder's office is a huge collection of paper records, often containing millions of title documents.

How can a later title searcher discover the O-A deed without examining every document? Each recorder's office maintains a book-like finding aid, known as an *index*. Most offices—about 75%—use the *grantor-grantee index*. In a grantor-grantee index, data about each deed or other title document is organized alphabetically according to the names of the parties involved and the year the transaction occurred. For example, if O's full name is Olivia P. Owner, information concerning the O-A deed will be entered into the grantor-grantee index under "Owner, Olivia P." in the volume that covers the year 2000, when the O-A deed was recorded. An entry normally lists:

(1)　the type of document (e.g., deed, lease, or mortgage),

(2)　the grantor's name,

(3)　the grantee's name,

(4)　the document number,

(5)　the recording date,

(6)　the location where the document can be found in the records (e.g., the book and page number), and

(7)　a brief legal description of the parcel.

The same information—organized under the name of the grantee—is contained in a counterpart index, called the *grantee-grantor index*.

Some recorder's offices utilize a *tract index*. In a tract index, information concerning each document is organized based on the legal description of the parcel involved.

§ 25.05　Procedure for Searching Title

[A]　Goals of Title Search

Prospective buyer A is thinking about purchasing Greyacre from Oscar Owner, its apparent owner. Before consummating the purchase, A prudently decides to investigate record title to Greyacre. A would probably retain an attorney, title company, or other agent to act on her behalf. But for the sake of simplicity, let us assume that A will personally perform the title search. We will further assume that A is not charged with actual, inquiry, or imputed notice of any adverse claim to Greyacre (*see* § 24.06).

What are A's goals in searching title? First, A wants to ensure that Owner owns the estate he purports to be selling—presumably fee simple absolute in Greyacre. If title to Greyacre is held by someone else, A will discontinue negotiations. Second, A wants to identify and evaluate any liens, easements, and other encumbrances on Owner's title that may affect the value or desirability of the land. For example, if Greyacre is encumbered by a recorded covenant that limits its use to growing crops—thereby precluding residential or commercial development—it may be worth far less than an unrestricted parcel. Under these circumstances, A will either offer a lower price for Greyacre or refuse to purchase it at all.

[B]　Title Search Using Grantor-Grantee Index

[1]　Overview

Assume that A's jurisdiction uses the grantor-grantee index. A will search title in three steps. First, A will search *backward* in time using the grantee-grantor index to locate each past conveyance of title, in order to find a historical starting point for the title search, as shown in Table 4. A will then search *forward* in time using the grantor-grantee index, examining each link in the chain of title shown in Table 4, to learn whether any grantor made any conveyances during his period of ownership other than the known conveyances. Finally, A will then read the documents discovered during her search of the grantor-grantee index and evaluate their legal significance.

[2]　Step One: Search Backward in Time in Grantee-Grantor Index

Where does A begin? A knows that Owner claims ownership of Greyacre. If so, then at some time a prior grantor must have conveyed Greyacre to Owner, as grantee. But when? A's first step is to locate the entry for that conveyance in the *grantee-grantor index*. Assume A's search begins in 2000. Because A is unsure when Owner received title, A will search the grantee-grantor index under Owner's name ("Owner, Oscar") as grantee for each year until she locates the entry. Suppose A searches the indexes for 2000, 1999, 1998, and finally locates the entry in the 1997 index. The index entry indicates that Owner acquired title to Greyacre from someone called Paula Pond in 1997.

A now repeats the process, searching the grantee-grantor index backwards in time, year by year, under Pond's name to determine when Pond obtained title. Suppose A finally locates an entry in the 1950 index that shows that Pond obtained title from Quentin Quan. A again repeats the process, searching the grantee-grantor index backwards under Quan's name until she discovers in the 1922 index that Quan acquired title from Rita Ramsey. A again searches the grantee-grantor index backwards each year, under Ramsey's name, and locates an entry in the 1878 index that indicates that Ramsey acquired title to the land from the United States, under the nineteenth-century homestead laws.

In theory, a searcher should examine title backwards until the point where the land was owned by a "sovereign"—the federal government, a state government, the English crown, or another foreign government. Yet many searchers routinely limit their searches to a period of 40 to 50 years, because (a) the cost and difficulty of searching are high and (b) "stale" claims are unlikely to pose a serious title challenge. Marketable title acts in force in many states now limit the required scope of search to between 20 and 40 years (*see* § 25.08). Having traced title to Greyacre back to the federal government—as shown in Table 4—A has gone far enough. She is now ready to shift her search to the grantor-grantee index.

TABLE 4: TITLE SEARCH USING GRANTOR-GRANTEE INDEX

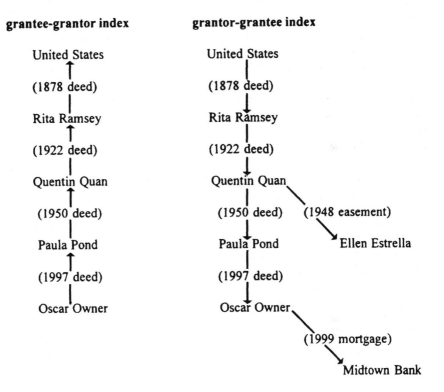

[3] Step Two: Search Forward in Time in Grantor-Grantee Index

A now searches the grantor-grantee index under Ramsey's name to determine whether Ramsey made any conveyances during the period she held title before the 1922 conveyance to Quan.[7] Thus, A will examine each index covering the period between 1878 and 1922 to locate any conveyances by Ramsey as grantor. Assume A finds that Ramsey made no conveyances before the 1922 deed to Quan. Should A search the indexes under Ramsey's name before 1878 (when Ramsey acquired title) or after 1922 (when Ramsey

---

[7] A might also search the grantor-grantee index to determine if the United States conveyed title to anyone other than Ramsey before 1878, but we will assume that A begins by searching under Ramsey's name.

conveyed title to Quan)? Most jurisdictions do not require such an extensive search (*see* § 25.07[B]), and we will assume that A's jurisdiction follows the majority approach.

A now repeats the process for each of the later grantors in the chain of title—Quan, Pond, and Owner—to determine whether any of them made any conveyances *during their respective periods of ownership* other than the known conveyances to each other. Thus, A searches the grantor-grantee indexes under Quan's name as grantor for each year between 1922 and 1950. Suppose A discovers an entry showing that Quan conveyed an easement over part of Greyacre to Ellen Estrella in 1948, before Quan conveyed title to Pond.

Continuing the search, A learns that when Pond held title between 1950 and 1997, Pond's only conveyance was the deed to Owner. Finally, A examines the grantor-grantee indexes between 1997 and the present to determine whether O conveyed any interest in Greyacre to anyone. To her surprise, she discovers a mortgage recorded in 1999 by which O mortgaged Greyacre to Midtown Bank to secure repayment of a $100,000 promissory note.

[4] Step Three: Read and Evaluate Documents That Affect Title

As shown in Table 4, A has located six documents that potentially affect title to Greyacre:

(1)   the 1878 deed from the United States to Ramsey (technically termed a *patent*),

(2)   the 1922 deed from Ramsey to Quan,

(3)   the 1948 easement from Quan to Estrella,

(4)   the 1950 deed from Quan to Pond,

(5)   the 1997 deed from Pond to Owner, and

(6)   the 1999 mortgage from Owner to Midtown Bank.

Using information provided in the index, A will now locate these documents in the deed books and read them thoroughly.

Does Owner own fee simple absolute in Greyacre? There is a clear chain of title from the United States to Ramsey to Quan to Pond to Owner. A will examine each deed to ensure that it conveys fee simple absolute, rather than some lesser estate or interest; that it is valid on its face; and that it properly describes Greyacre as the property being conveyed. If so, A will rightly conclude that O owns fee simple absolute in Greyacre.

Are there any liens, easements, or other encumbrances on Owner's title that may affect the value or desirability of the land? A's search has discovered two apparent encumbrances: (1) the 1948 easement to Estrella; and (2) the 1999 mortgage to Midtown Bank. In any jurisdiction—race, race-notice, or notice—Quan received title to Greyacre in 1950 subject to the 1948 easement; as successors to Quan, Pond and Owner also took title subject to this easement. A will examine the document that created the Estrella easement (presumably a deed of easement) to determine its validity, purpose, and scope. If the easement is minor in scope (e.g., for an underground water pipe that crosses through a corner of Greyacre for a few feet), it will have little or no impact on the value or desirability of the land. However, a prospective buyer like A would also take subject to the Midtown Bank mortgage, and this presents a problem. A will evaluate the validity of the mortgage. If the mortgage is valid, A will either refuse to complete the purchase or insist that the purchase price be reduced.

[C] Title Search Using Tract Index

Now suppose instead that A's jurisdiction uses a tract index. If so, her title search will be relatively easy. In a tract index, all entries are organized according to the identity of the parcel involved, regardless of the names of the parties. Thus, all conveyances involving Greyacre are listed on a particular page of the tract index. Once A locates this page, she will immediately discover the six documents that affect title to Greyacre and can then evaluate their legal significance (*see* [B][4], *above*).

§ 25.06 Recorded Documents That Provide Constructive Notice

In general, a recorded document provides constructive notice if four requirements are met:

> (1) it meets the formal requirements for recording (*see* § 25.04[A]),
>
> (2) it contains no technical defects (see § 25.07[A]),
>
> (3) it is recorded in the "chain of title" (*see* § 25.07[B]), and
>
> (4) it is properly indexed (*see* § 25.07[C]).[8]

In everyday life, attorneys and other professionals are usually involved in the sale, loan, and other transactions that produce recordable documents. They are able to ensure that such documents are properly prepared and recorded. Accordingly, the vast majority of recorded documents do provide notice to later purchasers.[9]

---

[8] *See also* Mountain States Tel. & Tel. Co. v. Kelton, 285 P.2d 168 (Ariz. 1955) (building contractor working on land had no duty to search title, and thus was not on constructive notice of recorded easement that referred to underground cable).

[9] In most jurisdictions, a later purchaser is also charged with constructive notice of certain records *outside* of the recorder's office, such as probate files, bankruptcy files, and tax records. A complete title search will include an examination of such records.

§ 25.07   Recorded Documents That Do Not Provide Constructive Notice

[A]   Defective Document

[1]   Invalid Acknowledgment

A recorded document that fails to meet the formal requirements for recording—and thus should never have been recorded in the first place— generally does not give constructive notice.[10] For example, if the acknowledgment is defective on its face or altogether absent, the document was not entitled to recordation, and is deemed unrecorded.[11]

A problem arises when the acknowledgment appears on its face to be valid, but suffers from a hidden defect. Suppose grantor G executes a deed in the absence of any notary; grantee E later convinces notary N to provide a certificate of acknowledgment, by which N falsely states that G personally acknowledged the deed in N's presence. The certificate appears valid on its face, but is technically invalid. E then conveys title to L, a bona fide purchaser; one week later, G purports to convey title to X, a purchaser for value.

Does the recorded G-E deed give constructive notice to X? In most states, the answer is "yes." A later purchaser like L has no reason to suspect any flaw in the acknowledgment; and the costs of investigating each acknowledgment in the chain of title would be high. In a few misguided states, however, the G-E deed is deemed unrecorded; accordingly, X is protected as a bona fide purchaser.[12] This result is contrary to the policies underlying the recording acts.

[2]   Incorrect Name

Similar difficulties arise when a recorded document contains significant errors in the names of the grantor or grantee. Suppose Greenacre is owned by Denise Berry. Berry conveys Greenacre to purchaser P, but the deed erroneously lists the grantor as "Denise Derry." The recorder's office will enter the B-P deed into the grantor-grantee index under the name "Derry, Denise." What if Berry now tries to sell Greenacre to X? Even if X diligently searches the grantor-grantee index under "Berry, Denise," he will not locate the B-P deed. The B-P deed is outside the "chain of title" (*see* [B], *below*), and thus does not provide constructive notice.[13] Suppose instead that the

---

[10] *See, e.g.*, Leasing Enter., Inc. v. Livingston, 363 S.E.2d 410 (S.C. Ct. App. 1987). However, some jurisdictions have adopted "curative acts," which retroactively cure minor defects in recorded documents—such as a defective acknowledgment or seal—after a period of years.

[11] *See, e.g.*, Hatcher v. Hall, 292 S.W.2d 619 (Mo. Ct. App. 1956) (obvious defects on face of supposed acknowledgment).

[12] *See, e.g.*, Messersmith v. Smith, 60 N.W.2d 276 (N.D. 1953).

[13] *See* Ball v. Vogtner, 362 So. 2d 894 (Ala. 1978) (recorded certificate that listed debtor as "Mary Morgan" did not give constructive notice of judgment lien to later purchasers from "Mary Collins").

B-P deed erroneously lists the grantor as "Denise Bery." In most jurisdictions, such a deed does give constructive notice. Why? A court would reason that both "Berry" and "Bery" begin with the same letter, and are pronounced in substantially the same way, so the minor spelling variation is unimportant. Under the doctrine of *idem sonans*, when an improperly spelled name sounds substantially like the true name, the spelling error is ignored. Thus, a title searcher must search not only under the correct name, but also under all variations that *sound like* the correct name.

Is this an excessive burden? A growing minority of states rejects the idem sonans approach. For example, one leading decision held that an abstract of judgment that wrongly identified the debtor as "William Duane Elliot" and "William Duane Eliot" did not give constructive notice to third parties that a judgment lien existed against property owned by "William Duane Elliott" (with two "t's" and two "l's").[14]

[3] Incorrect Property Description

A deed or other document that contains a materially defective property description does not give constructive notice.[15] In general, the description must be sufficiently accurate that a title searcher could both find the recorded document and determine that it concerned the land in question.

Luthi v. Evans[16] illustrates the point. There, Owens and others assigned their interests in various oil and gas leases to International Tours, Inc., pursuant to a written assignment that was later recorded. The assignment described the property subject to seven of these leases in great detail. It concluded with a sweeping "Mother Hubbard" clause, which provided that the "Assignors . . . by this instrument convey, to the Assignee all interest . . . in all Oil and Gas Leases in Coffey County, Kansas, owned by them whether or not the same are specifically enumerated above."[17] In fact, Owens owned an interest in an eighth oil and gas lease located in Coffey County, which she later transferred to Burris. The Kansas Supreme Court held that Burris was a bona fide purchaser because the earlier assignment did not describe the land subject to the eighth lease with sufficient specificity.

[B] Document Outside the "Chain of Title"

[1] The "Chain of Title" Generally

In general, recorded documents that cannot be located using the standard title search described above (*see* § 25.05[B]) are deemed "outside" the *chain of title*. As such, they do not provide constructive notice to later buyers. The four classic "chain of title" dilemmas are discussed below.

---

[14] Orr v. Byers, 244 Cal. Rptr. 13 (Ct. App. 1988).

[15] *See, e.g.,* Bowlin v. Keifer, 440 S.W.2d 232 (Ark. 1969) (no property description in document).

[16] 576 P.2d 1064 (Kan. 1978).

[17] Luthi v. Evans, 576 P.2d 1064, 1066 (Kan. 1978).

The chain of title concept is a judicially-invented limitation on the recording statutes. Consider a hypothetical "notice" statute that provides: "Every conveyance not recorded is invalid as against any subsequent purchaser in good faith and for a valuable consideration." Under the literal language of this statute, purchaser A takes priority over all later purchasers if she merely *records* her deed, even if the deed is difficult or even impossible for a later purchaser to find in the public records. Over time, courts interpreted such statutes to mean that a later purchaser was only charged with notice of documents that were recorded "in" the "chain of title" and thus could be discovered through a shorter title search. A document outside the chain of title is deemed "unrecorded."

Chain of title cases commonly focus on who should bear the notice burden—the prior purchaser or the later purchaser? The rationale of the typical case turns on which one is best situated to ensure that notice is received. Should the law require the prior purchaser to make sure that his or her deed is recorded in the chain of title, so that it can be easily located? Or should the later purchaser be required to conduct a more extensive search? In other words, where should the law draw the line between (a) protecting stability of ownership and (b) encouraging socially-beneficial transfers? The chain of title cases reflect a clear bias toward facilitating the transfer of land title to new owners.

[2] Prior Document Recorded Too Early

Suppose X owns title to Greenacre. O, who has no legal rights in Greenacre, conveys title to A in 1998; A records the O-A deed. In 1999, X conveys title to O, who records the X-O deed. In 2000, O conveys title to B; B records. Is B charged with constructive notice of the O-A deed?

TABLE 5: PRIOR DOCUMENT RECORDED TOO EARLY

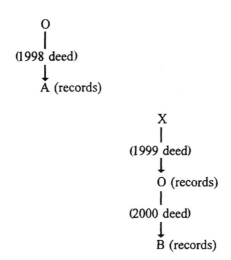

Most modern courts hold that a document recorded before the grantor obtained title—like the O-A deed—is not in the chain of title.[18] Why? The contrary rule would impose a difficult burden on title searchers and contribute to title uncertainty. A title searcher could locate the O-A deed only by searching the grantor-grantee index under O's name for every year of O's life before 2000. If O was born in 1950, for example, the title searcher would be required to search the index over a 50-year period, a heavy burden. On the other hand, the first grantee (here, A) can avoid the problem with minimal burden simply by rerecording the deed after his grantor (here O) receives title. Thus, under the majority approach a title searcher need only search the index during the period *after* the grantor obtained title, here only the years 1999 and 2000. Therefore, B is not charged with notice of the O-A deed. Of course, this rule is inapplicable in a jurisdiction that uses a tract index. There the O-A deed would be indexed under "Greenacre" and thus could easily be found.

[3] Prior Document Recorded Too Late

Suppose O acquires title to Greenacre in 1997. O conveys title to A in 1998, but A fails to record. In 1999, O conveys title to B, who immediately records; assume B has actual notice of the O-A deed and, accordingly, is not a bona fide purchaser. A records the O-A deed in 2000; in 2001, B

---

[18] *See, e.g.,* Sabo v. Horvath, 559 P.2d 1038 (Alaska 1976); Far West Sav. & Loan Ass'n v. McLaughlin, 246 Cal. Rptr. 872 (Ct. App. 1988); Palamarg Realty Co. v. Rehac, 404 A.2d 21 (N.J. 1979).

conveys to C and C immediately records. Is C charged with notice of the prior O-A deed?

TABLE 6: PRIOR DOCUMENT RECORDED TOO LATE

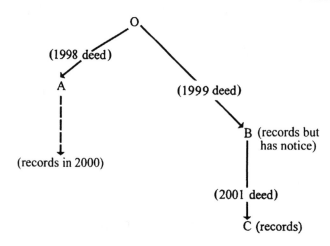

This "too late" scenario presents essentially the same issue as the "too early" scenario. Most courts resolve both in the same manner and for the same reason. In general, a prior deed recorded *after* the grantor conveyed title to a subsequent purchaser—like the O-A deed here—is not in the chain of title and does not give constructive notice.[19] C is charged with notice of conveyances from O that were recorded *during* O's ownership and *before* O's recorded transfer to B. Here, C would have to search under O's name only from 1997 to 1999 and would not be charged with notice of the O-A deed.

The rationale for the majority rule is the burden of searching title. A title searcher could locate the O-A deed only by searching the grantor-grantee index under O's name for every year after O received title. This presents only a minor burden in the example above; the searcher need only examine the index for two more years: 2000 and 2001. Yet in many cases the burden will be heavy. For example, suppose O acquired title in 1919, conveyed to A in 1920 (who failed to record), and then conveyed to B in 1921 (who recorded). Under the majority rule, a buyer like C in 2001 need only search the index under O's name for three years (1919 to 1921). Without this rule, C would be required to search title under O's name for 80 additional years (1921–2001). Again, use of a tract index would avoid this dilemma.

[4] Prior Deed from Grantor Outside Chain of Title

Suppose O owns Greenacre. In 1998, O conveys title to A, but A fails to record. In 1999, A conveys title to B, who immediately records. Finally, O

---

[19] *See, e.g.,* Rolling "R" Constr., Inc. v. Dodd, 477 So. 2d 330 (Ala. 1985); Palamarg Realty Co. v. Rehac, 404 A.2d 21 (N.J. 1979). *But see* Woods v. Garnett, 16 So. 390 (Miss. 1894) (following minority view).

conveys title to C in 2000 and C records. Is C charged with constructive notice of the prior A-B deed?

TABLE 7: PRIOR DEED FROM GRANTOR OUTSIDE CHAIN OF TITLE

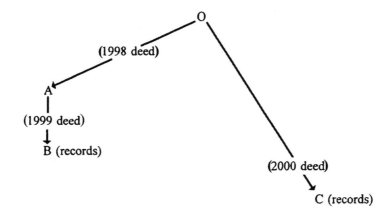

A prior conveyance from a grantor who is outside of the recorded chain of title—commonly called a *wild deed*—does not give constructive notice.[20] Even with the most thorough search, a later purchaser such as C could never discover the A-B deed in the grantor-grantee index. By definition, the A-B deed would be indexed under the name of the grantor, here A. But C, who is ignorant of A's existence, could only search the index under O's name. In theory, C could locate the A-B deed by reviewing each and every document ever recorded in the county land records. But this would impose an extraordinary burden on title searchers. In contrast, the search would be simple in a jurisdiction that utilizes a tract index.

[5] Deeds from Common Grantor of Multiple Lots

Suppose O acquires title to two adjacent properties, Blueacre and Greenacre, in 1998. In 1999, O conveys Blueacre to A and—by the same deed—covenants that Greenacre will only be used for growing crops. A records the O-A deed, but the responsible official in the recorder's office indexes the deed only using a property description of Blueacre. In 2000, O conveys Greenacre to B, without disclosing the restrictive covenant. Is B charged with constructive notice of the covenant in the O-A deed?

---

[20] *See, e.g.,* Board of Education v. Hughes, 136 N.W. 1095 (Minn. 1912).

TABLE 8: DEEDS FROM COMMON GRANTOR OF MULTIPLE LOTS

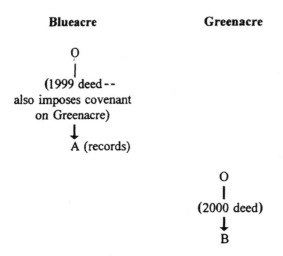

Blueacre   Greenacre

O
|
(1999 deed --
also imposes covenant
on Greenacre)
↓
A (records)

O
|
(2000 deed)
↓
B

This dilemma arises most frequently in the subdivision context, where the subdivider uses one deed to perform two functions: conveying title to a lot and imposing CC&Rs or an easement on the subdivider's retained land. A later purchaser may be charged with inquiry notice if there is visible evidence of the interest; for example, a road provides notice that an easement may exist (*see* § 24.06[D][2]). In the above hypothetical, the fact that crops are growing on Greenacre probably would not put B on notice of the restrictive covenant, unless farming is highly unusual in the area (e.g., if Greenacre is in New York City).

States are evenly divided on whether a later purchaser is charged with constructive notice in this situation. Courts that find notice typically stress that the earlier deed can be discovered simply by examining every convey-ance made by the grantor while he or she owned the property at issue.[21] Here, B could locate the restrictive covenant in the O-A deed by reading every deed from O that was recorded between 1998 and 2000, regardless of the property description used in the index. Another consideration is whether a state statute mandates the recorder's office to enter property descriptions in the index; without such a statute, some courts conclude that a title searcher cannot rely on any property description data that the recorder voluntarily chooses to include in the index.[22]

Conversely, courts that find no constructive notice usually emphasize the burden of searching title.[23] Suppose that O in the above example is an

[21] *See, e.g.,* Guillette v. Daly Dry Wall, Inc., 325 N.E.2d 572 (Mass. 1975).

[22] *See, e.g.,* Guillette v. Daly Dry Wall, Inc., 325 N.E.2d 572 (Mass. 1975).

[23] *See, e.g.,* Witter v. Taggart, 577 N.E.2d 338 (N.Y. 1991).

active real estate developer who has subdivided and sold thousands of residential lots. B might be required to examine thousands of deeds before discovering the covenant.

[C] Improperly Indexed Document

Suppose O conveys Greenacre to A. A duly records her deed, but a clerk in the recorder's office neglects to enter it in the index. Two years later, C conducts a careful title search and reasonably concludes that O owns Greenacre. O now conveys title to C. Is C charged with notice of the O-A deed?

In most states, a non-indexed document gives constructive notice.[24] Under this approach, C cannot qualify for bona fide purchaser status and, accordingly, A owns Greenacre. The same result follows if a document is indexed erroneously (e.g., using an incorrect grantor name or property description). The rationale underlying the majority approach is straightforward; the first-in-time buyer has done everything necessary to provide notice and should not be penalized by an unforeseeable clerical error. Yet this rule leads to an absurd result: later buyers like C are charged with knowledge of documents that they cannot find.

In a minority of states (including California and New York), an improperly indexed document is treated as unrecorded.[25] Under this approach, C is a bona fide purchaser and hence owns Greenacre. Legal scholars generally endorse this view, reasoning that the first-in-time buyer is in the best position to avoid the problem. A could easily check to ensure that the O-A deed is properly indexed. On the other hand, C has no reason to know that the O-A deed ever existed. C could discover the deed only by examining every document recorded in the county while O held title, an extraordinarily burdensome search.

§ 25.08 Effect of Marketable Title Acts

The traditional title search through the grantor-grantee index is often costly and time-consuming. And it may uncover dated or "stale" interests that—while unlikely to present a title problem—must nonetheless be investigated at substantial expense.

Broad *marketable title acts* enacted in 18 states address these concerns.[26] In a nutshell, if an owner has a clear record chain of title back to a *root of title* (that is, a deed or similar document that created or transferred title) for a specified period (commonly 20 to 40 years) then title is free from all rights or interests that were recorded before the root of title.[27]

---

[24] *See, e.g.,* Haner v. Bruce, 499 A.2d 792 (Vt. 1985).

[25] *See, e.g.,* Mortensen v. Lingo, 99 F. Supp. 585 (D. Alaska 1951); Rice v. Taylor, 32 P.2d 381 (Cal. 1934); Baccari v. DeSanti, 431 N.Y.S.2d 829 (App. Div. 1979).

[26] *See generally* Walter E. Barnett, *Marketable Title Acts—Panacea or Pandemonium?,* 53 Cornell L. Rev. 45 (1967).

[27] *See* City of Miami v. St. Joe Paper Co., 364 So. 2d 439 (Fla. 1978); Marshall v. Hollywood, Inc., 236 So. 2d 114 (Fla. 1970); Heifner v. Bradford, 446 N.E.2d 440 (Ohio 1983).

Suppose O acquires title to Blueacre, a vacant lot, in 1950. In 1952, O enters into a written agreement with his neighbor N, whereby O covenants that any building constructed on Blueacre will not exceed one story in height; the covenant is immediately recorded. In 1955, O conveys Blueacre to A, who records; and in 1991 A conveys title to B, who records. C now plans to purchase Blueacre from B. Assume that there is no recorded reference to the covenant after 1952. If the jurisdiction has a broad marketable title act, will C take title subject to the covenant? No. The 1955 O-A deed is deemed a root of title, because it transferred title more than 40 years before the present. Thus, C is *only* subject to interests that appear in the record *after* the 1955 deed. There is no later mention of the covenant and, accordingly, C's title will not be affected by it.[28]

The marketable title acts are certainly an overdue reform of an anti-quated system. In theory at least, a title searcher need only conduct a limited search—back to a root of title—thereby minimizing expense and delay. However, these acts contain so many exceptions that an extended search is usually still required. The exceptions always include interests held by the federal government and normally extend to such items as utility easements, mineral interests, and water rights. On balance, most commen-tators conclude that these acts have fallen far short of their laudable objectives.

Limited marketable title acts—typically directed toward one type of interest—are in force in many states. A typical statute concerns "ancient" mortgages, mineral rights,[29] or reversionary future interests (*see* § 13.05).[30]

§ 25.09 Technology and the Future of the Recording System

There is a clear—but agonizingly slow—trend toward computerization of public land title records. In a handful of recorder's offices, copies of newly-recorded documents are stored electronically and information about these filings is entered into a computerized index, usually a grantor-grantee index. Yet even these pioneers have made little effort to computerize previously-recorded documents. And the vast majority of recorder's offices still utilize the traditional system of paper records. Why? The costs of shifting to a computerized system are immense, while there is little public demand for modernization.[31]

The recording system of the future will probably center around a comput-erized tract index. Each tract of land will be assigned a unique identifying

---

[28] How could N have avoided this result? In such a jurisdiction, all who claim interests in land must periodically record a notice of claim or similar document (e.g., every 40 years). For example, if N had recorded such a notice in 1992, his covenant would survive.

[29] *See, e.g.,* Short v. Texaco, Inc., 406 N.E.2d 625 (Ind. 1980).

[30] *See, e.g.,* Presbytery of Southeast Iowa v. Harris, 226 N.W.2d 232 (Iowa 1975).

[31] Ironically, privately-owned title insurance companies already utilize computerized land record systems.

number, akin to the modern assessor's parcel number used for property taxation. All recorded documents will be stored electronically, based on the tract identification number. If X, a prospective buyer, wants to search title to Greyacre, the process will be quick, simple, and inexpensive. X will enter Greyacre's identification number into a computerized data base, and immediately retrieve copies of all recorded documents that affect title to the land.

The traditional chain of title rules will wither away in this new environment. These rules developed as judicially-crafted exceptions to the recording acts due to the search burden created by the paper record system. But the reason for these rules will disappear once the wild deed and similar items can readily be discovered through a computerized tract index.

Chapter 26

METHODS OF TITLE ASSURANCE

SYNOPSIS

§ 26.01　Title Assurance In Context

Although it is common to discuss the purchase of "land," in reality the buyer is purchasing something quite different: title to land.[1] Title is a set of intangible, legally enforceable rights relating to a specific parcel of land. While a layperson might think that S "owns" Blackacre, technically S merely owns an estate in Blackacre (*see* Chapter 9). Thus, if B contracts to purchase "Blackacre" from S for $400,000, B is actually purchasing title to Blackacre. If S's title is defective, B may ultimately receive nothing in exchange for her $400,000 purchase price. B is protected, of course, if she discovers a title defect *before* close of escrow; the express contract provisions concerning title (or alternatively, the implied covenant of marketable title) will presumably allow her to rescind the contract or use other remedies (*see* § 20.06[B]). But how can B protect herself against a title defect that is discovered *after* the close of escrow?

Three different methods of title assurance are widely used in the United States:

(1)　covenants of title in deeds;

(2)　title opinions and abstracts; and

(3)　title insurance.

Perhaps surprisingly, none of these methods offers absolute and complete protection of the buyer's title. Because each has its own weaknesses and limitations, title assurance methods are frequently combined in a single transaction. In the above purchase, for example, B might obtain both covenants of title from the seller and title insurance from a nationally recognized company, thereby minimizing the risk of later title defects. A fourth method of title assurance—registration of title—flourishes in a few regions.

An effective system of title assurance is crucial to the marketability of land. If potential buyers like B cannot obtain reasonable protection against unknown title defects, they will obviously be much less willing to purchase real property. On the other hand, the transaction costs of providing perfect title security to all buyers would be immense. The American system is essentially a compromise that provides adequate title assurance for the vast majority of buyers at a socially acceptable cost.

---

[1] *See generally* Jerome J. Curtis, Jr., *Title Assurance in Sales of California Residential Realty: A Critique of Title Insurance and Title Covenants with Suggested Reforms*, 7 Pac. L.J. 1 (1976); Arthur R. Gaudio, *Title Covenants for the Iowa Homeowner—Some Good News and Much Bad News*, 23 Drake L. Rev. 1 (1973); Quintin Johnstone, *Title Insurance*, 66 Yale L.J. 492 (1957). Joyce D. Palomar, *Title Insurance Companies' Liability for Failure to Search Title and Disclose Record Title*, 20 Creighton L. Rev. 455 (1987).

§ 26.02   Covenants of Title

[A]   What Are Title Covenants?

S conveys title to Greenacre to B, in return for the payment of $500,000. One day later, B discovers that S never owned any right, title, or interest in the property and—accordingly—neither does B. What are B's rights?

A deed usually contains express promises by the grantor about the state of title to the land being conveyed. These promises are known as *covenants of title* or *title covenants*. If one of these covenants is breached, the grantee (and sometimes his successors) may recover damages from the grantor. Here, depending on the language of the deed, B may be able to sue S for breach of the covenants of seisin and right to convey.

Title covenants originated in medieval England as a primitive method of title assurance. A prospective buyer could not readily search title before purchasing land in that era because England lacked an effective land record system. A buyer was forced to rely on the honesty and integrity of the seller. It became customary for the grantor to promise or covenant to the grantee that title was good by including express language in the deed. If title failed, the grantee could sue the grantor for damages.

Although title covenants are still used routinely, their importance as a source of title protection has waned in recent decades, particularly in commercial transactions. Other methods of title assurance—notably title insurance—offer better security to the modern buyer.

[B]   Scope of Title Covenants

[1]   The Six Title Covenants

American law has traditionally recognized six covenants of title:

    (1)   covenant of seisin,

    (2)   covenant of right to convey,

    (3)   covenant against encumbrances,

    (4)   covenant of warranty,

    (5)   covenant of quiet enjoyment, and

    (6)   covenant of further assurances.

A deed may contain all, some, or none of these covenants; and parties may invent new and different covenants. But these six listed covenants are customarily included in most deeds.

The first three covenants above are known as *present covenants*. They are breached, if at all, at the very instant the deed is delivered to the grantee. Accordingly, the statute of limitations for breach of a present covenant begins running when the deed is delivered.

The final three covenants are called *future covenants*. As the phrase suggests, they are concerned with future acts or omissions. A future covenant is breached, if at all, only when the grantee is actually or constructively evicted by someone holding superior title or suffers other damage. Thus, the statute of limitations for breach of a future covenant commences in the future, when the breach occurs.

[2] Discussion of Individual Covenants

[a] Covenant of Seisin

The *covenant of seisin* warrants that the grantor is the owner of the estate described in the deed. The covenant covers both the type of estate (e.g., fee simple absolute) and the quantity of land (e.g., 100 acres) being conveyed. Suppose O purports to convey fee simple absolute in Greenacre to B, using a general warranty deed. The covenant of seisin is breached, for example, if O owns a mere life estate in Greenacre, because O does not own the type of estate he attempted to convey. The covenant is similarly breached if O only owns fee simple absolute in the north half of Greenacre, because he does not own all of the land described in the deed.

What if O in fact owns fee simple absolute in all of Greenacre, but his title is encumbered by a mortgage in favor of M? This is not a breach of the covenant of seisin; O indeed owns fee simple absolute, the type of estate warranted. M's mortgage is merely an encumbrance on this title, and thus a breach of the covenant against encumbrances (*see* [c], *below*).

As a general rule, even a buyer who purchases with full knowledge of a title defect can recover damages for breach of the covenant of seisin. Suppose B is aware that title to Greenacre is uncertain because O and T both claim to be the sole owner. If O conveys his estate to B pursuant to a general warranty deed and the court later recognizes T's title, O is liable to B.

The covenant of seisin—as one of the three present covenants—guarantees the state of title only at the time of the conveyance. Thus, the covenant is breached—if at all—at the instant the conveyance is made and the statute of limitations begins running immediately. An illustrative decision is *Brown v. Lober*,[2] where the grantors purported to convey title to an 80-acre tract without exceptions, yet did not own two-thirds of the mineral rights. The grantors escaped liability for this clear breach of the covenant of seisin only because the grantees—apparently unaware of the title defect—failed to sue before the statute of limitations expired.

[b] Covenant of Right to Convey

The *covenant of right to convey* warrants that the grantor has the legal right to transfer title. Thus, this covenant overlaps substantially with the covenant of seisin. If F, having no right, title, or interest in Greenacre, purports to convey a life estate in Greenacre to G, F has breached both covenants. The covenant of right to convey is independently important only in a few situations. T, the trustee of a trust who attempts to convey title

---

[2] 389 N.E.2d 1188 (Ill. 1979).

to trust property in violation the trust, for example, owns the estate described in the deed but lacks the legal authority to convey title. Similarly, R might own fee simple absolute in a particular parcel, but lack the right to convey due to an express restraint on alienation in his chain of title. Like the covenant of seisin, the covenant of right to convey is a present covenant that is breached—if at all—at the time of conveyance.

[c] Covenant Against Encumbrances

[i] Nature of Covenant

The *covenant against encumbrances* warrants that there are no encumbrances on the land conveyed. What is an encumbrance? In this context, an encumbrance generally means a right or interest held by a third party—other than a present freehold estate or future interest therein—that reduces the value or restricts the use of the land. The typical encumbrance is a mortgage, easement, restrictive covenant, lease, tax lien, judgment lien, mechanic's lien, water right, or other interest in land of lesser legal status than a freehold estate.

Suppose O owns fee simple absolute in Greenacre; the land is burdened by an easement in favor of P, which allows a hidden, underground water pipe to cross Greenacre. O executes a general warranty deed conveying his estate in Greenacre to B. This conveyance does not breach the covenants of seisin or right to convey, because O owns this estate and has the right to convey it. But because P's easement is an encumbrance, the covenant against encumbrances is violated at the time of conveyance.

The scope of this covenant is controversial in two situations. Does the violation of a zoning ordinance, housing code, or other land use regulation constitute an encumbrance? And does the covenant extend to encumbrances that are obvious and visible on the land?

[ii] Ordinances and Regulations

Real property in the United States is widely subject to zoning ordinances, housing codes, and other land use regulations. All jurisdictions agree that the *existence* of such ordinances and regulations is not an encumbrance.[3] Assume, for example, that O conveys Greenacre, a vacant lot, to B pursuant to a general warranty deed. B later discovers that a local ordinance bars the building of a two-story structure on the land, and that a private covenant imposes the same restriction. Neither the ordinance nor the covenant has been violated, because the lot is vacant. The mere existence of the one-story ordinance is not a breach of the covenant against encumbrances. But the existence of the private covenant, which has the same effect, is considered a breach.

---

[3] Wilcox v. Pioneer Homes, Inc., 254 S.E.2d 214 (N.C. Ct. App. 1979) (stating rule); *cf.* Lohmeyer v. Bower, 227 P.2d 102 (Kan. 1951) (noting that existence of zoning ordinance that barred construction of residence within three feet of lot line was not an encumbrance for purposes of the marketable title doctrine).

Suppose instead that there is a four-story office building on Greenacre that already violates the ordinance when B acquires title. Does the *violation* of such an ordinance breach the covenant against encumbrances? Some courts find a breach in this situation, based on the risk of litigation or similar proceedings to compel compliance.[4] Conversely, other courts— probably a majority—conclude that such a violation does not breach the covenant against encumbrances because it merely creates a potential cause of action, not a present lien or other interest in land.[5] These courts reason that holding the seller liable for a latent violation of a land use ordinance, which could not be discovered by a title search or physical inspection of the premises, would be fundamentally unfair.

[iii] Obvious and Visible Encumbrances

Suppose O's property Greenacre is burdened with an obvious and visible defect that affects the physical condition of the land: a railroad track crosses the property. If O now sells his estate in Greenacre to B, is the covenant against encumbrances breached? The case law on the question is split into two approaches.[6] One view holds that permanent and readily visible improvements such as power lines, roads, and railroad tracks clearly indicate to any buyer that the land is subject to an easement. Accordingly, the buyer has presumably discounted the purchase price and cannot reasonably expect that the covenant against encumbrances will cover the defect.[7] But a number of courts still follow the traditional rule, insisting that the covenant extends to all encumbrances unless its language indicates otherwise.[8]

[d] Covenant of Warranty

Technically, the *covenant of warranty* is not a promise that the grantor has good title to convey. Rather, it is the grantor's promise to defend the grantee's title against other claimants; the grantor agrees to defend and indemnify the grantee who suffers an eviction or similar interference with possession of the land by a person who has superior or "paramount" title. This covenant covers both complete loss of title and the presence of an encumbrance on title. But—unlike the present covenants—it is breached only when someone holding superior title actually or constructively evicts

---

[4] Wilcox v. Pioneer Homes, Inc., 254 S.E.2d 214 (N.C. Ct. App. 1979) (violation of ordinance barring construction within 15 feet of lot line held an encumbrance); *cf.* Lohmeyer v. Bower, 227 P.2d 102 (Kan. 1951) (reaching similar result for purposes of the marketable title doctrine).

[5] *See, e.g.,* Frimberger v. Anzellotti, 594 A.2d 1029 (Conn. Ct. App. 1991) (filling of wetlands in violation of statute did not breach covenant); *cf.* Lick Mill Creek Apartments v. Chicago Title Ins. Co., 283 Cal. Rptr. 231 (Ct. App. 1991) (presence of hazardous substances on property in violation of federal law was not an encumbrance for purpose of title insurance).

[6] *See generally* Jones v. Grow Inv. & Mortgage Co., 358 P.2d 909 (Utah 1961).

[7] *Cf.* Leach v. Gunnarson, 619 P.2d 263 (Or. 1980) (rule was not met on facts of case because third parties' use of spring on grantor's land was not sufficiently open and notorious).

[8] Lockhart v. Phenix City Inv. Co., 488 So. 2d 1353 (Ala. 1986) (knowledge of encumbrance does not preclude action for breach); Bergstrom v. Moore, 677 P.2d 1123 (Utah 1984) (knowledge of utility easements did not exclude them from operation of covenant).

the grantee from the land.[9] In addition to compensatory damages, the grantor is also usually liable for the attorney's fees expended by the grantee in unsuccessfully defending against the superior title claim. For all practical purposes, the covenant of warranty is identical to the covenant of quiet enjoyment.

Suppose O conveys Blueacre, a 40-acre forest tract, to A in 1992; A immediately records his deed, but allows Blueacre to remain in pristine condition. In 1993, O conveys Blueacre to B under a general warranty deed. B, who failed to search title in advance, is ignorant of A's interest, and immediately takes possession of Blueacre by building a cabin there. B now learns about O's deed to A. All states will recognize A as the true owner of Blueacre on these facts, unless B has acquired title by adverse possession.

What must happen before B can assert a claim against O for breach of the covenant of warranty? A might actually evict B, for example, by using self-help to forcibly remove B from the land. But this scenario is unlikely to occur. A would probably first demand that B vacate Blueacre. Or A might simply sue B to recover possession. If B vacates Blueacre in response to A's demand or lawsuit—and A is indeed the true owner—most courts would view this as a constructive eviction that breaches the warranty.[10]

On the other hand, what if A never takes any action that threatens to interfere with B's possession? Here the covenant has not yet been breached, and thus suit by B is premature. *Brown v. Lober*[11] exemplifies the point. There, the grantors purported to convey fee simple absolute in 80 acres, but failed to convey two-thirds of the mineral rights, which were owned by another. But the mineral rights holder never challenged the grantees' title or possession. The Illinois Supreme Court observed that the mere *existence* of a paramount title was insufficient to breach the covenant of quiet enjoyment; rather, the grantees could not sue until someone holding superior title *actually interfered* with their possession (e.g., by beginning to remove minerals).

[e] Covenant of Quiet Enjoyment

The *covenant of quiet enjoyment* warrants that the grantee's possession and enjoyment of the property will not be disturbed by anyone holding superior title. The original distinction between this covenant and the covenant of warranty was slowly erased by case law and statutes. As a practical matter, this covenant is now identical to the covenant of warranty.

[f] Covenant of Further Assurances

The *covenant of further assurances* is a promise that the grantor will execute any additional documents and take any other actions that are reasonably necessary to perfect the grantee's title.

---

[9] *But cf.* Booker T. Washington Constr. & Design Co. v. Huntington Urban Renewal Auth., 383 S.E.2d 41 (W. Va. 1989) (covenant of warranty was breached when purchaser from grantee sued grantee for failure to deliver marketable title).

[10] *Cf.* Foley v. Smith, 539 P.2d 874 (Wash. Ct. App. 1975) (judgment of specific performance in favor of third party constituted a constructive eviction of grantees).

[11] 389 N.E.2d 1188 (Ill. 1979).

[3] Title Covenants in Standard Deed Forms

In theory, the buyer and seller are free to negotiate the nature and scope of the title covenants that will appear in the deed. Freedom of contract allows the parties to select any combination of title covenants (e.g., covenants of seisin and warranty only) or none at all. In practice, however, the parties customarily select one of three basic deed forms, each providing a different level of title assurance: the general warranty deed, the special warranty deed, and the quitclaim deed.

The *general warranty deed* contains all six standard title covenants discussed above and, accordingly, provides the most title protection (*see* § 23.03[B]). In some jurisdictions it is customary to expressly list each title covenant in the text of the deed. However, in most jurisdictions, the covenants are incorporated by reference into a short form deed through the use of shorthand terms (e.g., "warrant") usually pursuant to statutory authority.

Suppose O plans to convey Redacre to A, but is well aware that Redacre is encumbered by a title defect that cannot be removed—a recorded covenant that prohibits building a two-story structure on the land. O is unwilling to warrant title against this covenant. How can A obtain a general warranty deed? The answer is that parties can modify the title covenants in any deed simply by exempting known defects. Here, O's general warranty deed could expressly state that the title covenants do not apply to this particular covenant.

The *special warranty deed* contains the same six standard title covenants found in the general warranty deed, but applies them *only* to title defects caused by the acts or omissions of the grantor (*see* § 23.03[C]). Again, these covenants may be either listed on the face of the deed or incorporated by reference. The title protection afforded by the special warranty deed is quite limited, simply because it does not cover the acts or omissions of other parties. For example, suppose that O, holding fee simple absolute in Redacre, first executes a $100,000 mortgage in favor of A, and then conveys title to B. B, in turn, grants C an access easement across Redacre, and then conveys title to D, using a special warranty deed. D now learns that Redacre is encumbered by (1) A's mortgage and (2) C's easement. B is liable for breach of the covenant against encumbrances because she conveyed the easement to C. Because the special warranty deed warrants only against B's own conduct, however, B is not responsible for the mortgage created by O.

Finally, the *quitclaim deed* contains no title covenants at all (*see* § 23.03[D]). The grantor providing a quitclaim deed makes no warranties of any kind about the quality of his title, if any.

[C] Rights of Grantee's Successors

[1] Present Covenants

Suppose A conveys title to Redacre twice, first to B and then to C (who is not a bona fide purchaser), using a general warranty deed each time;

C immediately conveys title to D, using a mere special warranty deed. D has no warranty claim against C because C did not personally cause the title defect. Can D sue A for breach of the covenant of seisin in the A-C general warranty deed?

In a majority of states, the grantee's successor cannot sue the original grantor for breach of a present covenant, such as the covenant of seisin or covenant against encumbrances.[12] A present covenant is breached—if at all—when the deed is delivered. When the A-C deed was delivered, C immediately had a cause of action against A for breach, not a continuing covenant. The common law, fundamentally hostile to the assignment of a cause of action, refused to allow D to sue in C's place. This rule makes little sense today from a policy standpoint. Modern law allows the free assignment of causes of action. Why should the original grantor be relieved of liability merely because the grantee elects to transfer title?

A handful of states allow the successor to sue a remote grantor for breach of a present covenant. These states reason that the grantee's deed to a successor is an implied assignment of the grantee's existing cause of action against the grantor.[13]

[2] Future Covenants

On the other hand, future covenants do run with the land to the grantee's successors. Thus, the grantee's successors may sue the original grantor for breach of the covenants of quiet enjoyment, warranty, and further assurances.[14] Return to D's dilemma in the above hypothetical (*see* [1], *above*). Suppose D takes possession of Redacre from C at close of escrow; one week later, B forcefully removes D from the land. This actual eviction is sufficient interference with D's rights to breach the covenants of quiet enjoyment and warranty in the A-C deed. Thus, D could successfully sue A for breach of these future covenants.

[D] Remedies for Breach of Covenant

The grantor is liable for compensatory damages if any title covenant is breached. The appropriate measure of damages turns on which covenant is involved. As a general rule, however, the amount of recoverable damages cannot exceed the purchase price paid by the grantee.[15] The grantee who receives property as a gift through a warranty deed, for example, cannot recover against the donor-grantor in most states.

---

[12] *See, e.g.*, Proffitt v. Isley, 683 S.W.2d 243 (Ark. Ct. App. 1985) (covenant against encumbrances did not run to grantees' successors).

[13] *See, e.g.*, Rockafellor v. Gray, 191 N.W. 107 (Iowa 1922).

[14] *See, e.g.*, St. Paul Title Ins. Corp. v. Owen, 452 So. 2d 482 (Ala. 1984) (title insurance company, as subrogee to claims of insured mortgagee, may sue remote grantor for breach of covenants of quiet enjoyment and warranty).

[15] *Cf.* St. Paul Title Ins. Corp. v. Owen, 452 So. 2d 482 (Ala. 1984) (maximum recovery is purchase price paid).

The measure of damages for breach of most covenants—including the covenants of seisin and right to convey—is measured by the grantee's purchase price plus interest.[16] Suppose B purchases Greenacre from S for $150,000 pursuant to a general warranty deed; a court later holds that S's title was founded upon a forged deed, nullifies B's title claim, and orders that B be ejected from the land. Here S has breached the covenants of seisin, right to convey, warranty, and quiet enjoyment, entitling B to the return of his entire $150,000 purchase price. Alternatively, if B lost title to only 10% of Greenacre—a partial breach of covenant—he would receive a pro rata refund, here $15,000.

What if B loses title to all of Greenacre when its fair market value is $200,000, either due to appreciation or B's construction of improvements? In either situation, B's damages are restricted to the purchase price, $150,000. Why? Courts traditionally defend this result by explaining that value increases are unforeseeable, and contrary to the parties' contractual intent in establishing the purchase price. This rationale rings hollow in an era of increasing land values, particularly if the land—such as a residential building lot—is obviously destined to be improved.

Encumbrances present a different problem. Assume that after B purchases Greenacre from S for $150,000, he learns it is encumbered by: (a) a mortgage securing repayment of a $10,000 promissory note; and (b) an easement for an existing underground sewer pipe. The usual measure of damages for breach of the covenant against encumbrances is the amount paid by the buyer to remove the defect; if removal is impossible, the buyer's damages are measured by the diminution in the fair market value of the property caused by the defect on the purchase date. The same standard applies to breach of the covenants of warranty and quiet enjoyment when the title defect involved is an encumbrance. Here, B will almost certainly be able to eliminate the mortgage by paying the amount due on the secured note, probably now less than $10,000; he is entitled to reimbursement from S for this sum. On the other hand, it is unlikely that the holder of the sewer pipe easement will voluntarily relinquish his rights; if not, B's damages will be measured by the reduction in the value of Greenacre caused by the easement.[17]

A special limitation applies to the grantee's successor suing the original grantor for breach of future covenants. The measure of damages is limited by the purchase price paid by the original grantee.[18] Assume S conveys Greenacre to B for $150,000 by general warranty deed, and B later conveys the property to C for $200,000 by a quitclaim deed. If C is ultimately ejected from Greenacre due to S's lack of title, his maximum recovery for breach of the covenants in the S-B deed is $150,000 plus interest.

---

[16] *See, e.g.,* Hillsboro Cove, Inc. v. Archibald, 322 So. 2d 585 (Fla. Dist. Ct. App. 1975) (breach of warranty of seisin); Davis v. Smith, 5 Ga. 274 (1848) (breach of covenant of warranty).

[17] *See, e.g.,* Reed v. Rustin, 134 N.W.2d 767 (Mich. 1965).

[18] *See, e.g.,* Rockafellor v. Gray, 191 N.W. 107 (Iowa 1922); *see also* St. Paul Title Ins. Co. v. Owen, 452 So. 2d 482 (Ala. 1984).

[E]   Perspectives on Title Covenants

The unfortunate grantee who encounters a title defect after the close of escrow may also discover that the title covenants in the deed—even a general warranty deed—provide only limited protection. At best, the prudent buyer should rely on title covenants only to buttress another form of title protection, such as a title insurance policy.

First, the practical value of any title covenant hinges on the solvency of the grantor. If the grantor is bankrupt, dead, or simply unfindable, the luckless grantee will recover nothing even if the grantor is clearly liable. Suppose O conveys title to Greenacre to A, who moves onto the property but fails to record his deed. O then conveys Greenacre to B—who prudently conducts a title search but carelessly assumes A is merely a lessee—for $200,000 pursuant to a general warranty deed. O later promptly loses all of his money (including B's $200,000) while gambling at Atlantic City. Although O clearly breached deed covenants, B will recover nothing.

Second, the statute of limitations may bar any action against the grantor. Like the unfortunate plaintiff in *Brown v. Lober*,[19] the grantee may learn that an action on the present covenants is time-barred and an action on the future covenants is premature.

Finally, the damages awarded to the grantee who prevails in an action against a solvent grantor may not provide full compensation, particularly if the fair market value of the land has increased substantially or the grantee has built a home or other improvements.

§ 26.03   Title Opinions and Abstracts

Another method of title assurance is an attorney's opinion of title based on the examination of public records. Unlike early England, the United States has established a comprehensive system of public land records (*see* Chapter 25). It is accordingly possible for an American buyer to obtain title protection above and beyond the seller's covenants of title.

The process of obtaining a title opinion is simple. Suppose B is considering the purchase of O's property Goldacre and retains attorney A to provide a title opinion. A searches the public records affecting title to Goldacre, including not only the recorded documents found in the local recorder's office, but also applicable probate files, tax assessment records, and the like. Based on his examination of these records, A issues a written opinion on the state of title to Goldacre. The opinion identifies the holder of record title to Goldacre, lists any title defects revealed by the search, and states whether title is marketable.

Alternatively, A's title opinion might be based on an abstract of title. Under this approach, A does not examine the public records himself. Rather, A requests a nonlawyer who specializes in searching title (an *abstractor)* to prepare a written summary (an *abstract)* of the title to Goldacre. In

---

[19] 389 N.E.2d 1188 (Ill. 1979).

chronological order, the abstract briefly describes every deed, mortgage, judgment, and other document affecting title to Goldacre that has ever been entered into the public records. A then relies on the abstract to prepare his title opinion.

A title opinion serves two distinct functions, one before the close of escrow, and one thereafter. First, the prudent buyer will include a provision in the sales contract that conditions the obligation to purchase on the prior receipt of an acceptable title opinion or title insurance policy (*see* § 20.06). Thus, if the opinion discloses unacceptable title defects, the buyer can simply refuse to proceed with the purchase.

Alternatively, if the buyer purchases the property and later discovers that the title opinion was negligently prepared, he can recover compensatory damages by suing the attorney for malpractice.[20] If the abstractor caused the problem by performing a careless search, the attorney is not liable, but the buyer can generally sue the abstractor for negligence.[21] A problem arises, however, if the buyer did not directly employ the abstractor. Traditionally, the buyer had no claim if the abstractor was hired by another party (e.g., the seller) due to lack of privity. But modern courts usually find that the buyer's reliance on the abstract is reasonably foreseeable, and thus permit suit against the negligent abstractor even without privity.

The title opinion was the dominant method of title assurance in the United States during the nineteenth century and throughout much of the twentieth century. Today, however, the importance of this method is diminishing due to the widespread use of title insurance. The title opinion is the principal method only in a handful of jurisdictions (e.g., Iowa, Maine, Mississippi, North Dakota, and Vermont).

§ 26.04 Title Insurance Policies

[A] The Rise of Title Insurance

Title insurance is a uniquely American method of title protection.[22] Invented in the late nineteenth century, it remained relatively unimportant until the post-war boom of the late 1940s. Over the last 50 years, title insurance has become the dominant form of title protection in the United States. Most buyers obtain an owner's title insurance policy, instead of an attorney's opinion of title. Despite the continued trend toward title insurance, buyers still rely on title opinions in some regions, particularly in rural sections of the Midwest and South.

---

[20] *But cf.* Page v. Frazier, 445 N.E.2d 148 (Mass. 1983) (mortgagee's attorney who negligently prepared title opinion owed no duty of care to mortgagors).

[21] *Cf.* First Am. Title Ins. Co. v. First Title Serv. Co., 457 So. 2d 467 (Fla. 1984) (title company that relied on abstract in issuing title insurance policy could sue abstracter in negligence).

[22] *See generally* Jerome J. Curtis, Jr., *Title Assurance in Sales of California Residential Realty: A Critique of Title Insurance and Title Covenants with Suggested Reforms*, 7 Pac. L.J. 1 (1976); Quintin Johnstone, *Title Insurance*, 66 Yale L.J. 492 (1957).

What accounts for the modern popularity of title insurance? One reason is that title insurance offers better protection for buyers. For example: (1) title insurance covers "off-record" defects such as forgery or incapacity, while the title opinion assesses only record title; and (2) the title insurer is strictly liable for a covered defect, while the attorney is liable only for negligence. Ethical restraints also play a role; the rules of professional ethics bar attorneys from soliciting business, while title insurance companies are free from such limits.

But most authorities attribute the rise of title insurance to a third factor: the impact of the secondary mortgage market (*see* § 22.04[B]). Title insurance offers a uniform, national system for protecting title, which provides crucial protection for lenders buying mortgages in interstate commerce. Banks and other institutional lenders now routinely require that virtually all new residential mortgages be protected by title insurance, and this in turn leads buyers to obtain owner's policies protecting their own title.

[B]   What Is Title Insurance?

The title insurance policy is a contract of indemnity between the issuing company (the *insurer*) and the property owner or mortgagee (the *insured*). In the policy, the insurer promises to compensate or indemnify the insured against losses caused by covered title defects. Most types of insurance policies are prospective: they provide protection against contingent events that might occur in the future (e.g., a car accident or a flood). Title insurance, in contrast, is retrospective: it protects only against title defects that already exist at the time title is transferred, not those that may arise in the future.

[C]   Two Functions of Title Insurance

[1]   Title Assurance Before Close of Escrow

Like the title opinion, title insurance serves two related functions. Before close of escrow, it effectively tests the quality of the seller's title. The buyer will often condition the obligation to buy on the insurer's willingness to issue an adequate title insurance policy. If such a policy is available, the buyer will complete the purchase, knowing that he is protected if title defects are ultimately discovered. On the other hand, if such a policy cannot be obtained, the buyer is excused from performing the contract. Thus, before close of escrow, the availability of title insurance serves as a substitute for the buyer's examination of title.

Suppose B executes a contract to purchase Greenacre from S, contingent on obtaining title insurance. B applies to title insurance company T for a policy. Is T willing to ensure title to Greenacre? To answer this question, T, a prudent insurer, will examine the state of title to the property. Like many title insurance companies, T may maintain a computerized *plant* of land title records that parallels the public land record system; if so, T's employees will search this data base to locate recorded documents that affect title to Greenacre. Alternatively, T might base its analysis on a search of title performed by a local attorney or a professional abstractor. Based on this title examination, T will provide B with a *preliminary report, title report,* or similar document stating whether it will insure title to Greenacre and, if so, on what terms and conditions. T will normally exclude from coverage any title defect that is discovered during the search process. T is, after all, entitled to determine the nature and extent of the risk it is willing to take. If T and other insurers are unwilling to provide an adequate policy (e.g., because Greenacre is actually owned by X), the contract condition fails, and B is released from any obligation to buy Greenacre.

Or, as is more likely, suppose S owns fee simple absolute in Greenacre, but that the property is subject to a recorded encumbrance (e.g., an easement for a future freeway). T is willing to insure B's title to Greenacre in general, but will not insure against this known—and troublesome— defect. Such a policy would probably not satisfy the title condition in the B-S contract.

[2] Compensation After Close of Escrow

The second function of the title insurance policy is compensation. The standard policy imposes two basic duties on a title insurance company: the duty to defend and the duty to indemnify. The duty to defend obligates the company to incur the attorney's fees and costs necessary to defend the insured's title against legal challenge, subject to the policy terms. If this defense is unsuccessful, the company is required to either cure the defect or indemnify the insured.

Where a covered title defect is discovered after close of escrow, the insured buyer is entitled to recover for any actual loss that is proximately caused by the defect. This sum is usually measured by the lesser of (a) the amount needed to remove the defect from title or (b) the extent to which the defect reduces the fair market value of the land. The insured may also be able to recover foreseeable consequential damages (e.g., lost rental income, lost profits). In no event, however, can the insured's recovery exceed the policy limit specified in the policy itself.[23]

Assume, for example, that B obtains a title insurance policy upon her purchase of Blueacre, with a policy limit of $120,000. B later learns that Blueacre is encumbered by an enforceable restrictive covenant in favor of an adjacent neighbor, N, which restricts its use to farming. If N demands $100,000 to release the covenant, but the covenant only diminishes the value of Blueacre by $80,000, B's recovery is limited to the smaller of these two sums, here $80,000. Suppose instead that the farming-only covenant reduces market value by $150,000 and N demands $200,000 to remove it; here B's recovery is only $120,000, the limit she agreed to in purchasing her policy.

---

[23] The title insurance company that pays an insured's claim has a right of subrogation, that is, it may seek reimbursement from other parties liable to the insured. *See, e.g.,* Fidelity Nat'l Title Ins. Co. v. Miller, 264 Cal. Rptr. 17 (Ct. App. 1989).

[D]　Scope of Title Insurance Policy

[1]　Policy Provisions Generally

Most title insurers use standard policy forms developed by the American Land Title Association ("ALTA"). Insurers in a few states (notably California, New York, and Texas) utilize forms that are based on ALTA policies with regional modifications. The national trend, however, is toward uniformity.

There are two basic categories of ALTA forms: the owner's policy and the lender's policy. An insured may, of course, purchase special endorsements that expand the scope of coverage. The discussion below will focus on the terms of the standard ALTA owner's policy, the type most commonly purchased by property owners. ALTA also offers a "plain language" owner's policy that has broader coverage and is growing in popularity. Ironically, this innovative policy creates new problems of ambiguity. Unlike the standard ALTA owner's policy—which has generated an extensive body of interpretative case law—the plain language policy has little or no judicial track record.

The standard ALTA owner's policy has four parts:

(1)　the cover page (which describes the covered risks);

(2)　Schedule A (which states the name of the insured, the estate being insured, the policy premium amount, the policy limit, and the description of the property);

(3)　Schedule B (which lists the exclusions and exceptions to coverage); and

(4)　the Conditions and Stipulations (which impose various procedural requirements concerning the time, manner, and scope of claims).

Despite the increasing use of standard policy forms, ambiguities sometimes arise. In most jurisdictions, ambiguities are interpreted against the insurer and in favor of the insured. Thus, coverage clauses are construed expansively, while exclusionary clauses are construed narrowly.[24]

[2]　Covered Risks

The standard ALTA owner's policy covers four types of risks. Assuming no exception or exclusion applies, the title insurance company will compensate the insured owner if:

(1)　title to the estate is actually held by someone other than the insured owner;

(2)　there is a defect, lien, or encumbrance on the insured owner's title;

(3)　title to the land is unmarketable; or

---

[24] *See generally* White v. Western Title Ins. Co., 710 P.2d 309 (Cal. 1985).

(4)   the insured owner has no right of access to the land.

The first covered risk—if title is held by another—is straightforward. Suppose B obtains an ALTA owner's policy upon her purchase of Greenacre from S, showing that she holds fee simple absolute. B is entitled to compensation, for example, if fee simple absolute in all of Greenacre is actually vested in someone else (e.g., because S's title is founded upon a forged deed) or if another party holds fee simple absolute in part of Greenacre (e.g., because S conveyed away part of Greenacre by an earlier deed).

The scope of the next two covered risks is more troublesome. The policy protection against defects, liens, and encumbrances essentially safeguards the insured against any mortgage, easement,[25] restrictive covenant, lease, tax lien, assessment lien,[26] judgment lien, mechanic's lien, water right,[27] or other interest in land of lesser legal status than a freehold estate, much like the deed covenant against encumbrances (see § 26.02[B][2][c]). And the common law doctrine of marketable title (see § 20.06[B]) largely defines the meaning of "unmarketability" in the title insurance context as well. But—as illustrated by *Lick Mill Creek Apartments v. Chicago Title Insurance Co.*[28] —determining the scope of coverage is sometimes difficult.

Lick Mill was a collision between two different legal worlds: the traditional principles governing title insurance policies and the modern rules imposing strict liability for the cleanup of hazardous substances. In brief, plaintiffs obtained ALTA title policies upon their purchase of a 30-acre industrial tract. They later learned that the land was already contaminated by hazardous substances when they bought it and, accordingly, that they were strictly liable for cleanup costs under federal law (see § 29.10). Plaintiffs cleaned up the site and sought compensation from their title insurance companies.

Plaintiffs first argued that the presence of hazardous substances on the land rendered title unmarketable. But the court distinguished between marketable title, on the one hand, and marketable land, on the other. Here, the physical condition of the property was defective, which presumably impaired the marketability of the land; but plaintiffs' title was marketable. One can hold marketable title to valueless land. Next, plaintiffs asserted that because the transfer of the land carried with it the potential legal liability for future cleanup costs, this liability constituted an "encumbrance." The court rejected this argument, finding that when plaintiffs acquired title there was merely a potential for legal liability in the future—which had not yet crystallized into a judgment or recorded lien—not an existing property interest held by a third person. And the mere physical condition of land, the court reasoned, cannot constitute an encumbrance.

---

[25] *See, e.g.,* White v. Western Title Ins. Co., 710 P.2d 309 (Cal. 1985).

[26] *Cf.* Transamerica Title Ins. Co. v. Johnson, 693 P.2d 697 (Wash. 1985) (title insurance company compensated the insured buyers for loss caused by assessment liens and then sought indemnification from the seller).

[27] *See, e.g.,* White v. Western Title Ins. Co., 710 P.2d 309 (Cal. 1985).

[28] 283 Cal. Rptr. 231 (Ct. App. 1991).

The final covered risk—right of access to a public road—is strictly construed in most jurisdictions. The policy ensures only that a legal right of access exists, not that the route is usable or practical.[29]

[c]　Exceptions and Exclusions

The broad coverage afforded by the standard title insurance policy is limited by both *exceptions* and *exclusions*.[30]

Exceptions are actual or potential title defects that relate to the specific property, and are usually discovered during the insurer's search of title. Suppose B, a potential buyer, asks title company T to issue a policy insuring his title to Greenacre. While examining title to Greenacre, T learns that title is already encumbered with a road easement and a restrictive covenant. T will refuse to insure against these known defects, absent unusual circumstances. Accordingly, it will list them as exceptions to coverage in both its preliminary report and the eventual title insurance policy. Even though the standard policy provides coverage against encumbrances in general, then, these specific encumbrances are not covered. On occasion, a title insurance company will provide coverage against a known potential defect, usually when the risk of loss is remote and a party is willing to indemnify it against any loss; this process is known as *insuring over* or *insuring around* a defect.

Each policy also contains standard, preprinted exclusions, which apply to all properties. These are potential title defects that the title insurance company is unwilling to cover. Typical examples include:

(1)　matters that could be discovered through an inspection or survey of the land (e.g., adverse possession, encroachments, boundary disputes, and acreage shortages);[31]

(2)　problems created by the insured party (e.g., "matters created, suffered, assumed, or agreed to by the insured");

(3)　defects not shown by public records affecting land title;[32] and

---

[29] *See, e.g.,* Gates v. Chicago Title Ins. Co., 813 S.W.2d 10 (Mo. Ct. App. 1991) (legal right of access via route described as "goat path" suitable mainly for foot or horse travel was sufficient to preclude recovery).

[30] Other policy provisions known as "conditions and stipulations" may also affect the scope of coverage. *See, e.g.,* Stewart Title Guar. Co. v. Lunt Land Corp., 347 S.W.2d 584 (Tex. 1961) (policy provided that upon sale of property by insured, insurance company was liable only if insured was successfully sued by buyer on deed warranties).

[31] *See, e.g.,* Gates v. Chicago Title Ins. Co., 813 S.W.2d 10 (Mo. Ct. App. 1991) (exclusion barred recovery based on poor condition of access road); Walker Rogge, Inc. v. Chelsea Title & Guar. Co., 562 A.2d 208 (N.J. 1989) (exclusion barred recovery where survey would have disclosed property contained only 12.5 acres, not 19 acres as seller represented).

[32] *See, e.g.,* Ryczkowski v. Chelsea Title & Guar. Co., 449 P.2d 261 (Nev. 1969) ("wild" deed of easement, outside of chain of title, was excluded from coverage because it was not shown by the public records).

(4)   the impact of any law, ordinance, or regulation relating to the land (e.g., zoning violations, hazardous waste contamination, and building code violations).[33]

[E]   Liability of Title Insurer in Negligence

Suppose B applies to title insurer T for a policy insuring her title in connection with her pending purchase of Blueacre. While searching title to Blueacre, T's employees carelessly overlook a recorded pipeline easement. T provides a preliminary report to B that does not mention the easement. B purchases Blueacre, and at close of escrow T issues a standard ALTA owner's policy to B, which similarly fails to mention the easement. T is clearly liable to B in contract under the policy. But can B instead sue T in tort for negligently searching title? Phrased more broadly, is a title insurance company obligated to conduct a reasonably diligent search of title and to disclose any reasonably discoverable defects to the buyer?[34]

The national case law is split on this controversial issue. The dispute usually hinges on the nature of the preliminary report, title report, binder, commitment or similarly titled document provided by the insurer to the buyer before close of escrow. Is it a summary of title—like an attorney's title opinion—or merely a statement of the terms on which title insurance is offered?

The reason for the dispute is simple enough to identify: tort liability is much broader than contract liability. Any action for breach of contract is limited by the express terms of the policy, including the policy limit, the exclusions, and various procedural restrictions (e.g., a requirement that claims be made within 60 to 90 days after discovery of the loss). A negligence action avoids all these obstacles, potentially allowing a plaintiff like B to recover (a) more than the policy limit, (b) even though the defect is expressly excluded from coverage, and (c) even though she reported the claim too late. Similarly, a tort action may expose the title company to liability for emotional distress and punitive damages, which are not available under a contract theory.

Courts that impose negligence liability reason that the preliminary report is essentially a summary of title.[35] It is well-settled that an attorney or abstractor is liable in tort for a negligently prepared title opinion, abstract, or other summary of title. Thus, for example, if B had obtained a title opinion from attorney A that failed to list the pipeline easement, B could sue A for negligence. These courts explain that the preliminary report

---

[33] *Cf.* Lick Mill Creek Apartments v. Chicago Title Ins. Co., 283 Cal. Rptr. 231 (Ct. App. 1991) (refusing to decide whether this provision excluded coverage for hazardous substance contamination).

[34] *See generally* Joyce D. Palomar, *Title Insurance Companies' Liability for Failure to Search Title and Disclose Record Title*, 20 Creighton L. Rev. 455 (1987); Comment, *Title Insurance: The Duty to Search*, 71 Yale L.J. 1161 (1962).

[35] *See, e.g.,* Moore v. Title Ins. Co., 714 P.2d 1303 (Ariz. Ct. App. 1985). California adopted this approach through case law (*see, e.g.,* White v. Western Title Ins. Co., 710 P.2d 309 (Cal. 1985)), which was later overturned by statute (*see* Cal. Ins. Code § 12340.11).

serves the same function as the traditional title opinion or abstract. Indeed, most buyers appear to believe that the preliminary report is in fact a summary of the state of title, despite express disclaimers to the contrary. Thus, permitting suit in negligence protects the good faith expectations of the ordinary buyer.[36] As the New Jersey Supreme Court explained, "[t]he underlying notion is that the insured has the reasonable expectation that the title company will search the title."[37]

On the other hand, courts rejecting tort liability stress that the relationship between the insurer and the insured is essentially contractual.[38] From this perspective, the insured reasonably expects to receive a title insurance policy that imposes express limitations on the ability to recover damages (e.g., policy limits, exclusions, time limits). To allow the insured to sue in negligence—without these agreed-upon restrictions—would exceed his reasonable expectations. Although the title company routinely conducts a title search before agreeing to insure, this search is undertaken for its own benefit—to determine if it is willing to offer coverage—not for the benefit of the potential insured. Thus, the preliminary report is merely a statement of the terms and conditions on which the insurer is willing to issue its policy, not a representation about the state of title. Courts following this view also express an economic concern: the long-term effect of negligence liability would be to increase the overall cost of title insurance to buyers in general, because title companies would raise rates to compensate for the expanded risk.

[F] Perspectives on Title Insurance

Title insurance policies offer excellent title protection, particularly when compared to deed covenants or attorney opinions of title. The main advantage is solvency: title insurance companies maintain sufficient monetary reserves to satisfy potential claims, while deed covenants and attorneys' title opinions are effectively worthless if the seller or attorney is insolvent. And title insurance covers a broader range of title defects than either the attorney's opinion or the special warranty deed.

The principal criticism of title insurance is simply that it costs too much. During the 1980s, for example, the title insurance industry paid out only about 8% of its collected premiums to satisfy claims. In the same era, the comparable loss payout ratio for most casualty insurers was 80%. Why? Title insurers explain that a large percentage of each premium dollar is used to search and examine title, a cost not faced by other types of insurers.

---

[36] *See also* Transamerica Title Ins. Co. v. Johnson, 693 P.2d 697 (Wash. 1985) (even if insurer's preliminary report is deemed an abstract, the insurer is not liable to a noninsured party who failed to rely on the negligently prepared abstract).

[37] Walker Rogge, Inc. v. Chelsea Title & Guar. Co., 562 A.2d 208, 218 (N.J. 1989).

[38] *See, e.g.,* Walter Rogge, Inc. v. Chelsea Title & Guar. Co., 562 A.2d 208 (N.J. 1989); Greenberg v. Stewart Title Guar. Co., 492 N.W.2d 147 (Wis. 1992). The *Walter Rogge* court further suggested, however, that a title company might be held liable in tort if it voluntarily assumed an independent duty to the buyer (e.g., by performing escrow work for the sales transaction).

A secondary criticism is that the reasonable expectations of most insured buyers differ from the literal terms of their title insurance policies. The average buyer has little or no understanding about either the basic scope of coverage or the detailed exclusions from coverage. Rather, the buyer believes in general terms that the policy will protect against any title problem. Modern courts attempt to bridge this gap largely by construing policy ambiguities against the insurer, a process which presumes—incorrectly in most instances—that the insured actually read the policy form before purchase. The growing popularity of the "plain language" policy may alleviate this problem over time.

§ 26.05 Registration of Title

After studying the notable defects in the land title recording system discussed above, a neutral observer might suggest an alternative system: empower a government agency to determine who holds title.[39] Under such a title registration system—often called the *Torrens system* after its inventor—a government agency issues a *certificate of title* that establishes land title. The certificate identifies the current title holder and lists all easements, covenants, liens, mortgages, and other encumbrances on title.[40] While quite popular in England, the Torrens system is available only in a handful of states. Ironically, virtually all states use a Torrens-like system for the registration of automobiles.

An example illustrates the mechanics of the Torrens system. Suppose B is planning to purchase Redacre from O. B can search title to Redacre simply by inspecting the current certificate of title that is on file at the responsible agency. If the certificate states that O holds fee simple absolute in Redacre, free and clear of any encumbrances, for example, B can safely proceed with the purchase. B can perform this examination quickly and cheaply, without the assistance of a title insurance company, attorney, or abstractor. Once O conveys title to B, B will bring his deed to the agency so that it can issue a new certificate of title that lists B as the current owner.

What if the agency makes a mistake? Suppose, for example, that title to Redacre was actually vested in X at the time of the O-B sale, and thus the certificate of title should have identified X as the owner. In a situation like this, the certificate of title is still legally effective and, accordingly, B is the legal owner of Redacre. An indemnity fund compensates anyone whose property rights are lost through error; X's only remedy is to file a claim against this fund.

The future of the Torrens system in the United States is bleak. Scholars uniformly praise the system on efficiency grounds: it is both more accurate

---

[39] *See generally* C. Dent Bostick, *Land Title Registration: An English Solution to an American Problem*, 63 Ind. L.J. 55 (1987); John L. McCormack, *Torrens and Recording: Land Title Assurance in the Computer Age*, 18 Wm. Mitchell L. Rev. 61 (1992).

[40] *See, e.g.*, United States v. Ryan, 124 F. Supp. 1 (D. Minn. 1954), *rev'd*, 253 F.2d 944 (8th Cir. 1958) (judgment creating federal tax lien was never filed with registrar of titles in accordance with state law and thus did not encumber parcel registered under Torrens system).

and less expensive than the traditional recording system. During the twentieth century, 21 states adopted the Torrens system as an additional method of title assurance. But the promise of the system was never realized because only a small number of owners chose to register their titles. Custom, inertia, the initial cost of registration, and the vigorous opposition of title insurance companies undoubtedly contributed to this unhappy result. Many states accordingly abandoned the system. Although Torrens is still an available alternative in 10 states, it flourishes only in isolated pockets. The system is most successful in Hawaii, where about 45% of the land is registered.

Chapter 27

ADVERSE POSSESSION

SYNOPSIS

§ 27.01 "Title by Theft"?

Suppose O owns title to Blueacre, an unimproved 100-acre forest parcel. O accepts a post with the United Nations, and moves to Switzerland. Well aware that O will be absent for years, A takes possession of Blueacre; he posts several "No Trespassing" signs and builds a small cabin. Over the next ten years, A lives in the cabin each summer, harvests timber each fall, cuts a Christmas tree each winter, and gathers wild blueberries each spring. After 11 years, O returns. Who owns Blueacre? In many jurisdictions, A is now the owner by adverse possession.[1]

At first blush, adverse possession seems inconsistent with common sense. If O never agreed to transfer his title, how could he lose it? Even worse, why should A—who appears to be little better than a thief—acquire title? Indeed, the doctrine of adverse possession often strikes law students as "title by theft or robbery, a primitive method of acquiring land without paying for it."[2]

So why does adverse possession exist? The answer to this question tells us much about the policies underlying American property law. Property rights are defined by law, not by public expectations. For utilitarian reasons, our legal system normally respects the autonomy of landowners to use—or not to use—their land as they see fit. Yet, if private property exists to maximize the overall happiness of society, as utilitarian theory posits, then owner autonomy must be limited. Perhaps the clearest common law limit is adverse possession. Thus, the doctrine provides a window into the jurisprudential foundations of property law.[3]

§ 27.02 Evolution of Adverse Possession

As early as 2000 B.C., the Code of Hammurabi recognized a primitive form of adverse possession. A person who spent three years using a house, garden, or field owned by a soldier absent on military duty acquired title to the property, even if the soldier later returned.[4] This standard tended to keep land in productive use. Otherwise, the land might remain idle, awaiting the return of a presumably dead owner.

Scholars tracing the evolution of adverse possession in the Anglo-American legal system begin with the 1275 Statute of Westminster,[5] which limited actions for the recovery of land by precluding a suitor from alleging dated claims. In 1639, the Statute of Limitations required that suits to

---

[1] *See generally* Robert C. Ellickson, *Adverse Possession and Perpetuities Law: Two Dents in the Libertarian Model of Property Rights*, 64 Wash. U. L.Q. 723 (1986); R.H. Helmholz, *Adverse Possession and Subjective Intent*, 61 Wash. U. L.Q. 331 (1983); Thomas W. Merrill, *Property Rules, Liability Rules, and Adverse Possession*, 79 Nw. U. L. Rev. 1122 (1984–1985); John G. Sprankling, *An Environmental Critique of Adverse Possession*, 79 Cornell L. Rev. 816 (1994)

[2] Henry W. Ballentine, *Title by Adverse Possession*, 32 Harv. L. Rev. 135, 135 (1918).

[3] For discussion of adverse possession of personal property, see § 7.02.

[4] The Hammurabi Code and the Sinaitic Legislation 32–33 (Chilperic Edwards ed. 1904).

[5] Statute of Westminster I, 3 Edw. I, c. 39 (1275).

recover the possession of land be brought within 20 years.[6] In early England, land records were fragmentary; lengthy possession of land served as the best evidence of ownership. The prudent owner would presumably inspect his property regularly and eject any trespassers. Accordingly, if suit was not brought against an occupant acting like an owner, this absence of litigation could be reasonably interpreted as public acceptance of the occupant's claim to title.

Adverse possession flourished in the newly-independent United States. Land title conflicts in the new nation were widespread for several reasons. Undeveloped wilderness covered almost the entire land surface. Land was rarely surveyed, and boundary lines were usually unmarked. Land title was typically held by absentee speculators; but pioneer settlers without any title claims often appropriated vacant land, cleared timber, and started farms. These factors combined to create massive title confusion. As the Supreme Court observed in one early case, "[c]onflicts of title were unfortunately so numerous that no one knew from whom to buy or take lands with safety."[7] Over the course of the nineteenth century, American courts modified English adverse possession law to suit these uniquely American conditions.

§ 27.03 Requirements for Adverse Possession

[A] Overview

Adverse possession is a curious mixture of statutory and case law. Each state has a statute of limitations that establishes a time period for an owner to bring suit to recover possession of land from a wrongful occupant—typically 10, 15, or 20 years. However, most of the requirements for adverse possession are imposed by case law.

In general, an occupant acquires title to land by adverse possession if his possession is:

(1)   actual,

(2)   exclusive,

(3)   open and notorious,

(4)   adverse (or hostile) under a claim of right,

(5)   and continuous,

(6)   for the statutory period.[8]

Compliance with these elements is usually measured by a simple yardstick: the conduct of an average or "reasonable" owner given the location, nature, and character of the land. For example, if a reasonable owner would only use a remote desert tract for sheep grazing during a ten-week period each

---

[6] 21 Jam. I, ch. 16 (1623).

[7] Clark v. Smith, 38 U.S. (13 Pet.) 195, 202 (1839).

[8] *See generally* Teson v. Vasquez, 561 S.W.2d 119 (Mo. Ct. App. 1977); Chaplin v. Sanders, 676 P.2d 431 (Wash. 1984).

spring, the adverse possessor who uses the land in this manner for ten weeks annually is deemed to hold "continuous" possession.[9]

In some states, the traditional elements of adverse possession are modified or supplanted by legislation. For example, statutes in one group of states detail the precise actions that constitute actual possession (*see* [B][2], *below*). In other jurisdictions, statutes require the occupant to pay all taxes assessed against the land (*see* [H], *below*).

[B] "Actual" Possession

[1] Majority Approach

The adverse possessor must take *actual possession* of the land. Some authorities call this element *actual entry*, but this phrasing is misleading because more than mere entry is needed. Under the majority view, this element requires that the claimant must physically use the particular parcel of land in the same manner that a reasonable owner would.[10] Thus, the acts necessary to meet this requirement vary from parcel to parcel, depending on the nature, character, and location of the land, and the uses to which it may be devoted.[11]

Depending on the circumstances, this requirement may be satisfied by residence, cultivation, improvement, grazing, pasturing, hunting, fishing, timber harvesting, mining, or other economically-productive activities. For example, adverse possessor A1 can obtain actual possession of a house by residing there, because this is how an ordinary owner would use a residence. If A2 is attempting to adversely possess a 100-acre tract of farm land, however, A2 presumably must cultivate the land, just as an average owner would do. Yet adverse possessor A3, seeking to obtain title to a 1,000-acre parcel of wild, undeveloped land, need only perform the activities that are suited or adapted to the land in its natural condition, such as timber harvesting, mining, grazing, or the like.[12]

[2] Minority Approach

Statutes in ten states—including California,[13] Florida,[14] and New York[15]—specify the particular conduct that constitutes actual possession. When adverse possession is premised on a mere claim of right (*see* [E], *below*), the claimant must cultivate, improve, or substantially enclose the

---

[9] *See, e.g.,* Cooper v. Carter Oil Co., 316 P.2d 320 (Utah 1957).

[10] *See, e.g.,* Jarvis v. Gillespie, 587 A.2d 981 (Vt. 1991); *see also* Ewing v. Burnet, 36 U.S. (11 Pet.) 41 (1837).

[11] When mineral rights have been severed from surface ownership, however, occupancy of the land surface alone is not deemed actual possession of the underlying minerals.

[12] *Cf.* Failoni v. Chicago & North Western Ry. Co., 195 N.E.2d 619 (Ill. 1964) (plaintiff's occupation of land surface did not constitute possession of subsurface mineral estate).

[13] Cal. Code Civ. Proc. § 323.

[14] Fla. Stat. Ann. § 95.16.

[15] N.Y. Real Prop. Actions & Proc. L. § 522.

property.[16] The claimant who holds color of title (*see* [3], *below*), however, may also meet the actual possession requirement by cutting firewood or timber for fences.

These antiquated standards were developed to govern adverse possession of rural, undeveloped land, and have little application to urban property. For example, the adverse possessor who permanently resides in a Florida condominium presumably lacks the "actual" possession required by statute; he has failed to cultivate, improve, or enclose the property.

[3] Exception: Constructive Possession

In general, a claimant can acquire title only to the land he or she actually occupies. For example, if A cultivates five acres of the 500-acre farm known as Brownacre, and meets all other requirements for adverse possession, she obtains title only to the five cultivated acres, not all 500 acres.

A special rule applies if the claimant has *color of title*.[17] Color of title exists when an adverse possessor has a claim to the land based on a defective document that purports to transfer title, such as an invalid deed or will. The claimant with color of title who has actual possession of part of the land described in the deed or other document is deemed to be in *constructive possession* of the entire parcel. Thus, if A holds an invalid deed to Brownacre, she will acquire title to the entire property, even though she occupied only five acres.

[C] "Exclusive" Possession

The adverse possessor must hold *exclusive* possession. In effect, this means that possession must not be shared with either the true owner or the general public. Yet absolute exclusivity is not required. The claimant's possession must be as exclusive as would characterize an owner's normal use for such land.[18]

In order to interrupt the claimant's exclusive possession, the owner must retake possession of the property. How? Suppose adverse possessor A regularly cuts timber on Greenacre, an uninhabited 100-acre forest tract owned by O. O will not interrupt A's possession merely by visiting Greenacre on occasion. Rather, O must retake possession of Greenacre by using it in a manner that is suited to its condition (e.g., by removing firewood, cutting Christmas trees, or harvesting timber). On the other hand, if the property in question is a fifth-floor condominium unit, O can retake possession only by physically occupying the unit, changing the door locks to exclude A, or taking similar steps.[19]

---

[16] *See, e.g.,* Van Valkenburgh v. Lutz, 106 N.E.2d 28 (N.Y. 1952) (finding insufficient evidence of cultivation to justify adverse possession).

[17] *See* Powell on Real Property ¶ 1013[2][g] (Michael Allan Wolf ed., Matthew Bender).

[18] *See, e.g.,* Roche v. Town of Fairfield, 442 A.2d 911 (Conn. 1982).

[19] *Cf.* Mendonca v. Cities Serv. Oil Co., 237 N.E.2d 16 (Mass. 1968) (finding that owner's removal of fences and use of disputed strip for storage for three or four weeks interrupted occupant's exclusive possession).

In like fashion, isolated visits by third parties do not destroy exclusivity. An occasional hiker or hunter might cross through Greenacre, for example, without interrupting A's possession.[20] An adverse possessor must exclude third parties only to the extent that a reasonable owner would do so. It would be both difficult and expensive for a claimant to absolutely bar all third parties from trespassing on a large tract of unimproved land like Greenacre. Further, many hospitable owners of unimproved forest land routinely allow third parties to pick berries, dig clams, hunt, hike, fish, and conduct like activities.

An interesting question arises when two adverse possessors both occupy the same property. Suppose A1 and A2 both occupy Redacre, a farm owned by O. Arguably, neither A1 nor A2 has exclusive possession. Does the presence of A1 interrupt A2's exclusive possession or vice versa? In this rare situation, courts normally rule that two adverse possessors who hold joint possession will acquire title as tenants in common.

[D] "Open and Notorious" Possession

The claimant's possession must be *open and notorious*.[21] The acts of possession must be so visible and obvious that a reasonable owner who inspects the land will receive notice of an adverse title claim.[22] It is not necessary to show that the owner obtained actual knowledge of the claim,[23] or that the owner conducted an inspection; the owner is charged with the knowledge that a diligent inspection would reveal. On the other hand, furtive, secret, or hidden activities do not satisfy this requirement.[24]

Suppose O owns title to Greyacre, a 40-acre parcel of unimproved farm land. Adverse possessor A grows corn on the land for 15 years; A plows the land, plants seeds, sprays pesticides, nurtures the crop, and finally harvests the corn. On these facts, A's possession is open and notorious. If O inspected Greyacre, he would see clear evidence of A's activity on the land, and thus learn about A's title claim.[25] Now suppose instead that A never cultivates Greyacre. Instead, A merely visits Greyacre at night once a month in order to observe the stars. A is careful to show no light during these visits; and

---

[20] *Cf.* Nome 2000 v. Fagerstrom, 799 P.2d 304 (Alaska 1990) (allowing third parties to pick berries or fish did not destroy exclusive possession of remote parcel); Peters v. Juneau-Douglas Girl Scout Council, 519 P.2d 826 (Alaska 1974) (presence of occasional clamdiggers, picnickers, and others on beach area did not destroy exclusive possession of semi-wilderness parcel).

[21] This requirement is satisfied, however, if the owner has actual notice of the claimant's possession. *See* Chaplin v. Sanders, 676 P.2d 431 (Wash. 1984).

[22] *See, e.g.,* Porter v. Posey, 592 S.W.2d 844 (Mo. Ct. App. 1979); Jarvis v. Gillespie, 587 A.2d 981 (Vt. 1991); *see also* Marengo Cave Co. v. Ross, 10 N.E.2d 917, 920 (Ind. 1937) (the claimant "'must unfurl his flag' on the land, and 'keep it flying,' so that the owner may see, if he will, that an enemy has invaded his domains, and planted the standard of conquest").

[23] *But see* Mannillo v. Gorski, 255 A.2d 258 (N.J. 1969) (minor encroachment along common boundary is not open and notorious unless true owner has actual knowledge).

[24] *See, e.g.,* Marengo Cave Co. v. Ross, 10 N.E.2d 917 (Ind. 1937) (use of subsurface cave was not open and notorious).

[25] *See, e.g.,* Teson v. Vasquez, 561 S.W.2d 119 (Mo. Ct. App. 1977).

his activities leave behind no visible trace that O might discover aside from a few footprints. A's actions fail to meet this requirement.

What acts establish open and notorious possession? Activities such as residing on the land, building fences or other improvements, or cultivating crops are almost always sufficient. This requirement is especially troublesome, however, in cases involving wild, unimproved land such as forests, prairies, wetlands, or deserts. Almost by definition, the acts that constitute possession of such lands are often minor and infrequent, and most courts seem to accept a lower degree of openness and notoriety.[26] Depending on the circumstances, activities such as grazing livestock, cutting wild hay, harvesting timber, gathering firewood, clearing brush, fishing, hunting, posting "no trespassing" signs, or a combination of these actions may satisfy the requirement.[27]

[E]   "Adverse" or "Hostile" Possession Under "Claim of Right"

[1]   Overview

The most confusing element of adverse possession involves the adverse possessor's state of mind. There is little judicial agreement even about how to label this element. Some courts insist that possession be *adverse*, while others demand that possession be *hostile*. However, most authorities agree that these terms have the same meaning. Adding to this semantic chaos, many courts also formally insist that the adverse possessor have a *claim of right* or *claim of title*; but this is merely a component of adversity or hostility. Perhaps the most common phrasing is to require *adverse possession under a claim of right*.[28]

[2]   General Principles

[a]   Three Approaches

What state of mind must the adverse possessor have? There are three different approaches to the issue.[29] A growing majority of states follows

---

[26] *See, e.g.,* Alaska Nat'l Bank v. Linck, 559 P.2d 1049 (Alaska 1977); Nome 2000 v. Fagerstrom, 799 P.2d 304 (Alaska 1990); Chaplin v. Sanders, 676 P.2d 431 (Wash. 1984).

[27] *See, e.g.,* Nome 2000 v. Fagerstrom, 799 P.2d 304 (Alaska 1990) (building outhouse and other improvements, tree planting, camping, and related acts held open and notorious); Monroe v. Rawlings, 49 N.W.2d 55 (Mich. 1951) (building hunting cabin, visiting cabin six times each year, selling pulpwood, and related acts held open and notorious).

[28] *See* Powell on Real Property ¶ 1013[2][f] (Michael Allan Wolf ed., Matthew Bender).

[29] Van Valkenburgh v. Lutz, 106 N.E.2d 28 (N.Y. 1952) illustrates the judicial confusion concerning this element. The majority opinion first stated that the Lutzes could not adversely possess the land beneath a small shed because they knew they did not own the land; this suggests the court was using the good faith standard. Yet later, the same opinion rejected the Lutzes' claim to land underneath their encroaching garage, because they mistakenly thought the garage was entirely on their own land; this result reflects the intentional trespass standard. Finally, the dissent argued convincingly that New York law follows the objective test.

an *objective test*: the adverse possessor's state of mind is irrelevant. A number of states utilize a *good faith test*: the adverse possessor must believe in good faith that he owns the land. A few scattered decisions still reflect what might be called the *intentional trespass test*: the adverse possessor must know that he does not own the land and must intend to take title from the true owner.

However, all jurisdictions agree on one point: if the true owner authorizes or consents to the possession, it is not considered adverse or hostile.[30] For example, absent unusual circumstances, a tenant's possession is not deemed adverse or hostile toward the landlord. By definition, a landlord expressly consents to the tenant's occupancy. Similarly, possession by the owner's agent or a member of the owner's family is normally permissive, not adverse or hostile.

[b] Objective Test

In states that follow the majority view, the adverse possessor's subjective belief about who owns the land is irrelevant.[31] If the possessor uses the land as a reasonable owner would use it—*without permission from the true owner*—this element is satisfied. As one court explained, "[t]he 'hostility/ claim of right' element of adverse possession requires only that the claimant treat the land as his own as against the world throughout the statutory period."[32] The possessor's conduct is deemed objectively hostile and adverse, regardless of subjective intent. Under the objective test, any "claim of right" or "claim of title" is pure fiction; the possessor need not prove a rightful title claim or any actual intent to claim title at all.

In effect, the objective test asks only one question: did the true owner authorize the possession? If the possession is unauthorized and the other standard criteria are satisfied—actual, exclusive, open and notorious, and continuous possession for the statutory period—adverse possession is established.

Suppose A enters into possession of Greenacre, a 100-acre farm, fully aware that it is actually owned by O. Without O's permission, A resides in the farm house, cultivates the land, and takes related steps over a tenyear period that meet the other adverse possession criteria. Under the objective test, A's possession is deemed adverse and hostile under a claim of right, simply because she used the land as would a reasonable owner, without O's consent. The same result follows if A believed in good faith that she owned Greenacre or if she had no belief at all about who owned the land.

---

[30] *See, e.g.,* Charlton v. Crocker, 665 S.W.2d 56 (Mo. Ct. App. 1984) (no hostility where, inter alia, claimants asked permission of true owners before performing brush clearing on land and recorded a mechanic's lien against the property when the owners refused to pay for their services).

[31] *See, e.g.,* Nome 2000 v. Fagerstrom, 799 P.2d 304 (Alaska 1990); Peters v. Juneau-Douglas Girl Scout Council, 519 P.2d 826 (Alaska 1974); Chaplin v. Sanders, 676 P.2d 431 (Wash. 1984).

[32] Chaplin v. Sanders, 676 P.2d 431, 436 (Wash. 1984).

The justification for the objective test is straightforward. Under the dominant view, adverse possession is a specialized statute of limitations to recover possession of land (*see* § 27.06[B]). The occupant's conduct on the land—regardless of intent—affords notice to the true owner that triggers the running of the statutory period for filing suit. Hence, the occupant's subjective state of mind is irrelevant. The same result logically follows under most other theories used to explain adverse possession, although for varying reasons (*see* § 27.06). A secondary rationale is ease of administration. As the Pennsylvania Supreme Court observed, "discerning the mental state of an adverse possessor is, at best, an exercise in guesswork; and at worst, impossible."[33] The objective test provides the usual benefits of a "bright line" standard.

[c] Good Faith Test

In a dwindling minority of states, the adverse possessor must believe in good faith that he owns title to the land.[34] In other words, the possessor must innocently—but mistakenly—think that he is the true owner. Under this approach, the claim of right standard makes sense: the adverse possessor must indeed have a title claim that he subjectively believes is rightful. Why insist on good faith? This test reflects one of the secondary theories used to justify adverse possession: a method of curing minor title defects and thus protecting the title of the intended owner (*see* § 27.06[C]).

Assume that D initially owns Greenacre. D executes a deed that appears to convey title to A, but the deed is invalid due to lack of delivery. One week later, D dies intestate and all of his property—including title to Greenacre—descends by operation of law to O. If A holds possession of Greenacre under the good-faith belief that D conveyed title to her before his death, she satisfies this element of adverse possession. On the other hand, suppose A takes possession after learning from her attorney that the D-A deed is legally ineffective; in a state that follows the good faith test, she cannot acquire title by adverse possession.

The status of the good faith test is controversial. Most commentators agree that it remains a minority view.[35] However, although only a few courts expressly demand good faith, Professor Richard Helmholz argues that all modern courts implicitly require it.[36] Based on a survey of contemporary decisions, he concludes that only good faith occupants actually succeed in establishing title by adverse possession.

[d] Intentional Trespass Test

A few decisions suggest that the adverse possessor must (1) know that he does not actually own the land and (2) subjectively intend to take title

---

[33] Tioga Coal Co. v. Supermarkets Gen. Corp., 546 A.2d 1, 4 (Pa. 1988).

[34] *See, e.g.,* Carpenter v. Ruperto, 315 N.W.2d 782 (Iowa 1982).

[35] *See, e.g.,* Roger A. Cunningham, *Adverse Possession and Subjective Intent: A Reply to Professor Helmholz,* 64 Wash. U. L.Q. 1 (1986).

[36] R.H. Helmholz, *Adverse Possession and Subjective Intent,* 61 Wash. U. L.Q. 331 (1983).

from the true owner.[37] This "land piracy" approach to adverse possession effectively rewards intentional wrongdoers, while offering no protection to good faith occupants. Under this view, A can acquire Greenacre by adverse possession only if she affirmatively intends to wrest title from O, the true owner. This standard is both unjust and illogical. Although the intentional trespass test is—understandably—encountered only rarely, some states still use a variant of this standard in the specialized context of boundary line disputes (see [3], below).

[3] Special Problem: Boundary Line Disputes

Assume A and O own adjacent parcels of farm land. For 35 years, A believes that a wire fence marks the boundary line between the two parcels. During this period, A regularly cultivates all the land on his side of the fence and otherwise treats it as his own property. O commissions a survey that reveals that the true boundary line is 20 feet away from the fence, onto what A believed was his own land. Under cross-examination, A admits that he only intended to claim the land up to wherever the true boundary was located. Has A acquired title to the disputed 20-foot strip by adverse possession? Most jurisdictions apply the objective test (see [2][b], above) in this situation.[38] Under this approach, A's subjective intent is irrelevant. Because A occupied the strip without O's permission and met all other adverse possession elements, he owns the land.

However, a substantial minority of states follows a contrary view known as the "Maine doctrine."[39] In order to prove hostility in a boundary line dispute, the adverse possessor must intend to claim title to all the land up to a specific line (e.g., a fence, hedge, or road) *whether or not* it is the true boundary. Because A mistakenly believed that he owned the strip, he lacked the "claim of right" required for hostility under this view. The Maine doctrine is uniformly condemned by scholars and is slowly disappearing.

[F] "Continuous" Possession

[1] General Principles

The claimant must hold *continuous* possession during the statutory period. Yet this standard does not mandate that the claimant physically occupy the land every minute. The required continuity is measured by the location, nature, and character of the land.[40] Thus, the claimant's acts of possession need only be as continuous—or as sporadic—as those of a

---

[37] *Cf.* Van Valkenburgh v. Lutz, 106 N.E.2d 28 (N.Y. 1952) (suggesting that occupants' good faith belief that they owned land under encroaching garage precluded hostility).

[38] *See, e.g.,* Gilardi v. Hallam, 636 P.2d 588 (Cal. 1981); Brown v. Gobble, 474 S.E.2d 489 (W.Va. 1996); *cf.* Mannillo v. Gorski, 255 A.2d 258 (N.J. 1969) (adopting majority rule, but holding that true owner must have actual knowledge of minor encroachment along common boundary line in order for possession to be deemed open and notorious).

[39] *See* McQueen v. Black, 425 N.W.2d 203 (Mich. Ct. App. 1988).

[40] *See* Nome 2000 v. Fagerstrom, 799 P.2d 304 (Alaska 1990).

reasonable owner.[41] Depending on the nature of the land, possession may be deemed "continuous" even though there are long periods when the claimant does not use the land at all.

In the case of wild, unimproved land, for example, activities as rare as gathering firewood a few times each year or using the land for stock grazing for a few weeks may be sufficiently continuous if a reasonable owner would use the land in this manner. On the other hand, if the property in question is a single-family house in a residential suburb, the claimant presumably must reside in the house. Even in this situation, continuous possession does not mean constant presence. The reasonable homeowner usually leaves home to go to work, run errands, visit friends, take vacations, and so forth, and the adverse possessor may do the same.

Halfway between these two situations is the illustrative case of *Howard v. Kunto*,[42] involving adverse possession of a beach house property. For over 30 years, the Kuntos or their predecessors occupied the house during the summer, allowing it to remain vacant during the rest of the year, under the good faith belief that they owned title. A later survey revealed that the Kuntos in fact owned an adjacent lot, not the beach house. When the true owners of the beach house sued to quiet title, the Kuntos asserted the defense of adverse possession. The court held that seasonal occupancy was continuous possession because the average owner of similar property would use it in this way: "We reject the conclusion that summer occupancy only of a summer beach home destroys the continuity of possession required by the statute."[43]

The occupant's continuous possession may be interrupted by actions of the true owner. If the owner reenters the land and retakes possession in open and notorious manner, the required continuity (and exclusivity) ends in most states. Suppose O owns Blueacre, which is located in a jurisdiction that requires a ten-year period for adverse possession; A occupies Blueacre for eight years in a manner that satisfies all requirements except duration. When O retakes possession of Blueacre during the ninth year, this breaks A's continuous possession.[44] If A reenters Blueacre after O departs, he can acquire title only by ten more years of adverse possession.

[2] Exception: Tacking

Assume that O owns title to Redacre, a home located in a jurisdiction that requires a ten-year period for adverse possession. A1 takes possession of Redacre and meets all adverse possession requirements for seven years. A1 then conveys her interest in Redacre to A2, who similarly complies with all adverse possession elements for the next five years. If O now brings an

---

[41] *See, e.g.*, Jarvis v. Gillespie, 587 A.2d 981 (Vt. 1991) (holding sporadic use of unimproved parcel for uses such as cutting firewood, parking vehicles, cutting brush, storing wood, and cutting Christmas trees was continuous possession).

[42] 477 P.2d 210 (Wash. Ct. App. 1970).

[43] Howard v. Kunto, 477 P.2d 210, 213 (Wash. Ct. App. 1970).

[44] *Cf.* Mendonca v. Cities Serv. Oil Co., 237 N.E.2d 16 (Mass. 1968) (owner's occupancy of disputed strip for three or four weeks broke occupant's continuity of possession).

ejectment action, can A2 successfully assert adverse possession as a defense?

Successive periods of adverse possession by different persons may sometimes be combined together to satisfy the statutory duration requirement. This process is commonly known as *tacking*.[45] Tacking is permissible only if the successive claimants are in *privity* with each other. In this context, privity arises when one claimant transfers possessory rights to another. This transfer is most commonly made by deed (as in the A1-A2 deed above),[46] but can also be effected through devise or intestate succession.[47]

Conversely, no privity exists between successive trespassers. Suppose A1 simply abandons possession of Redacre after seven years. A2 watches A1 leave, and then immediately takes possession himself. If O later sues in ejectment, A2 cannot utilize tacking.

[G] For the Statutory Period

The requisite period for adverse possession varies substantially from state to state, ranging from 5 to 40 years. The vast majority of states, however, utilize periods of 10, 15, or 20 years. In general, western states tend to require a shorter period (10 years or less), northeastern states usually demand a longer period (20 years or more), and other regions fall somewhere in the middle.[48]

Special circumstances—for example, if the owner is a minor—may extend or "toll" the statutory period (*see* § 27.05[A]). And some jurisdictions shorten the period for adverse possession if the claimant holds color of title (*see* [B][3], *above*).

[H] Plus Payment of Taxes?

Statutes in some states impose an additional requirement: the adverse possessor must pay all taxes assessed against the property.[49] These statutes were apparently the product of lobbying efforts in the late nineteenth century by owners of large undeveloped tracts of western land—particularly railroads—who were concerned that squatters could readily meet the common law standards for adverse possession.

§ 27.04 Procedural Aspects of Adverse Possession

Adverse possession is sometimes described as a specialized statute of limitations. Yet this characterization is misleading. A statute of limitations

---

[45] *See, e.g.,* Carpenter v. Huffman, 314 So. 2d 65 (Ala. 1975); Porter v. Posey, 592 S.W.2d 844 (Mo. Ct. App. 1979).

[46] *See, e.g.,* Carpenter v. Huffman, 314 So. 2d 65 (Ala. 1975); Howard v. Kunto, 477 P.2d 210 (Wash. Ct. App. 1970); *cf.* Brown v. Gobble, 474 S.E.2d 489 (W. Va. 1996).

[47] *See, e.g.,* Belotti v. Bickhardt, 127 N.E. 239 (N.Y. 1920).

[48] *See* Powell on Real Property ¶ 1014 (Michael Allan Wolf ed., Matthew Bender).

[49] *See* Powell on Real Property ¶ 1013[2][h][i] (Michael Allan Wolf ed., Matthew Bender).

is merely a defense against litigation; it does not create any affirmative rights. However, successful adverse possession automatically extinguishes the former owner's title and creates a new title in the adverse possessor by operation of law.

Suppose A takes possession of Goldacre, a farm owned by O, and eventually satisfies all requirements for adverse possession. A now holds title to Goldacre. If O now sues to eject A from possession, A will assert his title as a defense to the action. In this setting, adverse possession functions much like an ordinary statute of limitations.

But what if O never files suit? As a successful adverse possessor, A now owns Goldacre; A may use the land as he wishes. A does confront a practical problem: O is still listed as the owner in the public land records. In order to correct record title—and thus allow A to easily transfer his rights—A will probably need to record a judgment or deed that confirms his ownership. A will either file a quiet title action against O or demand that O execute a quitclaim deed in A's favor.

§ 27.05 Special Restrictions on Adverse Possession

[A] Minor, Incompetent, or Imprisoned Owner

The limitations period for adverse possession is extended or *tolled* when the owner is unable to protect his interests due to a *disability*. Suppose adverse possessor A enters into possession of Goldacre in 1985 when O, the record owner, is only two years old. Statutes in all states afford special protection to a minor like O—who is incapable of suing to eject A—by extending the period required for successful adverse possession. Infancy[50] and mental incapacity[51] are recognized as disabilities in most states. In some states, imprisonment or absence from the jurisdiction also qualify as disabilities.[52]

How does a disability extend the limitations period? States differ. Some states toll the limitations period until the disability ends; others provide that the entire statutory period begins running only after the disability ends. However, the most common approach is to allow suit for a limited time after the disability ends.[53] For instance, in the Goldacre hypothetical above, assume the state's 15-year limitations period would normally end in 2000. But a state statute provides that a person under a disability may bring suit within ten years after the disability ends. If O is deemed an adult at age 21, O's disability ends in 2004; thus, O may bring suit to eject A until 2014.

In many states, a disability extends the period *only if* it already existed when the adverse possession began. Suppose that A enters into adverse

---

[50] *See, e.g.,* Adams v. Adams, 66 S.E.2d 809 (S.C. 1951).

[51] *See, e.g.,* Memmott v. Bosh, 520 P.2d 1342 (Utah 1974).

[52] *See* Powell on Real Property ¶ 1014[3] (Michael Allan Wolf ed., Matthew Bender).

[53] *See* Powell on Real Property ¶ 1014[3] (Michael Allan Wolf ed., Matthew Bender).

possession of Goldacre in 1985; O obtains title to the land by a 1988 devise. In this situation, O's disability is irrelevant. The 15-year limitations period expires in 2000.

[B] Government Entity As Owner

At common law, land owned by a government entity was immune from adverse possession. Why? Courts traditionally explain that government lands are held in trust for all citizens. Thus, the goal that adverse possession seeks to serve—the overall welfare of society—is best protected by retaining public ownership, not by transferring title to a private owner. Most states still follow this traditional rule. [54]

Statutes in some states authorize adverse possession of lands owned by state or local governments, usually with special restrictions. Several impose a longer period for adverse possession of such lands. Others apply the doctrine only to lands held in a "proprietary" capacity (e.g., state-owned farm land leased to a private farmer), not in a "governmental" capacity (e.g., a courthouse). [55]

Federal lands are subject to a statutory version of adverse possession. In 1986, Congress enacted legislation that overturned the traditional immunity rule in limited circumstances; to qualify, the claimant must occupy the land for over 20 years in good faith reliance on a claim of title and either cultivate the land or construct improvements. [56]

[C] Cotenant As Owner

Each cotenant has an equal right to occupy the property. Accordingly, possession by one cotenant is normally not considered adverse or hostile to other cotenants. In order to begin adverse possession, the cotenant in possession must unequivocally claim sole ownership of the land by either (1) physically ousting the cotenants or (2) taking other steps that clearly notify cotenants of the claim. [57] Absent physical ouster, many jurisdictions insist on actual notice to cotenants, while others simply require open and notorious actions that demonstrate hostility.

[D] Landlord As Owner

In general, the tenant who holds possession of leased premises with permission of the landlord cannot assert adverse possession. When the true owner authorizes possession, it is not adverse or hostile. However, the

---

[54] *See* Powell on Real Property ¶ 1015 (Michael Allan Wolf ed., Matthew Bender).

[55] *Cf.* Hinkley v. State, 137 N.E. 599 (N.Y. 1922) (discussing distinction); Jarvis v. Gillespie, 587 A.2d 981 (Vt. 1991) (allowing adverse possession of municipal lands not in public use).

[56] *See* 43 U.S.C. § 1068.

[57] *See, e.g.,* Mercer v. Wayman, 137 N.E.2d 815 (Ill. 1956); Shives v. Niewoehner, 191 N.W.2d 633 (Iowa 1971). *But see* Myers v. Bartholomew, 697 N.E.2d 160 (N.Y. 1998) (discussing New York statute that provides that after one cotenant holds possession for 10 years, continued possession is deemed adverse).

statutory period for adverse possession will begin running if the tenant unequivocally repudiates his status as a tenant and claims title to the land.

[E] Future Interest Holder As Owner

A future interest is immune from adverse possession until the interest holder is entitled to immediate possession of the land. Until that point, the interest holder has no right of action against the adverse claimant. Suppose L holds a life estate in Brownacre, followed by an indefeasibly vested remainder in R. Adverse possessor A occupies Brownacre in 1990 and remains in possession through 2000. Assuming that (1) the jurisdiction uses a ten-year period and (2) A meets the standard adverse possession requirements, A acquires only L's life estate in Brownacre in 2000.

The statutory period for A's adverse possession against R's remainder does not begin running until R is entitled to possession of Brownacre, that is, until L dies. Suppose L dies in 2001, ending the life estate. R now holds fee simple absolute in Brownacre. If A still holds possession of Brownacre when L dies, the period for adverse possession against R's title then begins to run.

§ 27.06 Policy Rationales for Adverse Possession

[A] Four Utilitarian Models

Adverse possession is premised on utilitarianism (see § 2.04); the doctrine seeks to maximize societal happiness in a broad sense. But what specific policies justify adverse possession? In other words, exactly what utilitarian benefits does it provide? There is surprisingly little agreement on the answers to these questions.

Scholars have identified four alternative theories that help explain adverse possession: the limitations model; the administrative model; the development model; and the efficiency/personhood model. No single theory adequately justifies all of American adverse possession law, but each theory provides valuable insights. Combined together, these four theories provide a range of policies that support the doctrine, just as four separate legs support the same chair.

Consider how these theories apply to a simple example. Suppose O holds record title to Redacre, a 500-acre tract of remote mountain land. Over a 15-year period, A visits the land to cut timber, mine gold, collect wild honey, hunt, fish, and occasionally camp; these are the usual activities that an owner of wild land might undertake. O never visits the land during this period. A acquires title to Redacre by adverse possession. Why?

[B] Limitations Model

Most authorities view adverse possession as a specialized statute of limitations to recover possession of land. Under this approach, the traditional common law elements of actual, exclusive, open and notorious, hostile, and continuous possession determine when the limitations period begins. This level of possession gives fair notice to the supposed owner of the occupant's apparent claim to title. The owner then has an opportunity to bring suit to eject the occupant. Under this view, A's activities are deemed notice to O that A claims a legal right to Redacre; O may now either challenge A's claim through litigation or acquiesce in A's ownership.

Two key policies underpin the limitations model. First, the limitations period minimizes the risk of judicial error in determining title, and thus helps to protect the true owner from frivolous claims. Over time, witnesses die, memories fade, and documentary evidence is lost. In general, as time passes, the trial of a title dispute between competing claimants is less and less likely to produce an accurate result; the risk of error increases with the years. Perhaps A is the true owner of Redacre, while O's title claim is frivolous.

Second, the limitations model provides repose for the successful adverse possessor. In particular, it guarantees the stability of the possessor's title, which in turn encourages the possessor to place the land in optimum productive use (see § 14.09). For example, if A knew that his title to Redacre might be challenged at any time—even 20, 50, or 100 years later—he would be reluctant to invest in the improvements necessary to maximize the productive value of the land.

[C] Administrative Model

Alternatively, we might view adverse possession as a useful method for curing minor title defects, thereby protecting the title of the possessor.[58] Mistakes often occur in the conveyancing process. For example, the chain of title to Redacre might contain a deed with an erroneous property description; or perhaps decades ago someone neglected to have the seller's spouse confirm her oral waiver of dower rights in a written instrument. Under these circumstances, lengthy possession by occupant A and his predecessors serves to demonstrate his title.

Under this approach, the common law elements are not intended to provide notice to anyone. Rather, they demonstrate the possessor's belief that he owns title to the land. In general, an adverse possessor must use the land in the same manner as a reasonable owner would, given its nature and character. Here, A used Redacre for timber harvesting, gold mining, and other activities that a reasonable owner would undertake. A's conduct evidences his ownership rights.

[D] Development Model

This model posits that the law governing adverse possession of wild, undeveloped lands is best explained as a tool to facilitate economic development.[59] During the nineteenth century, when the American law of adverse

---

[58] See Henry W. Ballentine, *Title by Adverse Possession*, 32 Harv. L. Rev. 135 (1918).

[59] See John G. Sprankling, *An Environmental Critique of Adverse Possession*, 79 Cornell L. Rev. 816 (1994).

possession evolved, forests, wetlands, grasslands, deserts, and other lands in their natural condition were seen as essentially worthless. By vesting title in the industrious settler—rather than the absentee landowner—adverse possession promoted rapid development of the nation's wilderness lands.

From this perspective, the common law elements have little to do with notice. Indeed, adverse possession results in the involuntary transfer of title based on inconspicuous, rare activities that are highly unlikely to give notice to the owner. Under the development model, these traditional elements test whether the adverse possessor or the true owner have placed the land in productive use. Here, A's timber and mining activities during the statutory period demonstrate his willingness to continue this productive conduct in the future; O's inactivity suggests that he will remain idle. A successfully asserts adverse possession because of his economic "track record." Adverse possession thus reallocates land to productive users.

[E]   Efficiency/Personhood Model

This model blends together diverse approaches that focus on avoiding injury to the adverse possessor. As Oliver Wendell Holmes explained, "[a] thing which you have enjoyed and used as your own for a long time . . . takes root in your being and cannot be torn away without your resenting the act."[60] Over time, the adverse possessor grows progressively more attached to the land, while the absentee owner becomes increasingly detached from it. The adverse possessor places a high personal value on the land, while the absentee owner has virtually abandoned it. Accordingly, at some point, it becomes appropriate to shift title to the adverse possessor, based on principles of efficiency, personhood, or reliance.

From this perspective, the common law elements measure the strength of the parties' respective attachments to the land. A, who satisfies all adverse possession requirements, has presumably established a close personal tie to Redacre. In contrast, absentee owner O who never uses the land has demonstrated his lack of interest. Justice is served by vesting title in A.

---

[60] Oliver Wendell Holmes, *The Path of the Law,* 10 Harv. L. Rev. 457, 477 (1897).

Chapter 28

TRANSFER OF PROPERTY AT DEATH

SYNOPSIS

§ 28.01 Death and Property

Suppose O suddenly dies. What happens to O's property?[1] The answer turns on whether O left a valid *will*. We must determine if O died *testate* (with a valid will) or *intestate* (without a valid will). In general, if O died testate, his property will ultimately be transferred according to the provisions of his will. The recipients will receive legal interests in the property or—if the will creates a *testamentary trust*—will receive equitable interests. On the other hand, if O died intestate, his property either (1) will be distributed to O's family members designated by the state laws governing *intestate succession* or (2) will *escheat* to the state if no such family members exist.

It is crucial to understand that these rules apply only to property owned by the decedent at the time of death. As a matter of prudent estate planning, a living person might elect to transfer property to others during her lifetime, using tools such as an inter vivos conveyance of real property (*see* Chapter 23) or a gift causa mortis (*see* Chapter 5). A similar tool is the *inter vivos trust*, which is discussed in this chapter together with the testamentary trust. Property so transferred before death is not part of the decedent's estate.

§ 28.02 The Will

[A] Nature of the Will

The will is a written instrument, effective only upon death, by which an owner disposes of property.[2] Somewhat more ornately, the Restatement (Second) of Property: Donative Transfers defines the will as a: "donative document of transfer intended to be legally operative to effect a transfer of property upon the donor's death."[3] The will can be revoked or amended at any time during the owner's life.

It bears repeating that a will can only transfer property that is still owned by the decedent at the time of death. Suppose W prepares a will in 1995, leaving her home Blueacre to M and her favorite horse, Ketchup, to N. W conveys Blueacre to O in 1998, and dies in 2000, still owning Ketchup. O owns Blueacre. Because W's will did not become legally effective until her death—a time when she no longer owned Blueacre—the attempted gift to M is invalid. However, the will does effectively transfer Ketchup to N.

---

[1] *See generally* Gregory S. Alexander, *The Dead Hand and the Law of Trusts in the Nineteenth Century*, 37 Stan. L. Rev. 1189 (1985); Harry D. Krause, *Equal Protection for the Illegitimate*, 65 Mich. L. Rev. 477 (1967); John H. Langbein & Lawrence W. Waggoner, *Reforming the Law of Gratuitous Transfers: The New Uniform Probate Code*, 55 Alb. L. Rev. 871 (1992); Orrin K. McMurray, *Liberty of Testation and Some Modern Limitations Thereon*, 14 Ill. L. Rev. 96 (1919); Eugene F. Scoles, *Succession Without Administration: Past and Future*, 48 Mo. L. Rev. 371 (1983).

[2] Some states allow oral wills under narrowly-defined circumstances, but only as to estates of relatively small value. *See, e.g.,* Kay v. Sandler, 718 S.W.2d 872 (Tex. App. 1986).

[3] Restatement (Second) of Property: Donative Transfers § 33.1 (1992).

[B] Terminology

The law concerning wills developed its own unique terminology over the centuries. The person making a will is called a *testator* (if male) or a *testatrix* (if female). At common law—and to some extent today—other key terms depend on whether real property or personal property is involved. A transfer of real property by will is known as a *devise*; the same term is also used as the verb to describe the transfer. The recipient of a devise is called a *devisee*. Thus, if O transferred his rights in the manor known as Greenacre to D through a will, we would technically say that O, a testator, devised Greenacre to D, a devisee. The gift of Greenacre to D is a devise.

In contrast, a transfer of personal property by will is known as a *legacy*, and the recipient of the legacy is termed a *legatee*. The verb used to describe the process is *bequeath*. Thus, if W transferred bonds through her will to S, we would say that O, a testatrix, bequeathed bonds to S, a legatee. The gift of the bonds to S is a legacy.

The law is gradually moving toward simplifying this terminology. For example, the influential Uniform Probate Code uses the term *devise* as both a noun and a verb, to describe the transfer of both real property and personal property. If X transferred the farm known as Greenacre, plus tractors and other farm equipment, to S through a will, the entire transfer is called a devise. An attorney would explain that X devised Greenacre and the equipment to S.

[C] Policy Rationales for the Will

It is a fundamental principle of American law that a person usually has the right at death to transfer property as he or she wishes. Why? Do the policy rationales that support the institution of private property in general (*see* Chapter 2) equally support unfettered freedom to control the disposition of property after death?

Utilitarian concerns dominate the arguments for and against freedom of testation. Proponents argue that it provides an incentive for productive labor. The average person will work harder and save more income—they suggest—if the law permits her to direct the disposition of property after death. Society in general will benefit from the resulting accumulation of wealth. Advocates also observe that the rule allows an owner to provide financial support for his or her family even after death, and to direct those assets to maximum advantage to meet the needs of individual family members; this freedom reduces the risk that family members may become financial burdens on the state. On the other hand, critics stress the social and economic dangers of complete testamentary freedom. The resulting concentration of wealth, they argue, leads to the social inequality that Thomas Jefferson and other founding fathers sought to prevent through the abolition of fee tail and related English doctrines. Moreover, the recipient of inherited wealth has no incentive to contribute productive labor to the national economy. Opponents further note that testamentary freedom offers no guarantee that the decedent will in fact support his or her family;

indeed, it permits the decedent to transfer his or her entire estate to a third person, potentially rendering the family destitute.

The policy objections to testamentary freedom have encountered only limited success. These concerns underlie the federal estate taxation system; the progressive taxation of large estates was originally intended to reduce the concentration of wealth and redistribute income to others. And the elective share (*see* § 11.03[D]) ensures that a surviving spouse (and, by extension, any children) will not be left penniless.

[D] Will Formalities

All states once required strict compliance with stringent formalities in order to create a valid will, and today many states still follow this view. In general, a will is effective if it is (1) in writing and (2) signed by the testator at the end, in the presence of two witnesses who themselves sign the will to attest to its execution. Yet even a minor deviation from these standards (e.g., if one of the witnesses was out of the room when the testator signed) renders the will invalid in some states.

This testamentary formalism seems increasingly archaic today. It stems from the Statute of Wills[4] of 1540 and the Statute of Frauds[5] of 1677, which imposed rigid requirements on wills in order to serve evidentiary and cautionary goals (*see* § 20.04[B][5]). The written will provides a clear evidentiary record of the testator's intent, thus avoiding potential fraud; and the formal process helps to ensure that the testator appreciates the nature and seriousness of his conduct. Modern critics, however, argue that the price for these benefits is often high: invalidating a will—and thus disregarding the testator's clear intent—due to an insignificant technical flaw. As a result, there is a recent trend toward simplifying the process, as reflected by the Uniform Probate Code.[6]

One historic exception to these requirements is the *holographic will*. In most states, a will that is entirely in the handwriting of the testator and signed by him is valid, even though it is not witnessed and does not comply with the other usual standards.[7] Courts reason that the holographic will serves the evidentiary and cautionary goals underlying the formal requirements. Fraud is avoided because the will is written, and the act of physically writing out testamentary wishes adequately assures that the testator appreciates the importance of his action. Finally, much like the gift causa mortis, the holographic will provides a quick and inexpensive substitute for a formal will.

---

[4] Statute of Wills, 32 Hen. 8, ch. 1 (1540).

[5] Statute of Frauds, 29 Car. 2, ch. 3, § 6 (1677).

[6] *See, e.g.,* Unif. Probate Code § 2-502, 8 U.L.A. 350 (permitting will to be signed on the testator's behalf by another person).

[7] *See* Powell on Real Property § 85.13[2] (Michael Allan Wolf ed., Matthew Bender).

[E] Probate and Administration

Suppose that S dies testate. It must be determined whether S's will is valid. And the property that comprises S's estate must be collected, managed, and distributed.

The judicial process for determining the validity of a will is known as *probate*. Typically, the decedent nominates an *executor* (or, if female, an *executrix*) in the will, and the named executor files a petition to establish the will's validity. The vast majority of probate proceedings are brief and uncontested. After appropriate notice to all potentially interested parties, the court conducts a brief hearing, receives evidence, and affirms the will. Of course, objections to the validity of the will (e.g., defective execution or lack of testamentary capacity) may result in a lengthy, trial-type proceeding.

The process of collecting, managing, and distributing the decedent's estate is called *administration*. Assuming the court approves the person nominated as executor in the will, the executor will perform this function. If the will fails to nominate an executor (or if the decedent died intestate), the probate court will appoint an *administrator* (or, if female, *administratrix*) to administer the estate. The executor, executrix, administrator, and administratrix are collectively described as *personal representatives*. Working under court supervision, the personal representative provides notice to the decedent's creditors, assembles and manages the decedent's property, represents the estate in litigation, pays the decedent's debts and taxes, and ultimately distributes the estate property as directed by the court.[8]

§ 28.03 The Trust

[A] Nature of the Trust

The trust involves a special fiduciary relationship in which one or more persons (the *trustees*) manage property on behalf of others (the *beneficiaries*).[9] The hallmark of the trust is that title to the trust property (the *corpus* or *res*) is divided, with the trustee and beneficiaries holding different interests. The trustee holds *legal title* to the trust property, while the beneficiaries hold beneficial or *equitable title*.[10] This split reflects the historic English separation between courts of law and equity. The *use*, protected by equity courts but not law courts, ultimately evolved into the modern trust.

---

[8] *See generally* Eugene F. Scoles, *Succession Without Administration: Past and Future*, 48 Mo. L. Rev. 371 (1983) (criticizing the prevailing system of estate administration as unduly lengthy and expensive).

[9] This chapter examines only the express private trust; resulting trusts, constructive trusts, and other specialized trusts are beyond the scope of this book.

[10] The Restatement (Second) of Trusts defines the express private trust as: "a fiduciary relationship with respect to property, subjecting the person by whom the title to the property is held to equitable duties to deal with the property for the benefit of another person, which arises as a result of a manifestation of an intention to create it." Restatement (Second) of Trusts § 2 (1959).

The person creating the trust is called the *settlor* (or sometimes *trustor*). Once the trust becomes irrevocable, the settlor has no further control over the trust property.

The trustee is obligated to manage the trust property in the best interests of the beneficiaries. Almost always, this property consists of income-producing assets (e.g., land, stock, bonds). The trustee must ensure that the property is productive; absent contrary instructions in the trust instrument, the trustee has the power to sell, lease, mortgage, and other-wise administer the property in order to maximize income to the trust, consistent with prudent judgment. At the same time, the trustee is under a duty to protect and preserve the trust property against loss or damage. The trustee typically pays the net trust income to the beneficiaries; depending on the trust instrument, the trustee may have discretion to determine the amount and timing of such payments. The trust instrument may also authorize the trustee to distribute all or part of the trust property to the beneficiaries

The beneficiaries, in contrast, are entirely passive. They have no right to manage or control the trust property, and merely receive income or principal payments from the trustee.

[B] The Testamentary Trust

[1] Creation

The *testamentary trust* is created as part of a will, and takes effect only at the death of the settlor. In order to create this trust, the settlor must execute a writing that: (1) expresses the intention to form a trust and identifies the trust property, beneficiaries, and purpose;[11] and (2) complies with all the formalities required for a valid will (*see* § 28.02[D]). A well-drafted trust specifies in detail the duties and powers of the trustee and the rights of the various beneficiaries. For centuries, the testamentary trust was the only recognized type of private trust. Almost all of the law of trusts was accordingly developed to fit this model. The other principal type of private trust is the *inter vivos trust*, which emerged only recently.

[2] Benefits

Why create a testamentary trust? The trust is most commonly used as an estate-planning tool to provide support for the settlor's family. In this setting, it offers several advantages over other forms of property ownership.

Assume that O, about to die, is planning the disposition of his sole asset: fee simple absolute in Redacre, an apple orchard. O has a wife, W, and two children, D (age 10) and S (age 3). O's goal is to provide support for W during her life, and then support for D and S during their lives, and finally to provide for any children D or S may have. O could meet this goal by convey-ing legal interests in Redacre: a life estate to W, followed by vested

---

[11] Restatement (Second) of Trusts § 54 (1959).

remainders for life in D and S, and a contingent remainder in fee simple absolute in the unascertainable class of future grandchildren. Alternatively, O could form a trust, creating the parallel equitable interests in W, D, S, and the future grandchildren, and vesting legal title in a trustee.

One advantage offered by the trust is flexibility to implement the settlor's intent. For example, suppose that the price of apples falls after O's death and, as a result, the income from Redacre is insufficient to support W. W wishes to sell Redacre, invest the sale proceeds, and live on the resulting income. If W merely holds a legal life estate, she cannot force the sale of fee simple absolute in Redacre over the objections of the remaindermen (*see* § 9.05[D][4]). Although W can sell her life estate, it will generate only a low price due to uncertainty about its duration. In this and similar situations, the split of title between the life tenant and remaindermen may produce stalemate. Unless all parties agree, it is difficult to sell, mortgage, or lease the property, or otherwise use it to maximum advantage. However, if Redacre is held in trust, then the trustee is empowered to sell, mortgage, lease, or otherwise dispose of the property in a manner that best carries out the intention of the settlor. Here, the trustee would be authorized—and probably required—to sell Redacre and reinvest the proceeds in a more profitable investment.

A second advantage of the trust is professional management. W, D, and S may lack the knowledge, skill, and diligence that are required to successfully operate an apple orchard. By vesting the management responsibility in a qualified trustee, O can be assured that the orchard will generate maximum profit for his family. This concern is particularly important where one or more of the beneficiaries are minors or suffer from mental disabilities.

A third advantage—perhaps less important today—is that the doctrine of restraints on alienation does not apply to equitable interests. Thus, if O wishes, he can have substantially greater control over post-death events if he creates equitable interests rather than legal interests (e.g., by preventing D and S from selling their interests).

Perhaps the most important advantage of the modern trust is purely financial. The well-drafted trust may lower the beneficiaries' income tax liability and also reduce the estate tax burden upon the beneficiaries' deaths.

[C] The Inter Vivos or "Living" Trust

[1] Creation

The *inter vivos trust* or *living trust* is relatively new. Unlike the testamentary trust, which is effective only at death, the inter vivos trust takes effect during the life of the settlor. In order to create an inter vivos trust, the settlor must either: (1) declare himself to be the trustee of property for a particular beneficiary; or (2) transfer property in trust to a third person as trustee for the beneficiary.

An oral trust is valid as to personal property in all but a few states.[12] A written instrument is uniformly required, however, to create an effective trust as to land; the Statute of Frauds mandates that any transfer of an interest in real property—including an equitable interest—must be in writing (*see* § 20.04[B]).

The inter vivos trust may be either *revocable* or *irrevocable*. The irrevocable inter vivos trust serves much the same function as the testamentary trust; it is a permanent disposition of the settlor's property. The revocable inter vivos trust, as the name suggests, may be revoked by the settlor at any time before death.

[2] Benefits

The revocable inter vivos trust has been popularized in recent decades as a will substitute that both (a) allows the settlor to exercise control over assets during his or her lifetime (unlike the irrevocable trust) and (b) avoids the delay and cost of estate administration (unlike the will).

Typically, the settlor serves as a trustee and receives income during his or her life; upon the settlor's death, the trust is administered by a new trustee, who distributes the income and principal to the beneficiaries pursuant to the terms of the trust. Because the trust property is not owned by the decedent upon death, it is not subject to the judicially-supervised process of estate administration. The revocable trust does not itself avoid estate taxation, but it does eliminate the executor's fee and other expenses incurred in administration; on the other hand, the trust is responsible for payment of a trustee's fee. While administration may consume two or more years, the revocable trust permits the trustee to manage the trust property on an ongoing basis. This continuity is particularly important where the trust involves a family business or other vulnerable asset. Another benefit of the inter vivos trust is privacy. Probate proceedings are open to the public, and the decedent's will becomes a public record. Because no judicial action is required in connection with an inter vivos trust, however, its terms can remain confidential.

[D] Special Problem: The Spendthrift Trust

[1] Nature of the Spendthrift Trust

Imagine that A's will creates a testamentary trust by which the trust income is payable to B for life, after which the trust principal is to be distributed to remainderman C; the trust provisions of the will further state that (a) B cannot transfer his interest in the trust and (b) B's creditors cannot attach this interest. B borrows $10,000 from D; later, B fails to repay the debt. Can D collect directly from the trust? This example raises the problem of the *spendthrift trust*. A spendthrift trust arises when the terms of the trust instrument provide both that the beneficiary may not transfer

---

[12] *See* Powell on Real Property ¶ 508[4] (Michael Allan Wolf ed., Matthew Bender).

his or her interest and that creditors cannot attach or otherwise reach that interest.

[2] General Validity of the Spendthrift Trust

English courts refused to countenance the spendthrift trust due to public policy concerns. However, late nineteenth-century American courts repudiated the English view and generally recognized this type of trust. Most states now generally permit the spendthrift trust, although many impose specific restrictions.[13]

Broadway National Bank v. Adams[14] exemplifies the American perspective. Decided by the Massachusetts Supreme Court in 1882, the case reflects the great stress on owner autonomy that characterized the late nineteenth-century judicial approach to private property.[15] One Adams created a spendthrift trust for his improvident (and presumably impecunious) brother, Charles. After Charles borrowed money from the plaintiff bank and failed to pay the debt, the bank sued the trustee to secure repayment directly from the trust. The court's starting point was the premise that an owner has an absolute right to dispose of his property on any conditions he chooses, unless contrary to public policy. The nature of the disposition here—a gift of financial support for a needy relative—was socially beneficial. The court brushed aside the plaintiff's assertion that the spendthrift trust violated public policy because it allowed a beneficiary to defraud creditors. It explained that a creditor could avoid loss by reviewing public records to investigate the customer's finances—and thus discover potential restrictions on income—before extending credit.

[3] Critique of the Spendthrift Trust

[a] The Diligent-Creditor Myth

The rationale of *Adams* and similar cases is widely criticized. At the most basic level, the court's apparent belief that the diligent creditor can readily discover spendthrift trust restrictions in advance is badly flawed.

A potential creditor (e.g., a bank) would encounter extreme difficulty in making such a search even today.[16] Why? There is no national index to spendthrift trusts. The spendthrift trust created under a will can be located only by inspecting probate records in the particular county where the will was subject to administration, and then only if the inspecting creditor knows the name of the settlor/decedent under which the probate file is listed. Suppose, for example, that the AAA Bank is considering a loan to B, a resident of Chicago, Illinois. B is the beneficiary of a spendthrift trust

---

[13] *See* Powell on Real Property § 42.25[5] (Michael Allan Wolf ed., Matthew Bender).

[14] 133 Mass. 170 (1882).

[15] *See generally* Gregory S. Alexander, *The Dead Hand and the Law of Trusts in the Nineteenth Century*, 37 Stan. L. Rev. 1189 (1985).

[16] *See generally* Willard M. Bushman, *The (In)Validity of Spendthrift Trusts*, 47 Or. L. Rev. 304 (1968).

created by settlor S, whose will was probated in Los Angeles County, California, but B fails to disclose this to the bank. How can the AAA Bank discover the trust and its limitations? The Bank is unaware that any trust exists, and thus is unaware of both its location and the name of the settlor. It could locate B's trust only by investigating every probate file ever opened in every county in the nation—an impossible task.

Further, the diligent-creditor explanation entirely collapses in other situations. Suppose B carelessly (or even worse, intentionally) injures C in an auto accident. Could C have investigated B's financial affairs before being injured? Or suppose B marries D, fathers children E and F, and then divorces D. Could E and F somehow have analyzed B's finances in advance of their birth?

The common law spendthrift trust doctrine presumably harms creditors and the public in general to some extent. The consensual creditor such as a bank or store will be able to pass on part of its losses to customers through increased prices. The tort victim or the beneficiary's impoverished family may ultimately turn to the state for assistance, thus shifting the financial burden to taxpayers. Yet there is little modern outcry to abolish the spendthrift trust, probably because it occurs so rarely that the social harm it causes is slight.

[b] Democratic Concerns

A more abstract concern is the impact of the spendthrift trust on democratic values. The young United States abolished fee tail in response to Jeffersonian fears that it would contribute to the development of a hereditary aristocracy that could control American political and social life (*see* § 9.05[C][5]). The spendthrift trust presents the same dangers. As the noted scholar John Chipman Gray lamented, the principle that "men not paying their debts should live in luxury on inherited wealth" is a doctrine "as undemocratic as can well be conceived."[17] The idle recipient of family wealth through a spendthrift trust is immune from creditors. The industrious wage earner, in contrast, must pay his debts.

[4] Exceptions to General Rule

Twentieth-century American law slowly carved out exceptions to the general enforceability of the spendthrift trust. The nature and pace of this evolution predictably varied widely from state to state. Thus, while some states still follow the common law rule, most states now recognize one or more exceptions that either limit the trust generally or favor particular creditors. In New York, for example, only that part of the beneficiary's income that is necessary for education and support is immune from a creditor's claims;[18] California, in contrast, shelters 75% of the beneficiary's income, but permits creditors to reach the remaining 25%.[19] Child support

[17] John Chipman Gray, Restraints on the Alienation of Property 246 (2d ed. 1895).

[18] N.Y. Est. Powers & Trusts Law § 7-3.4.

[19] Cal. Prob. Code § 15306.5.

claims, claims of creditors who provide necessary goods and services (e.g., medical care), and tax claims are permitted against the spendthrift trust in many states.[20]

§ 28.04 Intestate Succession

[A] The Problem

Over half of all Americans die intestate, without a valid will to control the disposition of their property. Others die partially intestate, meaning that the will does not cover all of their property. How should the law distribute decedents' property under these circumstances?

Broadly speaking, the modern laws governing intestate succession transfer the decedent's property to the closest living relatives, preferring the surviving spouse and children over more distant relatives. This system reflects two jurisprudential strands. Eighteenth-century theorists justified this approach on utilitarian grounds: it helped to provide support and security for the decedent's family. The more modern rationale—reflecting heightened concern for protecting owner autonomy—is that the system reflects the presumed intent of the decedent. In other words, the intestate succession rules seek to do what the decedent would have done if he or she had considered the matter.

[B] The English Foundation

The American law of intestate succession evolved from the English system. The dominant feature of English law was a sharp distinction between real property and personal property. The disposition of land was governed by feudal principles that favored the eldest male descendant. The transfer of tangible personal property was dominated by ecclesiastical law, which provided a share for the surviving spouse and equal shares for children regardless of gender.

Like the substantive law itself, the early terminology distinguished between land and personal property. A decedent's real property was said to *descend* to his *heir*. In the context of intestate succession, an *heir* is defined as a person who is designated by law to receive ownership of real property upon an intestate's death. Conversely, a decedent's personal property passed by *distribution* to his *next of kin*. In general, illegitimate and adopted children could not take as heirs or next of kin.

The inheritance of land was based on *primogeniture*: the oldest male descendant was the sole heir.[21] Suppose O owned fee simple absolute in

---

[20] *See* Powell on Real Property § 42.26 (Michael Allan Wolf ed., Matthew Bender).

[21] One exception to this general rule should be noted. Suppose D's surviving relatives at death were his two daughters, E and F, and G, D's grandson by a son who predeceased D. E and F would inherit in *coparceny*. When two or more female descendants were more closely related to the decedent than any living male descendant, they inherited jointly.

Blackacre, died intestate, and left a surviving spouse S and three surviving children, two sons and one daughter. O's oldest son received title to Blackacre; the other children obtained no right, title, or interest in the property. Similarly, because a spouse was not considered an heir at common law, O's widow S received nothing under the rules of intestate succession. Instead, S received a partial life estate known as dower (*see* § 11.02[D][1]).

What explains primogeniture? The preference for the oldest male descendant reflects, in part, the influence of feudalism. Feudal duties were easier to enforce when they were owed by a single, identifiable person; given the gender-based feudal mind-set, only a male could serve this function. Primogeniture also avoided the splitting of family lands, which might endanger the family's long-run wealth, power, and prestige. The oldest male descendant, like his ancestor, would presumably provide support for needy relatives. Given this archaic rationale, it is remarkable that primogeniture survived in England until 1925.

Personal property, in contrast, was traditionally subject to ecclesiastical law in England, which in turn was based on Roman law. As codified by the 1670 Statute of Distributions,[22] the law distributed personal property among the decedent's blood relatives according to a complex system that preferred close relatives—regardless of gender—over distant ones. For example, if the decedent left a surviving spouse S, two daughters, D and E, and a son, F, S received one-third of all personal property, while D, E, and F each received an equal share in the remaining two-thirds.

[C] Modern Rules

[1] Toward a Uniform System

The modern laws governing intestate succession vary somewhat from state to state, but are largely based on the 1670 Statute of Distributions. The historic split between real property and personal property has been eliminated, and the rules apply equally to both types of property. Further, there is broad agreement that the decedent's property should be distributed among members of the family, with a universal preference for close relatives (surviving spouse and children) over more distant relatives (e.g., grandparents or cousins). Primogeniture, like fee tail, was abolished in the young United States as inconsistent with social equality. Finally, the common law bias against adopted or illegitimate children has largely been overturned; illegitimate children are now accorded the same treatment as legitimate children, and there is a clear trend toward equal treatment for adopted children as well.

Jurisdictions still differ to some extent, however, on which family members should take priority over others. Under the influence of the Uniform Probate Code, which has been adopted by about one-third of the states, national law is gradually inching toward uniformity on this difficult issue.[23]

---

[22] Statute of Distributions, 22 & 23 Car. 2., ch. 10 (1670).

[23] Unif. Probate Code, 8 U.L.A. 1. Article II, Part 1, of the Uniform Probate Code, which covers intestate succession, was revised in 1990; some states follow the pre-1990 version, while others have adopted the 1990 revisions.

Even the traditional terminology is changing. The Uniform Probate Code, for example, defines *heirs* as the persons designated by law to inherit either real property or personal property.

[2] Rights of Spouse

In most jurisdictions, the rights of the surviving spouse turn on whether the decedent left *issue*. Issue in this context means lineal descendants of the decedent—children, grandchildren, great-grandchildren, etc. Most commonly, the surviving spouse takes the entire estate if there are no issue. But some states divide the estate between the spouse and the decedent's surviving parents in this situation.[24]

If the decedent leaves both a spouse and issue, the spouse typically receives one-half or one-third of the estate, and the remaining share is divided among the issue. The 1990 revisions to the Uniform Probate Code—now adopted in a few states—take a different approach under these circumstances. Studies demonstrate that the average testator usually leaves all of his property to the surviving spouse, even if there are living issue, probably because he believes his spouse will use these assets to support the issue. Presuming that the typical intestate decedent would have the same intent, the 1990 revisions provide that the surviving spouse takes the entire estate, even if there are living issue.[25]

[3] Rights of Issue

Where the decedent leaves issue, but no surviving spouse, the issue take the entire estate. Suppose O has five children before her spouse dies; O then dies intestate, survived by all five children. Distribution of O's estate is simple. Where all inheriting issue are in the same generation (here, all children of O), each receives an equal or *per capita* share (here, one-fifth).

Complexity arises when the inheriting issue are in different generations. Suppose now that when O dies, she is survived by only four of her five children (A, B, C and D), and by two grandchildren (F and G), who are the children of her deceased fifth child (E). The share of a predeceased child typically goes to his or her issue, if any, by *right of representation*. Thus, here A, B, C and D each receive a one-fifth share of the estate. The share that would have belonged to E is equally divided between F and G, each receiving a one-tenth interest.

[4] Rights of Parents

If the decedent leaves no surviving spouse or issue, the estate goes to the surviving parents. The decedent's brothers and sisters receive no share of the estate at this time, presumably because they may inherit it upon the parents' death. Some states permit other ancestors (surviving grandparents, great-grandparents, etc.) to inherit as well.[26]

---

[24] *See* Unif. Probate Code §§ 2-102, 2-103, 8 (Pt. I) U.L.A. 81, 83.

[25] *See* Unif. Probate Code § 2-102(1)(ii), 8 (Pt. I) U.L.A. 81.

[26] *See* Unif. Probate Code §§ 2-103(4), 8 (Pt. I) U.L.A. 83.

[5] Rights of Other Blood Relatives

Where no spouse, issue, or parents survive, the decedent's estate passes to *collaterals*. Collaterals are all blood relatives of the decedent other than issue and ancestors (e.g., brothers, sisters, cousins, nieces, nephews). The estate goes to the decedent's siblings and their issue or, if no such takers exist, to more distant collaterals.[27]

§ 28.05 Escheat

Suppose O, holding fee simple absolute in Blackacre, dies intestate without heirs. What happens to Blackacre? Under these circumstances, Blackacre escheats to the state in which it is situated. This process parallels the feudal incident of escheat (*see* § 8.03[B][3][b]), by which land reverted to the overlord if the tenant died without heirs. Modern law provides that the estate of an intestate decedent who has no heirs escheats to the state.[28] The doctrine of escheat similarly extends to abandoned property (e.g., unclaimed bank accounts).

The doctrine of escheat is purely utilitarian, reflecting the law's historic concern for ensuring the productive use of land. Escheat effectively returns "unowned" property to economic use, thus benefiting society as a whole. Rather than allowing O's former property Blackacre to remain idle and dormant, the state will sell the land to a private owner who will presumably use it to grow crops.

---

[27] *See* Unif. Probate Code § 2-103(3), 8 (Pt. I) U.L.A. 83.
[28] *See* Unif. Probate Code § 2-105, 8 (Pt. I) U.L.A. 84.

Chapter 29

NUISANCE

SYNOPSIS

§ 29.01   "An Impenetrable Jungle"?

A's factory emits foul odors onto B's farm; noise from C's tuba practice routinely pervades the quiet of D's bookstore; and E's smelter produces vibrations that make it impossible for F to sleep in her home.[1] Can B, D, and F assert any claim? As a general rule, an owner is free to use his land as he sees fit. But this freedom is not unlimited. For example, it is often said that one may not use land in a manner that injures the land of others.[2] This precept is the foundation of the law of nuisance, which governs the rights of B, D, and F.

The common law divided nuisances into two categories: private nuisances and public nuisances. Broadly speaking, a *private nuisance* arises when one uses his land in a manner that injures a private owner or occupant in the use or enjoyment of that person's land. The Restatement (Second) of Torts offers a more precise definition: "a nontrespassory invasion of another's interest in the private use and enjoyment of land."[3] A's odors, C's noise, and E's vibrations are all considered to be private nuisances under this standard. This chapter—and most of the law in the field—deals primarily with the private nuisance. Indeed, when judges, scholars, and attorneys use the term "nuisance," this is usually a shorthand reference to the private nuisance. In contrast, a *public nuisance* is an activity that interferes with the rights of the public in general, usually by threatening the public health, safety, or morals.

The modern law of nuisance is complex and confusing. As one authority observed, "[t]here is perhaps no more impenetrable jungle in the entire law than that which surrounds the word 'nuisance.'"[4] Two key issues arise: (a) what constitutes a nuisance? and (b) what is the appropriate remedy? Traditional English law was straightforward on these points: virtually any conduct that seriously injured another's land constituted a private nuisance and was automatically enjoined. American nuisance law has gradually moved away from this rigid, pro-owner view toward more flexible standards founded on utilitarian principles. The utility of the defendant's conduct is increasingly considered in determining whether nuisance liability exists; thus, for example, socially-beneficial conduct that clearly interferes with the plaintiff's use of land may not constitute a nuisance. And even if nuisance liability is found, the plaintiff may be unable to obtain an injunction against the offending conduct.

Before the widespread adoption of zoning ordinances in the early twenti-eth century, nuisance was the principal tool used to reconcile incompatible

---

[1] *See generally* Raymond R. Coletta, *The Case for Aesthetic Nuisance: Rethinking Traditional Judicial Attitudes,* 48 Ohio St. L.J. 414 (1987); Jeff L. Lewin, *Boomer and the American Law of Nuisance: Past, Present, and Future,* 54 Alb. L. Rev. 189 (1990); Edward H. Rabin, *Nuisance Law: Rethinking Fundamental Assumptions,* 63 Va. L. Rev. 1299 (1977); Stewart E. Sterk, *Neighbors in American Land Law,* 87 Colum. L. Rev. 55 (1987).

[2] This is a loose translation of the ancient Latin maxim that is the foundation of nuisance law—*sic utere ut alienum non laedas.*

[3] Restatement (Second) of Torts § 821D (1977).

[4] W. Page Keeton, et al., Prosser and Keeton on the Law of Torts § 86, at 616 (5th ed. 1984).

land uses. Indeed, nuisance law is sometimes called "judicial zoning." Its importance has diminished as land use regulation has expanded. As one observer summarized, nuisance law has been "relegated to marginal cases, involving small-scale, localized land use conflicts."[5] If the zoning process permits a use that neighbors dislike, nuisance law may provide a basis for attacking the use through litigation. And the doctrine also remains useful in rural regions that have little or no zoning.

Despite the declining importance of nuisance law, academic interest in the topic has grown in recent decades. In particular, the efforts of Guido Calabresi, Robert Ellickson, and other disciples of the law and economics movement to apply economic principles to this area have helped to shape the law's modern evolution.[6] Insights from law and economics scholarship have been especially useful on the question of the appropriate remedy for a private nuisance.

§ 29.02 What Is a Private Nuisance?

[A] Nuisance Defined

A leading authority once suggested that nuisance was "incapable of any exact or comprehensive definition."[7] The term "nuisance" simply means "harm" in old French. Of course, this literal definition is far too broad to be helpful. Centuries of legal evolution have produced a complex and unwieldy body of nuisance law that defies quick explanation.

Our starting point is the Restatement (Second) of Torts, which defines the private nuisance as "a nontrespassory invasion of another's interest in the private use and enjoyment of land."[8] Even this definition is overbroad: only *some* nontrespassory invasions of another's interest in the private use and enjoyment of land are private nuisances, not *all* such invasions (*see* § 29.04). However, the Restatement definition is useful because it focuses on the key factors that distinguish nuisance from other legal doctrines. First, nuisance involves a special type of harm—interference with the interest of an owner, tenant, or other land occupant in the *use and enjoyment of land.* Suppose F's factory emits an unpleasant odor. Although the odor may offend P, a pedestrian who walks by the factory, it does not affect P's use or enjoyment of his land; hence, P cannot bring a nuisance claim. Conversely, if the odor makes it difficult for N to live in his home which adjoins F's factory, N may be able to sue F in nuisance; the foul odor interferes with N's use and enjoyment of his home. Second, nuisance

---

[5] Jeff L. Lewin, Boomer *and the American Law of Nuisance: Past, Present, and Future,* 54 Alb. L. Rev. 189, 230 (1990).

[6] *See, e.g.,* Guido Calabresi & A. Douglas Melamed, *Property Rules, Liability Rules, and Inalienability: One View of the Cathedral,* 85 Harv. L. Rev. 1089 (1972); Robert C. Ellickson, *Alternatives to Zoning: Covenants, Nuisance Rules, and Fines as Land Use Controls,* 40 U. Chi. L. Rev. 681 (1973).

[7] W. Page Keeton, et al., Prosser and Keeton on the law of Torts § 86, at 616 (5th ed. 1984).

[8] Restatement (Second) of Torts § 821D (1977).

involves a special type of conduct—a *nontrespassory invasion*. A physical entry onto land owned or occupied by another is a trespass, not a nuisance. A nuisance involves conduct *other than physical entry*—such as producing dust,[9] fumes, gases, light, noise,[10] odors,[11] shadow,[12] smoke, or vibration—that interferes with the use or enjoyment of land.

[B] Distinguishing Nuisance from Trespass

The traditional distinction between nuisance and trespass hinges on the *nature of the intrusion*: is there a physical entry or not? A physical entry onto the land of another interferes with the occupant's right to possession and hence constitutes a trespass. For example, if F stands on his factory site and throws a rock into the back yard of N's adjacent house, this is a physical entry of N's land and thus a trespass. Any conduct that interferes with the use and enjoyment of land, other than a physical entry, is governed by nuisance law. Suppose F's factory routinely emits loud noises throughout the night, making it difficult for N to sleep. This noise is not a physical entry onto the land, and accordingly N's claim is governed by nuisance law.

However, scientific progress has blurred the once-clear boundary line between nuisance and trespass (*see* § 30.02[B]). Common law courts considered only a *visible* intrusion to be a physical entry. For example, throwing a rock onto N's land was a trespass, while emitting an invisible gas was a nuisance. This distinction reflected the primitive science of the era. Modern science teaches that odors, fumes, and other gasses consist of microscopic particles. Thus, we now know that when F's factory emits a smelly gas, small particles of matter physically enter N's land. Should such an intrusion be considered a trespass? Many courts now extend trespass liability to include air pollution, toxic contamination, and other entries by microscopic particles, effectively allowing the injured plaintiff to sue on either theory.

[C] Categories of Nuisances

[1] Nuisance *Per Se* or Nuisance *Per Accidens*?

Private nuisances are usually divided into two types: the nuisance *per se* and the nuisance *per accidens*. The nuisance *per se* is an act or condition that is always considered to be a nuisance, regardless of the surrounding

---

[9] *Cf.* Boomer v. Atlantic Cement Co., 309 N.Y.S.2d 312 (N.Y. 1970) (trial court found that emissions of dirt, smoke, and vibration from cement plant constituted a nuisance).

[10] *Cf.* Estancias Dallas Corp. v. Schultz, 500 S.W.2d 217 (Tex. Ct. Civ. App. 1973) (trial court found that noise from air conditioning equipment was a private nuisance).

[11] *Cf.* Spur Indus., Inc. v. Del E. Webb Dev. Co., 494 P.2d 700 (Ariz. 1972) (cattle feedlot that produced odors and attracted flies was a private nuisance).

[12] *See, e.g.,* Prah v. Maretti, 321 N.W.2d 182 (Wis. 1982) (observing that structure on adjacent land that blocks sunlight from plaintiff's solar heating system might be a nuisance). *But see* Fountainebleau Hotel Corp. v. Forty-Five Twenty-Five, Inc., 114 So. 2d 357 (Fla. Dist. Ct. App. 1959) (hotel project that cast shadow on beach of plaintiff's adjacent hotel was not a nuisance).

circumstances; most commonly, this is some type of activity that is prohibited by law (e.g., an illegal garbage dump). The nuisance *per accidens,* in contrast, is a nuisance only because of the surrounding circumstances, such as its location and manner of operation. For example, a hog farm in the city probably constitutes a nuisance, while a hog farm in a rural area may not. The bulk of private nuisance law—and of this chapter as well—concerns the nuisance *per accidens.*

[2] Temporary Nuisance or Permanent Nuisance?

The law also distinguishes between the *temporary* or *continuing nuisance* and the *permanent nuisance.* In general, a permanent nuisance exists where the nuisance is certain or likely to continue in the future due to the physical nature of the condition, the cost of abatement, or other factors; any other nuisance is deemed temporary. For example, if B's cement plant has emitted dust every day since its operations began 20 years ago and there is no technology available to remedy this problem, it is probable that the emissions will continue in the future. The cement plant is a permanent nuisance. On the other hand, if B's cement plant emitted dust for only two years—before modern air pollution control technology was installed—the plant was only a temporary nuisance. The distinction is important in two settings: (1) the appropriate measure of damages (*see* § 29.06[B]) and (2) the running of the statute of limitations.[13]

§ 29.03 Evolution of Nuisance Law

As it evolved in post-medieval England, the law governing private nuisances was relatively straightforward. Only one factor was considered to determine whether nuisance liability existed: the *gravity of harm* to the land owner or occupant. A nuisance occurred when a person used his land in a manner that caused substantial harm to another's use and enjoyment of land. And the remedy for a nuisance was equally simple: the court issued an injunction against the harmful conduct. For example, suppose F started a pig farm in the backyard of his city house; if the resulting odor was so offensive that F's neighbors could not reasonably live in their homes, they could obtain an injunction closing the farm.[14] Thus, the law strictly protected the neighbors' property rights to use and enjoy their lands free from any nuisance.

These simple rules made sense in an agricultural society, but proved unduly rigid as industrialization proceeded. The main problem was that this approach failed to consider the utility of the conduct in question, and

---

[13] For example, assume the jurisdiction has a three-year limitations period for bringing an action against a private nuisance. If the nuisance is permanent, the statute of limitations starts running on the first day the nuisance begins; thus, if such a nuisance began in 1997, a suit commenced in 2001 is too late. If the nuisance is temporary, the limitations period begins anew each day that the nuisance continues; a suit against a temporary nuisance that exists in 2001 is timely, regardless of when the nuisance began.

[14] *Cf.* Pendoley v. Ferreira, 187 N.E.2d 142 (Mass. 1963) (pig farm near residential subdivision was a nuisance).

thereby tended to prevent new development. For instance, a new railroad might be shut down merely because its noise caused one farmer's chickens to stop laying eggs. The benefits that the railroad provided to society in general were seen as irrelevant. In this manner, the law provided absolute protection for property rights regardless of the resulting social cost.

Early American courts accepted the English view. During the late nineteenth century, however, the law began to shift toward a more flexible approach: only an *unreasonable* land use would be considered a nuisance. The gravity of harm was important in assessing reasonableness, but courts tended to consider other factors as well (e.g., the locality of the use, the nature of the wrongful conduct). The evolution of American nuisance law during the twentieth century brought another major change, as courts gave increasing weight to *utility*. This affected both (1) the liability standard for determining when a private nuisance existed and (2) the appropriate remedy if a nuisance were found.

On the liability side, this change was sparked by the adoption of the first Restatement of Torts in 1939. The Restatement proposed a new liability standard known as the *balance of utilities* test: a use was unreasonable unless the utility of the actor's conduct outweighed the gravity of the harm.[15] The 1977 Restatement (Second) of Torts repeated this standard, but added an alternative basis for unreasonableness that ignores utility. Similarly, an injunction is no longer the automatic remedy once nuisance liability is established. Rather, most courts will *balance the equities* between the parties to determine if an injunction is appropriate; this process inevitably considers the utility of the defendant's conduct as a factor in the balance. Accordingly, the successful plaintiff may be awarded only damages.

§ 29.04 Elements of Private Nuisance

[A] Overview

The existence of a private nuisance is a question of fact that turns on the unique circumstances of each case. For instance, a halfway house for parolees might be deemed a nuisance under some circumstances, but not under others. Examples of land uses found to be nuisances on the facts of the particular case include: airports, bakeries, cement plants, cemeteries, dairies, dog kennels, feed lots,[16] funeral parlors, gas stations, halfway houses,[17] hog farms, hospitals, laundries, lumber mills, music stores, rifle ranges, roosters, slaughter houses, smelters, soup kitchens, stables, trees, and windmills.

Five elements are required to establish liability for a private nuisance. The plaintiff must prove that the defendant's conduct produced an

---

[15] Restatement of Torts § 826 (1939).

[16] *See, e.g.,* Spur Indus., Inc. v. Del E. Webb Dev. Co., 494 P.2d 700 (Ariz. 1972).

[17] *See, e.g.,* Arkansas Release Guidance Found. v. Needler, 477 S.W.2d 821 (Ark. 1972).

　(1)　intentional,[18]

　(2)　nontrespassory,

　(3)　unreasonable, and

　(4)　substantial interference

　(5)　with the use and enjoyment of the plaintiff's land.

The second element—a nontrespassory interference—has already been discussed (*see* § 29.02[B]). The remaining elements are discussed below.

[B] "Intentional" Interference

As the Restatement (Second) of Torts explains, a person's harmful conduct is deemed "intentional" if *either* (a) he acts for the purpose of causing the harm *or* (b) he knows that the harm is resulting or is substantially certain to result from his conduct.[19]

Suppose that E's factory routinely emits extremely loud noise that keeps N, the owner of an adjacent house, awake all night. N complains, but the noise continues. It is possible that E's conduct is motivated by malice; perhaps E desires to harm N. If so, E's conduct is considered "intentional" under the first prong of the Restatement test. It is more likely, however, that E does not actually intend to harm N. Yet under the second prong of the Restatement test, E's conduct is still deemed "intentional" because E knows from N's complaint that the noise from the continued operation of the factory will cause harm to N.

For instance, in *Morgan v. High Penn Oil Co.*[20] the defendant operated an oil refinery that periodically emitted nauseating gases and odors that sickened plaintiffs and other nearby landowners. Plaintiffs notified defendant about these problems and demanded that it stop the emissions. Thus, defendant knew that plaintiffs would be harmed, but continued to operate the refinery without stopping the emissions. Applying the second prong of the Restatement test, the North Carolina Supreme Court held that this conduct was intentional; the defendant "intentionally . . . caused noxious gases and odors to escape onto the nine acres of the plaintiffs to such a degree as to impair in a substantial manner the plaintiffs' use and enjoyment of their land."[21]

Under limited circumstances, a private nuisance may arise from unintentional conduct. The Restatement (Second) of Torts provides that nuisance liability may be premised on conduct that is "unintentional and otherwise

---

[18] Under narrow circumstances (*see* [B], *below*), liability for a private nuisance may be based on unintentional conduct.

[19] Restatement (Second) of Torts § 825 (1977).

[20] 77 S.E.2d 682 (N.C. 1953).

[21] Morgan v. High Penn Oil Co., 77 S.E.2d 682, 690 (N.C. 1953). *But see* Waschak v. Moffat, 109 A.2d 310, 316 (Pa. 1954) (emission of gas from coal processing facility that discolored paint on plaintiffs' house was not intentional interference because defendants "did not know, and had no reason to be aware, that this particular gas would be so emitted and would have the effect upon the painted house").

actionable under the rules controlling liability for negligent or reckless conduct, or for abnormally dangerous conditions."[22] In this special situation, it is not necessary to show that the defendant's conduct is either intentional or unreasonable. For example, if E stores a large quantity of explosives in the backyard of his suburban house, this is probably an abnormally dangerous condition—and hence a nuisance—regardless of E's intent or the reasonableness of his conduct.

[C] "Unreasonable" Interference

[1] Overview

If nuisance law is indeed an "impenetrable jungle," the heart of the jungle is the concept of unreasonable interference. In the typical case, the other nuisance elements are easily proven; thus, the outcome usually hinges on whether the interference was unreasonable.

[2] Traditional Approach

Many states still follow the traditional, pre-Restatement approach to unreasonableness.[23] Some seem to equate unreasonableness with serious injury to the plaintiff, a view that harkens back to the gravity of harm approach.[24] Others employ a multi-factor test to assess unreasonableness, although the factors considered vary widely from state to state. Sample factors include: the character of the neighborhood; the nature of the wrongful conduct; its proximity to plaintiff's property; its frequency, continuity, and duration; and the nature and extent of resulting injury to the plaintiff.[25] A number of states also consider the utility of the defendant's conduct as one factor.[26]

---

[22] Restatement (Second) of Torts § 822(b) (1977).

[23] *See generally* Jeff L. Lewin, Boomer *and the American Law of Nuisance: Past, Present, and Future,* 54 Alb. L. Rev. 189, 234–235 (1990) (concluding that 36 jurisdictions use a reasonableness test). *See also* Jost v. Dairyland Power Coop., 172 N.W.2d 647, 653 (Wis. 1969) (noting that whether the "economic or social importance" of defendant's power plant "dwarfed the claim of a small farmer is of no consequence in this lawsuit").

[24] *Cf.* Morgan v. High Penn Oil Co., 77 S.E.2d 682 (N.C. 1953); Estancias Dallas Corp. v. Schultz, 500 S.W.2d 217 (Tex. Ct. Civ. App. 1973).

[25] *See, e.g.,* Escobar v. Continental Baking Co., 596 N.E.2d 394 (Mass. App. Ct. 1992) (bakery that generated noise was not a nuisance, because it was located in a industrial district and existed before plaintiff moved into area); Bove v. Donner-Hanna Coke Corp., 258 N.Y.S. 229 (App. Div. 1932) (coke oven that produced steam, dust, gases, and odors was not an unreasonable use because it was situated in an industrial district); Blanks v. Rawson, 370 S.E.2d 890 (S.C. Ct. App. 1988) (neighboring family's dog pen, basketball goal, and ten-foot fence were not nuisances).

[26] *See* Powell on Real Property § 64.02[3][c] (Michael Allan Wolf ed., Matthew Bender).

[3] Restatement Approach

[a] Basic Test: Balance of Utilities

Under the basic Restatement approach—adopted in about one-third of the states—an intentional interference is deemed "unreasonable" if the "gravity of the harm outweighs the utility of the actor's conduct."[27] In order to apply this standard, a court must compare (a) the "utility" of the defendant's conduct with (b) the "gravity of the harm" that this conduct causes to the plaintiff.[28] Thus, unreasonableness is determined on a case-by-case basis after considering the particular facts of each dispute.

The Restatement lists eight factors to be used in this balancing process. Five factors bear on the gravity of harm: the extent of the harm (mainly in terms of degree and duration); the character of the harm (physical damage or personal discomfort); the social value of the plaintiff's use and enjoyment; the suitability of the particular use or enjoyment invaded to the character of the locality; and the burden on the plaintiff of avoiding the harm.[29] The remaining three factors help assess the utility of the defendant's conduct: the social value of the primary purpose of the defendant's conduct; the suitability of the conduct to the character of the locality; and the impracticability of preventing or avoiding the interference.[30]

Consider a hypothetical application of the Restatement standard. Suppose that A operates a cement factory in a rural and uninhabited area.[31] The factory regularly emits large quantities of cement dust into the atmosphere, and there is no technological method of preventing these emissions. B purchases a tract of land next to the factory, builds a home, plants a flower garden, and soon discovers that the cement dust stunts the growth of one particular type of flower.

Under the Restatement standard, this interference is not unreasonable. The overall gravity of harm to B is quite low. The extent of harm is minor because B can grow other types of flowers in the garden. Although the nature of the harm is physical damage, it is almost trivial in character, and B still has almost all of the use and enjoyment of the property. The area appears to be unsuitable for a residential flower garden; B might be better off trying to grow this type of flower inside his home or perhaps in a small

---

[27] Restatement (Second) of Torts § 826 (1977).

[28] *See, e.g.,* Hendricks v. Stalnaker, 380 S.E.2d 198 (W. Va. 1989) (using Restatement test to conclude that water well was not a nuisance); *cf.* Page County Appliance Ctr., Inc. v. Honeywell, Inc., 347 N.W.2d 171 (Iowa 1984) (discussing use of Restatement-like standard to determine whether computer that produced radiation interfering with television reception was a nuisance); Rose v. Chaikin, 453 A.2d 1378 (N.J. Super. Ct. Ch. Div. 1982) (applying variant of Restatement standard to conclude that noisy windmill in residential area was a nuisance).

[29] Restatement (Second) of Torts § 827 (1977).

[30] Restatement (Second) of Torts § 828 (1977).

[31] Of course, these facts are quite different from those at issue in the celebrated case of Boomer v. Atlantic Cement Co., 309 N.Y.S.2d 312 (N.Y. 1970). The trial court in *Boomer* apparently did not apply the Restatement standard for unreasonableness, while the Court of Appeals considered only the appropriate remedy, not liability.

greenhouse. On the other hand, the utility of A's conduct is high. Cement production is crucial to the construction of homes and other buildings; the uninhabited area is well-suited to cement production; and A is unable to prevent the emissions without closing the factory.

[b] Alternative Test: Severe Harm

In 1977, the Restatement (Second) of Torts added an alternative test for "unreasonableness" that seemed to turn the law back toward the traditional "gravity of harm" approach, and thereby generated extensive controversy. An intentional interference is deemed unreasonable under this test "if the harm resulting from the invasion is severe and greater than the other should be required to bear without compensation."[32] The utility of the defendant's conduct is irrelevant under this alternative test, but the plaintiff's remedy is limited to compensation.[33]

For example, imagine that N's steel factory produces noxious fumes that reach F's nearby farm, killing his entire corn crop. This harm is sufficiently severe to trigger the alternative test for unreasonableness, entitling F to compensatory damages if the other nuisance elements are established. It does not matter that (a) steel production is critically important to the national economy, (b) the factory is located in an appropriate locality, or (c) it is impossible for N to stop the fumes.

[D] "Substantial" Interference

Slight inconveniences or petty annoyances are insufficient to establish nuisance liability. "The law does not concern itself with trifles, and therefore there must be a real and appreciable invasion of the plaintiff's interests before he can have a cause of action for . . . a private nuisance."[34] If a normal person living in the community would regard the interference as strongly offensive or seriously annoying, then the level of interference is substantial enough to impose liability. However, nuisance law does not protect hypersensitive persons.[35]

Suppose L's lemon-processing factory occasionally emits a mild lemon odor that wafts over nearby homes. The odor does not disturb normal residents, and thus is not a substantial interference; nearby residents A, B, and C, for example, cannot sue L for a private nuisance. Moreover, even if the odor causes severe discomfort to resident D, who is allergic to lemons,

---

[32] Restatement (Second) of Torts § 829A (1977).

[33] *See also* Restatement (Second) of Torts § 826(b) (1977) (setting forth a similar alternative test); Crest Chevrolet-Oldsmobile-Cadillac, Inc. v. Willemsen, 384 N.W.2d 692 (Wis. 1986) (finding nuisance liability under § 826(b) test). *But see* Carpenter v. Double R Cattle Co., 701 P.2d 222 (Idaho 1985) (reversing court of appeal decision that endorsed § 826(b) test).

[34] Restatement (Second) of Torts § 821F cmt. c (1977). For example, most courts are unwilling to impose nuisance liability based only on aesthetic concerns.

[35] *See, e.g.,* Page County Appliance Ctr., Inc. v. Honeywell, Inc., 347 N.W.2d 171 (Iowa 1984) (where radiation emitted by defendant's computer interfered with television reception at plaintiff's appliance store, case was remanded to trial court for consideration of claim that appliance store was an unusually sensitive use).

D cannot sue L on a private nuisance theory either because D's discomfort stems from a unique sensitivity to lemons.

[E] Interference with "Use and Enjoyment of Land"

Nuisance liability arises only from interference with the interests of an owner, tenant, or other land occupant in the use and enjoyment of the land. This element is clearly met when the defendant's conduct causes physical injury to the land itself (e.g., if fumes from defendant's plant destroy plaintiff's apple orchard) or to tangible personal property located on the land (e.g., if the fumes ruin the paint on plaintiff's truck).[36] The same is true when the offending conduct causes death, bodily injury, sickness, or substantial discomfort or annoyance, to persons who are physically present on the land.[37]

§ 29.05 Defenses to Liability for Private Nuisance

[A] Generally

The range of defenses available in private nuisance cases is fairly broad. A plaintiff cannot recover if he consented or acquiesced to the nuisance. And the defense of laches may be available if the plaintiff seeks equitable relief. Similarly, if the defendant has continued the nuisance for a sufficiently long period to acquire a prescriptive easement for the conduct at issue, this is a complete defense. The statute of limitations may also bar the plaintiff's claim. Beyond this point, two additional defenses have special importance: the historic doctrine of "coming to the nuisance" and the modern "right-to-farm" statutes.[38]

[B] "Coming to the Nuisance"

Suppose B establishes a boat-manufacturing factory in a rural, uninhabited area; for 20 years, the factory routinely emits fumes, noise, and odors. H now purchases an adjacent parcel, builds a home on the land, and promptly complains that the emissions constitute a private nuisance. Can B assert any defense?

At one time, many courts recognized a defense known as "coming to the nuisance." A plaintiff like H who moved into the region after the offending conduct began was not entitled to recover; rather, the law protected the first-in-time use. Today, however, almost all courts reject this defense because it effectively allows first-in-time residents to stifle new development in the community.[39] Instead, a number of courts consider the

---

[36] *See also* Prah v. Maretti, 321 N.W.2d 182 (Wis. 1982) (suggesting that interference with plaintiff's right to receive sunshine for his solar heating system might be a nuisance).

[37] *See* Powell on Real Property § 64.02[4] (Michael Allan Wolf ed., Matthew Bender).

[38] *See* Powell on Real Property § 64.05 (Michael Allan Wolf ed., Matthew Bender).

[39] *Cf.* Carpenter v. Double R Cattle Co., Inc., 669 P.2d 643 (Idaho Ct. App. 1983). *But cf.*

plaintiff's "coming to the nuisance" as one factor in determining reasonableness. [40]

[C] Right-to-Farm Statutes

"Right-to-farm" statutes in over 35 states create a special defense to nuisance liability. [41] Although the details vary from state to state, the general approach of these statutes is the same: farms and other agricultural activities are immune from nuisance liability if the facts giving rise to the claim have existed for a specified period of time. The goal of these statutes is to protect farms in urbanizing areas against nuisance claims. [42] In a sense, these statutes revive the "coming to the nuisance" defense in the specialized context of agricultural nuisances. For example, suppose that F owns a large farm in an agricultural area; he installs an irrigation system and operates it for 25 years. Fleeing the pressures of urban life, C purchases an adjacent farm; C soon discovers that F's irrigation pumps emit ear-splitting noise during the early morning hours. When C complains, F informs her that the pumps have been making the same amount of noise for 25 years. In all probability, the state's right-to-farm statute will prevent C from successfully suing F on a private nuisance theory.

§ 29.06 Remedies for Private Nuisance

[A] Injunction

[1] "Balance of Equities" Approach

The traditional remedy in private nuisance cases was an injunction against the offending conduct. This rule reflected an absolutist view of property rights: every owner was entitled to enjoy his land free from any nuisance. If a person creating a nuisance could take away this right simply by paying compensation to the owner in the form of damages, this would be the equivalent of eminent domain—an owner would be compelled to sell the right over his objection. Because only the government has eminent domain power, courts reasoned that an injunction was necessary to protect the owner's right. The social utility of the defendant's conduct was seen as irrelevant.

This view began to break down in the late nineteenth century, as courts became increasingly concerned that it would disrupt industrial

---

Spur Industries, Inc. v. Del E. Webb Dev. Co., 494 P.2d 700 (Ariz. 1972) (suggesting that the defense would have barred recovery by developer who constructed new residential subdivision near existing cattle feedlot).

[40] See Powell on Real Property § 64.05[2] (Michael Allan Wolf ed., Matthew Bender).

[41] See, e.g., Tex. Agric. Code Ann. § 251.004. But see Bormann v. Board of Supervisors, 584 N.W.2d 309 (Iowa 1998) (holding right-to-farm law was a regulatory taking that violated the Takings Clause of the Fifth Amendment).

[42] See, e.g., Buchanan v. Simplot Feeders Ltd. Partnership, 952 P.2d 610 (Wash. 1998).

development.[43] In almost all jurisdictions today, the plaintiff no longer has an automatic right to an injunction. Instead, the court will use a balancing test—usually called "balancing the equities"—to determine if an injunction is appropriate on the facts of the case. By far, the single most important factor in this process is the relative economic impact of the injunction on the parties. All other things being equal, then, a court will issue an injunction only if the resulting benefit to the plaintiff is greater than the resulting damage to the defendant. However, the public interest in continuing or preventing the defendant's conduct is usually weighed in the balance as well. If an injunction is refused, the plaintiff receives compensatory damages (see [B], below).

For example, suppose a court determines that D's noisy dance studio is a nuisance. It will cost D $100,000 to install soundproofing materials to eliminate the noise. But the noise problem only lowers the value of P's land by $1,000. The social value of D's use is relatively low and no other neighbors are disturbed by the noise, so the public interest is a neutral factor. Granting an injunction here would impose $100,000 in costs on D, but only confer $1,000 in benefits on P. Because the costs outweigh the benefits, the court will deny an injunction and instead award $1,000 in damages to P.

[2] *Boomer v. Atlantic Cement Co.*

[a] Overview

The well-known New York decision of *Boomer v. Atlantic Cement Co.*[44] exemplifies the current approach. Before *Boomer* was decided in 1970, some courts had already adopted the "balance of equities" standard. But New York still followed the view that an injunction was automatic if a nuisance caused substantial continuing harm. In *Boomer,* the New York Court of Appeals adopted the emerging modern rule and thereby created a precedent that greatly influenced the evolution of nuisance law in other jurisdictions.

The facts of *Boomer* are simple. Defendant, Atlantic Cement Co., operated a large cement plant near Albany, New York. The facility emitted dirt, smoke, and vibration that injured lands owned by Boomer and other plaintiffs. Apparently without considering the utility of Atlantic's conduct, the trial court concluded that the plant was a private nuisance; but it refused to issue an injunction. Instead, the court awarded plaintiffs compensatory damages for their injuries to date and authorized them to bring suits in the future as further injury was suffered. For the guidance of the parties, however, the court determined that plaintiffs' total permanent damages were $185,000. Plaintiffs appealed.

[b] Rationale

The court of appeals stressed that compliance with the traditional rule would close the plant immediately. There was no known technological

---

[43] *See generally* Paul M. Kurtz, *Nineteenth Century Anti-Entrepreneurial Nuisance Injunctions—Avoiding the Chancellor,* 17 Wm. & Mary L. Rev. 621 (1976).

[44] 309 N.Y.S.2d 312 (N.Y. 1970).

method to control the dust and other by-products from the plant. Accordingly, the only way to comply with an injunction to abate the emissions would be to stop operations altogether. This would eliminate most of the value in Atlantic's $45,000,000 plant and put its over 300 employees out of work. With little analysis, the court announced that it was "fully agreed" to avoid the "drastic remedy" of closing the plant.[45] The court apparently reached this result by balancing the equities between the parties, although its opinion is remarkably vague. The harm to the defendant and the public caused by granting an injunction (loss of the $45,000,000 plant, elimination of 300 jobs, and—presumably—higher cement prices for the public) vastly outweighed the benefits to plaintiffs (avoidance of $185,000 in damages). As the court expressed it, there is "large disparity in economic consequences of the nuisance and of the injunction."[46]

Thus, the court considered alternative remedies that would avoid plant closure. One option was granting an injunction, but postponing its effect to allow research on technology that would prevent the emissions. But this technology was unlikely to be developed in the short run, and Atlantic had no ability to control the rate of research. In addition, such an injunction would give plaintiffs immense and unfair economic leverage over Atlantic. If research efforts were unsuccessful, Atlantic might be forced to pay plaintiffs a price far in excess of their actual damages in order to settle the case and thus eliminate the injunction. Accordingly, the court chose a second option: directing the trial court to grant an injunction to be vacated when Atlantic paid permanent damages to plaintiffs. In effect, this essentially awarded plaintiffs compensatory damages in lieu of an injunction.

[c] Reflections on *Boomer*

Boomer is probably the most celebrated decision in modern nuisance law. It generated immediate scholarly controversy which continues today;[47] and it is customarily included in property casebooks. Why?

The main reason is that *Boomer* marks a turning point in our approach to the appropriate remedy for a private nuisance. The basic scenario in *Boomer* —a socially-valuable factory causing comparatively minor damage to a small group of plaintiffs—was a common one. In many jurisdictions, pre-*Boomer* courts confronted with this scenario could choose from only two outcomes: (a) find no nuisance (thereby allowing the factory to continue harming plaintiffs) or (b) issue an injunction against the nuisance (thereby either closing the socially-valuable factory or, more likely, forcing the factory owner to pay plaintiffs a "windfall" settlement to eliminate the injunction). Neither option was entirely palatable. *Boomer* provided a third option—the payment of permanent damages in lieu of an injunction—essentially by shifting the "balancing" standard from liability analysis into

---

[45] Boomer v. Atlantic Cement Co., 309 N.Y.S.2d 312, 316 (N.Y. 1970).

[46] Boomer v. Atlantic Cement Co., 309 N.Y.S.2d 312, 315 (N.Y. 1970).

[47] *See, e.g., Symposium on Nuisance Law: Twenty Years After* Boomer v. Atlantic Cement Co., 54 Alb. L. Rev. 171 (1990).

remedy analysis. It became an important precedent that influenced other jurisdictions to adopt the same approach. [48]

At the same time, *Boomer* sparked new scholarly interest in the application of economic principles to nuisance law. The damages remedy is usually seen as a more efficient solution than an injunction because it helps to allocate resources to the most valuable use. The *Boomer* court properly concluded that a damages award was the cheapest method of resolving the conflict between the parties, thereby maximizing overall utility. It was more efficient to have Atlantic pay permanent damages to plaintiffs (estimated at $185,000) than to issue an injunction that would solve the problem by shutting down the factory (at the cost of the $45,000,000 plant, the 300 jobs, and higher cement prices to the public). But why not issue an injunction and then allow the parties to negotiate their way to a settlement, consistent with the Coase Theorem? Richard Posner explains that this approach would be inefficient due to high transaction costs. The parties in *Boomer,* he argues, were locked into a bilateral monopoly. Any price for settling the case between $185,000 and $45,000,000 would have benefited both sides more than if an injunction were issued. Because of this large bargaining range, "it would have paid each party to invest substantial resources to engross as much of it as possible." [49] For example, Atlantic might have spent $2,000,000 in attorneys fees to negotiate the settlement, while the Boomer side could have spent the same amount. The court's solution—an award of permanent damages—reached an efficient outcome without the need for the parties to incur such high transaction costs. Inspired in part by *Boomer,* an extensive body of law and economics scholarship has contributed to the continued evolution of American nuisance law.

[3] An Alternative Approach: The Compensated Injunction

Another remedial option is to issue an injunction against the nuisance, but require the plaintiff to compensate the defendant for costs of compliance. The pioneer decision adopting this alternative is *Spur Industries, Inc. v. Del E. Webb Development Co.* [50] Defendant Spur operated a commercial feedlot for up to 30,000 cattle in an agricultural area. Plaintiff later developed a residential community on nearby land, and sued to enjoin the feedlot as a nuisance because of the flies and odor that it produced. The Arizona Supreme Court agreed that the public interest justified an injunction closing the feedlot. Yet, because plaintiff was the direct cause of the problem, the court exercised its equitable powers to require plaintiff to indemnify the defendant for the costs of moving or shutting down. "It does not seem harsh to require a developer, who has taken advantage of the lesser land values in a rural area as well as the availability of large tracts

---

[48] As Joel Dobris summarized, "no *Boomer,* no change." *See* Joel C. Dobris, Boomer *Twenty Years Later: An Introduction, with Some Footnotes About "Theory,"* 54 Alb. L. Rev. 171, 172 (1990).

[49] Richard A. Posner, Economic Analysis of Law 71 (4th ed. 1992).

[50] 494 P.2d 700 (Ariz. 1972).

of land on which to build and develop a new town or city in the area, to indemnify those who are forced to leave as a result."[51] *Spur* is a controversial decision that has attracted much scholarly interest,[52] but has not been followed by other courts.

[B] Damages

The appropriate measure of compensatory damages turns on whether the nuisance is deemed permanent or temporary. If the nuisance is permanent, the plaintiff receives all damages—covering both past and future harm—in one lawsuit. Damages are measured by the extent to which the nuisance diminishes the fair market value of the affected property. For example, suppose the court determines that D's noisy smelter is a nuisance and further concludes that the noise will never be abated. If this permanent noise problem reduces the value of P's land from $200,000 to $150,000, P recovers $50,000 in damages.

On the other hand, if the nuisance is temporary or "continuing," the plaintiff only recovers damages that compensate for past harm; the plaintiff may bring successive lawsuits in the future as additional damages are incurred. In this setting, the plaintiff recovers damages equal to the diminished rental or use value of the property, together with any special damages. Suppose that D installs new noise suppression equipment at the smelter, completely eliminating the problem. If the noise problem lasted two years and reduced the rental value of P's land from $15,000 to $12,000 per year, P recovers $6,000 in compensatory damages.

§ 29.07 Public Nuisance

A *public nuisance* is "an unreasonable interference with a right common to the general public."[53] Although it sometimes overlaps with private nuisance law, the public nuisance doctrine is fundamentally different. A private nuisance merely interferes with the rights of a particular person or small number of persons in the use and enjoyment of their land. In contrast, the public nuisance doctrine involves conduct that interferes with the rights of the public in general, in situations that go far beyond the use and enjoyment of land. However, under some circumstances the same conduct may create both a public nuisance and a private nuisance.[54]

Virtually any intentional conduct that unreasonably interferes with the public health, safety, welfare, or morals may constitute a public nuisance. Factors that bear on unreasonableness include:

[51] Spur Indus., Inc. v. Del E. Webb Dev. Co., 494 P.2d 700, 708 (Ariz. 1972).

[52] *See* Jeff L. Lewin, *Compensated Injunctions and the Evolution of Nuisance Law*, 71 Iowa L. Rev. 775 (1986); *see also* Guido Calabresi & A. Douglas Melamed, *Property Rules, Liability Rules, and Inalienability: One View of the Cathedral*, 85 Harv. L. Rev. 1089 (1972).

[53] Restatement (Second) of Torts § 821B(1) (1977).

[54] *See, e.g.,* Spur Indus., Inc. v. Del E. Webb Dev. Co., 494 P.2d 700 (Ariz. 1972) (finding that cattle feedlot was both a public nuisance and a private nuisance).

(1)　whether the conduct "involves a serious interference" with the public heath, safety, peace, comfort, or convenience;

(2)　whether the conduct is prohibited by a statute, ordinance, or regulation; and

(3)　whether the conduct is continuing or permanent and has a "significant effect on the public right."[55]

Examples of conduct that normally constitutes a public nuisance include keeping diseased cattle, running a house of prostitution, operating an unlicensed casino, maintaining a vicious dog, holding a very loud rock concert, and detonating explosives on a residential street.

The typical plaintiff in a public nuisance action is a city or other governmental entity that brings suit on behalf of the general public and seeks damages, an injunction, or an abatement order. A private party may sue on this theory only if "special injury" can be demonstrated.[56] In this context, special injury means a "harm of a kind different from that suffered by the general public."[57] The rationale for the special injury rule is that it prevents a multiplicity of identical lawsuits from being filed against the same defendant, which is seen as an unfair burden.

Suppose F's factory routinely emits invisible radiation that completely disrupts television reception in Town T; as a result, no one in town can watch television. Because the radiation unreasonably interferes with the public welfare, it probably constitutes a public nuisance; Town T may accordingly sue F. Here, resident V has not suffered harm that is different in kind from the harm suffered by other residents; true, V cannot watch television, but neither can anyone else in town. Accordingly, V cannot demonstrate special injury and hence cannot bring suit. Suppose instead that the radiation tragically causes V to contract lung cancer. Because this harm is different in kind, V may sue F.

§ 29.08　Special Problem: Landowner Liability for Hazardous Substance Contamination

The United States enjoyed an unprecedented economic boom after World War II. But this post-war prosperity came at a price. Industries such as chemical manufacturing, plastics, petroleum refining, electronics, mining, and agriculture began generating large quantities of chemical wastes that threatened both human health and the environment. The vast bulk of these hazardous wastes were disposed of improperly, often through "midnight dumping" in remote regions. As a result, DDT, dioxin, PCBs, formaldehyde, vinyl chloride, and similar toxic substances contaminated the land surface and imperiled supplies of drinking water. Nuisance and other common law doctrines were blunt weapons against this new danger.

---

[55] Restatement (Second) of Torts § 821B(2) (1977).

[56] *See, e.g.,* Armory Park Neighborhood Ass'n v. Episcopal Community Servs., 712 P.2d 914 (Ariz. 1985) (neighbors of center that provided free meals to indigent had suffered special injury and thus had standing to maintain a public nuisance action).

[57] Restatement (Second) of Torts § 821C (1977).

Faced with a potential public health crisis, Congress enacted the Comprehensive Environmental Response, Compensation, and Liability Act of 1980 ("CERCLA").[58] CERCLA imposes *strict liability* for the cleanup of hazardous substances on four categories of persons:

(1)   the current "owner" or "operator" of the land;

(2)   persons who were owners or operators of the land at the time of disposal;

(3)   persons who arranged for disposal or treatment; and

(4)   persons who transported the substances to the land.

However, under limited circumstances, an owner may qualify for protection under the *innocent landowner* or *innocent buyer* defense.[59] This defense arises when the owner

(1)   acquires the land after the disposal of the hazardous substance,

(2)   conducts a pre-purchase investigation into the previous ownership and uses of the land "consistent with good commercial or customary practice in an effort to minimize liability,"[60]

(3)   has no reason to know about the contamination, and

(4)   meets various other criteria.

Suppose B, a developer, is considering the purchase of an abandoned industrial site owned by I. B walks across the land—which is covered with grass and wildflowers—and observes no contamination. She purchases the land for $100,000, begins grading the site in preparation for building a condominium project, and discovers toxic contamination in the soil from I's past operations. The federal Environmental Protection Agency investigates the site and estimates that the cleanup will cost $5,000,000. If EPA cleans up the site and then sues B for reimbursement, B will be personally liable for the entire cleanup cost as the current owner *unless* she qualifies for the innocent landowner defense. The main issue here is the adequacy of B's pre-purchase inspection. Given B's sophistication as a developer and the past industrial use of the land, her visual inspection was probably insufficient. Of course, if the I-B sales contract contains a warranty from I that the land is uncontaminated—and I is still solvent—B will be able to obtain indemnity from I. But B's indemnity right against I is not a defense to EPA's action for recovery of cleanup costs.

Now suppose that the toxic contamination on B's land pollutes the underlying groundwater; the plume of toxic groundwater eventually reaches and contaminates N's adjacent parcel. N might sue B for private nuisance. However, CERCLA also creates a cause of action in private parties. Therefore, N may prefer to cleanup the contamination and sue B for reimbursement under CERCLA.

---

[58] 42 U.S.C. §§ 9601–9675.

[59] 42 U.S.C. § 9601(35), 9607(b)(3).

[60] 42 U.S.C. § 9601(35)(B).

Chapter 30

TRESPASS

SYNOPSIS

§ 30.01   The Right to Exclude

The common law cherished an owner's virtually absolute right to exclude others from his land.[1] The law of trespass, which evolved to safeguard this right, was, as a result, extraordinarily broad.

Blackstone expressed this common law view by defining property as "that sole and despotic dominion which one man claims and exercises over the external things of the world, in total exclusion of the right of any other individual in the universe."[2] Blackstone's eighteenth-century approach was quite influential in the young United States. As the Supreme Court ultimately explained, the right to exclude is "one of the most essential sticks in the bundle of rights that are commonly characterized as property."[3]

Why prohibit trespass? The main reason is utilitarian. As Richard Posner explains, the law protects a landowner's right to exclusive possession in

---

[1] *See generally* David J. Bederman, *The Curious Resurrection of Custom: Beach Access and Judicial Takings*, 96 Colum. L. Rev. 1375 (1996); Curtis J. Berger, *PruneYard Revisited: Political Activity on Private Lands*, 66 N.Y.U. L. Rev. 633 (1991); Kelvin H. Dickinson, *Mistaken Improvers of Real Estate*, 64 N.C. L. Rev. 37 (1985); Thomas W. Merrill, *Trespass, Nuisance, and the Costs of Determining Property Rights*, 14 J. Legal Stud. 13 (1985); Richard R.B. Powell, *The Relationship Between Property Rights and Civil Rights*, 15 Hastings L.J. 135 (1963).

[2] Erlich's Blackstone 113 (J.W. Erlich, ed., Nourse 1959).

[3] Kaiser Aetna v. United States, 444 U.S. 164, 176 (1979).

order to maximize the efficient use of land.[4] Suppose farmer A plants wheat; he waters, weeds, and fertilizes his growing crop. When the wheat is ripe, T, a neighbor, enters the field, harvests the wheat, and sells it at market. In a world without trespass liability, A has no claim against T. Absent the protection afforded by the trespass doctrine, Posner argues, owners like A have no incentive to use their land productively. Why would A expend time and money in raising wheat if T or anyone else may appropriate the crop? By protecting owners like A, the trespass doctrine encourages an owner to undertake the investment necessary for optimum use of land. This results in maximum production of food and other goods that benefit society in general. Another important—but distinctly secondary theme—is that the trespass doctrine minimizes the risk of violence. If the law did not protect A's rights, he might be tempted to defend his wheat field through self-help (e.g., with a shotgun).[5]

In recent decades, the scope of the right to exclude—and consequently the trespass doctrine—has been curtailed for reasons of public policy. The productivity rationale underlying Posner's simple model has less force, for example, when applied to residential or commercial property. And other, countervailing policies have emerged. The absolutism of traditional trespass law is out-of-step with the needs of our increasingly crowded society. Thus, for example, the landlord's common law right to refuse to rent to a prospective tenant, or to evict an existing tenant, is no longer absolute (*see* §§ 16.02, 19.04). Similarly, a business open to the public cannot exclude potential customers based on discrimination.[6]

There is a clear movement toward crafting new exceptions to trespass liability in diverse areas, including beach access, migrant farmworker housing, and free speech activities in privately-owned shopping centers. As the New Jersey Supreme Court observed in *State v. Shack*, while overturning a criminal trespass conviction: "Property rights serve human values. They are recognized to that end, and are limited by it."[8] Courts are slowly building on this utilitarian sentiment by limiting the right to exclude in specialized situations.

§ 30.02 What Is a Trespass?

[A] Trespass Defined

At common law, any intentional and unprivileged entry onto land owned or occupied by another constituted a trespass.[9] The scope of this doctrine

---

[4] *See generally* Richard A. Posner, Economic Analysis of Law 32–35 (4th ed. 1992).

[5] *See* Jacque v. Steenberg Homes, Inc., 563 N.W.2d 154 (Wis. 1997) (affirming $100,000 punitive damages award against company that delivered mobile home by trespassing across plaintiffs' field, based in part on the law's policy against self-help remedies).

[6] 42 U.S.C. § 2000a–2000a-6; *see also* U.S. Jaycees v. McClure, 305 N.W.2d 764 (Minn. 1981) (effort of Jaycees club to exclude women members violated state law).

[8] 277 A.2d 369, 372 (N.J. 1971).

[9] *See* Restatement (Second) of Torts §§ 157–164 (1965).

was quite expansive, reflecting an absolutist view of property rights. The modern law of trespass—as reflected by the Restatement (Second) of Torts—largely follows the common law approach. Contemporary developments in the law have focused on carving out special exceptions to liability, not on changing the basic liability standards.

The element of intent has a special meaning in trespass law. A trespasser is strictly liable; good faith, knowledge, and fault are irrelevant.[10] T commits a trespass, for example, if he merely walks across O's land, mistakenly believing it to be his own. The trespass doctrine requires only that T intend to enter onto the land as a matter of free choice, not that he had a subjective intent to trespass or even knew he was trespassing. T's mistaken belief that he actually owns the land is not a defense, although it will presumably bar punitive damages.

Although trespass always involves a physical invasion, a trespass may occur without any personal entry by the trespasser. T will be liable in trespass, for example, if he causes a thing or a third person to enter O's land.[11] Further, although most trespass cases involve entry onto the surface of land, the doctrine also applies to entries below the land surface (e.g., through tunnels or caves)[12] and—at least partially—to entries in the air space over the land.[13]

A trespasser is liable even if the entry causes no actual damage.[14] A court will hold a trespasser like T liable to O for nominal damages and, upon O's request, will routinely enjoin any further trespass. The recent decision of *Jacque v. Steenberg Homes, Inc.*[15] illustrates the potential severity of this rule. The defendant, attempting to deliver a mobile home, discovered that the only road to the delivery site was nearly impassable. The road was covered with seven feet of snow, and contained a sharp curve that could be negotiated only with extensive labor. Defendant accordingly delivered the mobile home by crossing plaintiffs' snow-covered field, over their strong objection. Although the crossing caused no harm at all to the land, plaintiffs received $1 in nominal damages and $100,000 in punitive damages, a result affirmed by the Wisconsin Supreme Court.

[B] Distinguishing Trespass from Nuisance

The boundary between trespass and nuisance—once quite clear—is quite murky today. Traditionally, the distinction turned on the nature of the intrusion. Trespass protected the owner's right to exclusive *possession*. Any

---

[10] Restatement (Second) of Torts § 164 (1965).

[11] Restatement (Second) of Torts § 158 (1965).

[12] *Cf.* Edwards v. Sims, 24 S.W.2d 619 (Ky. Ct. App. 1929) (suggesting entry into cave beneath owner's property constituted a trespass).

[13] *But see* Geller v. Brownstone Condominium Ass'n, 402 N.E.2d 807 (Ill. App. Ct. 1980) (temporary construction scaffolding intruding into air space from adjacent land was not a trespass).

[14] Restatement (Second) of Torts § 163 (1965).

[15] 563 N.W.2d 154 (Wis. 1997).

physical entry onto another's land was deemed to interfere with possession, and was thus a trespass. For example, T could commit an actionable entry if (a) he crossed O's land, (b) he tossed rocks onto O's land, or (c) debris from his factory fell onto O's land.

Nuisance, on the other hand, protected the owner's *use and enjoyment* of land (*see* § 29.02). Any conduct—other than physical entry—that interfered with the use and enjoyment of land was accordingly governed by nuisance law. Thus, for example, if T emitted smoke, odors, noise, vibration, light, or gases onto O's property, this was a nuisance, not a trespass.

Today, many courts reject this simplistic distinction. In a very real sense—reflecting the limited scientific knowledge of the era—the common law distinction ultimately turned on *visibility*: were the invading particles large enough to be visible (usually a trespass), or so small as to be invisible (a nuisance)? Courts are now increasingly willing to stretch the boundary of trespass (e.g., in air pollution or toxic contamination cases) to encompass microscopic particles, usually by focusing on the nature of the harm caused, not the size of the particle. Thus, in borderline cases a plaintiff may choose to sue in either trespass or nuisance.

[C] General Exceptions to Trespass Liability

An entry under a legally-recognized privilege does not constitute a trespass. The classic example of a privileged entry is one made with the landowner's *consent*. If owner O invites plumber P onto O's land to fix a leaky pipe, for example, P's entry is privileged. The other main privilege may be broadly described as *necessity*. For example, a firefighter may enter private property to save an adjacent house from fire, just as a police officer may enter to arrest a suspect. Similarly, private persons are privileged to enter another's land in an emergency situation (e.g., while fleeing from an attacking bear).[16]

§ 30.03 Trespass and Rights of Migrant Farmworkers

O, a farmer, employs and houses migrant farmworkers on his property. P, a social worker, wishes to visit one of the farmworkers. Does the trespass doctrine permit O to exclude P from the farm?

This question was posed in the celebrated case of *State v. Shack*.[17] Two employees of government-funded organizations entered upon a privately-owned New Jersey farm in order to aid migrant farmworkers housed on the land. One, a health care provider, needed to remove sutures from a farmworker; the other, an attorney, wanted to discuss a legal problem with another worker. The farm owner, one Tedesco, confronted them with his shotgun and demanded that they leave the land. When they refused,

---

[16] *See generally,* Powell on Real Property ¶ 707[4] (Michael Allan Wolf ed., Matthew Bender).

[17] 277 A.2d 369 (N.J. 1971). *See also* Michele Cortese, Note, *Property Rights and Human Values: A Right of Access to Private Property for Tenant Organizers,* 17 Colum. Hum. Rts. L. Rev. 257 (1986).

Tedesco then summoned a state trooper to eject them and initiated a successful criminal prosecution for trespass. The New Jersey Supreme Court overturned the convictions, finding that defendants' entry was privileged. Refusing to reach defendants' constitutional claims, the court grounded its ruling in New Jersey law; "under our State law the ownership of real property does not include the right to bar access to governmental services available to migrant workers."[18]

The rationale for this decision, however, is far from clear. The court seemed to suggest that the traditional privileges of consent and necessity contributed to its ruling. Having opened up his property to house farmworkers, perhaps Tedesco impliedly consented to entries by at least some visitors. Similarly, the visits of the health care worker and the attorney were arguably prompted by considerations of necessity. Medical care, for instance, is a basic human necessity. On the other hand, why couldn't such services have been provided off Tedesco's land? Another view of the case relies on a federal preemption argument; the federal statutes creating the publicly-funded programs at issue implicitly established a right of access across private land in order to implement the program goals, which impliedly preempted the state law of trespass.

At bottom, however, *Shack* appears to rest on a more abstract utilitarian analysis. The court observed that rights are not absolute, but rather are relative. Thus, the law requires an accommodation between the right of a property owner and the "right of individuals who are parties with him in consensual transactions relating to the use of the property."[20] Trying to strike a fair adjustment of the competing needs of the parties, the court concluded that Tedesco could not isolate a farmworker "in any respect significant for the worker's well-being."[21] He was thus obligated to allow access by employees of government agencies and charitable organizations providing services to migrant workers.[22]

§ 30.04 Trespass and Freedom of Speech

[A] Rights Under Federal Constitution

Suppose P wishes to distribute Communist party literature to customers at a shopping center owned by O. Can O enjoin this conduct as a trespass? Or may P exercise her right of free speech on O's property?

The First Amendment protects the right of freedom of speech from state action, not private action. Accordingly, while P has a right to distribute her literature on public property, this right does not necessarily extend to private property as well. One might argue, of course, that O's shopping

---

[18] State v. Shack, 277 A.2d 369, 371–372 (N.J. 1971).

[20] State v. Shack, 277 A.2d 369, 374 (N.J. 1971).

[21] State v. Shack, 277 A.2d 369, 374 (N.J. 1971).

[22] *See also* Uston v. Resorts Int'l Hotel, Inc., 445 A.2d 370 (N.J. 1982) (partially relying on *State v. Shack* in holding Atlantic City casino could not exclude "card counter" from blackjack tables).

center should be subject to the First Amendment because it is the functional equivalent of a small town.[23] Like the business district of a small town, the typical shopping center has its own sidewalks, parking spaces, traffic controls, security force, fire protection, and so forth. Further, the shopping center serves both commercial and social functions. More than a mere collection of stores, it increasingly serves as a social meeting place. However, the Supreme Court rejected this argument in *Lloyd Corp. v. Tanner*,[24] reasoning that property does not lose its private character merely because the public is invited to use it for specific purposes. Thus, the First Amendment will probably not shelter P from trespass liability.

[B] Rights Under State Constitutions

The right to free speech contained in state constitutions, however, is sometimes broader than the First Amendment protection. A number of high-profile decisions have examined whether state constitutions allow citizens to exercise a right of freedom of speech at privately-owned shopping centers, with mixed results.[25] Although varying widely in other respects, these decisions typically focus on one issue: is today's shopping center the functional equivalent of yesterday's downtown business district? Answering "yes," courts in California, New Jersey, and certain other states interpret their state constitutions to protect such speech by P and other citizens. These decisions have prompted considerable litigation on the extent to which a shopping center owner may regulate the time, place, and manner of free speech activities.

The leading decision exploring this state constitutional right is *Prune-Yard Shopping Center v. Robins*.[26] The case arose when a group of high school students sought to enlist public support to oppose a pending United Nations resolution condemning "Zionism" by distributing literature and soliciting petition signatures in a privately-owned California shopping mall. Politely ejected from the mall by a security guard, they sued to obtain access. The California Supreme Court held that the state constitution protected the reasonably-exercised right of free speech even in private shopping centers. The mall owners subsequently attacked this decision before the United States Supreme Court, claiming, inter alia, that it constituted an illegal taking and violated their own federal right to freedom of speech. The Court found that no taking had occurred, reasoning that the owners lacked any evidence suggesting that such activity would unreasonably impair the value of their land as a shopping center. Any potential

---

[23] *See* Marsh v. Alabama, 326 U.S. 501 (1946) (First Amendment's guarantee of free speech applied to privately-owned "company town").

[24] 407 U.S. 551 (1972).

[25] *See, e.g.,* New Jersey Coalition Against War in the Middle East v. J.M.B. Realty Corp., 650 A.2d 757 (N.J. 1994) (New Jersey constitution protects right to distribute leaflets at shopping center); Western Pennsylvania Socialist Workers 1982 Campaign v. Connecticut Gen. Life Ins. Co., 515 A.2d 1331 (Pa. 1986) (Pennsylvania constitution does not protect right to collect signatures on nomination petition at shopping center).

[26] 447 U.S. 74 (1980). *See also* Curtis J. Berger, PruneYard *Revisited: Political Activity on Private Lands*, 66 N.Y.U. L. Rev. 633 (1991).

adverse impact, the Court observed, could be mitigated by reasonable time, place, and manner regulations. Nor did the ruling interfere with the owners' own freedom of speech. It was unlikely that patrons would conclude the owners were endorsing the views in question and, in any event, the owners could avoid this danger by expressly disclaiming any sponsorship.

§ 30.05   Trespass and Beach Access

[A]   Who Owns the Beach?

Roman law held that the ocean—and, by extension, ocean beaches as well—could not be privately owned, but rather was common property open to all. The *public trust doctrine* produces much the same result in the United States. It holds that state governments act as trustees over navigable waters and certain related lands in order to protect the public's right to use these areas for navigation, commerce, fishing, swimming, and other activities.

Under this doctrine, the public has a clear right to use wet-sand ocean beaches *below* the mean high tide line; these beaches are subject to the "ebb and flow" of the tide.[27] Suppose P, a member of the public, wishes to use the wet-sand beach. May P cross O's land—the dry-sand beach *above* the mean high tide line—to reach the wet-sand beach? Even better, may P use O's dry-sand beach? Or would such acts constitute trespasses?

[B]   Extending the Public Trust Doctrine

One judicial approach to these issues relies on the public trust doctrine itself, as illustrated by the New Jersey Supreme Court's decision in *Matthews v. Bay Head Improvement Association*.[28] There, the defendant association effectively controlled public access to most of the beach in the Borough of Bay Head, New Jersey; it owned the dry-sand parcels that separated the wet-sand beach from the ends of seven public streets, and leased or owned much of the rest of the dry-sand beach. Except for association members, no one could travel from these street ends to reach the wet-sand beach without the association's consent. The court first concluded that the public had a right of access across the association's dry-sand beach parcels. To deny public access, it reasoned, would seriously threaten or perhaps even nullify the public trust doctrine.

Extending this line of analysis, the *Matthews* court held that the public was entitled to use and occupy the dry-sand beach itself where this use was essential or reasonably necessary for enjoyment of the ocean. For example, it noted that swimming must be accompanied by periods of rest on land; during high tides, the effective exercise of this right required that a swimmer be allowed to rest on the dry-sand beach.

---

[27] *See, e.g.,* Phillips Petroleum Co. v. Mississippi, 484 U.S. 469 (1988); Matthews v. Bay Head Improvement Ass'n, 471 A.2d 355 (N.J. 1984).

[28] 471 A.2d 355 (N.J. 1984).

The result in *Matthews* rests heavily on the identity of the defendant, whose relationship with the Borough and virtual monopoly over the local beach gave it a quasi-public status. A city or other public entity—as a component of the state itself—is obviously restricted by the public trust doctrine. Just as a city would be obligated to provide general access to a city beach, the court ruled that the defendant association must provide beach access for members of the public, such as our hypothetical beach-lover P. *Matthews* offers little guidance, however, on whether the public trust doctrine imposes similar obligations on an ordinary private landowner.[29]

[C] Other Approaches

Two other approaches are utilized in access disputes where there is a long history of public use. Four states with extensive coastlines—Florida, Hawaii, Oregon, and Texas—rely on customary rights. In these states, lengthy and uninterrupted public use of the beach creates a perpetual right of access.[30]

Alternatively, a few states apply the prescriptive easement doctrine in these circumstances (*see* § 32.06). It is often difficult, however, to establish the elements of the doctrine in beach access cases. Continuous use by the public is hard to prove as a factual matter. And because many courts presume that the owner consented to prior public access, adverse use is rarely established.

§ 30.06 Encroachments

Suppose T mistakenly builds her new house in the wrong location: it extends two inches over her lot line onto the adjoining lot owned by O. What is O's remedy for this trespass?

A permanent or continuing trespass caused by the construction of a building or other improvement that *partially* extends onto another's land is known as an *encroachment*. The common law treated an encroachment just like any other type of trespass. Thus, under the traditional view, O had a choice. He could either (a) obtain an injunction forcing T to remove the encroachment or (b) recover damages from T.[31] This standard may produce harsh results. Suppose that removing the encroachment (by rebuilding part of the house) will cost T $10,000, while allowing the encroachment to remain will cause only minor damage to O, perhaps $500. Should the law permit O to inflict costs of $10,000 on T merely to save O $500?

---

[29] *Cf.* Nollan v. California Coastal Comm'n, 483 U.S. 825 (1987) (state's attempt to condition building permit for beachfront lot on owner's grant of beach access easement violated the Takings Clause of the Fifth Amendment).

[30] *See, e.g.,* State of Oregon *ex rel.* Thornton v. Hay, 462 P.2d 671 (Or. 1969).

[31] *See, e.g.,* Peters v. Archambault, 278 N.E.2d 729 (Mass. 1972) (house encroached 15 feet); Geragosian v. Union Realty Co., 193 N.E. 726 (Mass. 1935) (fire escape encroached 11 inches over plaintiff's land, and drain extended under land); Pile v. Pedrick, 31 A. 646 (Pa. 1895) (foundation wall encroached 1 3/8 inches).

Driven by concern for both equity and efficiency, most modern courts restrict the owner's remedy where the encroachment results from an innocent, good faith mistake. If the injury to the owner is minor compared to the cost of removing the innocent encroachment—as in the O-T example above—a court will deny the owner's requested injunction and award damages instead. Under this standard, O will receive $500. The common law view, however, still governs intentional encroachments. Accordingly, O could obtain an injunction compelling removal of the encroachment regardless of equity or efficiency if T's conduct was intentional.[32]

§ 30.07 Good Faith Improvers

What if an owner mistakenly builds a new house *entirely* on land owned by another? Suppose T intends to build on her own lot, but due to a survey error inadvertently builds her house on an adjacent lot owned by O. Because the owner of land is also deemed to own buildings on the land, O now owns the house. Yet O has been unjustly enriched by T's good faith mistake. Does T have any recourse?

English common law accorded only meager protection to the improver of another's land. In general, the improver was considered a trespasser subject to punishment, not a laborer entitled to compensation. In the United States, this standard still governs the fate of the "bad faith" improver who purposely builds on another's land; he loses ownership of the improvements without compensation.

Yet, to prevent unjust enrichment, most states afford limited relief to the *good faith improver*—one who improves land under the mistaken but good faith belief[33] that he owns it.[34] Case law in some states entitles the good faith improver to either (a) remove the improvements or (b) receive compensation equal to the amount by which the improvements increase the market value of the owner's land.[35] Other states—usually by statute—require the owner to either compensate the improver for the enhanced value produced by the improvements or to simply sell the land to the improver for its fair market value before improvement.[36]

---

[32] *See* Powell on Real Property ¶ 707.3[2] (Michael Allan Wolf ed., Matthew Bender).

[33] *But see* Raab v. Casper, 124 Cal. Rptr. 590 (Ct. App. 1975) (remanding case to trial court for determination on improver's possible negligence).

[34] *See generally* Kelvin H. Dickinson, *Mistaken Improvers of Real Estate*, 64 N.C. L. Rev. 37 (1985); John H. Merryman, *Improving the Lot of the Trespassing Improver*, 11 Stan. L. Rev. 456 (1959).

[35] *See, e.g.*, Madrid v. Spears, 250 F.2d 51 (10th Cir. 1957) (good faith improver can recover compensation measured by enhanced value of land); Hardy v. Burroughs, 232 N.W. 200 (Mich. 1930) (same); Somerville v. Jacobs, 170 S.E.2d 805 (W. Va. 1969) (good faith improver entitled to receive either enhanced value of land or conveyance of improved land in return for payment of land's value before improvement).

[36] *See* Powell on Real Property ¶ 707.3[1][c][iii] (Michael Allan Wolf ed., Matthew Bender).

Chapter 31

SURFACE, SUBSURFACE, AND AIR SPACE RIGHTS

§ 31.01 Attributes of Ownership

Suppose O holds fee simple absolute in Greenacre, a 500-acre tract of undeveloped land. O's basic rights are obvious:

    (1)   he is entitled to use Greenacre forever,

    (2)   he can exclude all other persons from the land, and

    (3)   he may freely transfer his rights to others.

But the nature and extent of other potential rights is less clear. For example, does O's ownership extend to the air space above Greenacre? Is O entitled to the oil, gas, and groundwater beneath Greenacre? Where is the boundary of Greenacre on the earth's surface? May O use water from the stream that flows across Greenacre?

This chapter examines doctrines that define various attributes of real property ownership: subsurface rights, air space rights, and miscellaneous surface rights.[1] If O owns title to Greenacre, what additional property rights does he hold beyond those already explored in this text? We might approach the same set of issues from another direction. If O owns legal rights in Greenacre, what physically comprises "Greenacre"?

A central theme in this chapter is the evolution of property rights. The common law doctrines governing surface, subsurface, and air space rights tended to favor "natural" uses of land, and were hostile to new development. These traditional rules usually vested absolute rights in the surface owner, regardless of the interests of others. Over the last two centuries, these doctrines have been increasingly reoriented toward encouraging land development; and much of the rigid common law absolutism has been replaced by a flexible, reasonableness standard that gives more deference to the needs of third parties and society at large.

§ 31.02 Water Rights

[A] Rivers, Lakes, and Other Watercourses

[1] Overview

Water rights in rivers, lakes, streams, and other watercourses are allocated through two basic systems. The *riparian system* dominates in eastern states, where water is usually abundant; the *prior appropriation system* prevails in western states, where water is typically scarce. The difference between the two is fundamental: the riparian system is based on the *location* of land, while the prior appropriation system is based on *first use* of water.

[2] Riparian System

A riparian system allocates water rights to the owner whose land adjoins a river, lake, stream, or other watercourse. Suppose A owns a tract of undeveloped land that borders the Green River. In a riparian jurisdiction, A holds the right to take water from the river simply based on the location of his property.

What is the extent of a riparian water right? There are two approaches to this question. Today virtually all riparian jurisdictions follow the *reasonable use doctrine*, sometimes called the "American rule." Under this approach, a riparian owner may take water for all reasonable uses that do not unreasonably interfere with the uses of other riparian owners.[2] Whether a particular use is deemed reasonable hinges on a number of factors, including the economic and social value of the use, the purpose of

---

[1] *See generally* Russell J. Adams, *Updating Groundwater Law: New Wine in Old Bottles*, 39 Ohio St. L.J. 520 (1978); Eric T. Freyfogle, *Context and Accommodation in Modern Property Law*, 41 Stan. L. Rev. 1529 (1989); Anthony Scott & Georgina Coustalin, *The Evolution of Water Rights*, 35 Nat. Resources J. 821 (1995).

[2] *See, e.g.,* Stratton v. Mt. Hermon Boys' School, 103 N.E. 87 (Mass. 1913).

the use, its suitability to the area, the harm caused to other users, the practicality of avoiding the harm, and so forth; domestic uses receive special priority. For example, presumably A may reasonably use water from the Green River to irrigate crops on his land.[3] On the other hand, A cannot divert most of the river's flow to create a lake where he can practice water skiing.[4] While the reasonable use standard facilitates the productive use of land—unlike the "natural flow" rule discussed below—it suffers from the usual defects in *ad hoc* tests: it is unpredictable in result and expensive to administer.

A few riparian jurisdictions still adhere to the historic *natural flow rule*. Under this view, the riparian owner may: (1) take an unlimited amount of water for "natural" uses (e.g., drinking, bathing, washing); and (2) take water for "artificial" uses (e.g., irrigation, mining) so long as the natural flow of the watercourse is not substantially diminished in either quantity or quality. As a practical matter, the natural flow rule tends to restrict new uses, and thus impedes development.

[3] Prior Appropriation System

The prior appropriation system is a variant on the familiar first-in-time rule. It allocates water rights to the first person to take water from a watercourse for a beneficial use. Suppose F, a farmer, constructs a pipe system that diverts water from the Blue River to his farm, located two miles away; F routinely uses the water to irrigate his crops. Under a prior appropriation system, this conduct is sufficient to create water rights in F because he was the first person to put the water to beneficial use. The fact that F's land does not adjoin the Blue River is irrelevant.

The rationale for the prior appropriation system is well-summarized in *Coffin v. Left Hand Ditch Co.*,[5] a nineteenth-century decision of the Colorado Supreme Court where a riparian owner challenged the validity of a nonriparian's prior appropriation. The court explained that in the arid west, artificial irrigation for agriculture was essential. Thus, "[i]t has always been the policy of the national, as well as the territorial and state governments, to encourage the diversion and use of water . . . for agriculture."[6] In reliance on the prior appropriation system, the court observed, landowners had built houses, constructed improvements, and brought thousands of acres under cultivation; "[d]eny the doctrine of priority . . . of right by . . . appropriation, and a great part of the value of all this property

---

[3] *See, e.g.,* Harris v. Brooks, 283 S.W.2d 129 (Ark. 1955) (following reasonable use standard); Borough of Westville v. Whitney Home Builders, Inc., 122 A.2d 233 (N.J. Super. Ct. App. Div. 1956) (same); *cf.* Pyle v. Gilbert, 265 S.E.2d 584 (Ga. 1980) (finding question of fact whether use of water for irrigation was reasonable).

[4] *See also* Game & Fresh Water Fish Comm'n v. Lake Islands, Ltd., 407 So. 2d 189 (Fla. 1981) (recognizing right of riparian owner to use surface of lake for access to island property); Johnson v. Seifert, 100 N.W.2d 689 (Minn. 1960) (recognizing right of riparian owner to use surface of lake for boating, fishing, etc.).

[5] 6 Colo. 443 (1882).

[6] Coffin v. Left Hand Ditch Co., 6 Colo. 443, 446 (1882).

is at once destroyed."[7] Beyond its role in fostering the productive use of land, the prior appropriation system has the usual virtue and vice of any capture rule: it provides a predictable "bright line" standard that is easily administered, but tends to encourage wasteful consumption.

The "beneficial use" requirement somewhat resembles the "reasonable use" standard in riparian jurisdictions. Beneficial use has two dimensions: purpose and quantity. Water may be taken only for a use that has a beneficial purpose (e.g., irrigation, recreation). And, in most states, only the quantity of water necessary for the beneficial use may be diverted.[8]

[4] Modern Rise of Permit Systems

Historically, water rights arose purely from private action, either by the acquisition of riparian land or the beneficial use of water. Today most states exercise administrative authority over the process of obtaining water rights, usually by requiring that a new user obtain a permit to divert surface water. In prior appropriation states, the criteria for issuance of permits are based on prior appropriation principles; riparian states follow riparian criteria.

[B] Diffused Surface Water

All surface water that is not confined in lakes, rivers, streams or other watercourses is known as *diffused surface water*. This includes water from flooding, rain, snow melt, springs, or seepage that flows across the land surface or gathers in temporary ponds or puddles. Conflicts rarely arise about rights to use diffused water; the surface owner clearly has the right to divert such water. Rather, in this area the law focuses on the problem of *too much* water. Suppose that rainfall runoff from A's land naturally drains downhill onto B's land. Is B obligated to accept this drainage or can she block it? Can A alter her land in a manner that increases the drainage burden on B's land?

Historically, American jurisdictions were divided into two diametrically opposed positions on these issues. In states adopting the *common enemy rule*, an owner was permitted to repel water from his land in any manner, without liability for any resulting injury to others.[9] Under this approach, for example, B could build a wall around her land to protect it from A's runoff, regardless of harm to A. Conversely, in states following the *civil law rule*, an owner could not interfere with the natural drainage of diffused water. In a jurisdiction utilizing this view, B must accept the natural runoff from A's land. But these rigid doctrines proved unworkable: the civil law rule effectively prohibited the development of land for new uses, while the common enemy rule allowed landowners to inflict severe injury on others.

The modern rule of *reasonable use* is a compromise between these two extremes. Roughly half of the states have flatly adopted the reasonable use

---

[7] Coffin v. Left Hand Ditch Co., 6 Colo. 443, 446 (1882).

[8] *See* Powell on Real Property § 65.07[3][c] (Michael Allan Wolf ed., Matthew Bender).

[9] *See, e.g.*, Argyelan v. Haviland, 435 N.E.2d 973 (Ind. 1982); Yonadi v. Homestead Country Homes, Inc., 127 A.2d 198 (N.J. Super Ct. App. Div. 1956).

standard: an owner may make reasonable use of the land, even though this alters the flow of diffused water in a manner that harms others.[10] Most other states have adopted the reasonableness standard indirectly, by using it to temper the application of the common enemy or civil law rules. The traditional common enemy and civil law rules persist only in a few states.[11]

[C] Groundwater

Groundwater—as the name suggests—is simply water located under the land surface. The law traditionally distinguishes between two categories of groundwater: (1) *underground streams* (water flowing underground in a defined channel), and (2) *percolating groundwater* (dispersed water that trickles or percolates through permeable subsurface layers).

When the law in this area began to develop, underground streams were seen as valuable sources of water for consumptive use, much like streams flowing on the surface. The rules governing surface watercourses (*see* [A], *above*) were accordingly extended to apply to underground streams as well. In contrast, during this formative period the law misjudged the importance of percolating groundwater. It was widely seen as a minor and unreliable water source that was difficult to exploit. Thus, under the *absolute owner-ship rule*, groundwater was considered to be part of the land itself, like soil, rock, or trees; whoever owned the land surface also owned the exclusive rights to the percolating groundwater under the land. For example, suppose O owned title to Greenacre. The absolute ownership rule allowed O to extract an unlimited amount of water from beneath Greenacre, even if this caused injury to adjacent landowners or others, unless O acted with malice or wasted the water.[12]

Over time, the increasing demand for water and the new realization that percolating groundwater was a highly productive source, led almost all jurisdictions to abandon the traditional rule. Today the law is splintered into four alternative approaches.[13] First, some states follow the American or "reasonable use" approach, which modifies the absolute ownership rule in two respects: (1) the water may be used only on the overlying land; and (2) the use must be reasonably related to the natural use of the land.[14] Second, a few states utilize a variant of the reasonable use approach found in the Restatement (Second) of Torts;[15] it determines whether a particular

---

[10] *See, e.g.,* Westland Skating Center, Inc. v. Gus Machado Buick, Inc., 542 So. 2d 959 (Fla. 1989) (adopting reasonable use standard); Heins Implement Co. v. Missouri Highway & Transp. Comm'n, 859 S.W.2d 681 (Mo. 1993) (same); Armstrong v. Francis Corp., 120 A.2d 4 (N.J. 1956) (same); Pendergrast v. Aiken, 236 S.E.2d 787 (N.C. 1977) (same).

[11] *See* Powell on Real Property § 65.12[2] (Michael Allan Wolf ed., Matthew Bender).

[12] *See* Finley v. Teeter Stone, Inc., 248 A.2d 106 (Md. 1968) (discussing common law rule); Friendswood Dev. Co. v. Smith-Southwest Indus., Inc., 576 S.W.2d 21 (Tex. 1978) (same).

[13] *See* MacArtor v. Graylyn Crest III Swim Club, Inc., 187 A.2d 417 (Del. Ch. 1963) (discussing different approaches); Prather v. Eisenmann, 261 N.W.2d 766 (Neb. 1978) (same); State v. Michels Pipeline Constr., Inc., 217 N.W.2d 339 (Wis. 1974) (same).

[14] *See* Powell on Real Property § 65.08[3][b][ii] (Michael Allan Wolf ed., Matthew Bender).

[15] Restatement (Second) of Torts § 858 (1977).

use is reasonable by balancing the equities and hardships among all users. Third, a handful of states utilize the "correlative rights" approach; it provides that all owners of land over a common pool of groundwater have equal rights to extract the water for beneficial uses on the overlying land.[16] Finally, an increasing number of states regulate groundwater rights through a statutory system, usually founded on the prior appropriation model; in these states, a permit is necessary before percolating groundwater can be extracted.[17]

§ 31.03 Public Trust Doctrine

The *public trust doctrine* is one of the most far-reaching and controversial rules defining the legal relationship between private owners and the environment.[18] Under this doctrine, navigable waters and closely-related lands are held by the sovereign in trust for use by the public in such activities as commerce, fishing, and navigation. If the sovereign conveys such property to a private owner, it remains encumbered by the trust and the rights of the owner are accordingly limited.

Suppose that State A conveys a parcel of ocean-front land, together with the adjacent beach, to B. B develops a private vacation resort on the land, and fences off the beach at each end to restrict access to his paying customers. Under the public trust doctrine, the public is entitled to use the wet-sand beach below the mean high tide line (*see* § 30.05). Thus, when B acquired his property rights in the beach, he did not receive all the metaphorical "sticks" that comprise fee simple absolute. B's title was subject to the public's preexisting rights under the public trust doctrine, including the right to use the wet-sand beach. As a result, B cannot exclude the public.

What property is subject to the public trust doctrine? The doctrine clearly applies to ocean waters, tidal wetlands,[19] the wet-sand ocean beach between the high and low tide lines,[20] navigable bodies of fresh water such as lakes and rivers,[21] the beds of navigable bodies of water (*e.g.*, the bed of a river),[22] and fresh water wetlands,[23] and may apply to other areas (*e.g.*, non-navigable tributaries of navigable waters) as well. However,

---

[16] *See* Powell on Real Property § 65.08[3][b][iii] (Michael Allan Wolf ed., Matthew Bender).

[17] *See* Powell on Real Property § 65.08[3][b][v] (Michael Allan Wolf ed., Matthew Bender).

[18] *See generally* Illinois Cent. R.R. Co. v. Illinois, 146 U.S. 387 (1892) (discussing doctrine); *see also* Richard J. Lazarus, *Changing Conceptions of Property and Sovereignty in Natural Resources: Questioning the Public Trust Doctrine*, 71 Iowa L. Rev. 631 (1986); Joseph L. Sax, *The Public Trust Doctrine in Natural Resource Law: Effective Judicial Intervention*, 68 Mich. L. Rev. 471 (1970).

[19] *See* Phillips Petroleum Co. v. Mississippi, 484 U.S. 469 (1988).

[20] *See* Matthews v. Bay Head Improvement Ass'n, 471 A.2d 355 (N.J. 1984) (extending the doctrine to dry-sand ocean beach).

[21] *See* National Audubon Soc'y v. Superior Court, 658 P.2d 709 (Cal. 1983).

[22] *See* Powell on Real Property, ¶ 160 (Michael Allan Wolf ed., Matthew Bender).

[23] *See* Just v. Marinette County, 201 N.W.2d 761 (Wis. 1972).

attempts to extend the doctrine to lands unrelated to water have enjoyed little success.

Most states have extended the doctrine to uses far beyond the traditional triad of commerce, fishing, and navigation. For example, swimming, hunting, bathing, boating, and other recreational uses are generally protected. In the landmark decision of *National Audubon Society v. Superior Court*,[24] the California Supreme Court observed that the public trust also encompassed the preservation of lands in their natural state to serve as open space, wildlife habitat, and ecological units for scientific study.

Is the public trust doctrine an essential tool for environmental preservation, a dangerous threat to private property rights, or both? Suppose O purchases a 100-acre tract of wetlands in County C that borders a navigable river. County C later rezones O's land into the newly-created "Open Space" zone, where the only permitted uses are nature study, harvesting naturally-growing crops (e.g., wild rice), and the like. If the rezoning leaves O with no economically viable use for the land, does it constitute a regulatory taking? Assuming that (a) O's wetlands are subject to the public trust doctrine and (b) the doctrine includes the preservation of lands for open space and wildlife habitat as *National Audubon* indicates, then O's title never included the right to develop the wetlands for a non-natural use. Because the law never gave this right to O in the first place, the rezoning "took" nothing from him (*see* Chapter 40).

§ 31.04 Right to Support

[A] Lateral Support

Suppose A and B own title to adjoining parcels of unimproved hillside land. A, the owner of the downhill parcel, excavates near the common boundary line in order to build the foundation for a new office building. The result is a landslide: B's uphill parcel slides down into A's excavation. What are B's rights?

Each landowner has a common law right to *lateral support*: the right to have the land in its natural condition supported by adjoining parcels of land. An adjoining owner who withdraws lateral support is strictly liable for all damage caused by the resulting subsidence. In the above hypothetical, A withdrew lateral support from B's unimproved land, causing the landslide. Therefore, A is strictly liable to B for the diminution in the value of B's land, or the cost of repairing the land, whichever is less. B may also secure an injunction to restrict A's future excavations.

The law governing the lateral support of land with buildings or other improvements, however, is less clear. Suppose that B's parcel in the above hypothetical is already improved with a house before A's excavation begins. Two situations are possible: (1) the landslide would have occurred even if B's land were in natural condition; or (2) the added weight imposed by B's

---

[24] 658 P.2d 709 (Cal. 1983).

house caused the landslide. In the first situation, most states apply the common law rule; here, A is strictly liable to B.[25] In the second situation, however, the majority of states use negligence principles. Accordingly, A is liable only if he failed to use due care to avoid injury to B's property (e.g., by failing to investigate soil conditions or using improper excavation methods).[26]

[B] Subjacent Support

Each landowner also has a common law right to *subjacent support*: the right to have the land in its natural condition supported by the earth below. Imagine that C owns title to the land surface, while D owns the subsurface mineral rights. D's mining activities withdraw subjacent support from C's land, causing it to collapse into a deep underground pit. If C's land is unimproved, D is strictly liable for the resulting damage.[27] In addition, even if C's land is improved with a house or other structure, D is probably still strictly liable in most jurisdictions because the added weight of the structure did not cause the subsidence—the land would have subsided even if unimproved. Compared to the weight of the overlying land, the weight added by any structure is usually minimal. As a result, most jurisdictions presume that improved land would have subsided even in natural condition.[28] In the rare instance where the added weight of a structure causes the subsidence, courts seem to apply negligence principles. Thus, if it can be clearly shown that the extra weight from C's structure caused the collapse, D is liable only if negligence is proven.

§ 31.05 Boundary Line Doctrines

[A] Land Boundaries: Agreed Boundary Line, Acquiescence, and Estoppel

O purchases title to Blueacre, a 100-acre farm surrounded by a fence, from S. O later commissions a survey of the land. The survey reveals that the fence on the farm's west side is not located on the actual boundary line between Blueacre and Redacre, the adjoining parcel owned by P. According to the deed description, the true boundary line is 20 feet west of the fence. In other words, a 20-foot wide strip of what appears to be Redacre is actually—according to the deed description—part of Blueacre. Where is the legal boundary line?

The common law developed four doctrines that may, under limited circumstances, establish the boundary line in a different location from that

---

[25] *See, e.g.,* Noone v. Price, 298 S.E.2d 218 (W. Va. 1982).

[26] *See, e.g.,* Spall v. Janota, 406 N.E.2d 378 (Ind. Ct. App. 1980) (discussing acts that constitute negligent excavation); *see also* Puckett v. Sullivan, 12 Cal. Rptr. 55 (Ct. App. 1961) (holding owner liable in negligence for excavation that removed support from noncontiguous land).

[27] Restatement (Second) of Torts § 820 cmt. b (1977).

[28] Restatement (Second) of Torts § 820 cmt. d (1977).

specified in the deed: agreed boundary line; acquiescence; estoppel; and adverse possession. Adverse possession is covered in Chapter 27. The remaining three doctrines—which courts often blend together—are discussed below. [29]

Agreed Boundary Line: The agreed boundary line doctrine requires:

(1)   initial uncertainty about the location of the boundary;

(2)   an express or implied agreement, written or oral, between adjacent owners to treat a particular line as the true boundary; and

(3)   in some states, possession by the parties up to the agreed line. [30]

For example, if S and P were uncertain about the location of Blueacre's western boundary, and orally agreed that the fence would serve as the boundary, the law will respect this agreement.

Acquiescence: The requirements for acquiescence differ widely from state to state. In general, when adjacent landowners mutually recognize and accept a fence or other clear line as the boundary between their parcels for a long period of time, this becomes the legal boundary. Most courts do not require either initial uncertainty or an actual agreement between the parties. Thus, for example, if S and P recognized the fence as the western boundary of Blueacre for 20 years before O's purchase, it became the legal boundary. [31]

Estoppel: Estoppel applies when one owner misleads a neighbor about the true location of the common boundary line, and the neighbor relies on the misrepresentation to his detriment. For example, suppose S constructed the fence himself, carelessly telling P: "The fence is right on the boundary line." If P relied on this misrepresentation (e.g., by building a barn on the affected strip of land), then the fence line became the legal boundary line through estoppel. [32]

[B] Water Boundaries: Accretion and Avulsion

Suppose that O and P own adjacent parcels and all deeds describe the boundary between their parcels as a body of water. For example, the deed conveying title to O might read, in part: "thence westerly to the middle of Bull Creek, thence northeasterly along the middle line of Bull Creek for 1,000 feet, thence easterly," etc. What happens to the boundary line if Bull Creek changes course?

Two deceptively-simple common law rules address this situation. *Accretion* occurs when the location of a boundary creek, river, lake, or other body of water moves slowly due to the gradual and imperceptible build-up of soil. A water boundary line shifts with accretion. [33] The opposite of accretion is

---

[29] *See generally* Olin L. Browder, Jr., *The Practical Location of Boundaries*, 56 Mich. L. Rev. 487 (1958).

[30] *See, e.g.,* Joaquin v. Shiloh Orchards, 148 Cal. Rptr. 495 (Ct. App. 1978).

[31] *See* Powell on Real Property § 62.02[3] (Michael Allan Wolf ed., Matthew Bender).

[32] *See* Powell on Real Property § 68.04 (Michael Allan Wolf ed., Matthew Bender).

[33] *See, e.g.,* Honsinger v. State, 642 P.2d 1352 (Alaska 1982).

avulsion: a sudden and perceptible change in the location of such a body of water, usually due to a flood or other major event. Avulsion does not change the boundary line. Though clear in concept, it is often difficult to apply these opposing rules to specific factual situations.

§ 31.06 Subsurface Rights

[A] Ownership: How Far Down?

The ownership of land has both horizontal and vertical dimensions. Suppose O owned fee simple absolute in Greenacre in 1700. At common law, O's ownership included:

(1)   the land surface of Greenacre,

(2)   the air space above the surface (*see* § 31.07), and

(3)   everything underneath the land surface down to the "center of the earth."[34]

In theory, then, O's property included a narrow column of soil and rock that extended downward from the surface thousands of miles below Greenacre to a point precisely in the middle of the planet.

Contemporary courts still protect the surface owner's absolute right to possession when third parties intrude into the subsurface, whether by mining, installing a pipeline, or otherwise. Perhaps the most famous decision is *Edwards v. Sims*,[35] a dispute involving ownership of the Great Onyx Cave.[36] Plaintiffs claimed that part of the cave was below their land and, accordingly, that they owned that part. The defendants, who owned the only cave entrance, claimed ownership of the entire cave. The trial court ordered surveyors to enter the defendants' property to survey the cave, and determine its location in relation to plaintiffs' land. When defendants petitioned for a writ of prohibition to prevent the survey, the court relied on the traditional rule: "[W]hatever is in a direct line between the surface of the land and the center of the earth belongs to the owner of the surface."[37] Therefore, the court reasoned, if plaintiffs could prove they owned the surface, they logically owned the cave beneath and the trial court properly exercised its equitable power in ordering the survey. An eloquent dissent protested against the absurdity of vesting property rights in surface owners who lacked any access to the cave itself: "It should not be held that he owns that which he cannot use and which is of no benefit to him, and which may be of benefit to others."[38]

---

[34] The oft-quoted Latin maxim is *"Cujus est solum, ejus est usque ad coelum ad infernos,"* loosely translated as "Whoever owns the soil also owns to the heavens and to the depths."

[35] 24 S.W.2d 619 (Ky. Ct. App. 1929).

[36] *See also* Marengo Cave Co. v. Ross, 10 N.E.2d 917 (Ind. 1937) (assuming surface owner owns underlying cave).

[37] Edwards v. Sims, 24 S.W.2d 619, 620 (Ky. Ct. App. 1929).

[38] Edwards v. Sims, 24 S.W.2d 619, 622 (Ky. Ct. App. 1929) (Logan, J., dissenting).

[B] Mineral Rights

Ownership of gold, coal, and other "hard" minerals is governed by the general common law rule: whoever owns the land surface also owns the minerals in place under the surface. Of course, it is possible—and quite common—to split off mineral rights from surface ownership. For example, O, owning title to Goldacre, might convey the subsurface mineral rights to M, while retaining ownership of the surface.[39]

Oil and natural gas do not fit neatly into the absolute ownership model because they are both "fugitive" minerals—they can move through porous underground strata, unlike hard minerals. Suppose R and T own adjoining parcels of land above a large pool of oil. If R begins pumping oil from her land, oil beneath T's parcel will naturally migrate toward R's well, be pumped to the surface, and end up in R's possession. If T "owns" the oil beneath his land, then he would inevitably sue R, creating lengthy and expensive litigation. It would indeed be difficult to prove whether R extracted T's oil and, if so, how much. Rather than face the inevitable lawsuits, owners like R might refrain from oil drilling altogether, thus diminishing the nation's supply of oil.

The law has developed two models of oil and gas ownership to deal with this dilemma and thereby encourage the production of these resources. Some states follow the *non-ownership* theory. Under this model, the surface owner does not own the oil and gas under the land. Instead, the surface owner merely has the right to extract or "capture" the oil and gas beneath the property, and acquires ownership only upon actual capture.[40] Under this rule of capture, T has no claim against R; R acquires ownership of the oil because she was the first person to "capture" it.[41]

A majority of states follow the *ownership-in-place* theory.[42] The owner of the land surface is deemed to own all the oil and natural gas in place under the surface, but will lose ownership if someone else extracts or "captures" the oil or gas first. Under this approach, T indeed "owns" the oil beneath his land, but still has no claim against R; R divested T's ownership by being the first to capture the oil. As a practical matter, there is no significant legal difference between these two theories aside from potential tax liability. In ownership-in-place jurisdictions, proven oil and gas reserves are deemed owned and thus subject to property taxation.

---

[39] *See, e.g.,* Pennsylvania Coal Co. v. Mahon, 260 U.S. 393 (1922) (involving dispute between surface owner and mineral estate owner); *see also* United States v. 3,218.9 Acres of Land, 619 F.2d 288 (3d Cir. 1980) (holding that government's condemnation of surface estate was not a taking of subsurface rights).

[40] *See, e.g.,* Barnard v. Monongahela Natural Gas Co., 65 A. 801 (Pa. 1907).

[41] What happens when natural gas is first extracted or "captured" and then injected into a natural underground reservoir for storage? Is it now available for capture by others, or is it still the property of the first captor? *Compare* Texas Am. Energy Corp. v. Citizens Fidelity Bank & Trust Co., 736 S.W.2d 25 (Ky. 1987) (still owned by captor), *with* Anderson v. Beech Aircraft Corp., 699 P.2d 1023 (Kan. 1985) (unowned and available for capture).

[42] *See, e.g.,* Wronski v. Sun Oil Co., 279 N.W.2d 564 (Mich. Ct. App. 1979); Elliff v. Texon Drilling Co., 210 S.W.2d 558 (Tex. 1948).

On the other hand, both the non-ownership and ownership-in-place theories are usually qualified by an important modern limitation: the overlying owner is entitled to a reasonable opportunity to extract a just and equitable share of the oil or gas in the pool.[43]

§ 31.07 Rights in Airspace: How High?

Common law courts confidently proclaimed that each landowner owned "to the heavens." Thus, in theory at least, each landowner held title to a column of air space that extended upward from the land surface for an infinite distance. Any intrusion that interfered with the owner's exclusive possession of this air space—such as an overhanging tree branch from a neighbor's yard—was deemed a trespass.[44]

This absolutist position collapsed with the invention of the airplane. As the Supreme Court explained in *United States v. Causby*, the rule would subject the operator of every transcontinental flight to "countless trespass suits."[45] In turn, this would "clog these highways [and] seriously interfere with their control and development in the public interest."[46] It was accordingly necessary to formulate a new approach to ownership of air space. Modern courts uniformly agree that an airplane overflight within "navigable air space," as defined by federal regulations, is not a trespass.[47]

More broadly, it is increasingly accepted that a landowner owns only the air space that is reasonably necessary for the use or enjoyment of the property.[48] Thus, for example, while landowner O owns enough air space above her land to accommodate a high-rise office building, her ownership rights do not extend infinitely upward.

---

[43] *See, e.g.*, Wronski v. Sun Oil Co., 279 N.W.2d 564 (Mich. Ct. App. 1979); Elliff v. Texon Drilling Co., 210 S.W.2d 558 (Tex. 1948).

[44] *See, e.g.*, Whitesell v. Houlton, 632 P.2d 1077 (Haw. Ct. App. 1981) (holding owner had right to cut away overhanging tree branches).

[45] 328 U.S. 256, 261 (1946).

[46] United States v. Causby, 328 U.S. 256, 261 (1946).

[47] *But cf.* United States v. Causby, 328 U.S. 256 (1946) (finding that frequent airplane overflights 83 feet above plaintiffs' land constituted a taking); Brown v. United States, 73 F.3d 1100 (Fed. Cir. 1996) (suggesting low, frequent overflights may be a taking).

[48] *See, e.g.*, Geller v. Brownstone Condominium Ass'n, 402 N.E.2d 807 (Ill. App. Ct. 1980) (finding that defendants' use of temporary scaffolding above plaintiff's land during construction of high rise building was not a trespass); *see also* County of Westchester v. Town of Greenwich, 745 F. Supp. 951 (S.D.N.Y. 1990) (suggesting airport may have acquired prescriptive easement for flights over defendants' land that requires defendants to trim their trees).

Chapter 32

EASEMENTS

SYNOPSIS

§ 32.01 The Easement in Context

A owns Whiteacre, a 100-acre tract that is "landlocked," meaning that it does not adjoin a public road.[1] Whiteacre is entirely surrounded by lands owned by B. How can A legally cross B's land to reach Whiteacre? How can A obtain the right to install electric, telephone, and cable television lines through B's land to reach Whiteacre? In each instance, A's best solution is to obtain an *easement*—a nonpossessory right to use land in the possession of another—from B.

The modern easement evolved in response to economic and social changes that began in sixteenth-century England. One major influence was the collapse of the "common field" system of agriculture. During the Middle Ages, most farm land was cultivated on a communal basis, by which

---

[1] *See generally* Susan F. French, *Toward a Modern Law of Servitudes: Reweaving the Ancient Strands,* 55 S. Cal. L. Rev. 1261 (1982); Uriel Reichman, *Toward a Unified Concept of Servitudes,* 55 S. Cal. L. Rev. 1179 (1982); Stewart E. Sterk, *Neighbors in American Land Law,* 87 Colum. L. Rev. 55 (1987).

individual peasants were assigned to work on rather small, separate fields; peasants could roam freely through the countryside to reach their designated fields. The adoption of more efficient farming methods during the sixteenth century led to the "enclosure" movement, which gradually created large, fenced farms in place of small, unfenced fields. Because farmers could no longer wander freely, the need arose for formalized rights of access through fenced agricultural land. A second influence was the Industrial Revolution, which created new demands for legally-protectable access rights for railroads, canals, and other improvements. These pressures created an extensive body of law governing easements, most of which was later inherited by the new United States.

Today the law recognizes five basic categories of easements, which are classified according to the manner of their creation:

(1)   express easements (*see* § 32.03),

(2)   easements implied from prior existing use (*see* § 32.04),

(3)   easements by necessity (*see* § 32.05),

(4)   prescriptive easements (*see* § 32.06), and

(5)   irrevocable licenses or "easements by estoppel" (*see* § 32.07).

The first type of easement—the express easement—arises only when a landowner agrees to burden his or her land. For example, B might voluntarily decide to grant an easement to A. But under limited circumstances, the law will impose an easement without consent of the burdened landowner. The remaining four types of easements all arise as a matter of law, *without any express agreement to create an easement.* In other words, the law might give A an easement over B's land despite B's objection. Why would the law create an easement against the will of the burdened landowner? The answer to this question provides a window into the basic policies that underpin American property law.

The law of easements is well-settled and provokes little academic controversy. However, the new Restatement (Third) of Property: Servitudes proposes significant changes in the rules governing the easement and its cousins, the real covenant (*see* Chapter 33) and the equitable servitude (*see* Chapter 34). Most importantly, the Restatement would simplify the law by combining all three doctrines into one: the servitude (*see* § 34.08).

§ 32.02 What Is an Easement?

[A] Defining the Easement

In general, an *easement* is a nonpossessory right to use land in the possession of another. This pithy definition has several elements. First, an easement does not give its holder any right to possession of land; in this sense, the easement is different from freehold and nonfreehold estates, which are possessory interests. The easement holder merely has the right to use the land for a limited purpose, most commonly for access to another parcel. Second, an easement is viewed as an interest in land, not simply a contract right; among other things, this means that the grant of an easement is subject to the Statute of Frauds. Finally, the easement burdens land that is possessed by another person, typically an owner; a person cannot hold an easement in his own land.

Consider a sample easement. Suppose C, the owner of Redacre, holds an easement that allows her to cross part of Greenacre, owned by D, in order to reach the nearest public highway. C is not entitled to possession of Greenacre; rather, she merely has a right to use a portion of the land for a narrow purpose: access between Redacre and the highway. D remains the fee simple owner of Greenacre, subject only to C's easement.

The law of easements has developed its own terminology over the centuries. The land benefited by an easement (here, Redacre) is known as the *dominant tenement, dominant estate,* or sometimes the *dominant land*; the easement holder (here, C) is sometimes called the *dominant owner.* Conversely, the land burdened by an easement (here, Greenacre) is variously called the *servient tenement,* the *servient estate,* or just the *servient land*; the person entitled to possession of the servient land (here, D) is often called the *servient owner.*

The distinctions between the easement and the following related doctrines are discussed elsewhere in this text:

(1)   license (*see* § 32.13),

(2)   profit a prendre (*see* § 32.14),

(3)   real covenant (*see* § 33.02[B]), and

(4)   equitable servitude (*see* § 34.02[B]).

[B]   Classifying Easements

[1]   Affirmative or Negative?

Every easement is classified as either affirmative or negative. An *affirmative easement* authorizes the holder to do a particular act on the servient land. The easement that allows C to cross D's land (*see* [A], *above*) is affirmative in character; it permits the holder (C) to do something on (to travel across) the servient land (D's land Greenacre). Most easements are affirmative. For example, easements that allow the holder to use the servient land for power lines, railroads, drainage, hunting, or boating are all affirmative. In contrast, a *negative easement* entitles the dominant owner to prevent the servient owner from doing a particular act on the servient land (*see* § 32.12).

[2]   Appurtenant or In Gross?

Every easement is also classified as either appurtenant or in gross. An *easement appurtenant* benefits the easement holder in using the dominant land. In other words, it benefits the holder in a special sense—as the owner of the dominant land. Under the law, it is seen as attached to the dominant land, not to any particular owner of that land. For example, C's right to cross D's land Greenacre is presumably an easement appurtenant, attached to Redacre. By definition, an easement appurtenant exists only when there is both dominant land and servient land.

Conversely, the *easement in gross* is personal to the holder. It benefits the holder in a personal sense, whether or not he owns any other parcels of land. Thus, it is attached to the holder, not the land. The easement in gross involves only servient land; by definition, no dominant land exists. For example, suppose utility company U holds an easement that allows it to maintain power lines that cross O's land. This easement does not benefit U in U's use of any particular parcel of land. Instead, it benefits U regardless of whether U owns land at all.

The intention of the parties determines whether a particular easement is appurtenant or in gross. A well-drafted express easement will specify the parties' intent. Absent such clear evidence, courts determine intent based on the circumstances surrounding the creation of the easement. For example, access easements are almost always appurtenant because they facilitate the holder's use of a particular parcel of dominant land.[2] In the same manner, if an easement contributes to the use or enjoyment of a particular parcel owned by the holder, it will usually be classified as appurtenant.[3] The law generally favors the easement appurtenant over the easement in gross because this result facilitates the productive use of land. Thus, if a court cannot determine the parties' intent, it will classify the easement as appurtenant.

The distinction between the easement appurtenant and the easement in gross is sometimes critical. For example, an easement appurtenant is automatically transferred when the dominant tenement is transferred, while an easement in gross remains with the holder (*see* § 32.10). Suppose O owns Bigmart, a retail store; O holds an easement that allows patrons of Bigmart to park on P's land, Parkacre. O now sells Bigmart to R pursuant to a deed that does not mention the easement; O then purchases another nearby store called Superstore. Who can park on Parkacre? If the easement is appurtenant (which it presumably is), it was automatically transferred to R along with title to Bigmart; thus, only Bigmart patrons may park there. If the easement is in gross, it remained with O, and only Superstore customers may park on the land.

---

[2] *See, e.g.*, Cushman Virginia Corp. v. Barnes, 129 S.E.2d 633 (Va. 1963); Green v. Lupo, 647 P.2d 51 (Wash. Ct. App. 1982).

[3] *See, e.g.*, Martin v. Music, 254 S.W.2d 701 (Ky. Ct. App. 1953); Michell v. Castellaw, 246 S.W.2d 163 (Tex. 1952); Corbett v. Ruben, 290 S.E.2d 847 (Va. 1982).

§ 32.03 Express Easements

[A] Nature of Easement

The *express easement* is voluntarily created in a deed, will or other written instrument. The vast majority of easements are express easements.

The express easement may arise either by *grant* or by *reservation*. The distinction between the two methods turns on who is obtaining the easement: the transferor or a transferee. As its name suggests, the easement by grant is typically created when a grantor conveys or "grants" an easement to another person. Suppose A owns Whiteacre and her neighbor B owns Blackacre. If A conveys an easement to B that allows B to install and maintain a water pipe across Whiteacre, this easement arises by grant.

The easement by reservation arises in a special situation: when a grantor conveys land to another, but retains or "reserves" an easement in that land. Suppose C owns both Greenacre and Blueacre; C conveys Greenacre to D, but reserves an easement for access across Greenacre to reach Blueacre. C's easement arises by reservation.[4]

[B] Creation of Easement

[1] By Grant

Creation of an express easement by grant is simple. The deed conveying the easement must comply with the same Statute of Frauds requirements applicable to all deeds (*see* § 23.04[A]).[5]

Briefly, it must

    (1) be in writing,

    (2) identify the grantor and grantee,

    (3) contain words manifesting an intention to create an easement,

    (4) describe the affected land, and

    (5) be signed by the grantor.

The usual exceptions to the Statute of Frauds—notably estoppel and part performance—apply here as well.

[2] By Reservation

The formal requirements for creating an express easement by reservation are identical to those governing the express easement by grant. The only

---

[4] The easement by *reservation* arises when a deed creates a wholly new easement that is retained by the transferor upon conveyance of land to another. But suppose that the land is already burdened by an easement before the conveyance; if the transferor retains this pre-existing easement, it is called an *exception*. However, in practice many courts use these terms interchangeably without acknowledging the distinction.

[5] *See, e.g.*, Berg v. Ting, 886 P.2d 564 (Wash. 1995).

controversial issue concerning the express easement by reservation is whether it can be created in a third person.

At common law, an easement could only be reserved in favor of the grantor. Any attempt to reserve an easement in favor of a third person was invalid. Influenced by the California Supreme Court's landmark decision in *Willard v. First Church of Christ, Scientist*,[6] many courts have abandoned the traditional rule. The *Willard* court justified its departure from centuries of precedent mainly by demonstrating that the original reason for the rule no longer existed. It reasoned that the rule arose in England during a transitional era when freehold estates could be transferred either by the historic ceremony of livery of seisin or by the newly-authorized deed. Common law courts refused to allow a reservation in favor of a third person in order to discourage use of the deed, and thus protect livery of seisin. Yet livery of seisin became obsolete centuries ago; and with its demise, the rationale for the rule ended. Today the deed is the standard method to transfer interests in real property, and there is no justification for ignoring the grantor's clear intent to create an easement.

[C] Policy Rationale

Why should the law recognize an express easement? Two major jurisprudential strands underpin this easement. At one level, enforcement of an express easement respects the personal liberty of landowners to act as they wish. More fundamentally, the law presumes that honoring such easements will facilitate the efficient use of land. If adjacent owners A and B agree to burden A's land in order to benefit B's land, their agreement presumably reflects a rational economic decision about how to maximize the value of their respective parcels. Further, B's knowledge that courts will enforce the easement in the future encourages her to invest in developing the long-term productivity of her land.

§ 32.04 Easements Implied from Prior Existing Use

[A] Nature of Easement

A purchases from B a parcel of industrial land that receives its electric power through lines that cross B's retained adjacent land. The B-A deed, which is duly delivered, makes no reference to an easement. Can B now remove the power lines from his property?

The common law answer to this dilemma is the *easement implied from a prior existing use*, sometimes loosely called an *implied easement* or *easement by implication*. Even though A and B never expressly agreed to create an easement, the court may infer such intent from the presence of an existing use (the power lines crossing B's retained land) and impose an easement by operation of law. The Statute of Frauds is inapplicable to this

---

[6] 498 P.2d 987 (Cal. 1972).

type of easement. Of course, if the parties affirmatively express their intent not to create an easement, this easement cannot arise.

The easement may be created either by grant or by reservation. Some states impose more rigorous requirements for the implied easement created by reservation. They reason that a reservation of an easement is inconsistent with the words of grant in the deed executed by the grantor. Most commonly, such states demand a heightened showing of necessity for an easement by reservation.

[B] Creation of Easement

[1] Required Elements

Three elements are required for an easement implied from a prior existing use:

(1)   *severance of title* to land held in common ownership,

(2)   *an existing, apparent, and continuous use* when severance occurs, and

(3)   *reasonable necessity* for the use at time of severance.[7]

In the B-A hypothetical (*see* [A], *above*), all three elements are satisfied. B conveyed part of his land to A, thus severing title. At the time of conveyance, B's retained land was already burdened with visible power lines that were used to benefit the portion he transferred to A. Finally, the easement for power lines is reasonably necessary for the use of A's industrial land.

[2] Severance of Title

The first element is severance of title. A tract of land held in common ownership must be divided into two or more parcels; at least one parcel must be transferred to a new owner and at least one must be retained by the original owner.[8] Consider a sample hypothetical. Suppose S owns Greenacre, a 100-acre tract of unimproved land that adjoins a public highway on its southern border. For years before the sale, S regularly reached the north half of Greenacre by using a gravel road that runs from the highway across the south half of the land. On January 1, S conveys the northern half of Greenacre to B. The severance of title requirement is met on these facts because S divided Greenacre into two parcels, selling one to B and retaining the other.

---

[7] The first Restatement of Property attempted to merge the two implied easements recognized at common law (by prior use and by necessity) into a single category, whose creation was regulated by eight criteria. Restatement of Property § 476 (1944). Most courts ignored this novel approach. *But see* Peterson v. Beck, 537 N.W.2d 375 (S.D. 1995) (applying Restatement criteria). The Restatement (Third) of Property: Servitudes abandons this experiment and returns to the common law distinctions.

[8] *See, e.g.*, Cordwell v. Smith, 665 P.2d 1081 (Idaho Ct. App. 1983); *see also* Schmidt v. Eger, 289 N.W.2d 851 (Mich. Ct. App. 1980) (holding that conveyance of leasehold estate was severance of title); Hellberg v. Coffin Sheep Co., 404 P.2d 770 (Wash. 1965) (same).

[3] Existing, Apparent, and Continuous Use

The second element is an apparent and continuous use of part of the tract for the benefit of another part, which already exists when title is severed. In other words, while the common owner still owns both parcels, he or she must use one parcel in a manner that benefits the other parcel. This pre-existing use must be so "apparent" and "continuous" that the parties presumably intended it to continue.

This second requirement is also satisfied in the S-B hypothetical (*see* [2], *above*). For years before the sale, S used the gravel road across part of his land (south Greenacre) to benefit another part (north Greenacre); the road is readily visible to any observer; and S's use has been continuous over the years. Therefore, on January 1, when title is severed, an existing, apparent, continuous use exists.[9]

S's use before severance of title does not create an easement as such; one cannot obtain an easement in one's own land. For the sake of having a convenient label, however, this type of use existing before severance of title is often described as a *quasi-easement*. Under this terminology, before severance of title, north Greenacre is termed the *quasi-dominant tenement* and south Greenacre is called the *quasi-servient tenement*.

Case law has substantially diluted the traditional requirement that the use be "apparent." The term was once limited to readily visible uses, such as roads, surface pipelines, and the like. But most courts have redefined the term to include uses that are discoverable through reasonable inspection, even if not readily visible. Predictably, this standard often creates difficult factual issues.

The main impetus leading to this transformation was the problem of the underground sewer pipe.[10] Suppose G's home is serviced by a sewer pipe that crosses underneath an adjacent unimproved lot also owned by G. G sells the lot to H who has no actual or record notice of the pipe; the G-H deed does not expressly reserve an easement. Is the underground pipe "apparent" such that G can claim an implied easement from prior existing use? Many courts would reason that although the pipe is not visible, it is connected to visible utilities at G's house, and therefore is discoverable by H.[11] Yet this argument has little connection with the main rationale for this implied easement—that it reflects the parties' mutual intent. Why should H assume that G's sewer line crosses under the lot, instead of taking some other route to the sewer main? Is it reasonable to expect a buyer like H to inquire about the location of underground sewer pipes? Rather than continuing to "torture the meaning of 'apparent,'" the Restatement (Third) of Property: Servitudes simply treats underground utilities as a special

---

[9] *Cf.* Granite Prop. Ltd. Partnership v. Manns, 512 N.E.2d 1230 (Ill. 1987) (driveway).

[10] For a helpful examination of the issue, see Joel Eichengrun, *The Problem of Hidden Easements and the Subsequent Purchaser Without Notice*, 40 Okla. L. Rev. 3 (1987).

[11] *See, e.g.,* Van Sandt v. Royster, 83 P.2d 698 (Kan. 1938); Romanchuk v. Plotkin, 9 N.W.2d 421 (Minn. 1943); Otero v. Pacheco, 612 P.2d 1335 (N.M. Ct. App. 1980); *cf.* Motel 6 v. Pfile, 718 F.2d 80 (3d Cir. 1983). *But see* Campbell v. Great Miami Aerie No. 2309, 472 N.E.2d 711 (Ohio 1984) (holding that underground sewer line was not apparent).

case.[12] It recognizes implied easements for such utilities regardless of whether they are discoverable, largely based on an efficiency rationale, not party intent.

In addition, most courts require that the use be continuous or permanent, as opposed to temporary, sporadic, or occasional.[13] This requirement is typically explained in terms of notice to the parties. The use must be sufficiently continuous so that the parties would reasonably expect that it will continue after severance of title.

[4] Reasonable Necessity

Most states only require a showing of *reasonable* necessity.[14] In other words, the easement must be convenient or beneficial to the use and enjoyment of the dominant tenement, but need not be absolutely necessary. This standard is usually met if the owner of the dominant tenement would be forced to expend substantial money[15] or labor in order to provide a substitute for the easement.[16]

Suppose, under the S-B road hypothetical (*see* [B][2], *above*), that B already has an express easement to reach north Greenacre via a narrow and steep road over land owned by X. It is not absolutely or "strictly" necessary that B secure an easement over S's retained land because B has legal access to north Greenacre. On the other hand, because this route is narrow and steep, it would be more convenient for B to use the wide gravel road over S's property, and accordingly reasonable necessity exists.[17]

[C] Policy Rationale

This easement is most commonly justified in terms of party intent. If an existing use is sufficiently apparent and continuous when a parcel is divided, the parties were on notice of the use and presumably expected—or should have expected—that it would continue. Under this view, the failure to grant or reserve an express easement is merely an oversight that the law rectifies by recognizing an implied easement. Using the B-A hypothetical (*see* [A], *above*), presumably both A and B intended that the power lines would continue to benefit A's parcel and burden B's parcel. Or at least they would have so intended if they had considered the issue.

---

[12] Restatement (Third) of Property: Servitudes § 2.12 cmt. g (Tentative Draft No. 1, 1989) ("Implying the servitude will normally impose a relatively slight economic burden, while the costs of relocating the utility lines will often be high.").

[13] *See, e.g.,* Cordwell v. Smith, 665 P.2d 1081 (Idaho Ct. App. 1983) (where roads were built and temporarily used to remove logs, and then left unused for years, there was no continuous use).

[14] A few states still require strict necessity, particularly for an easement by reservation.

[15] *See, e.g.,* Schmidt v. Eger, 289 N.W.2d 851 (Mich. Ct. App. 1980) (finding necessity for use of drainage ditch where replacement drain system would cost $30,000 or more); Adams v. Cullen, 268 P.2d 451 (Wash. 1954) (finding necessity for driveway where replacement "could only be done at great cost").

[16] Restatement (Third) of Property: Servitudes § 2.12 cmt. e (Tentative Draft No. 1, 1989).

[17] *But see, e.g.,* Whitt v. Ferris, 596 N.E.2d 230 (Ind. Ct. App. 1992) (no reasonable necessity).

In addition, under utilitarian theory this easement serves the policy goal of promoting the productive use of land. It reflects a bias in favor of continuing land uses that already exist, absent an affirmative objection by a party. Thus, we could also explain the doctrine as ensuring that A's parcel receives the electrical power that is critical to continuing the industrial use. Absent such an easement, A would be required to pay the significant cost of obtaining replacement power lines, at a minimum; at worst, A might be forced to cease operations altogether. Both options are likely to be inefficient.

§ 32.05 Easements by Necessity

[A] Nature of Easement

Suppose A owns Brownacre, a 200-acre parcel of wild and unimproved land, bordered by a public road only on its east side. A conveys the west half of Brownacre to B on January 1. Assume west Brownacre is now landlocked, without any legal access to a public road. The easement implied from a prior existing use is unavailable, because no prior use existed. How can B reach his land?

The common law solution is the *easement by necessity*, which will allow B access over A's land. Like its cousin, the easement implied from a prior existing use, this easement arises by operation of law based on the circumstances of the case, without any express agreement. Similarly, the doctrine is an exception to the Statute of Frauds. But the difference between the two easements is fundamental. The easement implied from a prior existing use requires—as the name suggests—an existing use before severance of title; the easement by necessity requires a high degree of necessity when title is severed—hence the name—but no prior use.

Virtually all decisions finding an easement by necessity involve road easements to reach landlocked parcels.[18] How could such a problem arise? Perhaps the most common scenario involves an amateur attempt to divide family-owned lands that inadvertently fails to provide legal access for one or more parcels. The law has long viewed road access as absolutely necessary. But, perhaps afflicted by a nineteenth-century mind set, courts have not extended the doctrine to easements for sewer pipes, water lines, electric power lines, or other modern utilities.

Two special rules minimize the burden that an easement by necessity imposes on the servient land. The servient owner is usually permitted to select the location for the road easement, as long as the route is reasonable. Further, the easement endures only for so long as the necessity itself. Once the necessity ends (e.g., the state builds a highway through the dominant land), an easement by necessity terminates.[19]

---

[18] *See, e.g.,* Roy v. Euro-Holland Vastgoed, B.V., 404 So. 2d 410 (Fla. Dist. Ct. App. 1981).

[19] *See, e.g.,* Fox Invs. v. Thomas, 431 So. 2d 1021 (Fla. Dist. Ct. App. 1983).

[B] Creation of Easement

[1] Required Elements

Two elements are generally required for an easement by necessity: (1) *severance of title* to land held in common ownership; and (2) *strict necessity* for the easement at the time of severance.[20] These elements are closely related to the criteria for an easement implied from a prior existing use. However, the standard for necessity in most jurisdictions is strict, not reasonable, and no pre-existing use is required.

Both elements are met in the A-B hypothetical (*see* [A], *above*). A conveyed the west half of Brownacre to B, thus severing title. At the time of the conveyance, access across A's retained land (east Brownacre) was absolutely necessary for travel to B's land (west Brownacre). B is entitled to an easement by necessity over A's land.

[2] Severance of Title

The first element—severance of title—merely requires ownership of a tract of land, followed by the conveyance of part of the tract to a new owner, as in the A-B hypothetical above. The discussion of severance of title in connection with easements implied by prior existing use (*see* § 32.04[B][2]) is equally applicable here.

[3] Necessity at Time of Severance

[a] Traditional View: Strict Necessity

Most courts still recite the traditional rule that strict necessity is required.[21] In order to establish an access easement under this approach, an owner must prove that the severance of title caused the property to be absolutely "landlocked." In other words: (a) the parcel must be entirely surrounded by privately-owned land, without touching any public road; and (b) the owner must not hold an easement or other legal right of access to cross the adjoining land to reach a public road.[22]

Under this view, if the owner has any legal means of reaching the land—regardless of how inconvenient, expensive, or impractical it may be—no strict necessity exists.[23] For example, suppose O has an easement that allows him to reach his land by hiking across P's land on a narrow and dangerous trail. O cannot prove strict necessity; he has a right of access,

---

[20] *See* Reese v. Borghi, 30 Cal. Rptr. 868 (Ct. App. 1963); Berkeley Dev. Corp. v. Hutzler, 229 S.E.2d 732 (W. Va. 1976).

[21] *See, e.g.,* Finn v. Williams, 33 N.E.2d 226 (Ill. 1941); Ward v. Slavecek, 466 S.W.2d 91 (Tex. Civ. App. 1971).

[22] A public entity that is authorized to acquire property by eminent domain can never establish necessity. It can always acquire an easement through condemnation.

[23] This doctrine evolved before the invention of the airplane. Accordingly, even if an owner can reach his or her landlocked parcel via helicopter, jet belt, or other air transportation, strict necessity still exists.

even if it is impractical to use. Or suppose that part of R's land adjoins a public road, but an impassible cliff in the middle of the land prevents R from reaching the rest of his land without building an expensive road; because R has legal access to his land, strict necessity does not exist. Another classic dilemma is the landlocked parcel that adjoins a lake, river, or other navigable body of water. Many early decisions held that water access precludes strict necessity, but it seems unlikely that a modern court would follow this antique approach.

The strict necessity must exist when title is severed. In the A-B hypothetical (*see* [A], *above*), A's conveyance to B both (a) severed title to Brownacre, and (b) created the necessity for an easement by landlocking B's new property, west Brownacre. Necessity is measured at the instant in time when the common ownership is severed, not later. For example, the 1950 decision of *Othen v. Rosier*[24] involved a severance of title that occurred in 1896. It was clear that plaintiff's parcel had been landlocked since at least 1900. But because plaintiff could not meet his burden of producing evidence about the access situation in 1896—presumably because the potential witnesses had died—the court refused to find an easement by necessity.

The easement by necessity doctrine does not apply to a parcel that becomes landlocked only after the severance of title.[25] Suppose that O's land Blueacre adjoins public roads on its north and south borders. O conveys north Blueacre to B. Strict necessity does not exist at this point, because B can access his land by the public road along his north boundary. One year later, after a bridge washes out, the county closes and abandons the public road along north Blueacre. Strict necessity now arises, but too late. B cannot obtain an easement by necessity.

[b]　Minority View: Reasonable Necessity

The minority view—endorsed by the new Restatement (Third) of Property: Servitudes[26]—only requires *reasonable* necessity for the easement.[27] The easement must be convenient or beneficial to the normal use and enjoyment of the dominant land. For example, in the O-P hypothetical (*see* [a], *above*), O's existing easement does not allow him to make normal use of his land because it only allows access by foot, not by automobile; under the reasonable necessity standard, O is entitled to an easement by necessity for automobile access. Similarly, because R (*see* [a], *above*) cannot utilize all of his land unless he builds an extremely expensive road, R has reasonable necessity for an easement to reach the rest of his property.

The new Restatement suggests that this standard might support recognition of easements by necessity for non-road purposes, such as easements for utility lines.[28] Electricity and telephone services are usually provided

---

[24] 226 S.W.2d 622 (Tex. 1950).

[25] However, statutes in a number of states authorize a private landowner to condemn an easement by necessity across surrounding lands, regardless of when the necessity arose.

[26] Restatement (Third) of Property: Servitudes § 2.15 (Tentative Draft No. 1, 1989).

[27] *See, e.g.*, Cordwell v. Smith, 665 P.2d 1081 (Idaho Ct. App. 1983).

[28] Restatement (Third) of Property: Servitudes § 2.15 cmt. d (Tentative Draft No. 1, 1989).

through power lines or cables. Depending on the circumstances, an owner whose land lacks access to such utilities might well be deprived of the beneficial enjoyment of the property. Once seen as luxuries, electricity and telephone service are now viewed as reasonably necessary to the modern home. On the other hand, with the development of wireless forms of communication (e.g., the cellular telephone) and alternative energy sources (e.g., solar panels), the need for utility line easements may decrease in future years. Nonetheless, as technological change converts the luxury of today into the necessity of tomorrow, the scope of easements by necessity will correspondingly enlarge.

[C] Policy Rationale

The policy rationale underpinning the easement by necessity has two strands: society's utilitarian interest in encouraging productive use of land and the parties' presumed intent. The relative importance of each strand has fluctuated over time.

The first strand originated in seventeenth-century England, where courts feared that landlocked parcels might remain idle and wasted. Judicial recognition of easements by necessity allowed the cultivation, improvement, and occupancy of these lands. This focus on society's interest in the efficient utilization of land gained renewed importance in the twentieth century.

The second strand—the presumed intent of the parties—has roots in thirteenth-century English law. But its modern prominence arose in the nineteenth century, as American courts gradually turned away from broad concerns of social policy toward implementing the intent of private owners. Under this view, a grantor presumably intends to convey everything that is necessary for the grantee to make beneficial use of the land. Thus, if grantor R conveys an apparently landlocked parcel of land to grantee E, the law presumes that R also intended to convey an access easement to E over R's retained land.

Although both approaches have shaped the doctrine, the party-intent approach is still the dominant influence.[29] It explains the traditional rules that the necessity (a) must be strict, and (b) must be caused by the severance; otherwise, there is no basis to infer intent. Moreover, if the parties clearly manifest an intent not to create an easement upon severance of title (e.g., by expressly disclaiming intent), an easement by necessity cannot arise. If the doctrine were based solely on the public policy in favor of productive land use, any landlocked parcel would be entitled to an easement by necessity, regardless of the surrounding circumstances.

---

[29] *See* Hurlocker v. Medina, 878 P.2d 348 (N.M. Ct. App. 1994).

§ 32.06　Prescriptive Easements

[A]　Nature of Easement

A owns Pineacre, a ten-acre mountain tract that adjoins Oakacre, a similar tract owned by B. The dirt driveway leading from A's house across Pineacre to the nearest public road is rough and narrow. But the driveway on Oakacre that connects B's garage to the public road is paved and wide. For 20 years, A regularly drives her car over to Oakacre and then down B's driveway in order to reach the road; she reverses the process when going home. Can B now install a gate on the driveway that blocks A's access? On these facts, A has probably acquired a prescriptive easement to use B's driveway.

The *prescriptive easement* is closely related to the doctrine of adverse possession (*see* Chapter 27). Both share the central concept that property rights in the land of another can be acquired by conspicuous, long-term use. Under the majority American view, both involve specialized applications of the statute of limitations.[30] And most of the modern law governing the prescriptive easement is borrowed from adverse possession, including the list of required elements and the principles of "tacking" and "tolling." As a practical matter, the main difference between the two doctrines today is the result. The adverse possessor receives title to the land, while the prescriptive easement holder merely receives an easement in land still owned by another.

Almost any type of affirmative easement can be acquired by prescription. The vast majority of cases involve easements for access over a road or driveway. Prescriptive easements can also be acquired for uses including power lines, drainage, encroaching buildings, bathing,[31] and airplane overflights. However, negative easements cannot be established through prescription.

[B]　Creation of Easement

[1]　Required Elements

The elements required for a prescriptive easement vary somewhat from state to state. The most common formula requires that the claimant's use be:

　(1)　open and notorious,

---

[30] Early American courts justified the prescriptive easement using the legal fiction of a supposed *lost grant*. Open, notorious, and continuous use throughout the prescriptive period created a presumption that the claimant had received an express easement by grant from the servient owner, but that the deed had somehow been misplaced or lost. *See* Dartnell v. Bidwell, 98 A. 743 (Me. 1916). Although traces of this approach still linger in a few states, almost all courts explain the prescriptive easement by analogy to adverse possession. *See* Powell on Real Property § 34.10 (Michael Allan Wolf ed., Matthew Bender).

[31] *See, e.g.,* Miller v. Lutheran Conference & Camp Ass'n, 200 A. 646 (Pa. 1938).

(2)   adverse and under a claim of right, and

(3)   continuous and uninterrupted for the statutory period.[32]

What about the other two standard elements for adverse possession—exclusive possession and actual entry or possession?[33] Some courts list *exclusive use* as a required element. However, as discussed below, this element has a special, narrow meaning when applied to prescriptive easements, and rarely becomes important. Only a few courts expressly require *actual use*. Certainly, the claimant must make some actual, physical use of a defined area of land;[34] but most courts seem to subsume this requirement within open and notorious use.[35]

[2] Open and Notorious Use

The first element is open and notorious use. The claimant's use must be sufficiently visible and apparent that a diligent owner who was present on the land at the time would be able to discover it. The use must not be concealed or hidden from view. But it is not necessary that the owner have actual knowledge of the use.[36]

This element is almost always satisfied in the typical prescriptive easement case, involving a claimed easement for access over a path, road, or driveway.[37] For example, in the A-B hypothetical (*see* [A], *above*), B could easily have seen A's car going up and down the driveway. In the same manner, improvements that permanently occupy the land surface (e.g., an encroaching garage) or airspace (e.g., an overhanging power line) usually constitute open and notorious uses. On the other hand, suppose that C owns two adjacent lots, Lot 1 and Lot 2. The sewage pipe from C's house on Lot 1 crosses underneath the surface of Lot 2 before connecting to the main sewer line. There is nothing on the ground surface such as signs, manhole covers, or gratings that would give anyone notice of the subsurface pipe. D purchases Lot 2, and 10 years later—after the limitations period has run—C claims a prescriptive easement. On these facts the pipe is not considered an open and notorious use.[38]

---

[32] *See, e.g.,* Warsaw v. Chicago Metallic Ceilings, 676 P.2d 584 (Cal. 1984); *see also* Restatement (Third) of Property: Servitudes §§ 2.16, 2.17 (Tentative Draft No. 3, 1993).

[33] A handful of courts also state that the use must be with the knowledge and acquiescence of the servient owner; this is a remnant from the outdated "lost grant" theory of prescriptive easements. *See, e.g.,* Berkeley Dev. Corp. v. Hutzler, 229 S.E.2d 732 (W. Va. 1976).

[34] *See* Othen v. Rosier, 226 S.W.2d 622 (Tex. 1950) (finding testimony about location of easement was too vague and uncertain to allow tacking on prior use); Community Feed Store v. Northeastern Culvert Corp., 559 A.2d 1068, 1071 (Vt. 1989) (location of easement need not be proven "with absolute precision, but only as to the general outlines consistent with the pattern of use").

[35] There is no requirement that the claimant pay property taxes, even in states that mandate that the adverse possessor pay taxes.

[36] *See* White v. Ruth R. Millington Living Trust, 785 S.W.2d 782 (Mo. Ct. App. 1990).

[37] *See, e.g.,* White v. Ruth R. Millington Living Trust, 785 S.W.2d 782 (Mo. Ct. App. 1990) (use of road on most weekends); Brocco v. Mileo, 565 N.Y.S.2d 602 (App. Div. 1991) (daily use of access way).

[38] *But cf.* Van Sandt v. Royster, 83 P.2d 698 (Kan. 1938) (suggesting that lot buyer was charged with inquiry notice of sewer pipe easement).

[3] Use That Is Adverse and Under Claim of Right

The most commonly litigated issue in prescriptive easement cases is whether the use was adverse and under a claim of right. The law on this element mirrors the familiar split in adverse possession doctrine between the majority *objective test* and the minority *subjective test* (*see* § 27.03[E]). Under the objective test, the claimant need only use the land as a reasonable owner would use it, without permission from the servient owner; the claimant's subjective intent is irrelevant.[39] A handful of states follows the subjective test, which requires that the claimant have a good faith belief that he or she is entitled to use the land.

This element is particularly interesting in the typical case where there is no evidence at all about whether the owner consented to the use—where the facts simply show long-term use by the claimant without objection by the owner. Should the law's "default standard" assume that the use was permissive or adverse? As a general rule, proof of the other elements—open, notorious, continuous, and uninterrupted use—creates a presumption that the use was adverse and under a claim of right.[40] This shifts the burden to the owner to prove consent, which is impossible in the common scenario outlined above. For example, in the A-B hypothetical (*see* [A], *above*), A's use is presumed to be adverse because she can easily prove the other elements for a prescriptive easement; B has no evidence to rebut this presumption. However, many states refuse to apply this presumption when the land is wild and unenclosed, assuming instead that the owner allowed the use as a neighborly accommodation.[41] And a minority of states reject the doctrine entirely, presuming that all use is permissive.

[4] Exclusive Use

Some courts require that the use be *exclusive*, mechanically borrowing the element from adverse possession doctrine. Yet courts that follow this view do not demand exclusivity in the adverse possession sense of the term.[42] Confusingly, a claimant's use may still be considered "exclusive" even though he is not the exclusive user (e.g., if he shares the use with the owner and with others). In this context, exclusivity means that the claimant's use is independent of uses by others. As a practical matter, in most cases this element merely requires that the use must be separate and distinguishable from uses by the general public.

---

[39] *See, e.g.,* Finley v. Botto, 327 P.2d 55 (Cal. Ct. App. 1958) (finding permissive use); Othen v. Rosier, 226 S.W.2d 622 (Tex. 1950) (finding permissive use where owners controlled access to road by installing gate and repaired road).

[40] *See, e.g.,* Plettner v. Sullivan, 335 N.W.2d 534 (Neb. 1983); Brocco v. Mileo, 565 N.Y.S.2d 602 (App. Div. 1991); Community Feed Store v. Northeastern Culvert Corp., 559 A.2d 1068 (Vt. 1989).

[41] *See, e.g.,* Hester v. Sawyers, 71 P.2d 646 (N.M. 1937).

[42] *See, e.g.,* Plettner v. Sullivan, 335 N.W.2d 534 (Neb. 1983) (holding use was sufficiently exclusive for prescriptive easement, but not for adverse possession).

[5] Continuous and Uninterrupted Use for the Statutory Period

Finally, the use must be continuous and uninterrupted for the statutory period. The first portion of this element—continuous use—focuses on the conduct of the claimant. Just as with adverse possession, continuous use does not mean constant use. The use need only be as frequent as is appropriate given the nature of the easement and the character of the land. Particularly in rural areas, occasional or seasonal use of an easement may be sufficient.[43]

In the A-B hypothetical (*see* [A], *above*), it is not necessary for A to drive up and down B's driveway every minute of every day. A seeks an access easement in order to travel between her home and the public road a few times each day. Thus, if A crosses B's driveway two or three times daily, this periodic use is sufficiently continuous. Conversely, if A normally travels on her own driveway, and only utilizes B's driveway one or two times each year, this sporadic use is not continuous.

The second part of this element—uninterrupted use—focuses on the conduct of the owner. As a general rule, if the owner succeeds in stopping the use—even for a short period of time—continuity ends. Suppose that after A uses B's driveway daily for three years, B chops down a tree that blocks the driveway for a month; this interrupts A's continuity. If B removes the tree, and A starts using the driveway again, an entirely new prescriptive period begins to run.

In almost all jurisdictions, the statutory period for adverse possession also applies to the prescriptive easement (*see* § 27.03[G]). Thus, between 10 and 20 years of continuous use are typically required to obtain such an easement.

[C] Policy Rationale

The prescriptive easement doctrine is supported by the same blend of utilitarian policies that underpin adverse possession (*see* § 27.06).[44] It facilitates the productive use of land by protecting the industrious claimant's use. As one court observed, "land use has historically been favored over disuse, and . . . therefore he who uses land is preferred in the law to he who does not, even though the latter is the rightful owner."[45] It also serves the goals of the statute of limitations—minimizing the risk of judicial error and allowing repose.

---

[43] *See, e.g.,* Block v. Sexton, 577 N.W.2d 521 (Minn. Ct. App. 1998) (holding use of farm road "several times each month between May and October" was continuous).

[44] *See also* Restatement (Third) of Property: Servitudes § 2.16 cmt. c (Tentative Draft No. 3, 1993).

[45] Finley v. Yuba County Water Dist., 160 Cal. Rptr. 423, 427 (Ct. App. 1979).

§ 32.07 Irrevocable Licenses or "Easements by Estoppel"

[A] Nature of "Easement"

A owns Blackacre, a landlocked parcel that adjoins Redacre, a parcel owned by B; Redacre adjoins a public highway. An old private road travels from the highway, across Redacre, and reaches Blackacre, but A has no right to use this road. Planning to build a vacation cabin on Blackacre, A asks permission to use the road for this purpose and B replies: "Sure!" With B's consent, A widens and improves the road. B observes A use the road to haul materials, machinery, and workers to the building site. A eventually spends $25,000 to build the cabin. Can B now block A from using the road?[46]

In some jurisdictions, A now holds an *irrevocable license* to use the road. B's oral consent gave A a *license* (*see* § 32.13) to use the road for access to Blackacre. Ordinarily, an owner who gives a license can revoke it at any time. However, under limited circumstances, a license may become irrevocable through estoppel. Under this approach, if the licensee expends substantial money or labor in reasonable reliance on the license and the licensor should reasonably expect such reliance, the licensor is estopped to revoke it.[47]

The irrevocable license is the functional equivalent of an easement for most purposes. Indeed, some courts loosely refer to the irrevocable license as an "easement by estoppel."[48] However, an irrevocable license endures only so long as necessary to allow the licensee to recover the value of his or her investment. For example, suppose A's cabin burns down. If the insurance company fully compensates A for the value of the cabin, the license ends because it is no longer needed to prevent inequity.

[B] Creation of Irrevocable License

[1] Required Elements

Three elements are commonly required to create an irrevocable license:

(1) a license, typically for access purposes;

(2) the licensee's expenditure of substantial money or labor in good faith reliance; and

(3) the licensor's knowledge or reasonable expectation that reliance will occur.

---

[46] The facts of this hypothetical are based on Holbrook v. Taylor, 532 S.W.2d 763 (Ky. 1976).

[47] *See, e.g.,* Camp v. Milam, 277 So. 2d 95 (Ala. 1973); Stoner v. Zucker, 83 P. 808 (Cal. 1906); Holbrook v. Taylor, 532 S.W.2d 763 (Ky. 1976).

[48] *Cf.* Ricenbaw v. Kraus, 61 N.W.2d 350 (Neb. 1953) (referring to irrevocable license as an "irrevocable easement"). In fact, easement by estoppel is a separate doctrine. Such an easement arises, for example, when (a) an owner fraudulently represents that a person holds an easement over his land and (b) the person reasonably relies on this representation to his or her detriment.

[2] License

The license may be either express or implied. The A-B example (*see* [A], *above*) involves an express license. In some states, an implied license can arise based solely on the conduct of the parties (e.g., if A never sought permission and B failed to object to A's continuing use of the road).

[3] Reliance by Licensee

The licensee's reliance often consists of improvements to the servient land that directly benefit the licensor, such as paving or repairing an access road.[49] Alternatively, the construction of a home, barn, or other improvement on the licensee's property may be sufficient, as in the A-B hypothetical above. But can extensive reliance on an informal oral statement ever be truly reasonable? One might argue that A's expenditure of $25,000 in reliance on B's offhand comment is inherently unreasonable, absent unusual circumstances (e.g., a long-term friendship or family relationship). Reliance is more likely to be found reasonable if the parties clearly intended to create a permanent right of access (e.g., where an oral easement is unenforceable due to the Statute of Frauds).

[4] Knowledge of Licensor

Finally, the licensor must know, or have reason to believe, that reliance will occur. In the A-B hypothetical above, B knew about A's plan to build the cabin when he orally consented to A's use of the road; and B also observed A using the road for this purpose.

[C] Policy Rationale

The policy rationale for the irrevocable license is usually explained in terms of equity: it would be unfair to allow the licensor to revoke the license after the licensee has substantially relied to his detriment. A secondary theme is that the doctrine facilitates the productive use of land. In the A-B hypothetical above, A's investment in Blackacre will be wasted unless A can use B's road for access. A law and economics scholar would put it somewhat differently: efficiency is served by allocating the right to A, who values it more highly than B does.

But two countervailing concerns lead most courts to construe the doctrine narrowly. First, it discourages neighborly conduct. B's land is now subject to an easement-like right in A because B was initially a "nice guy." Knowledgeable owners might well avoid the risk of licenses becoming irrevocable by refusing to grant them at all. Second, the irrevocable license undermines the policies served by the Statute of Frauds.

---

[49] *See, e.g.,* Shearer v. Hodnette, 674 So. 2d 548 (Ala. Civ. App. 1995) (maintaining access road and granting easement that allowed road improvement); Cooke v. Ramponi, 239 P.2d 638 (Cal. 1952) (improving access road).

§ 32.08   Other Types of Easements

Several other types of easements are also recognized. For example, an easement may be implied from a subdivision map or plat. If a subdivider conveys lots by reference to a subdivision map that depicts privately-owned streets, parks, or other common areas, each lot owner acquires an implied easement to use these areas.[50]

Easements may also be created through eminent domain. A governmental entity might condemn an easement for a highway or other public purpose. Similarly, statutes in many jurisdictions allow private owners of landlocked parcels to condemn private easements for access; but the constitutionality of such statutes is unclear in some states (*see* § 39.05).

Finally, an easement in favor of the public may arise by implied dedication. The contours of this doctrine are remarkably vague. In general, the landowner's conduct must show a clear intent to dedicate the property to public use. For instance, if the public regularly uses a path across A's land to reach the beach for 20 years, without any objection by A, an easement by implied dedication arises in some jurisdictions.[51]

§ 32.09   Scope of Easements

[A]   Manner, Frequency, and Intensity of Use of Easement

The scope of an easement may evolve over time as the manner, frequency, and intensity of use change. Broadly speaking, the scope of an easement turns on the intent of the original parties.[52] Courts consider a number of factors in determining this intent, including:

    (1)   the circumstances surrounding the creation of the easement;

    (2)   whether the easement is express, implied, or prescriptive; and

    (3)   the purpose of the easement.

Because it is usually difficult to ascertain the parties' actual intent, the law relies heavily on what might be called presumed intent. In general, the law presumes that the parties to an express or implied easement intended that the easement holder would be entitled to do anything that is reasonably necessary for the full enjoyment of the easement, absent evidence to the contrary. Accordingly, reasonable changes in the manner, frequency, or intensity of use to accommodate normal development of the dominant land are permitted, even if this somewhat increases the burden on the servient land.[53] On the other hand, the easement holder cannot

---

[50] *See, e.g.*, De Ruscio v. Jackson, 565 N.Y.S.2d 593 (App. Div. 1991); Putnam v. Dickinson, 142 N.W.2d 111 (N.D. 1966).

[51] Easements for beach access may arise under other theories as well, as discussed in § 30.05.

[52] *See, e.g.*, Sides v. Cleland, 648 A.2d 793 (Pa. Super. Ct. 1994) (limiting time and manner of use of trail based on parties' apparent intent to allow users to enjoy wilderness setting).

[53] *See generally* Restatement (Third) of Property: Servitudes § 4.10 (Tentative Draft No.

change the scope of the easement so as to impose an unreasonable burden on the servient land.[54] These principles stem more from the traditional policy favoring productive land use than from true concern about the parties' intent.[55]

For example, it is well-settled that the scope of an easement usually expands to accommodate technological change, on the theory that this is necessary for its full enjoyment. The access easement originally created for horse-drawn wagons before the invention of automobiles later extends to include trucks;[56] and the easement intended to provide electric, telephone, and telegraph service before the development of television eventually enlarges to accommodate cable television lines.[57]

Disputes about the scope of an easement frequently surface when the dominant parcel is subdivided. Suppose D owns Whiteacre, an unimproved five-acre tract that he visits on weekends. D holds an appurtenant easement by grant that allows him to use a road across E's farm Greenacre in order to reach Whiteacre. D now subdivides Whiteacre into five residential lots, planning that the lot buyers will also use the easement. This would increase the frequency of trips across Greenacre from two per week to perhaps 50 per week. Can E prevent this expanded use?

As a general rule, when the dominant land is subdivided, every lot owner in the subdivision is entitled to use any easement appurtenant to the dominant land. But this rule is tempered by the principle that the easement cannot be expanded so far that it unreasonably burdens the servient land. How far is too far? Most courts view the subdivision or other intensified use of the dominant land as acceptable development, absent evidence that it substantially interferes with the rights of the servient owner.[58] For example, if the road across Greenacre is a steep, narrow lane that E normally uses to move equipment from place to place on his farm, the

---

4, 1994) (noting that the "manner, frequency, and intensity of the beneficiary's use of the servient estate may change over time to take advantage of developments in technology and to accommodate normal development of the dominant estate" unless this imposes an unreasonable burden).

[54] *See, e.g.*, Preseault v. United States, 100 F.3d 1525 (Fed. Cir. 1996) (use of railroad easement for public hiking and biking trail imposed unreasonable burden on servient tenement).

[55] Similarly, the servient owner may not unreasonably interfere with the dominant owner's use of the easement. *See, e.g.*, Figliuzzi v. Carcajou Shooting Club, 516 N.W.2d 410 (Wis. 1994) (servient owner cannot interfere with hunting easement by building condominiums on servient land).

[56] *See* Glenn v. Poole, 423 N.E.2d 1030, 1033 (Mass. App. Ct. 1981) ("The progression from horse or ox teams to tractors and trucks is a normal development . . ."); *see also* Faus v. City of Los Angeles, 431 P.2d 849 (Cal. 1967) (easement for electric railways extended to encompass busses).

[57] *See* Henley v. Continental Cablevision, 692 S.W.2d 825 (Mo. Ct. App. 1985).

[58] *See, e.g.*, Martin v. Music, 254 S.W.2d 701 (Ky. Ct. App. 1953) (expansion of sewer easement due to residential development of dominant land did not impose unreasonable burden); Hayes v. Aquia Marina, Inc., 414 S.E.2d 820 (Va. 1992) (increase in road use caused by expansion of marina from 84 slips to 280 slips was not unreasonable burden); *cf.* Green v. Lupo, 647 P.2d 51 (Wash. Ct. App. 1982) (overturning injunction that banned motorcycle travel along easement to land developed as new mobile home park).

increased traffic produced by the subdivision might seriously interfere with E's rights. Unless such unusual circumstances exist, the law will probably permit the expanded use.

The prescriptive easement presents a special problem. Courts are often reluctant to permit expansion of a prescriptive easement because it has little connection to party intent.[59] The presumption that the parties intended the easement to expand to meet future needs is unavailable.

[B] Use of Easement to Benefit Land Other than Dominant Land

In general, an easement holder cannot use the easement to benefit any parcel other than the dominant land; the normal remedy for violation of this rule is an injunction.[60] Yet modern decisions have begun to erode this traditional standard.

For example, in *Brown v. Voss*[61] plaintiffs held an easement that entitled them to cross defendants' land ("Parcel A") in order to reach their own land ("Parcel B"), which was improved with a single-family house. Plaintiffs then purchased an adjacent parcel ("Parcel C"), planning first to demolish the house on Parcel B and then to build a new house that would straddle the boundary line between Parcels B and C. These changes would not increase the burden on Parcel A. Plaintiffs sued for the removal of obstructions defendants had placed within the easement area, and defendants counter-claimed for an injunction to limit plaintiffs' use of the easement to Parcel B. The Washington Supreme Court applied the standard rule and held that plaintiffs had no right to extend the easement to serve Parcel C. But the decision adopted an innovative remedy. On the facts of the case, the court exercised its equitable power to refuse defendants' request for an injunction; this limited the defendants' remedy to damages, here only $1.00. As a practical matter, plaintiffs won the case: they acquired the right to extend the easement to Parcel C.

In effect, the *Brown* court converted the traditional "bright line" rule into a rather mushy standard that requires case-by-case analysis. On balance, however, it may be a more efficient standard. This approach parallels developments in the law of private nuisance, where many courts have soft-ened traditional liability rules in the interest of efficiency by restricting some successful plaintiffs to damages instead of injunctive relief (*see* § 29.06[A]).

---

[59] *See, e.g.,* Aztec Ltd. v. Creekside Dev. Co., 602 P.2d 64 (Idaho 1979); S.S. Kresge Co. v. Winkelman Realty, 50 N.W.2d 920 (Wis. 1952). *But see* Glenn v. Poole, 423 N.E.2d 1030 (Mass. App. Ct. 1981).

[60] *See, e.g.,* Penn Bowling Recreation Ctr. v. Hot Shoppes, 179 F.2d 64 (D.C. Cir. 1949).

[61] 715 P.2d 514 (Wash. 1986).

[C] Change in Location or Dimensions of Easement

It is well-settled that the location or dimensions of an easement may be changed only if the owners of the servient and dominant lands all agree.[62] However, the new Restatement (Third) of Property: Servitudes would allow the servient owner to make reasonable changes in the location or dimensions of an easement if necessary for the normal use or development of the property, so long as the easement holder is not prejudiced.[63]

§ 32.10 Transfer of Easements

[A] Easements Appurtenant

The rules governing the transfer of an easement appurtenant are simple. By definition, an easement appurtenant is deemed attached to a particular dominant parcel. Any transfer of title to the dominant land also automatically transfers the benefit of the easement, unless there is a contrary agreement.[64] For example, suppose A owns Blueacre, which is benefited by an appurtenant access easement burdening B's property Redacre. A now conveys Blueacre to C, using a deed that fails to mention the easement. C now holds the easement because it was appurtenant to Blueacre.

In the same fashion, any transfer of title to the servient land usually transfers the burden of the easement. This rule does not apply if (a) the transferee qualifies for protection against an express easement as a bona fide purchaser (see § 24.03), or (b) the owner of the dominant land agrees to release the easement.

[B] Easements in Gross

The law regulating the transfer of easements in gross has progressed through three distinct stages. Early American courts were concerned that permitting the assignment of such easements might unfairly increase the burden on the servient land. For example, suppose that A holds an easement in gross to hunt ducks on B's land; if A can freely assign his easement to a duck club that has 500 members, this may greatly expand the burden of the easement. For this reason and others, the rule developed that easements in gross were not transferable.

In the second stage, courts created a distinction between commercial easements (e.g., easements for utilities, railroads or other economic purposes) and noncommercial easements (e.g., easements for hunting, fishing,

---

[62] *See, e.g.,* Umphres v. J.R. Mayer Enters., 889 S.W.2d 86 (Mo. Ct. App. 1994) (holder could not change location of easement); Cox v. Glenbrook Co., 371 P.2d 647 (Nev. 1962) (holder could not widen easement); Sakansky v. Wein, 169 A. 1 (N.H. 1933) (servient owner could not reduce height of easement); Clemson Univ. v. First Provident Corp., 197 S.E.2d 914 (S.C. 1973) (holder could not enlarge easement).

[63] Restatement (Third) of Property: Servitudes § 4.8 (Tentative Draft No. 4, 1994).

[64] *See, e.g.,* Nelson v. Johnson, 679 P.2d 662 (Idaho 1984).

boating or other personal purposes).[65] Influenced by the Pennsylvania Supreme Court's landmark decision in *Miller v. Lutheran Conference & Camp Association*[66] and similar cases, the first Restatement of Property provided that commercial easements in gross were freely transferable.[67] On the other hand, noncommercial easements in gross were usually not transferable.

Today the law is gradually moving into a third stage that discards the commercial/noncommercial distinction. An increasing number of decisions—and the new Restatement (Third) of Property: Servitudes—broadly recognize that any easement in gross is freely transferable, unless circumstances show that the parties "should not reasonably have expected" this result.[68]

§ 32.11 Termination of Easements

[A] In General

Easements can be terminated for a number of reasons, most of which also apply to real covenants and equitable servitudes. The new Restatement (Third) of Property: Servitudes would complete this process by providing a single set of methods to terminate the new unified "servitude" (*see* § 34.08[C]).

Under current law, for example, the creating parties might impose an express limitation on the easement (e.g., a provision limiting its duration to 50 years);[69] or the easement holder might voluntarily agree to release his or her rights to the servient owner. Alternatively, if one owner acquires both the dominant and servient lands, the easement is extinguished under the doctrine of merger.[70] And an easement may also be terminated by eminent domain or estoppel (*see* § 34.06[D][2]).[71] Finally, an express easement ends if the servient land is conveyed to a bona fide purchaser without notice of the easement; the weight of authority holds that such a conveyance does not end an implied easement by prior use or an easement by necessity, although the issue rarely arises because the buyer is usually charged with inquiry notice; and the law is quite clear that even a bona fide purchaser takes title subject to a prescriptive easement.

Three bases for termination merit special discussion: (1) abandonment; (2) misuse; and (3) prescription.

---

[65] *See, e.g.,* Crane v. Crane, 683 P.2d 1062 (Utah 1984).

[66] 200 A. 646 (Pa. 1938).

[67] Restatement of Property § 489 (1944).

[68] Restatement (Third) of Property: Servitudes § 4.6 (Tentative Draft No. 3, 1993).

[69] *See, e.g.,* Pavlik v. Consolidation Coal Co., 456 F.2d 378 (6th Cir. 1972).

[70] *See, e.g.,* Tract Dev. Serv. v. Kepler, 246 Cal. Rptr. 469 (Ct. App. 1988) (finding no merger on facts).

[71] *See, e.g.,* Lindsey v. Clark, 69 S.E.2d 342 (Va. 1952).

[B] Abandonment

An easement may be terminated through abandonment. What constitutes abandonment? Courts uniformly hold that mere nonuse of an easement does not meet this standard.[72] For example, suppose that E holds an access easement over S's servient land, but fails to use the easement for 25 years. Despite this extended period of nonuse, E has not abandoned the easement.

Abandonment hinges on the easement holder's intent: he must affirmatively intend to relinquish his rights. Courts generally use an objective standard to determine this intent, based on the circumstances of each case. Abandonment will be found if the holder both (a) stops using the easement for a long period and (b) takes other actions that clearly manifest intent to relinquish the easement.[73] For example, in *Preseault v. United States*[74] the court found abandonment of a railroad easement where the holder: (a) failed to use the easement for 26 years; and (b) removed the rails, switches, and all the other railroad equipment from the servient land, thus making future railroad use impossible.[75] Courts tend to be hostile toward the abandonment doctrine—because it may have a disastrous impact on the dominant owner—and hence it is usually difficult to terminate an easement on this basis.

[C] Misuse

Suppose easement holder E misuses his access easement over S's servient land: E regularly allows guests to park along the easement, which impedes S's own access. On these facts, S can probably secure an injunction to prevent such future misuse.[76] But what if an injunction is ineffective to prevent misuse? Some courts hold that misuse by the easement holder will extinguish the easement in cases where injunctive relief is wholly ineffective.[77] However, even in jurisdictions that accept this doctrine in theory, it is very rarely used.

[D] Prescription

Just as the dominant owner may acquire an easement by prescription, the servient owner may terminate an easement by prescription. The same

---

[72] *See, e.g.,* Lindsey v. Clark, 69 S.E.2d 342 (Va. 1952) (mere nonuse did not constitute abandonment).

[73] *See, e.g.,* Hickerson v. Bender, 500 N.W.2d 169 (Minn. Ct. App. 1993) (abandonment of access easement found based on lengthy nonuse and holder's failure to object to servient owners' obstruction of easement); Frenning v. Dow, 544 A.2d 145 (R.I. 1988) (abandonment of easement for water pipe established by (a) nonuse for 16 years and (b) other actions that included failing to maintain pipeline, allowing line to be blocked, and obtaining new water sources).

[74] 100 F.3d 1525 (Fed. Cir. 1996).

[75] *See also* Consolidated Rail Corp. v. Lewellen, 682 N.E.2d 779 (Ind. 1997).

[76] *Cf.* Reichardt v. Hoffman, 60 Cal. Rptr. 2d 770 (Ct. App. 1997).

[77] *See, e.g.,* Crimmins v. Gould, 308 P.2d 786 (Cal. Ct. App. 1957). *But see* Frenning v. Dow, 544 A.2d 145 (R.I. 1988).

prescriptive easement elements (*see* § 32.06[B]) generally apply to both situations, with one important difference. In order to obtain a prescriptive easement, the claimant's use need not be truly exclusive, nor need it interfere with the servient owner's use of the land; most easements—by their very nature—are nonexclusive. However, to extinguish an easement by prescription, the servient owner's conduct must substantially interfere with the holder's use of the easement, such as by blocking the holder from using the easement at all.[78] For example, suppose servient owner S builds a brick wall across E's access easement, completely preventing any use of the easement by E. If this blockage continues for the prescriptive period, it will terminate the easement.[79]

§ 32.12   Negative Easements

[A]   In General

A *negative easement* entitles the holder to prevent the owner of the servient land from doing a particular act on that land, much like a veto power. Suppose that A's farm Greenacre adjoins B's farm Redacre; an irrigation canal crosses Redacre, bringing water to Greenacre. If A holds the right to prevent B from blocking the canal on Redacre, the law would classify this right as a negative easement. A is not personally entitled to do anything on Redacre; but he can stop B from doing something on Redacre.

[B]   Traditional Approach

English courts were traditionally hostile to the negative easement for three reasons. First, they feared that it would restrict marketability and accordingly impair the productive use of land. For example, if C's farm Blueacre could be restricted by a negative easement that prohibited C and her successors from building any structures on the land, Blueacre could never be devoted to desirable commercial or industrial uses. Second, in England negative easements could be created by prescription, without the landowner's consent; this exacerbated concern that the negative easement might stifle development. Finally, under English law the purchaser of land took title subject to all existing easements whether or not he had notice of them. The risk of negative easements—which were often difficult to detect by inspection—tended to discourage land purchases.

Accordingly, English law recognized only four categories of negative easements. Suppose E owned Blackacre and his neighbor F owned

---

[78] *See, e.g.,* Tract Dev. Service v. Kepler, 246 Cal. Rptr. 469 (Ct. App. 1988) (fence across easement did not terminate it because users could pass through unlocked gate); Hickerson v. Bender, 500 N.W.2d 169 (Minn. Ct. App. 1993) (easement terminated by prescription where garage, stone barbecue, trees and other obstacles materially blocked easement).

[79] *But see* Castle Assoc. v. Schwartz, 407 N.Y.S.2d 717 (App. Div. 1978) (recognizing exception where easement has been created but no occasion has arisen for its use).

Whiteacre. At common law, E could hold negative easements that entitled him to prevent F from taking the following actions on Whiteacre:

(1)   blocking windows of Blackacre buildings,

(2)   blocking air that flowed to Blackacre in a defined channel,

(3)   blocking water that flowed to Blackacre in a defined channel, and

(4)   removing support from Blackacre buildings.

Early American courts blindly adopted the English limitations on the negative easement, even though the reasons for these limitations were largely inapplicable to American conditions. The United States was blessed with an abundance of undeveloped land; negative easements could not arise by prescription; and the bona fide purchaser doctrine protected innocent buyers against unknown easements.

[C]   Modern Approach

In recent decades, the negative easement has expanded beyond its historic boundaries. This expansion stems partly from judicial action. Modern courts recognize that the negative easement and other private land use restrictions may enhance the productive use of land (*see* § 33.03). As a result, some courts now accept a new negative easement that arises by grant—the easement of view.[80] If G, owner of Brownacre, grants an easement of view to H, owner of Blueacre, then H may stop G from doing anything on Brownacre that obstructs the view from Blueacre.

The bulk of this expansion, however, comes from legislative action. Statutes in many jurisdictions expressly authorize the creation of new types of negative easements by grant, including conservation and solar easements. The *conservation easement* is used to restrict development of the servient land, usually to protect its natural, scenic, historic or open space values.[81] Typically, the servient owner grants a conservation easement to a government entity or private charitable organization, and then continues to utilize the land to the extent permitted by the easement. Suppose A owns Greenacre, a 400-acre tract of farm land; A conveys a conservation easement to B (a non-profit entity dedicated to the preservation of agricultural land) that forever restricts the use of Greenacre to farming. With the easement in place, A and his successors can never utilize Greenacre for residential, commercial, or industrial purposes, but may continue to farm the land.

The *solar easement* is designed to protect a solar energy system on the dominant land. It stops the servient owner from constructing improvements or growing vegetation that obstructs the natural flow of sunlight across his land.

---

[80] *See, e.g.,* Petersen v. Friedman, 328 P.2d 264 (Cal. Ct. App. 1958).

[81] *See* Unif. Conservation Easement Act, 12 U.L.A. 163 (1981).

§ 32.13   Licenses

A *license* is informal permission that allows the licensee to use the land of another for a narrow purpose. The license is routinely encountered in everyday life. The spectator at a football game,[82] the guest at a New Year's Eve party, and the customer at a grocery store all hold licenses.[83]

Two features distinguish the license from the easement.[84] First, the license is generally not considered to be an interest in land. It is viewed as a personal privilege, usually temporary in nature. For example, the party guest who enters a home does not acquire any right in the land; rather, the guest has only temporary permission to enter the home for the limited purpose of attending the party. Accordingly, the Statute of Frauds does not apply to the license; a license can be created orally. Second, as a general rule, the licensor may revoke a license at any time; and it is automatically revoked if the licensor dies or conveys title to another.[85] However, a license may become irrevocable due to estoppel (*see* § 32.07). And a license coupled with an interest is similarly irrevocable. For example, if A purchases a truck from B, A has an irrevocable license to enter B's land and retrieve the truck.

§ 32.14   Profits a Prendre

The *profit a prendre* or *profit* is the right to enter the land of another and remove timber, minerals, oil, gas, gravel, game,[86] fish or other physical substances. Like the easement, it involves a right to use land in the possession of another person; but unlike the easement, it includes the right to sever and remove some substance from the land.

Profits are generally governed by the same rules that apply to easements. Indeed, the first Restatement of Property proposed that profits be treated as a type of easement and that the term "profit" be abandoned.[87] Yet the term lingered in common usage. The Restatement (Third) of Property: Servitudes continues to treat the profit as a specialized form of easement, but retains the term for convenience.[88]

---

[82] *Cf.* Marrone v. Washington Jockey Club, 227 U.S. 633 (1913) (holding ticket to race track was a license).

[83] *See, e.g.*, Baseball Publishing Co. v. Bruton, 18 N.E.2d 362 (Mass. 1938) (agreement allowing plaintiff to place an advertising sign on wall created an easement); Linro Equip. Corp. v. Westage Tower Assocs., 650 N.Y.S.2d 399 (App. Div. 1996) (agreement allowing plaintiff to install and maintain coin-operated laundry machines in residential complex created a license); Todd v. Krolick, 466 N.Y.S.2d 788 (1983) (same).

[84] *See generally* McCastle v. Scanlon, 59 N.W.2d 114 (Mich. 1953).

[85] *See, e.g.*, Mosher v. Cook United, Inc., 405 N.E.2d 720 (Ohio 1980).

[86] *See, e.g.*, St. Helen Shooting Club v. Mogle, 207 N.W. 915 (Mich. 1926).

[87] Restatement of Property § 450 cmt. f (1944).

[88] Restatement (Third) of Property: Servitudes § 1.2 (Tentative Draft No. 7, 1998).

Chapter 33

REAL COVENANTS

§ 33.01   The Birth of Private Land Use Planning

Suppose A owns fee simple absolute in two adjacent parcels, Greenacre (her home) and Blueacre (a vacant lot).[1] A plans to sell Blueacre to B, but wishes to restrict it to residential use in order to preserve the character of the neighborhood; B agrees to this restriction. Accordingly, A conveys Blueacre to B using a deed that provides: "B, his successors, heirs, and assigns shall use Blueacre only for residential purposes." B then conveys Blueacre to C, who opens a pig farm there. What rights does A have against C?

Under traditional English law, the answer was "none." If B had opened the pig farm, A could enforce B's promise as a *personal covenant,* like any other contract. But the personal covenant suffered from a fatal flaw: it did not burden or benefit the successors to the original contracting parties. In that era, contract rights and duties could not be assigned or delegated to successors. Thus, the personal covenant was hopelessly weak as a land planning device.[2]

Over time, the law developed two methods to address this problem: the *real covenant* or *covenant running at law* (discussed in this chapter) and the *equitable servitude* (discussed in Chapter 34). Both methods serve the same purpose: they extend the burdens and benefits of land use covenants to the successors of the original parties. Damages are recoverable for breach of a real covenant, while the equitable servitude is primarily enforced by injunction. These new doctrines facilitated long-term private land use planning.

Yet—much like twins separated at birth—the two doctrines evolved quite differently. The modern evolution of the real covenant occurred in the eighteenth-century English law courts, which were quite hostile to restrictions on the free use of land (*see* § 9.08[A]).[3] Reflecting this heritage, the real covenant is a rigid, narrow, and intricate device. The American law governing real covenants is so confusing that one text describes it as an "unspeakable quagmire."[4] In contrast, the equitable servitude developed during the nineteenth century in the English equity courts; these courts were more willing to tolerate private land use restrictions in order to avoid unfairness and inequity.[5] The law governing equitable servitudes is relatively simple and straightforward. Thus, the distinction between the two doctrines stems more from historical accident than from logic.

---

[1] *See generally* Lawrence Berger, *Unification of the Law of Servitudes,* 55 S. Cal. L. Rev. 1339 (1982); Susan F. French, *Toward a Modern Law of Servitudes: Reweaving the Ancient Strands,* 55 S. Cal. L. Rev. 1261 (1982); Uriel Reichman, *Toward a Unified Concept of Servitudes,* 55 S. Cal. L. Rev. 1177 (1982); William B. Stoebuck, *Running Covenants: An Analytical Primer,* 52 Wash. L. Rev. 861 (1977).

[2] A related planning device—the negative easement—was similarly ineffective because common law courts narrowly limited its scope. *See* § 32.12.

[3] *See* Spencer's Case, 77 Eng. Rep. 72 (1583).

[4] Edward H. Rabin & Robert R. Kwall, Fundamentals of Modern Property Law 447 (3d ed. 1992).

[5] *See* Tulk v. Moxhay, 41 Eng. Rep. 1143 (1848).

American courts have often blurred the boundary between the real covenant and the equitable servitude, and today there is a clear trend toward eliminating the distinction. As a practical matter, the real covenant is now used infrequently; instead, the equitable servitude dominates the field. Moreover, the new Restatement (Third) of Property: Servitudes proposes to combine the real covenant, the equitable servitude, and the easement into a single category—the *servitude* (*see* § 34.08). [6] This unified servitude would be enforceable either in damages or by injunction. Accordingly, the real covenant may be nearing extinction.

§ 33.02 What Is a Real Covenant?

[A] Defining the Real Covenant

A real covenant is a promise concerning the use of land that (1) benefits and burdens the original parties to the promise *and also their successors* and (2) is enforceable in an action for damages. Legal authorities usually recite that such a covenant "runs with the land," but this phrasing is merely a shorthand reference, not literal truth. A real covenant does not "run with the land"; rather, it "runs" with an estate in land. The promisor's successors in title are bound to perform the promise; and the promisee's successors in title are able to enforce the promise in an action to recover compensatory damages.

In a practical sense, both the real covenant and the equitable servitude are tools that allow a promise to be enforced by or against a successor owner under limited circumstances. Suppose adjacent landowners A and B jointly agree that B's property Blueacre will be restricted to residential use; A sells her land to C, and B sells Blueacre to D. If D now begins building an oil refinery on Blueacre, C has a choice of theories. C can enforce the promise against D *either* as a real covenant *or* as an equitable servitude, assuming all requirements are met. Note that A and B probably did not describe their original agreement as a "real covenant" or an "equitable servitude," nor is this necessary. If all requirements are satisfied, *a promise can be enforced either as a real covenant or as an equitable servitude.*

A real covenant may be an *affirmative covenant* (a promise to perform a particular act) or a *negative covenant* (a promise not to perform a particular act).

[B] Distinguished from Other Doctrines

How does the real covenant differ from its close relatives—the equitable servitude and the negative easement? The equitable servitude is quite similar to the real covenant; it is a promise concerning the use of land that benefits and burdens the original parties and their successors. But the traditional remedy for breach of the equitable servitude is an injunction, not damages; the requirements for creating a valid equitable servitude are

---

[6] Restatement (Third) of Property: Servitudes §§ 1.1, 1.4 (Tentative Draft No. 7, 1998).

far easier to satisfy; and a broader range of defenses are available against enforcement of an equitable servitude (*see* Chapter 34).

The distinction between the real covenant and the negative easement is harder to discern. Both may involve the owner's promise to refrain from performing an action on the land that the law otherwise permits; and the remedy of damages is available under both. Of course, the requirements for each differ. At a more practical level, American courts—like their English counterparts—recognize only a few types of negative easements, which limits the scope of the doctrine (*see* § 32.12).

§ 33.03 Policy Implications of Private Land Use Restrictions

The English law courts restricted the real covenant due to utilitarian fear that it would limit marketability and thereby impair the productive use of land. "[R]estrictive covenants [are disfavored] based upon the view that the best interests of society are advanced by the free and unrestricted use of land."[7] But modern American courts increasingly acknowledge that the real covenant and the equitable servitude can help to ensure that land is used efficiently. In other words, private land use restrictions may enhance productive use.

For example, consider the A-B covenant that limits Blueacre to residential use (*see* § 33.01). By enforcing this covenant between adjacent landowners, the law ensures that A's home—and presumably other neighborhood homes as well—are protected against noise, odors, and other nuisance-like impacts from industrial or other non-residential uses. Today private land use restrictions are most commonly created in connection with new residential "common interest communities"—tract home subdivisions, townhouse developments, or condominium projects (*see* Chapter 35). In this setting, restrictions both permit the operation of the community (e.g., by providing a method for collection of homeowner assessments) and protect the legitimate expectations of home buyers that the residential character of the development will be preserved (e.g., by limiting uses, reducing noise levels, and policing architectural design).

A second policy theme may be broadly described as individual liberty, incorporating both libertarian precepts and law and economics theory. By enforcing the A-B agreement, the law respects the autonomy of each owner to deal with land as he or she sees fit, with minimal state intervention. For libertarian theorists, this result comports with the goal of protecting the personal freedom of A and B; and law and economics scholars presume that market-driven decisions by rational economic maximizers like A and B will best ensure that land is used efficiently.

On the other hand, private land use restrictions can sometimes impair the productive use of land, particularly over the long term.[8] Suppose that

---

[7] Charping v. J.P. Scurry & Co., 372 S.E.2d 120, 121 (S.C. Ct. App. 1988).

[8] *See* James L. Winokur, *The Mixed Blessings of Promissory Servitudes: Toward Optimizing Economic Utility, Individual Liberty, and Personal Identity*, 1989 Wis. L. Rev. 1.

E and F agree in 1920 that E's farm Redacre will "forever be restricted to agricultural use." But by 2000, a growing city has literally surrounded Redacre; the farm is now an agricultural island in an urban sea. Redacre is now most valuable if it can be developed into a large apartment complex to meet the urgent housing needs of low-income residents. Should the law enforce the restriction?

§ 33.04   Creation of a Real Covenant

[A]   Perspectives on the Real Covenant

The law governing real covenants is—to put it charitably—confused. Courts tend to be imprecise in analyzing and describing the law; and even within a single jurisdiction, the case law is sometimes inconsistent. Moreover, modern cases involving real covenants are relatively scarce, because most plaintiffs prefer to enforce restrictions as equitable servitudes.

In approaching the real covenant, two points are crucial. First, the law distinguishes between the *original parties* to the covenant and their *successors*. Suppose A and B agree that B's property Blueacre will be restricted to residential use; B conveys Blueacre to C, and A conveys her retained property, Greenacre, to D. A (the promisee or "covenantee") and B (the promisor or "covenantor") are the original parties to the covenant; D and C, respectively, are their successors in title.

Second, each real covenant has two "sides." The promisor's duty to perform the promise is commonly called the *burden*; the promisee's right to enforce the promise is commonly called the *benefit*. In analyzing whether a real covenant is enforceable, it is usually helpful to approach the two sides separately. Why? Disputes involving real covenants fall into one of three basic scenarios, based on the identities of the plaintiff and the defendant; and the requirements for enforcement differ in each scenario. First, the original promisee might seek to enforce the covenant against the promisor's successor; here the issue is whether the *burden* runs. Second, the promisee's successor could try to enforce the covenant against the original promisor; here the issue is whether the *benefit* runs. Finally, the promisee's successor might seek to sue the promisor's successor; here both the *burden* and the *benefit* must run.

[B]   Original Promisee vs. Promisor's Successor: Does the Burden Run?

[1]   Requirements for Burden to Run

Suppose A owns fee simple absolute in two adjacent parcels, Blackacre (A's home) and Greyacre (a vacant lot). From the second story, A's home enjoys a view across Greyacre to a distant lake. A wants to sell Greyacre, but also wishes to protect this view. A agrees to sell Greyacre to B, and eventually conveys title to B pursuant to a deed that expressly states: "B, his successors, heirs, and assigns shall not allow construction on Greyacre of any building or structure that exceeds 12 feet in height." After the A-B deed is recorded, B in turn conveys Greyacre to C. C begins construction of a 30-foot high home that will block the view.

Can A recover damages from C for breach of the covenant? Here A, the original promisee, is seeking to enforce its benefit; it is not necessary to prove that the benefit runs to A's successors. The only issue is whether the covenant can be enforced against C, as B's successor. Thus, the question here is whether the *burden* of the covenant runs to C.

In order for the burden of a real covenant to "run with the land," and thereby bind the promisor's successors, American law traditionally requires that six elements be established:

(1) the covenant must be in writing,

(2) the original parties must intend to bind their successors,

(3) the covenant must "touch and concern" land,

(4) horizontal privity must exist,

(5) vertical privity must exist, and

(6) the successor must have notice of the covenant.

[2] Covenant in Writing

Almost all modern courts view the real covenant as an interest in land. Accordingly, a writing that complies with the Statute of Frauds is required to create an enforceable real covenant (*see* § 23.04[A][1]).[9] In practice, this requirement rarely poses a problem. Covenants are typically set forth in a deed, lease or other written instrument between the covenanting parties.[10] The hypothetical A-B covenant (*see* [B][1], *above*) obviously meets this requirement because it is contained in the deed from A to B. A different technique is commonly used to impose covenants on new subdivision projects; most states allow the developer to record a written "declaration" or a plat map that expressly imposes covenants on the entire subdivision project before any lots are sold.[11] Even an oral covenant is enforceable, however, if one of the standard exceptions to the Statute of Frauds—notably estoppel or part performance—can be proven (*see* § 20.04[B][4]).[12]

[3] Intent to Bind Successors

The original parties must intend that the covenant bind the promisor's successors. How can their subjective intent be determined? The requisite

---

[9] In addition, the covenant must satisfy the usual requirements for valid contract.

[10] A deed that imposes the burden of a covenant on the grantee is uniformly held to comply with the Statute of Frauds even though it is not executed by the grantee.

[11] *See, e.g.,* Citizens for Covenant Compliance v. Anderson, 906 P.2d 1314 (Cal. 1995).

[12] In contrast, the presence of a common plan or scheme may support enforcement of a restriction as an equitable servitude, without a memorandum that satisfies the Statute of Frauds (*see* § 34.05[B]).

intent is most commonly found in the express language of the covenant. Words such as "assigns" or "successors" usually evidence this intent. Intent is clearly shown in the hypothetical A-B covenant (*see* [B][1], *above*) because B's "successors, heirs, and assigns" are expressly included as parties bound by the height restriction.

Alternatively, an intent to bind successors may be inferred from the nature of the restriction, the situation of the parties, and the other circumstances surrounding the covenant, even if the covenant contains no express language.[13] Suppose the A-B covenant merely provided: "No building or structure in excess of 12 feet in height may be constructed on Greyacre." Does this covenant bind only B or B's successors as well? Since B is not expressly named, one might infer that the parties intended the covenant to mean that no such building or structure may "ever" be constructed on Greyacre, regardless of the lot owner's identity. This interpretation makes sense in light of the purpose of the covenant; in order to effectively protect the view from Blackacre, it is necessary that B's successors also be bound.

Can an intent to bind successors be inferred simply because the covenant restricts the use and enjoyment of land? Many courts appear to presume that any such covenant was intended to run with the land, absent affirmative evidence that the original parties intended to create only a personal obligation in the promisor.[14] Under this approach, the requirement of intent to bind successors is largely irrelevant. If the covenant meets the "touch and concern" requirement—and thus restricts the use and enjoyment of land—intent is found.

[4]   "Touch and Concern" Land

[a]   Defining "Touch and Concern"

[i]   Use of the Land

What types of promises should run with the land? Most of the required elements for a real covenant concern the status of the parties to the covenant. The only element that examines the content of the covenant is "touch and concern." The burden of the covenant must "touch and concern" land. Unfortunately, there is little modern agreement about what this requirement means. If the law governing real covenants is truly a quagmire, then "touch and concern" is its deepest and most dangerous part.

Certainly, the core of the "touch and concern" requirement is simple. Courts typically state that the burden of the covenant must relate to use of the land. As one court summarized, "the promise must exercise direct influence on the occupation, use or enjoyment of the premises."[15] This

---

[13] *See, e.g.,* Runyon v. Paley, 416 S.E.2d 177 (N.C. 1992) (finding intent based on overall circumstances despite absence of express language).

[14] *But cf.* Charping v. J.P. Scurry & Co., 372 S.E.2d 120 (S.C. Ct. App. 1988).

[15] Caullett v. Stanley Stilwell & Sons, Inc., 170 A.2d 52, 54 (N.J. Super. Ct. App. Div. 1961).

standard is easy to understand and apply when a physical use is involved. For example, consider the A-B covenant that restricts the height of future buildings on Greyacre (*see* [B][1], *above*). This covenant meets the "touch and concern" test because it limits the types of uses that are physically permitted on the land. At the other extreme, suppose that a covenant requires the promisor to perform an act that has no connection whatsoever to the land (e.g., dancing a jig in the village square on New Year's day). The burden of this covenant does not "touch and concern" the promisor's land.

What about covenants that have little connection with the physical use of the land, such as covenants to arbitrate lease disputes, to pay real property taxes, or to refrain from operating a competing business? Here the "touch and concern" requirement loses its clarity. Broadly speaking, many modern cases seem to recognize a sliding scale—a covenant is less likely to "touch and concern" as its connection to physical use of the land diminishes. As the New York Court of Appeals explained, "whether a covenant is so closely related to the use of the land that it should be deemed to 'run' with the land is one of degree, dependent on the particular circumstances of a case."[16] However, the "sliding scale" approach provides little practical guidance.

Various efforts have been made to fill this doctrinal vacuum.[17] Probably the most influential is a standard pioneered by Dean Harry Bigelow that focuses on how the covenant affects the fair market value of the respective parties' interests in land.[18] Under this approach if the covenant lessens the value of the promisor's interest in land, then the burden is deemed to "touch and concern" the land; and if the covenant increases the value of the promisee's interest, then the benefit will similarly "touch and concern."[19] Yet this standard is circular. Only a covenant that does "touch and concern" the land in the first place is enforceable, and only an enforceable covenant can affect market value.

[ii] Negative Covenants

The burden of a negative covenant that restricts the use of the promisor's land usually satisfies the "touch and concern" requirement.[20] Most of the covenants routinely encountered in residential subdivision or condominium developments fall into this category. For example, covenants to use the land

---

[16] Eagle Enters., Inc. v. Gross, 349 N.E.2d 816, 819–820 (N.Y. 1976).

[17] *See, e.g.*, Davidson Bros., Inc. v. D. Katz & Sons, Inc., 579 A.2d 288 (N.J. 1990) (considering "touch and concern" only as one factor to determine whether a covenant is "reasonable" and thus enforceable).

[18] *See, e.g.*, Gallagher v. Bell, 516 A.2d 1028 (Md. Ct. Spec. App. 1986) (endorsing *Bigelow* standard); Neponsit Property Owners' Ass'n, Inc. v. Emigrant Indus. Sav. Bank, 15 N.E.2d 793 (N.Y. 1938) (same); Abbott v. Bob's U-Drive, 352 P.2d 598 (Or. 1960) (same).

[19] Harry A. Bigelow, *The Content of Covenants in Leases,* 12 Mich. L. Rev. 639 (1914); *see also* Charles E. Clark, Real Covenants and Other Interests Which "Run With Land" (2d ed. 1947).

[20] *See, e.g.*, Runyon v. Paley, 416 S.E.2d 177 (N.C. 1992) (covenant restricting land to two residences).

only for residential purposes, to build any structure at least 30 feet behind the front lot line, or to build no more than two homes per acre all "touch and concern" the land.

Covenants not to compete present a more complex problem. Suppose C operates a wine store on Greenacre; when C conveys his adjacent property Blueacre to D, D covenants not to operate a business on the land that would compete with C's wine store. This covenant would seem to satisfy the "touch and concern" requirement with ease, because it restricts D's physical use of Blueacre. Yet—apparently concerned about potential monopolies—many nineteenth-century courts refused to enforce such anticompetitive covenants, reasoning that they did not sufficiently "touch and concern." Although this heritage may linger in a few states, almost all modern courts now conclude that covenants not to compete do meet the "touch and concern" requirement.[21]

[iii] Affirmative Covenants

Most of the controversy about the "touch and concern" requirement involves affirmative covenants—those that require the promisor to perform some affirmative act, usually the payment of money. Traditionally, courts were reluctant to enforce an affirmative covenant against the promisor's successors unless it was closely tied to the land. Suppose E and F, adjacent landowners, agree that F will keep the wooden fence on the E-F property line in good repair. This covenant clearly meets the "touch and concern" standard because it affects the physical use of the land.[22] On the other hand, what if F covenanted to buy a fire insurance policy on the fence? Would a court enforce this purely monetary obligation?

The traditional view is that covenants to pay money—for example, covenants to pay real property taxes, to purchase insurance,[23] to pay security deposits, or to pay homeowners association dues—do not "touch and concern."[24] Even here, however, there was one glaring exception: the tenant's promise to pay rent to the landlord was uniformly held to "touch and concern" the land. Modern courts have relaxed the traditional approach. There is a clear trend toward holding that monetary payments related to the land do "touch and concern."[25] Probably the clearest example of this trend involves covenants to pay homeowners association dues.[26] Today

---

[21] See, e.g., Whitinsville Plaza, Inc. v. Kotseas, 390 N.E.2d 243 (Mass. 1979).

[22] Cf. Moseley v. Bishop, 470 N.E.2d 773 (Ind. Ct. App. 1984) (covenant to improve and maintain a drainage ditch met test); see also Abbott v. Bob's U-Drive, 352 P.2d 598 (Or. 1960) (covenant to arbitrate lease disputes satisfied test).

[23] See, e.g., Burton v. Chesapeake Box & Lumber Corp., 57 S.E.2d 904 (Va. 1950) (holding that covenant to insure did not "touch and concern").

[24] Cf. Eagle Enters., Inc. v. Gross, 349 N.E.2d 816 (N.Y. 1976) (covenant to purchase water did not "touch and concern").

[25] See, e.g., Gallagher v. Bell, 516 A.2d 1028 (Md. Ct. Spec. App. 1986) (covenant to pay for building street and installing utilities did "touch and concern"). But see Caullett v. Stanley Stilwell & Sons, Inc., 170 A.2d 52 (N.J. Super. Ct. App. Div. 1961) (covenant requiring grantee to retain grantor to construct dwelling on land did not "touch and concern").

[26] See, e.g., Regency Homes Ass'n v. Egermayer, 498 N.W.2d 783 (Neb. 1993); Neponsit Property Owners' Ass'n, Inc. v. Emigrant Indus. Sav. Bank, 15 N.E.2d 793 (N.Y. 1938); cf. Streams Sports Club, Ltd. v. Richmond, 440 N.E.2d 1264 (Ill. App. Ct. 1982).

courts consistently hold that such covenants "touch and concern" the land; otherwise, common interest communities could not function.

[b] Special Problem: What if the Benefit Does Not "Touch and Concern"?

In general, the running of the burden and benefit are analyzed separately. Yet most states recognize an important exception to this rule: the burden does not run if the benefit is *in gross,* that is, if it fails to "touch and concern" land.

For example, in *Caullett v. Stanley Stilwell & Sons*[27] plaintiff purchased a building lot from the defendant-developer; the deed contained a covenant that gave defendant the right to "build or construct the original dwelling or building" on the land.[28] Plaintiff sued to quiet title, arguing that the restriction was not an enforceable covenant. The court agreed because, among other reasons, the benefit of the covenant was in gross. It did not "touch and concern" any property retained by the defendant; rather, it gave the defendant "a mere commercial advantage in the operation of his business."[29]

[5] Horizontal Privity

[a] Three Competing Views

The law traditionally requires that the original covenanting parties have a special relationship in order for the burden of a real covenant to run with the land. This relationship is known as *horizontal privity.* In determining whether horizontal privity exists, we consider only the relationship between the *original parties* to the promise, and ignore their successors (*see* Table 9).

---

[27] 170 A.2d 52 (N.J. Super. Ct. App. Div. 1961).

[28] Caullett v. Stanley Stilwell & Sons, Inc., 170 A.2d 52, 53 (N.J. Super. Ct. App. Div. 1961).

[29] Caullett v. Stanley Stilwell & Sons, Inc., 170 A.2d 52, 55 (N.J. Super. Ct. App. Div. 1961).

TABLE 9: HORIZONTAL AND VERTICAL PRIVITY

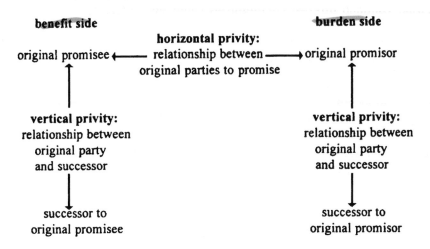

Under English law, only the privity of estate between landlord and tenant (*see* § 18.03[A]) satisfied this requirement. Accordingly, a real covenant could be created only between a landlord and a tenant. The practical effect of this requirement was to restrict the use of the real covenant, and thereby minimize its impact on productive land use. Suppose K and L, owners of adjacent English parcels, expressly agreed in 1800 that their respective lands would be limited "to agricultural use forever." Even if all other elements were met, the lack of a landlord-tenant relationship would prevent K and L from creating a valid real covenant.

The confusion over horizontal privity arises because American courts extended the doctrine far beyond its English confines, to relationships other than landlord-tenant. What relationships create horizontal privity under American law? There are three competing views. First, a few states insist on a landlord-tenant relationship or a similar relationship involving mutual interests in the same land. Second, a majority of states extend the doctrine farther to include all successive interests, including the grantor-grantee relationship. Finally, a number of states have abandoned the requirement altogether. It is difficult to determine the current status of the law on horizontal privity because modern decisions involving real covenants are rare.

[b] Mutual Interests

This approach finds horizontal privity between the promisor and promisee who hold mutual interests in the same land.[30] A landlord and tenant, for example, have mutual interests (respectively, a reversion and a nonfreehold estate) in the same property (the leased premises) at the same time (during the lease term). The other main example is the easement. The

---

[30] *See, e.g.,* Whitinsville Plaza, Inc. v. Kotseas, 390 N.E.2d 243 (Mass. 1979).

owners of the dominant and servient tenements have mutual interests (respectively, an easement and fee simple absolute) in the same property (the land burdened by the easement) at the same time (during the life of the easement).

Suppose landlord L and tenant T enter into a 10-year lease. The lease provides that T, "his successors and assigns" shall not permit hazardous waste to be stored on the property. T assigns the lease to A, who promptly opens a hazardous waste disposal site on the land. L sues A for damages under the lease. The horizontal privity requirement is met because the original covenanting parties—L and T—had mutual interests in the leased premises.

Consider again the height restriction imposed by the hypothetical A-B covenant above (see [B][1], above). A and B never held simultaneous interests in the burdened land, Greyacre. Rather, their interests were successive: A conveyed his interest to B. In a jurisdiction using the mutual interests standard, no horizontal privity existed between A and B. Thus, the burden of the height restriction did not run to B's successor C. A cannot recover damages from C.

[c] Successive Interests

This approach finds horizontal privity when a covenant is created in a transaction involving the conveyance of an interest in land between the covenanting parties.[31] Thus, the grantor-grantee relationship establishes horizontal privity, without any continuing relationship between the parties. In the A-B hypothetical (see [B][1], above), the covenant was created in the deed conveying fee simple absolute in Greyacre from A to B; horizontal privity accordingly arises. Assuming the other elements of a real covenant are present, then, A can recover damages against B's successor C. Although the case law is scant, this approach appears to be the majority view in the United States.[32]

Note that this approach incorporates the "mutual interests" approach as well. For example, the landlord who transfers a leasehold estate to the tenant, or the owner who grants a road easement to a neighbor, is conveying an interest in land.[33]

[d] No Horizontal Privity Required

In a growing number of states, horizontal privity is not necessary.[34] Legal scholars roundly condemn the requirement as a meaningless anachronism (see § 33.07). Moreover, because it can be easily circumvented through a "straw" transaction, it poses difficulty only for unsophisticated parties.

---

[31] See, e.g., Runyon v. Paley, 416 S.E.2d 177 (N.C. 1992).

[32] See, e.g., Runyon v. Paley, 416 S.E.2d 177 (N.C. 1992) (conveyance between original parties satisfied horizontal privity requirement).

[33] See, e.g., Moseley v. Bishop, 470 N.E.2d 773 (Ind. Ct. App. 1984) (easement created horizontal privity under "mutual or successive interest" standard).

[34] See, e.g., Gallagher v. Bell, 516 A.2d 1028 (Md. Ct. Spec. App. 1986).

There is a clear modern trend toward abolishing the requirement, as the new Restatement (Third) of Property: Servitudes advocates.

[6] Vertical Privity

Traditional law also requires *vertical privity* in order for the burden of a covenant to bind successors.[35] Vertical privity concerns the relationship between the original covenanting party and his successors (see Table 9). If the successor succeeds to the *entire estate* in land held by the original covenanting party, vertical privity exists. On the other hand, if the successor acquires *less than the entire estate,* no vertical privity arises.

In the A-B hypothetical (*see* [B][1], *above*) A conveyed fee simple absolute in Greyacre to B; the A-B deed imposes a height restriction on future buildings. B later transferred his fee simple absolute estate to C. Vertical privity exists between B and C simply because C acquired B's entire estate. The method of transfer—conveyance, devise, or intestate succession—is irrelevant.

On the other hand, if B had transferred less than his entire estate (e.g., a life estate or a term of years tenancy) to C, no vertical privity would arise. Accordingly, if C—as a tenant under a term of years tenancy—builds a home that exceeds the height limit, A cannot enforce the restriction against C as a real covenant. The same result follows if C acquires B's estate through adverse possession; here, no privity of any kind exists between B and C.

[7] Notice to Successors

In most instances, the successor must have notice of the covenant.[36] This requirement arises indirectly from the state recording statutes, not as a direct element of the real covenant. In general, a later purchaser who acquires an interest for value and without notice of a prior adverse claim is protected under the recording laws as a bona fide purchaser (*see* § 24.03). Accordingly, a real covenant is enforceable against a later purchaser for value only if the purchaser has notice of the covenant when acquiring the interest. The notice requirement is satisfied by:

(1)   actual notice,

(2)   record notice,

(3)   inquiry notice, or

(4)   imputed notice (*see* § 24.06).

However, one acquiring an interest by gift is not a bona fide purchaser. Accordingly, a devisee, heir, or other donee is bound by a prior covenant even without notice.

---

[35] *See, e.g.,* Moseley v. Bishop, 470 N.E.2d 773 (Ind. Ct. App. 1984); Runyon v. Paley, 416 S.E.2d 177 (N.C. 1992).

[36] *See, e.g.,* Bishop v. Rueff, 619 S.W.2d 718 (Ky. Ct. App. 1981).

[C] Promisee's Successor vs. Original Promisor: Does the Benefit Run?

[1] Requirements for Benefit to Run

Suppose that the promisee's successor seeks to enforce the covenant against the original promisor. Here, the only question is whether the *benefit* of the covenant runs to the promisee's successor. Reconsider the A-B hypothetical (*see* [B][1], *above*). A and B enter into a covenant limiting the height of future buildings on B's land Greyacre. Suppose that A conveys his land Blackacre to D; B now begins building a 30-foot-high house on Greyacre that will block the view. In order for D to enforce the restriction as a real covenant, he must demonstrate that the *benefit* of the covenant runs to him, as A's successor. It is not necessary to show that the *burden* also runs because here D seeks to enforce the covenant against B, the original promisor, not a successor to B.

Logic suggests that it should be easier to benefit successors than to burden them. The law reflects this approach. In order for the benefit of a real covenant to run to successors, only four elements are required:

    (1)   the covenant must be in writing (*see* [B][2], *above*),

    (2)   the original parties must intend to benefit successors (*see* [B][3], *above*),

    (3)   the benefit of the covenant must "touch and concern" land (*see* [B][4], *above*), and

    (4)   vertical privity must be present (*see* [B][6], *above*).

In most jurisdictions, neither horizontal privity nor notice is required.

The standard for vertical privity on the benefit side is greatly relaxed. In general, courts find vertical privity in successors even when they received less than their predecessors' entire interest. For example, assume L and K enter into a covenant that bans the sale of alcohol on K's land; L leases her land to M; and K starts selling alcohol. The benefit of the covenant runs to M, as L's successor, even though M did not acquire L's entire estate.

Suppose developer D creates a 100-lot residential subdivision; she records a declaration of restrictions against all the lots that (1) creates a homeowners association; (2) requires lot owners to pay assessments to the association; and (3) imposes various use restrictions. D sells lot 39 to E, and sells the other lots to various buyers. If E now refuses to pay the assessments, presumably any other lot owner is entitled to sue him. Because all lot owners are successors to D, vertical privity exists. But the homeowners association has no privity with D. Can it sue to collect the unpaid assessment? Most courts allow suit on the theory that the homeowners association is acting as an agent for the benefited lot owners.[37]

---

[37] *See, e.g.,* Neponsit Property Owners' Ass'n v. Emigrant Indus. Sav. Bank, 15 N.E.2d 793 (N.Y. 1938).

[2]   Example: The "Lawn Covenant"

Assume R and S own single-family residences on the same street; R, S, and the other homeowners on the street all enter into a written agreement that provides, in part: "In order to protect the visual appearance of the neighborhood, and protect property values, each owner agrees that at least 90% of the front yard of his or her property shall consist of a grass lawn that the owner will maintain in good condition. This agreement will bind and benefit all successors." One year later, R sells her home to T. S then removes all the grass from his front yard, and paves the entire area with asphalt, planning to store old cars there. Can T recover damages from S for breach of covenant?

Here, all the lots were simultaneously burdened and benefited by the restriction. But on these facts, T seeks the benefit of the covenant for himself, and wishes to enforce its burden against S. S is an original party to the covenant, so he is bound by its burden as a matter of contract law. The only question is whether the benefit of the covenant runs to T as a successor to R, an original promisee.

On these facts, the benefit runs to T. The covenant is contained in a writing, which we will presume complies with the Statute of Frauds; and the covenant expressly manifests the parties' intent to benefit and burden their successors. A modern court would undoubtedly hold that the covenant does "touch and concern" the land, because it restricts the physical use of S's property; S must devote 90% of his front yard to lawn. Finally, because R apparently conveyed her entire estate to T, the element of vertical privity is easily satisfied.

[D]   Promisee's Successor vs. Promisor's Successor: Do the Burden and the Benefit Both Run?

[1]   Requirements for Burden and Benefit to Run

Suppose that the promisee's successor attempts to enforce the covenant against the promisor's successor. In order for this claim to succeed, both the *burden* and the *benefit* must run. Consider the A-B height restriction hypothetical once more (*see* [B][1], *above*). Suppose that after A and B enter into the covenant, A conveys his land Blackacre to D and B conveys his land Greyacre to C. C now begins building a 30-foot high house on Greyacre. Can D, the promisee's successor, enforce the covenant against C, the promisor's successor? The answer to this question turns on the analysis already discussed above. If both the burden (*see* [B], *above*) and the benefit (*see* [C], *above*) run to successors, then D can enforce the restriction as a real covenant. If either the burden or the benefit fails to run, D's claim will fail.

[2]   Example: The "Lawn Covenant" Revisited

Consider again the "lawn covenant" among R, S, and their neighbors (*see* [C][2], *above*). Now suppose that after the covenant is created, R sells her home to T and S sells his home to U. U now replaces the front lawn with pavement. Can T recover damages from U? In order for T to prevail, both the benefit and the burden of the covenant must run to successors. We already established that the benefit runs to T (*see* [C][2], *above*). So, does the burden run to U?

Three of the six necessary elements (*see* [B][1], *above*) are easily met. As already discussed in connection with the benefit analysis (*see* [C][2], *above*), the covenant is in writing, manifests an intent to bind successors, and satisfies the "touch and concern" test. On the facts, vertical privity exists between S and U; it appears that S conveyed his entire estate to U. But no horizontal privity existed between the original parties to the covenant—R, S, and their neighbors; they did not have mutual or successive interests. Unless the jurisdiction has abandoned the horizontal privity requirement, the burden does not run. Notice presents another problem. No facts suggest that U had actual or record notice of the covenant. But did the uniform appearance of front lawns in the area put U on inquiry notice? This seems unlikely, because grass lawns are quite common in residential areas. On balance, the burden of the covenant probably does not run to U.

§ 33.05 Termination of Real Covenants

Traditional law provides only a few defenses to enforcement of a real covenant.[38] Of course, parties might create a covenant that according to its terms continues only for a fixed period (e.g., 30 years); or the party benefited by a covenant might agree to release his rights. Eminent domain or other governmental action might also end a covenant.[39] And when one party acquires ownership of all the land benefited and burdened by a covenant, it is extinguished by the doctrine of merger. Anti-discrimination statutes might also bar enforcement of a covenant (*see* § 34.06[B]). Beyond this point, the main potential defenses are: (1) abandonment; and (2) changed conditions.[40]

Abandonment occurs when the conduct of the person entitled to the benefit of the covenant demonstrates the intent to relinquish his or her rights.[41] For example, suppose that Redacre is a 100-lot subdivision subject to a recorded covenant that limits the height of all buildings to one story; the owners of 99 lots proceed to build two-story dwellings. The owner of the 100th lot would reasonably conclude that the conduct of the other lot

---

[38] In jurisdictions that provide equitable remedies for breach of a real covenant, the standard equitable defenses are also available (*see* § 34.06[D]).

[39] *But see* Lake Arrowhead Community Club, Inc. v. Looney, 770 P.2d 1046 (Wash. 1989) (tax sale did not terminate covenant requiring owner to pay share of costs for neighborhood recreational facilities).

[40] Additional defenses may arise in the specialized context of covenants, conditions, and restrictions that regulate residential condominium projects, single-family residential subdivisions, and other "common interest developments" (*see* Chapter 35).

[41] *But see* Pocono Springs Civic Ass'n, Inc. v. MacKenzie, 667 A.2d 233 (Pa. Super. Ct. 1995) (because real property cannot be abandoned under Pennsylvania law, owners could not avoid liability for assessments due under covenant by abandoning their lot).

owners constituted an abandonment of the restriction.[42] As one court explained, abandonment is found "when the average person, upon inspection of a subdivision and knowing of a certain restriction, will readily observe sufficient violations so that he or she will logically infer that the property owners neither adhere to nor enforce the restriction."[43]

Under the *changed conditions* doctrine, a covenant becomes unenforceable when conditions in the neighborhood of the burdened land have so substantially changed that the intended benefits of the covenant cannot be realized (*see* § 34.06[C]). This defense originated in equity, and is uniformly held applicable to the equitable servitude. Yet an increasing number of jurisdictions also apply this defense to the real covenant.

§ 33.06 Remedies for Breach of Real Covenants

The historic remedy for breach of a real covenant is compensatory damages. The successful plaintiff recovers damages equal to the difference between the fair market value of the property before and after the defendant's breach. For example, suppose A builds an oil refinery on his land in violation of a real covenant that permits only residential use; if this violation reduces the fair market value of B's adjacent home from $200,000 to $50,000, B is entitled to $150,000 in general damages. Special or consequential damages may also be recovered.

As a practical matter, the modern plaintiff has a choice of remedies. *Almost any restriction that can be enforced as a real covenant can alternatively be enforced as an equitable servitude (see § 34.04).* If so, the plaintiff can usually choose between (1) compensatory damages (by enforcing the restriction as a real covenant) or (2) an injunction against future conduct and damages for the past violation (by enforcing it as an equitable servitude).

§ 33.07 Scholarly Perspectives on Real Covenants

The real covenant has attracted much scholarly attention in recent years, undoubtedly encouraged by debate over the provisions of the new Restatement (Third) of Property: Servitudes. At this point, there is a general consensus in favor of simplifying the law. Most scholars agree that the requirements of "touch and concern," horizontal privity, and vertical privity should either be abolished or greatly relaxed.

The "touch and concern" requirement has sparked vigorous academic battle. Led by Richard Epstein, opponents charge that this requirement is vague and unpredictable, frustrates the intention of the parties, and fails to serve any useful function.[44] While conceding that some reform is

---

[42] *See also* Western Land Co. v. Truskolaski, 495 P.2d 624 (Nev. 1972) (sporadic violations of covenants were insufficient to constitute abandonment); *cf.* Pettey v. First Nat'l Bank, 588 N.E.2d 412 (Ill. App. Ct. 1992) (isolated failures to enforce covenants was not a waiver).

[43] Fink v. Miller, 896 P.2d 649, 653 (Utah Ct. App. 1995).

[44] *See* Richard A. Epstein, *Notice and Freedom of Contract in the Law of Servitudes,* 55 S. Cal. L. Rev. 1353 (1982).

appropriate, Uriel Reichman and other supporters argue that the requirement both (1) promotes the efficient utilization of land (by preventing burdens that impair marketability) and (2) protects the long-term expectations of owners (by ensuring that there is at least a minimal relationship between benefit and burden).[45] Opponents retort that individual owners are best able to determine whether their covenant promotes efficient land use, while the notice requirement already prevents unfair surprise to owners of burdened land.

In contrast, scholars uniformly agree that horizontal privity is obsolete and should be eliminated. Courts traditionally feared that real covenants would impair the productive use of land. In this climate, the horizontal privity requirement arguably served a function: it made the creation of real covenants more difficult, and thereby reduced the number of covenants that could arise. However, given the modern recognition that private land use restrictions can provide social benefits, the reason for this requirement no longer exists.

Further, critics note that the horizontal privity requirement can be easily circumvented through a "straw" transaction. Suppose that R and S, adjacent landowners, wish to prohibit industrial uses on R's property; but because they lack horizontal privity their agreement would not be enforced as a real covenant. A simple solution is available: R conveys her land to S, and S reconveys it to R pursuant to a deed that includes the desired use restriction. R and S now have successive interests, which satisfy the horizontal privity requirement in most jurisdictions.

Finally, the vertical privity requirement enjoys little scholarly support. The historic rationale for the requirement ended long ago. And its continued existence serves to frustrate party intent. Why should an owner lose the right to enforce a covenant against a successor merely because the owner of the burdened land chooses to transfer less than his entire estate?[46] If A and B enter into a real covenant that restricts B's land Greenacre to residential use, and B later leases Greenacre to C for a 99-year term, C should reasonably be bound by the covenant, just as if B conveyed fee simple absolute. At the other extreme, if B leases Greenacre to C for a very short term (e.g., to use as a fruit stand for a month during strawberry season), enforcement of the covenant against C—who probably lacks actual knowledge of the covenant—might well be inequitable.

§ 33.08 The Restatement (Third) of Property: Servitudes

The new Restatement (Third) of Property: Servitudes greatly simplifies the traditional law of real covenants and equitable servitudes (see § 34.08). It combines these two doctrines into one—the *servitude*. Unlike the real

---

[45] See Uriel Reichman, *Toward a Unified Concept of Servitudes*, 55 S. Cal. L. Rev. 1177 (1982); A. Dan Tarlock, *Touch and Concern Is Dead, Long Live the Doctrine*, 77 Neb. L. Rev. 804 (1998).

[46] See Uriel Reichman, *Toward a Unified Concept of Servitudes*, 55 S. Cal. L. Rev. 1177 (1982).

covenant, this new servitude is quite simple to create. Broadly speaking, a contract or conveyance creates a servitude if

    (1)   the parties intend it to do so;[47]

    (2)   it complies with the Statute of Frauds;[48] and

    (3)   the servitude is not illegal, unconstitutional, or violative of public policy.[49]

The Restatement abandons horizontal privity and "touch and concern" altogether, and greatly relaxes the requirement of vertical privity. This innovative approach reflects the utilitarian view—echoed by most legal scholars—that "servitudes are useful devices which people ought to be able to use without artificial constraints."[50] On the other hand, the Restatement acknowledges that particular servitudes may become inefficient, obsolete, or socially harmful over time. It accordingly provides new tools that make it easier to modify or terminate such servitudes.[51]

---

[47] Restatement (Third) of Property: Servitudes § 2.2 (Tentative Draft No. 1, 1989).

[48] Restatement (Third) of Property: Servitudes § 2.8 (Tentative Draft No. 1, 1989).

[49] Restatement (Third) of Property: Servitudes § 3.1 (Tentative Draft No. 7, 1998).

[50] Restatement (Third) of Property: Servitudes, ch. 2 intro. note (Tentative Draft No. 1, 1989).

[51] *See generally* Restatement (Third) of Property: Servitudes ch. 7 (Tentative Draft No. 6, 1997).

Chapter 34

EQUITABLE SERVITUDES

SYNOPSIS

§ 34.01   The Equitable Servitude in Context

The equitable servitude is the primary modern tool for enforcing private land use restrictions. It evolved because the real covenant (*see* Chapter 33) failed to satisfy the need for an effective method of binding successor owners to promises made by their predecessors. In a sense, the equitable servitude is a response to the shortcomings of the real covenant. Yet both doctrines reflect the law's effort to reconcile two opposing policy concerns: individual liberty and efficient use of land (*see* § 33.03).

Suppose A owns Redacre and B owns the adjacent parcel Orangeacre; both parcels are undeveloped, mountainous land.[1] A plans to create a vacation subdivision on Redacre where weary city residents can relax in peaceful quiet. A and B accordingly enter into an agreement whereby B promises that no industrial uses will be permitted on Orangeacre in exchange for a $50,000 payment from A. A develops the subdivision and conveys all the lots to buyers. B then leases Orangeacre to C for a term of 60 years and C builds a noisy lumber mill on the land. The lot owners (A's successors) cannot enforce the promise against C (B's successor) as a real covenant because both horizontal and vertical privity are missing. And even if the promise could be enforced as a real covenant, the remedy is inadequate: the lot owners could only recover damages, not an injunction to eliminate the noise.

This example illustrates the limitations of the real covenant. The traditional threshold for establishing a real covenant is quite high. As a result, many restrictions—like the A-B effort to prohibit industrial uses—cannot be enforced against successors. And the damages remedy is often inadequate.

The equitable servitude was invented in the nineteenth century to fill this doctrinal vacuum. It is generally easier to enforce a promise as an equitable servitude than as a real covenant because horizontal and vertical privity are not required. Accordingly, a broader range of restrictions can be enforced against successors. For instance, the lot owners in the above example could enforce B's promise against C as an equitable servitude. The

---

[1] *See generally* Lawrence Berger, *Unification of the Law of Servitudes,* 55 S. Cal. L. Rev. 1339 (1982); Susan F. French, *Toward a Modern Law of Servitudes: Reweaving the Ancient Strands,* 55 S. Cal. L. Rev. 1261 (1982); John C. Paulus, *The Equitable Servitude in Land Use Planning,* 2 Willamette L. Rev. 399 (1963); Uriel Reichman, *Toward a Unified Concept of Servitudes,* 55 S. Cal. L. Rev. 1177 (1982); Russell R. Reno, *The Enforcement of Equitable Servitudes in Land,* 28 Va. L. Rev. 951 (1942); Glen O. Robinson, *Explaining Contingent Rights: The Puzzle of "Obsolete" Covenants,* 91 Colum. L. Rev. 546 (1991).

usual remedy for violation of an equitable servitude is injunctive relief, which often provides more effective relief than compensatory damages. Here, the lot owners presumably could obtain an injunction forcing C to eliminate the noise.

The law of equitable servitudes is well-developed and relatively straight-forward, at least when compared to the confusion surrounding the real covenant (see § 33.07). This chapter focuses on the traditional rules that govern equitable servitudes. These rules somewhat overlap with the principles governing real covenants, already discussed in Chapter 33. This area of the law is in transition because the line between the real covenant and the equitable servitude—once quite clear—has blurred in recent decades. Accordingly, this chapter examines the proposal of the new Restatement (Third) of Property: Servitudes to combine the equitable servitude and the real covenant into a single, simplified doctrine.

§ 34.02   What Is an Equitable Servitude?

[A]   Defining the Equitable Servitude

In general, an equitable servitude is a promise concerning the use of land that (1) benefits and burdens the original parties to the promise *and their successors* and (2) is enforceable in equity. Like the real covenant, the equitable servitude is essentially a tool that allows a promise to be enforced by or against a successor party under limited circumstances (see § 33.02[A]). The same promise might be enforced either as a real covenant (if the plaintiff desires damages) or as an equitable servitude (if the plaintiff seeks an injunction), assuming all requirements are met.[2]

[B]   Distinguished from Other Doctrines

Three factors distinguish the equitable servitude from the real covenant. First, the standard for enforcing a promise as an equitable servitude is easier to meet than the parallel standard for a real covenant (see § 34.04). Second, a broader array of defenses applies to the equitable servitude (see § 34.06). Finally, the traditional remedy for violation of an equitable servitude is an injunction, not damages (see § 34.07).

The boundary between the equitable servitude and the negative easement is more difficult to locate. Both might involve a promise to refrain from performing an act on land that is otherwise allowed; injunctive relief may be available if either is breached; and, under the modern view, both are considered interests in land. Thus, under some circumstances, the same promise might be enforced either as an equitable servitude or an easement. However, the elements required to create a valid equitable servitude differ somewhat from those required for an easement, and the available defenses

---

[2] When discussing equitable servitudes and real covenants, it is common to refer to the underlying promise as a "covenant." To avoid confusion with the real covenant, this chapter generally uses the term "promise" or "restriction" in lieu of "covenant."

also vary. More fundamentally, the traditional judicial hostility toward negative easements still restricts the scope of that doctrine (*see* § 32.12).[3]

§ 34.03 Evolution of the Equitable Servitude

The equitable servitude was born in *Tulk v. Moxhay*,[4] a landmark 1848 decision of England's chancery court that vividly demonstrated the shortcomings of the real covenant. Tulk conveyed Leicester Square, a privately-owned park in London, to one Elms. Elms promised in the deed to maintain the property "in an open state, uncovered with any buildings."[5] Apparently, Tulk wanted this promise in order to benefit several houses he owned that fronted on the square; it ensured that Tulk's tenants could both use the park as a private, fenced garden and enjoy the view from their houses.

Moxhay eventually acquired title to the square with actual notice of the promise, but claimed that it did not bind him. This conclusion was quite correct under existing English law. The promise could not be enforced in the law courts as a real covenant against Moxhay, a successor, because no horizontal privity existed between Tulk and Elms, the original parties;[6] in England, only a landlord-tenant relationship created horizontal privity (*see* § 33.04[B][5][a]).[7]

Undaunted, Tulk sued in chancery court for an injunction and prevailed. The key to the ruling was that Moxhay had notice of the promise before his purchase. Given this advance notice, the court reasoned, it would be inequitable to permit Moxhay to violate the restriction. "[F]or if an equity is attached to the property by the owner, no one purchasing with notice of that equity can stand in a different situation from the party from whom he purchased."[8] Otherwise, the court suggested, an original purchaser (like Elms) could buy land at a price that was reduced due to a restrictive promise and then resell the land for a greater price to a successor (like Moxhay) who could freely ignore the promise.

Yet another theme may lurk below the surface of the opinion. Nineteenth-century London was already an urban metropolis where open parkland was rare. Allowing Moxhay to build on the square might be inefficient; it could potentially cause more damage to the value of Tulk's houses than it would increase the value of the square.[9] In this situation, enforcement of Elms's promise against his successor Moxhay promoted productive land use. The traditional concern of the law courts that restrictions would impair productivity was inapplicable.

---

[3] Indeed, if early courts had recognized a wider range of negative easements, there might have been no need for the equitable servitude.

[4] 41 Eng. Rep. 1143 (1848).

[5] Tulk v. Moxhay, 41 Eng. Rep. 1143, 1143 (1848).

[6] Nor could it be enforced as a negative easement, because it did not fall into one of the four categories of negative easements recognized by English courts (*see* § 32.12).

[7] *See* Spencer's Case, 77 Eng. Rep. 72 (1583).

[8] Tulk v. Moxhay, 41 Eng. Rep. 1143, 1144 (1848).

[9] Tulk's ownership of nearby houses was essential to the result. As later decisions made clear, the burden of an equitable servitude does not bind successors if the benefit is in gross. *See* London County Council v. Allen, 3 K.B. 642 (1914).

§ 34.04   Creation of an Equitable Servitude

[A]   Perspectives on the Equitable Servitude

The law governing equitable servitudes is closely related to the law of real covenants. Thus, two foundational rules—already discussed in connection with the real covenant—apply equally to the equitable servitude. First, it is important to distinguish between the *original parties* to the promise and their *successors* (*see* § 33.04[A]). While the original parties are generally bound as a matter of contract law, property law determines whether the burden and benefit of the promise run to their successors.

Second, each equitable servitude has two "sides," just like a real covenant (*see* § 33.04[A]). The promisor's duty to perform the promise is known as the *burden*, while the promisee's right to enforce the promise is called the *benefit*. The requirements for enforcement differ, based on the identities of the plaintiff and defendant, as discussed below.

[B]   Original Promisee vs. Promisor's Successor: Does the Burden Run?

[1]   Requirements for Burden to Run

In order for the burden of an equitable servitude to bind the promisor's successors, American law generally requires that four elements be satisfied:

    (1)   the promise must be in writing or implied from a "common plan";

    (2)   the original parties must intend to bind successors;

    (3)   the promise must "touch and concern" land; and

    (4)   the successor must have notice of the promise. [10]

Neither horizontal privity nor vertical privity is required.

[2]   Promise in Writing or "Common Plan"

Most jurisdictions view the equitable servitude as an interest in land. Thus, as a general rule, a writing that satisfies the Statute of Frauds is required to create an enforceable equitable servitude (*see* § 23.04[A][1]). But American courts recognize a special exception to this rule, known as the "common plan" or "common scheme" doctrine. As discussed below (*see* § 34.05[B]), where a developer manifests a "common plan" to impose uniform restrictions on a subdivision, most courts will find implied equitable servitudes even without a writing.

[3]   Intent to Bind Successors

The original parties must intend that the promise bind the promisor's successors in order for the burden to run. [11] The law governing intent to

---

[10] *See generally* Runyon v. Paley, 416 S.E.2d 177 (N.C. 1992).

[11] *But see* William B. Stoebuck, *Running Covenants: An Analytical Primer*, 52 Wash. L. Rev. 861, 895 (1977) (arguing that reported decisions do not require intent).

bind successors in connection with real covenants (*see* § 33.04[B][3]) applies equally here.

[4] Touch and Concern

The burden of the promise must "touch and concern" land in order for an equitable servitude to run, as in the case of a real covenant. Accordingly, the discussion of the "touch and concern" element for real covenants (*see* § 33.04[B][4]) is generally applicable here as well.[12] Courts sometimes neglect to list "touch and concern" as an element of the equitable servitude, fueling academic speculation that it is not required. However, these decisions tend to involve situations where the element is clearly met, such that discussion is unnecessary.[13]

Must the benefit of an equitable servitude "touch and concern" land in order for the burden to run?[14] Under English law, an easement in gross—that is, an easement not attached to a dominant tenement—was invalid. Analogizing the equitable servitude to a negative easement, English courts held that the burden of an equitable servitude did not run unless it benefited a specific parcel of land.[15] American courts are divided on the issue.[16] Although the rationale for the English approach does not apply here—because easements in gross are generally accepted in the United States—many jurisdictions insist that the benefit of an equitable servitude "touch and concern" land. Presumably this approach reflects the policy concern that land use restrictions are potentially inefficient; thus, in order to restrict one parcel, there must be an offsetting benefit to another parcel.

[5] Notice to Successors

In general, the successor must have notice of the promise before acquiring his interest. The celebrated English decision of *Tulk v. Moxhay* (*see* § 34.03) expressly requires notice as an element of the equitable servitude, apparently in all cases. Under the prevailing American view, however, the notice requirement arises indirectly from the state recording statutes, not as a direct element of the equitable servitude.

Broadly speaking, a later purchaser who acquires an interest for value and without knowledge of a prior adverse claim is protected under the recording statutes as a bona fide purchaser (*see* § 24.03). For example, suppose that A and B enter into an agreement by which B promises to restrict his land to single-family residential use only. Eventually, X, a bona

---

[12] *See, e.g.*, Runyon v. Paley, 416 S.E.2d 177 (N.C. 1992) (provisions restricting land to residential use and limiting density to two residences did "touch and concern" land).

[13] *See* Lawrence Berger, *Integration of the Law of Easements, Real Covenants, and Equitable Servitudes*, 43 Wash. & Lee L. Rev. 337, 362 (1986). *But see* Davidson Bros. v. D. Katz & Sons, 579 A.2d 288 (N.J. 1990) (holding that "touch and concern" is merely one factor in determining the overall reasonableness—and hence enforceability—of a covenant).

[14] *See* Christiansen v. Casey, 613 S.W.2d 906 (Mo. Ct. App. 1981).

[15] London County Council v. Allen, 3 K.B. 642 (1914).

[16] *See, e.g.*, Caullett v. Stanley Stilwell & Sons, 170 A.2d 52 (N.J. Super. Ct. App. Div. 1961) (no).

fide purchaser without notice of the promise, acquires title to B's land. When X begins construction of a shopping center, A seeks an injunction. Even if all the other elements of an equitable servitude are met, A cannot prevail because X took title free and clear of the prior covenant.

The only potential difference between the English and American rules involves the owner who acquires title by gift. A devisee, heir, or other donee cannot qualify for protection as a bona fide purchaser; under the American rule, a donee is bound by a prior promise even without notice. In contrast, *Tulk v. Moxhay* suggests that in England a promise is unenforceable against any successor who lacks notice, whether purchaser or donee.

The notice requirement can be satisfied by:

(1)   actual notice,[17]

(2)   record notice,[18]

(3)   imputed notice, or

(4)   inquiry notice (*see* § 24.06).

An example of inquiry notice is *Sanborn v. McLean*,[19] where a buyer purchased a home and lot in a residential area, and later started to build a gas station on part of the land. Neighbors sued for an injunction, arguing that the lot had been impliedly restricted to residential use by the subdivider. The Michigan Supreme Court held that the buyer was charged with inquiry notice of the implied promise due to the residential appearance of the neighborhood—the "uniform residence character given the lots by the expensive dwellings thereon."[20]

[6]   Example: The "Pornography Restriction"

Suppose A, B, and ten other owners of small businesses in a small resort town wish to attract vacationing families to the area, and thereby increase their sales revenues. In order to create a "family atmosphere," they jointly execute a written document entitled "Agreement" by which they all promise not to sell or distribute pornography on their respective properties; the Agreement provides that it is intended to benefit and bind all successors and assigns, and is duly recorded. B then leases his bookstore to C for a term of six months. C immediately begins selling pornographic books. Can A enjoin C?

Here, every parcel was both benefited and burdened by the restriction; every owner who agreed to the restriction was both a promisor and a promisee. But because A is seeking to enforce the promise against C, we classify A as the promisee and C as a successor to the promisor. Here, A (the original promisee) can enforce the promise as an equitable servitude against C (the

---

[17] *See, e.g.,* Cheatham v. Taylor, 138 S.E. 545 (Va. 1927).

[18] Difficult questions about the scope of record notice are presented where a common grantor (typically a subdivider) conveys multiple lots, but expressly restricts only some of them. *See* Bishop v. Rueff, 619 S.W.2d 718 (Ky. Ct. App. 1981); Sanborn v. McLean, 206 N.W. 496 (Mich. 1925); *see also* § 25.07[B][5].

[19] 206 N.W. 496 (Mich. 1925).

[20] Sanborn v. McLean, 206 N.W. 496, 498 (Mich. 1925).

promisor's successor). The burden runs to C because all four requirements are met. The agreement complies with the Statute of Frauds; it manifests a clear intent to bind successors; the burden of the promise does "touch and concern" land because it limits the manner in which successors like C may use the land; and C is charged with notice of the recorded agreement. The lack of horizontal and vertical privity is irrelevant.

[C] Promisee's Successor vs. Original Promisor: Does the Benefit Run?

Suppose the promisee's successor seeks to enforce the promise against the original promisor as an equitable servitude. Now our question is whether the benefit runs. Only three elements are required for the benefit of an equitable servitude to run to successors:

(1)   the promise must be in writing or implied from a "common plan" (*see* [B][2], *above*),

(2)   the original parties must intend to benefit successors (*see* [B][3], *above*), and

(3)   the promise must "touch and concern" land (*see* [B][4], *above*).

Consider again the "pornography restriction" among A, B, and other business owners (*see* [B][6], *above*). Suppose that after the Agreement is recorded, A sells his business to D; B immediately begins selling pornographic books at his bookstore. Can D (the promisee's successor) enforce the promise against B (the original promisor)? Here the benefit runs to D because all elements are satisfied: the Agreement meets the Statute of Frauds; the original parties intended to benefit successors; and the promise does "touch and concern" land.

The law increasingly allows persons other than successors to enforce equitable servitudes. The issue arises most commonly in the subdivision context where uniform restrictions are imposed on a deed-by-deed basis, but the subdivider does not expressly promise to restrict all lots. In this setting, courts routinely permit earlier buyers to enforce uniform restrictions against later buyers, even though earlier buyers are not technically successors (*see* § 34.05[C]). Some jurisdictions take the further step of allowing any third-party beneficiary to enforce a promise created for his or her benefit, even absent a common plan (*see* § 34.05[C]).[21]

[D] Promisee's Successor vs. Promisor's Successor: Do the Burden and the Benefit Both Run?

Suppose that the promisee's successor seeks to enforce the promise against the promisor's successor. In order for this suit to succeed, both the *burden* and the *benefit* must run to successors. Consider the "pornography restriction" example (*see* [B][6], *above*). Assume that after the Agreement

---

[21] *See generally* Restatement of Property, ch. 46 int. note (1944); *cf.* Rodgers v. Reimann, 361 P.2d 101 (Or. 1961).

is recorded, A sells his business to D, while B leases his bookstore to C; C begins selling pornographic books. D (the promisee's successor) can enforce the promise against C (the promisor's successor) because the burden (*see* [B][6], *above*) and the benefit (*see* [C], *above*) both run.

§ 34.05   Special Problem: Equitable Servitudes and the Subdivision

[A]   Creation of Subdivision Restrictions

Developers of "common interest communities" such as residential subdivisions typically impose uniform restrictions on every lot in order to protect the long-run desirability of the neighborhood, and thereby attract buyers (*see* Chapter 35). Buyer B, for example, is more likely to purchase a home site in developer D's tract Brownacre if all the lots may only be used for single-family residences[22] and related restrictions are imposed. In order for this to occur, all lots in D's subdivision must be both burdened and benefited by uniform restrictions. This allows each lot owner to enforce the restrictions against any other lot owner.

Suppose D wishes to impose uniform restrictions that burden and benefit all lots in Brownacre. Today the process is simple. In most jurisdictions, D need only record a properly-drafted document (commonly called a *declaration*) containing the restrictions (usually called *covenants, conditions, and restrictions* or *CC&Rs*) against all lots in Brownacre before any sales begin. All later lot buyers receiving title through D or his successors are bound by these previously-recorded restrictions.

Yet in the early days of subdivision development—roughly from the late nineteenth century through the mid-twentieth century—quite a different method was utilized. Subdivider S would insert the restrictions into each individual deed. For example, if S's development Silveracre had 100 lots, then S would ensure that all 100 deeds contained the restrictions. But what happened if a developer like S carelessly failed to insert the restrictions into a few deeds? Were those lots bound? And which lots were benefited by the restrictions under this system? In particular, were earlier buyers entitled to enforce the restrictions against later buyers? Over time, a large body of law developed to answer these and similar questions.

[B]   Implied Burden: The Implied Reciprocal Covenant and the "Common Plan"

Can an equitable servitude arise by implication? Suppose developer E subdivides a tract of land into 20 lots and proudly advertises that the

---

[22] Extensive litigation explores the meaning of "single-family residence" as used in such restrictions. *See, e.g.,* Hill v. Community of Damien of Molokai, 911 P.2d 861 (N.M. 1996) ("single-family residence" interpreted to include group home where unrelated people live together); *cf.* Groninger v. Aumiller, 644 A.2d 1266 (Pa. Super. Ct. 1994) (restriction limiting structures to "residential purposes" only affected appearance of structure and did not bar commercial uses).

subdivision "will be a quiet, single-family residential community." Each lot is sold in sequence to a different buyer. The deeds from E to the first 19 buyers all expressly provide: "Buyer promises to use the property only as a single-family residence." However, the deed from E to the last buyer, Buyer 20, contains no such promise. If Buyer 20 starts building a winery on his lot, can the first lot buyer (Buyer 1) secure an injunction? Is lot 20 burdened by the promise?

If Buyer 1 tried to enforce the promise as a real covenant, Buyer 20 would assert a simple defense: it is not contained in a writing that satisfies the Statute of Frauds, and is thus unenforceable. However, because Buyer 1 seeks to enforce the promise as an equitable servitude, a special exception applies.

If a developer manifests a *common plan* or *common scheme* to impose uniform restrictions on a subdivision, most courts conclude that an equitable servitude will be implied in equity.[23] The common plan or scheme is viewed as an implied promise by the developer to impose the same restrictions on all the retained lots.[24] Under this approach, every lot in the subdivision is both burdened and benefited by the restriction. No lot owner may violate the restriction; and any lot owner can enforce the restriction against another.

Here, when E sold the first lot (lot 1) to Buyer 1, the deed contained an express promise restricting lot 1 to single-family use only. Under the majority approach, the common plan is deemed an *implied* promise by E to Buyer 1 that the other lots E still owns at this time (lots 2-20) will be similarly restricted to single-family use. Thus, when later buyers (including Buyer 20) acquire their lots from E, the lots are already impliedly burdened by the promise.

The leading case on point is *Sanborn v. McLean*,[25] where developers apparently intended to create a 91-lot residential subdivision in Detroit. However, presumably due to carelessness, only 53 of the 91 deeds contained express language restricting the lots to residential use. About 20 years later, after houses had been built on all the lots, defendant McLean purchased one of the seemingly unrestricted lots and started to erect a gas station in its back yard. Plaintiff Sanborn and other lot owners brought suit to enjoin the construction. Responding to the defense argument that the restriction did not appear in the chain of title, the Michigan Supreme Court held that where "the owner of two or more lots . . . sells one with restrictions of benefit to the land retained, the servitude becomes mutual, and . . . the owner of the lot or lots retained can do nothing forbidden to the owner of the lot sold."[26] The *Sanborn* court described these implied

---

[23] *See, e.g.,* Turner v. Brocato, 111 A.2d 855 (Md. 1955); Evans v. Pollock, 796 S.W.2d 465 (Tex. 1990); Mid-State Equip. Co. v. Bell, 225 S.E.2d 877 (Va. 1976).

[24] *See also* Nelle v. Loch Haven Homeowners' Ass'n, 413 So.2d 28 (Fla. 1982) (developer's reservation of right to modify restriction did not negate existence of common plan); *but see* Suttle v. Bailey, 361 P.2d 325 (N.M. 1961) (because subdividers reserved right to modify subdivision covenant, it did not run with the land).

[25] 206 N.W. 496 (Mich. 1925).

[26] Sanborn v. McLean, 206 N.W. 496, 497 (Mich. 1925).

restrictions as "reciprocal negative easements" and this rather misleading usage lingers today. A more accurate label would be "implied reciprocal servitudes" or "implied reciprocal covenants."[27]

What evidence proves the existence of a common plan? One key factor is the percentage of deeds that contain the restriction. For example, if the restriction is present in only 20% of the subdivision deeds, a common plan is far less likely to be found than if it appears in 95% of the deeds.[28] Other relevant factors include the subdivider's oral representations to buyers, statements in written advertising, sales brochures, or maps given to buyers, and recorded plat maps or declarations.[29]

A minority of jurisdictions—including California[30] and Massachusetts[31]—refuse to imply equitable servitudes from a common plan, usually on the basis that this would violate the Statute of Frauds.

[C] Implied Benefit

Which subdivision lots are benefited by the promise? Suppose S creates a three-lot subdivision and sells the lots in sequence; buyer A buys lot 1 in 1998, buyer B buys lot 2 in 1999, and buyer C buys lot 3 in 2000. S takes care to ensure that each deed contains an express promise from the buyer that the lot is restricted to single-family residential use, which benefits "S, his successors, and assigns." But S does not expressly promise buyers that other lots will be burdened.

Suppose A now starts building an oil refinery on her lot. Both B and C, as successors to S, are entitled to sue, because the 1998 A-S promise expressly benefited S and his "successors." In short, it is simple to explain why a *later* buyer (as a successor to the subdivider) is entitled to sue an *earlier* buyer.

But what happens if an *earlier* buyer sues a *later* buyer? Assume that A and B comply with the promise, but C uses his lot as an oil refinery. A sues C. Note that S no longer owned A's lot in 2000 when the C-S promise was created. Thus, C will argue that the benefit of the C-S promise does not extend to a prior purchaser like A; rather, it extends only to S and his "successors"—those who bought from S in 2000 or later. In jurisdictions following the "common plan" approach, the answer to the question is straightforward. The existence of the common plan is seen as evidence of the subdivider's intent to benefit all lots.[32] Under this approach, the S-A

---

[27] *See also* Restatement (Third) of Property: Servitudes § 2.14 (Tentative Draft No. 1, 1989).

[28] *See, e.g.,* Steinmann v. Silverman, 200 N.E.2d 192 (N.Y. 1964) (no common plan where restriction appeared in 20% of deeds).

[29] *See* Warren v. Detlefsen, 663 S.W.2d 710 (Ark. 1984).

[30] Riley v. Bear Creek Planning Comm., 551 P.2d 1213 (Cal. 1976) (requiring writing that satisfies Statute of Frauds); Citizens for Covenant Compliance v. Anderson, 906 P.2d 1314 (Cal. 1995) (same).

[31] Sprague v. Kimball, 100 N.E. 622 (Mass. 1913); Snow v. Van Dam, 197 N.E. 224 (Mass. 1935); Houghton v. Rizzo, 281 N.E.2d 577 (Mass. 1972).

[32] *But see* Petersen v. Beekmere, Inc., 283 A.2d 911 (N.J. Super. Ct. Ch. Div. 1971) (insufficient evidence of common plan).

deed includes an implied promise by S to restrict his remaining lots for the benefit of A.

But what about the minority of states that rejects the common plan approach? The Massachusetts solution to this dilemma, inspired by dicta in *Snow v. Van Dam*,[33] stems from contract law: the third-party beneficiary doctrine. The inclusion of an express promise in a later deed (here, the S-C deed) demonstrates the implied intent of the parties to benefit all other lot owners as third-party beneficiaries, including earlier buyers (like A and B).

§ 34.06   Termination of Equitable Servitudes

[A]   Defenses in General

The law provides many defenses to enforcement of an equitable servitude. Foremost among these are (1) anti-discrimination protections and (2) changed conditions, which are discussed in detail below, along with various additional defenses. Four other defenses—release, abandonment,[34] merger, and eminent domain—are discussed in connection with real covenants (*see* § 33.05). Defenses with special application to condominiums and other "common interest communities" are discussed in Chapter 35.

[B]   Anti-Discrimination Protections

[1]   Racial Covenants

In the landmark case of *Shelley v. Kraemer*,[35] the Supreme Court barred the enforcement of racially restrictive covenants on constitutional grounds. The Shelleys, an African-American couple, purchased a Missouri home burdened with a restriction that prohibited occupancy by "any person not of the Caucasian race."[36] Neighboring owners sued for an injunction to force the Shelleys from their home, and won in state court.

The broad question before the Supreme Court was whether judicial enforcement of the restriction was unconstitutional. The Equal Protection Clause of the Fourteenth Amendment provides that no state may deny any person the "equal protection of the laws." For example, a state cannot discriminate among its citizens based on race; if Missouri had enacted a statute that purported to prevent African-Americans from living within its boundaries, the statute would obviously be unconstitutional. But the Equal

---

[33] 197 N.E. 224 (Mass. 1935).

[34] For illustrative cases discussing abandonment as a defense to enforcement of an equitable servitude, see B.B.P. Corp. v. Carroll, 760 P.2d 519 (Alaska 1988) (abandonment found where most owners failed to comply with restriction requiring destruction of certain tree species); Fink v. Miller, 896 P.2d 649 (Utah Ct. App. 1995) (abandonment found where roofs on 23 of 81 houses in subdivision violated restriction requiring wood shingles); and Mountain Park Homeowners Ass'n v. Tydings, 883 P.2d 1383 (Wash. 1994) (no abandonment found).

[35] 334 U.S. 1 (1948).

[36] Shelley v. Kraemer, 334 U.S. 1, 5 (1948).

Protection Clause does not limit purely private action. The case accordingly presented a relatively narrow issue: did judicial enforcement of a private promise constitute enough "state action" to trigger the Equal Protection Clause? The Court answered this question with a clear "yes." "[B]ut for the active intervention of the state courts . . . petitioners would have been free to occupy the properties in question without restraint."[37]

The logic of *Shelley* suggests that judicial enforcement of virtually any land use promise would be considered "state action," and accordingly limited by the Constitution. But later decisions seem to confine this approach to cases involving racial discrimination. For example, judicial enforcement of a promise barring religious uses is not state action that violates the First Amendment right to the free exercise of religion.[38]

Twenty years after *Shelley,* Congress adopted the Fair Housing Act of 1968, which prohibits discrimination in the sale or rental of housing based on race, color, religion, sex, national origin, familial status, or handicap (*see* § 16.02[B][1]). Accordingly, enforcement of a land use promise that causes such a discriminatory effect will violate the Act.

[2] "Single-Family Residence" Covenants and the Group Home

Suppose a restriction limits the use of all subdivision lots to "single-family residences only." Lot owner A now uses her house as a group home for mentally-handicapped children. Can A's neighbors secure an injunction to close the facility? Questions like this have generated extensive litigation in recent years.

Is a group home a "single-family residence"? Courts are divided on the question.[39] For example, the New Mexico Supreme Court held that operating a group home for four unrelated individuals with AIDS was a use for "single-family residential purposes" in *Hill v. Community of Damien of Molokai.*[40] The court reasoned that the purpose of the home was to give residents a "traditional family structure, setting, and atmosphere," with only limited administrative oversight.[41] Conversely, some decisions conclude that the language of such restrictions demonstrates that the parties intended to exclude group homes.[42]

A growing number of jurisdictions refuse to enforce such "single-family residence" restrictions against group homes on substantive grounds. Some

---

[37] Shelley v. Kraemer, 334 U.S. 1, 19 (1948). *But see* Conrad v. Dunn, 154 Cal. Rptr. 726 (Ct. App. 1979) (judicial enforcement of ban on radio antennas did not constitute state action in violation of First Amendment right to free speech).

[38] *See, e.g.,* Ginsberg v. Yeshiva of Far Rockaway, 358 N.Y.S.2d 477 (App. Div. 1974).

[39] *Compare* Blevins v. Barry-Lawrence County Ass'n, 707 S.W.2d 407 (Mo. 1986) (yes) and Rhodes v. Palmetto Pathway Homes, Inc., 400 S.E.2d 484 (S.C. 1991) (yes) *with* Omega Corp. v. Malloy, 319 S.E.2d 728 (Va. 1984) (no).

[40] 911 P.2d 861 (N.M. 1996).

[41] Hill v. Community of Damien of Molokai, 911 P.2d 861, 866 (N.M. 1996).

[42] *See, e.g.,* Omega Corp. v. Malloy, 319 S.E.2d 728 (Va. 1984).

courts reason that interpreting these restrictions to bar group homes is contrary to the public policy that favors integrating disabled individuals into the mainstream of society.[43] Other courts hold that such restrictions violate the Fair Housing Act's bar on discrimination against handicapped persons.[44] Finally, statutes in a few states expressly prohibit enforcement of such restrictions against group homes.[45]

[C] Changed Conditions

[1] Nature of Defense

The most commonly-asserted defense to enforcement of a promise as an equitable servitude is *changed conditions*. This doctrine applies when conditions in the neighborhood have so changed that the intended benefits of the restriction cannot be obtained in a substantial degree.[46] In other words, when there has been such a major change in conditions since creation of the restriction that its continuation "would be of no substantial benefit to the dominant estate,"[47] the restriction is unenforceable.

For example, *El Di v. Town of Bethany Beach*[48] involved a restriction that banned the sale of alcohol. The restriction was originally imposed about 1900 by a religious organization that planned to develop a 120-acre parcel as a church-affiliated residential community. By the 1980s, however, the area had become the commercial center of a busy tourist resort and defendant began selling alcoholic beverages at its restaurant. The Delaware Supreme Court refused to enforce the restriction because—given these changed conditions—it no longer benefited other property owners.

Two policy rationales support the changed conditions doctrine. Early courts reasoned that the doctrine implemented the intent of the original parties, and thus served the goal of individual liberty. Presumably, the parties would not intend a promise to continue running after its benefits were eliminated by changed conditions. The second—and more modern—rationale is purely utilitarian. Obsolete restrictions interfere with the productive use of land. If a restriction produces only small benefit to owner A but imposes a large burden on owner B and society in general, it should be terminated in order to allow efficient land use. Otherwise, A could

---

[43] *See, e.g.,* Crane Neck Ass'n v. New York City/Long Island County Servs. Group, 460 N.E.2d 1336 (N.Y. 1984); Rhodes v. Palmetto Pathway Homes, Inc., 400 S.E.2d 484 (S.C. 1991).

[44] *See, e.g.,* Hill v. Community of Damien of Molokai, 911 P.2d 861 (N.M. 1996) (group home for AIDS patients); Rhodes v. Palmetto Pathway Homes, Inc., 400 S.E.2d 484 (S.C. 1991) (group home for mentally-impaired adults).

[45] *See, e.g.,* Cal. Health & Safety Code § 1569.87 (group home for elderly deemed single-family residential use); *see also* Hall v. Butte Home Health, Inc., 70 Cal. Rptr. 2d 246 (Ct. App. 1997).

[46] *See, e.g.,* Trustees of Columbia College v. Thacher, 87 N.Y. 311 (1882) (invalidating residential-only restriction on land under elevated railway); *cf.* Orange & Rockland Util. v. Philwold Estates, 418 N.E.2d 1310 (N.Y. 1981).

[47] Restatement (Third) of Property: Servitudes § 7.10 cmt. c (Tentative Draft No. 6, 1997).

[48] 477 A.2d 1066 (Del. 1984).

demand an exorbitantly high price in return for releasing a restriction of little real value.

[2] Special Problem: The "Border Lot"

One typical scenario where the defense arises involves the vacant "border lot" in a residential subdivision. Most of these cases present the same factual pattern:

   (1)   all lots in the subdivision were restricted to residential use at a time when the region was relatively undeveloped;

   (2)   over time, development of the surrounding area creates traffic, congestion, noise, and other offensive conditions along the streets that border the subdivision (e.g., the quiet rural road becomes a high-speed, six-lane expressway);

   (3)   as a result, vacant lots on the border of the subdivision become unsuitable for residential use;

   (4)   the owner of one or more border lots wants to develop a commercial use; and

   (5)   when owners of interior lots sue to enforce the restriction, the border lot owner asserts the "changed conditions" defense. [49]

Under the majority view, changed conditions outside a subdivision that impact only border lots do not trigger the doctrine. [50] Courts reason that interior lots continue to receive substantial benefit from the restriction, even if border lots are harmed. [51] "Although commercialization has increased in the vicinity of the subdivision, . . . the restrictive covenants . . . are still of real and substantial value to those homeowners living within the subdivision." [52] Indeed, maintaining the restriction on border lots creates a buffer zone that protects the interior lots from these adverse conditions. If border lots were freed from the restriction, the next row of lots inside the subdivision would quickly become the new border and their owners would similarly seek to avoid the restriction. In this manner, "all other lots would fall like ten-pins, thus circumventing and nullifying the

---

[49] *See, e.g.,* Camelback Del Este Homeowners Ass'n v. Warner, 749 P.2d 930 (Ariz. Ct. App. 1987); DeMarco v. Palazzolo, 209 N.W.2d 540 (Mich. Ct. App. 1973); Western Land Co. v. Truskolaski, 495 P.2d 624 (Nev. 1972); Cowling v. Colligan, 312 S.W.2d 943 (Tex. 1958); *cf.* Pettey v. First Nat'l Bank, 588 N.E.2d 412 (Ill. App. Ct. 1992).

[50] *See, e.g.,* Western Land Co. v. Truskolaski, 495 P.2d 624 (Nev. 1972); Cowling v. Colligan, 312 S.W.2d 943 (Tex. 1958). *But see* DeMarco v. Palazzolo, 209 N.W.2d 540, 542 (Mich. Ct. App. 1973) (invalidating restriction on border lots but requiring that "green belt or fence area" be established to protect interior lots); Restatement (Third) of Property: Servitudes § 4.10 (Tentative Draft No. 6, 1997) (allowing court to modify servitude if changed conditions render servient estate unsuitable for any use permitted by the servitude, even if servitude still benefits dominant estate).

[51] Of course, this rule creates the risk of a "holdout." Even if 99 lot owners in a 100-lot subdivision agree the public interest is served by allowing non-residential use, the remaining lot owner seemingly holds veto power. *Cf.* Rick v. West, 228 N.Y.S.2d 195 (Sup. Ct. 1962).

[52] Western Land Co. v. Truskolaski, 495 P.2d 624, 626 (Nev. 1972).

restriction and destroying the essentially residential character of the entire area."[53]

On the other hand, the defense does apply if changed conditions outside the subdivision are so substantial and widespread that all lots in the subdivision are adversely affected to the point that the benefits of the restriction cannot be realized. For instance, if smoke and fumes from M's nearby smelter constantly pervade a subdivision—rendering all lots unsuitable for residential use—the residential-only restriction is unenforceable. Similarly, changed conditions occurring inside a subdivision may justify use of the doctrine.

[D] Other Defenses

[1] Acquiescence

The plaintiff who ignores violations of a promise by some owners, but then seeks to enforce the same promise against the defendant, will lose due to acquiescence. Suppose that all five lots in a residential subdivision are burdened and benefited by a restriction that requires all structures be located at least 40 feet behind the front lot line. The lots are purchased, respectively, by owners A, B, C, D, and E. A, B, and C build their houses within 30 feet of their respective lot lines, and E never objects. If D now builds her house one foot over the line (that is, within 39 feet of the front lot line), E cannot enforce the restriction against her because of acquiescence.

[2] Estoppel

If the plaintiff manifests an intention not to enforce a land use promise, and the defendant reasonably relies on this conduct to his or her detriment, the defense of estoppel is available. For example, suppose owner E in the above hypothetical (see [1], above) tells owner D: "Don't worry about the lot line restriction! Build wherever you want." If D builds her house one foot over the line in reliance on this statement, E is now estopped to enforce the restriction.

[3] Laches

The defense of laches arises when the plaintiff's unreasonable delay in enforcing a promise causes substantial prejudice to the defendant.[54] Suppose owner D starts building her house one foot over the line (see [1], above); owner E watches construction progress and never objects. Six months later, E completes her house at a cost of $500,000. If E now tries to enforce the restriction, his suit will be barred by laches.

---

[53] Cowling v. Colligan, 312 S.W.2d 943, 946 (Tex. 1958).

[54] See, e.g., Pettey v. First Nat'l Bank, 588 N.E.2d 412 (Ill. App. Ct. 1992); Chevy Chase Village v. Jaggers, 275 A.2d 167 (Md. 1971).

[4] Relative Hardship

As a general rule, courts traditionally consider the relative hardship to the parties in deciding whether the successful plaintiff will receive an injunction or other equitable relief. The plaintiff is entitled to an equitable remedy only if (among other things) the "balance of the equities" tilts in his or her favor; otherwise, the remedy is damages. Courts are divided about how the relative hardship doctrine should apply to the equitable servitude.[55] Some courts apply the doctrine as usual; they refuse to issue an injunction for breach of an equitable servitude if the resulting harm to the defendant is greater than the resulting benefit to the plaintiff. A court might not issue an injunction forcing D to remove the portion of her house that violates the lot line restriction (*see* [1], *above*) simply because the cost to D would vastly outweigh any benefit conferred on E. Other courts modify the doctrine in the equitable servitude context, granting an injunction unless the resulting benefit is substantially outweighed by the resulting harm; and still other courts seem to ignore the doctrine altogether.

[5] Unclean Hands

The doctrine of unclean hands prevents a plaintiff who has violated a promise from seeking to enforce it in equity against another party. If owner E breaches the restriction by building his house over the line (*see* [1], *above*), and then seeks to enforce the same restriction against owner D, his suit will be barred by unclean hands.

§ 34.07 Remedies for Breach of Equitable Servitudes

The standard remedy for breach of an equitable servitude is an injunction. For example, if C successfully enforces a residential-only restriction against D's oil refinery, C will obtain an injunction that bars D from operating the refinery in the future. The court might also award incidental compensatory damages to C for the past violation.

What about breach of a covenant to pay money? Here most courts will impose an equitable lien on the affected property, rather than award compensatory damages. If the obligation remains unpaid, the plaintiff may collect by foreclosing on the lien.[56]

§ 34.08 The Restatement (Third) of Property: Servitudes

[A] General Approach

The new Restatement brings the prospect of revolutionary change to the traditional rules governing equitable servitudes, real covenants, and

---

[55] *Cf.* Gaskin v. Harris, 481 P.2d 698 (N.M. 1971); Mohawk Containers, Inc. v. Hancock, 252 N.Y.S.2d 148 (Sup. Ct. 1964).

[56] *Cf.* Neponsit Property Owners' Ass'n v. Emigrant Indus. Sav. Bank, 15 N.E.2d 793 (N.Y. 1938) (action to foreclose lien).

easements.[57] Its overriding theme is simplification of prior law. Thus, the Restatement combines the equitable servitude, the covenant, and the easement into one doctrine: the *servitude*. It establishes a simplified, uniform set of rules for creating, modifying, terminating, and enforcing a servitude.

This approach reflects the policy view that "servitudes are useful devices which people ought to be able to use without artificial constraints."[58] Accordingly, the law should respect the parties' individual liberty to create a servitude, absent unusual circumstances. In addition to making it easier to create a servitude in the first place, the Restatement also makes it easier to modify or terminate a servitude that becomes harmful over time.

[B] Creation of Servitudes

[1] Basic Requirements

Under the Restatement approach, it is relatively simple to create a valid servitude. In general, a contract or conveyance creates a servitude if three elements are met:

(1) the parties intend to create a servitude;[59]

(2) the servitude complies with the Statute of Frauds;[60] and

(3) the servitude is not illegal, unconstitutional, or violative of public policy.[61]

Historic requirements such as "touch and concern" and horizontal privity are no longer necessary; the vertical privity requirement is greatly weakened; and lack of notice becomes a defense, not a creation element.

The first two elements—intent and compliance with the Statute of Frauds—are generally required under the traditional law governing real covenants and equitable servitudes. The Restatement generally follows the contours of existing law on these points. Thus, for example, intent may be either express or implied from circumstances;[62] and various exceptions to the Statute of Frauds (e.g., change of position based on reasonable reliance) apply.[63]

The third element is novel. It provides a set of specific, narrow rules for screening the substantive validity of servitudes, mainly in place of the

---

[57] *See* Susan F. French, *Toward a Modern Law of Servitudes: Reweaving the Ancient Strands,* 55 S. Cal. L. Rev. 1261 (1982); James L. Winokur, *Ancient Strands Rewoven, or Fashioned out of Whole Cloth?: First Impressions of the Emerging Restatement of Servitudes,* 27 Conn. L. Rev. 313 (1994).

[58] Restatement (Third) of Property: Servitudes, ch. 2 intro. note (Tentative Draft No. 1, 1989).

[59] Restatement (Third) of Property: Servitudes § 2.2 (Tentative Draft No. 1, 1989).

[60] Restatement (Third) of Property: Servitudes § 2.8 (Tentative Draft No. 1, 1989).

[61] Restatement (Third) of Property: Servitudes § 3.1 (Tentative Draft No. 7, 1998).

[62] Restatement (Third) of Property: Servitudes § 2.2 (Tentative Draft No. 1, 1989).

[63] Restatement (Third) of Property: Servitudes § 2.9 (Tentative Draft No. 1, 1989).

cumbersome "touch and concern" standard. The Restatement explains that these rules address "whether allowing the benefits or burdens to run with the land would create such risks of social harm that a servitude should not be permitted."[64] A servitude that violates a statute or government regulation,[65] or infringes a constitutional right, is invalid. A servitude is also invalid if it violates any one in a long list of specified public policies.[66] For instance, a servitude that imposes an unreasonable restraint on alienation,[67] trade[68] or commerce is unenforceable; and an arbitrary, spiteful, or capricious servitude is similarly invalid.

[2] Special Issues

Which successors are burdened and benefited by a servitude? The Restatement response hinges on the distinction between negative and affirmative covenants. In general, the benefit and burden of negative covenants automatically pass to all subsequent owners or possessors of the benefited and burdened land, just as in the case of easements. This includes lessees, adverse possessors, and persons who acquire title by foreclosure. On the other hand, the benefit and burden of affirmative covenants run only if vertical privity (*see* § 33.04[B][6]) exists.[69] Exceptions to this rule are provided for lessees, life tenants, and adverse possessors under certain circumstances.[70]

Servitudes in gross are expressly permitted. However, the beneficiary must demonstrate a "legitimate interest" in order to enforce such a servitude.[71]

[C] Termination or Modification of Servitudes

Over time, a servitude that once performed a useful social function may become harmful. While endorsing the traditional defenses to enforcement of a servitude, the Restatement also enhances the power of courts to modify or terminate harmful servitudes on a case-by-case basis. For example, it provides that a covenant to pay money terminates after a reasonable time if the instrument lacks a termination date or fails to state the total sum due.[72] In the same manner, a covenant to pay money or provide services may be terminated or modified based on undue burden—when the obligation becomes excessive, for instance, in relation to the value received by the burdened estate.[73]

---

[64] Restatement (Third) of Property: Servitudes § 3.1 cmt. a (Tentative Draft No. 7, 1998).

[65] *Cf.* Rhodes v. Palmetto Pathway Homes, Inc., 400 S.E.2d 484 (S.C. 1991).

[66] Restatement (Third) of Property: Servitudes § 3.1 (Tentative Draft No. 7, 1998).

[67] *Cf.* Procter v. Foxmeyer Drug Co., 884 S.W.2d 853 (Tex. Ct. App. 1994).

[68] *Cf.* Davidson Bros. v. D. Katz & Sons, 579 A.2d 288 (N.J. 1990).

[69] Restatement (Third) of Property: Servitudes § 5.2(2) (Tentative Draft No. 5, 1995).

[70] Restatement (Third) of Property: Servitudes §§ 5.3–5.5 (Tentative Draft No. 5, 1995).

[71] Restatement (Third) of Property: Servitudes § 8.1 (Tentative Draft No. 7, 1998).

[72] Restatement (Third) of Property: Servitudes § 7.11(1) (Tentative Draft No. 6, 1997).

[73] Restatement (Third) of Property: Servitudes § 7.11(2) (Tentative Draft No. 6, 1997).

[D] Remedies for Breach of Servitudes

Under the Restatement, a servitude may be enforced by any legal or equitable remedy, including compensatory damages, punitive damages, injunctions, restitution, imposition of liens, or declaratory relief.[74]

---

[74] Restatement (Third) of Property: Servitudes § 8.2 (Tentative Draft No. 7, 1998).

Chapter 35

CONDOMINIUMS AND OTHER COMMON INTEREST COMMUNITIES

SYNOPSIS

§ 35.01   A New Model of Home Ownership

The nature of home ownership in the United States has changed dramatically in recent decades.[1] Under the traditional model, a homeowner held title to a detached single-family house free from any private land use restrictions. Restrictions were imposed only on a small number of properties; and they usually dealt only with one issue (e.g., a height restriction). Yet today over 40 million Americans reside in condominiums or other

---

[1] *See generally* Gregory S. Alexander, *Dilemmas of Group Autonomy: Residential Associations and Community,* 75 Cornell L. Rev. 1 (1989); Robert C. Ellickson, *Cities and Homeowners Associations,* 130 U. Pa. L. Rev. 1519 (1982); Susan F. French, *The Constitution of a Private Residential Government Should Include a Bill of Rights,* 27 Wake Forest L. Rev. 345 (1992); *Symposium on the Law of Condominiums, Cooperatives, and Home Owner Associations,* 73 St. John's L. Rev. 1 (1999); James L. Winokur, *The Mixed Blessings of Promissory Servitudes: Toward Optimizing Economic Utility, Individual Liberty, and Personal Identity,* 1989 Wis. L. Rev. 1.

"common interest communities," where their properties are subject to comprehensive land use restrictions administered by private community associations. This trend toward the common interest community ("CIC")—which is expected to continue throughout the twenty-first century—poses new challenges that our property law system has yet to resolve fully.

What is a *common interest community*? The term includes various types of residential developments, including condominiums, cooperatives, and planned unit developments. Yet CICs usually share certain features:

    (1)   each owner is entitled to occupy a particular dwelling unit;

    (2)   all units are subject to comprehensive private restrictions that regulate land use and impose financial obligations;

    (3)   the development is governed by a private owners association;

    (4)   certain "common areas" are owned in common by all owners or by the association; and

    (5)   upon receiving title, each owner automatically becomes a member of the association and is obligated to comply with the restrictions.

The meteoric rise of the CIC has been fueled by several factors. It offers the opportunity of home ownership at a more affordable cost, because it usually utilizes less land per unit than a traditional development; this advantage is particularly important in rapidly-growing regions where land costs are high. The CIC typically provides desirable recreational amenities (e.g., tennis courts, swimming pool); and it offers the convenience of minimal maintenance and upkeep. On the negative side, the CIC has been criticized as a "private utopia" that erects barriers against the outside world, creating racial, ethnic, and cultural separations.

The benefits of communal living are made possible only by the surrender of individual freedom. "[I]nherent in the condominium concept is the principle that to promote the health, happiness, and peace of mind of the majority of the unit owners since they are living in such close proximity and using facilities in common, each unit owner must give up a certain degree of freedom of choice which he might otherwise enjoy in separate, privately owned property."[2] But how much freedom must the owner surrender? A growing body of law—augmented by the Uniform Common Interest Ownership Act[3] and the new Restatement (Third) of Property: Servitudes[4] —is devoted to answering this question.

---

[2] Hidden Harbour Estates v. Norman, 309 So. 2d 180, 181–182 (Fla. Dist. Ct. App. 1975).

[3] Unif. Common Interest Ownership Act, 7 U.L.A. 471.

[4] *See generally* Restatement (Third) of Property: Servitudes, Chapter 6 (Tentative Draft No. 7, 1998).

§ 35.02   Types of Common Interest Communities

[A]   Condominiums

Silveracre, a hypothetical condominium development, consists of a ten story residential building, parking lots, a swimming pool and tennis courts, all located on 15 acres of land.[5] There are three dwelling units on each floor of the building, for a total of 30 units. If O owns title to "Unit 24" on the eighth floor, exactly what does O own?

In a *condominium* development, each owner (1) holds fee simple title to an individual unit (usually in a multi-story building), and (2) also owns an undivided interest in the common area as a tenant in common with other owners.[6] The "individual unit" is essentially a cube of air: the air space enclosed by the walls, floor, and ceiling of the dwelling.[7] The building itself (including the exterior walls, roof, floors, lobby, ceilings, hallways, stairways, elevators, and heating, electrical, and mechanical systems), land under the building, recreational facilities, and parking lots are usually all considered "common area." Thus, our hypothetical unit owner O technically owns: (a) fee simple absolute in the air space inside Unit 24; and (b) a 1/30th undivided interest as a tenant in common in the building, facilities, and land that comprise Silveracre. O may also have an exclusive right to use portions of the common area (e.g., the right to use a particular parking space or balcony).

The basic idea of the condominium—separating ownership of air space from ownership of the land surface—is foreign to traditional Anglo-American property law. Condominiums only became popular in the United States during the 1960s, after all states adopted special enabling legislation that permitted their creation. Due to this history, condominiums are heavily regulated by statute.

A variant on the condominium is the *timeshare*. The typical timeshare arrangement involves a condominium unit used for vacation purposes (e.g., a beach front unit). Ownership of the unit is usually divided into multiple periods of time (e.g., one week each year) during which each owner has the right to exclusive occupancy; thus, the owner receives a form of freehold estate. Alternatively, the owner of a timeshare interest might not receive a freehold estate at all, but merely a lease or license. Though timeshare projects are often highly profitable for the developer, many owners later discover that their interests are difficult to resell.

---

[5] Condominiums may also be created for non-residential purposes, such as retail stores, business offices, parking spaces, and even boat slips.

[6] As a result, each unit owner may be liable for property damage caused by negligent maintenance of the common area. *See* Dutcher v. Owens, 647 S.W.2d 948 (Tex. 1983).

[7] Because the units in a condominium project are virtually identical, some courts reason that damages are an adequate remedy for the buyer's breach of a contract to buy a condominium unit and accordingly deny specific performance. *See, e.g.,* Centex Homes Corp. v. Boag, 320 A.2d 194 (N.J. Sup. Ct. Ch. Div. 1974).

[B] Cooperatives

The *cooperative* is essentially a legal dinosaur—a method for dividing ownership of multi-story apartment buildings that developed before the condominium era. New cooperatives are rarely created today. However, many cooperatives created before the 1960s still linger, principally in New York City.

The hallmark of the cooperative is that residents do not receive title to their units. Rather, a corporation owned by the residents usually holds title to the entire development, including the building, land under the building, recreational facilities, parking lots, and the like. Suppose O owns an interest in Goldacre, a cooperative. What does he own? O (a) owns shares of stock in the corporation that holds title to Goldacre, and (b) holds a long-term lease from the corporation that entitles him to exclusive occupancy of a particular unit. Due to this unusual legal structure, it is often difficult for an owner to sell or finance an interest in a cooperative.

[C] Planned Unit Developments

The *planned unit development* is a broad category that encompasses a variety of residential developments, ranging from a small cluster of tract homes to a "gated community" to a privately-owned town. It usually consists of detached single-family houses, row houses, or attached townhouses that rest on the land surface, together with roads, parks, and other recreational facilities. Each owner holds fee simple title to his unit and the land on which it sits, and may also own the front and back yards. Each owner is entitled to use the roads, parks, and recreational facilities, but title to this "common area" is usually held by the community association. For example, if O owns a unit in Blueacre, a planned unit development consisting of single-family residences, she owns (a) fee simple absolute in her house and the underlying land, and (b) an easement to use the common areas of Blueacre.

Although the appearance of a planned unit development often resembles that of an ordinary tract of detached single-family houses, its legal structure is quite different. Like all CICs, the planned unit development is subject to comprehensive restrictions, is governed by a private association to which all owners belong, and includes privately-owned common area.

§ 35.03 Restrictive Covenants and the Common Interest Community

[A] Role of the Declaration

A common interest community is typically created through a document called a *declaration*. The declaration imposes binding restrictions—usually enforceable as real covenants or equitable servitudes—on all units in the project. These restrictions are known in many regions as *covenants, conditions, and restrictions* or *CC&Rs* and in others are merely called *covenants.* Every potential buyer has the opportunity to read the declaration before purchasing a unit; accordingly, at least in theory, by purchasing a unit each owner voluntarily agrees to be bound by its provisions.

The typical declaration has four basic components. First, it identifies the units and common areas that comprise the CIC, and are subject to the declaration. Second, it contains provisions that create the owners association, enumerate the association's powers, and establish voting procedures. Third, it obligates all unit owners to pay regular assessments (usually monthly) and special assessments (as needed) which finance repairs, maintenance, and other expenses of the association.[8] Unpaid assessments usually are deemed to create a lien on the unit, which the association may collect through foreclosure.[9] Finally, the fourth component consists of detailed, comprehensive restrictions on the use, appearance, construction, and sometimes transferability of units. For example, a declaration might include provisions that:

(1)　limit the units to residential use;

(2)　prohibit satellite dishes;

(3)　mandate use of a particular fire-resistant roof;

(4)　restrict the exterior paint color of units;

(5)　ban all pets;

(6)　require association approval of any unit sale; and

(7)　prohibit all exterior signs, flags, or banners.

[B]　Validity of Covenants

[1]　The Policy Debate

Suppose the declaration for Greenville, a hypothetical CIC, includes the following restrictions: (1) the association must approve any unit sale; (2) no one may watch television; and (3) no flags may be displayed. Are such restrictions legitimate tools for building a cohesive community or invalid restraints on private property rights? This question has prompted vigorous debate, centered around whether the law should recognize new defenses to the enforcement of restrictions that unduly interfere with an owner's personal liberty.

Scholars who advocate minimal judicial review of CIC covenants typically stress two themes: (1) the owner's voluntary acceptance of the declaration; and (2) the legitimate interests of other unit owners. From this perspective, each owner voluntarily agrees to be bound by the declaration—like any other contract—and accordingly surrenders a certain degree of personal freedom. The owner who decides with hindsight that he or she has made an unwise decision—for example, by buying a unit in a "no television" development—can escape the restriction by selling the unit or by convincing

---

[8] *See, e.g.,* Regency Homes Ass'n v. Egermayer, 498 N.W.2d 783 (Neb. 1993).

[9] *See, e.g.,* Streams Sports Club v. Richmond, 440 N.E.2d 1264 (Ill. App. Ct. 1982).

other owners to amend the declaration. Further, the law must protect the legitimate interests of the other owners who purchased their units in order to enjoy the benefits of the no-television restriction (e.g., more participation in neighborhood social activities). This concern also extends to avoiding the expense and inconvenience of litigation about whether the covenants are enforceable in the first place.

On the other hand, scholars who support the creation of new defenses to enforcement: (a) argue that CIC covenants are more coercive than voluntary; and (b) emphasize the traditional importance of personal liberty within the home. From this viewpoint, the buyer's purchase of a unit is not a voluntary acceptance of the declaration, but more akin to an adhesion contract. Almost all buyers are far more concerned with the location, price, and amenities of the unit than with the terms of the declaration. Many buyers do not even read the declaration before they purchase, while those who do often fail to understand it fully. And because the declaration is presented on a "take-it-or-leave-it" basis, the occasional buyer who objects to a particular provision has no opportunity to negotiate changes. Further, American law has historically respected the sanctity of the home, and permitted an extraordinarily broad range of personal freedom inside its walls; as the old adage goes, "a man's home is his castle." Consistent with this tradition, the average buyer has a reasonable expectation that he will enjoy a high degree of autonomy in his new home. Under these circumstances, restrictions that violate the owner's fundamental rights or legitimate expectations should be invalid.

[2] Movement Toward a General Rule

American courts are slowly moving toward a new standard that strikes a balance between these competing policy arguments. CIC covenants are presumed to be valid. And the objecting owner who merely asserts that a particular provision is unpopular or unfair, that it provides little benefit to the community, or that he or she failed to read it, will obtain no relief. On the other hand, a growing minority of courts will invalidate a CIC covenant if it is arbitrary, violates a fundamental constitutional right, or violates public policy.[10]

The evolution of this new standard was particularly influenced by decisions in Florida and California. For example, in *Hidden Harbour Estates v. Basso*,[11] a Florida appellate court noted that use restrictions are valid unless they are "wholly arbitrary in their application, in violation of public policy, or . . . abrogate some fundamental constitutional right."[12] And in *Nahrstedt v. Lakeside Village Condominium Association*,[13] the

---

[10] Of course, the general defenses to the enforcement of real covenants and equitable servitudes discussed in Chapters 33 and 34 apply in this context as well.

[11] 393 So. 2d 637 (Fla. Dist. Ct. App. 1981); *see also* Noble v. Murphy, 612 N.E.2d 266 (Mass. App. Ct. 1993) (following *Hidden Harbour Estates*).

[12] Hidden Harbour Estates, Inc. v. Basso, 393 So. 2d 637, 640 (Fla. Dist. Ct. App. 1981).

[13] 878 P.2d 1275 (Cal. 1994).

California Supreme Court struck a similar theme, holding that a restriction would be enforced unless it "is arbitrary, imposes burdens on the use of lands it affects that substantially outweigh the restriction's benefits . . . or violates a fundamental public policy."[14]

The new Restatement (Third) of Property: Servitudes blends these approaches. It would invalidate any restriction or other servitude that

    (1)   is arbitrary,[15]

    (2)   unreasonably burdens fundamental constitutional rights,[16] or

    (3)   violates another public policy.[17]

A restriction is "arbitrary" if it lacks a legitimate purpose or the means adopted lack a reasonable relationship to accomplishing that purpose.[18]

[3]　Restrictions on Sale

One common provision—particularly in condominiums and cooperatives—is a restriction on the sale of units.[19] The usual explanation is that such provisions are necessary to screen out potentially disruptive occupants and thereby preserve a harmonious living environment for residents living in close quarters. The need for sale restrictions in cooperatives is understandable, given the lack of fee simple title to individual units; as a practical matter, all owners are jointly responsible for the project's financial survival. But in condominiums—where owners hold title to their units—the rationale for such restrictions is less clear and the risk of discrimination more pronounced.[20]

The two principal types of sale restraints are: (1) a requirement that the association pre-approve the sale of any unit; and (2) a provision that gives the association a right of first refusal or preemptive right to purchase the unit itself. Both types have been challenged, mainly under the common law doctrine of restraints on alienation. For example, one decision involved express language that permitted the condominium association to "arbitrarily, capriciously, or unreasonably" withhold its consent to any unit sale.[21] Reasoning that this provision allowed the association "to reject perpetually any unit owner's prospective purchaser for any or no reason,"[22] the court struck it down as an invalid restraint. On the other hand, if the provision does not specify any standard for granting or denying consent, a court may imply a requirement that the association act reasonably and uphold the

---

[14] Nahrstedt v. Lakeside Village Condominium Ass'n, 878 P.2d 1275, 1290 (Cal. 1994).

[15] Restatement (Third) of Property: Servitudes § 3.1(1) (Tentative Draft No. 7, 1998).

[16] Restatement (Third) of Property: Servitudes § 3.1(2) (Tentative Draft No. 7, 1998).

[17] Restatement (Third) of Property: Servitudes § 3.1 (Tentative Draft No. 7, 1998).

[18] Restatement (Third) of Property: Servitudes § 3.1 cmt. i (Tentative Draft No. 7, 1998).

[19] Restrictions on leasing are also common, and almost always upheld. See, e.g., City of Oceanside v. McKenna, 264 Cal. Rptr. 275 (Ct. App. 1989).

[20] See Restatement (Third) of Property: Servitudes § 3.4 cmt. g (Tentative Draft No. 2, 1991) (discussing special justifications for sale restraints in cooperatives and condominiums).

[21] Aquarian Found. v. Sholom House, 448 So. 2d 1166, 1167 (Fla. Dist. Ct. App. 1984).

[22] Aquarian Found. v. Sholom House, 448 So. 2d 1166, 1169 (Fla. Dist. Ct. App. 1984).

provision.[23] In *Laguna Royale Owners Association v. Darger*,[24] for instance, the court concluded that the denial of approval is reasonable if (a) the reason for disapproval is "rationally related to the protection, preservation or proper operation of the property and the purposes of the Association," and (b) the decision was made in a "fair and nondiscriminatory manner."[25] Our hypothetical Greenville restriction on sales (*see* [1], *above*) would probably be upheld on this basis as well.

The second type of sale restraint, providing a right of first refusal or preemptive right, is generally upheld as a reasonable restraint on alienation because it does not materially impair the owner's right to sell.[26] These provisions affect only the identity of the buyer; the association (or its nominee) becomes the new buyer, obligated to purchase the unit for the same price as the originally-intended buyer.

[4] Use and Building Restrictions

Restrictions that concern the use or construction of a unit are usually held valid.[27] For example, provisions that limit units to residential use, restrict noise levels, or impose architectural design controls are virtually always enforced, consistent with concern for the rights of other owners. On the other hand, what if a restriction bans purely personal conduct, such as television viewing within Greenville units? Restrictions that regulate personal conduct in the privacy of the home, without any direct impact on neighboring units, pose a more difficult problem and are the particular focus of the emerging minority approach to CIC covenants discussed above (*see* [2], *above*).

An intriguing example is the restriction that bans pets. Perhaps the most famous decision on this point is *Nahrstedt v. Lakeside Village Condominium Association*,[28] where a cat-loving condominium owner challenged a restriction that prohibited all animals other than small fish and birds.[29] Applying a state statute that provided all CIC covenants were enforceable unless "unreasonable," the California Supreme Court found that the pet ban was reasonable. The court interpreted the statute as meaning that such covenants are valid unless they are wholly arbitrary, violate a fundamental public policy, or impose a burden on the use of affected land that far outweighs any benefit.[30] In evaluating the pet ban, the court considered

---

[23] *But see* Lauderbaugh v. Williams, 186 A.2d 39 (Pa. 1962) (invalidating approval clause that lacked specific standards).

[24] 174 Cal. Rptr. 136 (Ct. App. 1981).

[25] Laguna Royale Owners Ass'n v. Darger, 174 Cal. Rptr. 136, 144 (Ct. App. 1981).

[26] *But see* Wolinsky v. Kadison, 449 N.E.2d 151 (Ill. App. Ct. 1983) (holding that unreasonable exercise of right of first refusal would be an invalid restraint).

[27] *But see* Portola Hills Community Ass'n v. James, 5 Cal. Rptr. 2d 580 (Ct. App. 1992) (refusing to enforce ban on satellite dishes).

[28] 878 P.2d 1275 (Cal. 1994).

[29] *See also* Winston Towers 200 Ass'n v. Saverio, 360 So. 2d 470 (Fla. Dist. Ct. App. 1978) (invaliding pet restriction); Noble v. Murphy, 612 N.E.2d 266 (Mass. App. Ct. 1993) (upholding pet restriction).

[30] Nahrstedt v. Lakeside Village Condominium Ass'n, 878 P.2d 1275, 1287 (Cal. 1994).

its impact on the CIC as a whole, not the facts specific to plaintiff's individual case. Plaintiff's pleas that her particular cats were always silent, kept indoors, and were not a nuisance—and thus in fact did not affect other unit owners at all—were irrelevant. Under this framework, the court had no difficulty in concluding that—as a general matter—the pet restriction was rationally related to health, safety, and noise concerns, and hence not arbitrary. Nor did any fundamental public policy justify keeping cats in a condominium unit. Finally, despite an eloquent dissent about the social value of cats, the majority found no facts suggesting that the restriction imposed an undue burden. [31]

[5]　Restrictions on Constitutional Rights

The Constitution safeguards fundamental rights against government action, not private action. For example, the First Amendment provides that Congress shall make no law abridging freedom of speech. Neither this clause nor other constitutional protections limit purely private conduct. Thus, absent a showing that "state action" is somehow involved, CIC covenants cannot be attacked on constitutional grounds. Consider the hypothetical Greenville restriction (*see* [1], *above*) that prohibits flags, presumably including the American flag. Does this provision violate the First Amendment protection for freedom of speech?

Almost all courts would find no state action on these facts, and uphold the restriction. [32] Following the Supreme Court's lead in *Shelley v. Kraemer* (*see* § 34.06[B][1]), a few courts might find that judicial enforcement of the restriction constitutes enough state action to trigger the First Amendment; but most courts confine this approach to cases involving racial discrimination. And state action might be found if the owners association was the functional equivalent of a local government, providing police, fire, recreation, and other traditionally public services, by analogy to the "company town," [33] although no decision has yet gone so far.

The Restatement (Third) of Property: Servitudes adopts a new approach to the issue. [34] It would invalidate a restriction that "unreasonably" burdens fundamental constitutional rights such as freedom of speech, press, religion, privacy, and association. [35] In evaluating whether a burden is unreasonable, the purpose of the restriction, its importance to the benefited parties, the extent to which it interferes with the right, and the extent to which the burdened party consented to the restriction, would all be considered. [36] The Greenville flag ban would probably be held invalid under this standard.

---

[31] *See generally* Carl B. Kress, *Beyond Nahrstedt: Reviewing Restrictions Governing Life in a Property Owner Association*, 42 UCLA L. Rev. 837 (1995).

[32] *Cf.* Conrad v. Dunn, 154 Cal. Rptr. 726 (Ct. App. 1979) (restriction that banned radio antenna did not violate First Amendment right to freedom of speech).

[33] *See* Marsh v. Alabama, 326 U.S. 501 (1946).

[34] *Cf.* Susan F. French, *The Constitution of a Private Residential Government Should Include a Bill of Rights*, 27 Wake Forest L. Rev. 345 (1992).

[35] Restatement (Third) of Property: Servitudes § 3.1 (Tentative Draft No. 7, 1998).

[36] Restatement (Third) of Property: Servitudes § 3.1 cmt. k (Tentative Draft No. 7, 1998).

[C] Amendment of Declaration

The declaration typically provides that it can be amended by a vote of the unit owners. Thus, new restrictions—for example, a ban on late-night parties—might be added after an owner buys a unit. Although a majority vote is occasionally sufficient, most declarations require some form of supermajority vote (e.g., a two-thirds vote) for an amendment.[37] Concerned that amendment might unfairly penalize a minority of unit owners, some courts impose additional constraints[38] on the process (e.g., a requirement that any change in restrictions affect all lots, not merely a few lots).[39]

§ 35.04 The Owners Association

[A] Nature of the Association

Every CIC is governed by an owners association, sometimes called the *community association, homeowners association,* or *condominium association.* There are now over 200,000 owners associations in the United States. As authorized by the declaration, the typical association:

(1) maintains and repairs the common area,

(2) hires and supervises staff,

(3) enforces the CIC restrictions,

(4) adopts and enforces rules or by-laws that bind all owners (*see* [B][3], *below*),

(5) collects monetary assessments from the owners,

(6) represents the CIC in dealing with the outside world, and

(7) generally takes such other actions as are necessary to operate the CIC.

The powers of the association are usually exercised by a board of directors or similarly-titled group; certain powers may be delegated to committees or to a management company. In a new project, the developer initially selects the members of the board. Once enough units are sold, the unit owners elect the board members.

---

[37] *See, e.g.,* Brown v. McDavid, 676 P.2d 714 (Colo. Ct. App. 1983) (66% vote required to modify or terminate covenants). *But see* Penney v. Ass'n of Apartment Owners, 776 P.2d 393 (Haw. 1989) (statute required unanimous vote before one owner could have exclusive use of part of common area).

[38] *See, e.g.,* McMillan v. Iserman, 327 N.W.2d 559 (Mich. Ct. App. 1982) (amendment does not apply to owner who justifiably relied on prior restrictions and would be prejudiced by amendment); Breene v. Plaza Tower Ass'n, 310 N.W.2d 730 (N.D. 1981) (amendment does not bind existing owner absent acquiescence).

[39] *See, e.g.,* Walton v. Jaskiewicz, 563 A.2d 382 (Md. 1989) (amendment must alter restrictions for all lots, not merely some); Montoya v. Barreras, 473 P.2d 363 (N.M. 1970) (same); Ridge Park Home Owners v. Pena, 544 P.2d 278 (N.M. 1975) (same).

[B]   Judicial Review of Association Decisions

[1]   In General

Courts have experienced difficulty in crafting an appropriate standard for judicial review of association decisions. This problem stems from the unique nature of the association: a private organization that performs quasi-governmental functions. Should it be considered a voluntary, private entity—like an ordinary corporation—whose internal decisions are largely immune from judicial review? Or should it be seen more as a quasi-governmental entity whose decisions are subjected to more intensive review, including constitutional scrutiny? Or is another model—such as a trust—more appropriate? Legal scholars differ widely on these fundamental questions.[40]

A clear majority of courts review association decisions under a reasonableness standard. As the new Restatement (Third) of Property: Servitudes provides, the association must "act reasonably in the exercise of its discretionary powers."[41] In effect, the association is held to the standard of a reasonably prudent person under the same circumstances. Unlike the majority approach, however, the Restatement places the burden of proving unreasonableness on the complaining owner. A minority of courts—more fearful than the majority about the burdens of costly and divisive litigation—apply the less-rigorous business judgment rule.[42] Borrowed from the corporate setting, this rule insulates the association from liability if its board reached the decision in good faith and rationally believed that the decision was in the best interest of the association.

[2]   Approval of Architectural Design

Suppose O owns an unimproved residential lot in a CIC governed by association A. The declaration requires that A's architectural review committee approve the design of any proposed structure before construction begins. O duly submits her proposed house plans for evaluation, but the committee denies consent. O sues. What standard of review should the court apply?

Almost all courts apply the reasonableness standard in this situation.[43] For example, decisions denying the owners' applications (a) to build a geodesic dome house in an area of conventionally-designed homes[44] and

---

[40] *Compare* Robert C. Ellickson, *Cities and Homeowners Associations,* 130 U. Pa. L. Rev. 1519 (1982) (voluntary private associations) *with* Richard T. Ford, *The Boundaries of Race: Political Geography in Legal Analysis,* 107 Harv. L. Rev. 1841 (1994) (coercive, quasi-governmental organizations).

[41] Restatement (Third) of Property: Servitudes § 6.13(1)(c) (Tentative Draft No. 7, 1998).

[42] *See, e.g.,* Levandusky v. One Fifth Ave. Apt. Corp., 553 N.E.2d 1317 (N.Y. 1990).

[43] *But see* Rywalt v. Writer Corp., 526 P.2d 316 (Colo. Ct. App. 1974) (applying business judgment rule).

[44] Smith v. Butler Mountain Estates Property Owners Ass'n, 367 S.E.2d 401 (N.C. Ct. App. 1988).

(b) to move a 30-year-old Spanish style, stucco house into a subdivision consisting mainly of modern ranch and split-level homes[45] were both upheld under this standard. In each instance, the proposed design differed radically from the existing houses in the neighborhood.

[3] Adoption of Rules and By-Laws

Suppose association A enacts a new rule that bars the consumption of alcohol in and around the common area swimming pool. Owner O, an inveterate beer drinker, sues to invalidate the rule, arguing that it was not included in the declaration when he purchased his unit. Can A enforce the rule against O?

As noted above, the declaration typically authorizes the board to adopt new rules or by-laws. While restrictions in the original declaration are substantially immune from later attack—on the theory that unit buyers voluntarily agreed to be bound—this rationale cannot apply to newly-enacted rules. Hence, virtually all courts—and the Restatement (Third) of Property: Servitudes[46]—agree that new rules must be reasonable in order to survive judicial review.[47] As one court summarized, "the board is required to enact rules . . . that are reasonably related to the promotion of the health, happiness and peace of mind of the unit owners."[48] The hypothetical "no-alcohol" rule above presumably satisfies this standard because it lessens the risk of drunken behavior in the pool area, thereby protecting the health and safety of swimmers and other users.[49]

---

[45] Rhue v. Cheyenne Homes, Inc., 449 P.2d 361 (Colo. 1969).

[46] Restatement (Third) of Property: Servitudes § 6.13(1)(c) (Tentative Draft No. 7, 1998).

[47] See, e.g., O'Buck v. Cottonwood Village Condominium Ass'n, 750 P.2d 813 (Alaska 1988); Riss v. Angel, 934 P.2d 669 (Wash. 1997); McHuron v. Grand Teton Lodge Co., 899 P.2d 38 (Wyo. 1995).

[48] Hidden Harbour Estates v. Basso, 393 So. 2d 637, 640 (Fla. Dist. Ct. App. 1981).

[49] Cf. Hidden Harbour Estates v. Norman, 309 So. 2d 180 (Fla. Dist. Ct. App. 1975).

Chapter 36

FUNDAMENTALS OF ZONING

SYNOPSIS

§ 36.01   The Land Use Revolution

Suppose that O owned fee simple absolute in Greenacre, a 500-acre tract of farm land, in 1900. Did government regulation affect O's ability to use Greenacre as he desired? The answer is a resounding "no." At the dawn of the twentieth century, there were essentially no government restraints on how a private owner could use land, except for the common law doctrine of nuisance. Land use was seen as a private matter, not a public concern. Thus, an owner like O enjoyed complete discretion to use his land as he saw fit, as long as no nuisance resulted.

Today, only a century later, almost every parcel of land in the United States is subject to *zoning*: a complex maze of ordinances, regulations, and statutes that restrict the use of land.[1] Comprehensive government regulation of private land use is now the norm. Urbanization, industrialization, population growth, technological change, and other economic and social forces have all contributed to this revolutionary change. Increasingly, land use is viewed as a public matter, not solely a private concern. Local governments regulate land use pursuant to the *police power*—the inherent government power to promote the public health, safety, welfare, and morals.

Suppose that O owns fee simple absolute in Greenacre today. Local ordinances probably restrict Greenacre to agricultural use only. For example, O cannot build a subdivision of tract homes, open a bookstore, start a school, or develop a factory on the land; indeed, he may not even be able sell his crops from a roadside stand on the property. While the law will probably allow O to build his personal residence on Greenacre, it may regulate such matters as the height, size, location, and design of the house. In short, modern law substantially restricts O's discretion about how Greenacre may be used.

§ 36.02 What Is "Zoning"?

The meaning of the term "zoning" evolved over the course of the twentieth century. During most of the century, zoning referred to the form of land use regulation that emerged in the 1920s—the division of communities into geographical districts or "zones" where particular types of land use were allowed, together with restrictions on the height, bulk, and density of buildings in the zone.

During the second half of the century, however, the nature of land use regulation expanded well beyond the concept of geographical zones. For example, today a city might regulate the architectural design of buildings, impose environmental restraints on new development, mandate the preservation of historic structures, or even ban new construction (*see* Chapter 38). Even though none of these controls relate to geographical zones, they are frequently grouped together under the traditional label of zoning. In effect, today "zoning" is often used to mean all forms of government land use regulation.

§ 36.03 The Birth of Zoning

[A] A Rural, Agricultural Nation

Before the twentieth century, there was virtually no government regulation of land use in the United States. Nor was such regulation needed.

---

[1] *See generally* Richard A. Epstein, *A Conceptual Approach to Zoning: What's Wrong with Euclid*, 5 N.Y.U. Envtl. L.J. 277 (1996); Charles M. Haar, *"In Accordance with a Comprehensive Plan,"* 68 Harv. L. Rev. 1154 (1955); Bradley C. Karkkainen, *Zoning: A Reply to the Critics*, 10 J. Land Use & Envtl. L. 45 (1994).

America was essentially an agricultural nation; and its predominantly rural population enjoyed an abundant supply of undeveloped land. In this era, land use restrictions arose—if at all—by private action.[2] Private parties could voluntarily impose restrictions on their lands by agreement. The rights of hypothetical owner O, holding fee simple absolute in Blueacre, might be limited by a real covenant, equitable servitude, or easement (*see* Chapters 32–34). And private parties could bring nuisance actions in response to egregious behavior by their neighbors (*see* Chapter 29). Thus, the government role in land use was normally restricted to judicial proceedings—courts enforced private agreements and adjudicated nuisance disputes.

Legislation restricting land use was both rare and fragmentary. Only a handful of large cities regulated land use at all. And the typical ordinance targeted only a single problem, such as limiting the height of buildings or restricting the location of one particularly noxious use (e.g., slaughterhouses).

[B] The Movement Toward Comprehensive Zoning

[1] An Urban, Industrial Nation

By the 1920s, the twin forces of industrial development and urbanization had transformed the United States. Two statistics symbolize this shift. In 1870, only 26% of Americans lived in urban areas; fifty years later, the figure was 51%. In 1900, automobiles were so unusual that auto registrations were not required; by 1920, over nine million autos were registered.

Living conditions in urban areas were often abysmal. Smoke, odors, noise, disease, filth, overcrowding, and other problems threatened the welfare of city residents. This crisis overwhelmed the traditional system of piecemeal, private land use planning. For example, the industrial properties responsible for much of the problem were not burdened by private land use restrictions. Nuisance litigation was similarly ineffective for a variety of reasons.

[2] Zoning As a Utilitarian Response

Zoning is best understood as a utilitarian response to these problems. It restricts the rights of private landowners in order to promote the health, safety, and welfare of the general public. In other words, zoning is a means to an end.

The pioneers of zoning reasoned that the evils of urban life could be overcome through comprehensive land use regulation. Two key principles—adapted from the "garden city" movement in England—guided this effort. First, the zoning pioneers assumed that separation of uses was desirable. Industrial, commercial, and residential uses should be located in different districts, rather than mixed together. Thus, for example, residential areas would be free from the nuisance-like impacts of industrial uses.

---

[2] *See* Robert C. Ellickson, *Alternatives to Zoning: Covenants, Nuisance Rules, and Fines as Land Use Controls*, 40 U. Chi. L. Rev. 681 (1973).

Second, early zoners firmly believed in the moral virtues of rural life. If the city was corrupt and artificial, the country remained pure and natural. Residential areas should consist of detached single-family houses, each standing alone in its own park-like garden, much like country cottages scattered around a village green. It was accordingly necessary to regulate the height, size, and location of houses, as well as the size and configuration of lots. The result, of course, was the modern housing tract—detached single-family residences in the middle of large lots.

[3] Impact of the Standard State Zoning Enabling Act

Comprehensive, standardized zoning spread quickly throughout the United States during the 1920s. In 1920, only New York and a few other cities had comprehensive zoning. Yet by 1930, over 1,000 municipalities had adopted zoning ordinances, almost all following the same pattern.

The catalyst that produced this rapid growth was the 1922 "Standard State Zoning Enabling Act," issued by the U.S. Department of Commerce as a model act for state legislatures to adopt. Cities and other local governmental entities possess no inherent police power that enables them to enact zoning ordinances. Zoning was possible only if states delegated police power to local governments for this purpose. The Standard State Zoning Enabling Act both (1) authorized local governments to enact a comprehensive zoning ordinance and (2) set forth the basic provisions of the standard ordinance to be enacted (see § 36.04). By 1930, most states had expressly adopted the Act, while others had enacted legislation patterned on the Act. As a result, municipalities across the nation had adopted zoning ordinances.

Today, zoning ordinances are in place in almost every American city. Most of these ordinances are based on the Standard State Zoning Enabling Act and, accordingly, are remarkably similar. This form of zoning is often called *Euclidean zoning*, named after the Euclid, Ohio zoning ordinance that the Supreme Court approved in its landmark decision *Village of Euclid v. Ambler Realty Co.*[3]

§ 36.04 A Sample Zoning Ordinance

[A] Enacting the Ordinance

The typical state zoning enabling act empowers a city council or other local legislative body to

(1) adopt a "comprehensive plan,"

(2) enact a zoning ordinance, and

(3) delegate administrative authority to an appointed board.

The adoption of a zoning ordinance is a legislative act. The ordinance is enacted by the city council or similar body in the usual course of business,

---

[3] 272 U.S. 365 (1926).

just like any other law or ordinance. It reflects a legislative judgment that its particular mix of land use restrictions will best serve the health, safety, welfare, and morals of local residents.

The Standard State Zoning Enabling Act required that zoning be "in accordance with a comprehensive plan," and this requirement led to a certain amount of confusion. The drafters of the Act apparently intended that the local legislative body would first prepare a comprehensive, long-term plan for its community, and then, in a second step, adopt a zoning ordinance that implemented the plan. Yet only a minority of jurisdictions—including California, Florida, and Oregon—require that zoning ordinances be consistent with a previously-adopted comprehensive plan.[4] In most jurisdictions, the local legislative body can enact zoning ordinances even though no comprehensive plan is in place. This result is defended on various grounds. Probably the most common explanation is that a detailed zoning ordinance itself constitutes a comprehensive plan, without any need for a separate document.

[B]   Use Regulations

Use regulation is the heart of zoning. Zoning theorists assumed that separation of uses was desirable: residential areas, commercial districts, and industrial regions, for example, should all be separated from each other. Thus, the typical zoning ordinance divides the community into separate regions or "zones," which are shown on detailed maps, and specifies the uses permitted in each zone.[5]

Zoning ordinances adopted in the 1920s were "cumulative" in nature, and many modern ordinances still reflect this approach. Under a cumulative zoning system, the relationship between use zones resembles a pyramid. At the top of the pyramid is a zone that only allows one use: detached single-family homes. The next zone might permit both duplexes and detached single-family homes; the third zone might allow duplexes, detached single-family homes, and also apartment buildings; the fourth zone might permit retail stores in addition to all "higher" uses, and so forth. At the bottom of this zoning pyramid is a district where heavy industrial uses (e.g., smelters, refineries) are permitted, together with all "higher" uses.

[C]   Height and Bulk Regulations

The typical zoning ordinance also imposes restrictions on the buildings that house each particular type of use. These restrictions are justified on a number of bases, including fire safety, density control, and protection of access to light and air.

Maximum height limits for buildings—measured in either stories or feet—are common. Buildings in a residential zone may be limited to one

---

[4] *See, e.g.,* Town of Jonesville v. Powell Valley Village Ltd. Partnership, 487 S.E.2d 207 (Va. 1997) (invalidating zoning ordinance due to lack of comprehensive plan).

[5] *See, e.g.,*Village of Euclid v. Ambler Realty Co., 272 U.S. 365, 379–384 (1926) (describing provisions of Euclid, Ohio ordinance).

story, for example, while a four-story structure might be allowed in a district zoned for office use. The standard ordinance also contains bulk regulations. These typically include:

(1)   minimum lot size requirements (e.g., each building lot in a residential zone must contain at least 5,000 square feet);

(2)   lot coverage requirements (e.g., no more than 50% of the lot may be occupied by a building);

(3)   minimum frontage requirements (e.g., each lot must have at least 50 feet of frontage on a public street); and

(4)   setback requirements (e.g., each building must be set back at least 30 feet from the street, 5 feet from each side lot line, and 20 feet from the rear lot line).

One modern alternative to the traditional height and bulk requirements is the floor-area ratio or "FAR."[6] Suppose an ordinance imposes a 1:2 FAR for commercial office buildings. Developer D can choose to build a one-story office building that covers half of the lot, a two-story building that covers one-quarter of the lot, and so forth.

[D]   Administering the Ordinance

The typical ordinance is administered by a local agency usually called a zoning board, board of zoning adjustment, or board of zoning appeals. The members of this board are appointed by the local legislative body (e.g., the city council).

The board has two basic functions. First, it considers appeals from decisions made by zoning officials. For example, if official G wrongly concludes that the roof of H's home exceeds the applicable height limit, H can appeal this ruling to the board. Second, and more importantly, the ordinance usually authorizes the board to approve landowner applications for *variances* (§ 37.03) and *special exceptions* (§ 37.04). Suppose that the strict application of the zoning law imposes a severe hardship on landowner L; L's residential lot is so oddly shaped that it is impossible to build a house that complies with all the setback requirements. Under these circumstances, the board may grant a variance—a special deviation from the strict enforcement of the ordinance—that allows L to build close to his lot lines.

§ 36.05   The Constitutionality of Zoning

[A]   The Issue

Is zoning constitutional? During the 1920s, opponents hoped to invalidate zoning on constitutional grounds. They argued that zoning (1) deprived owners of property without due process of law, (2) violated owners' rights

---

[6] *See, e.g.,* Raritan Dev. Corp. v. Silva, 689 N.E.2d 1373 (N.Y. 1997) (discussing FAR standards).

to the equal protection of the laws, and (3) took property without just compensation.

Zoning opponents raised attacks based on substantive due process and equal protection in a famous test case that challenged the zoning ordinance in Euclid, Ohio. Ironically, the Supreme Court's eventual decision in *Village of Euclid v. Ambler Realty Co.*[7] firmly established the constitutionality of zoning in general. The landmark *Euclid* decision is discussed below, while the argument that zoning is a taking of property without just compensation is addressed in Chapter 40.

[B] *Village of Euclid v. Ambler Realty Co.*

[1] Factual Setting

Plaintiff purchased a 68-acre tract of undeveloped land in the Village of Euclid, near Cleveland, Ohio. The southern edge of the land bordered Euclid Avenue, a major street, and was suitable for retail store uses. The balance of the land, which adjoined a railroad to the north, seemed destined to accommodate the growing regional demand for industrial property.

In 1922, the village adopted its first comprehensive zoning ordinance. The ordinance divided the village into six districts and restricted the uses permitted in each, in cumulative fashion (*see* § 36.04[B]). The only major use permitted in the U-1 district was single-family residences; the U-2 district was extended to include duplexes; the U-3 district allowed the U-1 and U-2 uses, together with apartments, public buildings, and the like. The U-4 district was further extended to include retail uses; the U-5 district added light industrial uses; and every use, including heavy industry, was permitted in the U-6 district. The ordinance also regulated building height and lot size.

The new ordinance substantially restricted the uses allowed on plaintiff's land, and thereby reduced its value. The southern one-third of the tract bordering Euclid Avenue was zoned U-2, while the northern half adjoining the railroad was zoned U-6; a thin strip in the middle was zoned U-3. According to plaintiff, the land was worth $10,000 per acre as industrial property, but only $2,500 per acre as residential property.

Plaintiff argued that the zoning ordinance violated its rights to substantive due process and equal protection. The federal district court struck down the ordinance, holding that the police power did not permit a municipality to "classify the population and segregate them according to their income or situation in life."[8]

[2] The Decision

In upholding the constitutionality of the Euclid ordinance, the Supreme Court established principles that still dominate American zoning law.

---

[7] 272 U.S. 365 (1926).

[8] Ambler Realty Co. v. Village of Euclid, 297 F. 307, 316 (N.D. Ohio 1924), *rev'd*, 272 U.S. 365 (1926).

Writing for the majority, Justice Sutherland focused on the new problems created by population growth and urbanization. Modern conditions justified regulations that would have been rejected as arbitrary and oppressive in the past. The source of local zoning authority was the police power—the power to protect the public health, safety, welfare, and morals. But how far did the police power extend? Sutherland answered this question by analogizing to nuisance law; after all, he observed: "A nuisance may be merely a right thing in the wrong place—like a pig in the parlor instead of the barnyard."[9] Sutherland accordingly found that the Euclid ordinance was facially constitutional because it essentially regulated nuisance-like impacts (see [3], below). For example, the provisions of the ordinance that separated industrial uses from residential uses protected homes from noise, smoke, fumes, and similar intrusions. This nuisance-control rationale had little impact on later cases, but the rules it initially justified still endure.

Three interrelated principles emerge from the majority opinion. First, a zoning ordinance is presumed to be constitutional. Second, the ordinance will be upheld against substantive due process and equal protection attacks unless it is arbitrary and unreasonable, having no substantial relation to the public health, safety, welfare, or morals. Finally, a court may not conduct an independent review of the wisdom or policy of a zoning ordinance; if the validity of the legislative classification is "fairly debatable, the legislative judgment must be allowed to control."[10]

[3]   Reflections on *Euclid*

Euclid is easily the most important decision in the evolution of American zoning law. With the Supreme Court's stamp of approval firmly in place, Euclidean zoning swept across the nation. Municipal officials and planners promoted Euclid-like ordinances, confident that they would withstand constitutional attack.

Yet from the perspective of the twenty-first century, the judicial reasoning underlying *Euclid* seems somewhat antique. The Court defends comprehensive zoning—in essence—as a method to prevent nuisance-like impacts. This analysis makes sense to a point. Certain types of industrial uses—for example, refineries, smelters, and tanneries—are likely to be nuisances if located in a residential district. Thus, the exclusion of industrial uses from the U-1, U-2, and U-3 zones is easily explained.

But the nuisance-control rationale collapses when the Court tries to explain why apartment houses are barred from the single-family residential zone. The Court's suggestion that an apartment house is "a mere parasite" whose coming destroys the "residential character of the neighborhood and its desirability as a place of detached residences"[11] implies reasons for zoning that go far beyond the nuisance doctrine. Zoning suddenly seems more like social engineering, which serves broad "quality of life" goals by

---

[9] Village of Euclid v. Ambler Realty Co., 272 U.S. 365, 388 (1926).

[10] Village of Euclid v. Ambler Realty Co., 272 U.S. 365, 388 (1926).

[11] Village of Euclid v. Ambler Realty Co., 272 U.S. 365, 394 (1926).

shielding single-family residential neighborhoods from change. And the Court ignores the toughest question: why exclude duplexes from the single-family residential zone. Could anyone seriously argue that a duplex is a nuisance?

[C] Post-*Euclid* Developments

As the leading Supreme Court decision on the constitutionality of zoning, *Euclid* became the foundation for American zoning law. In the wake of *Euclid*, federal and state courts routinely followed its mandate that comprehensive zoning *in general* was constitutional unless arbitrary and unreasonable, having no substantial relation to the public health, safety, morals, or general welfare.[12] Under this deferential standard of review, courts did not question the wisdom or necessity of zoning ordinances. These broad standards, of course, went far beyond the logic of nuisance-control. And later courts utilized them to uphold zoning ordinances that served quite different purposes, including protection of property values, preservation of neighborhood character, and controls on growth (*see* Chapter 38).

One reason for the extraordinary influence of *Euclid* is its isolation. The Supreme Court decided only two significant zoning cases before 1974: *Euclid* in 1926, and then *Nectow v. City of Cambridge*[13] in 1928.[14] *Euclid* stands alone as the leading case establishing the constitutionality of zoning *in general*. *Nectow* established the important principle that a zoning ordinance might be unconstitutional *as applied* to a particular parcel. There, part of plaintiff's land was restricted to residential use, even though adjacent industrial and railroad uses made the land highly undesirable for housing. At the trial level, a special master concluded that "no practical use can be made of the land in question for residential purposes."[15] Based on this record, the Court had no difficulty in holding that the application of the ordinance to plaintiff's land failed to promote the public health, safety, or welfare, and accordingly was unconstitutional.

§ 36.06 Zoning and the Nonconforming Use

[A] The Problem

Imagine a City that adopts its first zoning ordinance in 1925. Following the standard Euclidean zoning pattern, the ordinance neatly divides the City into zones where particular uses are allowed. One predominantly residential neighborhood, for example, is zoned for single-family residential use only. How does this new zoning ordinance affect an existing non-residential use in the neighborhood—for example, a bakery?

---

[12] *See, e.g.,* Messiah Baptist Church v. County of Jefferson, 859 F.2d 820 (10th Cir. 1988) (upholding ordinance that excluded churches from residential zone); Pierro v. Baxendale, 118 A.2d 401 (N.J. 1955) (upholding ordinance that excluded motels from residential zone).

[13] 277 U.S. 183 (1928).

[14] *See also* Gorieb v. Fox, 274 U.S. 603 (1927) (upholding ordinance imposing set back lines on residential and commercial lots).

[15] Nectow v. City of Cambridge, 277 U.S. 183, 187 (1928).

In general, zoning regulates only *future* development. Thus, from the 1920s onward, virtually all zoning ordinances allowed the prior *noncon- forming use* to continue.[16] A nonconforming use is a use of land that lawfully existed before the zoning ordinance was enacted, but that does not comply with the ordinance. It might be a type of land use that violates the use restrictions in the zone, such as the bakery example above. Or it might be a building that fails to comply with the ordinance restrictions on height, lot coverage, set back, lot size, frontage, or other similar items. A noncon- forming use may also arise when a zoning ordinance is amended (*see* § 37.02).

Why allow nonconforming uses to continue? The early advocates of zoning realized that nonconforming uses threatened the success of comprehensive land use regulation. Allowing a bakery in a residential zone, for instance, violated the zoning axiom that different uses should be geographically separate. However, zoning advocates understood that banning nonconform- ing uses could cause major problems. A flat ban might encourage public opposition to the adoption of zoning ordinances in general. And it would increase the vulnerability of zoning to constitutional attacks based on the Due Process and Equal Protection Clauses. Finally, it might constitute a regulatory taking under the Takings Clause.

[B] Restricting the Nonconforming Use

The pioneers of zoning anticipated that nonconforming uses would slowly wither away; the "weeds" in the Euclidean garden would eventually die. Zoning ordinances seek to accelerate this process by restricting the noncon- forming use.

Most ordinances bar the expansion of a nonconforming use.[17] For exam- ple, the nonconforming bakery in a residential zone will not be allowed to build a new addition that increases the area of the store. Under the same logic, if the bakery only operated between 8:00 a.m. and 8:00 p.m. before the zoning ordinance took effect, it cannot now operate 24 hours each day. In contrast, some jurisdictions allow the nonconforming use to expand in response natural or normal growth in demand.

Similarly, one nonconforming use cannot be transformed into a different nonconforming use.[18] The nonconforming bakery in a residential zone, for example, cannot be changed into a nonconforming video store. And although the owner of a nonconforming use can effect minor repairs, major alter- ations or structural repairs that will extend the duration of the use cannot be made.

---

[16] *See, e.g.,* City of Akron v. Chapman, 116 N.E.2d 697 (Ohio 1953).

[17] *See* Denver Police Protective Ass'n v. City & County of Denver, 710 P.2d 3 (Colo. Ct. App. 1985).

[18] *See, e.g.,* Town of Belleville v. Parrillo's, Inc., 416 A.2d 388 (N.J. 1980) (holding that nonconforming restaurant could not be converted into discotheque).

[C] Terminating the Nonconforming Use

[1] Abandonment or Destruction

Early zoners anticipated that the right to continue a nonconforming use would be lost either through abandonment or destruction. In most jurisdictions, abandonment occurs only if both (1) the owner intends to abandon the use and (2) the use is discontinued for a substantial period.[19] Some ordinances provide that discontinuance during a specific time period—usually six months or a year—is sufficient to end the use, regardless of the owner's intent.[20] Similarly, the destruction of a nonconforming use—or the structure containing the use—usually terminates the right to continue the use. In most jurisdictions, for example, if the building that houses a nonconforming bakery is entirely destroyed by an accidental fire, the bakery use ends.[21] However, many ordinances allow rebuilding if only partial destruction occurs.

[2] Amortization

Contrary to the expectations of the early zoners, many nonconforming uses not only survived abandonment and destruction, but actually flourished. Why? By barring new businesses from certain districts, zoning ordinances gave existing nonconforming uses an artificial monopoly. The only bakery in a residential zone, for example, enjoyed high demand and little competition. How could these persistent nonconforming uses be eliminated? During the 1950s, the new technique of *amortization* came into widespread use.

Amortization gives the owner of a nonconforming use a fixed period of time to operate the use; when the period ends, the right to continue the use ends.[22] Suppose B owns rights in a nonconforming billboard. The amortization provision of the local ordinance might give B a five-year period to continue the billboard use. During this period, B can continue to derive rental revenue from the billboard. The theory underlying amortization is that the owner will be able to recover his investment by continuing the nonconforming use for a reasonable period of time. Accordingly, the city or other government entity can later end the use without any constitutional obligation to compensate the owner. Suppose, for example, that B invested $10,000 to construct the billboard before the billboard ban took effect. If B receives net rents of $2,500 each year and is allowed to continue the billboard use for five years, he will receive $12,500, thus recovering more than his original investment.

---

[19] *See, e.g.,* A.T. & G., Inc. v. Zoning Bd. of Review, 322 A.2d 294 (1974).

[20] *See, e.g.,* Anderson v. City of Paragould, 695 S.W.2d 851 (Ark. Ct. App. 1985).

[21] *See, e.g.,* Weldon v. Zoning Bd. of Des Moines, 250 N.W.2d 396 (Iowa 1977).

[22] *See generally* Osborne M. Reynolds, Jr., *The Reasonableness of Amortization Periods for Nonconforming Uses—Balancing the Private Interest and the Public Welfare,* 34 Wash. U. J. Urb. & Contemp. L. 99 (1988).

In most jurisdictions, amortization is valid if the length of the amortization period is reasonable.[23] There is no fixed formula to calculate a reasonable period. Despite the precision that the term "amortization" suggests, courts normally do not determine whether the particular period mathematically allows the owner to recoup the investment. Rather, they assess reasonableness in a more general sense, examining factors such as the amount of the owner's investment, the nature of the nonconforming use, its remaining useful life, and the potential harm to the public if the use continues.

The leading decision of *City of Los Angeles v. Gage*,[24] for example, upheld the constitutionality of a five-year period to amortize a nonconforming plumbing business. The court noted that the ordinance merely required the defendants to move their nonconforming business to a new location only about a half-mile away; the moving cost was less than 1% of the gross income generated during the amortization period. In addition, the move would eliminate the noise and traffic burden that the business imposed on the surrounding residential neighborhood. Taken as a whole, the court found that the ordinance struck a proper balance between public gain and private loss. Conversely, in *PA Northwestern Distributors, Inc. v. Zoning Hearing Board*[25] a concurring justice observed that a 90-day amortization period for an adult bookstore was unreasonably short because, among other factors, it would not permit the owner to obtain a reasonable return on his investment.

A handful of jurisdictions hold that amortization is per se unconstitutional.[26] Thus, a nonconforming use can be eliminated only if it constitutes a nuisance or is abandoned, destroyed, or purchased through eminent domain.[27]

§ 36.07 Zoning and Vested Rights

Zoning ordinances mainly regulate future development. Suppose City amends its zoning ordinance on January 1, 2000 by banning fast food restaurants from its downtown district. Fast food restaurants that already exist before enactment of the ordinance are exempted as nonconforming uses (*see* § 36.06). And the zoning ordinance clearly applies to anyone who decides on January 1, 2000 or thereafter to establish such a restaurant.

But what law applies to a project caught in the middle? Suppose B's fast food restaurant is under construction—but not yet open for business—when

---

[23] *See, e.g.,* Village of Valatie v. Smith, 632 N.E.2d 1264 (N.Y. 1994) (upholding validity of amortization period that permitted nonconforming mobile home use until transfer of ownership of mobile home or underlying land).

[24] 274 P.2d 34 (Cal. Ct. App. 1954).

[25] 584 A.2d 1372 (Pa. 1991).

[26] *See, e.g.,* PA Northwestern Distribs., Inc. v. Zoning Hearing Bd., 584 A.2d 1372 (Pa. 1991).

[27] *Cf.* City of Akron v. Chapman, 116 N.E.2d 697 (Ohio 1953) (invalidating ordinance that allowed city council to discontinue any nonconforming use that had existed for a "reasonable time").

the amended ordinance takes effect on January 1, 2000. The answer to B's dilemma is the doctrine of *vested rights*.[28] In most states, the owner who obtains a building permit and makes substantial expenditures in good faith reliance on the permit obtains a vested right to the use, regardless of any later change in the law. States vary widely on the extent of the required reliance. Construction of the building foundation, or even mere excavation on the site, may suffice. On the other hand, the developer who expends large sums for architectural, engineering, and planning services—but never actually begins construction—is unlikely to acquire vested rights.[29]

[28] *See, e.g.,* Davidson v. County of San Diego, 56 Cal. Rptr. 2d 617 (Ct. App. 1996); H.R.D.E., Inc. v. Zoning Officer, 430 S.E.2d 341 (W. Va. 1993). *See also* Richard B. Cunningham & David H. Kremer, *Vested Rights, Estoppel, and the Land Development Process*, 29 Hastings L.J. 625 (1978).

[29] *See, e.g.,* Stone v. City of Wilton, 331 N.W.2d 398 (Iowa 1983) (holding that developer who spent $7,900 on architectural, engineering, and financing costs for planned multi-family housing project, but never started construction, did not acquire vested rights).

Chapter 37

TOOLS FOR ZONING FLEXIBILITY

SYNOPSIS

§ 37.01   A Modern Approach to Zoning

The American law of zoning is undergoing fundamental change.[1] The rigid Euclidean zoning system is slowly collapsing; at the same time, new

---

[1] *See generally* Carol M. Rose, *New Models for Local Land Use Decisions*, 79 Nw. U. L. Rev. 1155 (1984–1985); Carol M. Rose, *Planning and Dealing: Piecemeal Land Controls as a Problem of Local Legitimacy*, 71 Cal. L. Rev. 837 (1983); Ronald M. Shapiro, *The Zoning Variance Power—Constructive in Theory, Destructive in Practice*, 29 Md. L. Rev. 3 (1969); Ronald M. Shapiro, *The Case for Conditional Zoning*, 41 Temp. L.Q. 267 (1968).

methods of land use regulation are gaining acceptance. This chapter examines the techniques that bring flexibility to the traditional zoning system, while Chapter 38 explores the new purposes that contemporary zoning serves.

The national model for Euclidean zoning—the Standard State Zoning Enabling Act—grudgingly recognized three flexibility devices: the *zoning amendment,* the *variance,* and the *special exception.* But it was anticipated that these "loopholes" would be rarely used. Euclidean zoning rested on the assumption that the public interest is best served by a stable comprehensive plan. If zoning could be changed on a piecemeal, lot-by-lot basis, the comprehensive plan would gradually wither away, reviving the problems zoning sought to remedy.

Potential piecemeal zoning presented a second danger: zoning officials might betray the public trust for private gain.[2] One impact of Euclidean zoning was to create an economic scarcity of land zoned for particular high-value uses; this, in turn, increased the market value of land in certain districts. Suppose that only 50 acres in Town T were zoned for shopping center use, while O's 20-acre parcel was limited to agricultural use. O's land might be worth $2,000 per acre as farm land, but $100,000 per acre if it could be used as a shopping center site. If T's zoning officials had discretion to reclassify O's property into a shopping center zone, O might be able to affect their decision through ties of friendship, political pressure, or outright bribery. Zoning decisions based on self-interest, corruption or favoritism would injure the public interest.

The modern approach to land use regulation places less reliance on the comprehensive plan and more emphasis on discretionary, lot-by-lot zoning decisions. It recognizes that blind adherence to the comprehensive plan will impair the overall public interest in many instances. This approach values zoning decisions that are individually tailored to implement the public interest according to the unique circumstances of each case. Flexible zoning, in short, is seen as effective zoning. The risk of corruption or abuse of power, while still quite real, can be controlled through various techniques.

Accordingly, the three traditional flexibility devices—the zoning amendment, the variance, and the special exception—are used quite frequently today; and they have been expanded to situations that the founders of Euclidean zoning never imagined. Further two new layers of innovative regulatory devices have been added atop this historic foundation: (1) novel forms of zoning; and (2) the subdivision regulation process.

---

[2] *See, e.g.,* Schauer v. City of Miami Beach, 112 So. 2d 838 (Fla. 1959) (affirming rezoning decision even though councilman who voted for rezoning owned property that thereby increased in value by $600,000); Fleming v. City of Tacoma, 502 P.2d 327 (Wash. 1972) (overturning rezoning decision based on councilman's apparent conflict of interest).

§ 37.02 Zoning Amendments

[A] Role of the Amendment

A zoning ordinance may be modified by a *zoning amendment* adopted by the city council or other local governmental entity. Section 5 of the Standard State Zoning Enabling Act provides that "regulations, restrictions, and boundaries may from time to time be amended, supplemented, changed, modified, or repealed." In practice, state zoning acts routinely permit local governments to amend their ordinances.

There are two types of zoning amendments. First, the zoning map might be amended by placing certain land in a wholly different zone. Suppose O owns a 500-acre farm within the city limits of Smithville; the farm is currently in the A-2 zone, which allows only agricultural uses (e.g., crops, livestock). O wishes to construct and operate a grain elevator on his land. The Smithville city council might rezone O's farm into the A-3 zone, which allows grain elevators and other additional uses (e.g., feed mills, warehouses). Alternatively, the text of the zoning ordinance might be amended by changing the uses that are allowed in a particular zone. The city council might, for example, amend its ordinance by adding "grain elevators" to the list of uses permitted in the A-2 zone.

[B] Standards for Amendments

[1] Legislative Judgment

Traditionally, a zoning amendment is viewed as legislative action, just like the adoption of the initial zoning ordinance or any other type of legislation. The city council or other local legislative body decides in its sole discretion whether rezoning serves the public interest. Because the separation of powers principle requires judicial deference to legislative judgments, this decision is largely insulated from later judicial review.

A zoning amendment is presumed to be valid. Absent proof that the rezoning decision was arbitrary or unreasonable, courts will uphold the amendment against constitutional attack under the Due Process and Equal Protection Clauses.[3] As the Supreme Court observed in *Village of Euclid v. Ambler Realty Co.*, a zoning ordinance is valid unless "clearly arbitrary and unreasonable, having no substantial relation to the public health, safety, morals, or general welfare."[4]

But should a zoning amendment be treated with the same deference accorded to normal legislation? The founders of Euclidean zoning anticipated that amendments would (a) be rare, (b) affect many parcels owned

---

[3] *See, e.g.,* Stone v. City of Wilton, 331 N.W.2d 398 (Iowa 1983) (discussing standard); Karches v. City of Cincinnati, 526 N.E.2d 1350 (Ohio 1988) (holding zoning amendment was "unreasonable, arbitrary and confiscatory" and thus violated the Due Process and Takings Clauses); Anderson v. Island County, 501 P.2d 594 (Wash. 1972) (holding zoning amendment was "arbitrary and capricious").

[4] 272 U.S. 365, 395 (1926). *See also* Pharr v. Tippitt, 616 S.W.2d 173 (Tex. 1981).

by many owners, and (c) be initiated by local government. Yet in practice the rezoning power is used quite differently. Rezoning applications (a) are very common, (b) often affect only one parcel, and (c) are usually initiated by the owner of the parcel. In effect, many landowners view the rezoning power as a major "loophole" in the zoning system that may be utilized for private gain.

Improper rezoning decisions erode the very foundation of Euclidean zoning: comprehensive land use planning. If individual parcels can be rezoned on an ad hoc, case-by-case basis, then the comprehensive plan may become riddled with exceptions and slowly wither away. Further, abuse of the rezoning power serves the interests of individual landowners, at the expense of the community as a whole. Closely tied to this concern is the danger of corruption or other official misconduct.[5] Restricting the rezoning power helps to ensure that zoning officials will properly perform their duties.

As a result of these concerns, virtually all jurisdictions impose additional restrictions on the rezoning power. Most jurisdictions will invalidate a zoning amendment if it constitutes "spot zoning" (see [2], below), while a few jurisdictions follow the narrow "change or mistake" rule (see [3], below). Procedural constraints may also limit the rezoning power in some jurisdictions. The most common constraints are judicial review of zoning amendments as quasi-judicial action (see [C][1], below) and rezoning by initiative or referendum (see [C][2], below). A final restriction is that zoning amendments may not violate "vested rights" held by individual landowners (see § 36.07).[6]

[2] Spot Zoning

In practice, the main limitation on rezoning is the doctrine of *spot zoning*. If a zoning amendment violates this doctrine, it is generally held invalid.[7] The essence of spot zoning is simple: rezoning that confers a special benefit on a small parcel of land regardless of the public interest or the comprehensive plan.

Unfortunately, the case law interpreting the spot zoning doctrine is vague, confusing, and often wildly inconsistent. Courts commonly consider a number of factors when applying the doctrine, including:

(1)   the size of the parcel;

(2)   the benefits conferred on the parcel compared to surrounding parcels;

(3)   any injury or detriment to surrounding landowners and the public in general;

---

[5] *See, e.g.,* Fleming v. City of Tacoma, 502 P.2d 327 (Wash. 1972) (invalidating zoning amendment based on councilman's apparent conflict of interest).

[6] *See, e.g.,* Stone v. City of Wilton, 331 N.W.2d 398 (Iowa 1983) (plaintiff's expenditures for architectural and engineering services on future project were not substantial enough to create vested rights against rezoning).

[7] *See, e.g.,* Little v. Winborn, 518 N.W.2d 384 (Iowa 1994).

(4) any changed conditions in the area; and

(5) whether the rezoning is in accordance with a comprehensive plan.[8]

Yet many courts find spot zoning even if some of these criteria are not met. And other courts seem to find spot zoning only if the rezoning is inconsistent with the overall public interest, even if all other criteria are present.[9] Still other courts find spot zoning whenever a rezoning conflicts with the comprehensive plan regardless of other factors.[10]

Suppose A owns Blueacre, a vacant lot that is one-quarter acre in size and zoned for residential use only; the lot is located in the middle of a large tract of single-family homes. A convinces the city council to rezone Blueacre for commercial use, so that he can operate a video rental store. Most courts would agree that this action constitutes spot zoning. The rezoning affects only one small parcel. And it confers a special privilege—the right to operate a commercial enterprise—that the adjacent parcels do not share. The rezoning will presumably cause adverse traffic, parking, noise, and other impacts on neighboring owners, and cannot be justified by changed conditions. Finally, the action is inconsistent with the residential use contemplated by the comprehensive plan.

The importance of the spot zoning doctrine is slowly waning with the demise of Euclidian zoning. There is a clear trend toward more flexible forms of zoning and, accordingly, away from the rigidity of the Euclidean approach. The spot zoning doctrine is less relevant in this new climate. A rezoning that might have been condemned in the 1950s as illegal spot zoning may well be praised today as a shining example of innovative planning.

[3] "Change or Mistake" Rule

A few states follow the narrow "change or mistake" rule.[11] Under this view, rezoning is appropriate only (a) to correct a mistake made in the original zoning ordinance or (b) if physical conditions in the neighborhood have fundamentally changed since the ordinance was adopted.

[C] Other Constraints on Amendments

[1] Judicial Review of Quasi-Judicial Action

In *Fasano v. Board of County Commissioners*,[12] the Oregon Supreme Court pioneered a new approach toward curbing abuses of the rezoning

---

[8] *See, e.g.,* Pharr v. Tippitt, 616 S.W.2d 173 (Tex. 1981) (finding no spot zoning); Anderson v. Island County, 501 P.2d 594 (Wash. 1972) (finding spot zoning); Bell v. City of Elkhorn, 364 N.W.2d 144 (Wis. 1985) (finding no spot zoning).

[9] *Cf.* Bartram v. Zoning Comm'n, 68 A.2d 308, 311 (Conn. 1949) (no spot zoning where rezoning would "serve the best interests of the community as a whole").

[10] *See* Cannon v. Murphy, 600 N.Y.S.2d 965 (App. Div. 1993).

[11] *See, e.g.,* White v. Spring, 675 A.2d 1023 (Md. Ct. Spec. App. 1996).

[12] 507 P.2d 23 (Or. 1973).

power: treating zoning amendments as quasi-judicial action. The court reasoned that a rezoning decision by a local legislative body that affects only one parcel of land is essentially judicial, not legislative, in character. Legislative action connotes the *creation* of a general rule that is applicable to all citizens. But the single-parcel rezoning decision involves the *application* of a general rule to one owner's specific factual situation; this process, the court explained, is the hallmark of judicial action. And, as quasi-judicial action, the rezoning decision is subject to a more rigorous standard of judicial review. The court held that rezoning is appropriate only if the owner seeking approval proves both (a) there is a public need for the proposed change and (b) the need is best served by rezoning the particular parcel rather than other property.

The *Fasano* approach is controversial.[13] A handful of jurisdictions endorse the approach as an appropriate safeguard in single-parcel rezoning.[14] But most jurisdictions reject the *Fasano* view, relying on differing rationales.[15] One objection is that *Fasano* is out-of-step with the modern movement toward zoning flexibility; by imposing new hurdles on any rezoning application, it returns to the outdated notion of a timeless comprehensive plan. Another objection focuses on the institutional competence of the judiciary to make land-use planning decisions. The local legislative process, although imperfect, may be a superior method of reconciling the interests of competing constituencies. Further, if zoning amendments are characterized as quasi-judicial, then they are exempt from public scrutiny through an initiative or referendum. Finally, case-by-case determinations of whether particular land-use approvals are legislative or quasi-judicial action would produce substantial administrative costs.

[2] Zoning by the Electorate

Another potential solution to rezoning abuses is the ballot box. In some jurisdictions, the public may vote on zoning amendments, either through a referendum or an initiative. The issue arises most commonly when neighbors object to a developer's plan to build a high-density residential project on a large tract of vacant land. Suppose D intends to build a 400-unit apartment complex on a ten-acre parcel currently used for cattle grazing but already zoned for multi-family residential use. E and other neighbors may try to block the project by placing an initiative on the next ballot to rezone the land for non-residential use (e.g., agriculture only). Alternatively, suppose the land is currently restricted to agricultural use only; if the city council rezones the property for multi-family use, this decision may be subject to review through a referendum.

The leading case examining the review of zoning amendments by referenda is *City of Eastlake v. Forest City Enterprises, Inc.*[16] There, a developer

---

[13] *See generally* Jan Z. Krasnowiecki, *Abolish Zoning*, 31 Syracuse L. Rev. 719 (1980); Carol M. Rose, *New Models for Local Land Use Decisions*, 79 Nw. U. L. Rev. 1155 (1984–1985).

[14] *See, e.g.,* Board of County Comm'rs v. Snyder, 627 So. 2d 469 (Fla. 1993).

[15] *See, e.g.,* Arnel Dev. Co. v. City of Costa Mesa, 620 P.2d 565 (Cal. 1980).

[16] 426 U.S. 668 (1976).

obtained city council approval to rezone its eight-acre parcel from "light industrial" to high-rise residential use. The city charter required that any land use changes be approved by a referendum, but the developer leveled various constitutional attacks at this requirement. The Supreme Court ultimately upheld the charter provision, finding that it was not an unconstitutional delegation of legislative power because the state constitution expressly reserved this power to the electorate. Nor did the mere use of the referendum procedure to review a rezoning decision violate the Due Process Clause. The Court observed that the developer could challenge the referendum if it could demonstrate the result was clearly arbitrary and unreasonable. Three justices dissented, arguing that the referendum process is not an appropriate method to resolve issues affecting individual rights.

Subsequently, in *Arnel Development Co. v. City of Costa Mesa*,[17] the California Supreme Court rejected a due process challenge to rezoning by initiative. The case arose when plaintiff proposed to construct a 50-acre housing development, consisting of 127 single-family homes and 539 apartment units. A neighborhood group successfully campaigned for an initiative to rezone the land (and two small adjacent parcels) for single-family residential use only, and plaintiff challenged the result. Relying on *City of Eastlake*, the court held that (a) the use of the initiative process per se did not violate the Due Process Clause and (b) plaintiff could seek judicial invalidation of the rezoning if it was arbitrary or unreasonable. The court brushed aside plaintiff's claim that procedural due process mandated a hearing for the rezoning of small parcels. It noted that rezoning is legislative action, not subject to the notice and hearing requirements that restrict judicial action. In any event, the court concluded, the initiative process allows the landowner an opportunity for a "hearing" before the voters.

Is zoning by the electorate a good idea? Most legal scholars are sharply critical of the concept.[18] Voter turnout is typically low; and the voters who do participate generally fail to understand the issues. A high-profile media campaign may attract support for a poor project, while vigorous opposition by a few disgruntled residents may sabotage a worthy project. As a result, the electoral outcome is unlikely to reflect sound planning judgment. Even the foremost advocates of zoning flexibility condemn electoral zoning as the epitome of piecemeal zoning. Finally—despite *City of Eastlake* and *Arnel Development*—zoning by the electorate might violate the procedural due process rights of affected property owners. A "hearing" before the electorate may well lack the safeguards that our constitutional tradition requires.

---

[17] 620 P.2d 565 (Cal. 1980).

[18] *See, e.g.,* David L. Callies *et al., Ballot Box Zoning: Initiative, Referendum and the Law,* 39 Wash. U. J. Urb. & Contemp. L. 53 (1991); Ronald H. Rosenberg, *Referendum Zoning: Legal Doctrine and Practice,* 53 U. Cin. L. Rev. 381 (1984).

§ 37.03   Variances

[A]   Role of the Variance

Suppose O's vacant lot Blueacre is located in a zone that (a) allows residential use only and (b) requires a minimum lot size of 7,500 square feet.[19] But the total area of Blueacre is only 5,000 square feet. How can O develop his lot? The solution to O's dilemma is a *variance*—an authorized deviation from strict enforcement of the zoning ordinance in an individual case due to special hardship. In effect, a variance permits a particular parcel of land to be used in a way that would otherwise violate the ordinance. Here, O may be able to obtain a variance from the local zoning board that allows him to build a home on his undersized lot.[20]

At bottom, the variance is a "safety valve" in the basic zoning ordinance. It both protects the rights of individual property owners and helps to insulate the ordinance from attack as an unconstitutional taking of property. After all, if a zoning ordinance prohibited any economically beneficial or productive use of Blueacre, O might be able to recover damages for a regulatory taking (*see* § 40.08).

[B]   Types of Variances

There are two basic types of variances: the *area variance* and the *use variance*. The area variance allows modification of height, location, setback, size, or similar requirements for a use that is permitted in the zone.[21] For instance, suppose A plans to build an office building on her parcel, which is the only use allowed in the zone; because the parcel is triangular in shape, however, she cannot construct an office building that is large enough to be commercially viable under the current height (20 feet maximum) and setback (ten feet away from all property lines) requirements. She might obtain a variance that allows a higher building (e.g., 25 feet high) or a smaller setback (e.g., five feet away from property lines). Either one would be considered an area variance.

In contrast, the use variance allows a use that would normally be prohibited in the zone. Suppose, for example, that B owns a vacant corner lot that is zoned for residential use only, but wishes to build and operate a grocery store. A use variance, if available, would permit this commercial use in the residential zone.

The use variance is controversial. Statutes, ordinances, or case law prohibit the use variance in many jurisdictions based on the logic that it constitutes a rezoning of the parcel. While a variance is administratively

---

[19] *See generally* Ronald M. Shapiro, *The Zoning Variance Power—Constructive in Theory, Destructive in Practice*, 29 Md. L. Rev. 1 (1969).

[20] *See, e.g.,* Commons v. Westwood Zoning Bd. of Adjustment, 410 A.2d 1138 (N.J. 1980).

[21] *See, e.g.,* Commons v. Westwood Zoning Bd. of Adjustment, 410 A.2d 1138 (N.J. 1980) (involving application for variance from minimum lot size and minimum street frontage requirements).

issued by the local zoning board, the power to amend a zoning ordinance is vested solely in the local legislature. Even in jurisdictions that allow the use variance, a particular use variance may be held invalid if it resembles a rezoning in practice. For example, a use variance for a large parcel that substantially alters the character of the district—such as allowing a retail mall in the middle of a residential zone—will normally be disallowed. Because of these concerns, the burden of proof is usually greater for a use variance than for an area variance.[22]

[C] Standards for Variance

[1] General Rule

The birthplace of the variance was Section 7 of the Standard State Zoning Enabling Act (see § 36.03[B][3]). It empowered the local zoning board to authorize "in specific cases such variance from the terms of the ordinance as will not be contrary to the public interest, where, owing to special conditions, a literal enforcement of the provisions of the ordinance will result in unnecessary hardship, and so the spirit of the ordinance shall be observed and substantial justice done." Most modern statutes and ordinances still utilize this standard—or one similar to it—as the test for granting a variance. Broadly speaking, then, the prevailing variance standard focuses on two issues: (1) hardship to the property owner; and (2) overall protection of the public interest.[23]

[2] Hardship

What type of hardship is required for a variance? Most courts define hardship to mean that the owner cannot obtain a reasonable return under the existing zoning due to some special characteristic of the property itself that is not generally shared by other parcels in the district.[24]

The hardship must stem from the nature of the land, not from the owner's private need.[25] In other words, there must normally be an unusual physical condition on the land—such as mountainous terrain[26] or irregular lot size[27]

---

[22] See, e.g., Village Bd. v. Jarrold, 423 N.E.2d 385 (N.Y. 1981) (under New York law, use variance is available only if owner proves he cannot obtain a reasonable return from a permitted use).

[23] Cf. Topanga Ass'n for a Scenic Community v. County of Los Angeles, 522 P.2d 12 (Cal. 1974) (holding that issuance of a variance must be accompanied by administrative findings, supported by substantial evidence, showing that the requirements for a variance have been satisfied).

[24] See, e.g., Puritan-Greenfield Improvement Ass'n v. Leo, 153 N.W.2d 162 (Mich. Ct. App. 1967); Village Bd. v. Jarrold, 423 N.E.2d 385 (N.Y. 1981).

[25] See, e.g., Puritan-Greenfield Improvement Ass'n v. Leo, 153 N.W.2d 162 (Mich. App. 1967) (proximity of home to heavy traffic and closeness to business district were not sufficient hardships to justify converting home to dental and medical clinic).

[26] Cf. Topanga Ass'n for a Scenic Community v. County of Los Angeles, 522 P.2d 12 (Cal. 1974).

[27] See, e.g., Commons v. Westwood Zoning Bd. of Adjustment, 410 A.2d 1138 (N.J. 1980).

—that is not found on surrounding parcels. And, in most jurisdictions, the owner must prove that this condition precludes a reasonable return on the land when used in accordance with the current zoning. Suppose, for example, that B owns a ten-acre tract that is zoned only for agricultural use. But because the parcel is essentially a deep, rocky canyon, B cannot obtain a reasonable return by using it for agriculture. Under these unique circumstances, a use variance is appropriate. It should be noted that some jurisdictions utilize a less stringent test for the area variance, requiring only that the existing zoning create "practical difficulties" in using the parcel. [28]

Suppose that O owns a residential lot containing 10,000 square feet; the zoning ordinance requires a minimum lot size of 7,500 feet. O splits his lot into two parcels, one containing 7,500 feet and the other 2,500 feet, and constructs a house on the larger parcel. Can O now claim hardship to obtain a variance to build on the smaller parcel? The answer to this question is "no." O cannot take advantage of the hardship he created. [29]

Another variant on the theme of self-imposed hardship is the buyer who acquires undeveloped property with full knowledge of a zoning problem. Suppose the local zoning ordinance requires that each lot have 75 feet of street frontage; B purchases a vacant lot that has only 50 feet of street frontage and applies for a variance. Some courts will deny relief to a party such as B, reasoning that she created her own dilemma. [30] Presumably B paid a lower purchase price because of the zoning problem, and does not need a variance in order to receive a reasonable return on her investment. The majority approach, however, allows B to obtain the variance; otherwise, society loses the productive value of the land.

The owner's personal hardship is irrelevant. Suppose O owns a home in a zone where the height restriction permits only one-story homes. O has five children and applies for a height variance to add a second story. Here the hardship stems from O's personal needs, not from any unusual characteristic of her land. The variance is designed to ensure that each parcel in the zone receives equal treatment with other parcels, not a special advantage. O's application will be denied.

[3] Protection of Public Interest

The public interest standard focuses on the impact the variance will have on the neighborhood or zoning district. Is the variance consistent with the "spirit of the ordinance" and "substantial justice"? For most courts, the key question is whether the variance will alter the essential character of the area. For example, in *Commons v. Westwood Zoning Board of Adjustment* [31] the New Jersey Supreme Court noted that the zoning board could properly deny a variance to construct a home on an undersized parcel if it would

---

[28] *See, e.g.,* Kisil v. City of Sandusky, 465 N.E.2d 848 (Ohio 1984).

[29] *Cf.* LeBlanc v. City of Barre, 477 A.2d 970 (Vt. 1984).

[30] *See, e.g.,* Clark v. Bd. of Zoning Appeals, 92 N.E.2d 903 (N.Y. 1950).

[31] 410 A.2d 1138 (N.J. 1980).

adversely affect the "character of the neighborhood," considering its impact both on aesthetics and property values.

[D] Procedure for Obtaining Variance

The power to issue variances is typically delegated by ordinance to the board of zoning appeals or a similar agency. After the property owner applies for the variance, the board provides notice to the public and conducts a public hearing on the application. Most states allow the board to impose conditions on the use when granting a variance.[32] An administrative appeal—and eventually a challenge through litigation—is available to parties dissatisfied with the board's decision.

The issuance of a variance is an administrative decision, generally seen as "quasi-judicial" in nature. As a general rule, it is far easier to obtain a variance than to defend it successfully in later litigation. Courts often observe that variances should be sparingly granted.[33] Consistent with this approach, they rigorously review contested variances to ensure that all requirements are met, according little deference to administrative decisions.

§ 37.04 Special Exceptions (aka Conditional or Special Uses)

[A] Role of the Special Exception

The *special exception* is a use that is authorized by the zoning ordinance if specified conditions are met.[34] Typically, it is an unusual use—such as an airport, school, landfill, golf course, or hospital—that may injure the neighborhood. Potential problems include traffic congestion, noise, odors, population density, impact on property values, and similar concerns. The special exception reflects a legislative decision that while the particular use is appropriate in the zone as a *general* matter, certain restrictions are needed to ensure that it does not harm surrounding uses at its *specific* location. Thus, the zoning board reviews applications for special exceptions on a case-by-case basis to ensure the required conditions are met. Depending on the jurisdiction, the special exception may instead be called a conditional use, conditional use permit, special use, or special use permit.

For example, suppose owner O wishes to use her property Greenacre for a dump. The ordinance might allow this use in a particular zone only if O demonstrates to the zoning board that Greenacre meets certain predetermined criteria: (1) it is 50 acres or more in size; (2) it is at least 1,000 feet from the nearest residential use; and (3) it is at least 400 feet from any stream, river, or lake.

---

[32] *See, e.g.,* St. Onge v. Donovan, 522 N.E.2d 1019 (N.Y. 1988).

[33] *See* Matthew v. Smith, 707 S.W.2d 411, 413 (Mo. 1986) (citing numerous cases).

[34] *See generally* Kotrich v. County of Du Page, 166 N.E.2d 601 (Ill. 1960); Zylka v. City of Crystal, 167 N.W.2d 45 (Minn. 1969).

The special exception provides a flexible method for mitigating the impacts of desirable but unusual uses. Without this tool, a zoning ordinance could only prohibit a use (e.g., no dumps are allowed in the zone) or automatically authorize it (e.g., dumps are permitted everywhere in the zone).

[B] Special Exception Distinguished from Variance

Although the special exception is often confused with the variance, it is fundamentally different. The special exception involves a use authorized by the zoning ordinance; in contrast, the variance allows a use that deviates from the ordinance. And the concern underlying the special exception is to prevent harm to surrounding uses, while the variance serves to relieve the property owner from unusual hardship.

[C] Standards for Special Exception

The special exception originated in Section 7 of the Standard State Zoning Enabling Act (see § 36.03[B][3]). This section authorized the local zoning board "in appropriate cases and subject to appropriate conditions and safeguards, [to] make special exceptions to the terms of the ordinance in harmony with its general purpose and intent." It was originally intended that zoning ordinances would list detailed criteria for special exceptions. Thus, the zoning board would have little or no discretion in evaluating an application; it would simply determine whether the criteria were met. Many ordinances still follow this pattern. For example, in the dump hypothetical (see [A], above), O's application must be approved if Greenacre meets three specific tests, one relating to parcel size and two concerning location. Criteria for special exceptions may also relate to project design, noise levels, traffic impacts, parking impacts, and related issues.

On the other hand, many ordinances contain only vague, general criteria for approving special exceptions. An ordinance might authorize a special exception, for example, if it is "consistent with the public health, welfare, and safety." Courts are divided on the issue of whether such vague standards are valid.[35] Ordinances utilizing these standards vest extraordinarily broad discretion in zoning boards and similar administrative bodies. This discretion may allow a zoning board to perform its task more effectively, by carefully tailoring individual conditions to ameliorate the unique impacts of the project. At the same time, vague standards create the danger that decision-making may be arbitrary or unreasonable;[36] this undercuts the Euclidean goal of zoning in accordance with a comprehensive plan. Further, by vesting uncontrolled discretion in an administrative body, these standards may present concerns about separation of powers. While some

---

[35] See 7 Patrick J. Rohan, Zoning & Land Use Controls § 44.03[1] (Matthew Bender).

[36] See, e.g., Zylka v. City of Crystal, 167 N.W.2d 45 (Minn. 1969) (holding that city council's denial of application was arbitrary).

courts permit vague standards, others invalidate them as an improper delegation of legislative authority.[37]

[D] Procedure for Obtaining Special Exception

The procedure for obtaining a special exception involves the same application, notice, hearing, and appeal steps that govern the variance (*see* § 37.03[D]). Where litigation ensues, however, the judicial attitude toward special exceptions is much more favorable than it is toward variances. Because the special exception reflects a legislative decision that the use is permitted in the zone as a general matter, many courts effectively presume that the applicant is entitled to receive the exception.[38]

§ 37.05 New Zoning Tools

[A] Contract Zoning

Suppose O owns a house, Greyacre, located on a busy corner in a residential zone. He plans to convert Greyacre into a grocery store, and accordingly asks the city to rezone the property for commercial use. The neighborhood residents like the idea of having a corner grocery store conveniently nearby. But they are worried that O's store will sell alcohol late at night, which might produce drunken or rowdy behavior. Can O and the city accommodate this concern by entering into an agreement, under which the city consents to rezone Greyacre and O promises to record a covenant that bars his store from selling alcohol after 6:00 p.m.?

A number of decisions hold that such *contract zoning* is invalid. Some courts reason that contract zoning constitutes illegal spot zoning, while others rely on the principle that a public entity cannot contract away its police powers. Recent decisions, however, reflect a trend toward accepting contract zoning.[39]

[B] Conditional Zoning

Conditional zoning closely resembles contract zoning, but with a slight twist: the city or other governmental entity makes no official promise. It identifies the conditions that must be met before rezoning is approved, but—in theory—does not legally bind itself to rezone the land. The owner unilaterally fulfills the conditions, applies for the rezoning, and presumably receives approval.

Consider how conditional zoning might apply to O's effort to rezone Greyacre. The city informs O that he must record a covenant precluding the sale of alcohol after 6:00 p.m. as a condition to any future rezoning.

---

[37] *See, e.g.,* Cope v. Inhabitants of the Town of Brunswick, 464 A.2d 223 (Me. 1983) (ordinance deemed unconstitutional).

[38] *See, e.g.,* North Shore Steak House, Inc. v. Bd. of Appeals, 282 N.E.2d 606 (N.Y. 1972).

[39] *See generally* 1 Patrick J. Rohan, Zoning & Land Use Controls, Ch. 5 (Matthew Bender).

O duly records the covenant, and then reappears before the city council on his rezoning application. The city is free, in theory, to deny the application. But in practice, the application will invariably be granted. Both good faith and the fear of negative publicity will preclude the city from altering its position.

There is a clear national trend toward accepting conditional zoning. In the leading case of *Collard v. Incorporated Village of Flower Hill*,[40] the New York Court of Appeals upheld conditional zoning despite arguments that it constituted spot zoning and bargained away the defendant village's police power. The court reasoned that the test for spot zoning turned on the reasonableness of the rezoning in relation to neighboring uses; the standard for judging the validity of conditional zoning, then, was no different from that applied to unconditional zoning.

[C] Floating Zones

Another emerging tool is the *floating zone*. The city or other government entity approves the creation of a new zoning district with particular characteristics but does not specify its location. A developer can then apply for a rezoning to attach the floating zone to specific property. The main advantage of the floating zone is that it allows a city enhanced control over the location of shopping centers, industrial complexes, and other large-scale projects that may produce significant traffic, parking, and other impacts. Today the floating zone is valid in almost all states. A few states reject the concept, most commonly as either spot zoning or an illegal delegation of legislative power.[41]

[D] Cluster Zones

The *cluster zone* is an innovative approach to the design of the residential subdivision. The traditional zoning ordinance (1) requires that each single-family house be a detached, free-standing building on its own lot and (2) specifies exactly where the house may be built on each lot (e.g., at least 20 feet away from the front and rear lot lines, at least five feet away from each side line). Suppose developer D owns 25 acres zoned for single-family residential use; under the standard formula, she might devote five acres to roads, sideways, and the like, and divide the remaining 20 acres up into 80 lots, each one-quarter acre in size. D would then build 80 houses, one per lot, producing another ordinary suburb.

In contrast, cluster zoning merely imposes a limit on the density of a residential subdivision, allowing the developer to "cluster" the units on part of the land. This, in turn, allows the planned preservation of open space or the creation of new amenities for the development. Suppose D's land is located within a cluster zone that permits 80 housing units on 25 acres of land. D can still build only 80 units, but now she can arrange them in a

---

[40] 421 N.E.2d 818 (N.Y. 1981).

[41] *See generally* 2 Patrick J. Rohan, Zoning & Land Use Controls, Ch. 13 (Matthew Bender).

manner that produces maximum benefit. For example, D might opt to cluster all 80 units on ten acres (e.g., using small lot sizes and common walls), in order to preserve a small lake and surrounding wetlands that occupy the remaining 15 acres.

[E] Planned Unit Developments

The *planned unit development* or *PUD* is the very antithesis of Euclidean zoning, saved from condemnation as "spot zoning"—if at all—by the large size of the typical parcel.[42] In a sense, the PUD is simply the expansion of cluster zoning to include non-residential uses. Within general guidelines, the owner is allowed to master-plan the specific details of a large-scale development project, including the types and locations of permitted uses. The final plan is then presented to zoning authorities for approval.

A PUD ordinance might provide, for example, that no more than 70% of the tract may be devoted to residential use, no more than 15% may be devoted to commercial or retail uses, and at least 10% must be preserved as open space. Within these parameters, the developer is free to select the type and location of housing units, shopping centers, commercial facilities, and other improvements. In effect, the PUD technique permits a private entrepreneur to plan an entire community or neighborhood in a comprehensive manner.

§ 37.06 The Subdivision Process

Although this chapter focuses on zoning, land use controls may also be imposed through a separate and independent method: the subdivision approval process. Suppose E, an entrepreneur, wishes to develop Greenacre, a 500-acre tract of farm land, into a residential subdivision. E confronts two hurdles. First, he must convince the local zoning authority to rezone Greenacre for residential use. Second, he must obtain permission from the planning commission or local legislative body to subdivide Greenacre into separate lots. In order to obtain subdivision approval, E must comply with conditions and restrictions specified by the approving agency; and in some jurisdictions, the agency has broad discretion to deny subdivision applications altogether. The subdivision approval process is thus a second method for ensuring comprehensive land use planning.[43]

A subdivision is simply the legally-recognized division of one parcel of land into multiple parcels, typically four or more lots. Virtually every residential housing tract requires subdivision approval. The typical residential developer seeks to subdivide a large tract of "raw land"—usually agricultural property—into separate lots that accommodate individual houses. Subdivision approval is also required for certain commercial developments (e.g., industrial parks).

---

[42] *See, e.g.,* Cheney v. Village 2 at New Hope, Inc., 241 A.2d 81 (Pa. 1968).

[43] *See generally* Youngblood v. Board of Supervisors, 586 P.2d 556 (Cal. 1978).

Modern subdivision regulation addresses three basic issues: design review; infrastructure financing; and overall acceptability. At the most basic level, local ordinances govern the design or physical layout of the tract to ensure that lots, streets, and utilities are situated in the appropriate locations.

The standard ordinance also requires the developer to construct the streets, sidewalks, storm drains, lighting, parks, and other public infrastructure improvements necessitated by the development. It may also force the developer to mitigate the effect of the project on other public facilities such as schools, libraries, and police and fire services by dedicating land for public use or by paying impact fees. The government power to compel such *exactions* is in turn limited by the Takings Clause of the Fifth Amendment. As the Supreme Court concluded in *Dolan v. City of Tigard*,[44] such exactions must bear a "rough proportionality" to the impacts caused by the development (*see* § 40.08).

In many jurisdictions, the responsible agency is obligated to approve each subdivision application that meets the minimum standards imposed by local ordinance. In some jurisdictions, however, the agency has discretion to deny the application or delay the project, if required by the public health, safety, or welfare (e.g., if the project would cause unreasonable off-site traffic impacts).[45] There is a clear national trend toward authorizing such discretionary denial in order to enhance planning flexibility.

---

[44] 512 U.S. 374 (1994).

[45] *See, e.g.*, Durant v. Town of Dunbarton, 430 A.2d 140 (N.H. 1981) (subdivision application properly denied because project posed threat of flooding and contamination of groundwater by sewage).

Chapter 38

MODERN ZONING CONTROVERSIES

§ 38.01   The Transformation of "Zoning"

The pioneer zoners of the 1920s would undoubtedly be shocked by our modern system of land use regulation.[1] Particularly in recent decades, the

---

[1] *See generally* Robert C. Ellickson, *Alternatives to Zoning: Covenants, Nuisance Rules, and Fines as Land Use Controls*, 40 U. Chi. L. Rev. 681 (1973); Bradley C. Karkkainen, *Zoning: A Reply to the Critics*, 10 J. Land Use & Envtl. L. 45 (1994); Bernard H. Siegan, *Non-Zoning is the Best Zoning*, 31 Cal. W. L. Rev. 127 (1994).

simple world of Euclidean zoning has yielded to a complex universe of pervasive land use restrictions. The goals and the nature of "zoning" have fundamentally changed.

In its classic 1926 decision of *Village of Euclid v. Ambler Realty Co.*,[2] the Supreme Court justified a typical zoning ordinance as little more than a nuisance control measure; the ordinance minimized the adverse effects of smoke, fumes, noise, and other problems. Today, land use regulation serves a broad array of additional social and economic goals. These new goals include

(1)   protecting property values (particularly for single-family homes),

(2)   preserving the "character" of neighborhoods,

(3)   preventing environmental degradation,

(4)   enhancing the property tax base, and

(5)   encouraging tourism and other economic development.

The nature of zoning has evolved over time to serve these expanded goals. Euclidean zoning merely regulated the geographic location of particular uses; the basic question was *where* a use could be placed. But modern land use regulation prohibits various uses, even those that are not common law nuisances. Increasingly, we ask *if* a particular use (or sometimes, a particular user) should be allowed at all within the municipality. At its outer edges, the transformation of zoning raises difficult questions about individual liberty, economic efficiency, public welfare, democratic theory, and social justice. For example, should Town A be allowed to bar unrelated persons from living together? May City B prohibit all apartments and other multi-family housing, thereby excluding low-income residents? Can Village C ban an unusually-designed house? And may Town D proscribe all new residential development? In short, how far can a democratically-elected city council or other local legislature go in exercising its land use regulation power?

Questions like these have generated extensive litigation since the 1970s. Challenges to land use regulations based on the federal Constitution, state constitutions, and the Fair Housing Act in particular have enjoyed occasional but limited success. The resulting case law is dominated by a small number of well-known decisions—mainly from the Supreme Court—that provide only limited guidance. Thus, this area requires the careful study of individual decisions that illuminate the broad contours of the law, but in fact resolve fairly narrow issues.

Will our current system of land use regulation undergo major change in the foreseeable future? Probably not. A handful of legal scholars—led by Robert Ellickson and Richard Epstein—urge that the system should be either abolished or dramatically curtailed. Epstein's laissez faire approach would largely rely on market forces to make efficient land use decisions, on the model of Houston—the only major United States city without

---

[2] 272 U.S. 365 (1926).

zoning.[3] In contrast, Ellickson argues that a blend of private covenants, nuisance law, and administrative fines—together with minimal land use regulations—would minimize the negative externalities that Epstein's model permits.[4] Yet there is no widespread demand for abolition or radical change. Indeed, in all likelihood, land use regulation will become even more pervasive in future decades, as government confronts the increasing demands placed on our finite land surface by population growth, economic development, technological change, environmental degradation, and other pressures.

§ 38.02   Zoning and the Constitutional Framework

[A]   Federal Constitution

[1]   Overview

The Constitution is the ultimate constraint on the zoning power. A short (and admittedly simplistic) overview of relevant provisions will help the reader to understand the balance of the chapter. Zoning challenges most frequently involve the Equal Protection, Due Process, and Takings Clauses (*see* Chapter 40) and the First Amendment protection for freedom of speech.[5]

[2]   Equal Protection

The Equal Protection Clause of the Fourteenth Amendment provides that no state shall "deny to any person within its jurisdiction the equal protection of the laws."[6] Equal protection challenges to land use regulations are usually reviewed under either the "strict scrutiny" or "rational basis" standard. The more searching standard—*strict scrutiny*—applies when an ordinance or other regulation discriminates against a "suspect class" (e.g., a class based on race, alienage, or national origin) or infringes a "fundamental right" (e.g., freedom of speech or religion). Under this standard, the ordinance is valid only if it is supported by a compelling state interest; the party seeking to uphold the ordinance has the burden of proof.

Otherwise, the regulation is presumed to be valid and is reviewed under the deferential *rational basis* test. "When social or economic legislation is at issue, the Equal Protection Clause allows the States wide latitude, . . . and the Constitution presumes that even improvident decisions will

---

[3] *See* Richard A. Epstein, *A Conceptual Approach to Zoning: What's Wrong with* Euclid?, 5 N.Y.U. Envtl. L.J. 277 (1996).

[4] *See* Robert C. Ellickson, *Alternatives to Zoning: Covenants, Nuisance Rules, and Fines as Land Use Controls,* 40 U. Chi. L. Rev. 681 (1973).

[5] Land use regulation occasionally triggers review under the Free Exercise Clause of the First Amendment, which guarantees freedom of religion (e.g., where a municipality refuses to rezone land to allow operation of a church). *See, e.g.,* Messiah Baptist Church v. County of Jefferson, 859 F.2d 820 (10th Cir. 1988).

[6] U.S. Const. amend. XIV.

eventually be rectified by the democratic processes."[7] Under this standard, a regulation will be upheld if it is rationally related to a legitimate state interest—usually the public health, safety, or welfare. And the party challenging the regulation has the burden of establishing that no rational relationship exists. As one authority noted, this traditional standard is so deferential to the local legislature that it "approximates a rule of non-review."[8] There is some suggestion that the Supreme Court is moving toward a more rigorous version of the rational basis test, dubbed "rational basis with bite."[9] In practice, the applicable review standard usually determines the outcome of an equal protection challenge. Courts rarely find a compelling state interest, but usually find a rational basis.

[3] Due Process

The Due Process Clause of the Fourteenth Amendment provides that no state shall "deprive any person of life, liberty, or property, without due process of law."[10] Due process has two prongs: procedural and substantive. Procedural due process focuses on the fundamental fairness of the procedures used to deprive a person of life, liberty, or property. For example, procedural due process ordinarily requires that the state provide notice and an opportunity for a hearing before depriving an owner of his or her property rights.

Substantive due process, in contrast, is a rather vague and ill-defined doctrine. Since the early nineteenth century, the Supreme Court has been reluctant to apply substantive due process to economic and social legislation. This has contributed to uncertainty about the meaning of the doctrine. Substantive due process examines the substance or content of the governmental decision, as opposed to the procedure by which the decision was reached. It provides a safeguard against arbitrary, capricious, or unreasonable decisions. In general, the basic test for substantive due process seems to be the same used for equal protection: unless a fundamental right is involved, a land use regulation will be upheld if it has a rational relationship to the public health, safety, or welfare, or another legitimate governmental interest. If a fundamental right is involved, the regulation will be subject to strict scrutiny review.

[4] Freedom of Speech

Government regulation of forms of speech—such as signs and sexually-oriented businesses[11] —may invoke review under the First Amendment.[12]

---

[7] City of Cleburne v. Cleburne Living Ctr., Inc., 473 U.S. 432, 440 (1985).

[8] Julian C. Juergensmeyer & Thomas E. Roberts, Land Use Planning and Control Law 468 (1998).

[9] See City of Cleburne v. Cleburne Living Ctr., 473 U.S. 432 (1985) (applying more rigorous "rational basis" standard).

[10] U.S. Const. amend. XIV.

[11] See, e.g., City of Renton v. Playtime Theatres, 475 U.S. 41 (1986); Buzzetti v. City of New York, 140 F.3d 134 (1998).

[12] U.S. Const. amend. I.

The key distinction is between land use restrictions that regulate the content of speech ("content-based") and those that do not ("content-neutral"). Content-neutral regulations on the time, place, and manner of speech are upheld when (a) the government interest is "substantial," (b) the regulation directly advances that interest, and (c) the regulation is no broader than necessary to serve that interest.[13] Especially in the context of sexually-oriented businesses, courts emphasize that the regulation must not unreasonably limit alternative avenues of communication. On the other hand, a content-based regulation is valid only if the government demonstrates that the regulation serves a "compelling" interest rather than a mere substantial interest, and also establishes the final two criteria above.

[B] State Constitutions

State constitutions usually include provisions that parallel the federal Constitution, such as rights to equal protection, due process,[14] privacy, and freedom of speech. Yet state courts are free to construe these provisions more broadly than their federal counterparts. Because a state's own supreme court holds the ultimate authority to interpret its state constitution, a decision based on state constitutional grounds cannot be overturned by federal courts. For example, a land use regulation might be invalidated under the state equal protection clause, even though it satisfies the federal Equal Protection Clause. And state courts are far more willing than federal courts to strike down regulations based on substantive due process.

§ 38.03 "Family" Zoning

[A] The Issue

Town A's zoning ordinance permits only one type of residential use—"single-family dwellings." The ordinance defines "family" as "one or more persons related by blood, adoption, or marriage, or a group of two persons who are not related by blood, adoption, or marriage." In effect, such zoning excludes groups of unrelated people. Suppose that college student E wishes to share a house in Town A with three unrelated students. And N, a charitable association, plans to open a "group home" in the town that will shelter ten mentally-ill children. Can E or N successfully attack A's ordinance?

Family zoning is usually justified on the basis that it reduces traffic, noise, congestion, overcrowding, and other problems related to density, and—more vaguely—protects the family or residential character of a neighborhood. For example, consider two adjacent single-family homes: one is occupied by 20 members of a motorcycle gang, while a nuclear family consisting of two parents and two children resides in the other. All other things being

---

[13] Central Hudson Gas & Elec. Co. v. Public Serv. Comm'n, 447 U.S. 557 (1980).

[14] *See, e.g.,* Guimont v. Clarke, 854 P.2d 1 (Wash. 1993) (invalidating ordinance under due process clause in state constitution).

equal, we would reasonably expect more density problems from the first house. Of course, a city might deal with such problems by simply imposing a reasonable maximum occupancy limit regardless of any relationship among the occupants.

Challenges to the validity of family zoning surface most frequently in the two scenarios outlined above: (a) a group of unrelated persons—typically college students—decides to live together as roommates; or (b) a non-profit organization seeks to establish a group home for persons in need of special supervision. As a general matter, courts tend to uphold family zoning against attacks based on the federal or state constitutions; thus E will probably not prevail. On the other hand, in the specialized context of group homes for the handicapped, there is a clear trend in the other direction. N's challenge will probably be successful, based either on constitutional principles or the federal Fair Housing Act.

[B] Unrelated "Families" Generally

[1] *Village of Belle Terre v. Boraas*

In 1974, the Supreme Court upheld "family" zoning against due process and equal protection challenges in *Village of Belle Terre v. Boraas*.[15] The Village of Belle Terre is a community near the New York State University at Stony Brook. Apparently hoping to exclude college students, the Village enacted a typical "family" zoning ordinance. The ordinance permitted only one-family dwellings, expressly barring fraternity houses and similar uses. "Family" was defined as "[o]ne or more persons related by blood, adoption, or marriage" or up to "two (2) [persons] . . . not related by blood, adoption, or marriage."[17] In effect, only two unrelated persons could inhabit a particular dwelling, but an unlimited number of related persons could occupy the adjacent house. The case arose when six unrelated students leased a house together; the Village objected; the landlords and tenants jointly sued for a declaratory judgment that the ordinance was unconstitutional.

The pivotal question before the Court was the applicable standard of review. Writing for the majority, Justice Douglas blended the equal protection and due process issues together. He viewed the ordinance as mere social and economic regulation that did not involve either a fundamental right or a suspect class.[18] Under these circumstances, the ordinance would be upheld if it was reasonable and not arbitrary, having a rational relationship to a permissible state objective. Douglas concluded that the ordinance

---

[15] 416 U.S. 1 (1974).

[17] Village of Belle Terre v. Boraas 416 U.S. 1, 2 (1974). Courts may circumvent less precise ordinances through interpretation, without the need to confront constitutional issues. *See, e.g.,* Borough of Glassboro v. Vallorosi, 568 A.2d 888, 889 (N.J. 1990) (construing "traditional family unit or the functional equivalency [sic] thereof" to include ten unrelated college students living together).

[18] It is well-settled that the Constitution does not create any right to housing. Lindsey v. Normet, 405 U.S. 56 (1972). And wealth is not considered a suspect classification under the Equal Protection Clause. San Antonio Indep. School Dist. v. Rodriguez, 411 U.S. 1 (1973).

easily met this deferential standard because it reduced the traffic, parking, noise, and other urban problems caused by group living arrangements. "The police power is not confined to elimination of filth, stench, and unhealthy places. It is ample to lay out zones where family values, youth values, and the blessings of quiet seclusion and clean air make the area a sanctuary for people."[19]

Dissenting, Justice Marshall argued that the ordinance unreasonably burdened two fundamental rights—the rights of association and privacy—and thus was subject to "strict scrutiny" review. "The choice of household companions . . . involves deeply personal considerations as to the kind and quality of intimate relationships within the home. . . . The instant ordinance discriminates on the basis of just such a personal lifestyle choice as to household companions."[20] The ordinance certainly would have been struck down under strict scrutiny review. Marshall reasoned that as a means to control density problems, the ordinance was both underinclusive (e.g., because it did not limit the total number of persons who could live in a house) and overinclusive (e.g., because it barred groups such as "three elderly and retired persons").[21]

[2] Developments After *Belle Terre*

After *Belle Terre,* challenges to "family" zoning mainly focused on state constitutional theories. State courts are split on the issue. Following the lead of *Belle Terre,* a majority hold that their state constitutions do not prohibit "family" zoning.[22] States that reject this approach—often employing a more rigorous standard of review—stress Justice Marshall's point that the means are not rationally related to the end of controlling density-related problems. "Under the instant ordinance, twenty male cousins could live together, motorcycles, noise, and all, while three unrelated clerics could not."[23] Two interesting examples of the minority view are decisions from New Jersey[24] and Michigan,[25] both invalidating "family" zoning in cases involving Christian groups who live together as nontraditional families because of their religious beliefs.

In 1977—three years after *Belle Terre*—the Supreme Court addressed a related issue in *Moore v. City of East Cleveland.*[26] The East Cleveland zoning ordinance provided that only a "family" could occupy a dwelling, but defined the term so narrowly that some blood relations were excluded. Defendant Moore lived in a single-family residence with three relatives: one of her sons (Dale) and two of her grandchildren (Dale, Jr. and John, Jr.).

---

[19] Village of Belle Terre v. Boraas, 416 U.S. 1, 9 (1974).

[20] Village of Belle Terre v. Boraas, 416 U.S. 1, 16 (1974) (Marshall, J., dissenting).

[21] Village of Belle Terre v. Boraas, 416 U.S. 1, 19 (1974) (Marshall, J., dissenting).

[22] *See, e.g.,* City of Ladue v. Horn, 720 S.W.2d 745 (Mo. Ct. App. 1986).

[23] Charter Township of Delta v. Dinolfo, 351 N.W.2d 831, 841 (Mich. 1984).

[24] State v. Baker, 405 A.2d 368 (N.J. 1979).

[25] Charter Township of Delta v. Dinolfo, 351 N.W.2d 831 (Mich. 1984).

[26] 431 U.S. 494 (1977).

The City filed criminal charges against Moore on the basis that John, Jr.—
the son of Moore's nonresident son John—was not a family member as
defined by the ordinance. While acknowledging that substantive due
process was a "treacherous field," a divided Court struck down the ordinance on this basis.[27] The plurality opinion distinguished *Belle Terre* as
involving only unrelated individuals, while the East Cleveland ordinance
directly interfered with "the sanctity of the family."[28] Under the more rigorous scrutiny triggered by this distinction, the ordinance failed. While the
ordinance was intended to serve legitimate goals (e.g., reducing traffic,
parking, and other density-related problems), in fact it did little to advance
these goals.

In the wake of *Belle Terre* and *Moore,* could a city constitutionally bar
an unmarried couple from a "family" zone? The *Belle Terre* majority had
no need to reach this issue because the ordinance expressly permitted two
unrelated persons to cohabit. Concern for the rights of privacy and association might well be greater if an ordinance barred all unrelated cohabitants.
On the other hand, *Moore* seemed to reinforce the traditional definition of
a family by sharply distinguishing between blood relations and unrelated
persons. Accordingly, one lower federal court upheld such an ordinance; it
acknowledged the "governmental interest in marriage and in preserving
the integrity of the biological or legal family," but found no parallel interest
in "keeping together a group of unrelated persons."[29]

[C] Group Homes

[1] Nature of Group Homes

The typical group home is a small non-profit facility for the treatment
or rehabilitation of persons who need special care, such as battered women,
teenage delinquents, elderly persons, persons infected with AIDS, drug
addicts, paroled prisoners, mentally-ill persons, and alcoholics. Thus, the
group home serves persons who might otherwise be placed in hospitals,
asylums, prisons, or similar public institutions.

Controversy has flared in recent years over the development of group
homes in single-family residential neighborhoods. Supporters stress that
the group home provides better care than large institutions and at a smaller
cost; in particular, the residential neighborhood surrounding a group home
helps to create a comfortable atmosphere that facilitates effective treatment. Opponents complain about (1) noise, traffic, and other density-related
problems, (2) the heightened risk of violence or other criminal activity, and
(3) the reduction of property values. Once the local legislative body weighs
these competing policy arguments and renders a decision on a proposed
group home, the losing side frequently turns to litigation.

---

[27] Moore v. City of East Cleveland, 431 U.S. 494, 502 (1977).

[28] Moore v. City of East Cleveland, 431 U.S. 494, 503 (1977).

[29] City of Ladue v. Horn, 720 S.W.2d 745, 752 (Mo. Ct. App. 1986).

[2] Equal Protection

The landmark Supreme Court decision in the area is *City of Cleburne v. Cleburne Living Center, Inc.* [30] Plaintiffs wished to open a group home for 13 mentally-retarded persons in a single-family residence. The residence was located in a district that allowed apartment houses, boarding houses, most hospitals, and similar multi-occupant uses as a matter of right; however, a special use permit was required for any hospital for the "feeble-minded." Plaintiffs brought suit after their use permit application was denied, claiming that the ordinance on its face and as applied violated the Equal Protection Clause.

In a rather curious decision, the Court invalidated the ordinance. Concluding that the mentally retarded were not a suspect class or "quasi-suspect class," it recited that the ordinance should be reviewed under the rational basis standard. Yet the Court seemed to apply a form of heightened scrutiny—later dubbed "rational basis with bite"—by imposing the burden of proof on the party seeking to uphold the ordinance, contrary to traditional practice. For example, the city had objected to the facility in part based on its location: across the street from a junior high school and in a flood plain. One might easily find a "rational basis" here for treating mentally retarded persons differently from others; they are more likely to be harassed by teenage students, and are less able to care for themselves during a flood emergency. But the Court brushed aside these concerns, seemingly because the city had failed to provide proof that supported the differential treatment.

[3] Fair Housing Act

During the last decade, the federal Fair Housing Act has become the principal weapon against zoning ordinances that exclude group homes for the handicapped. The 1998 amendments to the Act extend its anti-discrimination protections to handicapped persons, defined to include persons with "a physical or mental impairment which substantially limits one or more of such person's major life activities." [31] Under the Act as amended, it is unlawful to make housing "unavailable . . . because of a handicap" [32] or to refuse to make "reasonable accommodations in rules [or] policies" to allow handicapped persons to occupy a dwelling. [33] Although the Act is primarily aimed at discriminatory conduct by private persons (mainly sellers and landlords), these provisions also apply to zoning ordinances and other governmental activities that effectively exclude group homes for the handicapped. [34]

---

[30] 473 U.S. 432 (1985).

[31] 42 U.S.C. § 3602(h)(1).

[32] 42 U.S.C. § 3604(f)(1).

[33] 42 U.S.C. § 3604(f)(3).

[34] *See* Doe v. City of Butler, 892 F.2d 315 (3d Cir. 1989) (discussing whether ordinance that precluded group home shelter for abused women and children was discrimination based on "familial status" that violated Fair Housing Act).

The Supreme Court brushed aside one potential roadblock to such application of the Fair Housing Act in *City of Edmonds v. Oxford House, Inc.* [35] Under the zoning ordinance in Edmonds, Washington, a single-family dwelling could be occupied by (1) an unlimited number of persons related by genetics, adoption, or marriage or (2) five or less unrelated persons. When the city brought criminal charges against Oxford House—which operated a group home for 10-12 recovering alcoholics and drug addicts in a single-family zone—it raised the Fair Housing Act as a defense. Yet the Act expressly does not apply to any "reasonable . . . restrictio[n] regarding the maximum number of occupants permitted to occupy a dwelling."[36] The city then filed a separate action seeking a declaratory judgment that its ordinance was entirely exempt from the Act on this basis, which eventually wound up before the Court. The Court flatly held that the ordinance was not a maximum occupancy restriction because it did not cap the total number of persons who could live in a dwelling; it clearly allowed occupancy by an unlimited number of related persons. The ordinance was intended to preserve the family character of a neighborhood, not to control density-related problems.

Although the *City of Edmonds* court expressly refused to decide the broader question—whether the ordinance in fact violated the Fair Housing Act—a number of lower courts have applied the Act to invalidate similar ordinances[37] and this seems to be the modern trend.[38]

§ 38.04 Exclusionary Zoning

[A] The Issue

City B zones 90% of its land for single-family residential use only, with a required minimum lot size of five acres; the remaining land is zoned for commercial, industrial, or governmental purposes. No land is zoned for apartments or other multi-family residential uses. O wishes to construct an apartment complex for low-income tenants. Can O successfully challenge B's zoning plan?

Exclusionary zoning refers to land-use controls that tend to exclude low-income and minority groups.[39] The most obvious example is the refusal to

---

[35] 514 U.S. 725 (1995).

[36] 42 U.S.C. § 3607(b)(1).

[37] *See, e.g.,* Association for Advancement of the Mentally Handicapped, Inc. v. City of Elizabeth, 876 F. Supp. 614 (D.N.J. 1994). *But see, e.g.,* Oxford House-C v. City of St. Louis, 77 F.3d 249 (8th Cir. 1996) (upholding ordinance).

[38] *See also* Larkin v. Michigan Dep't of Social Servs., 89 F.3d 285 (6th Cir. 1996) (invalidating ordinance provisions that mandated 1,500 foot separation between group homes and required notice to municipality before beginning operation). *But see* Familystyle of St. Paul, Inc. v. City of St. Paul, 923 F.2d 91 (8th Cir. 1991) (upholding rules requiring a one-quarter mile separation between group homes).

[39] *See generally* Martha Lamar, *et al.,* Mount Laurel *at Work: Affordable Housing in New Jersey, 1983-1988,* 41 Rutgers L. Rev. 1197 (1989); Lawrence G. Sager, *Tight Little Islands: Exclusionary Zoning, Equal Protection and the Indigent,* 21 Stan. L. Rev. 767 (1969).

allow high-density, low-income housing, as in the above hypothetical. Other exclusionary zoning techniques include requirements for large lot sizes and minimum floor space, and prohibitions on the use of manufactured housing. Whatever the technique, the result is the same: the cost of housing becomes so high that low-income residents are priced out of the housing market. And—because minority residents are more likely to be poor—these techniques tend to foster racial discrimination.[40]

Three justifications for exclusionary zoning are commonly advanced. First, it protects open space and aesthetic values by ensuring low-density development. Second, such zoning upholds property values by restricting low-cost development. Finally, it promotes high-quality public services at a minimal tax cost, by limiting the number of residents who utilize schools and other governmental services. A simplistic example illustrates this final point. Suppose a $500,000 single-family home in a city with exclusionary zoning adds two children to the local school system. In contrast, assume that a $500,000 apartment complex with 10 units in an ordinary city adds 20 children to the system. Assuming a property tax rate of 1% in both cities, each property will yield $5,000 in tax revenue each year. If the entire amount is devoted to education, schools in the first city receive $2,500 per student, while those in the second receive only $250 per student.

Is exclusionary zoning a legitimate use of the zoning power? In the wake of the landmark *Village of Euclid v. Ambler Realty Co.* decision (*see* § 36.05), American courts were extremely deferential to local legislative zoning decisions, even if they had exclusionary effects. Yet the underlying rationale for such deference—respecting the will of voters who selected the legislative body—had less force when applied to exclusionary zoning because potential residents excluded by this practice were not entitled to vote. In the modern era, exclusionary zoning ordinances have been invalidated in suits premised on state constitutions or the federal Fair Housing Act; but challenges based on the federal Constitution have been less successful.

[B] Exclusion of Multi-Family Housing

[1] Federal Decisions

[a] *Village of Arlington Heights v. Metropolitan Housing Development Corporation*

The most influential decision on the constitutionality of exclusionary zoning is *Village of Arlington Heights v. Metropolitan Housing Development Corporation*,[41] where the Supreme Court upheld a rezoning denial against

---

[40] A related problem is the placement of waste treatment plants and other undesirable land uses in poor or minority communities, often attacked as *environmental racism. See, e.g.,* Coalition of Concerned Citizens Against I-670 v. Damian, 608 F. Supp. 110 (S.D. Ohio 1984) (refusing injunction against highway project); Bean v. Southwestern Waste Management Corp., 482 F. Supp. 673 (S.D. Tex. 1979) (refusing injunction against solid waste facility).

[41] 429 U.S. 252 (1977).

an equal protection challenge in 1977. The defendant Village, an over-whelmingly-white suburb of Chicago, was mainly zoned for single-family residences. Plaintiff planned to develop a federally-subsidized, racially integrated housing project for low and moderate-income residents; the project site was a 15-acre parcel in a neighborhood zoned for single-family use only. The Village denied plaintiff's application to rezone the land for multi-family use, consistent with its policy that multi-family uses were permitted only as a buffer zone between single-family and industrial uses. Plaintiff sued, alleging that the denial was based on racial discrimination that violated (a) the Equal Protection Clause of the Fourteenth Amendment and (b) the Fair Housing Act.

The pivotal question before the Court was the applicable standard of equal protection review. It refused to apply the strict scrutiny standard because there was insufficient proof that discriminatory *intent* was a motivating factor in the Village's decision. The discriminatory *effect* of the decision—standing alone—did not trigger such review. The Court observed that a racially discriminatory effect could be considered in assessing intent where, for example, facially-neutral government action reflected a depar-ture from official policy or produced "a clear pattern, unexplainable on grounds other than race."[42] However, the Court found that neither situa-tion was present. The facts demonstrated that the Village had consistently applied its "buffer zone" policy in the past. Yet the Court failed to explain why a "clear pattern" of discriminatory effect was absent. Racial minorities constituted 18% of Chicago area residents; but African-American residents comprised only about 1/20th of 1% of the Village's population (27 of 64,000 residents). The Court implicitly accepted the district court's conclusion that the rezoning denial was valid under the "rational basis" standard. It re-manded the Fair Housing Act claim, however, for further consideration below.

Arlington Heights effectively closed the door to exclusionary zoning challenges based on the Equal Protection Clause. Absent unusual circum-stances, it is impossible to prove that an exclusionary zoning ordinance was motivated by discriminatory intent.

[b] Fair Housing Act

With *Arlington Heights* looming as a roadblock to equal protection challenges, attention shifted in the late 1970s to challenges based on the Fair Housing Act of 1968 (*see* § 16.02[B][1]). The Act is mainly aimed at discrimination in the sale or rental of housing, and thus focused on actions of sellers and landlords. But the Act also provides that it is unlawful to "otherwise make unavailable or deny, a dwelling to any person" because of covered discrimination, and federal courts have utilized this provision to invalidate exclusionary zoning ordinances.

Lower federal courts generally agree that proof of a racially discrimina-tory *effect* is sufficient to establish a prima facie case that a zoning decision

---

[42] Village of Arlington Heights v. Metropolitan Housing Dev. Corp., 429 U.S. 252, 266 (1977).

violates the Act, even without evidence of discriminatory *intent*. As a result, the Act has become a powerful weapon against exclusionary zoning.

The leading case on point is *Huntington Branch, NAACP v. Town of Huntington*,[43] whose facts are quite similar to those in *Arlington Heights*. Plaintiffs planned to construct a racially integrated housing project for low-income residents in a neighborhood that was 98% white. Because the project site—like almost all residential land in the town—was zoned for single-family residences only, plaintiffs requested that the site be rezoned for multi-family use. The town board denied the application, citing traffic, health, and other concerns. The Second Circuit found that the decision had racially discriminatory effects because (1) it perpetuated segregation and (2) it disproportionately affected African-American residents, who had a greater need for low-income housing than did white residents. This established a prima facie case of discrimination under the Act, and shifted the burden to the town (1) to present legitimate justifications for its action and (2) to demonstrate that less discriminatory alternatives were unavailable. Because the town was unable to meet this burden, the court ordered that the site be rezoned.

[2] State Decisions

Even before *Arlington Heights*, exclusionary zoning had been successfully attacked under state constitutional law. The state court attack on exclusionary zoning is dominated by twin decisions of the New Jersey Supreme Court—both entitled *Southern Burlington County NAACP v. Township of Mt. Laurel*—commonly called *Mt. Laurel I*[44] and *Mt. Laurel II*.[45] Based on the New Jersey Constitution, the court held that almost every local government was obligated to meet its "fair share" of the regional need for low and moderate-income housing. This "fair share" approach has been followed in other jurisdictions, notably New Hampshire,[46] New York,[47] and Pennsylvania.[48]

In 1975, when *Mt. Laurel I* was decided, the Township of Mt. Laurel was a developing suburb within commuting distance of both Camden, New Jersey and Philadelphia, Pennsylvania. Only about 35% of the township's 14,000 acres had been developed, mainly in the form of detached single-family residences. Mt. Laurel effectively excluded all low-income housing because virtually the entire township was zoned for industrial use (29%), detached single-family residences (70%), and retail uses (1%). Multi-family housing developments were simply not allowed anywhere under the basic

---

[43] 844 F.2d 926 (2d Cir.), *aff'd* 488 U.S. 15 (1988).

[44] 336 A.2d 713 (N.J. 1975).

[45] 456 A.2d 390 (N.J. 1983).

[46] *See, e.g.,* Britton v. Town of Chester, 595 A.2d 492 (N.H. 1991).

[47] *See, e.g.,* Berenson v. Town of New Castle, 341 N.E.2d 236 (N.Y. 1975). *But see* Asian Americans for Equality v. Koch, 527 N.E.2d 265 (N.Y. 1988) (refusing to apply *Mt. Laurel* standard to New York City).

[48] *See, e.g.,* Surrick v. Zoning Hearing Board, 382 A.2d 105 (Pa. 1977); Fernley v. Board of Supervisors, 502 A.2d 585 (Pa. 1985).

zoning ordinance.[49] Although a substantial number of apartments and townhouses were included in three planned unit developments, the ordinance required the developers to provide various amenities that increased the price of these units beyond the reach of low- and moderate-income families.

In *Mt. Laurel I,* the New Jersey Supreme Court concluded that the township's zoning ordinance violated the equal protection and due process provisions of the state constitution. The court attributed Mt. Laurel's zoning plan to the state's tax structure, which created a fiscal incentive for developing communities to exclude the poor: "Almost every one acts solely in its own selfish and parochial interest and in effect builds a wall around itself to keep out those people or entities not adding favorably to the tax base."[50] Yet, because a municipality exercises zoning power delegated by the state, the court concluded that it was restricted in the same manner as the state. Thus, a community like Mt. Laurel was obligated to consider the general welfare of all persons in the region, not simply the parochial interests of its current residents. As a result, the court held that every developing municipality has a presumptive obligation to provide "an appropriate variety and choice of housing," including low- and moderate-income housing, to satisfy its fair share of the regional need.[51] On the facts, Mt. Laurel failed to establish "valid superseding reasons"[52] that would overcome this presumption. The court accordingly ordered Mt. Laurel to correct its zoning ordinance within 90 days or such additional time as the trial court permitted.

An outraged New Jersey Supreme Court revisited the controversy eight years later. Despite the court's order in *Mt. Laurel I,* the township's zoning ordinance continued to exclude the poor; only 20 acres had been rezoned for low-income housing. Determined to "put some steel into that doctrine," the *Mt. Laurel II*[53] court crafted a 120-page opinion that expanded the "fair share" principle in three important ways. First, it held that all municipalities designated by the state as growth areas were bound by the doctrine, not merely "developing" municipalities; this extended the doctrine to almost all of New Jersey other than urban areas. Second, it required municipalities to take affirmative measures to encourage construction of low- and moderate-income housing. The court reasoned that merely eliminating obstacles like exclusionary zoning ordinances was insufficient. Rather, municipalities were obligated to

---

[49] Indeed, such exclusionary zoning appeared to be valid under prior New Jersey law. *See, e.g.,* Vickers v. Gloucester Township, 181 A.2d 129 (N.J. 1962) (upholding zoning ordinance that banned mobile homes).

[50] Southern Burlington County NAACP v. Township of Mt. Laurel, 336 A.2d 713, 723 (N.J. 1975).

[51] Southern Burlington County NAACP v. Township of Mt. Laurel, 336 A.2d 713, 731 (N.J. 1975).

[52] Southern Burlington County NAACP v. Township of Mt. Laurel, 336 A.2d 713, 730 (N.J. 1975).

[53] Southern Burlington County NAACP v. Township of Mt. Laurel, 456 A.2d 390, 410 (N.J. 1983).

(1)   help developers obtain state and federal subsidies for low- and moderate-income housing projects,

(2)   provide incentives to developers to build such housing (e.g., allowing increased density),

(3)   require that developers include a minimum amount of low- and moderate-income housing in any future housing project, and/or

(4)   utilize other affirmative methods for meeting the fair share requirement.

Actual success—not merely good faith effort—was required. Finally, the court authorized an innovative procedure known as the *builder's remedy*; if a municipality refused to allow construction of a housing project in violation of its "fair share" obligation, a trial court could allow the project to proceed unless it "is clearly contrary to sound land use planning."[54]

By adding teeth to the toothless *Mt. Laurel I*, *Mt. Laurel II* generated extraordinary controversy.[55] Ultimately, New Jersey supplanted part of the holding through legislation[56] that created a new agency to grapple with the low-income housing problem and suspended the builder's remedy. Yet it was not until 1997—22 years after *Mt. Laurel I*—that the Township of Mt. Laurel finally approved its first low-income housing project.

[C] Other Exclusionary Zoning Techniques

Other zoning techniques—such as minimum lot size requirements, minimum floor space requirements, and bans on manufactured housing—can produce the same exclusionary effect as an outright prohibition on multi-family housing. By increasing the cost of housing, they price low-income families out of the community. Yet attacks on such exclusionary techniques have produced mixed results.

Large minimum lot size requirements in residential zones (e.g., 5,000 square feet, two acres, or five acres) are usually upheld as appropriate methods to reduce traffic congestion, sanitation problems, fire danger, and density concerns. Minimum floor space standards (e.g., 1,400 square feet) have proven somewhat more vulnerable to challenge. Particularly when no limit is placed on the number of residents, it is difficult to justify such standards as necessary to protect the health, safety, or general welfare. Finally, although bans on manufactured housing have long been upheld, the law is gradually changing. Most courts still reason—as in the past—that concerns based on aesthetics, protection of property values, and health and safety risks are sufficient to bar mobile homes and other forms of manufactured housing. However, a number of states have enacted legislation that curtails the ability of local governments to ban or restrict such housing.

---

[54] Southern Burlington County NAACP v. Township of Mt. Laurel, 456 A.2d 390, 452 (N.J. 1983).

[55] The principles of *Mt. Laurel II* have not been adopted by other jurisdictions. *But cf.* Britton v. Town of Chester, 595 A.2d 492 (N.H. 1991) (upholding trial court's use of builder's remedy).

[56] *See generally* Hills Dev. Co. v. Township of Bernards, 510 A.2d 621 (N.J. 1986) (upholding constitutionality of legislation).

§ 38.05 Aesthetic Zoning

[A] The Issue

C, a small western village, seeks to attract tourists and thereby support local businesses; the village council enacts an ordinance that mandates that all new buildings must utilize an architectural design "consistent with those found in small towns in the western United States between 1860 and 1880." O now wishes to build a geodesic dome home on his undeveloped lot. Is C's ordinance enforceable?

Land use restrictions based on aesthetics—loosely known as *aesthetic zoning*—are controversial.[57] One issue dominated the debate for much of the twentieth century: does the police power permit municipalities to regulate aesthetics? The law has evolved in three distinct stages. Early twentieth-century courts held flatly that the police power could not be exercised based on aesthetic considerations alone; thus, ordinances that attempted to regulate the visual impact of billboards, for example, were deemed to violate substantive due process. By the 1960s, the law had progressed to the point where aesthetic zoning was upheld if it furthered some legitimate governmental purpose other than pure aesthetics (e.g., traffic safety, fire safety, preservation of property values, or promotion of tourism), and some jurisdictions still follow this approach.[58] Under this view, C's ordinance is presumably valid because it serves the economic goal of encouraging local tourism.

By 1980, a majority of American courts had embraced yet a third position—holding that aesthetics alone was an appropriate governmental purpose.[59] As Justice Douglas explained in a related context: "The concept of the public welfare is broad and inclusive. . . . The values it represents are . . . aesthetic as well as monetary. It is within the power of the legislature to determine that the community should be beautiful as well as healthy . . . ."[60] Under this approach, C's ordinance is valid simply because it serves aesthetic goals.

As a general matter, municipalities are now empowered to regulate billboards, junkyards, and other unsightly uses based on aesthetic considerations alone. In recent decades, attention has accordingly shifted to other constitutional constraints on aesthetic zoning, notably the First Amendment guarantee of freedom of speech.

---

[57] *See generally* Samuel Bufford, *Beyond the Eye of the Beholder: A New Majority of Jurisdictions Authorize Aesthetic Regulation*, 48 UMKC L. Rev. 127 (1980); Raymond R. Coletta, *The Case for Aesthetic Nuisance: Rethinking Traditional Judicial Attitudes*, 48 Ohio St. L.J. (1987); John Nivala, *Constitutional Architecture: The First Amendment and the Single Family House*, 33 San Diego L. Rev. 291 (1996).

[58] *See, e.g.*, Village of Hudson v. Albrecht, 458 N.E.2d 852 (Ohio 1984).

[59] *See, e.g.*, State v. Jones, 290 S.E.2d 675 (N.C. 1982) (adopting majority view, with slight modifications).

[60] Berman v. Parker, 348 U.S. 26, 33 (1954).

[B] Structures

One widespread form of aesthetic zoning is the architectural design review ordinance. The usual ordinance establishes an administrative board that evaluates the design of proposed single-family residences and other structures in light of particular criteria. Typical criteria include:

(1)　the appearance of the surrounding area;

(2)　specified design standards; and

(3)　impact on the property value of nearby parcels.[61]

If the board rejects a particular design, the affected owner cannot obtain a building permit for the project.

State ex rel. Stoyanoff v. Berkeley[62] —a 1970 decision by the Missouri Supreme Court—illustrates the concept. The city of Ladue, a wealthy suburb of St. Louis, adopted a design review ordinance. It required all structures to "conform to certain minimum architectural standards of appearance and conformity with surrounding structures, and that unsightly, grotesque and unsuitable structures . . . be avoided, and that appropriate standards of beauty and conformity be fostered and encouraged."[63] After petitioners' application to build a pyramid-style home in a neighborhood of Colonial, French Provincial and English Tudor houses was rejected, they sought a writ of mandate to compel the city to issue a building permit on the basis that the ordinance violated the state constitution's due process clause. The Missouri Supreme Court upheld the ordinance as a legitimate exercise of the police power, using essentially the same "rational basis" standard applied to the federal Due Process Clause. Following the minority approach, the court refused to rest its decision on aesthetics alone. Rather, it reasoned that the proposed home would adversely affect property values and otherwise disrupt the general welfare of area residents; thus, the decision was neither arbitrary nor unreasonable.[64] In a sense, of course, this reasoning is circular. The pyramid house would affect property values and community welfare *because of* its unusual appearance, i.e., its aesthetics.

Is architecture a form of speech safeguarded by the First Amendment? Although the Supreme Court has never considered the issue, some scholars suggest that architecture should be so protected. Under this view, an ordinance that prohibits a particular architectural style might be seen as a form of content-based censorship, not merely a restriction on the time, place, or manner of expression. For instance, might the pyramid-style

---

[61] A recurring problem is whether such criteria provide sufficient guidance to applicants or are void for vagueness. *Compare* State *ex rel.* Stoyanoff v. Berkeley, 458 S.W.2d 305 (Mo. 1970) (sufficient) *with* Anderson v. City of Issaquah, 851 P.2d 744 (Wash. Ct. App. 1993) (void).

[62] 458 S.W.2d 305 (Mo. 1970).

[63] State *ex rel.* Stoyanoff v. Berkeley, 458 S.W.2d 305, 306–307 (Mo. 1970).

[64] *See also* Reid v. Architectural Board of Review, 192 N.E.2d 74, 77 (Ohio Ct. App. 1963) (upholding board's disapproval of design for one-story home consisting of twenty modules in neighborhood of two and one-half story "dignified, stately, and conventional" structures).

architecture in *Stoyanoff* be construed as a cultural or political statement and thereby be entitled to First Amendment protection?

[C] Signs

Signs are a traditional form of speech. Accordingly, controls on signs pose obvious First Amendments concerns. And the city of Ladue—already familiar to the reader from the discussion of *State ex rel. Stoyanoff v. Berkeley* (*see* § 38.04[B])—has contributed to the evolution of the law in this area as well. In general, municipalities may regulate signs under the police power. Yet, as the Supreme Court explained in *City of Ladue v. Gilleo*,[65] a sign ordinance might be invalid because it (a) "simply prohibit[s] too much protected speech" or (b) discriminates based on the content of the sign's message[66] and hence "in effect restricts too little speech."[67]

City of Ladue arose when the city adopted an ordinance that banned all signs, except those falling into one of ten exemptions. For example, "for sale" signs on residences, signs for religious institutions, and commercial signs were all exempt from the ban. The ordinance was accompanied by legislative findings that it was necessary to avoid "ugliness, visual blight and clutter," diminution of property values, safety and traffic hazards, and threats to the "special ambience" of the city.[68] In 1991, during the Gulf War era, plaintiff Gilleo posted an 8½ by 11-inch sign in the window of her home that stated: "For Peace in the Gulf." When the city refused to allow the sign, plaintiff challenged the ordinance as a violation of her right to freedom of speech.

A unanimous Court struck down the ordinance because it entirely foreclosed a traditional and important medium of expression: residential signs. Just as the ordinance barred plaintiff from expressing her political views about the Gulf War, it similarly prohibited signs for particular political candidates, and other political, religious, and personal statements. The Court rejected the claim that the ordinance merely regulated the time, place, and manner of speech, because substitute methods of speech were inadequate. Displaying a sign at one's own residence is cheap, convenient, and uniquely identifies the speaker, features that other alternative methods do not possess. Finally, the Court noted that Ladue's legitimate regulatory concerns could be satisfied through a more narrowly-tailored ordinance.

§ 38.06 Growth Control and Zoning

In rapidly-growing Town D, over 200 homes have been built annually in recent years. The result is increased traffic congestion, crowded schools, a

---

[65] 512 U.S. 43 (1994).

[66] For example, in Metromedia, Inc. v. San Diego, 453 U.S. 490 (1981), the Court held a sign ordinance invalid because it treated commercial signs more favorably than some noncommercial signs, and thereby discriminated based on the content of the message.

[67] City of Ladue v. Gilleo, 512 U.S. 43, 50–51 (1994).

[68] City of Ladue v. Gilleo, 512 U.S. 43, 47 (1994).

shortage of sewage treatment capacity, and loss of the small-town ambience that its citizens have long valued. The town council adopts an ordinance that restricts the rate of development to 50 homes per year. Each developer may file an annual application for a permit to build new homes, and permits will be allocated based on objective criteria that measure the impacts of the proposed project (e.g., amount of added traffic). Subdivider S wishes to build 400 homes this year in the town. Can S successfully challenge D's ordinance?

Growth control ordinances[69] are generally upheld against due process and equal protection attacks.[70] The pioneering decision is *Golden v. Planning Board of Town of Ramapo*,[71] where the New York Court of Appeals upheld a "phased growth" ordinance somewhat like the hypothetical ordinance above. Due to rapid growth, the infrastructure of Ramapo was inadequate to provide the sewage, school, recreation, road, and fire service facilities necessary to continue the recent rate of development; the ordinance allocated permits for new homes based on the availability of these services. Reviewing the ordinance under the deferential "rational basis" standard, the court found that the circumstances easily justified the growth restriction.

The Ninth Circuit went even farther in *Construction Industry Association of Sonoma County v. City of Petaluma*.[72] The court rejected a substantive due process attack on an ordinance that limited growth in order to "preserve [the city's] small town character, its open spaces and low density of population, and to grow at an orderly and deliberate pace."[73] The *Petuluma* court relied in part on the Supreme Court's decision in *Belle Terre*, concluding that the ordinance served the legitimate governmental interest of preserving quiet residential neighborhoods.

Of course, an ordinance intended to regulate growth might conceivably be so restrictive as to constitute a regulatory taking (*see* Chapter 40). For example, in *Lucas v. South Carolina Coastal Council*[74] the Supreme Court held that a state statute that effectively prevented any development or other beneficial use of two residential lots was a compensable taking, absent proof that background principles of property and nuisance law justified the ban.

---

[69] *See generally* Robert C. Ellickson, *Suburban Growth Controls: An Economic and Legal Analysis*, 86 Yale L.J. 385 (1977).

[70] *See, e.g.,* Associated Home Builders v. City of Livermore, 557 P.2d 473 (Cal. 1976) (finding insufficient facts to overcome the presumption of constitutionality under the "rational basis" test).

[71] 285 N.E.2d 291 (N.Y. 1972).

[72] 522 F.2d 897 (9th Cir. 1975).

[73] Construction Industry Ass'n of Sonoma County v. City of Petaluma, 522 F.2d 897, 909 (9th Cir. 1975).

[74] 505 U.S. 1003 (1992).

Chapter 39

EMINENT DOMAIN

SYNOPSIS

§ 39.01   Eminent Domain in Context

O owns fee simple absolute in a ten-acre tract of land where the federal government plans to build a post office. O refuses to sell even though the government offers a fair price. Can the government "take" the property over O's loud and vigorous protests? Yes. Federal, state, and local governments have the inherent power to take private property for public use over the owner's objection, through a process known as *eminent domain* or *condemnation*.[1] Although this chapter will discuss the eminent domain power mainly

---

[1] *See generally* Lawrence Berger, *The Public Use Requirement in Eminent Domain*, 57 Or. L. Rev. 203 (1978); Thomas W. Merrill, *The Economics of Public Use*, 72 Cornell L. Rev. 61 (1986); Frank I. Michelman, *Property, Utility, and Fairness: Comments on the Ethical Foundations of "Just Compensation" Law*, 80 Harv. L. Rev. 1165 (1967); William B. Stoebuck, *A General Theory of Eminent Domain*, 47 Wash. L. Rev. 553 (1972); Comment, *The Public Use Limitation on Eminent Domain: An Advance Requiem*, 58 Yale L.J. 599 (1949).

in connection with real property, it may also be used to acquire personal property.

Eminent domain was an uncontroversial—and indeed dull—subject until the middle of the twentieth century. Until this point, the exercise of the power was relatively infrequent. More importantly, its exercise was almost always limited to acquiring land for uses that were purely governmental in character (e.g., military bases, post offices, highways, parks, or schools). But attempts in recent decades to extend the eminent domain power to new arenas such as urban renewal, land redistribution, and commercial development have sparked vigorous controversy. In turn, the controversy has focused attention on how the Constitution limits this power.

This chapter examines the formal eminent domain process. Chapter 40 explores the closely related issue of when government land use regulation goes "too far" and thus becomes a regulatory taking for which compensation must be paid.

§ 39.02 The Takings Clause of the Fifth Amendment: "Nor Shall Private Property Be Taken For Public Use, Without Just Compensation"

[A] Scope of the Takings Clause

The Constitution does not expressly grant eminent domain power to the federal government. Apparently, the framers viewed this power as an essential element of sovereignty. Just as the British Crown had the inherent power to take private property, the framers assumed that the new United States would possess this power. Instead, the Constitution *restricts* the eminent domain power.[2]

The key provision is the final sentence of the Fifth Amendment, commonly called the Takings Clause. It states: "[N]or shall private property be taken for public use, without just compensation." Literally, the Takings Clause only restricts the federal government. But its provisions have been held equally applicable to state and local governments through the conduit of the Fourteenth Amendment. In addition, all state constitutions contain parallel provisions that directly bind state and local governments.

The Takings Clause applies only when *private property* (see § 39.03) is *taken* (see § 39.04). It imposes two restrictions on the eminent domain power. Government (1) may take private property only for *public use* (see § 39.05) and (2) must pay *just compensation* to the owner (see § 39.06).

---

[2] *See generally* William M. Treanor, *The Original Understanding of the Takings Clause and the Political Process*, 95 Colum. L. Rev. 782 (1995); William M. Treanor, Note, *The Origins and Original Significance of the Just Compensation Clause of the Fifth Amendment*, 94 Yale L.J. 694 (1985).

[B] Origin of the Takings Clause

Under English law, a landowner whose property was physically taken by the sovereign had no right to compensation. However, even before the Revolutionary War, the custom in the American colonies was quite different. Although not legally obligated to pay, the colonies usually provided compensation when taking land for public use. The main exception to this practice involved the condemnation of rural land for a public highway or road, where payment was rarely provided. Yet even here the affected landowner received indirect compensation: the new highway typically increased the value of his or her remaining land.

In light of this background, the origin of the Takings Clause is somewhat murky. Citizens of the new United States could reasonably anticipate that the colonial practice of paying compensation would continue. Even in the feverish debate that preceded the ratification of the Constitution, little public concern was expressed about the lack of a clause requiring compensation for government takings. In this sense, the Takings Clause stands out from the rest of the Bill of Rights. Every provision ultimately included in the Bill of Rights was specifically requested by two or more states, except for the Takings Clause. Not a single state demanded such a clause.

History reflects that James Madison drafted and proposed the Takings Clause as one of several suggested amendments to the Constitution. But Madison's motivation is unclear. It has been suggested that Madison was responding to popular outcry against a frequent practice of the American army during the Revolutionary War: seizing privately-owned food, supplies, and other personal property necessary for the war effort without compensation. Yet Madison's writings suggest that the Takings Clause was intended to serve broader economic and political goals.[3] It would protect large property owners against government-mandated redistribution of wealth and other arbitrary actions. Even if poor or impoverished citizens someday formed a majority, they could not use the machinery of government to confiscate property without payment. Similarly, Madison firmly believed that the ownership of property was fundamental to political freedom. Democracy could prosper only if individuals were sufficiently independent from government pressure and influence to act in the best interests of the nation. In Madison's vision, this political independence stemmed from private property: the landowner who could support his family by growing crops on his own land had no reason to sacrifice the national good for personal gain. By protecting private property, the Takings Clause would help to safeguard democracy.

[C] Modern Rationale for the Takings Clause

In recent decades, the Supreme Court has stressed that one of the principal purposes of the Takings Clause is "to bar Government from forcing some people alone to bear public burdens which, in all fairness and justice,

---

[3] *See generally* William M. Treanor, Note, *The Origins and Original Significance of the Just Compensation Clause of the Fifth Amendment*, 94 Yale L.J. 694, 710–713 (1985).

should be borne by the public as a whole."[4] This rationale combines two key themes that reflect Madison's concerns. First, the Takings Clause is seen as a check on arbitrary government action. Government cannot capriciously single out certain individuals or groups for disparate treatment. Second, the Takings Clause ensures that all citizens bear their fair share of public burdens. One citizen cannot be unfairly forced to assume obligations that all citizens should meet.

§ 39.03 "Nor Shall Private Property . . ."

Any type of private property may be acquired through eminent domain. The vast majority of cases involves the condemnation of a possessory estate in land, almost always fee simple absolute. All possessory estates (both freehold and nonfreehold)[5] and other interests (e.g., easements, CC&Rs, and future interests) in real property may similarly be condemned. Tangible and intangible personal property is also subject to condemnation.[6]

§ 39.04 ". . . Be Taken . . ."

In the standard eminent domain case, a state or other government entity takes permanent physical possession of a particular parcel of land. For example, State A might condemn 10 acres of O's land in order to build a new state prison; when the process is complete, O's possessory rights will be extinguished. As the Supreme Court explained in *Loretto v. Teleprompter Manhattan CATV Corp.*,[7] any permanent physical occupation of property authorized by government is deemed a compensable taking.

Beyond this point, however, the definition of a "taking" is extraordinarily uncertain.[8] Under some circumstances, a temporary physical "invasion" of land authorized by government or an overly-restrictive land use regulation may be compensable takings, as discussed in Chapter 40.

§ 39.05 ". . . For Public Use . . ."

[A] The Problem of Defining "Public Use"

American courts have struggled for over two centuries to define "public use."[9] The phrase implies that condemnation is permitted only if the

---

[4] Dolan v. City of Tigard, 512 U.S. 374, 384 (1994) (quoting Armstrong v. United States, 364 U.S. 40, 49 (1960).

[5] *See, e.g.,* Almota Farmers Elevator & Warehouse Co. v. United States, 409 U.S. 470 (1973) (condemnation of leasehold estate).

[6] *See, e.g.,* City of Oakland v. Oakland Raiders, 646 P.2d 835 (Cal. 1982) (suggesting city had right to condemn professional football franchise).

[7] 458 U.S. 419 (1982).

[8] *See, e.g.,* Rubano v. Department of Transp., 656 So. 2d 1264 (Fla. 1995) (elimination of U-turn and other changes in traffic flow caused by highway construction, which did not significantly impair access to petitioners' properties, was not a taking).

[9] *See generally* Lawrence Berger, *The Public Use Requirement in Eminent Domain,* 57 Or. L. Rev. 203 (1978); Comment, *The Public Use Limitation on Eminent Domain: An Advance Requiem,* 58 Yale L.J. 599 (1949).

affected land will be physically used or occupied by members of the public (e.g., as a public park or library). Under this approach, public use is defined by the *identity* of the future land users or occupiers. This "physical use" standard was adopted by nineteenth-century courts, but withered away during the twentieth century under the pressure of changing political and social conditions. As government undertook new and expanded functions—such as housing development and urban renewal—the physical use test proved unduly restrictive.

[B] The Public Purpose Test

[1] Shift to a New Standard

Two landmark Supreme Court decisions—*Berman v. Parker*[10] and *Hawaii Housing Authority v. Midkiff*[11] —signaled the shift to a new standard: the *public purpose* test. Under this approach, public use is defined by the *purpose* underlying the government action. As long as property is taken for a legitimate public purpose—that is, a purpose within the scope of the government's police power—the public use requirement is satisfied. Today virtually all courts utilize the public purpose test.

[2] *Berman v. Parker*

The public purpose test gained prominence in the 1954 Supreme Court decision of *Berman v. Parker*. The case arose when the District of Columbia condemned plaintiffs' department store in a "blighted" area as part of a large-scale urban renewal program to eliminate unsafe, unsanitary, and unsightly buildings. The District intended to resell the land to entrepreneurs who would build privately-owned projects consistent with the urban renewal plan. Plaintiffs sued to enjoin the condemnation, arguing that it was merely "a taking from one businessman for the benefit of another businessman,"[12] in other words, a taking of private property for private use.

Writing for the Court, Justice Douglas focused on the purpose for the government action, not the identity of the future land users. If government has the right to exercise the police power for a particular public purpose, he reasoned, then it has the right to condemn property as well. He observed: "Once the object is within the authority of Congress, the right to realize it through the exercise of eminent domain is clear. For the power of eminent domain is merely the means to the end."[13] Here, the District sought to upgrade housing conditions for an entire neighborhood through a comprehensive redevelopment plan, rather than through a piecemeal, structure-by-structure approach. This goal was a legitimate public purpose and, accordingly, the condemnation was for a "public use." In effect, Douglas

---

[10] 348 U.S. 26 (1954).

[11] 467 U.S. 229 (1984).

[12] Berman v. Parker, 348 U.S. 26, 33 (1954).

[13] Berman v. Parker, 348 U.S. 26, 33 (1954).

suggested that the scope of the government's eminent domain power was coextensive with the police power.

[3] *Hawaii Housing Authority v. Midkiff*

In 1984, *Hawaii Housing Authority v. Midkiff*[14] posed a more challenging question: could the state of Hawaii condemn land from a landlord and then convey it to his tenant? The issue arose because fee simple ownership of private land in Hawaii was highly concentrated in a few owners. For example, 22 owners held 72.5% of all fee simple land on the island of Oahu. Residents could easily lease land, but found it difficult to purchase fee simple title. The Hawaii legislature adopted a statute that sought to remedy this problem. It authorized tenants living in single-family homes to petition a state agency to condemn these properties, and then resell them to the tenants. Plaintiffs, trustees of a charitable trust that owned extensive lands, sued to invalidate the statute as authorizing an unconstitutional exercise of the eminent domain power. The Ninth Circuit agreed. It construed the statute as permitting a taking for purely private use, referring to the statute as "a naked attempt . . . to take the private property of A and transfer it to B solely for B's private use and benefit."[15]

In upholding the constitutionality of the Hawaii statute, the Supreme Court broadened the scope of the public purpose test in two important respects. First, Justice O'Connor, writing for the majority, confirmed what *Berman* had suggested: the public use standard is coterminous with the scope of the police power. The *Midkiff* plaintiffs argued that the public use standard included a requirement that government possess and use the land at least temporarily, just as the District of Columbia had temporarily possessed the land condemned in *Berman*. In contrast, the state of Hawaii had never held possession of the lands condemned in *Midkiff*; rather, the private tenants had always retained possession. The Court's holding that this distinction was irrelevant extinguished any lingering traces of the "physical use" test. Under the Fifth Amendment, public use is now defined by the purpose underlying the government action, not by the identity of the land user.

Second, *Midkiff* established that condemnation decisions are judicially reviewed under the deferential "rational basis" standard. Thus, when a particular exercise of the legislature's eminent domain power is attacked, the appropriate question is not whether *in fact* the condemnation serves a public purpose. Rather, a court may only inquire whether the decision is rationally related to a conceivable public purpose. In other words, could the legislature *rationally have believed* that the condemnation would serve a permissible public purpose?

---

[14] 67 U.S. 229 (1984). *See generally* Susan Lourne, Comment, Hawaii Housing Authority v. Midkiff: *A New Slant on Social Legislation: Taking from the Rich to Give to the Well-to-Do*, 25 Nat. Resources J. 773 (1985).

[15] Midkiff v. Tom, 702 F.2d 788, 798 (9th Cir. 1983), *rev'd sub nom.* Hawaii Housing Authority v. Midkiff, 467 U.S. 229 (1984).

Applying its expanded public purpose test to the *Midkiff* facts, the Court found no difficulty in upholding the Hawaii statute. Regulating a land oligopoly to reduce its social and economic evils was seen as a classic exercise of the police power. The scarcity of fee simple land both artificially increased its price and precluded many residents from enjoying the economic and social benefits of owning their own homes. The statute was a rational approach to correcting what the Court perceived as a malfunctioning land market.

[4] Significant State Court Decisions

Two state court decisions—*Poletown Neighborhood Council v. City of Detroit*[16] and *City of Oakland v. Oakland Raiders*[17] —further illustrate the evolution of the public purpose test. It is important to note that these cases were decided before the Supreme Court's 1984 decision in *Hawaii Housing Authority v. Midkiff* (*see* [B][3], *above*). Yet both *Poletown* (1981) and *City of Oakland* (1982) demonstrate the broad interpretation that state courts had already given to the public purpose test.

Poletown Neighborhood Council v. City of Detroit[18] held that Detroit could condemn homes in an ordinary residential neighborhood and then transfer the land to General Motors to build a Cadillac assembly factory.[19] Unlike the situation in *Berman v. Parker* (*see* [B][2], *above*), the neighborhood was not a slum or other blighted area that presented health and safety concerns. The Michigan Supreme Court found that the taking served a public purpose because it would benefit the public by providing employment and revitalizing the economic base of the community. Although General Motors would benefit as well, this private benefit was seen as merely incidental.[20] One dissenting justice criticized the "extraordinary" decision as having "seriously jeopardized the security of all private property ownership."[21]

In *City of Oakland v. Oakland Raiders*,[22] the California Supreme Court suggested that Oakland's attempted condemnation of the Oakland Raiders

---

[16] 304 N.W.2d 455 (Mich. 1981).

[17] 646 P.2d 835 (Cal. 1982).

[18] 304 N.W.2d 455 (Mich. 1981). *See generally* John J. Bukowczyk, *The Decline and Fall of a Detroit Neighborhood:* Poletown v. G.M. & the City of Detroit, 41 Wash. & Lee L. Rev. 49 (1984).

[19] *But see In re* City of Seattle, 638 P.2d 549 (Wash. 1981) (holding Seattle could not condemn land for project that included a shopping center, museum and park, because project served private purpose as well as public purpose).

[20] *But see* City of Lansing v. Edward Rose Realty, Inc., 502 N.W.2d 638 (Mich. 1993) (ordinance allowing condemnation of easements for cable television services to apartment complexes was unconstitutional because the dominant benefit was a private benefit to the cable company, not a public benefit).

[21] Poletown Neighborhood Council v. City of Detroit, 304 N.W.2d 455, 464, 465 (Mich. 1981) (Ryan, J., dissenting).

[22] 646 P.2d 835 (Cal. 1982). *See generally* Lisa J. Tobin-Rubio, Note, *Eminent Domain and the Commerce Clause Defense:* City of Oakland v. Oakland Raiders, 41 U. Miami L. Rev. 1185 (1987).

football team might be a taking for public use. The court observed that a city certainly could condemn land to construct a sports stadium because this served the public purpose of providing recreational benefits to city residents in the form of spectator sports. The court further intimated there was no difference between owning the stadium and owning the team that played in the stadium, but remanded the case to the trial court for further proceedings on the issue.

[C] Reflections on the Public Use Standard

Is the public use requirement now meaningless? Almost, but not quite. In the wake of *Hawaii Housing Authority v. Midkiff* (*see* [B][3], *above*), scholars generally agree that the public use clause has little impact as an independent restriction on government action.[23] If the police power permits a city or other government entity to take a particular action, then it is automatically authorized to use the eminent domain power to implement that decision.

Except in unusual cases, virtually every taking can be defended as an action that conceivably provides a public benefit and thus serves a public purpose. While *Midkiff* notes that a "purely private taking" would violate the public use requirement, this situation is unlikely to occur because it would presumably exceed the government's police power authority in the first place.

§ 39.06 ". . . Without Just Compensation"

[A] Defining "Just Compensation"

[1] The Fair Market Value Standard

An unbroken line of Supreme Court decisions defines "just compensation" as the fair market value of the property when the taking occurs. "Fair market value," in turn, means the amount that a willing buyer would pay in cash to a willing seller.[24] The goal is to put the owner in as good a monetary position as if the property had not been taken, but rather voluntarily sold on the open market. Fair market value is usually established by evidence concerning recent sales of the property at issue or sales of comparable properties.[25] If the type of property involved is so rarely sold that fair market value is difficult to ascertain, the court may apply other just and equitable standards (e.g., the cost to acquire substitute facilities).[26]

---

[23] *See, e.g.,* Thomas W. Merrill, *The Economics of Public Use*, 72 Cornell L. Rev. 61 (1986).

[24] Almota Farmers Elevator & Warehouse Co. v. United States, 409 U.S. 470 (1973).

[25] *Cf.* J.J. Newberry Co. v. City of East Chicago, 441 N.E.2d 39 (Ind. Ct. App. 1982) (measure of damages for condemnation of leasehold interest was determined by fair market value of the unexpired term minus the future rent due under the lease, not by capitalization of income method of valuation).

[26] *See generally* United States v. 564.54 Acres of Land, 441 U.S. 506 (1979) (concluding alternate standard was not appropriate on facts of case); United States v. 50 Acres of Land, 469 U.S. 24 (1984) (same).

[2] Impact of Owner's Sentimental Attachment or Special Need

What if an owner places sentimental or subjective value on the property? Suppose O owns fee simple absolute in Greenacre, a home where her family has lived for 200 years. The state now condemns the home to build a new sewage disposal plant. The fair market value of Greenacre to an objective buyer is $200,000. From O's perspective, however, Greenacre is a unique family treasure. Moreover, she is not a "willing seller." It is quite possible that she would never voluntarily sell the property; in this sense, it is "priceless" to O. If O were forced to place a dollar value on Greenacre, it would be far more than $200,000, perhaps $1 million. Yet, by definition, fair market value is measured only by the market. It does not consider the sentimental or subjective value that the property may have for any particular owner. O will thus receive $200,000, not $1 million.

Similarly, fair market value does not necessarily compensate the owner for the full economic value of the land. For example, in one case the federal government condemned three church-owned summer camps with a fair market value just under $500,000.[27] The cost to develop replacement camps, however, was almost $6 million, because the new camps would have to comply with expensive regulatory requirements from which the existing camps were exempt. The Supreme Court held that fair market value does not include the special value of property to the owner arising from its adaptability to a particular need.

[B] Future Land Uses

In a free market transaction, the prudent buyer of land will evaluate the future uses for which the property may be suitable. Suppose B contemplates purchasing a 400-acre turnip farm owned by S. In negotiating a sales price, both B and S will assess the possibility that the land may someday be desirable for another use (e.g., residential development), and therefore be more valuable than ordinary agricultural property. To what extent must future expectancies be considered in setting the fair market value of condemned property?

As a general rule, property must be valued at the *highest and best use* for which it could be adapted, not merely its existing use. But the potential future use must be reasonably probable; the owner's fantasy or speculation about possible uses is irrelevant. Three factors are typically important in making this determination:

(1) the physical condition of the land (including location, topography, etc.),

(2) the current and reasonably probable future zoning of the parcel, and

(3) the market demand for the particular future use.

---

[27] United States v. 564.54 Acres of Land, 441 U.S. 506 (1979).

Controversy often focuses on the likelihood of a future zoning change (e.g., a rezoning from agricultural to residential use). In most jurisdictions, only zoning changes that are reasonably probable may be considered.[28]

The Supreme Court addressed the expectancy issue in *Almota Farmers Elevator & Warehouse Co. v. United States*,[29] where the federal government brought an eminent domain action to acquire a term of years leasehold in a grain elevator complex. The government asserted that the property being taken consisted only of the tenant's rights during the remaining 7½ years of the lease; thus, it argued that it was not required to pay additional value because of the *possibility* that the lease might be renewed at the end of the term. The Court concluded, however, that a willing private buyer in a free market transaction would consider the likelihood of lease renewal, particularly since renewal seemed probable on the facts of the case. Observing that eminent domain should not place the tenant in a worse position than if it had voluntarily sold its leasehold to a private buyer, the Court reasoned that the government should not escape paying what a willing buyer would pay for the same property.

[C] Goodwill

The condemnation of a business presents a special problem. Assume the state condemns O's grocery store in order to build a government office building on the site. The state obviously must compensate O for the fair market value of the property taken. But is the property taken defined as (1) the lot and store building regardless of the current use or (2) the lot and store building as an ongoing, profitable business? The difference between the two is *goodwill*, that is, the going-concern value of a business. Must the state compensate for the loss of goodwill?

In most jurisdictions, the condemning agency is not required to compensate for goodwill.[30] This result stems from the apparent assumption that goodwill is portable, i.e., that the displaced business owner can readily relocate the business to new premises. Yet frequently the success of a business is produced more by its unique location than by the owner's personal abilities. In such a situation, this rule effectively prevents the owner from receiving full compensation.[31]

---

[28] *See, e.g.,* State of New Jersey v. Caoili, 639 A.2d 275 (N.J. 1994) (trial court properly allowed jury to consider evidence that use variance could be obtained to change property from residential to commercial use because variance was reasonably probable).

[29] 409 U.S. 470 (1973).

[30] *See generally* Lynda J. Oswald, *Goodwill and Going-Concern Value: Emerging Factors in the Just Compensation Equation,* 32 B.C. L. Rev. 283 (1991).

[31] *But see* City of Detroit v. Michael's Prescriptions, 373 N.W.2d 219 (Mich. Ct. App. 1985) (evidence as to going-concern value of pharmacy was properly admitted before trial court, because business value stemmed in part from unique location and could not be transferred to new location).

[D] Partial Takings

The law governing the measure of damages for partial takings is particularly complex. Suppose the state condemns 50 acres from O's 120-acre farm in order to build a new freeway interchange. The state must compensate O for the fair market value of the 50 acres so taken. Further, if the taking reduces the value of O's remaining 70 acres (e.g., by cutting off irrigation water), the state must pay O *severance damages* to compensate for this loss.[32]

On the other hand, what if the taking of O's 50 acres actually *increases* the value of his remaining parcel? O's 70 acres may now be suitable for commercial use (e.g., gas stations, fast food restaurants) and thus far more valuable than farm land. Where the owner's retained property receives a *special benefit* from the new project—that is, one that directly affects the particular property, not merely one enjoyed by the public at large—most states allow the condemning agency to offset this special benefit against any severance damages due the owner. For example, suppose the condemnation of O's 50 acres causes $50,000 in severance damages to O's remaining land, but also increases the value of that land by $100,000; in most jurisdictions, O will receive no severance damages.

The more difficult question is whether the condemning agency can offset a special benefit against the compensatory damages otherwise due to the owner for the land physically taken. Suppose now that the fair market value of O's 50 acres is $150,000, O suffers no severance damages, and the freeway project provides a special benefit that increases the value of O's 70 acres by $100,000. Must the agency still pay O $150,000 (fair market value) or can it pay only $50,000 (fair market value less the special benefit conferred on the remaining land)? Although the federal rule allows an agency to offset any special benefit in these circumstances,[33] most states do not permit such an offset.

§ 39.07 Eminent Domain Procedure

The procedure for eminent domain varies widely from state to state. The process usually begins with the government's effort to negotiate a voluntary purchase from the owner. Statutes in many states require such negotiations, often on the basis of an appraisal performed by the condemning agency and provided to the owner.[34] If negotiations fail, the agency will typically file suit to condemn the property.

At its core, an eminent domain action is simply a specialized form of litigation, involving essentially the same pleading, motion, discovery, and trial stages found in ordinary civil ligation. The issues involved, however, are quite limited. On occasion, the agency's right to take becomes an issue, such as where the affected owner can overcome the deferential "public use"

---

[32] *See, e.g.,* State Dept. of Transp. & Dev. v. Regard, 567 So. 2d 1174 (La. Ct. App. 1990).

[33] *See, e.g.,* Acierno v. State of Delaware, 643 A.2d 1328 (Del. 1994) (allowing offset).

[34] *See, e.g.,* Texas-New Mexico Power Co. v. Hogan, 824 S.W.2d 252 (Tex. Ct. App. 1992).

standard (*see* § 39.05) to demonstrate that the taking is for a private purpose or where the agency lacks the eminent domain power. But in the vast majority of cases, the only issue is the fair market value of the property. Market value is determined directly by the trial judge or jury in some states. In a slightly larger group of states, a commission, master, or referee makes the initial determination of value; this decision may then be appealed to a judge or jury.[35] Thus, the central focus of the garden-variety eminent domain action is a battle between expert appraisal witnesses on the issue of fair market value.

---

[35] *See* 6 Julius L. Sackman, Nichols on Eminent Domain, Ch. 26D (Matthew Bender).

Chapter 40

LAND USE REGULATION AND THE TAKINGS CLAUSE

§ 40.01   The Takings Problem

When does land use regulation become a "taking" of private property?[1] The Takings Clause of the Fifth Amendment provides: "[N]or shall private property be taken for public use, without just compensation."[2] At some point, regulation may so restrict an owner's rights as to become a taking—thus requiring payment of compensation—even though government does not physically occupy the land. Defining when such a regulatory taking occurs is one of the most controversial issues in property law today.

An example illustrates the problem. Assume L's 1,000-acre tract is one of the last undeveloped forest parcels in County, a fast-growing suburban county, but is zoned for residential development. County wishes to keep the forest land within its borders in natural condition in order to protect views, preserve open space, and minimize adverse impacts from development (e.g., additional traffic and air pollution). How should County proceed? Undoubtedly, County could use its eminent domain power to acquire title to L's land upon payment of just compensation (*see* Chapter 39). But can County secure the same public benefits through regulation? Suppose that County instead rezones L's parcel into the newly-created "Forest Preservation" zone, where the only permitted uses are harvesting wild hay, livestock

---

[1] *See generally* Richard A. Epstein, Takings: Private Property and the Power of Eminent Domain (1985); Robert Meltz, et al., The Takings Issue: Constitutional Limits on Land-Use Control and Environmental Regulation (1999); J. Peter Byrne, *Ten Arguments for the Abolition of the Regulatory Takings Doctrine,* 22 Ecology L.Q. 89 (1995); Frank I. Michelman, *Property, Utility, and Fairness: Comments on the Ethical Foundations of "Just Compensation" Law,* 80 Harv. L. Rev. 1165 (1967); Joseph L. Sax, *Takings and the Police Power,* 74 Yale L.J. 36 (1964); William M. Treanor, *The Original Understanding of the Takings Clause and the Political Process,* 95 Colum. L. Rev. 782 (1995).

[2] U.S. Const. amend. V. The Takings Clause is made applicable to state and local governments by judicial interpretation of the Fourteenth Amendment. *See* Chicago, Burlington & Quincy R.R. Co. v. Chicago, 166 U.S. 226 (1897).

grazing, and camping. This regulation is an effective substitute for acquiring title to L's land by eminent domain; under either approach, L's forest is preserved. Yet the rezoning greatly lowers the market value of L's land. Must County now compensate L?

The Supreme Court's landmark 1922 decision in *Pennsylvania Coal Co. v. Mahon*[3] established that regulation will be recognized as a taking if it "goes too far."[4] But how far is too far? Although the Court has addressed this question in a number of major decisions, it has never provided a clear answer. The Court has offered various tests for determining when a regulatory taking occurs. But these tests—and the results of their application—are all too often uncertain, confusing, and inconsistent. Rather than proceeding in a uniform direction from case to case, the law of regulatory takings resembles a roller coaster: it lurches, jerks, spins, whirls, loops, and reverses direction, leaving the dazed rider unable to predict the next turn. The resulting body of case law is variously described as a "mess," a "muddle," and a "swamp."

In order to understand takings law, the reader must examine the key Supreme Court decisions in detail and fit them together—like pieces of a jigsaw puzzle—to form a recognizable picture. Two clues are helpful in this process. First, the Court's modern decisions generally agree on the purpose underlying the Takings Clause: "to bar Government from forcing some people alone to bear public burdens which, in all fairness and justice, should be borne by the public as a whole."[5] Second, despite different phrasing and emphasis, all of the Court's various takings tests involve one or more of only three core variables. The variables are:

(1)   the economic impact of the government action on the owner,

(2)   the nature of the public interest underlying the government action, and

(3)   whether the government action involves physical intrusion or merely regulation.

One consistent theme emerges from this puzzling body of case law: a regulation is not a taking simply because it somewhat reduces the market value of an owner's land. Why not? As the Court explained in *Pennsylvania Coal*: "Government could hardly go on if to some extent values incident to property could not be diminished without paying for every such change in the general law."[6]

---

[3] 260 U.S. 393 (1922).

[4] Pennsylvania Coal Co. v. Mahon, 260 U.S. 393, 415 (1922).

[5] *See, e.g.,* Dolan v. City of Tigard, 512 U.S. 374, 384 (1994) (quoting Armstrong v. United States, 364 U.S. 40, 49 (1960)).

[6] Pennsylvania Coal Co. v. Mahon, 260 U.S. 393, 413 (1922).

§ 40.02 The Foundation Era of Regulatory Takings: 1776–1922

[A] Original Intent and the Takings Clause

Did the framers intend the Takings Clause to apply to regulations that restrict the use of private property? The answer to this question is a resounding "no!"[7] Although the origin of the Takings Clause is somewhat murky, "one thing is clear: the draftsmen were not troubled by any issue involving regulation of the use of land."[8] Colonial law occasionally restricted the use of land; for example, an early New York City ordinance effectively banned all slaughterhouses.[9] But land use regulation generated no controversy during this era.

Legal scholars agree that the Takings Clause was originally intended to apply only if government physically seized or occupied property.[10] Two concerns—both involving physical takings—apparently contributed to the adoption of the clause (see § 39.02[B]). First, during the turmoil of the Revolutionary War, the American army had often taken privately-owned food, livestock, and other supplies without making any payment; some feared this practice might return. Second, and more fundamentally, James Madison—the principal author of the clause—was seemingly motivated by fear that populist democracy might lead to the forced redistribution of land from the rich to the poor.

[B] Early Decisions

[1] The "Nuisance" or "Noxious Use" Exception

Consistent with the framers' intent, American courts followed a clear rule during the foundation era: regulation of land use under the police power was not a taking. The police power authorizes government to regulate the use of land to protect the public health, morals, safety, and welfare; and early courts viewed the Due Process Clause as the only constitutional check on this power. A land use regulation would be upheld against substantive due process attack if it had a rational relationship to a legitimate government interest, such as public health or safety (see § 38.02[A][3]). Thus, if government used its police power to regulate a nuisance or other harm to the public caused by the use of land, the affected landowner was not entitled

---

[7] See generally William M. Treanor, The Original Understanding of the Takings Clause and the Political Process, 95 Colum. L. Rev. 782 (1995).

[8] Fred Bosselman, et al., The Taking Issue: An Analysis of the Constitutional Limits of Land Use Control 104 (1973).

[9] Fred Bosselman, et al., The Taking Issue: An Analysis of the Constitutional Limits of Land Use Control 82-84 (1973).

[10] See, e.g., William M. Treanor, The Original Understanding of the Takings Clause and the Political Process, 95 Colum. L. Rev. 782 (1995); see also Lucas v. South Carolina Coastal Council, 505 U.S. 1003, 1028 n.15 (1992) ("[E]arly constitutional theorists did not believe the Takings Clause embraced regulations of property at all.").

to compensation under the Takings Clause.[11] Two early Supreme Court decisions—*Mugler v. Kansas*[12] in 1887 and *Hadacheck v. Sebastian*[13] in 1915—illustrate this approach.

Mugler v. Kansas[14] arose when Kansas adopted a statute prohibiting the manufacture of alcohol. Mugler, who owned a profitable brewery, argued that the law greatly reduced the market value of his property; the brewery buildings and machinery were of "little value" for any purpose other than making beer.[15] The Court saw this as a simple case. All property in the nation, it reasoned, is held under the implied obligation that the owner's use will not harm the community. Thus, "[a] prohibition simply upon the use of property for purposes that are declared, by valid legislation, to be injurious to the health, morals, or safety of the community, cannot . . . be deemed a taking or an appropriation of property for the public benefit."[16] The police power "is not . . . burdened with the condition that the State must compensate such individual owners for pecuniary losses they may sustain, by reason of their not being permitted, by a noxious use of their property, to inflict injury upon the community."[17] Here, the property had not been seized or physically taken away. Mugler was free to devote it to any use he desired, except for making alcohol—the particular "noxious use" banned by the statute.

The Court confronted a similar situation in *Hadacheck v. Sebastian*.[18] Hadacheck purchased land containing a valuable bed of clay and established a profitable brick-manufacturing factory; at the time, the property was in an undeveloped area outside of Los Angeles. Later, the area became a residential district that was annexed to the city. The city adopted an ordinance that prohibited brick manufacturing in the region and thereby reduced the value of Hadacheck's land from $800,000 to $60,000. Evidence in the record showed that Hadacheck's factory emitted "fumes, gases, smoke, soot, steam, and dust" that "caused sickness and serious discomfort to those living in the vicinity."[19] On these facts, the Court easily concluded that the police power allowed the city to regulate the offensive effects of the factory, thereby protecting the health and comfort of the community. Hadacheck's resulting financial loss was seen as essentially irrelevant: "There must be progress, and if in its march private interests are in the way, they must yield to the good of the community."[20]

---

[11] *See also* Raymond R. Coletta, *Reciprocity of Advantage and Regulatory Takings: Toward a New Theory of Takings Jurisprudence*, 40 Am. U. L. Rev. 297, 305–319 (1990) (discussing "reciprocity of advantage" theme in early case law).

[12] 123 U.S. 623 (1887).

[13] 239 U.S. 394 (1915).

[14] 123 U.S. 623 (1887).

[15] Mugler v. Kansas, 123 U.S. 623, 657 (1887).

[16] Mugler v. Kansas, 123 U.S. 623, 668–669 (1887).

[17] Mugler v. Kansas, 123 U.S. 623, 669 (1887).

[18] Hadacheck v. Sebastian, 239 U.S. 394 (1915).

[19] Hadacheck v. Sebastian, 239 U.S. 394, 408 (1915).

[20] Hadacheck v. Sebastian, 239 U.S. 394, 410 (1915).

In short, the *Mugler-Hadacheck* line of cases held that police power regulation that prevents harm to the public is not a taking. Although this doctrine is often called the "nuisance" or "noxious use" exception, its scope is broader than these terms imply.[21]

[2] "Reciprocity of Advantage"

A secondary doctrine sometimes used to uphold comprehensive zoning ordinances and other regulation during the foundation era was *reciprocity of advantage*, sometimes called *average reciprocity of advantage*. The gist of the doctrine was that the reciprocal benefits or "advantages" of regulation compensate for its burdens. A regulation was justified when the burdens it imposed on landowners were offset by the benefits it conferred on them. For example, suppose a local ordinance provides that no building may exceed two stories in height. The ordinance burdens landowner K because he cannot build, for instance, a three-story structure on his parcel. But, at the same time, the ordinance benefits K because the adjacent lots owned by his neighbors J and L are similarly restricted. J, for example, cannot construct a five-story house that would block light and air from reaching K's land. The ordinance is constitutional because it provides reciprocity of advantage.

§ 40.03 The *Pennsylvania Coal Co. v. Mahon* Revolution and Its Aftermath: 1922–1978

[A] Birth of the Regulatory Takings Doctrine

The Supreme Court's 1922 decision in *Pennsylvania Coal Co. v. Mahon*[22] is generally recognized as the birthplace of the regulatory takings doctrine.[23] The Court struck down a state statute as unconstitutional under the Takings Clause—thus establishing the rule that mere regulation could be a taking—but offered little guidance about what constitutes a taking.

[B] Facts of *Pennsylvania Coal*

The case arose in the coal country of northeastern Pennsylvania, a region long troubled by surface subsidence. Subsurface mining removed the coal supporting the surface; the land surface then collapsed, sometimes causing personal injury and property damage. The Pennsylvania Coal Company conveyed a parcel of land to plaintiffs' predecessor in title, but reserved in the deed the right to remove all the coal under the land surface. The

---

[21] *See, e.g.,* Miller v. Schoene, 276 U.S. 272 (1928).

[22] 260 U.S. 393 (1922). *See also* Carol M. Rose, Mahon *Reconstructed: Why the Takings Issue is Still a Muddle,* 57 S. Cal. L. Rev. 561 (1984).

[23] A minority of scholars reject the view that *Pennsylvania Coal* is a takings case at all, instead arguing that it rests on substantive due process. *See, e.g.,* Robert Brauneis, *"The Foundation of Our 'Regulatory Takings' Jurisprudence": The Myth and Meaning of Justice Holmes's Opinion in* Pennsylvania Coal Co. v. Mahon, 106 Yale L.J. 613 (1996).

plaintiff Mahons later purchased the property (apparently with notice of this restriction) and moved into the house built on the land.

In the interim, the state adopted a statute that prohibited the mining of coal under residential areas in a manner that caused the subsidence of any dwelling. In effect, the statute required that pillars of coal be left in place underground to support the land surface. When the coal company warned the Mahons that its future mining operations would soon cause their home to subside, they sought an injunction pursuant to this statute. In reply, the coal company argued that the statute was an unconstitutional taking of its mineral rights.

[C] Holmes's Majority Opinion

Writing for the majority, Justice Holmes concluded that the statute was a taking of the coal company's property rights. He conceded that "[g]overnment could hardly go on if to some extent values incident to property could not be diminished without paying for every such change in the general law."[24] On the other hand, "if regulation goes too far it will be recognized as a taking."[25] Holmes found that the Pennsylvania statute indeed went "too far." But the test he used to reach this result was far from clear.

Holmes emphasized that "[o]ne fact" for consideration was the "extent of the diminution," that is, the extent to which the regulation diminished the fair market value of the property.[26] At the time, Pennsylvania law divided subsurface mineral rights into two separate estates in land: (a) the mineral estate (ownership of minerals that can be removed without disturbing the land surface) and (b) the support estate (ownership of minerals that remain in place to support the land surface). Holmes found that the extent of the taking was "great," because the statute took the coal company's *entire* support estate; "[i]t purports to abolish what is recognized in Pennsylvania as an estate in land—a very valuable estate."[27]

In addition, Holmes considered the extent of the public interest served by the statute. He stressed that the case involved damage only to a single private house, which could not be viewed as a public nuisance or as damage to the public in general. Implicit in this analysis was the assumption that plaintiffs knowingly purchased the surface rights only, aware that they had no right to support of their house or the land surface itself. Moreover, the statute was not necessary to protect the plaintiffs' personal safety because the mining company could provide advance notice of its intention to mine, as indeed had happened here. Based on this analysis, Holmes found that the "plaintiffs' position" did not create "a public interest sufficient to warrant so extensive a destruction of the defendant's constitutionally protected rights."[28]

---

[24] Pennsylvania Coal Co. v. Mahon, 260 U.S. 393, 413 (1922).

[25] Pennsylvania Coal Co. v. Mahon, 260 U.S. 393, 415 (1922).

[26] Pennsylvania Coal Co. v. Mahon, 260 U.S. 393, 413 (1922).

[27] Pennsylvania Coal Co. v. Mahon, 260 U.S. 393, 414 (1922).

[28] Pennsylvania Coal Co. v. Mahon, 260 U.S. 393, 414 (1922).

In the balance of the opinion, Holmes proceeded to discuss the general validity of the statute regardless of "plaintiffs' position." He failed to explore the possible public interest in favor of preventing personal injury or property damage caused by surface subsidence generally, nor did he discuss the *Mugler-Hadacheck* rule.[29] Rather, he focused only on diminution in value. Because the statute made it illegal to mine the pillars of coal that supported the surface, this had "very nearly the same effect for constitutional purposes as appropriating" the coal.[30]

[D] Brandeis's Dissenting Opinion

Dissenting, Justice Brandeis argued that the case was clearly controlled by the *Mugler-Hadacheck* rule: a "restriction imposed to protect the public health, safety or morals from dangers threatened is not a taking."[31] The statute merely prohibited a "noxious use"—subsurface mining that endangered the public.

Brandeis then opened a debate that remains alive today. Assuming that the "diminution in value" of property is relevant, to what "property" does this standard apply? Holmes had viewed the "property" as only the pillars of coal left in place to support the surface. Brandeis argued, however, that the relevant "property" was the whole property owned by the coal company; thus, the extent of diminution in value could be determined only by comparing (a) the "value of the coal kept in place" with (b) the "value of the whole property."[32]

For example, suppose the coal company could comply with the statute by removing 98% of the underground coal (the mineral estate) and leaving only 2% of the coal (the support estate) in pillars to support the surface. On these facts, Brandeis would argue that the statute diminished the value of the "whole property" only by 2%, which would be a minor impact. Holmes, in contrast, would argue that the statute eliminated all value from the support estate (the 2% of coal left in place), causing "total taking:" a 100% diminution in the value of the "property." The Brandeis approach to this issue has prevailed in later decisions (*see* § 40.04[B]).

[E] Aftermath of *Pennsylvania Coal*

The *Pennsylvania Coal* decision left the law of regulatory takings in confusion. A regulation could indeed be a taking if it went "too far," but exactly what did this mean? Legal scholars even failed to agree on what test Holmes had applied. Many interpreted the decision as creating a *diminution in value test,* in which the only relevant factor was the extent to which the regulation diminished the value of the property; these scholars

---

[29] Holmes mentioned—but quickly dismissed—reciprocity of advantage, implicitly finding that the statute conferred no reciprocal advantage on the coal company.

[30] Pennsylvania Coal Co. v. Mahon, 260 U.S. 393, 414 (1922).

[31] Pennsylvania Coal Co. v. Mahon, 260 U.S. 393, 417 (1922) (Brandeis, J., dissenting).

[32] Pennsylvania Coal Co. v. Mahon, 260 U.S. 393, 419 (1922) (Brandeis, J., dissenting).

focused on Holmes's observation that when diminution "reaches a certain magnitude, in most if not in all cases there must be . . . compensation."[33] Other scholars argued that Holmes had actually used a *balancing test,* comparing the extent of the public interest with the extent of diminution; this approach placed great weight on Holmes's conclusion that the statute did not manifest a public interest "sufficient to warrant so extensive a destruction."[34] So, what was the test? And how much diminution in value was too much? Equally troublesome was the relationship between the new *Pennsylvania Coal* test (whatever it was) and the historic "nuisance" or "noxious use" standard. Had the Court superseded the historic standard or merely created an additional test?

Over 50 years elapsed before the Supreme Court revisited the takings issue in its 1978 decision of *Penn Central Transportation Co. v. New York City.*[35] During this period, the meaning of *Pennsylvania Coal* remained unclear. The Court failed to even cite the decision in its next two important zoning cases—*Village of Euclid v. Ambler Realty Co.*[36] in 1926 and *Nectow v. City of Cambridge*[37] in 1928—although it later characterized both as "takings" cases. Over the ensuing decades, *Pennsylvania Coal* was rarely cited by any court and the law of regulatory takings became dormant. Takings claims were infrequent, and almost always dismissed under the "nuisance" or "noxious use" test. Regulations enacted to prevent harm to the public were deemed valid under the police power, while—as a matter of logic—regulations enacted to benefit the public might presumably require compensation under the Takings Clause. But the weakness of this approach, often called the *harm-benefit test,* was apparent: almost any regulation could be seen as either harm-preventing or benefit-conferring, depending on one's perspective.[38]

Another chapter in the *Pennsylvania Coal* saga was written in 1987, when the Supreme Court reached the opposite result in an almost identical case, *Keystone Bituminous Coal Ass'n v. DeBenedictis.*[39] The case concerned a later Pennsylvania surface subsidence statute that—like its predecessor—effectively required coal companies to leave pillars of coal in place to support the land surface. Applying its modern test (*see* § 40.05), the Court held that the statute was not a regulatory taking. The Court found that the newer statute was supported by a broader range of policies than its predecessor, including the public interest in health, the environment, and the fiscal integrity of the region, and prevented mining activity that was akin to a public nuisance. More importantly, the Court followed Justice Brandeis's approach to the question of defining the relevant "property." The statute

---

[33] Pennsylvania Coal Co. v. Mahon, 260 U.S. 393, 413 (1922).

[34] Pennsylvania Coal Co. v. Mahon, 260 U.S. 393, 414 (1922).

[35] 438 U.S. 104 (1978).

[36] 272 U.S. 365 (1926).

[37] 277 U.S. 183 (1928).

[38] *See, e.g.,* Just v. Marinette County, 201 N.W.2d 761 (Wis. 1972) (zoning ordinance that prevented filling of wetlands seen as harm-preventing).

[39] 480 U.S. 470 (1987).

required coal companies to leave less than 2% of their coal in place, and the Court found this 2% diminution in the value of the whole property to be insignificant.

§ 40.04 Overview of the Modern Era in Regulatory Takings: 1978–Present

[A] Current Takings Tests

After 56 years of silence, the Supreme Court reentered the takings arena with its 1978 decision in *Penn Central Transportation Co. v. New York City*.[40] Since then, the Court has further developed its regulatory takings jurisprudence in a number of other key decisions. These decisions have established a series of new (and somewhat inconsistent) standards for determining when a regulatory taking occurs. Although echoes of the Court's earlier tests may linger, they have been largely swept aside by these new standards. Thus, the "nuisance" or "noxious use" test, the "reciprocity of advantage" approach, and the *Pennsylvania Coal* test have all apparently been superseded. But they remain helpful in understanding the current law, and indeed are still used or cited occasionally, together with more modern standards.

What are the current takings tests? Although generalizations about takings law are notoriously risky, there appear to be four independent tests. The Court opened the modern era by adopting an "ad hoc" approach in *Penn Central*. Justice Brennan explained that the Court had "been unable to develop any 'set formula' for determining when 'justice and fairness'" required compensation.[41] Thus, each future takings case was to be decided under a new multi-factor balancing test (*see* § 40.05[C]). The three relevant factors are:

(1)   the economic impact of the regulation on the claimant,

(2)   the extent to which the regulation interferes with the claimant's distinct investment-backed expectations, and

(3)   the character of the governmental action.

However, the Court's subsequent opinion in *Agins v. City of Tiburon* has cast some doubt on the role of the *Penn Central* test (*see* § 40.05[E]).

In later decisions, the Court crafted three more-or-less "bright line" rules that supplement the *Penn Central* standard. Greatly oversimplified, these "categorical" rules provide that a taking will be found:

(1)   if government authorizes a *permanent physical occupation* of land (*Loretto v. Teleprompter Manhattan CATV Corp.*) (*see* § 40.06);

(2)   if regulation causes the loss of *all economically beneficial or productive use of land*, unless justified by *background principles*

---

[40] 438 U.S. 104 (1978).

[41] Penn Central Transp. Co. v. New York City, 438 U.S. 104, 124 (1978).

of property or nuisance law (Lucas v. South Carolina Coastal Council) (see § 40.07); or

(3)　if government demands an exaction that either lacks an *essential nexus* with a legitimate state interest or lacks *rough proportionality* to the impacts of the proposed project (*Nollan v. California Coastal Commission—Dolan v. City of Tigard*) (*see* § 40.08).

Accordingly, four different tests might potentially apply to a takings problem. So—as a practical matter—when does each one apply? The conventional wisdom is as follows. First, determine if the regulation is a taking under any of the three special rules (*Loretto, Lucas,* and *Nollan-Dolan*). If not, proceed to a second step: determine whether the regulation is a taking under the *Penn Central* standard. Of course, the only safe prediction about the future of regulatory takings jurisprudence is that the law will continue to change. The four tests of today may well evolve into a quite different set of standards in the near future.

[B]　Defining the Relevant "Property"

What "property" do these standards apply to? Suppose O buys an undeveloped parcel of land that contains 100 acres, and later government action adversely affects five acres of the parcel. Do we apply the takings tests to the 100-acre parcel or the five-acre parcel? First discussed in *Pennsylvania Coal*, this question is called the "denominator" or "conceptual severance" issue.

The law is clear when the government action is a physical occupation. Under *Loretto,* any permanent physical occupation of land authorized by government is a taking (*see* § 40.06[C]). For example, if the county constructs a public school on five acres of O's property, this is clearly a taking of the five acres even though O retains possession of the remaining 95 acres.

On the other hand, when the government action is mere regulation—without any physical occupation—the "whole parcel" is considered.[42] Suppose O's 100-acre parcel is initially zoned for low-density residential development (e.g., one house for every 10 acres), but the county rezones five acres of the parcel into a "Rural Agriculture" district where no development of any kind is permitted. As *Penn Central* makes clear, we would apply its takings criteria to the 100-acre parcel (*see* § 40.05[C]). Thus, at worst the economic effect of the rezoning is a 5% loss in value of the 100-acre parcel, not a 100% loss in value of the five-acre parcel.

---

[42] Two further issues arise. If the same owner sold adjacent parcels before the regulation took effect, are these considered together with the affected parcel as the "whole property"? Probably not, although some contrary authority exists. *Compare* Deltona Corp. v. United States, 657 F.2d 1184 (Ct. Cl. 1981) (yes) *with* Loveladies Harbor, Inc. v. United States, 28 F.3d 1171 (Fed. Cir. 1994) (no). And are other contiguous or noncontiguous parcels owned by the same owner as of the claimed taking date considered part of the "whole property"? There is a split of authority on this point as well. In particular, the Supreme Court seemed to indicate in Lucas v. South Carolina Coastal Council, 505 U.S. 1003, 1016–1017 n.7 (1992), that noncontiguous parcels—at least—would not be included.

§ 40.05   Basic Modern Standard for Regulatory Takings: *Penn Central Transportation Co. v. New York City* (1978)

[A]   *Penn Central* in Context

The single most important modern decision about regulatory takings is *Penn Central Transportation Co. v. New York City*.[43] The takings test it established brought much-needed coherence to the law and signaled renewed judicial interest in the topic. The *Penn Central* test is admittedly vague and imprecise, sometimes leading to unpredictable results; but it is an improvement over the mystifying *Pennsylvania Coal* approach. Although the three "bright line" rules later created by the Court have somewhat reduced the role of the *Penn Central* test, it remains the basic standard used to resolve most regulatory takings cases today.

[B]   Facts of *Penn Central*

One of the most famous buildings in New York City—Grand Central Terminal—was designated a "landmark" under the city's Landmarks Preservation Law. Constructed in 1913, the eight-story terminal was considered a "magnificent example of the French beaux-arts style."[44] Under the landmarks law, any change in the exterior architectural features of a landmark, or construction of any exterior improvement on its site, required advance approval from a city commission. However, city ordinances also allowed the owner of a landmark to transfer unused development rights from the landmark parcel to other nearby parcels.

The owners of the terminal property—Penn Central Transportation Co. and affiliated companies ("Penn Central")—leased the airspace above the terminal to UGP Properties, Inc. ("UGP") for a 50-year term. Even without the lease, the existing terminal use provided Penn Central with a reasonable return on its investment; the lease would provide millions of dollars in additional income each year. UGP's plan to construct a 55-story office building in the airspace over the terminal required approval from the landmarks commission. The commission rejected both the initial design proposal and 53-story alternative proposal, based mainly on aesthetic considerations. For example, the commission stated: "To balance a 55-story office tower above a flamboyant Beaux-Arts facade seems nothing more than an aesthetic joke. Quite simply, the tower would overwhelm the Terminal by its sheer mass."[45]

At this point—without submitting a proposal for a smaller office building or trying to transfer development rights to another parcel—Penn Central and UGP filed suit, alleging that the application of the landmarks law to the property was a taking. Plaintiffs made two main arguments. First, the

---

[43] 438 U.S. 104 (1978).

[44] Penn Central Transp. Co. v. New York City, 438 U.S. 104, 115 (1978).

[45] Penn Central Transp. Co. v. New York City, 438 U.S. 104, 117–118 (1978).

law constituted a total taking of their property rights in the airspace, just as the statute in *Pennsylvania Coal* took the coal company's entire support estate. Second, in the alternative, considering the property as a whole, the law substantially diminished the value of the land in order to confer the benefits of landmark preservation on the public; the *Mugler-Hadacheck* rule was inapplicable because the law was not intended to prevent public harm.[46]

[C] The *Penn Central* Balancing Test

In a 6-3 decision, the Supreme Court held that no taking had occurred. Writing for the majority, Justice Brennan quickly dismissed the plaintiffs' first argument that the law was a total taking of their airspace rights. "'Taking' jurisprudence does not divide a single parcel into discrete segments and attempt to determine whether rights in a particular segment have been entirely abrogated."[47] The Court would consider the impact of the law on "rights in the parcel as a whole—here, the city tax block designated as the 'landmark site,'" not merely its impact on the airspace rights.[48] This language clearly repudiated the Court's contrary suggestion in *Pennsylvania Coal* (*see* § 40.03[C]).

Brennan characterized the Court's past takings decisions as "essentially ad hoc, factual inquiries" based on several factors, without any "set formula."[49] He then proceeded to create a new multi-factor balancing test for determining when a regulation constituted a taking. The factors were:

(1) "[t]he economic impact of the regulation on the claimant";

(2) "particularly, the extent to which the regulation has interfered with distinct investment-backed expectations"; and

(3) "the character of the governmental action."[50]

Applying this test to plaintiffs' second argument, Brennan found that all three factors supported the conclusion that no taking existed. First, the economic impact of the law on plaintiffs was not severe. Even without the office building, Penn Central could derive a reasonable return on its investment by operating the terminal. Moreover, plaintiffs could still seek to construct a smaller office building in the airspace or transfer the valuable development rights to another parcel. Nor did the law interfere with Penn Central's primary investment-backed expectation concerning use of the parcel: operating the terminal as it had been used for the last 65 years. Finally, turning to the character of the government action, the landmarks law was found to be a regulation reasonably related to the promotion of the general welfare, not a physical invasion by government.

---

[46] A third argument was that reciprocity of advantage did not justify the law. It affected only a few buildings—all separated from each other—which were singled out and treated differently from the surrounding buildings, and accordingly produced no reciprocal benefits.

[47] Penn Central Transp. Co. v. New York City, 438 U.S. 104, 130 (1978).

[48] Penn Central Transp. Co. v. New York City, 438 U.S. 104, 130–131 (1978).

[49] Penn Central Transp. Co. v. New York City, 438 U.S. 104, 124 (1978).

[50] Penn Central Transp. Co. v. New York City, 438 U.S. 104, 124 (1978).

[D] Exploring the *Penn Central* Factors

[1] "Economic Impact of the Regulation on the Claimant"

The most important factor appears to be the economic impact of the regulation on the claimant. Yet the Court provided little information about how this factor should be applied. Suppose a regulation reduces the fair market value of B's land from $500,000 to $25,000—a 95% reduction in value. Is this a taking? Presumably, if a regulation eliminates all economically viable use of the land or reduces its fair market value to zero, the economic impact on the claimant would be seen as extremely severe.

On the other hand, the Court made it quite clear that even when a regulation causes significant "diminution in property value," it is not a taking if the regulation is "reasonably related to the promotion of the general welfare."[51] It observed, for example, that neither the "87½% diminution in value" in *Hadacheck v. Sebastian* nor the "75% diminution in value" in *Village of Euclid v. Ambler Realty Co.* constituted a taking because the regulations at issue met this standard.[52] But because almost every land use regulation meets the highly-deferential "rational relationship" standard, this language literally seems to mean that a regulation that causes even an extreme reduction in market value (e.g., a 95% reduction or more) would not be a taking. Adding more confusion, the Court later suggested in *Lucas v. South Carolina Coastal Council* that a 95% reduction in value might result in a taking under the *Penn Central* test.[53]

Another approach to this factor focuses on whether the regulation prevents the owner from obtaining a "reasonable return" from the land. The Court stressed that Penn Central could obtain a reasonable return on its investment by continuing to use the land as a terminal, regardless of any transferable development rights.[54]

[2] "Extent to Which the Regulation Has Interfered with Distinct Investment-Backed Expectations"

This rather confusing factor examines the owner's reasonable "investment-backed" expectations about the use of his or her land.[55] The scant case law on point seems to distinguish between existing uses and potential future uses. In most instances, the buyer who purchases land already

---

[51] Penn Central Transp. Co. v. New York City, 438 U.S. 104, 131 (1978).

[52] Penn Central Transp. Co. v. New York City, 438 U.S. 104, 131 (1978).

[53] Lucas v. South Carolina Coastal Comm'n, 505 U.S. 1003, 1019 n.8 (1992).

[54] *See also* Keystone Bituminous Coal Ass'n v. DeBenedictis, 480 U.S. 470 (1987) (mine owner failed to show that regulation rendered mine operation unprofitable).

[55] *See* Frank I. Michelman, *Property, Utility, and Fairness: Comments on the Ethical Foundations of "Just Compensation" Law*, 80 Harv. L. Rev. 1165, 1233 (1967) (suggesting the "investment-backed expectations" standard later adopted in *Penn Central*); *see also* Daniel R. Mandelker, *Investment-Backed Expectations in Taking Law*, 27 Urb. Law. 215 (1995) (discussing standard).

devoted to a legally-permitted use has a reasonable investment-backed expectation that the use will continue. For example, the *Penn Central* Court stressed that the landmarks preservation ordinance did not interfere with the owner's "primary expectation"—continuing the existing terminal use.[56] Suppose buyer B purchases a 40-acre shopping center complex—a use clearly allowed by the local zoning ordinance—consisting of retail stores, parking lot, and related facilities. If the city council now rezones part of the parking lot into a district where only "urban recreational uses" (e.g., skateboarding) are permitted, curtailing parking for shopping center customers, the shopping center might no longer be profitable. This would be a severe interference with B's investment-backed expectations.

On the other hand, if a parcel of land is already subject to a zoning ordinance or other land use regulation at the time of purchase, the buyer probably cannot have a reasonable investment-backed expectation that he or she will be able to violate the law.[57] Suppose B wants to build a new shopping center on vacant land; he purchases a 40-acre parcel located in an "open space" zone where no building is permitted. Under these circumstances, all courts would agree that the ordinance does not interfere at all with B's reasonable expectations. B either knew—or, as a prudent investor, should have known—about the use restriction.[58]

[3] "Character of the Governmental Action"

The final factor is the character of the government action. The Court explained that a taking is more likely to be found if the government interference is a "physical invasion . . . than when interference arises from some public program adjusting the benefits and burdens of economic life to promote the common good."[59] This factor became less important when the Court adopted its *Loretto* rule that any permanent physical occupation authorized by government is a taking. So what does this factor mean after *Loretto*?

The Court's phrasing of the factor suggests that a benefit-conferring regulation is less likely to be a taking than a physical invasion. Indeed, in a famous footnote, the Court seemed to abandon the harm-benefit test entirely. It explained that the *Mugler-Hadacheck* line of cases was best understood not as turning on any "noxious" use of land, but rather "on the ground that the restrictions were reasonably related to the implementation of a policy . . . expected to produce a widespread public benefit and applicable to all similarly situated property."[60] Therefore, in the *Penn Central* context, this factor seems to mean that a regulation that is reasonably related to the public health, safety, or welfare is not a taking

---

[56] Penn Central Transp. Co. v. New York City, 438 U.S. 104, 136 (1978).

[57] *But cf.* Nollan v. California Coastal Comm'n, 483 U.S. 825 (1987).

[58] What about owners who acquire their interests by gift, descent, or devise? Whether such owners can have investment-backed expectations is "dubious." Irving v. Hodel, 481 U.S. 704, 715 (1987).

[59] Penn Central Transp. Co. v. New York City, 438 U.S. 104, 124 (1978).

[60] Penn Central Transp. Co. v. New York City, 438 U.S. 104, 134 n.30 (1978).

even if it substantially diminishes the value of the affected land; it is irrelevant whether the regulation is harm-preventing or benefit-conferring.

Yet the Court clearly backs away from this broad interpretation in later cases, leaving the modern significance of this factor somewhat unclear.[61] In all probability, a nuisance-prevention regulation is less likely to be viewed as a taking than one that—like the historic preservation ordinance in *Penn Central*—is mainly oriented toward benefiting the public.

[E]　Aftermath of *Penn Central*

Two years later, the Court threw a potential monkey wrench into the *Penn Central* test when deciding *Agins v. City of Tiburon*.[62] Rejecting a facial takings attack on a zoning ordinance, the *Agins* Court seemed to adopt a new and different basic test for determining when a taking occurred. Under the *Agins* standard, a generally applicable zoning law effects a taking if the ordinance "does not substantially advance legitimate state interests . . . or denies an owner economically viable use of his land."[63] The first prong of this test stems from the historic standard for substantive due process (*see* § 38.02[A][3]), while the second prong is arguably linked to the first two *Penn Central* criteria. In practice, however, this second prong is so vague as to be almost meaningless.

The Court has never explained how the vague *Agins* standard relates to the *Penn Central* test. Is it a shorthand reference to the more detailed *Penn Central* criteria, or is it intended to replace them? In some post-*Agins* decisions, the Court seems to follow the *Penn Central* test, while in others it appears to use the *Agins* standard.[64] Indeed, one authority concludes that the Court "could do all affected groups a service by jettisoning the *Agins* . . . criteria in favor of" the *Penn Central* test.[65] Yet the Court primarily seems to use the *Agins* standard as support for its growing list of categorical rules, implying that *Penn Central* continues to apply where the categorical rules do not.

---

[61] *See, e.g.,* Hodel v. Irving, 481 U.S. 704 (1987) (where statute prohibited Native Americans from devising small undivided interests in reservation lands, the "extraordinary" character of the government regulation supported finding a taking).

[62] 447 U.S. 255 (1980).

[63] Agins v. City of Tiburon, 447 U.S. 255, 260 (1980).

[64] *See also* 152 Valparaiso Assocs. v. City of Cotati, 65 Cal. Rptr. 2d 551 (Ct. App. 1997) (suggesting that rent control ordinance might be taking under *Agins* if ordinance fails to advance its stated purposes).

[65] Robert Meltz, et al., The Takings Issue: Constitutional Limits on Land Use Control and Environmental Regulation 139 (1999).

§ 40.06 Special Rule for Permanent Physical Occupations: *Loretto v. Teleprompter Manhattan CATV Corp.* (1982)

[A] A "Bright Line" Rule

Suppose H owns 200 acres of vacant land destined for future residential development. Without obtaining H's consent, the U.S. Post Office installs a permanent mailbox on the edge of H's land. Embedded in a concrete slab, the mailbox occupies about four square feet of land, less than.00005% of the total surface area of H's parcel. Is this a taking?

The answer is clearly "yes" under *Loretto v. Teleprompter Manhattan CATV Corp.* [66] In *Loretto,* the Supreme Court established a special exception to the ad hoc *Penn Central* approach. For the first time, the Court recognized a bright line rule: any "permanent physical occupation authorized by government is a taking without regard to the public interests that it may serve." [67] Here, the mailbox is a permanent physical occupation of H's land, and hence a taking, regardless of the public interest that its placement on the land might promote.

Loretto only applies to physical takings. It can be classified as a regulatory takings case only in the narrow sense that government had authorized the permanent physical occupation of land by a third party. Yet *Loretto* is crucial to understanding the development of regulatory takings jurisprudence.

[B] Facts of *Loretto*

Loretto revolves around the installation of cable television equipment at a New York City apartment building. In 1970, the building owner permitted the local cable television company to install and maintain a "crossover" line on the building roof. This crossover line had three parts: (1) a thin cable about 36 feet long; (2) two "directional taps," each one a 4-inch cube; and (3) two metal boxes, each approximately 18" by 12" by 6" in size. The crossover line was part of a cable "highway," which served other buildings on the block, not this particular building. Loretto purchased the building in 1971, unaware that the crossover line existed.

In 1973, New York enacted a statute that (a) authorized cable television companies to install cables and related facilities on residential rental property without the landlord's consent and (b) provided that the landlord would receive a "reasonable" payment in return, as determined by a state commission; the commission later found that a one-time payment of $1.00 was reasonable. Shortly thereafter, the local cable television company installed a "noncrossover" cable line at Loretto's building; this line provided cable television service to Loretto's tenants. Loretto later sued, claiming that the state law was a taking of property without just compensation.

---

[66] 458 U.S. 419 (1982).

[67] Loretto v. Teleprompter Manhattan CATV Corp., 458 U.S. 419, 426 (1982).

[C] The *Loretto* Test

The Court held flatly that any "permanent physical occupation" of land is a taking, regardless of "whether the action achieves an important public benefit or has only minimal economic impact on the owner."[68] It made no difference whether government occupied the property itself, or merely—as here—authorized a third party to do so. The Court reasoned that such an occupation effectively destroys all of the owner's basic property rights: the rights to possess, use, and dispose of property. "[T]he government does not simply take a single 'strand' from the 'bundle' of property rights: it chops through the bundle, taking a slice of every strand."[69] Moreover, the Court observed, in such an extreme case "the property owner entertains a historically rooted expectation of compensation."[70] After reviewing more than a century of precedent, the Court concluded that its decisions had uniformly found a taking in such circumstances.[71]

Under this standard, the cable installation on Loretto's building was a taking. The cables and related facilities were attached to the building with bolts and screws and thus were permanent; this equipment constituted a physical occupation because it occupied space on and above the roof, and along the exterior wall of the building. Although the extent of the occupation was admittedly small, this was relevant only in assessing the amount of compensation due for the taking.

The Court stressed that not all physical intrusions were takings under this standard. It distinguished sharply between a "permanent physical occupation" and a mere "temporary invasion."[72] A temporary invasion— such as an occasional demonstration at a shopping center[73] or intermittent flooding of agricultural land—is a much smaller interference with an owner's property rights. It does not wholly eliminate the owner's right to use, or exclude others from, the land.[74] Thus, the *Penn Central* balancing test applies to "cases of physical invasion short of permanent appropriation."[75]

---

[68] Loretto v. Teleprompter Manhattan CATV Corp. 458 U.S. 419, 435 (1982).

[69] Loretto v. Teleprompter Manhattan CATV Corp., 458 U.S. 419, 435 (1982).

[70] Loretto v. Teleprompter Manhattan CATV Corp., 458 U.S. 419, 441 (1982). *But see* Yee v. City of Escondido, 503 U.S. 519 (1992) (rent control ordinance that severely restricted landlords' ability to evict tenants was not governed by *Loretto* rule because the tenants were initially invited onto the property by the landlords, not forced upon them by government).

[71] *See also* United States v. Causby, 328 U.S. 256 (1946) (low altitude flights by air force planes through air space above owner's land constituted a taking).

[72] As the dissent points out, it is difficult in many cases to distinguish between a "permanent physical occupation" and a "temporary physical invasion." Loretto v. Teleprompter Manhattan CATV Corp., 458 U.S. 419, 447–448 (1982) (Blackmun, J., dissenting).

[73] *See, e.g.,* PruneYard Shopping Center v. Robins, 447 U.S. 74 (1980).

[74] If government compels a landowner to provide a non-exclusive easement for public access, this is apparently considered a "permanent physical occupation" and thus governed by the *Loretto* rule. *See* Nollan v. California Coastal Comm'n, 483 U.S. 825 (1987).

[75] Loretto v. Teleprompter Manhattan CATV Corp. 458 U.S. 419, 433 n.9 (1982).

[D] Reflections on *Loretto*

The core of *Loretto* is uncontroversial. The concept that government seizure or occupation of privately-owned land constitutes a taking is the historic foundation of the Takings Clause. And, logically, it should make no difference whether the occupation is performed, or merely authorized, by government.[76]

But should this rule extend to trivial and insignificant occupations? For example, as the dissent noted, New York law requires landlords to supply mailboxes for their tenants; in effect, a landlord is compelled to purchase and install mailboxes at his or her own expense. Yet, under the *Loretto* standard, if the state purchases mailboxes and installs them at its own expense in a landlord's building, this is a permanent physical occupation and hence a taking. Is this distinction of constitutional significance? The dissent argues that an "intelligible takings inquiry must also ask whether the *extent* of the State's interference is so severe as to constitute a compensable taking."[77] Indeed, it seems doubtful that the framers originally intended the Takings Clause to apply to trivial intrusions. However, these concerns may be more theoretical than real. Cases involving de minimis occupations are unlikely to be brought because the small amount of damages at stake will not warrant the expense of litigation.

Suppose M illegally dumps hazardous wastes on her rural property, creating a toxic nightmare that will endanger human life for years to come. In order to protect the public, the state installs a brick fence around the contaminated area and erects large warning signs on steel posts. Is this a taking, such that the state must pay M for the land occupied by the fence and signs? Seemingly, yes. The fence and signs are as permanent as the cable equipment in *Loretto*; and they physically occupy space on M's land. The *Loretto* rule is apparently applied regardless of the nature of the public interest at stake—or the culpability of the landowner—so the strong public interest in protecting human health and safety here is irrelevant. Of course, if the occupied land has little or no value—as seems likely—a token payment to M may satisfy the just compensation requirement.

§ 40.07 Special Rule for Loss of All Economically Beneficial or Productive Use: *Lucas v. South Carolina Coastal Council* (1992)

[A] A "Bright Line" Rule?

Suppose R owns 20 acres of desert land in pristine natural condition. The state adopts a desert preservation statute that designates R's land and

---

[76] *See also* United States v. Sioux Nation of Indians, 448 U.S. 371 (1980) (1877 statute that abrogated treaty with tribe, thereby legitimatizing settlers' occupancy of Indian lands, was a taking).

[77] Loretto v. Teleprompter Manhattan CATV Corp., 458 U.S. 419, 453 (1982) (Blackmun, J., dissenting).

similar undeveloped desert property as "conservation zones." In order to "protect the fragile desert ecosystem for future generations," the statute provides that land in conservation zones may be used only for one purpose: nature study. Assume that the statute reduces the fair market value of R's land from $20,000 to zero. Is this a taking?

In *Lucas v. South Carolina Coastal Council*, the Supreme Court adopted a "categorical" takings rule: a taking will always be found if regulation eliminates "all economically beneficial or productive use of land," unless the regulation is justified under background principles of property or nuisance law.[78] Under this standard, the desert preservation statute would be considered a taking. By reducing the value of R's land to zero, the statute eliminates all economically beneficial or productive use; and no previously-existing rule of property or nuisance law would justify this intrusion.

[B]   Facts of *Lucas*

Lucas, a real estate developer, paid $975,000 for two beachfront lots in a residential development located on a barrier island off the coast of South Carolina. At the time, a state statute required that owners of certain coastal lands—including beaches and areas adjacent to sand dunes—obtain a permit before developing their property. Because Lucas's lots were 300 feet away from the beach when he purchased, they were not covered by this statute. However, for many years in the recent past, the lots had been either part of the beach or flooded regularly by the ebb and flow of the tide.

Two years after Lucas's purchase, South Carolina adopted a more comprehensive statute to preserve its shoreline and beaches. The state legislature explained, among other things, that by preserving the beach/dune system as a barrier to hurricanes and other storms, the statute would protect life and property from serious injury. Accordingly, the statute prohibited all construction along a long stretch of shoreline, including both of Lucas's lots. Concluding that the statute reduced the value of Lucas's lots to zero, the trial court found a regulatory taking had occurred and awarded over $1,200,000 in compensatory damages. The South Carolina Supreme Court reversed, finding that the statute was a valid exercise of the police power to prevent nuisance-like activities under the *Mugler-Hadacheck* standard.

[C]   The *Lucas* Test

Writing for the Court, Justice Scalia carved out a special exception to the *Penn Central* standard. Acknowledging that the Court generally preferred to resolve takings cases on an ad hoc basis—as in *Penn Central*—he nonetheless identified two "categories" where a taking could be found without a fact-specific inquiry: (a) "regulations that compel the property owner to suffer a physical 'invasion' of his property" (as in *Loretto*) and (b)

---

[78] 505 U.S. 1003, 1005 (1992).

regulations that deny "all economically beneficial or productive use of land."[79]

This second standard—which governed the outcome in *Lucas*—is clearly linked to the Court's early *Pennsylvania Coal* approach and to the *Agins* standard. Under the *Lucas* test, a regulation that denies the landowner all economically beneficial or productive use of his land is a taking, *unless* the regulation is justified by "background principles of the State's law of property and nuisance."[80] Applying its new test, the Court held that the statute clearly eliminated all economically beneficial or productive use of Lucas's land. But it remanded the case to determine if the statute could be justified under background principles of South Carolina law, which it appeared to doubt. "It seems unlikely that common-law principles would have prevented the erection of any habitable or productive improvements on petitioner's land; they rarely support prohibition of the 'essential use' of land."[81]

[D] Exploring the *Lucas* Factors

[1] Loss of "All Economically Beneficial or Productive Use of Land"

The first prong of the *Lucas* test is quite rigorous: the regulation must deprive the owner of *all* economically beneficial or productive use of land. This standard was met in *Lucas* because the trial court found that the construction ban rendered the lots totally valueless—a clear case. But market value may not be the only relevant yardstick. The test concerns whether land can be *used* in a manner that is economically beneficial or productive. And the meaning of "economically beneficial or productive use" is far from clear.

For example, is a use "economically" beneficial or productive if it generates *any* income at all, even if less than a reasonable return on investment? Suppose that O purchases a tract of wild land for $100,000; later, the county adopts an "open space" ordinance that requires that the land be kept in its natural condition. Mining, timber harvesting, agriculture, residential development, and all other uses that might provide a reasonable return on O's investment (e.g., $5,000 per year) are all prohibited. However, assume that O could rent the land to C, a veteran camper, for $100 per year; C will use the land for recreational camping. Do these facts trigger the *Lucas* test? Presumably not. Here O retains an economically beneficial and productive use because the land produces rental income. The *Lucas* test apparently does not mandate a "profitable" use, and the Court noted that its rule would apply only in "relatively rare situations."[82] On the other hand, the Court suggested that "requiring land to be left substantially in its natural state" was a typical example of regulation that deprived an owner of all economically beneficial or productive options for land use.

---

[79] Lucas v. South Carolina Coastal Council, 505 U.S. 1003, 1015 (1992).

[80] Lucas v. South Carolina Coastal Council, 505 U.S. 1003, 1029 (1992).

[81] Lucas v. South Carolina Coastal Council, 505 U.S. 1003, 1031 (1992).

[82] Lucas v. South Carolina Coastal Council, 505 U.S. 1003, 1018 (1992).

Certainly, the precise factual situation before the Court—a statute that (purportedly) reduced the property value to zero—is highly unlikely to recur. Even if a law now prohibits all use of a particular parcel of land, a speculator would probably be willing to purchase it at a low price because the prohibition might well be lifted or relaxed in the future.

[2] Unless Justified by "Background Principles of the State's Law of Property and Nuisance"

Having established a new "categorical" rule, the Court immediately proceeded to create a huge exception. In a rather confusing turnabout, Justice Scalia first condemned the harm-benefit test as unworkable, and then revived the *Mugler-Hadacheck* nuisance exception in modified form.

If the first prong of the *Lucas* test is met, Scalia explained, this creates a presumption that a taking has occurred, without the need for fact-specific inquiry into the public interest that underlies the regulation. This presumption shifts the burden to the government. In order to avoid takings liability, the government must now show that the prohibited use would violate the "background principles of the State's law of property and nuisance" that govern land ownership.[83] In other words, it must be proven that the right to engage in the particular use was not in the "bundle of rights" that the owner acquired when purchasing the land.

What are the relevant "background principles"? While state nuisance law is obviously included, the exception also seems to encompass all aspects of the particular state's body of property law. This would include, for example, the public trust doctrine and the right to destroy property without compensation in emergency situations. Because these "background principles" differ from state to state, the scope of the exception will vary in each state. The exception also extends to regulations based on federal law, according to another section of the opinion.

Yet the scope of this exception remains somewhat unclear on two key points: (a) which types of law are considered? and (b) when is the relevant date for determining the law? Referring often to "common-law" principles, the Court certainly implies that only case law is relevant, not statutes, voter-adopted initiatives, administrative regulations, or state constitutional provisions. In effect, a legislature cannot adopt a statute that eliminates all economically beneficial and productive use *unless* courts could already reach the same result under common law principles. And the Court suggests that the restriction must be a "pre-existing limitation" on the owner's title, presumably existing when the owner acquired title or at some undefined earlier point. Does this standard "freeze" the state's law in the past or are courts (or legislatures) able to craft new rules in response to changing conditions? The majority hints that "changed circumstances or new knowledge" may justify new regulation.[84] If the relevant law is frozen at the time

---

[83] What about the reverse? Perhaps *Lucas* also stands for the proposition that a regulation based on background principles of property or nuisance law can *never* be a taking.

[84] Lucas v. South Carolina Coastal Council, 505 U.S. 1003, 1031 (1992).

each owner acquires title, then—even within a single state—the scope of the exception will vary for every owner.

Scalia stressed the narrow context in which this exception operates. A property owner, he reasoned, "necessarily expects the uses of his property to be restricted, from time to time, by various measures newly enacted by the State in legitimate exercise of its police powers."[85] But regulation that eliminates all economically valuable use after an owner buys his or her land has an extraordinarily severe impact on the owner. Thus, it can be justified only if this restriction already exists in the law when the owner acquires title.[86]

[E] Significance of *Lucas*

Although *Lucas* ignited scholarly controversy, its practical effect has been quite limited. State courts and lower federal courts tend to interpret *Lucas* narrowly, stressing that it applies only to the unusual situation where regulation eliminates *all* economically beneficial or productive use. Thus, one study of state court opinions concluded that *Lucas* "has not resulted in more than a trivial number of constitutional invalidations of state and local regulations."[87] However, the *Lucas* saga is far from over. As the case law continues to evolve, the *Lucas* standard may be applied to wetland-preservation laws or similar regulations that seek to protect environmentally-sensitive lands.

Lucas may be more significant as a compass—an indication of the direction that the Court's future takings decisions will follow. For example, the majority opinion suggests that a 95% diminution in market value might constitute a "categorical" taking under the *Lucas* test. This hint might ultimately lead to a decision that substantially broadens the *Lucas* approach (e.g., a decision holding that regulation that reduces property value by 80% is a taking, regardless of the public interest that it serves).

The *Lucas* majority also signals interest in reopening the "conceptual severance" debate, which *Penn Central* had seemingly resolved. If a regulation forces a developer to leave 90% of a rural parcel in its natural condition, for example, the Court opined that "it is unclear whether we would analyze the situation as one in which the owner has been deprived of all economically beneficial use of the burdened portion of the tract, or as one in which the owner has suffered a mere diminution in value of the tract as a whole."[88]

---

[85] Lucas v. South Carolina Coastal Council, 505 U.S. 1003, 1027 (1992). On remand, the South Carolina Supreme Court found no background principles of state law that justified the statute and accordingly instructed the trial court to award compensatory damages to Lucas. Lucas v. South Carolina Coastal Comm'n, 424 S.E.2d 484 (S.C. 1992).

[86] *See, e.g.,* Hunziker v. State, 519 N.W.2d 367 (Iowa 1994) (holding *Lucas* test inapplicable because statute in question was enacted before the plaintiff owners purchased the land).

[87] *See* Ronald H. Rosenberg, *The Non-Impact of the United States Supreme Court Regulatory Takings Cases on the State Courts: Does the Supreme Court Really Matter?*, 6 Fordham Envtl. L.J. 523, 548 (1995).

[88] Lucas v. South Carolina Coastal Council, 505 U.S. 1003, 1016–1017 n.7 (1992).

§ 40.08   Special Rule for Exactions: The *Nollan-Dolan* Duo (1987/1994)

[A]   The Problem of Exactions

Suppose developer D hopes to build 200 homes on a 50-acre parcel that is currently zoned for residential use. D needs subdivision approval from County in order to proceed with the project. In all probability, County will either (a) deny D's application or (b) grant the application subject to certain conditions known as exactions. An *exaction* is a requirement that the developer provide specified land, improvements, payments, or other benefits to the public to help offset the impacts of the project. Why demand exactions? Exactions shift the financial burden of accommodating new development from local government to the private developer, thereby avoiding the need for additional taxes or other public revenues. And the developer typically shifts this cost to buyers through higher prices.

For example, D's project will require construction of roads, sidewalks, storm drainage, and other public facilities on the 50-acre site. County will undoubtedly require D to provide these "on-site" improvements. In order to do this, D will *dedicate* the necessary land to public use, meaning that D will convey the land to County for these purposes; D will also construct the improvements at his own expense. County might also require D to provide "off-site" improvements (e.g., installing traffic lights at the intersection that adjoins the site in order to mitigate the impact of extra traffic) or to pay "impact" fees that compensate for other effects of the project (e.g., to help finance construction of additional school, water, and sewage facilities). The logic of these requirements is apparent: since D's project generated the need for these improvements, D should provide them. D can presumably pass on these costs to future residents of the project by increasing the sales prices of the homes.

What happens if County demands an exaction that has little or no relationship to the impacts of D's project? For example, suppose County insists that D convey 10 acres of his land to County for a public park as a condition of subdivision approval. This park is far bigger than needed to serve D's development. In effect, County is forcing D to provide a free park for the general public, instead of using its eminent domain power to purchase the land for this purpose (*see* Chapter 39). Courts applying state law generally require that exactions have a "reasonable relationship" with the project in question, but this is a fairly deferential test. Can D instead challenge this exaction as an unconstitutional taking?

[B]   *Nollan v. California Coastal Commission*: An "Essential Nexus" (1987)

The Supreme Court first addressed the exaction issue in *Nollan v. California Coastal Commission*.[89] The Nollans owned a beachfront lot in

---

[89] 483 U.S. 825 (1987).

Southern California. A dilapidated house covered part of the lot; the rest of the lot—between a seawall and the mean high tide line—consisted of a "dry sand" beach. California law required that the Nollans obtain a special coastal development permit in order to build a new home on the lot. The state coastal commission granted the Nollans' permit application subject to a condition: the Nollans were required to "dedicate" or grant an easement that allowed the public to cross the portion of their lot on the ocean side of the seawall. Such an easement would, for example, allow the public to walk along the beach even at high tide, by crossing through the "dry sand" part of the Nollans' lot. The Nollans argued that the easement condition was a taking, and the Supreme Court agreed by a 5-4 vote.

Writing for the majority, Justice Scalia first considered a hypothetical: assuming the Nollans had never applied for a permit, could the state force them to provide an easement for public use without compensation? The answer to this question was clearly "no." Under the *Loretto* standard, this would be the equivalent of a permanent physical occupation authorized by government, and hence a taking. Thus, the question became whether requiring the easement as a condition for a land-use permit changed this result.

Under one prong of the *Agins* standard, a land use regulation is a taking if it does not "substantially advance legitimate state interests." Scalia reasoned that a regulation substantially advances a state interest only if there is an "essential nexus" between an exaction and a state interest that the exaction is intended to serve. In other words, there must be a sufficient connection between the end (the state interest) and the means used to achieve that end (the exaction).

Here, the commission claimed that three state interests supported the easement condition: protecting the public's ability to see the beach; helping the public overcome a "psychological barrier" to using the beach; and avoiding beach congestion. But on the facts of the case, Scalia found that the easement had no relationship at all with these state interests. Although the Nollan's new house might adversely affect these state interests, the easement condition did not prevent or mitigate this problem. For example, if the planned house would block the public's prior view of the beach from the street in front of the house, then the commission could legally impose a height limit or other condition to protect the view. But the easement condition had no logical connection to this "view from the street" problem; it merely provided easier travel for people who were *already* walking on the beach and who thus already enjoyed an unimpaired view of the beach.[90] Thus, the requisite "essential nexus" did not exist.

---

[90] *See also* Blue Jeans Equities West v. City & County of San Francisco, 4 Cal. Rptr. 2d 114 (Ct. App. 1992) (refusing to apply *Nollan* standard to ordinance requiring payment of transit impact fee as approval condition).

[C] *Dolan v. City of Tigard*: The "Rough Proportionality" Test (1994)

In *Dolan v. City of Tigard*, the Court answered an issue left unresolved in *Nollan*: "[W]hat is the required degree of connection between the exactions . . . and the projected impacts of the proposed development?"[91]

Dolan, who owned a plumbing and electric supply store in Oregon, planned to double the size of her store, pave the existing gravel parking lot, and build an additional retail building on her land. The city granted Dolan's application for a building permit, but imposed two key conditions that effectively required her to convey or "dedicate" about 10% of her land to the city. First, because the project would increase the amount of impervious surface on the land—thus increasing storm-water runoff into the adjacent creek—Dolan was required to dedicate the part of her land lying within the creek's 100-year floodplain. Second, because the expanded store would attract additional customers—thus increasing traffic congestion on local streets—the city insisted that Dolan also dedicate an easement for a pedestrian/bicycle pathway over a 15-foot strip of her land.

The Court found an unconstitutional taking on these facts—again by a 5-4 vote—because the dedications demanded by the city lacked the required degree of connection with the impacts of the project. Chief Justice Rehnquist, writing for the majority, quickly concluded that the conditions satisfied the *Nollan* "essential nexus" standard. Limiting development within the floodplain promoted the city's interest in preventing floods; and providing the pedestrian/bicycle pathway served its interest in minimizing traffic congestion. Rehnquist then explored the degree of connection needed between the conditions and the impacts of Dolan's project, based on the *Nollan* premise that exactions must "substantially advance" such interests. He concluded that the Fifth Amendment required "rough proportionality": "[T]he city must make some sort of individualized determination that the required dedication is related both in nature and extent to the impact of the proposed development."[92] Although based on the state court "reasonable relationship" test, the "rough proportionality" standard is somewhat more stringent. Moreover, contrary to traditional law, it shifts the burden of proof to government to justify the exaction.

Under this new standard, no evidence in the record before the Court justified the floodplain dedication. Rehnquist suggested that the city's interest in flood control could be satisfied by a less intrusive condition— allowing Dolan to retain title to the floodplain land, but prohibiting any future development. Similarly, he found no evidence that the pedestrian/bicycle path easement was adequately related to the increased traffic that the project would cause. The record merely reflected that the path "could" offset some of the increased traffic, not that it "would" offset this traffic.

---

[91] Dolan v. City of Tigard, 512 U.S. 374, 377 (1994).

[92] Dolan v. City of Tigard, 512 U.S. 374, 391 (1994).

[D] Aftermath of *Nollan-Dolan*

Both *Nollan* and *Dolan* involved conditions that compelled an owner to convey an interest in land to the public in exchange for a discretionary land use approval. In order to withstand constitutional scrutiny under the Takings Clause, such an exaction must satisfy two separate tests:

(1)   there must an "essential nexus" between the exaction and a legitimate state interest that it serves, and

(2)   the exaction must be "roughly proportional" to the nature and extent of the project's impact.

In light of the *Loretto* rule that a permanent physical occupation is always deemed a taking, the *Nollan-Dolan* standards are not particularly surprising.

But do these standards apply to impact fees or other types of non-possessory exactions? In both *Nollan* and *Dolan,* the Court stressed the special nature of the condition at issue: the conveyance of an interest in land. A conveyance completely eliminates the owner's right to exclude others, "one of the most essential sticks in the bundle of rights that are commonly characterized as property."[93] The Court repeated this theme in a 1999 decision: "[W]e have not extended the rough-proportionality test of *Dolan* beyond the special context of exactions—land-use decisions conditioning approval of development on the dedication of property to public use."[94] Focusing on this distinction, most state courts and lower federal courts refuse to extend *Nollan-Dolan* to non-possessory exactions.

A notable exception is *Erlich v. City of Culver City,*[95] where the California Supreme Court applied the *Nollan-Dolan* standards to a monetary exaction. The owner of a private tennis club planned to demolish the club and build a residential condominium project in its place; the city conditioned project approval on the owner's payment of a $280,000 mitigation fee to compensate for the loss of recreational facilities. The *Erlich* court reasoned that the purpose underlying the *Nollan-Dolan* approach—avoiding illegitimate government demands that unfairly burden individual owners—applies equally to conveyances and monetary exactions. Although finding an "essential nexus" between the mitigation fee and the public interest in providing recreational facilities, the court held that the "rough proportionality" test was not met. The record before the court "was devoid of any individualized findings to support the required 'fit' between the monetary exaction and the loss of a parcel zoned for commercial recreational use."[96]

---

[93] *See, e.g.,* Dolan v. City of Tigard, 512 U.S. 374, 393 (1994) (quoting Kaiser Aetna v. United States, 444 U.S. 164, 176 (1979)).

[94] City of Monterey v. Del Monte Dunes, 119 S.Ct. 1624, 1635 (1999).

[95] 911 P.2d 429 (Cal. 1996).

[96] Erlich v. City of Culver City, 911 P.2d 429, 448 (Cal. 1996)

§ 40.09 Remedies for Regulatory Takings

[A] First English Evangelical Lutheran Church v. County of Los Angeles

Suppose that City adopts a land-use ordinance in 1997 that prevents O from constructing a planned shopping center on his vacant land. O sues City. In 2000, when O's takings case finally comes to trial, the court concludes that the ordinance is a taking. What remedy will O receive?

After decades of uncertainty, the law is now fairly straightforward: the remedy for a regulatory taking is compensatory damages. For decades, many believed that the appropriate remedy was a judgment invalidating the regulation at issue or similar equitable relief. The Supreme Court clarified the law in 1987 with its decision in *First English Evangelical Lutheran Church v. County of Los Angeles.*[97] The Court explained that the Takings Clause is designed "not to limit the governmental interference with property rights *per se*, but rather to secure *compensation* in the event of an otherwise proper interference amounting to a taking."[98] In short, the Constitution requires compensation for a taking.

Under *First English*, the successful plaintiff always receives compensation for the "temporary taking" of property at least for the period between (a) the date the regulation first adversely affected the land and (b) the date of judgment. But the owner has no right to demand that a "temporary taking" be made permanent, for this might force government to use its eminent domain power against its will. Rather, the government has a choice. "Once a court determines that a taking has occurred, the government retains the whole range of options already available—amendment of the regulation, withdrawal of the invalidated regulation, or exercise of eminent domain."[99] If the government elects to keep the regulation in place, the owner is entitled to compensation for a permanent taking. Alternatively, if the government chooses to cancel the regulation, the owner only receives compensation for the temporary taking that occurred during the period when the regulation was effective.

[B] Measure of Damages for Permanent Taking

For example, suppose that City elects to keep its ordinance in force. The measure of damages for a permanent taking is well-established. Just as in the case of eminent domain, the owner is entitled to receive the fair market value of the property on the date of the taking (*see* § 39.06). Thus, O will receive the fair market value of his land as of 1997, plus interest on this sum.

---

[97] 482 U.S. 304 (1987).

[98] First English Evangelical Lutheran Church v. County of Los Angeles, 482 U.S. 304, 315 (1987).

[99] First English Evangelical Lutheran Church v. County of Los Angeles, 482 U.S. 304, 321 (1987).

[C] Measure of Damages for Temporary Taking

On the other hand, if City rescinds its ordinance in 2000, O will receive compensation only for the temporary taking of his land between 1997 and 2000. Under *First English,* the measure of damages for a temporary taking is the fair market value of the use of the property during the takings period. Although clear in theory, this standard is usually difficult to apply. The typical regulatory takings case involves a government restriction on the future use of vacant land. For instance, but for the city's ordinance, O would have tried to build his planned shopping center. The fair rental value of O's property in its undeveloped condition is not adequate compensation for the loss of revenues from a shopping center. Conversely, the shopping center might not have been successful, and hence any potential lost profits are too speculative to provide a basis for damages.

In this situation, most courts determine the difference in the value of the land with and without the regulation in place, and then compute damages based on this differential. Suppose that O's property is worth $300,000 burdened by the ordinance, and $1,000,000 without it, a differential of $700,000. One common approach is to provide a market rate of return on the value differential. If a reasonable rate of return is 8%, for instance, O will receive $168,000 in damages (8% of $700,000 per year for three years).

TABLE OF CASES

[References are to sections and footnotes.]

[References are to sections and footnotes.]

[References are to sections and footnotes.]

[References are to sections and footnotes.]

[References are to sections and footnotes.]

[References are to sections and footnotes.]

[References are to sections and footnotes.]

G

[References are to sections and footnotes.]

[References are to sections and footnotes.]

[References are to sections and footnotes.]

[References are to sections and footnotes.]

[References are to sections and footnotes.]

[References are to sections and footnotes.]

[References are to sections and footnotes.]

Q

R

[References are to sections and footnotes.]

[References are to sections and footnotes.]

T

[References are to sections and footnotes.]

U

V

INDEX

[References are to sections.]

C

[References are to sections.]

[References are to sections.]

[References are to sections.]

[References are to sections.]

[References are to sections.]

N

[References are to sections.]

[References are to sections.]

[References are to sections.]

[References are to sections.]